Centre and Periphery, Roots and Exile

CENTRE AND PERIPHERY, ROOTS AND EXILE

Interpreting the Music of István Anhalt, György Kurtág, and Sándor Veress

FRIEDEMANN SALLIS, ROBIN ELLIOTT,
AND KENNETH DELONG, EDITORS

with assistance from Aaron Dalton

WILFRID LAURIER UNIVERSITY PRESS

We acknowledge the support of the Canada Council for the Arts for our publishing program. We acknowledge the financial support of the Government of Canada through the Canada Book Fund for our publishing activities.

Library and Archives Canada Cataloguing in Publication

Centre and periphery, roots and exile : interpreting the music of István Anhalt, György Kurtág, and Sándor Veress / Friedemann Sallis, Robin Elliott, and Kenneth DeLong, editors.

Majority of essays initially presented at the symposium Centre and periphery, roots and exile, at the University of Calgary, 22–25 January, 2008. Cf. Introd.
Includes bibliographical references and index.
Also available in electronic format.
Most essays in English; includes 3 essays in French
ISBN 978-1-55458-148-1 (hardcover).— ISBN 978-1-55458-582-3 (paperback)

1. Anhalt, István, 1919–. 2. Kurtág, György. 3. Veress, Sándor, 1907–1992. 4. Composers—Hungary—Biography. 5. Immigrants—History—20th century. 6. Music—History and criticism. I. Sallis, Friedemann II. Elliott, Robin, 1956– III. DeLong, Kenneth, 1944–

ML390.C397 2011   780.92'2   C2011-902745-3

Electronic monograph.
Also available in print format.
Most essays in English; includes 3 essays in French.
ISBN 978-1-55458-172-6 (PDF)

1. Anhalt, István, 1919–. 2. Kurtág, György. 3. Veress, Sándor, 1907–1992. 4. Composers—Hungary—Biography. 5. Immigrants—History—20th century. 6. Music—History and criticism. I. Sallis, Friedemann II. Elliott, Robin, 1956– III. DeLong, Kenneth, 1944–

ML390.C397 2011b   780.92'2   C2011-902746-1

Cover design by Sandra Friesen. Cover photo of István Anhalt by Walter Curtin, reproduced with the permission of the Walter Curtin Estate. Cover photo of György Kurtág by Sibylle Ehrismann, reproduced with the permission of the photographer. Cover photo of Sándor Veress reproduced with the permission of Claudio Veress. Text design by C. Bonas-Taylor.

© 2011 Wilfrid Laurier University Press
Waterloo, Ontario, Canada
www.wlupress.wlu.ca

Every reasonable effort has been made to acquire permission for copyright material used in this text, and to acknowledge all such indebtedness accurately. Any errors and omissions called to the publisher's attention will be corrected in future printings.

No part of this publication may be reproduced, stored in a retrieval system or transmitted, in any form or by any means, without the prior written consent of the publisher or a licence from The Canadian Copyright Licensing Agency (Access Copyright). For an Access Copyright licence, visit www.accesscopyright.ca or call toll free to 1-800-893-5777.

To István Anhalt
on the occasion of his ninety-second birthday

CONTENTS

List of Examples ix

List of Plates and Figures xiv

List of Tables xvii

Acknowledgements xviii

Introduction • FRIEDEMANN SALLIS 1

FIRST WORD

1 István Anhalt: A Character Sketch • JOHN BECKWITH 29

2 Kurtág, as I Know Him • GERGELY SZOKOLAY 37

3 "A Kind of Musical Autobiography": Reading Traces in Sándor Veress's *Orbis tonorum* • CLAUDIO VERESS 45

PLACE AND DISPLACEMENT

4 Of the Centre, Periphery; Exile, Liberation; Home and the Self • ISTVÁN ANHALT 57

5 István Anhalt's Kingston Triptych • ROBIN ELLIOTT 73

6 István Anhalt's *The Tents of Abraham*: Where Music Cannot Heal, Let It Be Restored • WILLIAM BENJAMIN 89

7 Which Displacement? Tracing Exile in the Postwar Compositions of István Anhalt and Mátyás Seiber • FLORIAN SCHEDING 111

8 Letters to America • RACHEL BECKLES WILLSON 129

9 Roots and Routes: Travel and Translation in István Anhalt's Operas • GORDON E. SMITH 175

10 Le fonds István Anhalt (MUS 164) à Bibliothèque et Archives Canada : auto-construction du compositeur et rôle du lieu dans son œuvre • RACHELLE CHIASSON-TAYLOR 199

Perspectives on Reception, Analysis, and Interpretation

11 Sewing Earth to Sky: István Anhalt and the Pedagogy of Transformation • AUSTIN CLARKSON 219

12 György Kurtág's *Játékok:* A "Voyage" into the Child's Musical Mind • STEFANO MELIS 241

13 Arracher la figure au figuratif : la musique vocale de György Kurtág • ALVARO OVIEDO 265

14 Dirges and Ditties: György Kurtág's Latest Settings of Poetry by Anna Akhmatova • JULIA GALIEVA-SZOKOLAY 279

15 Interpreting György Kurtág and George Crumb: Through the Looking Glass • DINA LENTSNER 303

The Presence of the Past and Memory in Contemporary Music

16 György Kurtág et Walter Benjamin : considérations sur l'aura dans la musique • JEAN-PAUL OLIVE 327

17 What Presence of the Past? Artistic Autobiography in György Kurtág's Music • ULRICH MOSCH 345

18 "Listening to inner voices": István Anhalt's *Sonance • Resonance (Welche Töne?)* • ALAN GILLMOR 371

19 Music Written from Memory in the Late Work of István Anhalt • FRIEDEMANN SALLIS 395

Final Word

20 On Doubleness and Life in Canada: An Interview with István Anhalt 423

The Contributors 433

Index 439

LIST OF EXAMPLES

The editors have identified the typeset music and diagrams, whether previously published or not, as *examples* (in English) and *exemples* (in French). Scans of manuscript material, whether published in facsimile or not, are identified as *plates* (in English) and *figures* (in French). Music in which both printed and manuscript symbols are used (as in György Kurtág's *Játékok*) are categorized as *examples*.

Example 2-1 Sándor Weöres, "Orbán," Sándor Weöres and Amy Károlyi, *Tarka forgó 120 vers az év tizenkét hónapjára* [Coloured Windwheel: 120 poems for the twelve months of the year] (1958) ... 38

Example 2-2 György Kurtág, *Játékok* I [Games I] (1973–78) "Hommage à Csajkovszkij" 40

Example 2-3 György Kurtág, *Játékok* I [Games I] (1973–78), "Hommage à Beethoven" 42

Example 3-1 Sándor Veress, *I. Quartetto per 2 Violini, Viola e Violoncello*, 24, ending of movement I 46

Example 3-2 Sándor Veress, *Orbis tonorum per orchestra da camera*, 108. Open ending of movement VIII 46

Example 7-1 István Anhalt, *Fantasia* for piano (1954), m. 1 117

Example 7-2 István Anhalt, Sonata for Violin and Piano, basic tone row 119

Example 7-3 Mátyás Seiber, *Ulysses*, Movement 3, basic tone row 119

Example 7-4 István Anhalt, Sonata for Violin and Piano (1954), mm. 1–3 120

Example 7-5 Mátyás Seiber, *Ulysses*, Movement 1, mm. 1–10 120

Example 8-1 Sándor Veress, *Sinfonia Minneapolitana*, Movement 1, mm. 19–23, Theme 1 138

Example 8-2 Sándor Veress, *Sinfonia Minneapolitana*, Movement 2, mm. 191–97, version of Theme 1 138

Example 8-3 Sándor Veress, *Sinfonia Minneapolitana*, Movement 3, mm. 278–91, version of Theme 1 138

Example 8-4 Sándor Veress, *Sinfonia Minneapolitana*, Movement 1, mm. 101–8, Theme 2 139

Example 8-5 Béla Bartók, *Cantata profana*, Movement 2, mm. 180–88, string parts 143

Example 8-6 Béla Bartók, Concerto for Orchestra, Movement 1, mm. 39–50, trumpets 147

Example 9-1 Istvan Anhalt's Operas 177

Example 9-2 Intersecting Concepts and István Anhalt's Music ... 179

Example 12-1 György Kurtág, *Játékok* I [Games I] (1973–78), "Totyogós" ["Toddling"], with clusters delineated and numbered ... 243

Example 12-2 The mental representation of musical images 246

Example 12-3 György Kurtág, *Játékok* I [Games I] (1973–78), "Totyogós" ["Toddling"], clusters 1, 2, 7, and 8 247

Example 12-4 György Kurtág, *Játékok* I [*Games* I] (1973–78), "Totyogós" ["Toddling"], structural diagram showing the chiastic arrangement 249

Example12-5 György Kurtág, *Játékok* I [Games I] (1973–78), "Hommage à Paganini" 251

Example 12-6 György Kurtág, *Játékok* I [Games I] (1973–78), "Unottan" ["Bored"] 253

Example 12-7 György Kurtág, *Játékok* I [*Games* I] (1973–78), "Unottan" ["Bored"], diagram of the first formal section 254

Example 12-8 György Kurtág, *Játékok* I [*Games* I] (1973–78), "Unottan" ["Bored"], diagram of the second formal section 256

Exemple 13-1 György Kurtág, *Kafka-Fragmente*, Op. 24 (1985–87), pour soprano et violon, « Sonntag, den 19. Juli 1910 (Berceuse II) », Début du fragment I-11 268

Exemple 13-2 György Kurtág, *Kafka-Fragmente*, Op. 24 (1985–87), pour soprano et violon, « Die Guten gehen im gleichen Schritt », Début du fragment I-1 269

Exemple 13-3 György Kurtág, *Kafka-Fragmente*, Op. 24 (1985–87), pour soprano et violon, « Der begrenzte Kreis », fragment III-6 ... 270

Exemple 13-4 György Kurtág, *Kafka-Fragmente*, Op. 24 (1985–87), pour soprano et violon, « Einmal brach ich mir das Bein », début du fragment I-13 270

Exemple 13-5 György Kurtág, *Kafka-Fragmente*, Op. 24 (1985–87), pour soprano et violon, « Ruhelos », fragment I-4 274

Example 14-1 György Kurtág, *Four Songs to Poems by Anna Akhmatova*, Op. 41 (1997–2008), "Пушкин" ["Pushkin"], mm. 1–10 288

Example 14-2 György Kurtág, *Four Songs to Poems by Anna Akhmatova* Op. 41 (1997–2008), "Александру Блоку" ["To Alexander Blok"], mm. 1–5 290

Example 14-3 György Kurtág, *Four Songs to Poems by Anna Akhmatova*, Op. 41 (1997–2008), "Плач-причитание" ["The Wailing Lament"], mm. 1–20 294

Example 15-1 Rimma Dalos, "Сон" ["Dream"], concentration of sibilants in the semantic field "inside, inner, near" 306

Example 15-2 Rimma Dalos, "Сон" ["Dream"], pro-/pri- alliteration in the text 306

Example 15-3 Rimma Dalos, "Сон" ["Dream"], the sound bridge between the beginning and the end of the last line 307

Example 15-4 Rimma Dalos, "Сон" ["Dream"], graphic representation of the sequence of the events in the poem 307

Example 15-5 György Kurtág, *Сцены из Романа. 15 Песен на Стихи Риммы Далош* [Scenes from a Novel. 15 Songs to Poems by Rimma Dalos], Op. 19, "Сон" ["Dream"], the division of the vocal line into four phrases 308

Example 15-6 György Kurtág, *Сцены из Романа. 15 Песен на Стихи Риммы Далош* [Scenes from a Novel. 15 Songs to Poems by Rimma Dalos], Op. 19, "Сон" ["Dream"], the two-layered construction of the soprano part 309

Example 15-7 György Kurtág, *Сцены из Романа. 15 Песен на Стихи Риммы Далош* [Scenes from a Novel. 15 Songs to Poems by Rimma Dalos], Op. 19, "Сон" ["Dream"], the interrelationship between four melodic phrases 311

Example 15-8 György Kurtág's interpretation of Rimma Dalos's poem, as revealed though a backward reading 312

Example 15-9 Federico García Lorca, "Gacela de la muerta oscura" ["Gacela of the Dark Death"], symmetrical structure of the text . . . 314

Example 15-10 Federico García Lorca, "Gacela de la muerta oscura" ["Gacela of the Dark Death"], corresponding pairs of the words within symmetrical structure 314

Example 15-11 Federico García Lorca, "Gacela de la muerta oscura" ["Gacela of the Dark Death"], the diachronic *r*-sound progression 315

Example 15-12 Federico García Lorca, "Gacela de la muerta oscura" ["Gacela of the Dark Death"], superimposed synchronic and diachronic aspects of the text 315

Example 15-13 George Crumb, *Madrigals, Book III*, No. 2, "Gacela de la muerto oscura" ["Gacela of the Dark Death"], the links between sections in the setting 318

Example 15-14 George Crumb, *Madrigals, Book III*, No. 2, "Gacela de la muerto oscura" ["Gacela of the Dark Death"], vertical/horizontal scheme of the madrigal with the resulting harmonic structure 318

Example 15-15 George Crumb, *Madrigals, Book III*, No. 2, "Gacela de la muerto oscura" ["Gacela of the Dark Death"], overlapping synchronic and diachronic compositional processes in the madrigal 319

Example 16-1 György Kurtág, *Hommage à Mihály András*, Op. 13 (1977–78), « 12 Microludes pour quatuors à cordes », n° 1 338

Example 16-2 György Kurtág, *Hommage à Mihály András*, Op. 13 (1977–78), « 12 Microludes pour quatuors à cordes », n° 6 339

Example 16-3 György Kurtág, *Hommage à Mihály András*, Op. 13 (1977–78), « 12 Microludes pour quatuors à cordes », n° 5 340

Example 16-4 György Kurtág, *Hommage à Mihály András*, Op. 13 (1977–78), « 12 Microludes pour quatuors à cordes », n° 12 342

Example 17-1 György Kurtág, *Játékok III* [Games III] (1973–78), "Hommage à Servánszky," version for piano solo (1975) 353

Example 17-2 György Kurtág, *Officium breve in memoriam Andreae Szervánszky* (1984–89), Op. 28, for string quartet, movement XII . . . 356

Example 17-3 György Kurtág, *Játékok III* [Games III] (1973–78), "Hommage à J.S.B." 358

Example 17-4 György Kurtág, *Játékok I* [Games I] (1973–78), "Hommage à Beethoven" 359

Example 18-1 Ludwig van Beethoven, String Quartet, Op. 132, Movement 5, Allegro appassionato, mm. 1–19 378

Example 18-2 Ludwig van Beethoven, Ninth Symphony, Movement 3, Adagio molto e cantibile, mm. 49–51 386

Example 19-1 István Anhalt, *Four Portraits from Memory* (piano version), III, formal divisions of the first segment of *Portrait* III, mm. 1–56 407

LIST OF PLATES AND FIGURES

Plate 2-1 György Kurtág, *Szokolay Cauuanyi első karácsonyára* [For Alexander Szokolay's first Christmas] for violin solo (15–17 December 2002) 41

Plate 4-1 István Anhalt, *Kantáta Előpatakon* [Cantata in Előpatak] (1943), typescript with handwritten corrections, recto 69

Plate 4-2 István Anhalt, *Kantáta Előpatakon* [Cantata in Előpatak] (1943), typescript with handwritten corrections, verso 70

Plate 8-1 Sándor Veress, *Sinfonia Minneapolitana*, Movement 1, mm. 137–40, breaking up of Theme 2 140

Plate 8-2 Sándor Veress, *Sinfonia Minneapolitana*, Movement 1, mm. 179–90 144

Plate 8-3 Sándor Veress, second autobiographic statement 151

Plate 8-4 Sándor Veress, third autobiographic statement 158

Plate 9-1 István Anhalt, dedication page from the score of *Traces (Tikkun)* (1994) 183

Plate 9-2 István Anhalt, *Traces (Tikkun)* (1994), "Arrival" (I) and opening of "Questions" (II), mm. 1–7, score page 1 185

Plate 9-3 István Anhalt, *Traces (Tikkun)* (1994), final page of the "Labyrinth" (III) and the opening page of "Oasis" (IV), mm. 165–73, score pages 46–47 188

Plate 9-4 István Anhalt, *Traces (Tikkun)* (1994), "In the Highdome" (VII), mm. 428–31, score page 100 190

Plate 9-5 István Anhalt, *Traces (Tikkun)* (1994), "The Answer" (X), mm. 648–54, score page 156 192

Figure 10-1 István Anhalt, *Traces (Tikkun)* (1994), esquisse (1992–93) 207

Figure 10-2 István Anhalt, *Traces (Tikkun)* (1994), esquisse
(1992–93) 208

Figure 10-3 István Anhalt, *Traces (Tikkun)* (1994), esquisse
subséquente du même passage présenté dans les figures
10-1 et 10-2 209

Figure 10-4 István Anhalt, *Traces (Tikkun)* (1994), manuscrit de
la page couverture (18 juillet 1993) 210

Figure 10-5 István Anhalt, *Traces (Tikkun)* (1994), corrections
aux textes (version du 18 juillet 1993) 211

Plate 17-1 György Kurtág, "Hommage à Szervánszky" (1975),
version for violin and cello or viola 354

Plate 18-1 István Anhalt, "Series 1" from sketches for *Sonance•Resonance (Welche Töne?)* (1989) 377

Plate 18-2 István Anhalt, *Sonance•Resonance (Welche Töne?)* (1989),
mm. 1–2 377

Plate 18-3 István Anhalt, *Sonance•Resonance (Welche Töne?)* (1989),
strings only, mm. 113–16 379

Plate 18-4 István Anhalt, *Sonance•Resonance (Welche Töne?)* (1989),
mm. 117–20 380

Plate 18-5 István Anhalt, *Sonance•Resonance (Welche Töne?)* (1989),
mm. 170–74 381

Plate 18-6 István Anhalt, *Sonance•Resonance (Welche Töne?)* (1989),
mm. 227–34 382

Plate 18-7 István Anhalt, *Sonance•Resonance (Welche Töne?)* (1989),
woodwinds and brass only, mm. 291–97 384

Plate 18-8 István Anhalt, *Sonance•Resonance (Welche Töne?)* (1989),
mm. 328–30 385

Plate 18-9 István Anhalt, *Sonance•Resonance (Welche Töne?)* (1989),
mm. 376–80 387

Plate 18-10 István Anhalt, *Sonance•Resonance (Welche Töne?)* (1989),
mm. 523–27 388

Plate 19-1 István Anhalt, *Four Portraits from Memory* (piano version),
I, mm. 1–12 399

Plate 19-2 István Anhalt, *Four Portraits from Memory* (piano version), II, mm. 1–28 400

Plate 19-3 István Anhalt, *Four Portraits from Memory* (piano version), IV, mm. 1–26 401

Plate 19-4 István Anhalt, *Four Portraits from Memory* (piano version), III, correction mm. 107–10 402

Plate 19-5 István Anhalt, *Four Portraits from Memory* (piano version), III, mm. 98–109 402

Plate 19-6 István Anhalt, *Four Portraits from Memory* (orchestral version), III, mm. 98–112 403

Plate 19-7 István Anhalt, *Four Portraits from Memory*, adaptation of the orchestral version for piano by John Beckwith, III, mm. 99–112 404

Plate 19-8 István Anhalt, *Four Portraits from Memory* (piano version), III, mm. 1–63 406

Plate 19-9 István Anhalt, *Four Portraits from Memory* (piano version), III, draft 409

Plate 19-10 István Anhalt, *Four Portraits from Memory* (piano version), III, sketch 410

LIST OF TABLES

Table 14-1 György Kurtág, Russian works written between 1976 and 2008 280

Table 14-2 Anna Akhmatova, original and translated texts in György Kurtág's Opus 41 284

Table 15-1 Rimma Dalos, "Сон" ["Dream"], transliterated and translated text 306

Table 15-2 Federico García Lorca, excerpt from "Gacela de la muerta oscura" ["Gacela of the Dark Death"], transliterated and translated text 313

Table 15-3 George Crumb's version of Federico García Lorca's text with the word repetition 316

ACKNOWLEDGEMENTS

The editors of this book would like to sincerely thank the Faculty of Fine Arts and the Department of Music of the University of Calgary, and the Institute for Canadian Music of the University of Toronto. Without their support this book could not have been published. We are indebted to the Paul Sacher Foundation (Basel) and Library and Archives Canada for allowing us to publish documents from their holdings, which have considerably enriched the content of this book. We heartily thank Michelle Arbuckle, head librarian at the Canadian Music Centre, for her help with source material. Jennifer Wlodarczyk also deserves our gratitude for her assistance. Finally, we reserve our warmest thanks for Aaron Dalton. His scrupulous proofreading (in both English and French) and rigorous comments have been of enormous benefit throughout the entire editorial process.

INTRODUCTION

FRIEDEMANN SALLIS

What it means to be a refugee cannot be described in the simple terms of finding a job and adjusting to foreign customs. It is a way of being, constantly lingering between arrival and departure. —Henry Pachter[1]

Today, after more than a century of electric technology, we have extended our central nervous system itself in a global embrace, abolishing both space and time as far as our planet is concerned. —Marshall McLuhan[2]

Where are we at all? And whenabouts in the name of space? I don't understand. I fail to say. I dearsee you too. —James Joyce[3]

Centres and Peripheries

This book brings together essays that examine how ideas of place and identity impinge on the creation, analysis, and interpretation of twentieth-century art music. These are not new topics. On the contrary, they have been much discussed, and with reason.[4] The twentieth century witnessed an unprecedented increase in the number of people leaving their homeland, more often than not motivated by desperate conditions brought on by economic collapse, oppression, war, and genocide. According to Eric Hobsbawm, this resulted in the greatest mass migration in history. "Men and women migrated not only across oceans and international frontiers, but from country to city; from one region of the same state to another—in short from 'home' to the land of strangers and, turning the coin around, as strangers into others' home."[5] This movement was facilitated by massive technological innovation. Travel and communication have been made faster and easier in ways that were unimaginable a century ago, and, as Marshall McLuhan predicted, the impact has been enormous. As a result, old certitudes have been, at the very least, destabilized, if not completely overthrown, and new ways of conceiving and creating music have been produced in astounding abundance, greatly complicating the task of understanding and interpreting it. What used to be known as Western art music no longer circulates in the comfortably close-knit, relatively homogeneous social strata dominated by the haute bourgeoisie, as was the case just one hundred years ago.[6] On the contrary, it now resonates across the globe in highly diverse, multicultural, multi-ethnic contexts, characterized by widely divergent expectations and value judgments. In our attempts to evaluate music in this new environment, we actively look for the "extraterritorial" and "cross-cultural" components of music, and in so doing, we appear to have left older, apparently simpler categories behind us. Homi Bhabha observes that the "very concepts of homogeneous national cultures, the consensual or contiguous transmissions of historical traditions, or 'organic' ethnic communities—as the grounds of cultural comparativism—are in a profound process of redefinition."[7] Writing against the grain on this point, Ian Biddle and Vanessa Knights argue that we need to recapture the middle ground (i.e., that imagined or real place which enables the discursive existence of regional or national identities). They confidently predict that "we should not be surprised to find that new forms of nationalism continue to emerge and the force of the nation as a cultural trope continues to adapt to new political and material conditions."[8] However, the closer one examines the idea of national and regional identities, the more illusionary it seems. Consider Darius Milhaud's statement: "Je suis un Français de Provence, de religion israélite."[9] In a few words, Milhaud's national identity unfolds to reveal a "métissage" of various linguistic, regional, and religious identities.[10] How the art music tradition will find its "place" in this new, extraordinarily fluid environment remains an open question.

David Beard and Kenneth Gloag have recently identified "place" as a key musicological concept. They suggest that it has only entered musicological discourse since the mid-1980s; however, as will be shown below, place has been implicitly part of the critical discussion of music since the nineteenth century.[11] Indeed, the related binary models centre-periphery, mainstream-margin, and universal-particular (or global-local, if one prefers the more up-to-date terms) are so thoroughly embedded in this discourse that they have been, and in many quarters still are, taken for granted. Each pair should be understood as two sides of the same conceptual coin, providing musicologists with logical tools to enable specific musical facts to be set in coherent contexts. To decide whether a music practice is central or peripheral, it must be set within some broader environment, which bears either a sustaining or conflicting relation to it. According to Reinhard Strohm, the main problem that arises when applying this model is the implied value judgment. "Only what is central is significant to us. Even if we can rarely prove (for lack of proper criteria) that music originating outside of the centres was less skilfully composed, music history has in any case adopted the model of centres and peripheries, at least for convenience's sake."[12] Thus as methodologically useful, and indeed as indispensable, as these models are, they have become increasingly controversial, fraught with significant aesthetic, historical, and political ramifications. It is instructive to briefly sketch how the use of these models has evolved over the past two centuries.

The centre-periphery model is of course bound up with the traditional and still ubiquitous habit of treating the art music of Germany, France, and Italy as central, and thus supposedly universal, while designating the music of all other places as national and consequently peripheral. This distinction has always been misleading. On the one hand, during the nineteenth century, nationalism was as much a factor in the central nation-states as anywhere else. On the other hand, the idea of "national" music has been approached almost exclusively from the perspective of *writing* national histories of music, which usually emphasize what is nationally unique and distinctive, rather than what is common and shared.[13] Be that as it may, the widespread uncritical acceptance of this model reinforced the notion of a musical "mainstream" of canonical works flowing more or less directly out of nineteenth-century music (one of the primary sources being the work of Ludwig van Beethoven). The idea of a musical mainstream was revisited and indeed rejuvenated in the mid-twentieth century by Theodor Adorno.[14] His theory of musical material, first comprehensively set down in his *Philosophie der neuen Musik* (1949), proposed nothing less than a kind of musical impulse of Hegelian proportions that reveals itself as a history of compositional technique.[15] For Adorno, the true subject of music history is neither the composer nor his work, but rather the historical process itself, which, through the "tendency of material," preordained what an aesthetically meaningful and successful work, compositional technique, or musical concept could be. Furthermore, Adorno left no doubt concerning the cultural and indeed geographic perspective from which his *Philosophie* was being formulated.[16] Following the Second World War, historical determinism reached its high-water mark, and under its influence many composers, particularly those involved in the Darmstadt summer courses where Adorno's *Philosophie* had a strong impact, saw themselves as agents acting out their own historical moment.[17] Pierre Boulez succinctly captured this certainty when he proclaimed the "uselessness" of all composers not directly involved in the serial project.[18] By the early 1960s, the belief that integral serialism constituted the logical next step in the development of musical material had faded, and as the influence of historical determinism subsided, the existence of a musical "mainstream" was also called into question. In one of his more poetic moments, John Cage observed, "We live in a time I think, not of mainstream, but of many streams or even, if you insist upon a river of time, that we have come to [a] delta, maybe even beyond [the] delta to an ocean which is going back to the skies."[19]

During the twentieth century, the universal-particular model also came to be used in ways that could hardly have been foreseen a century earlier. Since the early nineteenth century, the musical work of art was normally set in a dialectic between the specificity of its origins and its role as a vehicle allowing the listener to attain what Gustav Mahler called that other world "in which things are beyond classification into time and place."[20] For the Romantics, this relationship was thought of as complementary, underwriting the corollary assumption that, whereas great music serves to mediate the local and the universal, lesser music remains perforce contained within its local sphere. In his 1836 review, Robert Schumann famously observed that Fryderyk Chopin was a great composer because he was able to transform the raw musical characteristics of his national (i.e., local) heritage into individual works of universal value. For Schumann, national stylistic traits constituted a point of departure, "a source of energy, a substance on which the creative artist can feed, but they should not be his ultimate aesthetic authority."[21] In the twentieth century this subtle and ultimately very productive model was turned on its head and distorted with ever-increasing frequency. Johann Gottfried Herder's thesis that the "spirit of the people" [*der Volksgeist*] constituted the true source of creative human endeavour was recuperated by totalitarian regimes of all stripes.[22] In the Soviet Union, just as in Nazi Germany, national and regional characteristics were mobilized so as to resist the "antipopular," "rampantly individualistic," and "formalistic" trends in music that supposedly endangered its very future.[23] These so-called cosmopolitan influences were to be cleansed politically through administrative fiat, and in so doing the former dialectical relationship was reduced to a simple, dead dichotomy. For good or ill, this politicized use of the universal-particular model proliferated throughout the twentieth century, and not only in totalitarian regimes. In 1906, Zoltán Kodály publicly called for the performance of Hungarian folk songs in Hungarian concert halls, and in so doing, explicitly demanded the exclusion of "inferior foreign music-hall songs."[24] At the other end of the century, colleagues in ethnomusicology and popular music studies have produced a significant body of work based on the global-local model. In its extreme form, this work tends towards a reactive, one-sided attempt to set local musical practices of whatever sort in opposition to the homogenizing impulse of globalization. The result has been an idealization of both terms. The local or human is seen as inherently subversive, oppositional, and authentic, and an inverse figuration of the global or corporate, which is always already artificial, conformist, and inauthentic.[25] In all cases, the perceived musical common sense of the people, representing some kind of local place or particular identity, has been conscripted in the service of a political goal: to undermine the presumed privileged positions of illegitimate musical establishments. To paraphrase Giselher Schubert, this (ab)use of the global-local/universal-particular model is symptomatic of an unfortunate twentieth-century tendency to subsume aesthetics within a political function.[26]

István Anhalt, György Kurtág, and Sándor Veress

Few twentieth-century composers have not been affected in one way or another by the network of problems and issues related to these binary models, but the impact was particularly strong on the composers whose work will be examined in this book. Most received their training at the Franz Liszt Academy in Budapest. The primary objects of study will be compositions by István Anhalt (1919–), György Kurtág (1926–), and Sándor Veress (1907–92).[27] The former was born in Budapest, the latter two in what is now Romania. Veress was born in Kolozsvár, the major urban centre of Transylvania, which was then part of the Austro-Hungarian Empire. His family relocated to Budapest before the end of the First World War. Kurtág was born to Hungarian parents in Lugoj Romania. He spoke Hungarian at home and, from the age of six, Romanian at school. In 1946 he moved to Budapest, acquiring Hungarian citizenship in 1948. As well as their Hungarian mother tongue, the three composers have much in common. All received their professional training at the Liszt Academy. Veress and Anhalt studied composition with Kodály (1923–32 and 1937–41 respectively); Kurtág studied with Kodály's students, beginning with

Veress (1946–48) and completing his studies in composition with Ferenc Farkas (1948–55).[28]

Also, as one would expect, the Second World War had a profound impact on their careers.[29] In 1939 Veress found himself in London. He felt compelled to return to Budapest, where he succeeded in establishing himself as one of Hungary's leading composers. In 1943 he was named professor of composition at the Liszt Academy, and immediately following the war he was appointed to the Hungarian Arts Council. In 1948, feeling uncomfortable with the evolving political situation, he left Hungary and never returned. The following year he took a position as guest professor at the University of Bern in Switzerland. He would reside there for the rest of his life, pursuing a successful career as both a composer and an academic. For both Anhalt and Kurtág the war years were very different. Indeed, both belong to that group of writers, artists, and musicians who proved that poetry, art, and music could be created after Auschwitz. During the war Anhalt was forced to do hard labour for the Hungarian Army in what amounted to a form of legalized slavery because he was Jewish.[30] After the war he worked for a year as an assistant conductor at the Budapest Opera (1945–46). However, it seems that even before the war, he had come to the conclusion that he could not pursue his career as a composer in Hungary.

> While I greatly admired him [Kodály] for what he stood for, early enough it became clear to me that his programme could not have the same relevance for me as it held for most of my fellow students ... In the centre of Kodály's life-work stood the ideal of Hungary's cultural renaissance. Unquestionably a most admirable goal, I thought. But for me this presented a problem. How could I, I told myself, regarded, as I was at the time, in the country where I was born, as a person not fully acceptable in the political sense (and soon after increasingly also in the social sense), for the sole reason of belonging to a certain minority religious faith, how could I make this goal also mine?[31]

In 1946 he went to Paris, where he continued his studies in composition with Nadia Boulanger, and in 1949 he migrated to Canada, becoming a citizen in 1955. From 1949 to 1971 Anhalt taught at the Faculty of Music of McGill University. In 1971 he moved to Kingston, Ontario, where he became head of the recently founded Department of Music at Queen's University.[32] Little is known of Kurtág's wartime experience, though, being Jewish, he, like Anhalt, was lucky to survive. During the traumatic months of the failed Hungarian revolution (1956), Kurtág considered leaving

Hungary together with his friend and colleague György Ligeti. In the end, Kurtág and his wife Márta hesitated and as a result spent most of the next thirty years of their professional careers behind the Iron Curtain. Kurtág eventually took a position at the Liszt Academy, where he went on to an illustrious career as professor of chamber music.

As composers, Veress, Anhalt, and Kurtág developed along different but nevertheless related lines, as one would expect given their shared point of departure. In varying degrees, the work of all three composers was influenced by dodecaphonic technique: Veress and Anhalt during the 1950s and Kurtág in the early 1960s. Whereas Anhalt produced a number of electro-acoustic works during the 1960s, neither Veress nor Kurtág showed much interest in this medium. As their work matured, both Anhalt and Veress tended to write works for traditional large-scale ensembles; Kurtág's work is written primarily for soloists and small chamber ensembles. Ligeti has observed that it is focused on "rugged fragments" (*zerklüfteten Bruchstücken*), which are then welded together into powerfully expressive forms.[33] All three pursued distinguished careers as music pedagogues: Anhalt and Veress as university professors and Kurtág as professor of chamber music at the Liszt Academy, but the personal trajectories that each followed after the Second World War are drastically different. When Veress left Hungary in 1948, he could not have imagined that he would never return. He was grateful to have found refuge in Switzerland, where he remained an exile in more than one sense.[34] First, he would be officially classified as a "stateless" person for the next forty-two years. He was only granted a Swiss passport in 1991, a few months before he died.[35] Second, as a composer, Veress quickly found himself marginalized in relation to what became the postwar avant-garde. Notwithstanding the enormous contribution he made as a professor and composer in Switzerland, his postwar compositions never achieved the success that his pre-war compositions seemed to portend. John Weissman astutely summed up Veress's situation in 1955 when he wrote, "From his Swiss vantage point he has surveyed the European scene with the objective detachment of a visitor from another planet, untainted by the recently formed traditions and unburdened by the dangerous conventions of the day."[36] Veress's work has been recognized and honoured with numerous prizes in both Hungary (the Kossuth Prize in 1949 and the Bartók-Pásztory Prize in 1985) and Switzerland (the Bern Canton Prize in 1976). Anhalt has consistently reported that he experienced his departure from Hungary as a form of liberation, not an exile, and he adapted to his new home in Canada with seeming ease and remarkable success. The impact that he has had in

Canada as a composer, professor, researcher, writer, and builder of university music departments has been outstanding, and his contribution has been recognized with numerous prizes, awards, and honours, the most recent of which was his election to the Academy of Arts of the Royal Society of Canada in 2007. As professor at the Liszt Academy, Kurtág was clearly part of the local musical establishment. He nevertheless managed to maintain a critically important distance between himself and the political and administrative centres of power. Indeed, by carefully positioning himself on the periphery of the Hungarian musical establishment, Kurtág used his compositional and pedagogical activity to "re-centre" a significant portion of the new music scene in Budapest around his "official silence."[37] His work has received numerous awards both in Hungary and abroad, including the Ernst von Siemens Prize for music (1998) and the Grawemeyer music prize (2006). Today Kurtág is widely held to be Hungary's greatest living composer. He currently resides in France and has held dual Hungarian-French citizenship since 2002.[38]

Given these differences in their career trajectories, why have we decided to focus on the work of these three composers? Had we chosen to produce a monograph on one or the other, the relationship between music and place would have been fairly conventional. Anhalt's work could be "placed" in Canada's Saint Lawrence River valley, where both Kingston and Montreal are situated and where he has lived and worked for the past fifty years.[39] Veress's work would be located primarily in Switzerland; but of course it is difficult to come to terms with his compositions without relating them to his Hungarian past. Notwithstanding his recent move to France, Kurtág and his work would surely have been centred in Budapest. By bringing all three composers together as objects of study in the same book, such one-dimensional schemas are necessarily short-circuited and give way to an open network or field of possible relationships, reminding us of Umberto Eco's description of *Finnegans Wake*: a sort of topological maze in which everything is centred and peripheral at the same time.[40] James Joyce's own description of this network is particularly apt and worth citing:

> Because … every person, place and thing in the chaosmos of Alle anyway connected with the gobblydumped turkey was moving and changing every part of the time: the traveling inkhorn (possibly pot), the hare and the turtle pen and paper, the continually more and less intermissunderstanding minds of the anticollaborators, the as time went on as it will variously inflected, differently pronounced, otherwise spelled, changeably meaning vocable scriptsigns.[41]

When Anhalt immigrated to Canada, he did not merely move to another place in the Western world, he entered into a new kind of environment in which technology was redefining (and continues to redefine) old relationships between culture and a sense of place. The impact of technological change was probably felt more keenly in North America, and particularly in Canada, because the weight of accumulated cultural traditions was and continues to be far less important.[42] Of course, this is not to say that the relationship between culture and a sense of place has disappeared or been technologically erased. Art and music have and will continue to have tangible relationships to place, but the nature of these relationships will have to be re-evaluated and reconceptualized. Veress, Anhalt, and Kurtág were born into a culture that was clearly perceived as peripheral. Their achievements now circulate in a world in which judgments such as this seem rooted in another age. The authors of this book employ ideas of place, identity, culture, history, and memory in order to circumscribe what they feel is important to the object of study they are dealing with. In other words, they will be drawing peripheries around the centres of their choosing. Thus we invite the reader to enter into one small Hungarian-Canadian-Swiss corner of what one might be tempted to call the current musicological "chaosmos." We hope that you will find it as fascinating as we do.

The majority of the texts published here were initially presented at an international symposium that bore the same title as this book and that took place 22–25 January 2008 at the Faculty of Fine Arts of the University of Calgary. The book contains chapters in English and French, reflecting the bilingual nature of the symposium. The texts have been written by authors from a variety of cultural and linguistic backgrounds (Argentina, Canada, France, Germany, Hungary, Italy, Russia, and the United Kingdom). As a result, approximately one-third were written in the author's second language. On the one hand, the editors have rigorously imposed proper linguistic standards in both English and French. On the other hand, we have consciously avoided reducing the style of the diverse contributions to a characterless, generic North American academese. On the contrary, we have actively sought acceptable ways to retain and indeed highlight national accents and specific cultural approaches to the study of music. We feel that this decision provides for a richer, more diverse outcome. The book is organized in three thematic groups: "Place and Displacement," "Perspectives on Reception, Analysis, and Interpretation," and "The Presence of the Past and Memory in Contemporary Music." They are preceded by a section entitled "First Word": three short chapters, each written by a person close to Anhalt, Kurtág, and Veress that provide the reader with a portrait of the man behind each composer's public persona. The first is a character sketch of the book's dedicatee by John Beckwith. Anhalt and Beckwith met in the mid-1950s and have remained close friends and colleagues ever since. As composers, writers, teachers, and administrators, they have been at the centre of efforts to create an art music culture cut loose from the colonial habits, attitudes, and practices that were still well entrenched in mid-century Canada. Their achievement has been tremendous, and this country owes both an enormous debt of gratitude. The second was written by Gergely Szokolay, a professional pianist of Hungarian origin now living and working in Toronto, who studied piano with Kurtág and is the composer's godson. Kurtág's role as a pedagogue is legendary, but discussion of it is relatively rare.[43] Szokolay's text opens a brief but nevertheless fascinating window on this aspect of Kurtág's career. The chapter also includes the facsimile of an unpublished manuscript of a short piece for violin solo that the composer wrote for Szokolay's daughter Sophia. This type of piece has been at the centre of the composer's output for the past forty years at least. The Kurtág Collection of manuscripts, housed at the Paul Sacher Foundation, contains hundreds of pieces like this that were initially sent as messages of condolence or celebration to close friends and acquaintances. Notwithstanding the private nature of their content, many of these pieces have since been published in collections such as the eight-volume *Játékok* [Games] series and *Signs, Games and Message for Strings* and *Games and Messages for Winds*.[44] In the third chapter, Claudio Veress reads the movements of one of his father's last works, *Orbis tonorum* for chamber ensemble (1986), as a kind of musical autobiography. The main stylistic and technical characteristics of each of the eight movements are briefly introduced and adroitly linked to various aspects of the composer's life story and personality. The reader is thus efficiently introduced to a composer who is not as well known as he should be in the English-speaking world. We also become acquainted with a man whose career is intimately bound up with Hungary's fate in the twentieth century, even though he spent half of his life in exile.

Place and Displacement

The first group of essays begins with the text Anhalt submitted as a keynote address for the symposium. In it he carefully examines how the binary models centre-periphery, exile-liberation, and home-self relate to his personal history and to the places where he lived and worked: from Budapest, via Paris and Montreal, to Kingston, Ontario, where he now resides. One of the most poignant events along this trajectory took place in the Transylvanian village of Előpatak. There on 1 August 1943 Anhalt wrote a luminous poem originally entitled "Kantáta Előpatakon" ("Cantata in Előpatak") on love and the sheer joy of existence captured in an ephemeral moment during one of the darkest periods of the Second World War.[45] The poem evokes an ideal place, where friendship and communion are possible: a place conducive to the creative activity that Anhalt later found in Kingston.[46] The composer has remained very attached to this text ever since, and for that reason the earliest surviving document containing the original Hungarian text, conserved in the Anhalt Fonds of Library and Archives Canada, has been published in facsimile as an appendix to Anhalt's essay.

This book neither covers over significant differences of opinion nor shies away from controversial positions. In his chapter, Robin Elliott explores the significant relationships obtaining between Anhalt and Kingston, Ontario, the place where he has resided since 1971. Elliott suggests that this town, halfway between Montreal and Toronto, and comfortably situated at the eastern end of Lake Ontario, is not merely a pleasant backdrop for artistic activity. On the contrary, he insists that the category of place can apply even to a small Ontario city like Kingston; he demonstrates how this place became a substantive part of the triptych of orchestral compositions Anhalt wrote there between 2002 and 2005. William Benjamin complements this view in his examination of the extra-musical content of the second work of the Kingston Triptych: *The Tents of Abraham (A Mirage-Midrash)* (2003), arguably one of Anhalt's most successful works.[47] Few know the composer and his work better than Benjamin, and he uses this knowledge to scrutinize the relationships between Anhalt's Jewish identity, the content of *The Tents of Abraham*, and the place where this programmatic work was written.[48] He concludes that a reciprocal relationship was indeed established between the composer, the musicians, and the local audience such that Anhalt can and should be described as a Kingston composer. Florian Scheding, Rachel Beckles Willson, and Gordon E. Smith respond indirectly to these claims by accentuating displacement rather than place, movement between locales rather than the locales themselves. Scheding reminds us that a composer's biography and work history constitute different and often very distinct narratives: changing one's passport is one thing; dispensing with compositional training or a musical heritage is something entirely different. Scheding compares the biographies and work histories of Mátyás Seiber (1905–60) and Anhalt, which in many ways are quite similar: both studied with Kodály, in both cases anti-Semitism in Hungary compelled them to leave (though Seiber left much earlier than Anhalt), and both eventually settled in territories of the British Commonwealth.[49] Scheding focuses on the turn that both composers made towards serialism following the Second World War and how this change in compositional technique can be related to their displacement. Beckles Willson follows with "Letters to America," in which she examines the case of Sandór Veress, one of Hungary's leading composers, who fled to Switzerland in 1949 for political reasons. She presents a close reading of two versions of an autobiographical statement prepared by Veress in the mid-1950s as part of his failed attempts to migrate to the United States. In her study, she carefully teases apart layers of meaning and innuendo in the documents themselves (both of which are presented in facsimile in an appendix to her text), as well as in correspondence pertaining to the writing and rewriting of the autobiographical statements. In so doing, she demonstrates how, in the context of the Cold War, a composer's identity could be reconfigured according to the place he was striving to reach. Beckles Willson then shows what these documents have to say about Veress's music, specifically the *Sinfonia Minneapolitana* (1952–53), first performed in Minneapolis in 1954 under the direction of Antal Doráti. Gordon E. Smith reinforces Scheding's position in an examination of Anhalt's four operas. Using James Clifford's discussion of dwelling and travel as a point of departure, Smith examines the "routes and roots" of Anhalt's oeuvre. He brings his training as an ethnomusicologist to bear on Anhalt's deeply autobiographical third opera *Traces* (*Tikkun*) (completed in 1995), which is both a product of and a reflection on displacement.

The first goal of Rachelle Chiasson-Taylor's chapter is to present a much-needed update of Helmut Kallmann's introduction to the István Anhalt Fonds conserved in Library and Archives Canada.[50] In the second part of her essay, Chiasson-Taylor picks up a theme first introduced by Beckles Willson and reflects on how composers' legacies are auto-constructed, not only in the content of their work, but also through the manner in which document collections are selected and organized and how such constructions can be related to a sense of place. Finally, this essay is significant because it represents one of the first French-language texts on Anhalt and his work. Anhalt spent over twenty years working as professor at the Faculty of Music of McGill University and as such made a significant contribution to art and culture in Montreal. Consequently, we believe that it is high time that Anhalt's work be recognized and received in Quebec, as well as in the wider French-speaking world.

Perspectives on Reception, Analysis, and Interpretation

In the next group of essays the discussion moves to the work of György Kurtág and examines how cultural perspectives can impinge on the reception and interpretation of music. To begin, Austin Clarkson and Stefano Melis look at pedagogical aspects of the work of Anhalt and Kurtág respectively. Clarkson comes back to Anhalt's Jewish heritage and the strong impact it has had on Anhalt's hermeneutic doctrine: i.e., a triangular relationship between the artwork, the context of its presentation, and the aesthetic experience it produces. According to Clarkson, Anhalt's aesthetic is based on the assumption that interpretation is the prerogative of neither the author nor the expert critic, but rather is distributed among those listeners who are actively engaged in the aesthetic experience. Thus, for Anhalt, the purpose of art goes beyond the aesthetic object and resides in the awakening of the creative imagination of those who respond to the work. Melis takes a close look at the pedagogical aspects embedded in Kurtág's *Játékok* [Games], eight volumes of pieces for piano, piano four-hands, and two pianos that Kurtág began to compose in the early 1970s. In these pieces, compositional technique and pedagogical goals are so intertwined that they become all but indistinguishable. In his analysis, Melis shows how selected pieces from volume I of this collection can be interpreted as voyages into the child's mind.

This middle section ends with three analytical studies of Kurtág's vocal music. Alvaro Oviedo takes a close look at the relationship between text and music and notes that in Kurtág's compositions one encounters a balance of contradictory forces. Whereas madrigalisms or word painting are a consistent feature of these scores, the composer systematically destabilizes the musical figure at the very moment that it emerges, creating the fluid impression of suggested images that never really become manifest. This ephemeral relationship that lies at the centre of Kurtág's vocal style is illustrated with examples taken primarily from the *Kafka-Fragmente*, Op. 24 (1985–87), for soprano and violin, one of the composer's major achievements. Oviedo brings his chapter to a close with a strikingly original comparison between Kurtág's musical figures and figuration in Francis Bacon's studies of Popes.

The last two essays of the middle group are written by two Russian-trained musicologists currently working in North America and focus on Kurtág's vocal works set to Russian texts. Vocal music constitutes a major portion of the composer's output. The majority of these compositions are set to the work of Hungarian poets. However, beginning in the late 1970s,

Kurtág's choice broadened to include texts in Russian, German, French, Italian, English, Latin, ancient Greek, and most recently Romanian. Among these, Russian clearly predominates. For example, one finds Russian in no less than 10 per cent of the 5977 documents contained in the composer's 106 sketchbooks conserved in the György Kurtág Collection (held by the Paul Sacher Foundation). Furthermore, Russian occurs in the pages of these sketchbooks three times more often than all other foreign languages combined.[51] Julia Galieva-Szokolay begins with an overview of Kurtág's settings of Russian texts: eighteen titles composed between 1976 and the present. She notes in passing that during the 1970s and 1980s, Kurtág's fascination for Russian literary culture conflicted with the prevailing resentment among Hungarian dissident circles (with whom he was also associated) for all things Russian. Galieva-Szokolay then takes a closer look at Kurtág's recently completed cycle *Four Poems by Anna Akhmatova* [*Анна Ахматова: Четыре стихотворения*], Op. 41 (1997–2008), for soprano and ensemble and shows how sensitive it is to the complex layers of cultural meaning embedded in these texts. In her detailed analysis of prosody in selected songs from *Scenes from a Novel*, Op. 19 (1979–82), for soprano, violin, cimbalom, and double bass, Dina Lentsner seeks to dissolve the boundary between music and poetry. In so doing she identifies what she believes to be the true centre of Kurtág's work. Lentsner applies structuralist principles taken from Yuri Lotman's literary theory to this music and reveals Kurtág's remarkable sensitivity to the linguistic nuances of the texts he has chosen to set. She then underscores the broader significance of this methodology by applying the same analytical technique to the prosody of songs by George Crumb on Spanish texts by Federico García Lorca taken from Crumb's *Madrigals* (Book III, 1969) for soprano, harp, and percussion.

Presence of the Past and Memory in Contemporary Music

The final four chapters examine the impact that time and memory can have on notions of place and identity in music. Notwithstanding our new technologically saturated environment, which tends to underscore the *hic et nunc* of existence, temporal perspectives continue to substantiate relationships between music and place, as though endowing them with a sense of gravity. The first chapters by Jean Paul Olive and Ulrich Mosch look at how traces of the past inflect and articulate the content of Kurtág's ephemeral sounds. Jean Paul Olive begins by quoting Arnold Schoenberg, who asks,

"What makes it possible that a second tone should follow a first, a beginning tone?"[52] Embedded in the question is anxiety about how a composer can move forward following a break with tradition. This question has been at the heart of Kurtág's compositional endeavour since he emerged out of a period of self-imposed silence in the years following the traumatic events of the failed Hungarian uprising.[53] Olive then introduces the concept of "aura," Walter Benjamin's term for that special quality of art: "its presence in time and space, its unique existence at the place where it happens to be."[54] Olive applies Adorno's reading of this concept to selected movements from *Hommage à Mihály András 12 Microludes for String Quartet*, Op. 13 (1977–78). In so doing he explains how ephemeral relationships between past and present are at once maintained and disrupted in these musical aphorisms. In the following chapter, Ulrich Mosch asks how the past manifests itself in Kurtág's work in terms of compositional technique and how this is related to the evolution of his dual career as a composer and as a pianist. In answering these questions, Mosch carefully explains how arrangement, quotation, recourse to models, and allusion can be differentiated in specific pieces or movements, notably from *Játékok* and *Officium breve in memoriam Andreae Szervánszky*, Op. 28 (1984–89), for string quartet. Special attention is given to the idea of homage. Kurtág has written over one hundred such pieces in which he expresses his gratitude to composers, musicians, and other worthy individuals. Mosch then sets these aspects of Kurtág's work in a broader perspective by comparing them with those of three contemporaries: Bernd Alois Zimmermann (1918–70), Helmut Lachenmann (1935–), and Wolfgang Rihm (1952–).

Alan Gillmor and Friedemann Sallis draw upon themes from the previous chapters and apply them to compositions from Anhalt's late work. Beginning with the observation that all living art taps into the personal and collective past, Gillmor examines this aspect of Anhalt's *Sonance•Resonance (Welche Töne?)* for orchestra (1989).[55] His careful study of quotation and allusion in this work reveals links between it and events that marked Anhalt's development fifty years earlier; it allows Gillmor to raise fascinating questions concerning the interrelatedness of the compositional subject (the composer in the work) and the biographical subject (the composer of the work), considerations first raised in this book by Florian Scheding. In his study of Anhalt's last composition, *Four Portraits from Memory* (piano version, 2005–7), Sallis looks at how memory intersects with both compositional technique and content in the third of the four portraits. He also takes another look at Anhalt's *Alternative Voices* (1984) and suggests ways in which this important contribution to theory can be seen as a kind of manifesto in which Anhalt announced many of the themes that would preoccupy him as a composer, one of these being the significance of memory.⁵⁶

Fittingly, the book ends with a Final Word from István Anhalt. On 6 July 2008, Robin Elliott interviewed Anhalt in his home in Kingston, Ontario. The discussion's point of departure was Lydia Goehr's article "Music and Musicians in Exile: The Romantic Legacy of a Double Life."⁵⁷ Anhalt takes issue with Goehr's dialectic methodology and her assertion that the nineteenth-century idea of a double life pervades our thinking about exiled artists and intellectuals. He suggests that Goehr's focus on "doubleness" is distorting and that "multipleness" would be more appropriate for understanding the impact migration can have on artists and their work.⁵⁸ He then reflects on how composers deal with memory and are able, or not able, to make "peace with their past."

Notes

1. Henry Pachter, "On Being an Exile: An Old-Timer's Personal and Political Memoir," in *The Legacy of German Refugee Intellectuals*, ed. Robert Boyers (New York: Schocken, 1972), 21–22.
2. Marshall McLuhan, *Understanding Media: The Extensions of Man*, ed. Terrence Gordon (Corte Madera, CA: Gingko Press 2003), 5.
3. James Joyce, *Finnegans Wake* (Harmondsworth: Penguin, 1976), 558.
4. Over the past twenty years this topic has been discussed most vigorously by popular music scholars. For a concise survey of this literature see Ian Biddle and Vanessa Knights, "Introduction. National Popular Musics: Betwixt and Beyond the Local and Global," *Music, National Identity and the Politics of Location: Between the Global and the Local*, ed. Ian Biddle and Vanessa Knights (Aldershot: Ashgate, 2007), 1–3. Over the past two decades exile theory has become an area of musicological discourse in which place and displacement are much discussed, particularly in German. English-language contributions, especially those published on this continent, have tended to focus on the migration of Europeans to the United States; see Reinhold Brinkmann and Christoph Wolff, eds., *Driven into Paradise: The Musical Migration from Nazi Germany to the United States* (Berkeley: University of California Press, 1999). Contributions in other languages tend to take a broader, more multilateral approach. See, for example, Ferdinand Zehentreiter, ed., *Komponisten im Exil: 16 Künstlerschicksale des 20. Jahrhunderts* (Berlin: Henschel Verlag, 2008), which also takes note of composers such as Hans Eisler, Isang Yun, and Iannis Xenakis, all of whom moved in other directions. Composers are also addressing this aspect of their careers in their work: see for example reference to Vinko Globokar's *Les Émigrés* (1982–86) and *Élégie balkanique* (1992) in Sigrid Konrad, "« Das Vergessen ist ausgeschlossen ». Vinko Globokar und der Balkan," *dissonanz/dissonance* 92 (December 2005): 8–11. For recent Canadian contributions see Paul Helmer,

Growing with Canada: The Émigré Tradition in Canadian Music (Montreal and Kingston: McGill-Queen's University Press, 2009), and Sylvain Caron and Michel Duchesneau, eds., *Musique, art et religion dans l'entre-deux-guerres* (Lyon: Symétrie, 2009).
5 Eric Hobsbawm, *Age of Extremes: The Short Twentieth Century 1914–1991* (London: Abacus, 1994), 119.
6 The contributions of composers such as Iang Yun (1917–95), Tōru Takemitsu (1930–96), and Franghiz Ali-Zadeh (1947–), to mention only three, has meant that the term "Western" should now be considered a historically contingent term for the qualification of art music.
7 Homi Bhabha, *The Location of Culture* (London and New York: Routledge, 2006), 7.
8 Biddle and Knights, "Introduction," 11.
9 Darius Milhaud, *Ma vie heureuse* (Bourg-la-Reine: Zurfluh, 1998), 9.
10 Marie-Noëlle Lavoie has pointed out that the study of Milhaud's music has tended to downplay the importance of his religion in his work and that this aspect of his identity must also be understood as an evolving rather than a static phenomenon. Marie Noëlle Lavoie, "Identité, emprunts et régionalisme: judaïcité dans les oeuvres de Milhaud durant l'entre-deux-guerres," *Musique, art et religion dans l'entre-deux-guerres*, 68–69.
11 David Beard and Kenneth Gloag, *Musicology: The Key Concepts* (London and New York: Routledge, 2005), 131–33.
12 Reinhard Strohm, "Centre and Periphery: Mainstream and Provincial Music," in *Companion to Medieval and Renaissance Music*, ed. Tess Knighton and David Fallows (Berkeley: University of California Press, 1992), 55.
13 Carl Dahlhaus, *Nineteenth-Century Music* (Berkeley: University of California Press, 1989), 90 (Dahlhaus's emphasis). Ironically the universal/nationalist model has taken firmest root in North America, one of the erstwhile "peripheral" regions and a cultural backwater (except for a few urban centres on the eastern side of the continent) until well into the twentieth century. David Beveridge, writing at the end of the twentieth century, observed that this model remained a determining factor in many of the most widely read American histories of music still in use today. David Beveridge, "Dvořák's 'Dumka' and the Concept of Nationalism in Music Historiography," *Journal of Musicological Research* 12 (1993): 304.
14 The use of the metaphor was of course widespread. A typical example can be found in Josef Rufer's lecture entitled "Arnold Schoenberg" presented at Darmstadt in June 1949. "Wir sehen, es finden sich langsam immer mehr Musiker, die mit Schoenberg gegen den Strom schwimmen, und es ist vielleicht heute nicht mehr so vermessen zu sagen, daß diese Gegenströmung auch einmal Hauptströmung warden kann." Rufer cited in Doris Lanz, "'Es ist aber nur Mittel, nicht "Ziel"' Zur Rolle der Zwölftontechnik bei Sándor Veress und Wladimir Vogel um 1950," in *Sándor Veress. Komponist—Lehre—Forscher*, ed. Doris Lanz and Anselm Gerhard, Schweizer Beiträge zur Musikforschung Vol. 11, ed. Anselm Gerhard, Hans-Joachim Hinrichsen, Laurenz Lütteken, and Klaus Pietschmann (Kassel: Bärenreiter, 2008), 88. Rufer's complete text can be found in Josef Rufer, "Arnold Schoenberg [1949]," in *Im Zenit der*

Moderne: Die Internationalen Ferienkurse für Neue Musik Darmstadt 1946–1966, Vol. 3, ed. Gianmario Borio and Hermann Danuser (Freiburg i.Br.: Rombach Verlag, 1997), 43–57.

15 "The diminished seventh chord, which sounds false in salon music, is correct and filled with expression at the beginning of Beethoven's Sonata opus 111. Not only is the chord not patched in here, not only does it emerge from the constructive layout of the phrase, but the *niveau* of Beethoven's technique as a whole, the tendency between the most extreme dissonance that was possible for him and the consonance, the harmonic perspective assimilating all melodic events, the dynamic conception of tonality as a whole, all confer on this chord its specific weight. However, the historical process through which this chord has lost its weight is irreversible." Theodor W. Adorno, *Philosophy of New Music*, ed. and trans. Robert Hullot-Kentor (Minneapolis: University of Minnesota Press, 2006), 33. For an excellent summary of this aspect of Adorno's work in English, see Max Paddison, *Adorno's Aesthetics of Music* (Cambridge University Press, 1997), 65–107.

16 For example, towards the end of the section entitled "Stravinsky and the Restoration," Adorno reminds his reader that for those listeners schooled in German and Austrian music, among whom Adorno clearly situates himself, the experience of frustrated expectation in the music of Debussy is familiar. Adorno, *Philosophy of New Music*, 138.

17 Carl Dahlhaus, "Geschichte und Geschichten," *Die Musik der fünfziger Jahre. Versuch einer Revision*, ed. Carl Dahlhaus, Veröffentlichung des Instituts für Neue Musik und Musikerziehung, Vol. 26 (Mainz: Schott, 1985), 9–10. This idea that composers could see themselves as "actors" in an otherwise "historicially determined" process was contradictory and constitutes a misreading of Adorno's *Philosophy*. In a response written in 1950 to a polemical critique of his book, Adorno stated, "As a consequence of the philosophy for which I am responsible, I have implicitly applied to music a concept of objective spirit that asserts itself over and above the heads of individual artists as well as beyond the merits of individual works." Theodor Adorno, "'Misunderstandings': Adorno's Response to the Commentary on *Philosophy of New Music* (1950)," in *Philosophy of New Music*, 165. Of course history shows that ideologically motivated composers rarely allow mere logical contradictions to get in their way.

18 "Tout compositeur est *inutile* en dehors des recherches sérielles." Pierre Boulez, *Relevés d'apprenti* (Paris: Seuil, 1966), 271 (Boulez's emphasis).

19 John Cage, radio interview with Charles Amirkhanian, KPFA, Berkeley, 14 January 1992, cited in *Writings through John Cage's Music, Poetry, and Art*, ed. David W. Bernstein and Christopher Hatch (Chicago: University of Chicago Press, 2001), 1.

20 Mahler cited in Dahlhaus, *Nineteenth-Century Music*, 366.

21 Carl Dahlhaus, *Between Romanticism and Modernism: Four Studies in the Music of the Later Nineteenth Century* (Berkeley: University of California Press, 1980), 85.

22 For example, in his address to the All Union Congress of Composers in January 1948, Andrei Zhdanov, claiming to cite Mikhail Glinka, stated, "Music is created by the people, we artists only arrange it." Andrei A. Zhdanov, *Essays*

on *Literature, Philosophy, and Music* (New York: International Publishers, 1950), 83. For an exhaustive account of the so-called Zhdanovshchina (the musical show trials orchestrated by Zhdanov), see Alexander Werth, *Musical Uproar in Moscow* (London: Turnstile Press, 1949).

23 Zhdanov, *Essays*, 93–95.
24 Zoltán Kodály, "Hungarian Folksongs," in *The Selected Writings of Zoltán Kodály*, ed. Ferenc Bónis, trans. Lili Halápy and Fred Macnicol (London: Boosey & Hawkes, 1974), 10.
25 Biddle and Knights, "Introduction," 3.
26 Giselher Schubert, "The Aesthetic Premises of a Nazi Conception of Music," in *Music and Nazism: Art under Tyranny, 1933–1945*, ed. Michael H. Kater and Albrecht Riethmüller (Laaber: Laaber Verlag, 2003), 73.
27 The inquisitive reader might wonder why we have not included articles on one of Hungary's most famous exiles after Béla Bartók, György Ligeti. The main reason is precisely because there is such a wealth of secondary literature on this aspect of Ligeti's career. Consequently, we have decided to focus our book on other composers. Indeed Ligeti has himself contributed to this topic in numerous interviews and articles: see, for example, György Ligeti, "György Ligeti," in *Mein Judentum*, ed. Hans Jürgen Schultz (Berlin: Kreuz Verlag, 1978).
28 Kurtág also acknowledges Pál Járdányi's contribution to his training as a composer. Bálint András Varga, "A Brief Biography of György Kurtág," *György Kurtág: Three Interviews and Ligeti Homages*, compiled and edited by Bálint András Varga (Rochester: University of Rochester Press, 2009), 115.
29 For more on Veress's impact as a teacher of composition, see Simone Hohmaier, "'Veress war ein Vorbild, aber kein gutter Lehrer.' Zur Frage einer kompositorischen Veress-Rezeption bei Kurtág und Ligeti," and Friedemann Sallis, "Teaching as a Subversive Art. Sándor Veress's '*Billegetőmuzsika* (Fingerlarks)' and György Kurtág's '*Játékok* (Games),'" both in *Sándor Veress. Komponist—Lehrer—Forscher* 142–58 and 159–71 respectively.
30 For a moving account of how he survived, see Mordecai Paldile, "Antal, János Hungary," in *The Righteous among the Nations* (Jerusalem: Jerusalem Publishing House and Yad Vashem, 2007), 15–17.
31 István Anhalt, "What Tack to Take? An Autobiographical Sketch (Life in Progress …)," *Queen's Quarterly* 92/1 (1985 spring): 101.
32 For more information on Anhalt's biography, see *Istvan Anhalt: Pathways and Memory*, ed. Robin Elliott and Gordon E. Smith (Montreal and Kingston: McGill-Queen's University Press, 2001).
33 György Ligeti, "Laudatio auf György Kurtág," in Ligeti, *Gesammelte Schriften*, vol. 1, ed. Monika Lichtenfeld (Mainz: Schott and the Paul Sacher Foundation, 2007), 488. For more on this aspect of Kurtág's career, see François Polloli, "La continuité fragmentée: un chemin allant du *Quartetto per archi* op. 1 vers les *Kafka-Fragmente* op. 24," in *Gestes, fragments, timbres: la musique de György Kurtág*, ed. Márta Grabócz and Jean Paul Olive (Paris: L'Harmattan, 2008), 95–115; and Friedemann Sallis, "La musica di camera di György Kurtág (1950–2005). Dall'estetica del frammento ai 'programmi da concerto,'" *Rivista di Analisi e Teoria Musicale* 16/1 Kurtág e l'*Hommage* a Schumann: frammento e citazione, construzione formale e ascolto (2010): 7–24.

34 In a letter to Ligeti written in 1957, Veress noted that he had not planned on settling in Switzerland when he left Hungary. However, by 1957, he was very happy that things had worked out that way. Veress, cited in Friedemann Sallis, "'We play with the music and the music plays with us': Sándor Veress and His Student György Ligeti," in *Remembering Ligeti*, ed. Louise Ducheneau and Wolfgang Marx (Suffolk: Boyden and Brewer, forthcoming).

35 Rachel Beckles Willson, "A New Voice and a New Twentieth Century? An Experiment with Sándor Veress," in *Sándor Veress. Komponist—Lehrer—Forscher*, 14–15.

36 John Weissman, "Guide to Contemporary Hungarian Composers. (1) The Early Decades of the Twentieth Century," *Tempo* 35 (1955): 30.

37 For more on this aspect of Kurtág's career, see Rachel Beckles Willson, *Ligeti, Kurtág and Hungarian Music during the Cold War* (Cambridge and New York: Cambridge University Press, 2007), 127–62.

38 Varga, "A Brief Biography of György Kurtág," 115.

39 The Saint Lawrence River originates at the outflow of Lake Ontario between Kingston, Ontario, on the north bank, and Cape Vincent, New York, on the south bank.

40 Umberto Eco, *The Aesthetics of Chaosmos: The Middle Ages of James Joyce*, trans. Ellen Esrock (Cambridge, MA: Harvard University Press, 1989), 70. See also Eco, *The Role of the Reader: Explorations in the Semiotics of Texts* (Bloomington: Indiana University Press, 1984), 72–76.

41 Joyce, *Finnegans Wake*, 118.

42 Indeed, a significant Canadian thread running through Anhalt's creative and scholarly achievements is his concern for how the individual engages with this new environment, relating his work to that of Marshall McLuhan, Jean Le Moyne, Glenn Gould, and Paul Théberge, to name only a few.

43 The exception that proves the rule is Beckles Willson's examination of Kurtág's presence in Budapest as a composer and pedagogue. Beckles Willson, *Ligeti, Kurtág and Hungarian Music during the Cold War*, 137–62.

44 For more on this aspect of Kurtág's work see Friedemann Sallis, "Fleurs recyclées. Sur les traces de relations souterraines dans l'*Officium breve in memoriam Andreae Szervánszky* opus 28 pour quatuor à cordes de György Kurtág," *Circuit. Musiques contemporaines* 18/1 La frabrique des oeuvres (2008): 47–54.

45 The original title "Kantáta Előpatakon" [Cantata in Előpatak] was later changed to "Délibáb Előpatakon" [Mirage in Előpatakon] and has since been published under this title in English translation. See István Anhalt, "From 'Mirage' to *Simulacrum* and 'Afterthought,'" in *Pathways and Memory*, 421–23.

46 In a letter written to George Rochberg on 7 February 1982, Anhalt commented on his move to Kingston ten years earlier and drew an indirect relationship between place and compositional practice. "The composition work just continued here. It does not depend on *locus* as far as I am concerned.... I found out I was able to listen better here to my inner voices, and the character of this historical city awoke in me interests that were slumbering for a while before." Alan M. Gillmor, ed., *Eagle Minds: Selected Correspondence of Istvan Anhalt and George Rochberg 1961–2005* (Waterloo, ON: Wilfrid Laurier University Press, 2007), 122.

47 Anhalt was presented with a Juno Award for this composition in 2005.
48 Shortly after having completed *The Tents of Abraham*, Anhalt wrote that the work emerged from his reflections on the origins of the "awful situation existing between Israelis and Palestinians.... The outcome of all of this is the new piece, quite likely my 'rounding-out' statement about wanderers/searchers ... a 'role' and 'type' I have known only too well." Anhalt to Rochberg, 1 October 2003, Gillmor, ed., *Eagle Minds*, 403.
49 Whereas Seiber moved to the United Kingdom in 1935, Anhalt eventually settled in Canada in 1949. At the time, the Dominion of Canada was still seen by many people, including anglophone Canadians, as a kind of ex-colonial extension of Great Britain.
50 Helmut Kallmann, "The István Anhalt Fonds," in *Pathways and Memory*, 234–54. In 2004 the National Library of Canada and the National Archives of Canada were amalgamated and became Library and Archives Canada. This change has had a considerable impact on the musical collections of both former institutions.
51 After Russian, the foreign language that occurs most frequently in these pages is German, which comes a distant third at 1.8 per cent. Friedemann Sallis, "La classification et la gestion des manuscrits musicaux de la Collection György Kurtág conservée à la Fondation Paul Sacher," in *Gestes, fragments, timbres*, 46–47.
52 Arnold Schoenberg, "Problems of Harmony 1934," in *Style and Idea*, ed. Leonard Stein, trans. Leo Black (Berkeley: University of California Press, 1984), 270.
53 In an interview given in 1993, Kurtág explained that during his stay in Paris in 1956–57 he sought help from Marianne Stein, a psychologist whose specialty was helping artists find their way back to creative activity. She turned Schoenberg's question into a therapeutic tool, admonishing him to compose step by step using two notes at a time. György Kurtág, "Komponisten-Portrait György Kurtág entwickelt im Gespräch mit Ulrich Dibelius," in *Ligeti und Kurtág in Salzburg*, Programmbuch des Salzburger Festivals, ed. Ulrich Dibelius (Zurich: Residenz Verlag, 1993), 90–91.
54 Walter Benjamin, "The Work of Art in the Age of Mechanical Reproduction," in *Essays and Reflections*, ed. Hannah Arendt (New York: Schocken Books, 1969), 220.
55 In many ways this essay can be seen as a sequel to Alan M. Gillmor, "Echos of Time and the River," in *Taking a Stand: Essays in Honour of John Beckwith*, ed. Timothy J. McGee (Toronto: University of Toronto Press, 1995), 5–44.
56 István Anhalt, *Alternative Voices: Essays on Contemporary Vocal and Choral Composition* (Toronto: University of Toronto Press, 1984).
57 Lydia Goehr, "Music and Musicians in Exile: The Romantic Legacy of a Double Life," in *The Quest for Voice: On Music, Politics and the Limits of Philosophy*, The 1997 Ernest Bloch Lectures (Oxford: Clarendon Press, 1998), 174–207. The essay is reprinted in a somewhat modified form in Brinkmann and Wolff, eds., *Driven into Paradise*, 66–91.
58 Goehr does concede this point in her text. She notes that her use of doubleness "as a technique of philosophical description" should not be understood as arbitrarily limiting the scope of the migrant artist's relationships with his or

her context. Indeed migration implies that the person is "multiply situated," i.e., taken beyond the limits of the familiar and obliged to recognize that "there is more than one way to see the world." Goehr, *The Quest for Voice*, 203.

Bibliography

Adorno, Theodor W. *Philosophy of New Music*. Edited and translated by Robert Hullot-Kentor. Minneapolis: University of Minnesota Press, 2006.

Anhalt, István. *Alternative Voices: Essays on Contemporary Vocal and Choral Composition*. Toronto: University of Toronto Press, 1984.

———. "What Tack to Take? An Autobiographical Sketch (Life in Progress ...)." *Queen's Quarterly* 92/1 (1985 spring): 96–107.

Beard, David and Kenneth Gloag. *Musicology: The Key Concepts*. New York: Routledge, 2005.

Beckles Willson, Rachel. *Ligeti, Kurtág and Hungarian Music during the Cold War*. Cambridge and New York: Cambridge University Press, 2007.

———. "A New Voice and a New Twentieth Century? An Experiment with Sándor Veress." *Sándor Veress. Komponist—Lehrer—Forscher*. Edited by Doris Lanz and Anselm Gerhard. Schweizer Beiträge zur Musikforschung Vol. 11. Edited by Anselm Gerhard, Hans-Joachim Hinrichsen, Laurenz Lütteken, and Klaus Pietschmann, 14–19. Kassel: Bärenreiter, 2008.

Benjamin, Walter. *Essays and Reflections*. Edited by Hannah Arendt. Translated by Harry Zohn. New York: Schocken Books, 1969.

Bernstein, David W. and Christopher Hatch, eds. *Writings through John Cage's Music, Poetry, and Art*. Chicago: University of Chicago Press, 2001.

Beveridge, David. "Dvořák's 'Dumka' and the Concept of Nationalism in Music Historiography." *Journal of Musicological Research* 12 (1993): 303–25.

Bhabha, Homi. *The Location of Culture*. New York: Routledge, 2006.

Biddle, Ian and Vanessa Knights, eds. *Music, National Identity and the Politics of Location: Between the Global and the Local*. Aldershot: Ashgate, 2007.

Boulez, Pierre. *Relevés d'apprenti*. Paris: Seuil, 1966.

Brinkmann, Reinhold and Christoph Wolff, eds. *Driven into Paradise: The Musical Migration from Nazi Germany to the United States*. Berkeley: University of California Press, 1999.

Caron, Sylvain and Michel Duchesneau, eds. *Musique, art et religion dans l'entre-deux-guerres*. Lyon: Symétrie, 2009.

Dahlhaus, Carl. *Between Romanticism and Modernism: Four Studies in the Music of the Later Nineteenth Century*. Translated by Mary Whittal. Berkeley: University of California Press, 1980.

———. "Geschichte und Geschichten." *Die Musik der fünfziger Jahre. Versuch einer Revision*. Edited by Carl Dahlhaus, Veröffentlichung des Instituts für Neue Musik und Musikerziehung, Vol. 26, 9–20. Mainz: Schott, 1985.

———. *Nineteenth-Century Music*. Translated by J. Bradford Robinson. Berkeley: University of California Press, 1989.

Eco, Umberto. *The Aesthetics of Chaosmos: The Middle Ages of James Joyce*. Translated by Ellen Esrock. Cambridge, MA: Harvard University Press, 1989.
———. *The Role of the Reader: Explorations in the Semiotics of Texts*. Bloomington: Indiana University Press, 1984.
Elliott, Robin and Gordon E. Smith, eds. *Istvan Anhalt: Pathways and Memory*. Montreal and Kingston: McGill-Queen's University Press, 2001.
Gillmor, Alan M., ed. *Eagle Minds: Selected Correspondence of Istvan Anhalt and George Rochberg 1961–2005*. Waterloo, ON: Wilfrid Laurier University Press, 2007.
———. "Echos of Time and the River." In *Taking a Stand: Essays in Honour of John Beckwith*, edited by Timothy J. McGee, 5–44. Toronto: University of Toronto Press, 1995.
Goehr, Lydia. *The Quest for Voice: On Music, Politics and the Limits of Philosophy*. The 1997 Ernest Bloch Lectures. Oxford: Clarendon Press, 1998.
Helmer, Paul. *Growing with Canada: The Émigré Tradition in Canadian Music*. Montreal and Kingston: McGill-Queen's University Press, 2009.
Hobsbawm, Eric. *Age of Extremes: The Short Twentieth Century 1914–1991*. London: Abacus, 1994.
Hohmaier, Simone. "'Veress war ein Vorbild, aber kein gutter Lehrer.' Zur Frage einer kompositorischen Veress-Rezeption bei Kurtág und Ligeti." In *Sándor Veress. Komponist—Lehrer—Forscher*. Edited by Doris Lanz and Anselm Gerhard. Schweizer Beiträge zur Musikforschung Vol. 11. Edited by Anselm Gerhard, Hans-Joachim Hinrichsen, Laurenz Lütteken and Klaus Pietschmann, 142–58. Kassel: Bärenreiter, 2008.
Joyce, James. *Finnegans Wake*. Harmondsworth: Penguin, 1976.
Kodály, Zoltán. *The Selected Writings of Zoltán Kodály*. Edited by Ferenc Bónis. Translated by Lili Halápy and Fred Macnicol. London: Boosey & Hawkes, 1974.
Konrad, Sigrid. "« Das Vergessen ist ausgeschlossen ». Vinko Globokar und der Balkan." *dissonanz/dissonance* 92 (December 2005): 8–11.
Kurtág, György. "Komponisten-Portrait György Kurtág entwickelt im Gespräch mit Ulrich Dibelius." In *Ligeti und Kurtág in Salzburg*, edited by Ulrich Dibelius, 88–94. Programmbuch des Salzburger Festivals. Zurich: Residenz Verlag, 1993.
Lanz, Doris. "'Es ist aber nur Mittel, nicht "Ziel"' Zur Rolle der Zwölftontechnik bei Sándor Veress und Wladimir Vogel um 1950." In *Sándor Veress. Komponist—Lehrer—Forscher*. Edited by Doris Lanz and Anselm Gerhard. Schweizer Beiträge zur Musikforschung Vol. 11. Edited by Anselm Gerhard, Hans-Joachim Hinrichsen, Laurenz Lütteken and Klaus Pietschmann, 88–106. Kassel: Bärenreiter, 2008.
Lavoie, Marie Noëlle. "Identité, emprunts et régionalisme: judaïcité dans les oeuvres de Milhaud durant l'entre-deux-guerres." In *Musique, art et religion dans l'entre-deux-guerres*, edited by Sylvain Caron and Michel Duchesneau, 57–70. Lyon: Symétrie, 2009.

Ligeti, György. "Laudatio auf György Kurtág." In Ligeti, *Gesammelte Schriften*, Vol. 1, edited by Monika Lichtenfeld, 485–89. Mainz: Schott and the Paul Sacher Foundation, 2007.

———. "György Ligeti." *Mein Judentum*. Edited by Hans Jürgen Schultz. Berlin: Kreuz Verlag, 1978.

McLuhan, Marshall. *Understanding Media: The Extensions of Man*. Edited by Terrence Gordon. Corte Madera, CA: Gingko Press, 2003.

Milhaud, Darius. *Ma vie heureuse*. Bourg-la-Reine: Zurfluh, 1998.

Pachter, Henry. "On Being an Exile: An Old-Timer's Personal and Political Memoir." In *The Legacy of German Refugee Intellectuals*, edited by Robert Boyers, 12–51. New York: Schocken, 1972.

Paddison, Max. *Adorno's Aesthetics of Music*. Cambridge University Press, 1997.

Paldile, Mordecai. *The Righteous among the Nations*. Jerusalem: Jerusalem Publishing House and Yad Vashem, 2007.

Polloli, François. "La continuité fragmentée: un chemin allant du *Quartetto per archi* op. 1 vers les *Kafka-Fragmente* op. 24." In *Gestes, fragments, timbres: la musique de György Kurtág*, ed. Márta Grabócz and Jean Paul Olive, 95–115. Paris: L'Harmattan, 2008.

Rufer, Josef. "Arnold Schoenberg [1949]." *Im Zenit der Moderne: Die Internationalen Ferienkurse für Neue Musik Darmstadt 1946–1966*, Vol. 3, edited by Gianmario Borio and Hermann Danuser, 43–57. Freiburg i.Br.: Rombach Verlag, 1997.

Sallis, Friedemann. "La classification et la gestion des manuscrits musicaux de la Collection György Kurtág conservée à la Fondation Paul Sacher." In *Gestes, fragments, timbres: la musique de György Kurtág*, edited by Márta Grabócz and Jean Paul Olive, 39–50. Paris: L'Harmattan, 2008.

———. "Fleurs recyclées. Sur les traces de relations souterraines dans l'*Officium breve in memoriam Andreae Szervánszky* opus 28 pour quatuor à cordes de György Kurtág." *Circuit. Musiques contemporaines* 18/1 La frabrique des oeuvres (2008): 45–58.

———. "La musica di camera di György Kurtág (1950–2005). Dall'estetica del frammento ai 'programmi da concerto.'" *Rivista di Analisi e Teoria Musicale* 16/1 Kurtág e l'*Hommage* a Schumann: frammento e citazione, construzione formale e ascolto (2010): 7–24.

———. "Teaching as a Subversive Art. Sándor Veress's '*Billegetőmuzsika* (Fingerlarks)' and György Kurtág's '*Játékok* (Games).'" In *Sándor Veress. Komponist— Lehrer—Forscher*. Edited by Doris Lanz and Anselm Gerhard. Schweizer Beiträge zur Musikforschung Vol. 11. Edited by Anselm Gerhard, Hans-Joachim Hinrichsen, Laurenz Lütteken and Klaus Pietschmann, 159–71. Kassel: Bärenreiter, 2008.

———. "'We play with the music and the music plays with us': Sándor Veress and His Student György Ligeti." In *Remembering Ligeti*, edited by Louise Ducheneau and Wolfgang Marx. Suffolk: Boyden and Brewer, forthcoming.

Schoenberg, Arnold. *Style and Idea*. Edited by Leonard Stein. Translated by Leo Black. Berkeley: University of California Press, 1984.
Schubert, Giselher. "The Aesthetic Premises of a Nazi Conception of Music." In *Music and Nazism: Art under Tyranny, 1933–1945*, edited by Michael H. Kater and Albrecht Riethmüller, 64–74. Laaber: Laaber Verlag, 2003.
Strohm, Reinhard. "Centre and Periphery: Mainstream and Provincial Music." In *Companion to Medieval and Renaissance Music*, edited by Tess Knighton and David Fallows, 55–59. Berkeley: University of California Press, 1992.
Varga, Bálint András. "A Brief Biography of György Kurtág." *György Kurtág: Three Interviews and Ligeti Homages*. Compiled and edited by Bálint András Varga, 115–16. Rochester: University of Rochester Press, 2009.
Weissman, John. "Guide to Contemporary Hungarian Composers. (1) The Early Decades of the Twentieth Century." *Tempo* 35 (1955): 24–30.
Werth, Alexander. *Musical Uproar in Moscow*. London: Turnstile Press, 1949.
Zehentreiter, Ferdinand, ed. *Komponisten im Exil: 16 Künstlerschicksale des 20. Jahrhunderts*. Berlin: Henschel Verlag, 2008.
Zhdanov, Andrei A. *Essays on Literature, Philosophy, and Music*. New York: International Publishers, 1950.

First Word

ONE

István Anhalt: A Character Sketch

John Beckwith

As secretary of the newly formed Canadian League of Composers in the mid-1950s, I made several trips to Montreal in order to meet with colleagues there. On one of these occasions—it was, I think, in 1954—my hosts were Beate and István Anhalt. Our conversations about music and composing were intense; Anhalt's personality had a strong impact, and I was deeply impressed when he played for me his then-new Piano Fantasia. I later wrote about this and other pieces of his from that decade in the *University of Toronto Quarterly* and the *Canadian Music Journal*.[1] His performance came back to my memory more recently when I had the moving experience at the Anhalts' home in Kingston of hearing him read at the piano another brand-new score, *Four Portraits from Memory*.

In those writings of the 1950s, I observed that Anhalt's works had a common trait of starting with an outburst of dense information and proceeding with a kind of unravelling of its implications. On reflection, this corresponds to his approach to topics of study, and to creative projects as well. His initial enthusiasms led him to not only devour the literature but also to contact, by letter or in person, the known international experts. When planning the first McGill electronic-music studio (in the early 1960s in a coach house at the rear of the Faculty of Music building), he felt compelled to visit Hugh LeCaine in Ottawa, the fledgling University of Toronto studio, Max Matthews and Lejaren Hiller in the United States, and various exponents in France, Germany, and England. Nothing of significance was allowed to escape those penetrating eyes of his. For him, this wasn't cultural tourism or dabbling, but the road to mastery—in-depth mastery.

One night in 1959 he rang me in great excitement. He had just come from conducting the dress rehearsal of his Symphony No. 1 and was bursting to tell me about it. He said it was one of the really high-level musical experiences of his life, and the animation in his voice confirmed this. I later learned that he had been so keyed up during rehearsals that he required emergency medical attention for a sore shoulder.

In only a few years we had formed a close and enduring friendship. Between 1956 and the end of 2007 I have received 181 letters from him (not counting the years 1997 through 2004 for which the files are at present missing). My letters to him may number close to that. (He keeps copies of the letters he writes; I don't keep copies of mine.) As with his extensive correspondence with another composer, George Rochberg, the letters trace mutual professional concerns, the course of our respective creative and scholarly projects, family news, and commentary on reading preoccupations (exceptionally voluminous on Anhalt's part) and on the state of the world. In the published letters to and from Rochberg,[2] the more personal parts have been largely edited out; that's understandable, but to my mind it's a pity that the editor, Alan Gillmor, while retaining the warm salutations of both composers ("George, dear friend," "My dear Isty"), has omitted the sign-off line, which in Anhalt's case I'm sure was always "Love, István." Anhalt has always been direct in sending his long-time friends, regardless of gender, his "fondness," "affection," and, yes, his "Love." It's just part of his wholehearted, generous nature. He is a loving person.

Our friendship is sustained not just in the correspondence but in regular phone chats and in many visits involving our respective families. I can recall not only shared times with our wives and growing children in Toronto, but also similar meals and outings on Montreal Mountain, on another mountain overlooking Barton, Vermont, and in the Anhalts' Montreal home, as well as later adventures with them at their sabbatical digs in Cambridge and their beautiful Kingston residence. One of the Montreal dinner parties in the late 1960s centred around an intense discussion of the psychology of artists; at another I was licking my wounds after a disastrous first rehearsal, and felt supported and soothed by the understanding of my friends. In Vermont in 1971, István and I climbed to the top of one hill together, talking of the burdens and also the rewards of our lives. I remember that climb as a vivid and existential episode. On a later occasion, in Kingston, one evening around the fire, he read aloud an early draft of what would later become the *Winthrop* libretto.

His letters convey how thoroughly organized he always is, but not the extent to which in social and family situations he is always an *organizer*. "Now look here" is a characteristic opening phrase in the planning of expeditions—not in the sense of an autocratic command but in the sense of "let's get this show on the road" or "let's organize ourselves." In conversation, almost as in writing, he will begin an observation or an account with "Consider the following"—after which you can almost hear "colon" and "pause" before he goes on with a discourse that is always organized.

His research on Anhalt genealogy and his contacts during return visits to Hungary have roused memories, expressed in the odd article as well as in his letters. While at Library and Archives Canada in Ottawa a few years ago, working on the Anhalt orchestral repertoire, I was permitted to read the script of his play *Oppenheimer*, originally planned as an opera libretto. (It really should be performed by some enterprising Canadian theatre company.) I also read his unpublished autobiography, which filled in some of the gaps in the reminiscences he has often been moved to include in his letters. The standard versions of his CV rightly emphasize the horrors he faced in the Second World War and its aftermath. We may too easily forget the less dramatic early parts of his story; he grew to early maturity in a rich pre-war cultural milieu. Its intellectual stimulus is obvious; a more unexpected strain is the attraction he says he felt for thirties movies and music. As a teenager he adored the Rogers and Astaire films, and tried to notate their music by ear. The vocal trio of *La Tourangelle* owes at least some of its texture and harmony to his memories of the Andrews Sisters in early recordings. He once startled me by singing almost the whole of the sentimental Al Jolson hit "Sonny Boy." Growing up then in Budapest, US pop culture represented exoticism.

I wasn't in Montreal for the Symphony premiere, but later heard the work at the 1960 composers' conference in Stratford, where it had a profound effect. This is also where he and I both encountered George Rochberg for the first time. In 1969 I went to Buffalo for the first performance of *Foci* at the Albright-Knox Gallery. He now claims it was an unsatisfactory performance, but it came across powerfully in the unique performance space with a visual component in the form of projections. In the early '70s came the premiere in Toronto of *La Tourangelle* under Marius Constant, and I could appreciate up close how Anhalt's adrenalin starts to flow under rehearsal pressure. This phenomenon came into even closer view when I played one of the keyboard parts in the Toronto performance of *Foci*. (The second keyboardist was John Hawkins.) On the podium, Anhalt was not just keyed up, but at times almost frantic. His musical control never wavered, but he couldn't hide his impatience with performers and details of production in this complicated score (the little mouth organ, the offstage "hammer-man," the recorded multilingual voices—they all had to be perfect). There was concentration, a lot of tension, but in the end I felt quite thrilled to be so involved. On one occasion Kathleen McMorrow asked Anhalt what language he swore in, noting that Hungarian is a language especially rich in profanity, and he said English. In rehearsals I can't say I ever heard him swear. His spoken and written English has a special flavour. In a letter of 1997 his love of polysyllables reached its peak: "We are both," he writes, "awfully (and happily) unencapsulatable in words. Let's not even try." And after the seven-syllable neologism, as if astonished at his own invention, he inserts in parentheses "(a *Wow* word!)." Once at a concert reception in Toronto I found him in deep conversation with an Anglican priest, Reverend Brian Freeland. Shortly afterwards he asked me, "What is the name of that man of the cloth?" The locution "man of the cloth" is, I think, rare among native English speakers, but it seemed just right coming from István. In a reminiscent passage in one letter he mentioned what a pleasure it was in pre-war years to admire the figures of the young women of Budapest. I replied that I thought Canadian men were no less appreciative of feminine beauty than Hungarian men, to which he wrote back that he would concede the point, "if not *a priori* at least *a posteriori*."

About his generosity: once, at a composers' gathering at Queen's, he chaired a panel whose members included Jean Coulthard and John Weinzweig. Anhalt was so generous in recounting their achievements and describing his own appreciation of their music that he used up more than twenty minutes introducing them—and then greatly amused his audience by tapping his watch when one of the panelists started to run over his allotted time. His manner is to cover the topic *in full*, no matter whether it takes twenty minutes of conference time or twenty pages of a letter (and some of his letters are that long). The phone conversations may run on in a similarly generous and full-throttled way, whether about an item in the daily press or a concert or a book on the Kabbalah or a novel by Hardy or Balzac. Sometimes I have to interrupt, in my househusband role, and tell him to wait because I have something on the stove. When I receive a letter, I know I have to either reply or call him, or else there will be his voice on the phone: "Did you get my letter?"

That is not meant as a complaint. During my work on the chapter which I was invited to contribute to the Anhalt symposium-publication *Pathways and Memory*,[3] I had a number of really long and enormously valuable phone talks with him about the formative background of his orchestral repertoire, especially the remarkable "first triptych" of the late 1980s.

He answered all my questions with care, and delved into his researches and composing processes in ways that illuminated for me the richness of reference in these pieces. In a letter a few years after that time, commenting on my frequent use of the phrase "referential content," he quoted the anthropologist Bronislaw Malinowsky: "There is no context-free meaning." His creativity is fundamentally musical but the thoughts are developed in both words and notes. Just last year, in another letter, he reflected on his own work habits in this regard: "I seem to hold, still, that words (if not too many, or too pretentious) *could* help a listener to find his/her way to a composition." The notes, or perhaps the *sounds*, that also give form to his thoughts can be illustrated by the collection of scrap metal pieces which he once proudly showed me in his garage. He had picked them up in a local scrap metal yard and was assembling them for the "destruction of the idols" passage of *The Tents of Abraham*, described in Robin Elliott's review as "a resounding racket."

A few years ago we were in an auto accident together. István offered to drive me to my train after a reception in Kingston. It was dark, and perhaps snowing, and he hit a signpost on the median and smashed the windshield. Neither of us was hurt, but I had a hard time persuading him to stop; he was intent that I had to get to the station, come what may. Eventually we did stop, and, though it was again hard to persuade him, it seemed to me imperative that we call the police since there was evident damage not only to the car but also to city property. When they came, Anhalt kept insisting that priority should be given not to him or his car but to my transportation. Breathalyzer, okay, but I wasn't to miss my train. The solution turned out to be for one of the cops to drive me. (I should add that neither of us had over-imbibed.)

By an accident not of traffic but of fate, we have shared what I call the Composer's Operation. In the early 1990s, a mutual composer friend, Udo Kasemets, had a nasty fall and developed a subdural hematoma, a pressure of blood on his brain which had to be relieved surgically. Then, in 1995, Anhalt, while travelling in Austria, had a similar nasty fall and had to have the same procedure. Not to be outdone, since 2000 I have had it *twice*—I hope never again. Comparing notes on this experience has been another bond between us.

Having had over the years a certain amount of experience in writing and editing, I'm sometimes asked by publishers to assess manuscripts under their consideration. In the early 1980s, the University of Toronto Press approached me concerning the first draft of Anhalt's book *Alternative Voices*.[4] I knew he had been working on this study of new vocal-music devices for some years, dating back to *Cento* and including discussions with not only composers but also philologists, linguists, and others—yet another example of his in-depth immersion in a topic. Despite uneasiness over possible conflicting interests, I agreed to review it. I was struck by the wide range of his findings and the novelty of his concepts, but at the same time found the manuscript disconnected and in need of some polishing in its expression: so, I had to say this in my report. I advised the editors not to publish it until it was revised. I also said that when they sent the report to Anhalt they needn't preserve the usual anonymity of the assessor. (I figured István would recognize my voice anyway.) After they relayed it to him, I anxiously awaited his reaction, fearing I might have put too much of a strain on our friendship. But when it came, that reaction turned out to be one of his most generous. I had tried to present my criticisms constructively, and, by some miracle, far from being hurt by them, he thanked me.

I wonder if my image of a complicated explosion or outburst followed by a working out of its implications, applied to his earlier compositions, applies also to his life. If the outburst is the political stress of his youth in wartime Hungary, the working out could be the gradual unfolding of his studies, his immigration, his immersion in the cultural history of North America, and his still-later immersions in his family background and in Jewish lore. A remarkable series of links makes up that life chain. Our correspondence continues. My letters are typed, but his are always meticulously handwritten in pen and ink, as are his scores. After the harrowing experience of hole-in-the-head surgery he has now had to undergo major eye surgery, but the penmanship remains steady. The phone calls suffer from my loss of hearing, but we continue those too. Returning to Toronto by car from Ottawa in July, Kathleen and I had the spontaneous idea of dropping in on Beate and István, and when we called ahead they said it would be okay. What we discovered on our arrival is that a few days earlier István had gone through a sudden and drastic eye operation. He was recovering from the shock and seemed in a low state, though glad of our visit. His subsequent return to health and vigour has been amazing. In less than a month he was already, as he wrote me, "learning to do things with one eye," talking about his coming premiere by the Kingston Symphony, and telling Friedemann Sallis how to organize the symposium.

I habitually sign my letters to István with "Love, John."

Notes

1. John Beckwith: "Composers in Toronto and Montreal," *University of Toronto Quarterly* 26/1 (October 1956): 47–69; "Recent Orchestral Works by Champagne, Morel, and Anhalt," *Canadian Music Journal* 4/4 (Summer 1960): 44–48.
2. Alan Gillmor, ed., *Eagle Minds: Selected Correspondence of István Anhalt and George Rochberg, 1961–2005* (Waterloo, ON: Wilfrid Laurier University Press, 2007).
3. Robin Elliott and Gordon E. Smith, eds., *István Anhalt: Pathways and Memory* (Montreal and Kingston: McGill-Queen's University Press, 2001).
4. István Anhalt, *Alternative Voices: Essays on Contemporary Vocal and Choral Composition* (Toronto: University of Toronto Press, 1984).

Bibliography

Anhalt, István. *Alternative Voices: Essays on Contemporary Vocal and Choral Composition*. Toronto: University of Toronto Press, 1984.

Beckwith, John. "Composers in Toronto and Montreal." *University of Toronto Quarterly* 26/1 (October 1956): 47–69.

———. "Recent Orchestral Works by Champagne, Morel, and Anhalt." *Canadian Music Journal* 4/4 (Summer 1960): 44–48.

Elliott, Robin and Gordon E. Smith, eds. *István Anhalt: Pathways and Memory*. Montreal and Kingston: McGill-Queen's University Press, 2001.

Gillmor, Allan, ed. *Eagle Minds: Selected Correspondence of István Anhalt and George Rochberg, 1961–2005*. Waterloo, ON: Wilfrid Laurier University Press, 2007.

TWO

Kurtág, as I Know Him

GERGELY SZOKOLAY

GYURIBÁCSI, THE WAY MANY Hungarian musicians of my generation call Kurtág, is my godfather, a close friend of the family.[1] My father, Sándor Szokolay, studied composition together with Kurtág in Ferenc Farkas's class at the Franz Liszt Academy.[2] My parents met at one of Kurtág's Saturday gatherings, organized as an informal language and literature club. In the early 1950s Kurtág and his wife Márta used to host the regular semi-private reading sessions at Szondi utca 95[3] to present great works of literature preferably in their original language, such as Thomas Mann's *Tonio Kröger* in German or Constantin Stanislavski's *An Actor Prepares* in Hungarian.[4] As my mother Sári Szesztay recalls, the handful of literary enthusiasts were mostly students at the Academy, drawn to Kurtág's charismatic personality and driven by an urge to share and thus enhance their artistic experience.[5]

Literature and poetry have always been intimately linked to Kurtág's persona. Not surprisingly, my first encounter with him was also connected to literature. I think I might have been about five, when one afternoon Gyuribácsi came over to our place to read poems from a newly published, wonderfully illustrated children's book. His reading was an unforgettable experience. I can recall one particular poem in detail, with his gestures, funny mimics, expressive movements, and his most serious involvement with the silly, yet multi-layered symbolist story in the poem. Kurtág managed to captivate me so deeply that the imprint of his presence has preserved its original freshness over fifty years later. The word-for-word English translation of the poem is given in example 2-1.[6]

EXAMPLE 2-1 Sándor Weöres, "Orbán," Sándor Weöres and Amy Károlyi, *Tarka forgó 120 vers az év tizenkét hónapjára* [Coloured Windwheel: 120 poems for the twelve months of the year], with illustrations by Piroska Szántó (Budapest: Magvető Könyvkiadó, 1958), p. 25.

"ORBÁN"	"ORBÁN"
Alva jár az Orbán,	Orbán walks in slumber,
tornyot visz az orrán,	on his nose a tower,
trombitások ülnek benne	trumpeters are seated within
három szekér polyván,	on three cartloads of chaff,
– hú! – trombitások	ah! trumpeters
három szekér polyván.	on three cartloads of chaff.
Fújják egyre többen,	More join in the blowing
polyva szerteröppen,	and send the chaff agoing
rémes álmot lát az Orbán	Orbán sees a terrible dream
polyva-fellegekben,	in a chaff cloud appearing,
– hú! – rémes álmot	ah! a terrible dream
polyva-fellegekben.	in a chaff cloud appearing.

This poem was so unlike the fairy tales my grandmother used to read me while cuddled up in bed! Performed by Kurtág, Weöres's verses were a revelation: the brightness of images, the play of words, the intensity of expression, and most importantly, the unpredictable twists of the narrative created an open-ended soundscape that fascinates me to this day. It was like music! I was not told a story; rather I felt as though some unknown magical force had set me up to improvise, allowing me to create my own version of "Orbán" using words, visual images, gestures, and musical sounds. Perhaps this intuitive realization of the connection between spoken word and music was what Kurtág intended to impart. In any case, the experience doubtless played a role in my later decision to become a musician. Long before that, he taught me another important lesson. Gyuribácsi's son, kis Gyuri [little Gyuri], frequently played with my younger brother, Tamás, and I. When the Kurtágs came for a visit, the three of us enjoyed boisterous games and lively wrestling tournaments right in the middle of our apartment, adding an extra degree of excitement to an already tumultuous atmosphere, inevitable in a family of several busy musicians. At some point the grown-ups always had to interfere. When asked to be our referee, öreg Gyuri [old Gyuri] always refused to declare a winner, firmly claiming that we were all winners or losers. Only many years later, when confronted with questions about fairness in partnership and teamwork, did I fully understand the wisdom of this position.

My relationship with Kurtág has always been situated between two well-balanced modes: parental attentiveness to my personal matters and artistic guidance. Since leaving Hungary I have occasionally written letters asking for his opinion or advice. His short written responses, often in the form of references to specific literary works, such as Rilke's *Letters to a Young Poet* or Chekhov's *Ariadne*, offered insightful solutions to difficult situations. For years they remained memorable signposts that shaped my ability to see and understand my experiences in a larger perspective and I was able to use them constructively.

Studying chamber music with Kurtág at the Franz Liszt Academy and playing solo works for him formed the second mode of my relationship with him. Among the many wonderful hours spent together, two projects stand out: work on his Eight Piano Pieces, Op. 3, and on the piano duo version of Stravinsky's *Petrouchka*, which I performed with my brother Balázs for the Hungarian Radio in 1994. One of the most striking aspects of Kurtág's teaching method was its economy of means. He would often reduce a passage to one essential note and then show how it is ornamented by others. By joining it with other similarly reduced passages, we often ended up returning to the same note. This technique resulted in the linking of a number of passages containing widely different types of musical content. He always compared this to rhyme in poetry. Intervals could also be understood as essential elements in a passage. Connecting notes separated by wide intervals is a key to properly performing his compositions. When I worked on his Op. 3, he often asked me to practise leaps by gradually exceeding their distance, while keeping their singing quality. This exercise was not only revealing with regard to the dramatic quality of the intervals in question, but it opened a new way to learn the geography of the instrument.

Shortly before I was to begin my postgraduate studies at the Tchaikovsky Conservatory in Moscow in 1978, I asked him for a warm-up exercise that would remind me of our work together. The provision that I received from him for the journey was "Hommage à Csaijkovszkij," from the first volume of *Játékok* [Games] (see example 2-2). The clusters in this piece, imitating the opening strides of Tchaikovsky's First Piano Concerto, provide a sense of wholeness and flexibility to the palms, setting up the hands to play chords with majestic and noble sound, without harshness or angularity. Furthermore, the large gestures of this piece stimulate blood circulation in the arms, warming up not only the fingers, but the whole body and with it our whole being. The approximate pitch notation offers playful freedom and is intended to connect the performer with the child in each of us, thereby preparing the ground for the building of confidence with regard

EXAMPLE 2-2 György Kurtág, *Játékok* I [Games I] (1973–78) "Hommage à Csajkovszkij" © Editio Musica Budapest.

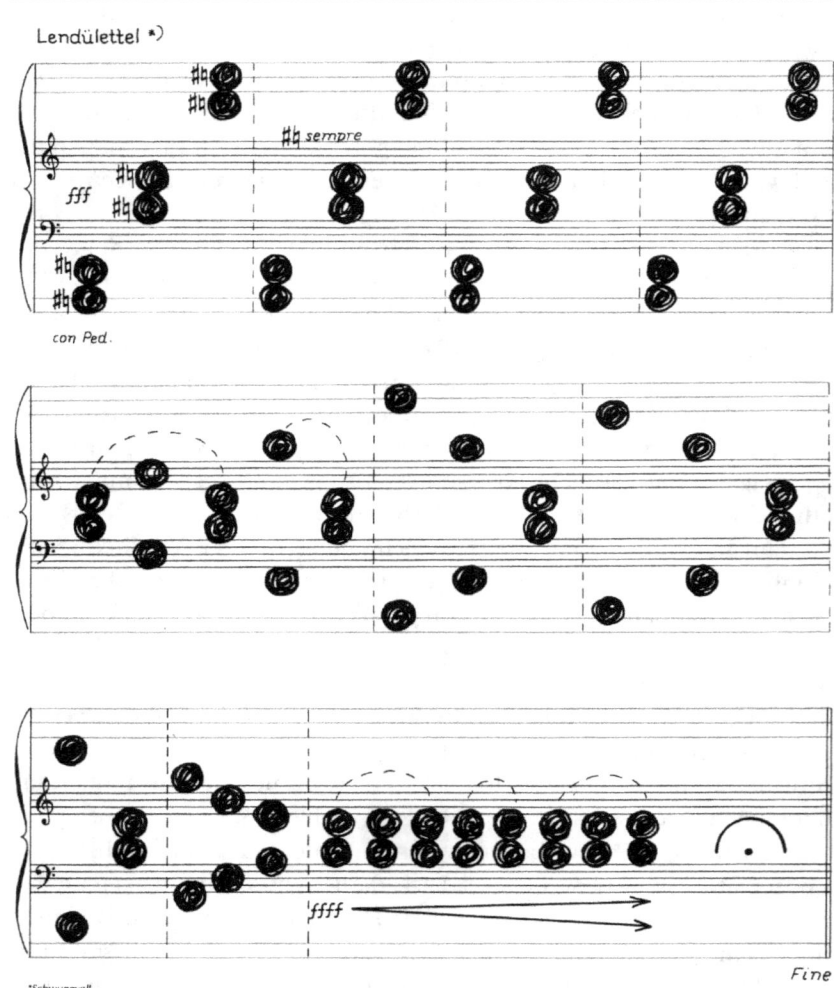

to performance. During lessons, Kurtág often emphasized the importance of sincerity and originality of expression, by daring us to be the child we once were. Sessions with Kurtág left me with the impression that the desired results would be achieved by stirring up all of the details and bringing them to a boiling point, and this underscores the holistic approach that he took to the teaching of music and performance.

EXAMPLE 2-2 (conclusion)

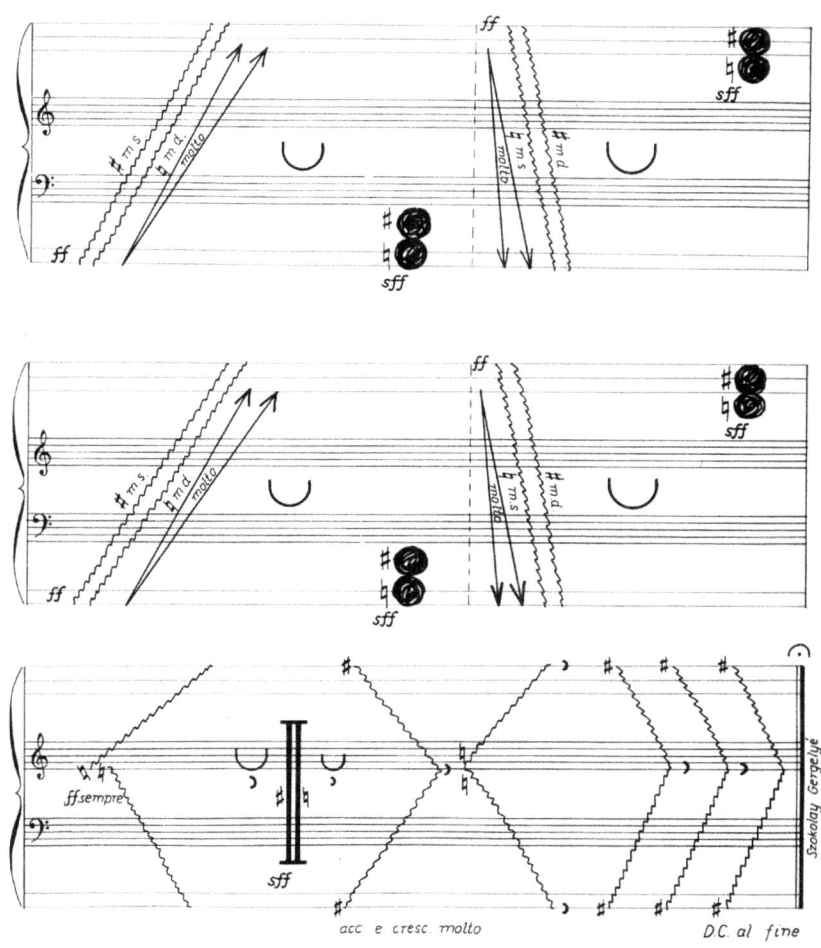

Kurtág dedicated "Hommage à Beethoven," published in the same volume of *Játékok*, to me as well (see example 2-3). This piece refers to the second movement (*adagio cantabile*) of Beethoven's Sonata in C minor op. 13 "Pathétique." Kurtág views his "Hommage" as an exercise, the goal of which is to achieve a restful position of the hands while working on the dexterity of the fingers to produce a beautiful, even sound for the performance of

EXAMPLE 2-3 Plate 2-2: György Kurtág, *Játékok* I [Games I] (1973–78), "Hommage à Beethoven." © Editio Musica Budapest.

moving melodic lines. During one lesson on the "Pathétique," Kurtág pointed out the resemblance between the first movement's opening motive and Chopin's "Revolutionary" Étude, Op. 10, No. 12. His technical advice for approaching the second movement was nearly identical to Chopin's own definition of piano technique. In the collection of notes now known as "Projet de Méthode" Chopin wrote, "One needs only to study a certain positioning of the hand in relation to the keys to obtain with ease the most beautiful quality of sound, to know how to play long notes and short notes and [to attain] unlimited dexterity ... A well-formed technique, it seems to me, [is one] that can control and vary [*bien nuancer*] a beautiful sound quality."[7] According to Karol Mikuli, this is achieved by "*souplesse* [suppleness] and with it independence of the fingers."[8] Based on his thorough knowledge of the piano literature and his mastery of the instrument, Kurtág was able to transmit a complete history of the piano and its performance practice in his lessons. His "Hommage à Beethoven" opens a modest window on his amazing grasp of the network of relationships that link Beethoven's music to that of Schubert, Chopin, Liszt, and others, including composers working today.

After settling in Canada and on the occasion of the birth of our son Alexander in November 2002, Kurtág wrote a solo violin piece for our older daughter Sophia, who studies the instrument (see plate 2-1). The piece was sent to us by fax on Christmas day. In spite of the hatching caused by the fax transmission, Kurtág's handwriting readily conveys the expressive qualities of the music. The second word in the title, *Cawanyi* combines Alexander's Russian nickname *Cawa* (Sasha written in Cyrillic, in reference to my wife, Julia Galieva's Russian background) with its Hungarian version *Sanyi* (from Sándor), which is also my father's nickname—*Sashanyi*. The subtlety of the multilingual wordplay attending to three generations of our family and the gesture to involve our first child in the celebration of our second reflect Kurtág's sensitivity to the complexity of

PLATE 2-1 György Kurtág, *Szokolay Cauuanyi első karácsonyára* [For Alexander Szokolay's first Christmas] for violin solo (15–17 December 2002), published with kind permission of the composer.

identity, his caring relationship with people close to him, and his credo of impartiality that I learned from him in my childhood.[9] This title is also symptomatic of music conceived as a rich fabric, interwoven with intricate cross-relations and references, one of the enduring traits of his compositional technique. The composer's final instruction at the end of the piece, *sognando* [dreamily], is evocative of Sophia's Russian nickname, Sonia, the way she prefers to be called.

Kurtág's presence in my life is a rare gift, and sharing this experience brings me immense joy.

Notes

1. Gyuribácsi is an affectionate nickname that expresses an important difference in age.
2. Sándor Szokolay (1931–) is one of the leading Hungarian composers of his generation. He began his studies early and obtained his diploma in composition from the Liszt Academy in 1957. He has received numerous prizes and honours, including the Kossuth Prize in 1966 for his opera *Vérnász* [Blood Wedding].
3. "For five years I lived with my wife Márta at my aunt's place, in the tiny servant's chamber beside the kitchen with cockroaches at night. The room was four meters long by two meters wide." Bálint András Varga, *Kurtág: Three Interviews and Ligeti Homages*, compiled and edited by Bálint András Varga (Rochester, NY: University of Rochester Press, 2009), 93.
4. Constantine Stanislavski, *A szinész munkája* [An Actor Prepares], trans. András Áchim (Budapest: Művelt Nép Kiadó, 1951).
5. Sári Szesztay (1927–) is a pianist, music educator, and amateur sculptor.
6. I would like to thank Margit Szesztay for her assistance in translating this poem.
7. Jean-Jacques Eigeldinger, *Chopin: Pianist and Teacher as Seen by His Pupils*, ed. Roy Howat, trans. Naomi Shohet with Krysia Osostowicz and Roy Howat (Cambridge and New York: Cambridge University Press, 2006), 16–17.
8. Ibid., 29. Karol Mikuli (1821–97) was a pupil and disciple of Chopin.
9. During our visit to Budapest in February 2006, he generously offered to coach this piece to Sonia, who was ten years old at that time.

Bibliography

Eigeldinger, Jean-Jacques. *Chopin: Pianist and Teacher as Seen by His Pupils*. Edited by Roy Howat. Translated by Naomi Shohet with Krysia Osostowicz and Roy Howat. Cambridge and New York: Cambridge University Press, 2006.

Stanislavski, Constantine. *A szinész munkája* [An Actor Prepares]. Translated by András Áchim. Budadpest: Művelt Nép Kiadó, 1951.

Varga, Bálint András. *György Kurtág: Three Interviews and Ligeti Homages*. Compiled and edited by Bálint András Varga. Rochester, NY: University of Rochester Press, 2009.

THREE

"A Kind of Musical Autobiography": Reading Traces in Sándor Veress's *Orbis tonorum*

Claudio Veress

It [time] advances much faster than these two hands—and then, suddenly, it is gone.[1]

ONE OF MY FATHER'S last completed compositions, *Orbis tonorum* for chamber ensemble, was premiered in the "Grosser Saal" of the Bern Conservatory on 9 November 1986. The work's title consciously plays with a reference to Johann Amos Comenius's illustrated pedagogical encyclopedia of 1658, *Orbis sensualium pictus*. In his *Orbis*, however, Sándor Veress does not adopt the objective, typically scientific, third-person perspective used by Comenius, but clearly prefers the subjective first-person perspective. In his own text written for the first performance, Veress expresses his wish to direct the attention "intra muros"[2] and not (or at least not exclusively) "extra muros." One may even meaningfully complete this quote with a metaphor from Augustine, an author Veress openly admired, and say: intra muros of the *ingens aula memoriae*.[3] The composer explicitly characterizes his work as "a kind of musical autobiography,"[4] and if one enters the realms of association suggested in the titles of its eight movements, the past dominates almost every movement. The first movement, *Tempi passati*, and the last movement, *Tempi da venire ...?* are (at least conceptually) linked by the same subject, which directs its attention either backwards or forwards. Before the *sempre diminuendo e morendo* receding drum beats of the work's open end, this subject takes its leave with a final signature—the

EXAMPLE 3-1 Sándor Veress, *I. Quartetto per 2 Violini, Viola e Violoncello* (Milano: Edizioni Suvini Zerboni, 1953), 24, ending of movement I.

EXAMPLE 3-2 Plate 3-2: Sándor Veress, *Orbis tonorum per orchestra da camera* (Milano: Edizioni Suvini Zerboni, 1986), 108. Open ending of movement VIII.

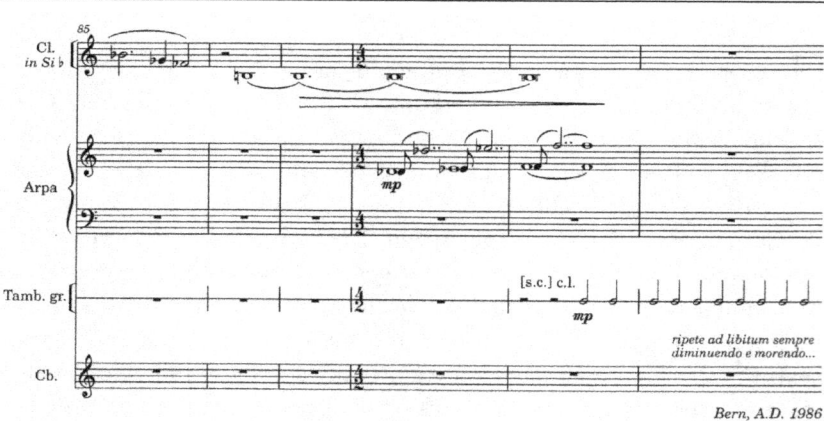

harp octave arpeggio sequence D flat – E flat – F beginning in bar 88—which can be read both as a last shadowy reference to the whole tone passage of this movement's "comforting melody"[5] and as a variation of a three-tone figure (octave arpeggio sequence in the second violin) from the opening movement of Veress's first string quartet composed in 1931 (compare examples 3-1 and 3-2). In his later years, Veress considered this work as his actual Opus 1; thus the idea easily arises that *Orbis* can be understood not only as an autobiographical reflection, but also as an opus ultimum.[6]

Veress's characterization of *Orbis* as a "musical autobiography" invites the assumption that the work could be interpreted as a report of his creative process as a composer or perhaps even as the story of his life.[7] The basic legitimacy of such a process could be underlined by the interdependence between life path and creative path, which Veress himself retrospectively evoked around the time of his eightieth birthday.[8] But this admittedly does not assure the possible success of such an attempt, and such a task would certainly lead beyond the scope of this chapter. Nevertheless, the reflexive atmosphere of *Orbis* allows me to dwell upon certain important traces in the score that will serve to explore the author's physiognomy, as I encountered it.

A word perhaps on the basic compatibility of "psychology" and "score" in the given case: Veress dedicated the eight movements of his piece to ten members of the Bern Music Society Committee of 1979. In his detailed dedicatory text—due to the commissioning conditions—he gives a few hints of a characterizing nature.[9] The mischievous irony he uses in this context makes it difficult to exploit the hermeneutic dimension, but a game with character masks before a mirror is nonetheless suggested.

tempi passati / tempi da venire ...? (Orbis tonorum I / VIII)

The diachronic, or more precisely, historical, perspective found in this piece generally plays an important role in Veress's work: His father was a historian who, among other things, studied the relationship between the Hungarian Kingdom and the Holy See in the Middle Ages and early modern era. From an early age, Veress learned what it meant to strive for historical understanding as a way of life. He loved England—his wife's country of origin, where he worked for decades as juror at the *Llangollen Eisteddfod*—for its Gothic quality and the art of William Turner, but beside this, the country he most regularly visited was Italy. He considered Italian art the absolute paradigm of beauty[10] and could read its history like an open book. The Italian terminology in his musical notation is not only the expression of an anti-Germanic tendency (common to new Hungarian music and many other national reaffirmations in recent European musical history) nor is it simply a specific understanding of *musica perennis*; rather it appears as an obvious homage to the country in which he most directly experienced aesthetic history.

The question mark in *tempi da venire ...?* refers to a particular colour in Veress's historical imagination, marked by the catastrophic developments before his emigration: the fall of the Austro-Hungarian Empire in the First World War, the Treaty of Trianon,[11] the German occupation of Hungary and the Arrow Cross Party's seizure of power in 1944, the Red Army's laborious liberation of Budapest, the short-lived political utopia destroyed by the pressure of Stalin's regime after 1948, and finally, on a personal level, disillusionment following his failed attempt to migrate to the United States during the escalating Cold War, and a continuously ambivalent attitude towards his exile in Bern.[12] Based on these experiences, Veress's political speculations were generally skeptical, not to say pessimistic. He saw no hope in the emerging communist experimentations of various democratic countries in Western and Southern Europe during the 1970s: To him, Marxism had failed politically and philosophically through its unforgivable manifestation in the "existing socialism" of the Soviet Union and its Eastern European satellites, which he considered irretrievably Stalinist.

The score of *Orbis* presents a clearly emphasized sense of catastrophic rupture: after bar 34 of the *Siciliano nostalgico* (*Orbis tonorum* II), and tutti *triple forte* beat (a dynamic which appears only once within the work), nothing is as it was.

alla maniera del Signor Tinguely (*Orbis tonorum* V, bar 117ff.)

A certain parallel can be drawn between Veress's historical pessimism and his relation to science and technical progress, although with more affirmative aspects. Veress's paternal grandfather, Sándor the elder, was an engineer who contributed importantly to the development of the Romanian railway line after 1878. Some of this engineering spirit lived on in Sándor the younger: He loved to watch the steam engines of the passenger ferries that continue to cross Swiss lakes to this day. Unscathed by war and uniquely maintained, they ecstatically recalled his crossing of the Atlantic on the fastest boat of all time, the *SS United States*, in 1965. But at the same time he belonged to a generation old enough to critically reflect on the first use of atomic bombs; early on he realized the different potentials *homo faber*'s machinations could unleash. Accordingly, one of the books that preoccupied him intensively, around the NATO Double-Track Decision of 1979 was Karl Jaspers's 1958 *The Atomic Bomb and the Future of Mankind*.

Veress's reference to Jean Tinguely's manner ("maniera") in the fifth movement of *Orbis*, entitled *Verticale e orizzontale*, expresses this ambivalent feeling towards science and the technical world. The joyful playfulness (bars 117ff.) that arrives at the end of this piece reveals the conflict between two incommensurable principles. In terms of classical aesthetic categories these could be described as: *mechanism* (illustrated by the frame sections of the movement, where thirty-one different tone orders come together "vertically" without consideration)[13] versus *teleology* (illustrated by the middle sequence, in which an almost folk-music-like bicinium of sensitive melodic profile is developed "horizontally"). Only with the unexpected coda is the antagonistic constellation finally resolved through the ironic parody of machinery. Similarly, Tinguely's automats (such as the spectacular water fountain in front of the Basel Theatre) break through the terror of "blind" causality by freeing themselves from the confinement of technical instrumentalization and organizing their constituent elements into an aesthetic, playful ensemble of "purposefulness without purpose."[14]

Intermezzo silenzioso (*Orbis tonorum* IV)

"Silence is a rare phenomenon in our time of hellish noise."[15] With this phrase the composer describes movement IV, a piece consisting of slow melodic movement above a static harmonic substrate. Veress was an introvert who needed "timeless time" to be able to work, and could also on occasion be very quiet in communicative situations. He tended to use sentences sparingly—just as he sternly censored every next note as a composer. He thus suffered correspondingly from the—not only acoustic—violence of modern cities. When the lease on his studio at Gerechtigkeitsgasse 57 was cancelled at the end of the seventies after he had spent many decades in the fifteenth-century patrician house in one of the oldest parts of Bern, he suffered a profound existential crisis. After a long search he found a small apartment on the fifth floor at Aarbergergasse 10, but the protected atmosphere of his old workshop was forever lost. His new neighbourhood in Bern belonged architectonically and historically to the old town, but its proximity to the main station transformed it into a hub of activity and commerce, with all the negative symptoms this presupposes. Until his death, Veress never quite came to terms with this situation.

Intermezzo turbolento (*Orbis tonorum* VII)

Orbis tonorum VII is a rapid virtuoso piece. Its perfectly coherent internal organization is covered by a multitude of sixteenth notes, thus creating a superficial impression of chaotic discontinuity. This noisy turbulence is clearly not a naive affirmation opposing a quiet ideal; rather it is a hyperbolic—and therefore somewhat scurrilous—portrayal of a concretely menacing phenomenon that the composer wished to banish from his surroundings as much as possible. The expression of this ban through a process of aesthetic irony reveals the composer's unusually heightened sensitivity towards natural forms of the grotesque. Extraordinary morphological appearances, peculiarities in animal behaviour, and counterintuitive physical phenomena could exert a lasting fascination on him. I remember a day when he came back from a shopping tour in the city with not only the necessary ingredients to fill the fridge, but also a gyroscope, a small machine that enables surprising balance experiments thanks to the stabilizing effect of a revolving metal disc. All the possibilities of this instrument were immediately tested. The primal, childlike quality of his amazement in such situations was both obvious and infectious. He maintained his capacity for wonderment in old age, and it remained certainly one of the sources of his creativity.

con spirito e leggerezza (Orbis tonorum VI)

The performance indication of this movement, entitled *Capriccio delizioso. Piccolo Concerto per Xilorimba, Arpa e Percussione*, calls for two dispositions: *spirit and lightness*. This can be read as a manifestation of Veress's concept of music as play:[16] the solo part of this "triple-concerto" is technically rather demanding, so the composer's comment intimates that the "happy smile" of this *capriccio* variation can only shine after, not during, the actual work of rehearsing and performing is done.[17] In any case, the indication undeniably demands that the *sonorous performance* of the score—though it be art—should give the impression of being a second nature whose artifices remain hidden. This brings us to an essential idea in Veress's (musical) pedagogy: the musician (and human being!) who has developed in freedom, even if he is only an interpreter, cannot perform a piece without contributing his own creative input.[18]

But Veress was not only convinced of this utopian and subversive[19] ideal as a music pedagogue; he was filled with it as well as a composer, and in the last productive decade of his life, the ideal of freedom that he had struggled for so many years to find became real. He often used the metaphor of walking through a vast and blooming field to express this. The dominant serenity of the *Orbis* music, even where the irretrievable—the *tempi passati*—becomes thematic in its irretrievability (because what is heard as an immediate melody must be recognized in its revelation as a twelve-tone series), may be a sign of this late reconciliation with his own history.[20]

Translated from the German by Laura Möckli

Notes

1 Sándor Veress, 29 September 1989, in a letter to the author accompanying the gift of a wall clock.
2 Sándor Veress, *Sándor Veress, Orbis tonorum* [program of the first performance] (Bern: Bernische Musikgesellschaft, 1986), 5.
3 Augustine, *Confessiones*, X, 8, 14: "Intus haec ago, in aula ingenti memoriae meae." In English, "This I do within myself in the immense court of my memory"; Augustine, *The Confessions*, trans. Maria Boulding, OSB (New York: Vintage Spiritual Classics, 1998), 206.
4 Veress, *Sándor Veress, Orbis tonorum*, 5.
5 Andreas Traub and Claudio Veress, eds., *Sándor Veress zum 85. Geburtstag. Begleitheft zu den Berner Veranstaltungen vom 31. Januar und 1. Februar 1992* (Bern: Lobsiger & Sohn, 1992), 9.
6 Veress composed another work after *Orbis*: the *Tromboniade* for two trombones and orchestra. This is the only later work apart from two fragmental scores of *Geschichten und Märchen* (1988) and *Concertotilinkó* (1991). This other final composition is the consequence of an exceptional commission and Veress's decision to take up the work despite his cancer (the diagnosis of which was made in August 1986, during the last phase of the composition of *Orbis*). Also, while *Orbis* quotes Veress's first valid compositional beginning, the *Tromboniade*, in turn, quotes the *Tempi passati* melody of the *Orbis* at a decisive point! A clearer statement can hardly be made of a feeling that life and work had "gone beyond." See Andreas Traub, "(K)ein Konzert für zwei Posaunen und Orchester," *Dissonanz/Dissonance* 84 (December 2003): 27.
7 Veress, *Sándor Veress, Orbis tonorum*, 6: "One should see the eight movements as mirrors for individual artistic phases that were effective at a given time on the path of creativity." ("[Man] soll die acht Sätze als Spiegel einzelner Phasen des künstlerischen Tuns betrachten, die auf dem Pfad der Kreativität in einem gegebenen Zeitsektor aktuell waren.") Concerning this, with special focus on compositional problems in *Orbis*, see Andreas Traub, *Zeitschichten. Zum, Orbis tonorum' (1986) von Sándor Veress* (Saarbrücken: Pfau, 1999), fragmen no. 28.
8 Andreas Traub, "Sándor Veress. Lebensweg—Schaffensweg," in *Sándor Veress. Festschrift zum 80. Geburtstag* (Berlin: Haseloff, 1986), 22–119.
9 See Veress, *Sándor Veress, Orbis tonorum*, 3.
10 Concerning this ideal, see an excerpt from a letter from Venice: "Here, one could not debate about beauty and what defines it—here it exists." ("Hier könnte man über Schönheit, was sie sei, nicht debattieren—sie *ist*.") Quoted in Andreas Traub, "Einleitung," in Sándor Veress, *Concerto per clarinetto e orchestra* (Milano: Edizioni Suvini Zerboni, 1982).
11 The Treaty of Trianon (1920), between the Allies of the First World War and Hungary, dramatically refined the latter's borders, reducing Hungary's territory by

over 70 per cent. For example, Transylvania, where Veress was born, was ceded to Romania.
12   Veress had become a member of the Hungarian Communist Party in 1945 and never rescinded his membership. For a closer look at this complex, see Rachel Beckles-Willson's "Letters to America" in this volume and Claudio Veress, "Komponieren im Zeichen skeptischer Parteilichkeit. Der Film 'Talpalatnyi föld' im Kontext der letzten ungarischen Jahre von Sándor Veress," in *Sándor Veress. Komponist—Lehrer—Forscher*, ed. Doris Lanz and Anselm Gerhard (Kassel: Bärenreiter, 2008), 41–45.
13   In his study of *Orbis*, Andreas Traub supposes that Veress may be alluding to Democritus's theory of "free falling atoms" (Traub, *Zeitschichten*, 15). What Kant and his contemporaries called *mechanism* [of nature] is similar to Democritus's materialism in that it is devoid of all teleological consideration.
14   Immanuel Kant, *Kritik der Urteilskraft*, 2nd ed. (Berlin: Lagarde, 1793), 44.
15   Veress, *Sándor Veress, Orbis tonorum*, 6.
16   Sándor Veress, "Folk Music in Musical and General Education," *Journal of the International Folk Music Council* 1 (1949): 40–43.
17   Veress, *Sándor Veress, Orbis tonorum*, 7.
18   See Veress's "Introductory Words" in the bilingual first edition of *Billegetőmuzsika / Fingerlarks* (Budapest: Cserépfalvi, 1947).
19   See Friedemann Sallis, "Teaching as a Subversive Art. Sándor Veress's 'Billegetőmuzsika (Fingerlarks)' and György Kurtág's '*Játékok* (Games),'" and Andreas Traub, "Verlust und Utopie. Bemerkungen zum Lebens- und Schaffensweg von Sándor Veress"; both articles are found in *Sándor Veress. Komponist—Lehrer—Forscher*, 159–71 and 77–87.
20   The *tempi-passati* theme of *Orbis tonorum* I is an ornamented melody of ten bars in a fragile A tonality whose first six bars may (and must) be read at the same time as a twelve-tone series. See Veress, *Sándor Veress, Orbis tonorum*, 6: "In *Tempi passati* a simple small melody is articulated which looks back to a broad past, to a time when melody was the leading principle of music. Here, however, it is put into the context of another perspective, i.e. a twelve-tone tonality, not an old diatonic scale." ("In *Tempi passati* wird eine einfache kleine Melodie angetönt, die als solche auf eine weite Vergangenheit zurückblickt, auf eine Zeit nämlich, als die Melodie noch das Leitprinzip der Musik war. Sie ist hier allerdings in einen anderen Aspekt gestellt, indem sie in die 12-Ton-Tonalität eingebettet erscheint anstatt in irgendeine alte diatonische Skala.")

Bibliography

Augustine. *The Confessions*. Translated by Maria Boulding, OSB. New York: Vintage Spiritual Classics, 1998.
Kant, Immanuel. *Kritik der Urteilskraft*. Second edition. Berlin: Lagarde, 1793.
Sallis, Friedemann. "Teaching as a Subversive Art. Sándor Veress's '*Billegetőmuzsika* (Fingerlarks)' and György Kurtág's '*Játékok* (Games).'" *Sándor Veress. Komponist—Lehrer—Forscher*. Edited by Doris Lanz and Anselm Gerhard, 159–71. Kassel: Bärenreiter, 2008.

Traub, Andreas. "Einleitung." In Sándor Veress, *Concerto per clarinetto e orchestra*. Milano: Edizioni Suvini Zerboni, 1982.

———. "(K)ein Konzert für zwei Posaunen und Orchester." *Dissonanz/Dissonance* 84 (December 2003): 22–27.

———. "Sándor Veress. Lebensweg—Schaffensweg." In *Sándor Veress. Festschrift zum 80. Geburtstag*. Berlin: Haseloff, 1986.

———. "Verlust und Utopie. Bemerkungen zum Lebens- und Schaffensweg von Sándor Veress." *Sándor Veress. Komponist—Lehrer—Forscher*. Edited by Doris Lanz and Anselm Gerhard, 77–87. Kassel: Bärenreiter, 2008.

———. *Zeitschichten. Zum, Orbis tonorum' (1986) von Sándor Veress*. Saarbrücken: Pfau, 1999.

Traub, Andreas and Claudio Veress, eds. *Sándor Veress zum 85. Geburtstag. Begleitheft zu den Berner Veranstaltungen vom 31. Januar und 1. Februar 1992*. Bern: Lobsiger & Sohn, 1992.

Veress, Claudio. "Komponieren im Zeichen skeptischer Parteilichkeit. Der Film 'Talpalatnyi föld' im Kontext der letzten ungarischen Jahre von Sándor Veress." *Sándor Veress. Komponist—Lehrer—Forscher*. Edited by Doris Lanz and Anselm Gerhard, 36–76. Kassel: Bärenreiter, 2008.

Veress, Sándor. "Folk Music in Musical and General Education." *Journal of the International Folk Music Council* 1 (1949): 40–43.

———. "Introductory Words." *Billegetőmuzsika / Fingerlarks*. Budapest: Cserépfalvi, 1947.

———. *Sándor Veress, Orbis tonorum* [program of the first performance]. Bern: Bernische Musikgesellschaft, 1986.

Place and Displacement

FOUR

Of the Centre, Periphery; Exile, Liberation; Home and the Self[1]

István Anhalt

The process of acquiring, ever so gradually and slowly, a sense of "centeredness" appears to me to be a "life-project." In its course, the notions of "centre" and "periphery" might, and for some do, take on meanings observable through visible and audible evidence. In the course of the journey from Budapest to Kingston, via Paris and Montreal, I have learned that the lessons are manifold and indispensable for an understanding of that halfhidden "central I," or this "I here-and-now."

I WOULD LIKE TO BEGIN by expressing my thanks to all who are present, to those who will participate as speakers and/or performers, and to those who will listen to them. I am also signalling my deep appreciation to Dr. Friedemann Sallis, who conceived the idea of this event and who worked tirelessly to make it a reality. I am also expressing my thanks to his institution, the University of Calgary, for making it possible.

I regret not being present at this gathering. I regret not seeing my colleague György Kurtág, whom I recall meeting briefly in 1972 in Budapest. Our interaction then made a deep impression on me. I wish I could know his music better; all opinions I hear about it indicate that his is a strongly personal compositional voice. Perhaps the record of this symposium will provide information in printed text and recorded sound, compensating somewhat for this unrealized opportunity.

The themes announced for this assembly are these: Roots vs. Exile and Centre vs. Periphery. These I shall approach from a perspective formed by the following related themes: (1) Scope for choice, (2) Thrown-ness (Heidegger),[2] (3) Walls and cracks in the walls, (4) Horizon (Gadamer), (5) The "I" in the world, and, finally, (6) A situation when "Eye" imposes its centrality upon the "I."

In a recent telephone conversation, Mrs. Klára Devecseri (she speaking in Budapest, I in Kingston) referred to her place of domicile, the capital of Hungary, as being the locus of a musical "world power." She didn't feel the need to justify her view. She counted on my familiarity with, and shared views regarding, the world importance of Bartók, and perhaps also, coming a close second, of Kodály as both a composer and as an educator.

I must now digress and tell you of that remarkable circle of young people who formed what then (about 1938–42) was referred to as the Devecseri circle. It consisted of about two dozen or so young (ages eighteen to twenty-six) university students: students of philology, the classics, mathematicians, poets (several of them sons of the then-living greatest poets in Hungary: Frigyes Karinthy and Zoltán Somlyó). I was (together with Klára) the only music student in the group. The weekly gatherings, on Saturday evenings, constituted an immensely diverse and enriching experience and a strong influence on me, who by then started to sense the intellectually narrow scope of an education confined to music only. Thus my friends in the Devecseri circle opened for me a broad vista on the world of the intellect, and I feel their influence to this day. For example, among my three most recent orchestral works there are two that revisit the classical worlds of Athens and Rome. I couldn't have done this without recalling the lasting inspiration of such early friends as Devecseri himself and that of János-György Szilágyi, who still is, at the age of eighty-nine, not only a great classical scholar but also a world authority on Etruscan art. The lives of those then-young persons were put in jeopardy by the political upheavals of the period 1933–39, leading to the devastation of the Second World War and the tragedy of the Holocaust. As a result, millions of people perished, and millions of others felt the need to seek other places for living than those where they almost lost their lives. These forces and the resultant relocations deeply affected the perceptions of home vs. centre, relocation, emigration, periphery for a large number of people. I was one of them.

In 1945 in war-torn Budapest, living a marginal existence professionally as an unpaid *répétiteur* in the Hungarian National Opera, while often enough encountering evidence of a still-alive propensity for anti-Semitism, I sensed the need for leaving that country. Was this a self-imposed "exile" or a "liberation?" I think it was the latter. I was able to accomplish this in January 1946, and soon I was on my way to Paris, where I arrived in March of that year. Within a month I became a student in the Conservatoire National de Musique (conducting), a private student of Nadia Boulanger (composition), and a piano student of Soulima Stravinsky. A Lady Davis Fellowship enabled me to realize a dream: immigration to Canada in January 1949 and a temporary teaching position at McGill University. With a number of changes in status, I taught at McGill until 1971 and attained the rank of full professor in January 1967.

My interest in electronic music, which began around 1957, took me to Germany (Cologne), where I met another stimulating group of people, all composers who were attracted to that city by its famous Electronic Music Studio, located on the premises of the West German Radio, where Herbert Eimert, Karlheinz Stockhausen, and Gottfried Michael Koenig worked to spectacular effect, drawing composers from other lands, including György Ligeti from Hungary, Mauricio Kagel from Argentina, and myself from Canada. It was a very stimulating situation. Also among the group was the novelist-composer Hans Helms, who made a claim (to me personally) that Cologne, despite the continuing presence of debris from the Second World War in some of the streets of the outlying districts, was a world centre for "new music" at that time, an allegation to be sustained by the innovatory contributions of Stockhausen in works such as *Gesang der Jünglinge*, his *Gruppen* (for three orchestras), and *Zeitmasze*.

Returning from Cologne to Montreal, I headed immediately to Ottawa to visit Hugh LeCaine at the National Research Council, who by then had a sophisticated facility for the production of electronic music, which included several of his own inventions. My collaboration with LeCaine lasted nearly two decades, until his premature death in 1977. His contributions to electronic music composition gave lie to the assertion that one had to go to Cologne or Paris to access electronic-musical technology. It was available right here in Canada! So much for leaping to conclusions regarding "centres" and "peripheries."

Locating the geographical centrality and importance of diverse music cultures over time becomes an immensely complex exercise if one accepts the inevitability of considering such diverse evidences of culture as, for example, the evolution of Gregorian chant, or the masterworks of the Netherlands Schools, those of sixteenth-century Italy, those of the German Baroque masterpieces, but also the marvellous musics of the island of Bali, or the musical traditions of North India, to mention just two of a multiplicity of Asian musical cultures. Even such a superficial listing makes it clear that the world of music over time is an immense interplay of juxtaposed, wonderfully rich centres! Yes! But human limitations make it inevitable that one has to choose. One thus finds oneself with a limited acquaintance with a limited corpus, X, which becomes one's central repertory. All else will sit on the edge of this domain, as if on a "periphery," with an increasing sense of dimness, lack of clarity, as one moves "outward."

And now allow me to revisit some "markers" in my compositional pathway. The 1950s were given to a slow acquisition of twelve-tone techniques. Three works aimed at this: a *Fantasia* for piano (1953), a Violin Sonata (1954), and a Symphony (1958) (premiered late in 1959), which turned out to be a landmark in my professional life. The 1960s saw the composition of three major works: *Cento*, *Foci*, and *Symphony of Modules*, which further explored innovative techniques. With these behind me, and confronted by the felt necessity to compose an opera, my first, about the Quebec mystic Marie de L'Incarnation, a complex liberating idea appeared as a chief inspirational force. *Everything is potentially relevant* if it can serve the purpose of depicting truthfully the complex persona of Marie. In other words, the emphasis no longer was on stylistic innovation, experimentation, but on truthful and appropriate expression. Her soul's and my mind's capabilities were to determine what was to appear in this score—in other words, the central "I" of Marie through the central "I" of myself, her "composer." And with this realization I am at a point where it is necessary for me to tell you how I have thought about this "I" ever since my childhood, however dimly.

In that uncertain past I became aware of the thought that (1) the "centre" is where I am, and (2) I will have to work in the course of much of my life on who this "person" is to whom I had assigned the word "I." To put it even more bluntly: the "centre" and the "I" have merged in my mind in a way that has "liberated" this "I" from the notion of a kind of "centre," any "centre," because the two, the "I" and the "centre" (of self-awareness), became one and the same—not unlike a snail and the shell it carries on its back.

Of course the self is responsive (it has to be) to the forces around it (things alongside the periphery). What we regard as "life," "action," and the like, is the stream of events that occur as the central "I" interacts with its surrounding periphery. A special kind of interaction is present if obstacles (even danger) appear before the central "I" in relation to its periphery. And there one sees the central "I" overcoming obstacles with the help of "cracks" in the "forbidding walls" that enable one to "get through."

My, or should I say our, lives seemed ideal over the decades of the '50s and '60s: increasingly fulfilling musical events, new works performed to satisfactory response. But then dark clouds appeared on the horizon. The two major ethnic and linguistic populations of Montreal began to show increasingly irresolvable antagonisms toward one another. I was worried on account of this: anxious regarding both groups. As a result, I found myself writing a parable entitled *The Bridge*. It was meant to be a warning for the antagonists, who slipped into behaviours that included even the murder of a leading politician and the kidnapping of a British consul. The opening paragraph of this parable is as follows:

> The bridge is no more. The pillars in the river are crumbling. Only the shouts are heard from the opposing shores in languages reciprocally no longer comprehensible. But the meaning of the gestures alongside the water is clear enough: the imploding fists, the windmills of the arms and the faces frozen in crooked masks. The walkways by the river are no longer tended: the trees are overgrown and the lawns trampled into mud. The patterned pavement, a favourite walking-path for lovers, for mothers, nannies pushing prams, a safe place, before, for racing children, is now broken up, its missing parts having served as projectiles aimed at the opposite shore. Only the sewer outlets remain true to the purpose for which they were built, although the intense stench seems to indicate that even the workers at the purification plant are, at times, absent from their shifts, having joined the swelling, shouting, crowd. Since a while there appears to be confusion in the minds of mothers. Some urge the children to join the heaving mob and live what in future years will, no doubt, become lessons of history. Others, propelled by fear, or encumbered by bitter memories, by oft-repeated warnings by an older, or long-deceased, relative, lock the doors, press the children to their aprons, offer them sweets as distraction, and wonder if they should not begin to board up the windows, as well. One overheard talk that the crews of the fire brigade were also seen standing by the river bank, adding their shouts to the overall din. What if ...? is the silent question in many minds, and the palms get moist and the stomachs tighten in apprehension. Other fears are also spreading around. Since the bridge is gone, there is no way of knowing what happened, or might happen, to those dear ones who got caught on the other side.

This text was never published anywhere. One could ask: why? But alongside this I had the practical problem and the related question: What am I to do in the face of this seemingly irresolvable situation? I was responsible for a family of five, including my two children, my wife, and my mother, who came to live with us after my stepfather passed away in 1963. The outcome of these thoughts took us from Montreal (and McGill) to Kingston (and Queen's University).

It soon became clear that it was a good move, as Queen's/Kingston proved to be conducive to fruitful activity and a welcoming social/professional life. Kingston, then a smallish city of about 60,000, has doubled in size since we came in 1971, and its amenities have also diversified remarkably. It is a fine, peaceable place that, at times, seems to replicate the image of an ideal environment that appeared to me as a quasi-dream, as described in a poem I wrote in 1943 in a dusty Transylvanian village on a hot Sunday afternoon, entitled "Miráge in Előpatak." I now cite this poem, translated by me from the Hungarian:

> Mirage in Előpatak
>
> Strolling happy friends with wit abounding,
> Thoughtfully smiling, invite you to join:
> Come along, pal, if it suits you;
> Surely you know us—forever calling,
> Yet also keeping you at a distance …
> Familiar? Of course. You also play by the same rule.
>
> Look: the sage is resting in the shady gardens,
> Streams of flushed-faced young
> Press towards him—the hub—
> Along the spokes of the wheel,
> With thirsty lips gently curving,
> Spirits alight
> To await word of the coming dawn.
>
> Ideas flow following idea
> Trust from the past welding onto offspring;
> An unringed migrating crane—leading
> At the apex of a swift winging v …
> Oh, what a splendid morning!
>
> Lo: safely nesting in his roomy basket
> Contentedly the just-fed infant coos,
> Delighting all with the primeval song.
> Soup on the stove; the bubbles are bursting,
> Tiny pea-balls dance in the sweet-smelling stream
> Tender shoots blending into flavour,
> Surrendering self to form a whole
> For the mid-day meal of a scorching day.
> So the soul fuses all that is worthwhile to keep.
>
> Reflecting the pane, by the window, a brother is speaking:
> Do you accept this? Something in which you could share?
> A magical call: to excel by doing well

The job at hand, yearning for mastery,
As the distant spires of shape
Urge you on to find the right place.

You uncatchable slippery buddy of mine
Time, all cartwheels, tumbles and twirls;
You are full of tricks.
You make me dizzy
As you turn the "now" into "past"
What will you do to the moment about to arrive?

The minute-hours roll by on the wheels of substance.
The view is rewarding, never twice the same.
On and onward towards the Crystal City
Until, in a well-guarded courtyard—we hear it—
The great bell is sounding;
The word of the king, the voice of the sun.
Noon!

If that's what you need: well … then rest.
Stretch out your limbs in the hollows of hills
By the edge of the darkly-pensive woods
Where you just might catch, unexpectedly,
A few words resounding from a generous spring:

"On the grassy plains you feed me, my Lord,
And even by the rim of the abyss you are my shepherd …"
Comes from a distance.
Then … silence
The voiceless word echoes as long as you hear the thought.

The heat of the hour wets palm and fingers.
For a while it is an effort to move.
But slowly the disc descends along its arc
And life returns to the squares and streets.
The multitude moves … each looking for something,
Peeking, peering as far as the eye can see.

The afternoon gardens prepare for the evening,
Distilling scents for the feast ahead
To please the dearest ones:
You, darling Ágicám.
In the waning warmth of the dusk
Your firm back trustingly fills the bay of my caress
And your peach-tasting lips chase
The last specks of dust from our content and joy.[3]

After having settled in Kingston I became struck by the many resemblances between my present home and that dreamed-up community in the poem. So much so that I came to think of our move to Kingston/Queen's as a kind of "homecoming"; in other words, I have found the ideal community in Kingston, and within it Queen's, that I envisioned in that dreamy, very hot Sunday afternoon sixty-four years ago!

At this point, I had to interrupt writing this because I had to go for a medical appointment with a retinal specialist. In the course of this I became aware of a change in the concentration of my thoughts. The "central I," I felt, is undergoing a change, a sort of shrinkage. In my mind's focus suddenly appeared my problem eye, the left one, with the rest of my concerns shunted over to the peripheries of that "I." This told me something new: namely that the centre, oft referred to here, can be experienced as having a "super centre" (in case my affected left eye and the rest of my concerns, including work on the present text, were shunted aside towards the "periphery" of that "centre"). Hence the conclusion: the notions of "centre" and "periphery" are perhaps to be thought of as being relative in relation to each other. What does that mean? Frankly, I do not know. It might take the experience of a student of ontology to penetrate this enigma. Perhaps a Heidegger ... This reminded me of his concept of *Geworfenheit* (thrown-ness). If I understand it well, it might mean that a "being" is thrown by an outside force into a situation which requires the coping with elements beyond the normal life-space (with its customary centres and periphery); or, to put it differently, being thrown thus imposes a change of centre/focus relationship, at variance with the "normal" pattern of priorities of a person. Complicating this, I thought, was the possibility that I am here misinterpreting the concept of *Geworfenheit*. Leaving this possibility aside, I was confronted by a drastic shift in the possible interpretation of the relationship between the notions of "centre" and "periphery." My left eye, taken as "granted," as a problem-less part of my body, suddenly claimed *central* attention because of the difficulties I had encountered with it. My whole "horizon" had changed thereby! A new *horizon*, in effect, may enlarge a field that contains new relationships involving new peripheries and new choices for focuses. The master student of this is, of course, Hans-Georg Gadamer. In his *Truth and Method* he writes:

> The horizon is ... something into which we move and that moves with us. Horizons change for a person who is moving. Thus the horizon of the past, out of which all human life lives, and which exists in the form of tradition, is always in motion. The surrounding horizon is not set in motion by historical consciousness. But in it this motion becomes aware of itself.[4]

I now have to backtrack to another key pair of concepts set forth as themes for this gathering, namely "roots vs. exile." I can say without hesitation that I have *never* regarded my move from my native Hungary as moving into "exile." I moved away from there of my *free volition*, behind which there was the clear view that by this I am *liberating myself* as if from some bondage. The multiple escapes (which I have related in a different text) were *stations* in my *self-liberation*. The final station in this (let us call it a sort of odyssey) had proved to be Kingston, our more than welcoming home for the past thirty-six years. Here we found, finally, peace, a framework for family development and professional activity. Here I undertook composing my first opera, *La Tourangelle*, followed by three other operatic works, all four receiving their premieres on CBC Radio, a factor that influenced their nature—works expressed in terms of *sound* only, the visual complement being only *suggested* and left to the listener's imagination. I came to call these four works *mind-operas*, and their themes and character were well summarized and commented upon in an essay by Gordon Smith in 2006.[5] Kingston's welcoming attitude towards my music has been generously realized by the four commissions I received from the Kingston Symphony's splendidly enterprising music director Glen Fast. As a result of this, my three premieres by this orchestra add up to what Robin Elliott came to call the "Kingston Triptych": *Twilight~Fire*, *The Tents of Abraham*, and, finally, *... the timber of those times ... (a theogony)*.

With hindsight it is now clear that each and all of these works is concerned with the relationship between the notions of *ethos* and *ethnos* based on a shared communal belief/repertory. In other words, this triptych explores the process of community formation and value systems. This second triptych follows an earlier one composed during the period 1987–89. The third piece of this set is the work entitled *Sonance•Resonance (Welche Töne?)* which will be heard, as played by the Calgary Philharmonic, in the course of this symposium. A key to this work is expressed through its Beethovenian allusions and its subtitle: "*Welche Töne?*" "Oh Friends ... Not these sounds ..." Which sounds should be suppressed? Making this question universal, I suggest one should scrutinize when and why we suppress any statement, or act. My interest (a mild word this ...) in matters related to what's "right" or "wrong" was an early concern. I may relate this to the tragic story of the Balinese dancer Sampih which forms the first movement of the composition *Comments*, a three-movement piece for contralto, piano, violin, and cello that I composed in the mid-1950s. Sampih was murdered upon his return to Bali after a European tour. The story imposed a question regarding the reasons for the tragic fate of this young dancer. The implication behind this is the conjecture that Sampih, through some act or another, might have violated a communal code of ethics, and for this transgression he had to pay with his life! An ethical conflict animates the fourth movement of *La Tourangelle* also. In it one hears a violent communal conflict between Marie and the city-folk of Tours, castigating her for abandoning her young son by migrating overseas to do missionary work. The dramatic climax of my second opera, *Winthrop*, is the trial of Anne Hutchinson, who holds a different theological/political position from that of Winthrop, for which she is being punished by expulsion from Boston, which was, in the context of the place at that time, tantamount to a death sentence. The third opera, *Traces*, re-enacts events close to those that I had experienced in my slow "progress" towards finding in Kingston a true home, perhaps the first one I ever had! I complete this set of comments by reference to the fourth and last of the operas, *Millennial Mall*; it also questions place and action from a communal, quasi-ethical, point of view. Perhaps not so surprisingly the enactments in this piece show ambivalence. Even doubt, as if the actors (and their inventor the librettist/composer himself) would no longer be at peace in taking up a judgmental position. Until close to the end, the voices seek refuge in ambivalence. But at the conclusion the piece finally finds its equilibrium while seeking to find a meaning for some central concerns.

At this point I had better return to the set theme: centre vs. periphery. By now I hope that I've made it clear that my *felt* centre is where *I am*. In other words, my centre is my own being, wherever I am and whatever I'm doing, including dreaming up music over the years. As life progresses, this central "I," my being, also mutates. But apart from its "periphery," what else is there, what *else* is relevant? Of course, it is my family: First, my dear wife Beate, my companion, love, and helpmate for more than fifty-eight years, then our two loved and loving daughters Helen-Jennifer and Carol. They also are close to this central "I" of myself, as are our three grandchildren: Walker, Astrid, and Claudia, all steadily working their way to maturity. Who else is there in this "I-centre" I am alluding to in a synchronous manner? Is this all there is?

I got to this question in a surprising way while reading André Schwartz-Bart's remarkable book, *The Last of the Just*, a few years ago. He tells a gripping tale spanning close to nine and a half centuries, from the late 900s to the mid-twentieth. It consists of a panorama, and it is a tragic one, of the doings of so-called "just men," all belonging to a single family, over a large expanse of time. Suddenly I was confronted with the reality of a series of "I"s, all acting out of a felt ethical necessity, a predicament that often energized me to write, yet now here imposed itself as a diachrony of similar "I"s, serving as a single ethical imperative. On one page of the book Schwartz-Bart tells of an old Jew (his family is Jewish) who refers to an imperative: all aging Jewish males have an obligation, namely, to gather information about the ancestry of their families. Reading this, I was struck deeply. Why? Because I hadn't done *anything to this end yet!* This I must rectify, I felt. The result of this obligation was a circa ten-year-long genealogical search which yielded a surprisingly rich bounty of information, some from such distant points in time and space as early eighteenth-century Habsburg Austria, and a place in the Prussian-occupied part of Poland after the third partition of that land. Many persons in family relations to each other emerged from the distant corners of history, all living, surviving, acting in sundry ways, all contributing to the possibility that I should be able to write these lines from the vantage point of my "I." These actors, female as well as male, were survivors in a turbulent stretch of Central European history, which now continues in Canada. All these past turbulences are viewed from the perspective of my old age, in the marvellously peaceable city of Kingston! The lessons of such a genealogical account are manifold and indispensable for the understanding of one's *now* and *here*. And yes, this "now" and "here" are the determinants of one's centre, the centre of the "I" I spoke about earlier.

To understand in necessary depth that half-hidden, half-submerged "central I," or this "I here-and-now," it helps to be able to put it in a temporal context. This might be close to Gadamer's *horizon*. It might also suggest that one must be seen as an actor in this saga of an extended family, over considerable spans of time, over large distances. This "centre-I" that is at work when I put notes on lined paper has two *chronotopes*: one contemporary with the act itself, the other doubly non-synchronous (the first non-synchrony derived from one's personal past, the second non-synchrony embedded in one's genetic makeup). In this way, I am suggesting here, one might look for backgrounds, even root causes, for what was done, and what was bypassed or omitted. One might even find clues to changes which suggest a relocation from "periphery" to "centre," showing that as long as something appears in *either* location, a relocation is possible, and, if it occurs, warrants questioning as to why it has occurred. An "I" is immensely complex. It may, as a result of illness, yield *centrality* to a specific part of one's struggling body, in this case an "Eye," that for a while may usurp the role of centrality in one's ongoing flow of time. But, hopefully, not for long ... Work remains to be done. A keynote address has to be composed ... Time is pressing ... Deadlines urge ... I have to compose that so-called keynote address ... Oh ... by the way ... how am I doing with it ...?[6]

Appendix: Kantáta Előpatakon [Cantata in Előpatak]

The following pages show the recto and verso sides of a folio containing the typescript of a poem written by István Anhalt in the Transylvanian village of Előpatak on 1 August 1943. The typescript was produced by Anhalt's mother and is now conserved in the István Anhalt Fonds at Library and Archives Canada. The recto contains two handwritten additions by the author. The first is Anhalt's signature written with a fountain pen in black ink. The signature is written in the usual Hungarian manner (surname first) which suggests that he signed this page before leaving Hungary in 1949. The second, written in blue ink with a ballpoint pen, was no doubt added much later, probably in Canada. The Fonds also conserves photocopies of this typescript on which Anhalt changed the title, crossing out the word Kantáta and replacing it with Délibáb [Mirage]. Since then an English translation of the poem has been published under the title "Mirage in Előpatak."[7]

At the time he wrote the poem, Anhalt was part of a three-hundred-man unit made up of Hungarian Jews who had been conscripted to do forced labour for the Hungarian army.[8] Anhalt remembers that once he had finished writing he was quite surprised with himself. This was the first poem he had ever written, and the words seemed to come of their own volition in a moment of intense creative activity. As he was contemplating what he had just achieved, his young commanding officer happened to walk by. This man had a university education and because of his social status, his rank and the nature of the unit, had held himself aloof from the men under his charge. Anhalt informed him that he had just written a poem and asked him if he would be interested to read it. The officer agreed, and once he had finished he sat down to talk about what he had just read. To Anhalt's utter astonishment, the officer recognized him as a human being for the first time. Of course, this experience had no impact whatsoever on the dreadful conditions under which Anhalt was living at that time. However the experience remained etched in Anhalt's memory because it demonstrated in a real and tangible way the power of poetry to transcend difference, establish lines of communication, and transform human relationships, even in the worst possible circumstances.[9]

OF THE CENTRE, PERIPHERY; EXILE, LIBERATION; HOME AND THE SELF • ANHALT   69

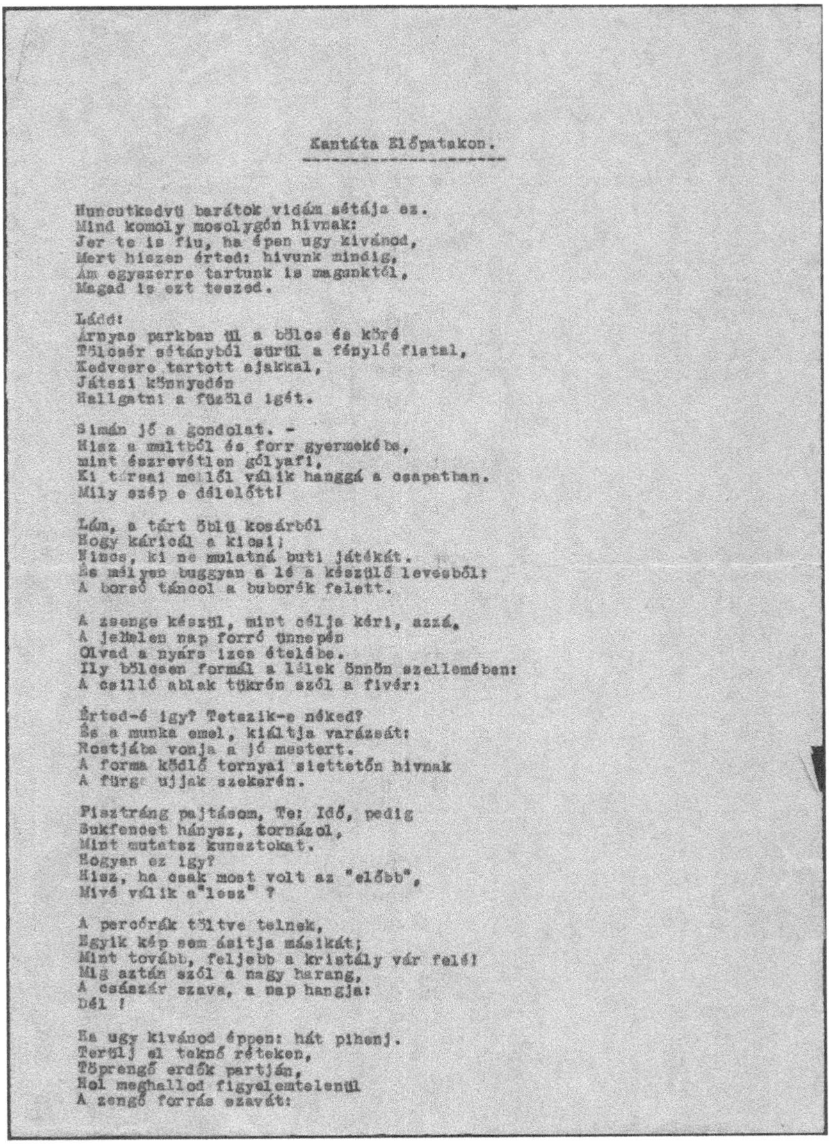

PLATE 4-1 István Anhalt, *Kantáta Előpatakon* [Cantata in Előpatak] (1943), typescript with handwritten corrections, recto, Library and Archives Canada, MUS164/F42,92, with kind permission of the composer and of Library and Archives Canada.

PLATE 4-2 István Anhalt, *Kantáta Előpatakon* [Cantata in Előpatak] (1943), typescript with handwritten corrections, verso, Library and Archives Canada, MUS164/F42,92, with kind permission of the composer and of Library and Archives Canada.

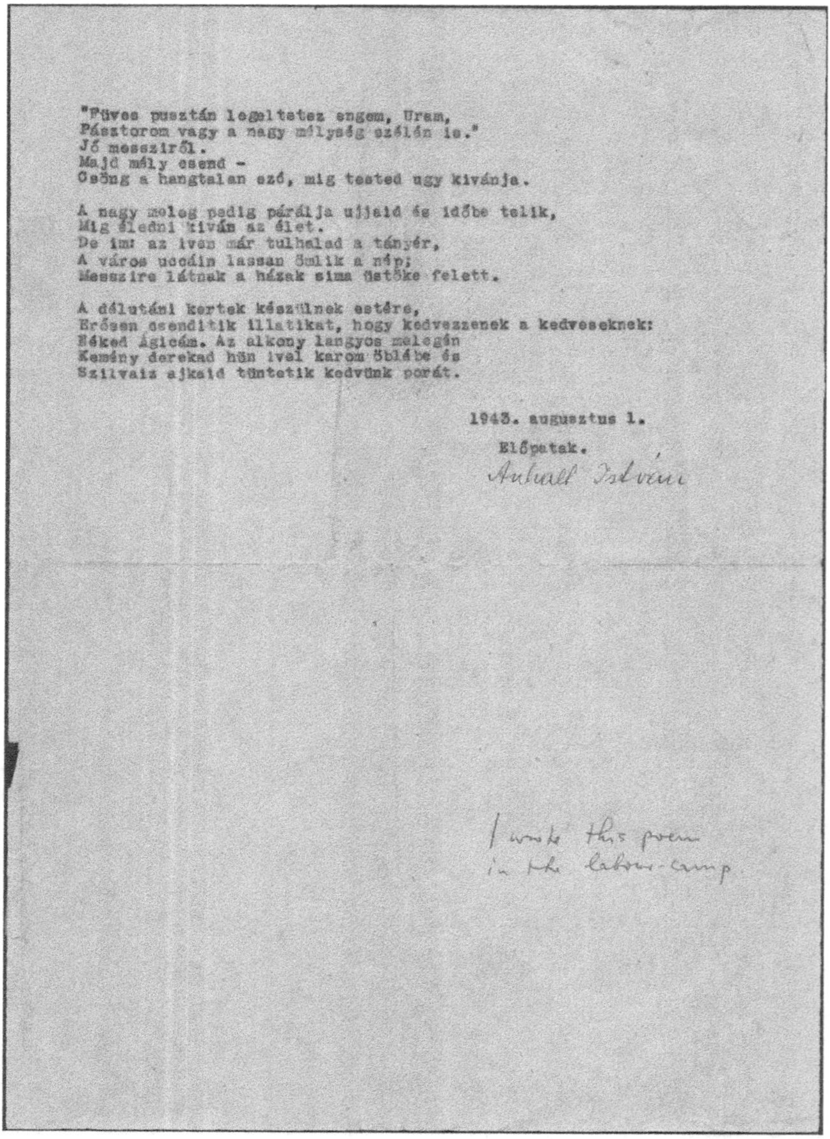

"Füves pusztán legeltetsz engem, Uram,
Pásztorom vagy a nagy mélység szélén is."
Jő messziről.
Majd mély csend -
Csöng a hangtalan szó, mig tested ugy kivánja.

A nagy meleg pedig párálja ujjaid és időbe telik,
Mig éledni kíván az élet.
De im: az ivan már tulhalad a tányér,
A város uccáin lassan ömlik a nép;
Messzire látnak a házak sima üstöke felett.

A délutáni kertek készülnek estére,
Erősen csenditik illatikat, hogy kedvezzenek a kedveseknek:
Néked Ágicám. Az alkony langyos melegén
Kemény derekad hün ivel karom öblébe és
Szilvaiz ajkaid tüntetik kedvünk porát.

1943. augusztus 1.

Előpatak.

Anhalt István

I wrote this poem
in the labour-camp

Notes

1 Keynote address of the conference "Centre and Periphery, Roots and Exile: Interpreting the Music of István Anhalt and György Kurtág," University of Calgary, 2008.
2 For the second-century Gnostic references to ideas related to "thrown-ness," see Hans Jonas, *The Gnostic Religion: The Message of the Alien God and the Beginnings of Christianity*, 2nd revised edition (Boston: Beacon Press, 2001), 45 and 64 respectively. (N.B.: Martin Heidegger was Hans Jonas's doctoral adviser.)
3 Editor's note: In the appendix to this essay we have published a facsimile of the earliest surviving document of the complete text in Hungarian; see plates 4-1 and 4-2.
4 Hans-Georg Gadamer, *Truth and Method*, 2nd revised edition, translation revised by Joel Weinsheimer and Donald G. Marshall (New York: Continuum, 2000), 304.
5 Gordon E. Smith, "From New France to a 'Millennial Mall': Identity Paradigms in Istvan Anhalt's Operas," *American Music* 24/2 (2006): 172–93.
6 With many thanks to Alan Gillmor for his important editorial and related help. I.A.
7 István Anhalt, "Mirage in Előpatak," in *Istvan Anhalt: Pathways and Memory*, ed. Robin Elliott and Gordon E. Smith (Montreal and Kingston: McGill-Queen's University Press, 2001), 421–23.
8 For more on the context and the history of the Hungarian labour service system, which was nothing other than an odious form of legalized slavery, see Robin Elliott, "Life in Europe," in *Istvan Anhalt: Pathways and Memory*, 12–13.
9 Anhalt related the events surrounding the writing and reading of his poem in a telephone conversation with Friedemann Sallis on 2 April 2009. The above text was transcribed from that conversation and then sent to Anhalt for corrections. He approved this text in a letter dated 27 April 2009.

Bibliography

Gadamer, Hans-Georg. *Truth and Method*. 2nd revised edition. Translation revised by Joel Weinsheimer and Donald G. Marshall. New York: Continuum, 2000.

Heidegger, Martin. *On Time and Being*. Translated by Joan Stambaugh. New York: Harper and Row, 1972.

Jonas, Hans. *The Gnostic Religion: The Message of the Alien God and the Beginnings of Christianity*. 2nd revised edition. Boston: Beacon Press, 2001.

Schwartz-Bart, André. *The Last of the Just*. Translated by Stephen Becker. New York: Atheneum, 1960.

FIVE

István Anhalt's Kingston Triptych[1]

ROBIN ELLIOTT

ISTVÁN ANHALT MOVED TO Kingston in 1971 at the age of 52.[2] His reputation as a heavyweight composer of challenging new music preceded him, but in Kingston his compositional idiom would change dramatically. It is arguable that this change was due, at least in part, to the influence of Kingston on him, both as a man and a musician.

Anhalt has written on several occasions about how much Kingston has meant to him, on both a personal and a professional level. "We found peace of mind here in Kingston," he stated in 2005. "Kingston provided us with a very congenial and reciprocally accepting environment."[3] Anhalt regards Canada as his home rather than a place of exile, and he has found contentment and security in Kingston that have enriched his life significantly.

In the darkest days of his youth, while serving a sentence in a Hungarian forced-labour battalion during the Second World War, Anhalt dreamed of a better future and wrote about it in a poem, "Mirage in Előpatak."[4] The poem was written in August 1943 in the village of Előpatak in Transylvania,[5] and in it Anhalt pictures himself living an idyllic existence in an imaginary place called Crystal City. Writing to George Rochberg about this poem in 1985, Anhalt said: "It is remarkable how close Kingston ... comes to that imaginary community whose mirage—the evocation of which—filled me with hope and strength that I felt I needed for the ordeal still ahead."[6] One of Anhalt's strongest statements about Kingston was in his keynote address for the conference "Centre and Periphery, Roots and

Exile," in which he called Kingston "a true home, perhaps the first one I ever had!"[7]

To say that Anhalt would have written very different music and developed in other ways as a composer if he had never moved to Kingston seems obvious, but this is also an assertion which can neither be proved nor disproved, for we have no valid grounds for comparison. There is no Anhalt who stayed in Montreal instead of moving to Kingston, nor one who decided to remain in Europe rather than immigrate to Canada. We can imagine the sorts of Anhalts that might have resulted from those alternative peregrinations, but we cannot do more than that. We only have the Anhalt that did move to Kingston, and analyzing what effect Kingston has had on that Anhalt remains a matter of conjecture rather than proof. Nevertheless, I feel that the nature of Anhalt's relationship to Kingston is worth exploring, and I propose to do this mainly through the lens of the three orchestral compositions that he wrote between 2001 and 2005 for the Kingston Symphony Orchestra.

Music and Place

When Anhalt moved to Kingston, he had for some time been recognized as one of the most important Canadian representatives of the international new music scene. This scene constituted what might be called an ethnoscape, to use Appadurai's term—a transnational association of like-minded composers, performers, scholars, promoters, broadcasters, and their acolytes.[8] The Canadian composer R. Murray Schafer coined the related term "soundscape" long before Appadurai colonized the "-scape" suffix for anthropologists. This is a good example of the centre-vs.-periphery paradigm in academia; as Appadurai pointed out over twenty years ago, the theoretical power of academic ideas depends in part upon "the institutional prestige of the founding author."[9] Appadurai was trained at the University of Chicago and has held a series of academic appointments at leading US universities, including Yale, Chicago, Michigan, Columbia, and NYU. Other academics respect his ideas and quote them frequently. Schafer developed the idea of the soundscape at Simon Fraser University and subsequently left academia altogether; his ideas have been stripped of institutional power and circulate on their own merit, without the imprimatur of an elite university. Most anthropologists and ethnomusicologists cite Appadurai's work, rather than Schafer's, even when speaking of soundscapes. Kay Kaufman Shelemay in the prefatory matter for her textbook *Soundscapes*, for instance, mentions Schafer's use of the word in passing but discusses

Appadurai's idea of the ethnoscape at length.[10] If the world of academic discourse is so beholden to the centre vs. periphery paradigm, and if the influence of place is so important to the world of ideas, it seems reasonable to suggest that the world of music is no less subject to these same sorts of influences.

Music scholars have only recently begun to pay serious attention to the idea of place and how it affects the creation and reception of music. We have lagged behind other disciplines in this regard: anthropology, sociology, cultural geography, and urban studies have all devoted much time and energy to theoretical considerations of place and space and how they influence sound and music, whereas the first theoretically informed important studies of music and place by music scholars are only now being published.[11] As Chris Gibson and John Connell note, "In a world of intensified globalization, links between space, music and identity are increasingly tenuous, yet places give credibility to music ... and music is commonly linked to place through claims to tradition, 'authenticity,' and originality."[12] Gibson and Connell's point that places give credibility to music is certainly germane to the world of contemporary art music. A complex web of composers, performers, impresarios, artist management firms, critics, scholars, and media outlets sustains the new music scene in major urban centres and ensures that the wider world takes notice of it. Simply put, new music composed and premiered in New York City has a better chance of being termed "significant" than does new music created in Kingston.

Much of the work being done on music and place by music scholars is taking place in the field of popular music studies. There is a good deal of scholarship, for instance, about the distinctive pop music sound that has arisen in cities such as Seattle, Memphis, and Liverpool. However, to say that there is such a thing as a "Kingston sound," and that this sound in turn has influenced Anhalt's music, would be both superficial and misleading. Nevertheless, in a recent article in *Kingston Life* magazine titled "City of Musical Artists," the author did attempt to do just that—to find a link connecting a group of twenty-three local professional musicians, including Sarah Harmer, the Tragically Hip, and Ryan Malcolm.[13] Anhalt was included in this article, and the incongruity between his music and that of the pop music artists listed is striking, even to the casual listener.

I would caution against the opposite viewpoint, though, which would maintain that contemporary art music is devoid of geographical reference points or influences. The international new music scene of the 1950s and 1960s, for instance, consisted of several specific centres of production, each of which had its own sphere of influence. Paris contributed the musique concrète idiom developed by Pierre Schaeffer and his colleagues, Cologne the elektronische Musik developed by Eimert and others in the studio of the Nordwestdeutscher Rundfunk. Earlier in the century particular new music idioms had also arisen in Budapest and Vienna, propagated through the efforts of Kodály and Bartók in the former and by Arnold Schoenberg and his pupils in the latter. When Anhalt arrived in Kingston in 1971, he brought with him first-hand, in-depth, ongoing experience of each of these new music places and the musical idioms associated with them. He had also lived for twenty-two years in Montreal, perhaps Canada's most cosmopolitan city at the time, and itself a leading centre for new music in this country thanks in part to Anhalt's efforts as a composer and educator at McGill University.[14] Initially these places from Anhalt's past and the new music associated with them found little resonance outside of the confines of his activities as a composer and music theorist at Queen's University. In order for Anhalt's musical world to come into alignment with Kingston's, some adjustments would be necessary on each side.

Kingston and the Kingston Symphony Orchestra

The nature of Kingston as a cultural and musical centre must be understood before we can determine whether it has had any influence on Anhalt's work. By North American standards, Kingston is a historic city. European settlement in the area began in 1673 with the establishment of the French outpost Fort Frontenac, located at the confluence of Lake Ontario with the St. Lawrence and Rideau rivers. Fort Frontenac was captured by the British in 1758, and, with the arrival of significant numbers of United Empire Loyalists in the aftermath of the American Revolution, it was renamed Kingston in honour of King George III. During the War of 1812 the development of a military and naval presence in Kingston in response to the perceived threat of an American invasion bolstered the local economy and population. With 12,000 inhabitants by mid-century, Kingston was the largest town in Upper Canada, and in 1846, at the instigation of the local lawyer John A. Macdonald (who was later to become Canada's first prime minister), it was incorporated as a city. In the second half of the nineteenth century, though, for a variety of political, geographic, and economic reasons, the growth of the city stalled.

Today, downtown Kingston, where Anhalt lives, retains much of the ambience of a nineteenth-century commercial-institutional town, though not perhaps as self-consciously as Quebec City or as artificially as Niagara-on-the-Lake. The local economy is protected from external market forces, supported as it is by the presence of significant institutional operations: a large military base, three post-secondary educational institutions, and an extensive network of government offices, including a large number of federal penitentiaries. The suburban sprawl surrounding Kingston is as anonymous and ugly as that of any North American city, but the inner core retains a lively sense of the city's past, thanks to the presence of over 700 buildings designated as being of historical or architectural interest and importance. Those who have lived in Kingston for any period of time often remark on the "town and gown" nature of local social and cultural life. Much of the city's reputation in the area of cultural activities, especially of a high-art nature, derives from university-inspired or -supported organizations, such as the Agnes Etherington Art Centre (which has two Rembrandt paintings in its collection) and the Kingston Symphony Orchestra (KSO).

The KSO was founded in 1953 by the Queen's University music professor Graham George.[15] In 1967 Alexander Brott was hired as the conductor and an expansion of activities was initiated, including the hiring of a core of professional wind and string players. Brott's mandate, which he fulfilled scrupulously and with considerable talent, was to build the orchestra from a purely amateur group into one with professional aspirations in terms of repertoire. Under Brott, the KSO attained such milestone achievements as its first performance of a Mahler symphony (No. 4, in 1978) and concerts with leading soloists such as Ravi Shankar, Ida Haendel, and Igor Kipnis. New works by Canadian composers were a comparative rarity, though the orchestra gave the first performance in 1976 of *Fantasy on a Theme*, a challenging work by Brott's McGill colleague Kelsey Jones. With the departure of Brott in 1981, Brian Jackson took over the baton and introduced concert performances of operas and for the first time programmed a Strauss tone poem (*Don Juan*, in 1983) and repertoire by Bartók and Stravinsky. Jackson in turn was succeeded by the Vancouver native Glen Fast in 1991. Fast has worked hard to cultivate local support for the KSO. "An orchestra is not only a collection of musicians and choristers," he has stated, "it's a community of people concerned with putting on concerts and listening to them."[16] As part of this mandate to create and sustain a sense of community around the KSO, Fast often invites local soloists to perform with the orchestra, and he regularly performs and commissions works by local composers, among them Kristi Allik, John Burge, F.R.C. Clarke, Clifford Crawley, Alfred Fisher, David Keane, and Marjan Mozetich, in addition to Anhalt.

The KSO and Anhalt

Throughout the decades of growth for the Kingston Symphony there was little overlap between its world and Anhalt's. Anhalt recalls attending KSO concerts on occasion—a Verdi *Requiem* under Brott and selected performances under Jackson and Fast.[17] He recognized that the orchestra was a cultural asset for Kingston but never considered writing for it.[18] One day in the mid-1990s, though, Anhalt met Glen Fast at a public event in the Agnes Etherington Art Centre. The two men fell into conversation and Fast asked Anhalt to write a piece for the KSO. There would be no commission, but the prospect of a local premiere of one of his works proved to be sufficient incentive for Anhalt to begin work on what would become *Twilight~Fire*. Up to that point, his career as a composer and his life as a Kingstonian had existed in two separate worlds: there had never been a work of his premiered, or even performed to my knowledge, in Kingston. The successful performance of *Twilight~Fire* on 29 September 2002 led to the request for a second work for the KSO, *The Tents of Abraham (A Mirage Midrash)*, premiered on 11 January 2004. At that time Eitan Cornfield was in the midst of preparing a CD documentary on Anhalt for the Canadian Music Centre's *Composers Portraits* series.[19] The performance of *The Tents of Abraham* was included in this two-CD release, and the work won the Juno Award for Best Canadian Classical Composition in 2005.

The KSO then got money from the Canada Council to commission a third orchestral work from Anhalt, *... the timber of those times ... (... a theogony ...)*, which was completed in 2005 and premiered on 23 April 2006. And finally, on 4 November 2007, a fourth Anhalt premiere was given by the KSO—*Four Portraits from Memory*, a series of four slow movements originally written for solo piano in 2005–6.[20] Of the four works by Anhalt premiered by the Kingston Symphony only *... the timber of those times ...* came about as the result of a traditional commissioning process. Anhalt recalls getting some money for *The Tents of Abraham* as well—likely through the Centrediscs recording project rather than from the orchestra—but *Twilight~Fire* and *Four Portraits* resulted in no income for Anhalt whatsoever. Notwithstanding this lack of financial compensation, Anhalt has been very pleased with the entire collaborative process with the KSO; in particular, he has enjoyed working with Glen Fast, whose abilities as a conductor deserve to be much more widely known and celebrated, in Anhalt's opinion.

Two Triptychs

The three orchestral works that Anhalt had written during the 1980s—*Simulacrum* (1987), *SparkskrapS* (1988), and *Sonance•Resonance (Welche Töne)* (1989)—were premiered by the National Arts Centre Orchestra of Ottawa, the Esprit Orchestra of Toronto, and the Toronto Symphony respectively. Writing for orchestras of this level of professional ability entailed little or no constraints upon Anhalt's writing process. Any level of technical difficulty and all manner of musical challenges were permitted. All three works were heard on national broadcasts by CBC Radio and were reviewed in the national media, and *SparkskrapS* was released on a CBC CD recording.[21]

In deciding to collaborate with the Kingston Symphony, Anhalt knew that he would be foregoing this level of national exposure and writing for a different level of orchestra from those he had worked with before. The Kingston Symphony is a Classical-sized ensemble and currently has about fifty-five players on its roster, but only a dozen or so are on contract as fully professional musicians. The rest are hired on a per-service basis; most work at a different day job and their level of playing ability varies. Anhalt set himself the challenge of respecting these limitations without compromising his own artistic ideas. *Twilight~Fire* was written for a complement of forty-four players, with doubled winds including two horns and two trumpets, one percussionist, one keyboard player (piano, celesta), plus harp and strings. The scoring includes a considerable amount of solo string writing. (Anhalt was exploring the capabilities of the orchestra, and was clearly unsure as to the level of playing ability that he could call upon in the back desks of the strings.) The violins are rarely required to go beyond third position, and anything past fifth position appears only in solos for Gisèle Dalbec, the orchestra's concertmaster.

With *The Tents of Abraham*, Anhalt evidently felt that he could experiment with a larger orchestra and a more advanced level of orchestral playing. That score calls for fifty-five players, with an expanded wind complement and four percussionists playing about thirty instruments, as opposed to just one percussionist covering a handful of instruments in *Twilight~Fire*. One compositional problem this posed was the issue of how to maintain a proper balance between the winds and strings, given that there were ten more wind players but the same number of strings as had been used in *Twilight~Fire* (8/6/6/6/3—a total of twenty-nine players). There were a number of ways in which Anhalt tried to achieve this balance. Octave doubling is often used in the strings, both within and between sections, to achieve a weightier sound. There is also more double stopping and greater use of the lower range of the instruments—the C and G strings in the violas and cellos and the G and D strings in the violins. A judicious amount of tremolo is called for in the strings in sections where they must compete with tutti wind writing at a loud dynamic level. Anhalt was evidently pleased with the results of this new orchestral sound, because he calls for almost the identical complement in ... *the timber of those times* ..., adding only a tuba and some extra doublings (piccolo, oboe d'amore and English horn, bass clarinet, contra-bassoon, and bass trombone).

From the Kingston Symphony's perspective, there were advantages and disadvantages to consider in choosing to premiere works by Anhalt. One advantage was that, whereas many audience members will have heard better performances of the Beethoven symphony or Mozart concerto on a KSO program, this was not the case with the Anhalt works, none of which had ever been heard before. The presence of the composer in the audience on each occasion lent an aura of authenticity to the event that is necessarily lacking in the performance of works from the standard repertoire, no matter how well played. On the other hand, Anhalt's compositional idiom, though more accessible now than during his high modernist phase of the 1950s through the 1970s, remains for many listeners at best unfamiliar and at worst incomprehensible. In the end, though, the support for a local composer was the more important element in the reception of Anhalt's works, all four of which met with a warm standing ovation from the KSO audience.

Anhalt refers to the first three of his pieces premiered by the Kingston Symphony as a triptych and has noted parallels with the three orchestral works of the 1980s. He writes that the three "S" works all focus on "the individual 'thisness' of persons as they try to come to terms with deeply personal matters and related memory layers. When these musics intimate societal matters and groups of persons, still the vantage points that suggest themselves appear to be those of individual 'actors' who react, in a variety of ways, to 'public' events."[22] John Beckwith, William E. Benjamin, and Alan Gillmor have written about the personal references embedded in these works and have shown how these compositions may be read as musical documents that are, at least in part, autobiographical in nature.[23]

A number of questions spring immediately to mind, then, about the more recent triptych. In what way are the three "T" works related to one another? How does the *Four Portraits from Memory* relate to these other three works? Are there autobiographical influences or other deep themes that relate the two triptychs to one another? What are the interrelationships as far as musical style and compositional technique are concerned?

To begin with, it is worth noting some important differences between the two triptychs. The titles of the "S" works all refer to intangible concepts, whereas the titles of the "T" works all refer to concrete objects. The "T" triptych is more concerned with the behaviour of a community than the inner life of an individual. If there is an underlying concept to the three works, it is the Greek concept of ethnos, rather than ethos, although, as Anhalt has remarked, those two words are closely linked both etymologically and hermeneutically.[24] The "T" works are on the whole more programmatic in nature than the "S" works, and this in turn leads to the observation that the "T" works are written in a musical language that is generally more comprehensible, and thus more accessible, than the "S" works. On the other hand, in the "T" triptych there are to my knowledge no direct quotations from earlier works, whereas such references abound in the "S" works, especially, of course, *Sonance•Resonance*, which is a close intertextual commentary on Beethoven's Ninth Symphony.

Two of the "T" works are derived from ancient Greco-Roman mythology. *Twilight~Fire* takes as its inspiration the story of Baucis and Philemon, as related in the Eighth Book of Ovid's *Metamorphoses*. This story of an elderly married couple who are rewarded for giving shelter and sustenance to the disguised gods Jupiter and Mercury (or Zeus and Hermes in the Greek version of the myth) obviously presented itself as an attractive subject to Anhalt, who was writing the work for his wife Beate on the occasion of their fiftieth wedding anniversary. The subtitle of the third work, "a theogony," refers to Hesiod's poem of that name, written ca. 700 BC, which deals with the origin and genealogy of the ancient Greek gods. The intention, as in Anhalt's earlier work *Millennial Mall*, was to demonstrate the relationship between, in Anhalt's words, "an ancient chronotope [and] the ongoing reality of one's own environment."[25]

The Tents of Abraham seems, on the surface, to be the odd one out in this triptych, as it takes us to the Middle East in ancient Biblical times and reflects upon the legacy of Abraham and his sons Isaac and Ishmael, born to his wife Sarah and his concubine Hagar respectively. But Anhalt has pointed out that this work, too, deals with "ethical matters, but from a different ethical *background* (the Hebrew one; while nos. 1. and 3. refer to the Graeco/Roman point of view)."[26] Both *The Tents of Abraham* and ... *the timber of those times* ... are in five movements (together with *Four Portraits* they are the only multi-movement orchestral works Anhalt has written), are scored for almost identical orchestral forces, and feature overtly descriptive writing.

Four Portraits from Memory is clearly intended as a separate work from the three works of the Kingston triptych. The title does not start with a "T," and the work was originally written for piano solo. The orchestral forces required—just twenty-six players in all—are half the size of those called for in two of the three works in the Kingston triptych. *Four Portraits* is a series of slow movements, each one a tribute to a recently deceased friend or relative; programmatic elements are non-existent and the musical language is sombre and elegiac throughout. Though not closely related to the other works in the Kingston triptych, *Four Portraits* was written for and premiered by the KSO and is in a musical language that is similar to the works of the Kingston triptych.[27]

Anhalt's Commentaries on the Triptych

The writing of a major composition for Anhalt has characteristically been followed by extensive reflections upon it in writing. In the case of *Twilight~Fire*, Anhalt has written three essays on the work to date. The first, "Memo to Myself," was written before he had finished composing *Twilight~Fire*.[28] In this essay, Anhalt describes sharing stories from ancient Greek mythology with his grandchildren, and specifically recalls telling them the story of Baucis and Philemon as related in Ovid's *Metamorphoses*. The second essay was written just over a month after the composition was completed, and it is one of the most detailed analyses of any of his works that Anhalt has offered.[29] He goes through the score bar by bar and describes in detail the use of symmetrical pitch structures, pentatonic, modal, and diatonic pitch collections, nested augmented triads, and so on in a clear and forthright fashion. But for all the detailed descriptions offered, there is little by way of interpretation or even analysis. The horn melody beginning at bar 63 is described as suggesting "the voice of a bard singing of 'times past,'"[30] but that is the only explicit link to an extra-musical idea in the entire essay. Otherwise, beyond purely musical descriptors, Anhalt offers only generalized suggestions of extra-musical references such as "a mood of contemplation," "a quasi-fanfare," or "pastoral in tone." The third text on *Twilight~Fire* offers the autobiographical information that Anhalt served part of his forced-labour battalion service in the Second World War in the Carpathian Mountains not far from where Ovid lived in exile at the end of his life after being banished by Augustus, and that Anhalt and his wife had recently visited Phrygia (now in Turkey), which is where the story of Baucis and Philemon takes place.[31]

Just days after completing ... *the timber of those times* ..., Anhalt wrote a brief essay about the composition of this work.[32] In it he explains that the word "timber" in the title refers to "the composite *stuff* which the 'world' of a cultural epoch (all epochs, perhaps) is made of ... the *basic substance of a culture.*"[33] He offers descriptive remarks on each movement, explaining that the lame wizard of the third movement is Hephaestus, and the mechanical bride is Pandora (she is represented by a solo violin figuration somewhat reminiscent of Vivaldi), that the title of the fourth movement refers to Ares the war god and Aphrodite, goddess of beauty, and that the "guide of souls" in the fifth movement is Hermes. In a postscript to this essay, Anhalt explains his own relationship to ancient Greek mythology. In his student days in Budapest, Anhalt was friends with two young pupils of the great Hungarian classics scholar Károly Kerényi. He also mentions travels to antiquities museums in Europe and visits to Turkey, Greece, Italy, and Israel as having contributed to his immersion in and fascination with the world of ancient Greek mythology.[34]

Anhalt's two brief writings on *The Tents of Abraham* date from September 2002 and May 2003.[35] The work is subtitled "a mirage midrash." As it is told in music, the story is present in hazy outlines, like a desert mirage. A midrash is an interpretation or exegesis; the music thus also presents a particular interpretation of the story of Abraham, told in order to inform our present-day understanding of the relationship between Judaism and Islam.[36] Once again, we see that for Anhalt the workings of the ancient world are of continuing relevance, and in reflecting upon them, we can come to a deeper understanding of present conditions. The same urge to understand the human condition motivates Anhalt to read both historical and philosophical treatises, and also the daily newspaper. In his creative work as a composer, he often searches for ways to relate the one to the other.

Conclusion: Composer and Community

I would like to conclude by returning to the questions posed at the beginning of this essay: in what way or ways has Kingston informed or influenced the triptych of works composed for the KSO? We can answer this question in various ways. Friedemann Sallis stakes out one extreme position when he writes "To suggest that Kingston has anything whatsoever to do with the music of *The Tents of Abraham* is a complete distortion ... Associating a magnificent work like *The Tents of Abraham* with a place, merely because it was composed and first performed there, is trivial. It does a disservice not only to the composer's legacy but also to the promotion of serious music in Canada."[37] Sallis wrote this in reaction to the CD documentary on Anhalt prepared by Eitan Cornfield, which, in Sallis's opinion, spends too much time offering superficial observations about the Kingston cityscape and not enough time delineating Anhalt's musical education and influences.

But I do not believe that we can dismiss out of hand the "Kingston-ness" of this trilogy. Kingston has afforded Anhalt the peace of mind to contemplate both his own history and inner life as a human being, which he did in the orchestral works of the 1980s, and also to think about bigger issues relating to history, religion, and the general human condition, which are the subject of the Kingston trilogy. The three "T" works were written for Glen Fast and the KSO, and in the course of composing the three works, Anhalt came to know these musicians well and to write with their specific abilities and qualities as performers in mind. To some degree this was a limitation, as we have seen in examining the orchestral writing of *Twilight~Fire*. But art without limitations can be indulgent and superficial; writing for the KSO forced Anhalt to simplify his musical language and to communicate his ideas clearly and directly, and it could be argued that his music is the stronger for that.

Personal circumstances and inspirations certainly are present in the Kingston works: a wedding anniversary (*Twilight~Fire*), the composer's religious heritage (*The Tents of Abraham*), and the deaths of loved ones (*Four Portraits from Memory*). But at heart the Kingston works are about the relationship between individual and community values, or more personally, they are artistic manifestations of Anhalt's search for the "Crystal City." In this sense, then, Kingston is not only the place where the works were composed and premiered, it is in some sense the fundamental inspiration that underlies each of them.

But there is something further that calls for recognition, some intangible influence that Kingston has had on Anhalt's music. Perhaps it can be found in the 700 heritage buildings within walking distance of his downtown Kingston home. As an avid walker, Anhalt has passed by virtually every one of those buildings, and while doing so I suspect that he has reflected upon how the past and the future are both intimately connected through this thin sliver of time that we call the present. The many professional and personal associations that he formed at Queen's University—with students and fellow faculty members alike—are another thread binding this place to this music. To overstate the influence of Kingston on Anhalt's most recent music would indeed be facile and simple-minded, but to remove it from the equation altogether would be doing a disservice both to Anhalt and to the community that has sustained and nurtured him for the past thirty-seven years and has finally embraced his music as its own.

Notes

1 This is an expanded version of a talk given on 24 January 2008 at the University of Calgary for the symposium "Centre and Periphery, Roots and Exile: Interpreting the Music of István Anhalt and György Kurtág." I would like to thank Friedemann Sallis for organizing this event and inviting me to speak at it. I also thank István Anhalt for his written comments on the original conference paper (in a letter to me dated 3 February 2008) and his oral comments on this expanded version of it (given to me during a meeting at his house in Kingston on 6 July 2008).
2 I first met Anhalt in Kingston in 1973 when we were neighbours, living just a block from each other on Johnson Street in Kingston (he at no. 273 and I at no. 221). The final version of this article was completed shortly after I myself turned 52, the same age that Anhalt was when he moved to Kingston.
3 Kay Langmuir, "Juno Nomination for Professor Istvan Anhalt," Queen's News Centre press release, http://qnc.queensu.ca/story_loader.php?id=4224db8a42 68a (accessed 27 June 2008).
4 The poem was written in Hungarian and translated into English by Anhalt in the 1980s. It is published in *Istvan Anhalt: Pathways and Memory*, ed. Robin Elliott and Gordon E. Smith (Montreal and Kingston: McGill-Queen's University Press, 2001), 421–23. It also appears in chapter 4 of this volume.
5 The village belonged to Hungary until 1944; it is now the village of Vâlcele in Romania.
6 Alan M. Gillmor, ed., *Eagle Minds: Selected Correspondence of Istvan Anhalt and George Rochberg (1961–2005)* (Waterloo, ON: Wilfrid Laurier University Press, 2007), 162.
7 Istvan Anhalt, "Of the Centre, Periphery; Exile, Liberation; Home and the Self," keynote address for "Centre and Periphery, Roots and Exile: Interpreting the Music of István Anhalt and György Kurtág," University of Calgary, 23 January 2008; corrected and expanded version—a fourteen-page typescript, copy in the author's possession. The quoted passage is on p. 11 of the typescript. The essay is published as chapter 4 of this volume.
8 Arjun Appadurai defines his neologism "ethnoscape" in *Modernity at Large: Cultural Dimensions of Globalization* (Minneapolis: University of Minnesota Press, 1996), 48. He had been using the term in print for at least five years prior to this book publication.
9 Arjun Appadurai, "Theory in Anthropology: Center and Periphery," *Comparative Studies in Society and History* 28/2 (1986): 359.
10 Kay Kaufman Shelemay, *Soundscapes: Exploring Music in a Changing World* (New York: W.W. Norton, 2001): xviii–xix. Her discussion of Schafer and Appadurai is essentially the same in the preface to the second edition of the textbook (2006: xvii), but she does add more information on Schafer later on (p. xxxiv).
11 An important recent example is Adam Krims, *Music and Urban Geography* (New York: Routledge, 2007).
12 Chris Gibson and John Connell, *Sound Tracks: Popular Music, Identity and Place* (New York: Routledge, 2003), i.

13 Ken Cuthbertson, "City of Musical Artists," *Kingston Life* 6/2 (2004): 60–75. The author quotes sometime-Kingston-area resident Dan Aykroyd (60), who states "My theory is that the past generation, through the strong military presence ... brought British music hall and swing band records to town. That mix, along with the area's exposure to American Black and White radio, has fostered the development of ... musical artists who are extremely knowledgable and talented." The influence of the repertoires that Aykroyd cites on the music of Anhalt has been negligible to non-existent.

14 See my article "István Anhalt and New Music at McGill," in *Compositional Crossroads: Music, McGill, Montreal*, ed. Eleanor Stubley (Montreal and Kingston: McGill-Queen's University Press, 2008), 33–55.

15 The Kingston Symphony Orchestra is run by the Kingston Symphony Association, which also oversees the Kingston Choral Society, the Kingston Youth Orchestra, the Kingston Youth Strings, and the Kingston Community Orchestra; all of these activities are overseen by a board of directors and supported by a volunteer committee.

16 Paul Gurnsey, "The Gift of Music [Kingston Symphony Association's 50th Anniversary]," *Kingston Life* 5/4 (2003–4): 28.

17 Information in this paragraph and the next is derived from a telephone conversation with Anhalt on 19 January 2008.

18 During his time as head of the Department of Music at Queen's University (1971 to 1981), Anhalt cooperated with the KSO in numerous ways; at that time, he regarded the idea of putting himself forward as a composer for the orchestra as something that would have been close to a conflict of interest (letter to the author, 3 February 2008).

19 *Canadian Composers Portraits: Istvan Anhalt*, Centrediscs CMCCD 10204, released in 2004.

20 The first public performance of the piano version of *Four Portraits from Memory* was given by Charles Foreman on 22 January 2008 in Eckhardt-Gramatté Hall, Rozsa Centre, University of Calgary, on the occasion of the conference "Centre and Periphery, Roots and Exile: Interpreting the Music of István Anhalt and György Kurtág." See Friedemann Sallis's article in this volume for further information on *Four Portraits from Memory*.

21 *Iridescence*, Esprit Orchestra conducted by Alex Pauk, CBC SMCD5132, released in 1994.

22 Istvan Anhalt, "A Pair of Orchestral Triptychs, from 1987 to 1989 and from 2002 to 2005: A Preliminary Account," five-page typescript, dated 4–6 September 2005 (quoted passage is on p. 3); copy in the author's possession. The second triptych was begun in 2001, not 2002; the score of *Twilight~Fire* is dated "Kingston / July 11, 2001" after the final bar. The score of *The Tents of Abraham* is not dated precisely beyond "© 2003"; the score of ... *the timber of those times* ... is dated "February 15, 2005, on Bea's birthday" after the final bar (Bea is Beate Anhalt [née Frankenberg], who was born in Düsseldorf on 15 February 1924, emigrated with her family to Montreal in August 1939, and married Anhalt on 6 January 1952). All three scores are in manuscript; copies in the author's possession.

23 John Beckwith, "Orchestral Works," and William E. Benjamin, "Alternatives of Voice: Anhalt's Odyssey from Personalized Style to Symbolic Expression," in *Istvan Anhalt: Pathways and Memory*, ed. Robin Elliott and Gordon E. Smith (Montreal and Kingston: McGill-Queen's University Press, 2001), 111–31 and 164–307; Alan M. Gillmor, "Echoes of Time and the River," in *Taking a Stand: Essays in Honour of John Beckwith*, ed. Timothy J. McGee (Toronto: University of Toronto Press, 1995), 15–44.
24 Anhalt, "A Pair of Orchestral Triptychs," 3–4.
25 Istvan Anhalt, "The Way to ... *the timber of those times* ... (... *a theogony* ...)," ten-page typescript dated 19 February 2005 (quoted passage is on p. 8); copy in the author's possession.
26 Istvan Anhalt, letter to the author, 3 February 2008 (Anhalt's emphasis).
27 It is worth noting that the fourth movement of the work was written in memory of the Austrian-born Kingston painter Ingeborg Mohr. Anhalt owns some of Mohr's paintings, including her last oil painting, which hangs over his piano; some of her work is also in the Agnes Etherington Art Centre. The other movements are tributes to Anhalt's half-sister Judit Anhalt, the composer George Rochberg, and Anhalt's friend Andras Kelemen. See Istvan Anhalt, "About *Four Portraits from Memory*," five-page typescript dated 16 May 2007; copy in the author's possession.
28 Istvan Anhalt, "Memo to Myself," eight-page typescript dated 27 May 2001, to which is appended a photocopy of the story of Baucis and Philemon from Book VIII of *The Metamorphoses of Ovid* in the translation by Mary M. Innes (Harmondsworth: Penguin, 1955), 195–98; copy in the author's possession.
29 Istvan Anhalt, "About *Twilight~Fire (Baucis' and Philemon's Feast)*," nineteen-page typescript dated 20 August 2001; copy in the author's possession.
30 Ibid., 3.
31 Istvan Anhalt, "*Twilight~Fire (Baucis' and Philemon's Feast)*," twelve-page typescript dated 5 April 2008; this is the text of a talk given at the Agnes Etherington Art Centre for the Eastern Ontario Regional Seminar of The Academies of Arts, Humanities and Sciences of Canada [The Royal Society of Canada], at Queen's University; copy in the author's possession. Anhalt was elected as a Fellow of the Royal Society of Canada in 2007.
32 Anhalt, "The Way."
33 Ibid., 3 (Anhalt's emphasis).
34 Ibid., 9–10. In a letter to the author (3 February 2008), Anhalt suggested contemporary parallels of these mythological topics, viz. Pandora / a woman who 'over-uses' plastic surgery; Ares / Arnold Schwarzenegger.
35 Istvan Anhalt, "About *The Tents of Abraham*," six-page typescript, dated 22 September 2002; and "*The Tents of Abraham (A Mirage ~ Midrash)*," one-page typescript, dated 24 May 2003; copies in the author's possession.
36 See the essay by William E. Benjamin in this volume for a detailed critical commentary on this aspect of *The Tents of Abraham*.
37 Friedemann Sallis, "Review of *Canadian Composers Portraits: Istvan Anhalt*," *CAML Review* 33/1–2 (2005): 43–44.

Bibliography

Appadurai, Arjun. *Modernity at Large: Cultural Dimensions of Globalization*. Minneapolis: University of Minnesota Press, 1996.

———. "Theory in Anthropology: Center and Periphery." *Comparative Studies in Society and History* 28/2 (1986): 356–74.

Beckwith, John. "Orchestral Works." In *Istvan Anhalt: Pathways and Memory*, edited by Robin Elliott and Gordon E. Smith, 111–31. Montreal and Kingston: McGill-Queen's University Press, 2001.

Benjamin, William E. "Alternatives of Voice: Anhalt's Odyssey from Personalized Style to Symbolic Expression." In *Istvan Anhalt: Pathways and Memory*, 164–307.

Cuthbertson, Ken. "City of Musical Artists." *Kingston Life* 6/2 (2004): 60–75.

Elliott, Robin. "István Anhalt and New Music at McGill." In *Compositional Crossroads: Music, McGill, Montreal*, edited by Eleanor Stubley, 33–55. Montreal and Kingston: McGill-Queen's University Press, 2008.

———, and Gordon E. Smith, eds. *Istvan Anhalt: Pathways and Memory*. Montreal and Kingston: McGill-Queen's University Press, 2001.

Gibson, Chris and John Connell. *Sound Tracks: Popular Music, Identity, and Place*. New York: Routledge, 2003.

Gillmor, Alan M., ed. *Eagle Minds: Selected Correspondence of Istvan Anhalt and George Rochberg (1961–2005)*. Waterloo, ON: Wilfrid Laurier University Press, 2007.

———. "Echoes of Time and the River." In *Taking a Stand: Essays in Honour of John Beckwith*, edited by Timothy J. McGee, 15–44. Toronto: University of Toronto Press, 1995.

Gurnsey, Paul. "The Gift of Music [Kingston Symphony Association's 50th Anniversary]." *Kingston Life* 5/4 (2003–4): 28–35.

Krims, Adam. *Music and Urban Geography*. New York: Routledge, 2007.

Sallis, Friedemann. "Review of *Canadian Composers Portraits: Istvan Anhalt*." *CAML Review* 33/1–2 (2005): 43–44.

Shelemay, Kay Kaufman. *Soundscapes: Exploring Music in a Changing World*. New York: W.W. Norton, 2001.

SIX

István Anhalt's *The Tents of Abraham*: Where Music Cannot Heal, Let It Be Restored

WILLIAM BENJAMIN

THE TENTS OF ABRAHAM (2003) is the middle work in István Anhalt's second orchestral triptych.[1] The first of these work-series, dating from the mid- to late 1980s, deals with the role of episodic (personal-life) memory in consciousness.[2] The second triptych, dating from the decade just ended, turns to ancient narratives and their potential reverberations into our collective present.[3] In its own way too, then, the second series is about memory, though collective rather than individual, but it differs from the first in making political ramifications more explicit.[4]

The two triptychs are connected in another way: the second work in each records a stage in the composer's increasingly open engagement with his public as a Jew. Anhalt's first orchestral work, the Symphony of 1958, was dedicated to "The Bi-centenary of Canadian Jewry," but this was an afterthought, occasioned by some support from the Canadian Jewish Congress for the premiere of an already completed, completely abstract piece. *Simulacrum* (1987), the first piece in the first orchestral triptych, includes Sephardic Jewish melodies that refer to the composer's early experiences of his grandfather's devoutness,[5] but the work's other musical references are to European culture in general, in one case, to music with disturbingly anti-Semitic associations.[6] *Traces (Tikkun)*, completed in 1995, is the penultimate of Anhalt's four large dramatic works, of which the first three deal with a hero who is engaged in a spiritual search that is connected with physical displacement. It is described by the composer as having a sophisticated "European-born Jew who has settled ... in Canada" as its hero-protagonist,[7] but, as he tellingly writes, "the word 'Jew' does not appear in the text [his own libretto], thus allowing for greater generality."[8]

Anhalt has obviously struggled with the questions of how and how much to identify as a Jew, but it seems to have become important to him, belatedly, to at least make known his identification with the Jewish people in their persistent refusal to dissolve in successive waves of majority culture.[9] At the same time, anything touched with rank sectarianism, with undue tribal partisanship, appears to strike him as having no place in the discourses in which he participates, no place in his public stance, at any rate. Thus the middle work of the first triptych, *SparkskrapS* (1988), attempts a musical translation of memories that are only intermittently of specifically Jewish content, via a symbol system drawn from Kabbalah, the hermeneutic approach to Hebrew scripture that is least connected to traditional Jewish practice;[10] and *The Tents of Abraham*, while prompted by Anhalt's frustration with attitudes toward Israel in the academic community and the mainstream media, is in no sense a Zionist tract.[11] It is, rather, a peace offering, dedicated, as the composer writes, to "the peace-seeking descendants and friends of Isaac and Ishmael."[12] The composer was motivated, no doubt among other factors, by a desire that his work might provide listeners with the opportunity to contemplate the sickening and seemingly intractable Israeli-Palestinian morass, and to see its origins in the travails of a fractured family 4000 years ago.[13] His larger purpose is presumably borrowed from ancient tragedy via twentieth-century therapy; namely, to promote the possibility of recovery from psychic wounds by way of confronting their original "causes," and thus to bring about the restoration of a proper fraternality between Israeli and Arab.[14]

From the deeply idealistic venture that is *Tents*, a sophisticated balancing act necessarily emerges, one in which the desire to acknowledge his passionate concern with Israel's (and thus the Jewish people's) right to exist weighs alongside Anhalt's deeply ingrained secular humanism and social progressivism, traits that mandate a striving for fairness, a disengagement from anything that smacks too much of national particularism, even a certain attempt at moral neutrality, in which it is bad form to choose sides too openly. Therefore, while political concerns form part of the intentional basis of the work's creation, of the guise in which it addresses itself to the world, and of its claim on the public's interest, these concerns are freighted with contradictions that undermine the potential to mitigate conflict that Anhalt, in moments of creative optimism, might have hoped *Tents* would have.

Still, *Tents* is so far the strongest work of what may turn out to be Anhalt's last decade as a regularly active composer. While it is arguably a virtue in a work when its aesthetic interest is coupled with features that symbolize and perhaps contribute to the resolution of social tensions, there are other, perhaps more basic, ways in which music can have deep social effects.[15] In the second part of this paper, after a discussion that explains the likely failure of *Tents* as a vehicle of reconciliation, I will say something about the work's success in engaging a particular group of performers and their public; its rare ability to reach an ordinary, if well-disposed and reasonably sophisticated audience, in a society like Canada's, that is not inclined to have its artistic tastes dictated from above. The success of the work, when performed by a semi-professional orchestra in Ontario before a disinterested audience with no need to pretend to like it, which led to its winning the 2005 Juno Award as best classical composition of the year,[16] seems to require more than passing comment, especially in view of the near total neglect of Anhalt's work by performers and concert audiences during the preceding fifty-four years of his life in his adopted country. I think this success can be explained, both in terms of qualities inherent in the work and by way of certain artistic and personal choices the composer made during the past thirty-five years. Ironically, it is these choices and their consequences that link up significantly with elements of the Abraham myth in ways that the vicissitudes of the contemporary Arab-Jewish saga do not. And, even more ironically, what Anhalt has achieved as a composer, in a context prevailingly indifferent or hostile to his art, carries a more direct lesson for the antagonists in Israel/Palestine than any recourse to Holy Writ. Justifying this strange seeming claim will occupy the latter parts of this paper. But I turn first to the work's ambitious but inherently clouded political agenda.

Problems with the Scriptural Sources

In *The Tents of Abraham*, as in his other orchestral works since the 1980s, Anhalt evokes a series of scenes. The musical processes that serve to call up these scenes represent their content without the aid of an internal text or any associated visual imagery, but rely on an implicit program in a manner that recalls some nineteenth-century music.[17] Operating in extremely varied ways, these processes attempt to conjure up a place in its totality, or to indicate the actions of characters in a story as well as the emotions connected to these actions. In other cases, musical patterns are meant to stand iconically for certain sounds: some real to a place, others imagined by the characters, or produced by their actions. Still other sonic complexes in this large work are intended to symbolize, in ways characteristic of much of Anhalt's later music, certain modes of consciousness in the characters, states of mind too abstract to be reckoned as emotions or feeling states. Examples might be meditating on a question, preparing to face the unknown, or resigning oneself to one's fate. Symbols of this last kind, as well as being complex, stand at times for the music's ability to induce in the listener what they symbolize, to get her to brood, him to steel himself, or another to feel as if accepting what must be borne.[18]

The story referred to in *Tents* is composed of episodes in the life of Abraham, taken from Genesis and from compilations of Jewish homiletical narrative known collectively as midrash, which date mostly from the first millennium of the common era.[19] The work is in fact subtitled "a mirage-midrash." The characters are Abraham, his wives Sarah and Hagar, his sons Ishmael and Isaac, and God. Since there can be no need for me to recount the story, I will say only that Anhalt focuses on certain aspects, among them the midrashic (and secondarily the quranic)[20] story of Abraham establishing his bona fides by shattering the idols in his father's workshop, the conflict between the women and the damage it causes, and the promises made by God to Abraham in return for his fidelity: to make him the father, through Isaac, of a great and model nation that will inherit Canaan, and to create a second line leading from him, through Ishmael, to another great nation. To this the composer adds an episode out of his imagination: he depicts the sons at rough play, although the biblical text represents Ishmael as having been banished as a teenager just after Isaac was weaned and scarcely in a position to do more than crawl, let alone roughhouse.[21]

Anhalt's first problem in attempting to speak to both sets of antagonists is his necessary reliance on Jewish texts as diegetic sources. The promise that God makes to Abraham in Genesis 15, and elaborates as a full-blown covenant in Genesis 17:4, provides the foundation for various Jewish claims on the land of Israel, incompatible as they may be: the claim that the Jews' present possession of Israel is a fulfillment of the promise, even if He who has promised is taken, post-theistically, as a projection of the national will; the modern Orthodox (Jewish) claim that this possession is necessary to prepare for a Messianic future; and, just as surely, the Ultra-Orthodox claim that by acting prematurely, in advance of explicit Divine sanction, Jews are imperilling that Messianic future and their own security. The centrality of this promise, in the text, forces Anhalt to skirt it by referring in the title of the last movement to "two promises." But what is the second promise? Presumably the assurance given to Hagar in Genesis 16, and repeated both to Hagar and to Abraham himself in Genesis 21, that Ishmael's seed shall also proliferate into a great nation, an assurance perhaps implied in Genesis 17:4, where God designates Abraham (until then Abram) as the "father of a multitude of nations."[22] The two promises have one thing in common, to be sure: the idea of one thing becoming a great many (an idea that is ingeniously represented by canonic textural accretion, brilliantly realized in orchestral terms, in mm. 536–65 [movement 5]). But Genesis can scarcely be thought to treat the promises as equivalent, since it differentiates the two sons in the most brutal terms. It is Isaac with whom God is prepared to establish his covenant (Genesis 17:19 and 17:21), while Ishmael, though destined to sire "twelve princes," is described contemptuously as a "wild ass of a man," someone whose "hand shall be against every man, and every man's hand against him" (Genesis 16:12), in other words, an outlaw.

The Hebrew Bible provides just as little support for Anhalt as he navigates his way through other episodes, seeking to find common ground for today's opposed camps. The third movement, "A Contest; Wife and Concubine," must face the fact that, while the Torah sheds a tear for Hagar, it does nothing to raise her to Sarah's level. Sarah dies and is buried with care and ceremony, while Hagar disappears into the thin air of the desert. But Anhalt, overcompensating, produces a contest that is no contest, since the sinuous third movement turns out to be a representation of a singular feminine sexuality, quite clearly in the singular. There is no duality of themes here, only a unitary flow of melody, and how could it be otherwise given that Sarah was in her eighties and hardly a competitor for Hagar, the voluptuous agent of Abraham's implied beguilement?[23] Likewise, the moral equivalence between the two boys depicted by the heterophonically tinged homophony of repetitively rhythmicized two- and three-tone chords in the fourth movement ("The Two Sons: Boys' Games")—the effect is of two figures so intertwined in their play as to be indistinguishable—besides being anachronistic (see above), goes against the sharp distinction between the boys that Genesis (not to mention the midrashic exegesis) hammers in at every opportunity.

My point is not that Anhalt has no right to tamper with the script. Of course, that is his prerogative. But one-half of the audience that he is trying to reach, the "peace-seeking descendents of Isaac," could well be put off by any attempt to equate the two promises made to Abraham when only one of the sons is described in the sources they know rather well as his true heir, the inheritor of his covenant with God, and the legatee of the land that goes with this covenant. Nor will the purported equation of the young lads or the overshadowing of Sarah by Hagar, effective as these are in purely dramatic terms, sit well with this crowd.

The Bible's recalcitrance to his purposes might have led Anhalt to the Quran as a parallel source, especially since he includes a quotation from that book in the score's front matter, opposite one from the Bible. Unfortunately, though, the Quran is not, by and large, a narrative text and thus offers very little to a composer intent upon deriving musical images from a story. Muslims read of Ibrahim, Ishaq, and Ismail in their holy writ but find there no soap opera, no competition between pushy mothers, and no displacement of the first-born by a golden child. The Quran makes no mention of Hagar at all; both boys may as well have emerged from one mother. And it mentions the two sons, almost always in tandem, as following in their father's dutiful footsteps. Even where one would think a singling out would be necessary, as in the episode of the binding of Isaac, the Quranic text opts for anonymity, allowing most Islamic authorities to claim that Ishmael was the chosen victim.[24]

One option for the composer would have been to concentrate on those episodes where the two traditions agree in some measure. The story of Abraham's destruction of the idols is one such (see note 20), while another is the sacrifice of the "only child," which forms the content of the Torah reading on Judaism's holiest day (Yom Kippur) and the subject of the Islamic festival of Eid al-Adha. The third, and potentially most effective, is the reconciliation of the brothers upon the occasion of the joint burial of their father at the Cave of Makhpelah, next to Sarah (Genesis 25:9–10).[25] As noted above, Anhalt foregrounds the story of the idols in the second movement, entitled "The Wanderer; Iconoclast—Visionary (Lekh Lekha)," but he takes no advantage of the other two possibilities.[26] It is easy to see why he avoided the sacrifice, which might well have overshadowed everything else with its content, searingly painful as it is and, as far as both traditions are concerned, deeply enigmatic from a moral standpoint as well. Moreover, a depiction of the sacrifice would have forced Anhalt to make God an independent player in his scenario, something he apparently had no desire to do. As for the burial of Abraham, perhaps Anhalt failed to see adequate dramatic or pictorial possibilities in a funeral. But by opting to concentrate on the sources of the conflict in their elemental forms of sexuality and inheritance, and to omit any reference to the biblical resolution with its potential to move hearts, Anhalt may have missed opportunities to support what he was trying to do.

This point about avoiding God as a real actor in the drama touches on a much larger difficulty for the composer in his desire that his music might get both sides thinking. I ask the reader to bear with me here and to assume a class of ideal listener-exegetes, who not only know the music well, but have also formed their interpretations by becoming aware of appropriate sources and carefully considering their relationship to the musical text.[27] Among such listener-exegetes, committed Jews might resist Anhalt's version of the story, as I have explained, but few would object on theological grounds to his portrayals of God and of the relationship between Abraham and God. And what are these? To answer this it is necessary to explain that, as in many of Anhalt's later works, there is a duality of musical idioms on offer here.[28] Some parts of the score explore various combinations of the basic transpositionally symmetrical collections (augmented triads, diminished seventh chords, and whole-tone scales) with the twelve-tone aggregate as the frame of reference, while others resort to an interaction of diatonic or quasi-diatonic music with passages situated in the chromatic scale but using harmonic collections that are relatively small, in many cases traditional, and generally connected by semitonal voice leading. Some passages cannot be easily located in either of these categories, but together they subsume much of the score. From a cognitive standpoint, one might want to argue that the first kind of music is more abstract, less easy to remember, and more apt to be taken in colouristically or in terms of its rhythmic, timbral, and textural evocation of an emotional atmosphere. The second kind of music is more traditional and singable, easier to remember in detail, and thus more prone to be absorbed quasi-syntactically. If this much can be allowed, perhaps one might hypothesize that the first kind of music represents the extra-human, the being of things that lie outside of what we ordinarily identify as characteristic of our lives and our consciousness, while the other music represents the human, that in which we recognize ourselves and our ways of being in the world. A rough and ready classification of episodes seems to support this interpretation; for example, the land is portrayed in movement 1 by means of large chords, with the octatonic and enneadic collections (Messiaen's modes 2 and 3 respectively) playing referential roles, while the love music of movement 3 enacts the birth of sexual attraction via the waltz topic, including a paradigmatic chromatically descending bass over which recognizable harmonies progress in chromatic contrary motion (mm. 257–70). What is striking in *Tents* is that when Anhalt comes round to depicting God's voice[29] in the last movement, he does so with melodic-harmonic materials that are notably traditional and that allow for every detail in mm. 470–530 to be readily absorbed, despite the lovely freshness of the harmonic connections and the spontaneously through-composed character of the whole. Only when it comes to the content of the actual promise (which is that the seed of Abraham shall be as the stars in the sky and the sand upon the seashore) does the material revert to the abstract, chromatic type, recognizing that the process of sexual generation and the metaphorical tokens of innumerableness are part of nature and not distinctively human. Two other substantial passages relate strongly to the portrayal of God's voice in terms of musical substance. These are, first, the lilting motions that seem to represent an alluring bodily gait, ostensibly Hagar's (mm. 286–99), and second, the portrayal of Abraham's and Hagar's arrival at erotic contact and fulfillment (mm. 313–40). These parallels, taken in the larger symbolic context, might suggest that we realize our full humanity in a certain level of erotic and emotional relationship— the Bible makes it clear that Abraham's feelings for Hagar were of the deepest sort, despite her lowly status—and also that God speaks to us as a being fully human or, more reasonably, that our imaginations project God at their fullest, that is, when functioning at a level that marks us as fully human. The other possible suggestion, that God and Eros should be equated, is not one I believe to be intended or relevant and is, in any case, vitiated by substantive differences between the passages involved, a discussion of which there is no need to enter into here. What the passages have in common is that they express something essential about us, something that differentiates us from nature: meaning, from land, idols (impersonal gods), procreation, or the less fully human state associated with social rejection (as in the end of movement 3, where Hagar's brokenness is portrayed).[30]

This amounts to arguing that Anhalt's take on the Abraham myth tends to the full-blown humanistic variety, though knowledge of the composer's oeuvre also suggests that the expressed humanism folds over into a mystical sense of divine immanence in creation. God is no transcendent, abstract being here—also no judge, merciful or vengeful. He is neither unimaginable nor terrifying. Instead, Abraham envisions him in response to a need to be understood and validated, using imaginative powers that are also enlisted, though in a different way, in forming the strongest bonds between persons. God's voice is made elusive by heterophonic techniques that braid the melody variously, taking up shifting numbers and qualities of strands, but instead of distancing this voice, or obscuring its origin, this elusiveness speaks of the need to protect the voice's source, which is Abraham's visionary consciousness. God speaks here in the "still, small voice" heard by Elijah in 1 Kings 19:11–12, a lyrical voice, and one profoundly sympathetic, standing not for transcendence, but for our situation: that of broken shards, confident of our worth only through intimations of reunification.

This view of the divine is hardly rabbinic in the classical sense but is arguably compatible with a body of modern, liberal Jewish thought. In denying God's transcendence, it also resonates with the mythic irrationality of Kabbalah, and thus with Anhalt's first foray into Judaism via the upper-storey entryway reconstructed by Gershom Scholem instead of the rabbinical ground floor.[31]

What now of committed Muslims among our class of ideal listener-exegetes? How might they react to this portrayal of the relation between Abraham and God, and thus between human and divine? The quotation from the Quran that Anhalt places at the front of the score of *Tents* is telling in this respect, but what it tells us is not auspicious. It reads, "Abraham was not a Jew nor yet a Christian; but he was true in Faith, and he bowed his will to God's (Which is Islam), and he joined not gods with God."[32] The key characteristic ascribed here to Abraham, and metonymically linked to the religion of Islam, is submission. Indeed, the word "Islam" is related by common root to the Arabic verb that means "to accept, surrender, or submit." The sacrifice of Isaac can be read as indicating Abraham's submission to a God he cannot understand, but as I have pointed out, this episode is missing from *Tents*, and for good reason. The Abraham we have in *Tents* (and arguably in Genesis) is anything but submissive; he is vulnerable of course, but in his need, perhaps intensified through the loss of Hagar and Ishmael, he intuits a loving God as the potential unity of the created with the creator. Thus, the relationship between Abraham and God as portrayed in *Tents* cannot be conceived in terms appropriate to servant and sovereign. It is a question, therefore, whether today's "descendants of Ishmael" would recognize Abraham and Allah in the characters portrayed by this music, one that, if answered largely in the negative, suggests a bigger obstacle to the work's achieving its intended aim than any affront to Jewish particularism.[33]

Anhalt's Ongoing Work, and Abraham's

I will turn from what Anhalt evidently tried to do in *Tents* to what I think he actually manages to do, perhaps without wanting or needing to acknowledge it. A growing corpus of biographical work exists dealing with the three phases of his life (in Europe, Montreal, and Kingston),[34] and Anhalt himself has provided an extensive account, spread over several sources, of his personal and artistic odyssey.[35] The letters to and from Rochberg are now published,[36] and a body of excellent critical work is accumulating. But in what follows, I rely less on what he has written about himself and on what others have written about him, than on my own impressions of the man gathered over forty-six years of regular, if intermittent, contact and on my considerable familiarity with most of his work in all its forms. Accordingly, I accept the blame for any inaccuracies, misrepresentations, or absences of appropriate qualifiers. I felt reassured, though, hearing his remarkably candid address to a conference at the University of Calgary in January 2008, since it confirmed the pertinence of much of what I say here.[37]

The Tents of Abraham clearly aims at, and succeeds in, putting us in mind of certain things as we listen, and still others become apparent once we absorb the composer's program. Just as importantly though, and more fundamentally, the piece causes us to follow its musical processes with attentive entrainment and the full panoply of our memorative capacities, rather as any other worthwhile music might be expected to do by an open-minded, well-disposed, but professionally disinterested concertgoing Western audience, for whom this music is certainly intended. Indeed, the tasks of absorbing, memorizing, and being able to anticipate what happens in this work are facilitated for any listener who has even casually immersed himself in Anhalt's orchestral corpus since *Simulacrum* (1987), because the composer uses many of the same harmonic and formal schemata in one work after another. In other words, he has an identifiable compositional voice, and one accessible to the listener as a medium of exchange.

With this assessment we come to the nub of the issue, that being the cultural work being done here without being advertised by a program at any level. For there is too little ambitious music composed in recent decades that maintains its highly personal idiom, avoids all pandering to a taste for the predictable, yet fully engages such an audience in this way. Of course, this is a point that has been made and lamented countless times, usually from the standpoint—misguided in my view—that new music needs to regain something like the "language" music once had. I would state the problem rather differently. The music of late modernism, with which Anhalt's work retains some substantive links, typically does not aim at such engagement to start with. Anhalt's music is significantly mimetic of things we have all experienced (places, sounds, gestures, concepts, and feelings); it calls to mind and perhaps engenders the emotions that give our lives their rhythm and texture (love, jealousy, sadness, pride, fear, exuberance, and awe); and its harmonic and melodic schemata are susceptible of being followed and memorized in considerable detail by an attentive, ordinary musical mind. It is no object of late modernist music, in general, to be this way. So much of the music of late modernism—in which I include much that is termed postmodern—addresses itself to anything but that which can be termed a part of ordinary subjectivity, preferring instead to conjure up all that is strange, inscrutable, sensorily assaulting, self-contradictory, without purpose, and basically sub- or super-human, in forms that can be apprehended only by non-subjects who register jolting impressions without remembering enough about them to relate them in meaningful ways, rather in the way an electroshock victim might register a series of earth tremors. And it is in this context—as a music that has, so to speak, survived the experience of late modernism—that *Tents*, and indeed much of Anhalt's music over the past twenty years at least, needs to be received and evaluated, with respect to the cultural work it is doing on behalf of a non-professional audience that is willing to devote its time to music that rewards attention and effort.

I say an audience, but of course I really mean performers and their audience, since what marks *Tents* and most of Anhalt's music over the past decade is that it was written for particular players and their particular public in a particular place, that place being Kingston, Ontario. This brings me to my central point, and it will lead me presently back to the Abraham myth with which I started.

When Anhalt left Europe to come to Montreal in 1949, he did not see himself as being in exile.[38] True, his new hometown was peripheral in artistic matters, even in the North American context, but he had not the slightest intention of returning to Europe, nor any desire to do so. From the start, he saw Canada as being for him a place of much greater possibility.[39] This may seem like self-deception, given that his musical roots remained in Europe and that he continued to look to new developments in Western Europe as his principal compositional models right up to the end of the 1960s, taking little notice of the potent sources in jazz, popular music, and non-Western music that were beginning to prompt North American composers in new directions. His attitude toward Canada has a simple explanation, however, and lies in his extreme antipathy to nationalism of the traditional European type, based on a triad of blood, soil, and faith that, by definition, made his continuing identification with a European state impossible and, for that matter, ruled out any possibility of his identifying deeply with Israel.[40] This applied not only to Hungary, his removal from which he regarded as an escape, but also to France or

Germany, where he might reasonably have chosen to try to make a go of it, and might certainly have benefited from more in the way of institutional support, much as his compatriot Ligeti did some few years later.

Anhalt's economic situation in Montreal remained precarious for many years, and he remained a respected but largely unheralded (let alone celebrated) figure for even longer. As well, he cannot have been unaware of the history of anti-Jewish prejudice in Canada, and especially in Quebec. But his optimistic take on his adopted country was that it had given him a chance to be himself, personally and artistically, with no fear that the decisions he made would be held against him as issuing from a foreign sensibility, or that important doors, open to others born here in the right circles, would be closed to him. Nothing he experienced during his first decade and a half in Montreal would cause him to feel this confidence had been misplaced.

It is hard to say how Anhalt's career might have unfolded had Canada lived up entirely to his expectations. Certainly Europe was changing in the postwar period, groping towards the secular, multinational federation that is now being achieved. And since his stylistic antennas were finely tuned towards Western Europe, it is possible to imagine him, almost fluently quadrilingual as he is, having made connections with the European new music community and, in due course, having developed a career and a self-concept that spanned two continents. But something crucial happened in Canada in the 1960s. This was the emergence of a Quebec nationalism that, for all its secularity, gave every sign of being capable of excluding, and perhaps likely to exclude, someone of his background. Anhalt had maintained close, even warm, relationships with established French-Canadian composers who were his peers: for example, Jean Papineau-Couture.[41] But things were changing as slightly younger composers, caught up in the nationalist mood and armed with public funds and with new dogmas from their sojourns in Paris, formed performance societies and other organs for the dissemination of new music that, deliberately or not, blocked out the voices of composers from other Canadian (and even Quebec) communities, including even those whose interests in new European developments ran parallel to theirs. Thus, Anhalt's masterly *La Tourangelle* (1974), a paean to the burning spirituality that sustained New France against all odds, and a work that John Beckwith has called "the most profound musical treatment of a subject from the era of New France,"[42] was premiered by the CBC in Toronto but—disgracefully, it has to be said—was never taken up by the Societé de Musique Contemporaine du Québec or any comparable Quebec group.[43]

The fact was—and Anhalt recognized this—that a genuine artistic community based on shared preoccupation with the challenges of avant-garde music was impossible where it had to contravene the barriers erected by nationalism and, in Canada, of regionalism as well. Modernism, which in music and the other arts claimed to be a way of thinking that transcended the parochial, turned out to be its opposite, a way in which artists of one culturally based interest group could band together to reinforce one another and keep others out. Nor was this surprising reversal confined to Quebec, though its manifestations were particularly acute there. It showed itself in all of Canada, where orchestras, while obliged to play Canadian music, have completely neglected the new music of any other country to this day; in North America as a whole (Quebec interestingly excepted), where new European music is only now trickling into the programs of some orchestras and smaller groups; and in Europe, where American music, aside from jazz and the work of a fringe of notable cult figures, is held in utter disregard.

When I say that Anhalt realized this, it is not clear that he would be prepared to openly admit it, even to himself. After all, he too has benefited over the years from the protectionism I've just described. But, unusually for a Canadian composer of his stature, a surprising percentage of his works have originated without commissions, born of his following a creative impulse without consideration for the context in which the work might be realized or disseminated. In any event, what is absolutely the case is that his removal from Montreal to Kingston in 1971 neatly coincides with the beginnings of his rejection of the avant-garde and his invention of an approach that was fully developed by the late 1980s, one that I have characterized above as mimetic, connected to the emotional life of a traditional subjectivity, and concerned with the spinning out of musical processes residing in schemata that can be followed, memorized, and anticipated.

I believe that with the move to a small city in English-speaking Canada, one with scant cultural resources and thus largely off the radar screen of any bureaucrat seeking to make his or her mark, Anhalt began to accept the full implications of his removal from Europe. If he was to reject the status of exile, there was no reason to take guidance from Europe any longer. If new music had no real spiritual centre, only places where more bureaucrats were spending more money on more supplicants, there was also no periphery. There were only places in which one was free to start over, and, to a degree, the smaller the better, since in small places one was removed from national adjudication committees, broadcast network mandarins, and multinational juries, and relieved of the constraints these imposed. To start over, then, could only mean one thing: reaching out to the musicians who were one's plausible colleagues, whose predispositions and potentials one could get to know, and, more fundamentally, to the highly cultured but musically conventional audiences with whom one shared one's daily life. In Anhalt's case, this reaching out happened very gradually and actually occurred in the reverse order. First he progressively restricted his musical resources, re-engaging with the Romantic and early modernist expressive traditions in which he had been reared, without entirely relinquishing the technique he had accumulated in twenty-odd years as a late modernist. Then, only ten years ago, he connected with the musicians of the Kingston Symphony and their conductor, Glen Fast, and has since developed a relationship with them that has given them a place unique among the semi-professional orchestras in Canada, and unusual for those of North America as a whole.[44]

This takes us back to the story of Abraham, for what really drew Anhalt to this story, in my view, is that Abraham's is the primordial case of starting over, of removal from a great cultural centre to somewhere that seems to be nowhere. Abraham, more resolutely than Anhalt, is absolute in his rejection of what he leaves behind. He is unconcerned with being out of the loop, interested only in the accommodations that need to be made to protect his kin and to be free to begin to build the basis of a new spirituality. Abraham's is a more radical trajectory than those of Marie de l'Incarnation or John Winthrop, the heroes of Anhalt's first two dramatic works. Whereas they were looking for more fertile fields in which to plant the religious seeds harvested from their European experience, Abraham relocates somewhat blindly, not really knowing what he will be required to do when he gets to his destination. He knows only that he can no longer bear the weight of inauthenticity that is his birthright. Only progressively, and sometimes uncertainly, does he assemble the seeds suitable for planting in the unpromising soil of Canaan. The parallel is surely inexact—and I shrink from the apparent foolishness, if not the blasphemy, of making comparisons between any contemporary, however worthy, and the father of nations—but surely it is the point of myth to invite such parallels in our own lives and the lives of those we cherish. Anhalt, realizing that he could not be a disciple of Kodály, and later that he could not be *musicien français* or Québécois, or for that matter a committed Zionist or a Jewish composer, understood that he had to find an authentic way of being a composer in Canada. It took him a quarter-century (after leaving Montreal) to finally discover that this could only mean helping to shape a community of players and listeners who, through their determination to get to know his music, would prove that they valued it. Thus he became a Kingston composer.

Enactment as a Modelling Activity

In the above analysis I have tried to show why, even assuming an idealistic attitude about music's performative potential in the social dimension, *Tents* carries little prospect of working to bridge the ideological and emotional gaps between the warring parties in Israel/Palestine. At the same, it has functioned marvellously well to forge a connection between its sophisticated musical materials, a semi-professional performance group, and a Western audience with no special connection to new art music. Having done so, it works to restore music to its historic role in the West, lost since the Second World War, of using large performing resources to engage receptive but untrained audiences at emotional and intellectual levels by stimulating both musical memory and pictorial imagery. One might say, then, that the piece succeeds in performing important social work, if not precisely the kind of work the composer has chosen to foreground in his public utterances.

All the same, there is an ironic sense in which *Tents* does have something important to say to the antagonists in the Middle East, ironic because it implies the value of forgetting what the work seems to ask them to remember. If Anhalt's life in Canada is justly spoken of as a kind of re-enactment of the Abraham story, then its climax is the composition of a new kind of music, of which *Tents* is the most eloquent instance. In composing this music, Anhalt found a way of sidestepping assumptions that held sway over many composers for decades, which led them to compose in ways that profoundly alienated their potential audiences. Overcoming these assumptions meant adopting a new, less abstract, and more eclectic operating procedure, and also required that Anhalt distance himself from the canonical texts (musical and verbal) of modernism and the quasi-religious baggage they entail. On one level, *The Tents of Abraham* asks people to remember an old story. On another level, as a creative act, it models forgetting what has been learned too well. What more pertinent example could a composer offer to peoples so desperately in need of forgetting parts of a heritage that have become dangerously oppressive, and learning to start over?

Notes

1 Anhalt identifies these two series of works as triptychs. This identification is documented in his unpublished essay, "A Pair of Orchestral Triptychs (from 1987 to 1989 and from 2002 to 2005): A Preliminary Account," dated 4–6 September 2005. In this essay he links the six works in the two series with the appellation "idea-pieces," saying that they are "individually engaged to address an idea, or group of related ideas." The concept of an artwork of ideas has its precursors in the Central European "Weltanschauungsmusik" of the early twentieth century, as discussed in Carl Dahlhaus, *Nineteenth-Century Music*, trans. J. Bradford Robinson (Berkeley: University of California Press, 1989), 360–68.

2 Anhalt writes of the first series, in "A Pair of Orchestral Triptychs," 3, that these three works might be regarded "as focusing on the 'thisness' of persons as they try to come to terms with deeply personal matters and related memory layers." Anhalt calls these three works—*Simulacrum, SparkskrapS, and Sonance-Resonance (Welche Töne?)*—his "S pieces." See also John Beckwith, "Orchestral Works," in *Istvan Anhalt: Pathways and Memory*, ed. Robin Elliott and Gordon E. Smith (Montreal and Kingston: McGill-Queen's University Press, 2001), 120–30.

3 This preoccupation with the present-day mirroring of ancient themes begins already with the "voice-drama" *Millennial Mall (Lady Diotima's Walk)*, for orchestra, choir, and soprano soloist (1999). See Gordon E. Smith, "From New France to a 'Millennial Mall': Identity Paradigms in Istvan Anhalt's Operas," *American Music* 24/2 (2006): 185–89.

4 Anhalt writes, in "A Pair of Orchestral Triptychs," 3, that in these "'T' pieces"—as he styles *Twilight~Fire, The Tents of Abraham,* and ... *the timber of those times* ...—the individual "appears as an actor in a momentous societal event, or in a vastly important societal framework."

5 Istvan Anhalt, "From 'Mirage' to *Simulacrum* and 'Afterthought,'" in *Istvan Anhalt: Pathways and Memory*, 417.

6 A chorus from the *St. Matthew Passion* in which Pilate asks what should be done with Jesus.

7 Istvan Anhalt, "An Operatic Triptych in Multiple Texts," in *Istvan Anhalt: Pathways and Memory*, 371.

8 Ibid., 370.

9 I make this claim based on countless private conversations with Anhalt, going back to the 1960s, that touched on Jewish matters over the course of which his growing preoccupation with these matters became evident to me. While Anhalt's public identification with Jewish concerns remains limited, he took a significant step, acknowledging that *Tents* is linked to the current threat to Israel, in remarks he made at a Holocaust Memorial Service held at Beth Israel Synagogue in Kingston, Ontario, on 16 April 2007. He wrote, for this occasion, that *Tents* has "an indirect relevance [to the *Shoah*] inasmuch as ... a significant part of the community of Jews is, once again threatened by enemies, principally in the Near East."

10 A detailed technical and hermeneutic analysis of this work is found in William Benjamin, "Alternatives of Voice: Anhalt's Odyssey from Personalized Style

to Symbolic Expression," in *Istvan Anhalt: Pathways and Memory*, 164–307. The rehabilitation of Kabbalah, by Gershom Scholem, whom Anhalt read extensively in the 1980s, was intended as an antidote to the long prevailing rationalism of rabbinic Judaism, which in its liberal, post-1850 developments became explicitly allied to humanism.

11   In another unpublished essay, composed in September 2002, Anhalt returns to explore the significance of *Tents* in greater detail. In this essay, titled simply "About *The Tents of Abraham*," Anhalt explains (p. 1) that he felt compelled to write this work after being goaded, by gentile colleagues, to take a critical stance, as a progressive intellectual, against Israeli policies, something he was not prepared to do.

12   These are the words of the dedication in the score.

13   In writing of Anhalt's motivations or intent, I am aware of engaging with a problem in humanistic research that has occasioned much debate over the years; namely, the so-called intentional fallacy. In its most objectionable form, and the form originally objected to by Wimsatt and Beardsley in their eponymous article of 1946 (rev. 1954), this involves *evaluating the success* of a work on the basis of its creator's stated or inferred intentions. Since, in this paper, I describe Anhalt as largely unsuccessful in his political intentions but as having produced a very successful work, I can hardly be accused of committing the fallacy in this egregious form. Nevertheless, some scholars may object to any interpretation of a work that relies, in large part, on what the creator says he or she was trying to do. My own view, as a music theorist, is that while analysis or interpretation can scarcely limit itself to what the composer says about the meaning of the work or about its structure, it certainly benefits from taking such information into account. I have written about this in "When Are Musical Structures of Aesthetic Relevance?" *Tijdschrift voor Muziektheorie* [Dutch Journal of Music Theory] 8/2 (2003): 95–101. I would also point out, as a way of begging the indulgence of scholars who may be more scrupulous in these matters than I am, that this is a special case: I spent many hours talking with Anhalt about his motivations for *The Tents of Abraham* while he was writing it and afterwards. This gives me confidence in taking what some may regard as a naive stance; to wit, that what Anhalt told me he wanted to do was, at least, a significant part of what he wanted to do. I also hope I am justified in believing that, in this paper, I have substantiated the relevance of his stated intentions with observations derived from the score.

14   In the remarks for the 2007 Holocaust Memorial Service (see note 9), he writes, "Is it possible that by revisiting the story of Abraham and his family, one just might find insights that might lead to a better understanding of the present conflict and potentially also to its peaceful resolution?"

15   This claim is substantiated by all of Anhalt's dramatic works since the 1960s, both those set in history, like *La Tourangelle* and *Winthrop*, and those dealing with an imagined present, like *Traces (Tikkun)* and *Millennial Mall (Lady Diotima's Walk)*. It would be interesting to compare his perspective on the issue with that of Adorno, with whose pessimism and determinism he would surely part company to a significant degree.

16 The Juno Awards are presented annually by members of the Canadian Academy of Recording Arts and Sciences to Canadian individuals and groups who have produced recordings during the preceding year that are judged to be of the highest technical and artistic merit.

17 The program is nowhere proposed in written form as part of the artwork, in the manner of the *Symphonie fantastique*, for example. The closest nineteenth-century precursors are works loosely based on literary models, like Liszt's *Hamlet*, Strauss's *Macbeth*, or Tchaikovsky's *Romeo and Juliet*, in which reference is made to a loose array of personality traits, moods, plot episodes, musical topics, and real sounds. Anhalt's program can be inferred with certainty and precision from his unpublished essays that deal with the work and from program and liner notes that he approved. See, for example, the notes to the two-CD set dedicated to Anhalt in the series *Canadian Composers Portraits*, issued in 2004 by the Canadian Music Centre under its Centrediscs label (CMCCD 10204). As a theorist, I am not disposed to think that music's impact is significantly via its program, but Anhalt is a composer who believes and operates out of the conviction that music can be quite transparent as to its ideational content. He composes everything—register, tone colour, harmony, melody, rhythm, etc.—with a symbolic purpose, and this makes the program basic to understanding his music.

18 The question as to whether music's emotional power is merely representational or actually inductive of feelings or states of mind in listeners is a time-honoured and vexing one in aesthetics. My view is that it can be both. An expressionist work, like Schoenberg's *Erwartung*, seems to me to aim at both depiction and arousal, though perhaps not of exactly the same states of mind. Notable examples of passages with a performative power (in inducing the state they are depicting) in Anhalt's later music include the opening of *Simulacrum*, which evokes a sense of gradually waking up and regaining awareness; the final passage of *SparkskrapS*, which depicts a dissolution of bodily energies and a loss of consciousness; and of course the final passage of *Tents*, which induces the listener to feel as if meditating on the many angles of a question that may have no answer, by presenting a musical figure that hangs in the air, mobile-like, always changing in thought-provoking ways, but coming to no resolution.

19 The collection of *midrashim* (exegeses often in the form of homiletical tales) most relevant to Anhalt's take on the story is *Genesis Rabbah*, the first book of *Midrash Rabbah*, a large collection of line-by-line exegesis for ten different books of the Hebrew Bible. The redaction of *Genesis Rabbah* is generally dated to 400 CE or slightly later. See Jacob Neusner, *Confronting Creation: How Judaism Reads "Genesis": An Anthology of "Genesis Rabbah"* (Columbia: University of South Carolina Press, 1991), 13–22.

20 In the Quran, verses 51–71 of Sura 21 ("The Prophets") deal entirely with a version of the story, as does chapter 38 of *Genesis Rabbah*. Modern scholarship, which recognizes the earlier provenance of the Jewish source, identifies the Quranic version as a retelling of a rabbinic tale that must have achieved considerable currency among Jews, but this conflicts with the Muslim belief in the Quran as completely revealed to Mohammed.

21 Anhalt was probably influenced here by the *Jerusalem Bible*, which was his source for the text. Chapter 21, verse 9, reads: "Now Sarah watched the son that Hagar the Egyptian had borne to Abraham, playing with her son Isaac." The Hebrew does not admit of this translation, in my view. The adjectival phrase with which the verse ends is a single Hebrew gerund (*m'tzachek*), which means "fooling around." There is no reference to Isaac (though his name comes from the same root as the gerund). It can also mean "mocking," and *Genesis Rabbah* (chapter 53), seeking to justify Sarah's wrath and to denigrate Ishmael, interprets it variously as implying fornication, idolatry, and even murder. See Neusner, *Confronting Creation*, 203–5.

22 The added "ha" stands for "hamon," the Hebrew for "multitude." The context of chapter 17 seems to imply, quite clearly, that the multitude falls within the covenant proposed there, which would mean that the "nations" are in fact tribes or clans within Israel. While the nations could also include the descendants of Ishmael and of the six sons of Keturah (the wife Abraham took after Sarah's death), all of whom are listed in Genesis 25, this is contradicted by God's bestowing on Sarah the title of "mother of nations" (chapter 17, verse 16), even though Sarah had only one child.

23 *Genesis Rabbah* (chapter 58) accounts for the redundancy in the description of Sarah's death at "one hundred years and twenty years and seven years (Genesis 23:1)" by saying that, at the age of one hundred, she was as innocent as at twenty, and as beautiful at age twenty as she was at age seven. The rabbis' concept of beauty is charmingly asexual, but even they do not claim beauty for Sarah at one hundred.

24 Many websites argue the identity of the son of the sacrifice. See, for example, the essay "The Sacrificial Son – Ishmael or Isaac (Ismail or Ishaq)?" by Ebrahim Saifuddin (9 April 2007, http://ebrahimsaifuddin.wordpress.com/2007/04/09/the-sacrificial-son-ishmael-or-isaac-ismail-or-ishaq/ (accessed 20 June 2008).

25 Anhalt has spoken repeatedly to me about this passage as the model for what he would like to see in Israel/Palestine today, most recently in a conversation that took place on 13 June 2008.

26 *Lekh-Lekha*, literally "get thee going," is the divine imperative with which the story of Abraham is initiated in the Hebrew Bible (Genesis 12:1).

27 I am under no illusion that most listeners, however well disposed, will readily intuit much of what is explained here. This does not make it less relevant to imagine how an ideal listener-exegete would react to such intuitions.

28 This is explored, with reference to *SparkskrapS*, in William Benjamin, "Alternatives of Voice," in *Istvan Anhalt: Pathways and Memory*, 241–42.

29 Anhalt writes in his 2007 Beth Israel Synagogue address (see note 9) about how he struggled with how to depict God's voice, saying that he decided that "Abraham also must have had some role in imagining what he came to identify as the voice of God."

30 This intention was personally communicated to me by Anhalt on 13 June 2008 and on earlier occasions.

31 Anhalt had very little in the way of a traditional Jewish education. In the 1980s, when he became interested in reading about things Jewish, it was not

the enormous corpus of rabbinic literature that drew his attention, but the writings of Gershom Scholem (1897–1982), the German-Jewish scholar who, beginning after the First World War and continuing upon his immigration to Palestine in 1923, single-handedly instigated a re-evaluation of the Kabbalistic tradition, which had been relegated by most Jewish authorities to the dustbin of history. See also note 10.

32 The quotation, of Surah 3:67, is from the translation of Abdullah Yusuf, 1963.

33 The image of servant and sovereign is also basic to classical Jewish prayer. But the theology it represents is being marginalized in many strains of modern Jewish religious practice.

34 In addition to the pioneering essays by Robin Elliott and Gordon E. Smith in *Istvan Anhalt: Pathways and Memory*, we now have Robin Elliott, "Istvan Anhalt and New Music at McGill," in *Compositional Crossroads: Music, McGill, Montreal*, ed. Eleanor V. Stubley (Montreal and Kingston: McGill-Queen's University Press, 2008), 33–55.

35 Istvan Anhalt, "What Tack to Take? An Autobiographical Sketch (Life in Progress ...)," *Queen's Quarterly* 92/1 (spring 1985): 96–107. See also chapters 14, 15, and 16 in *Istvan Anhalt: Pathways And Memory*, in which Anhalt inserts many autobiographical comments in discussions of his music. Anhalt's talk, read at the conference from which the present volume issues ("Centre and Periphery, Roots and Exile: Interpreting the Music of István Anhalt and György Kurtag"), printed herein, and entitled "Of the Centre, Periphery; Exile, Liberation; Home and the Self," is notable for its frank account of his strongly negative reaction to Quebec nationalism.

36 See Alan M. Gillmor, ed., *Eagle Minds: Selected Correspondence of Istvan Anhalt and George Rochberg (1961–2005)* (Waterloo, ON: Wilfrid Laurier University Press, 2007).

37 See note 35. This talk was read for him in his absence by Alan Gillmor. Of particular significance, in my view, is Anhalt's inclusion in this talk of "The Bridge," a parable he wrote in 1991, which reflects in a prophetic mode on the English-French divide in Quebec.

38 This is directly confirmed in "Of the Centre, Periphery: Exile, Liberation; Home and the Self" (see chapter 4).

39 Anhalt's optimism, with its ready accoutrement of rose-coloured glasses, is in evidence in his comments about his first forays into the streets of Montreal, as described in "What Tack to Take? An Autobiographical Sketch (Life in Progress ...)," 103. From personal knowledge, I can attest to the fact that, unlike Anhalt, Europeans recently arrived from Europe's bigger cities were unimpressed by Montreal in those days.

40 As he was quoted in Leslie Thompson, "The Inspiration of a Composer," *Music Magazine* 3/2 (March/April 1980): 26; and secondarily in Robin Elliott, "Life in Montreal (1941–71)," in *Istvan Anhalt: Pathways and Memory*, 34: "I immediately felt very good here. At that time there was no flag, no national anthem that everybody could sing. Also, people made fun of nationalism in those days, which was very refreshing, and I felt that nobody could really do any harm to me under these conditions."

41 Elliott, "Life in Montreal," 39.

42 John Beckwith, *Music Papers: Articles and Talks by a Canadian Composer* (Ottawa: Golden Dog Press, 1997), 127.
43 The anti-clericalism of the new Quebec may have played a role here.
44 Anhalt has related to me how he was reluctant during his years as the head of the Department of Music at Queen's to impose himself on the Kingston Orchestra, as well as being dubious about its capabilities. Thus, it was only after more than a decade had passed since his retirement in 1984 that he met Glen Fast at a social occasion and responded to the latter's evidently sincere invitation to write something for the orchestra to play, an invitation that resulted in *Twilight~Fire* and three subsequent works.

Bibliography

Anhalt, István. "About The Tents of Abraham." Unpublished essay, September 2002.

———. "From 'Mirage' to Simulacrum and 'Afterthought.'" In *Istvan Anhalt: Pathways and Memory*, edited by Robin Elliott and Gordon E. Smith, 412–25. Montreal and Kingston: McGill-Queen's University Press, 2001.

———. "An Operatic Triptych in Multiple Texts." In *Istvan Anhalt: Pathways and Memory*, 369–99.

———. "A Pair of Orchestral Triptychs (from 1987–1989 and from 2002 to 2005): A Preliminary Account." Unpublished essay, 4–6 September 2005.

———. "What Tack to Take? An Autobiographical Sketch (Life in Progress …)." *Queen's Quarterly* 92/1 (Spring 1985): 96–107.

Beckwith, John. *Music Papers: Articles and Talks by a Canadian Composer*. Ottawa: Golden Dog Press, 1997.

———. "Orchestral Works." In *Istvan Anhalt: Pathways and Memory*, 111–31.

Benjamin, William. "Alternatives of Voice: Anhalt's Odyssey from Personalized Style to Symbolic Expression." In *Istvan Anhalt: Pathways and Memory*, 164–307.

———. "When Are Musical Structures of Aesthetic Relevance?" *Tijdschrift voor Muziektheorie* [Dutch Journal of Music Theory] 8/2 (2003): 95–101.

Dahlhaus, Carl. *Nineteenth-Century Music*. Translated by J. Bradford Robinson. Berkeley: University of California Press, 1989.

Elliott, Robin. "Istvan Anhalt and New Music at McGill." In *Compositional Crossroads: Music, McGill, Montreal*, edited by Eleanor V. Stubley, 33–55. Montreal and Kingston: McGill-Queen's University Press, 2008.

———. "Life in Montreal (1941–71)." In *Istvan Anhalt: Pathways and Memory*, 33–64.

Gillmor, Alan M., ed. *Eagle Minds: Selected Correspondence of Istvan Anhalt and George Rochberg (1961–2005)*. Waterloo, ON: Wilfrid Laurier University Press, 2007.

Neusner, Jacob. *Confronting Creation: How Judaism Reads "Genesis": An Anthology of "Genesis Rabbah."* Columbia: University of South Carolina Press, 1991.

Salfuddin, Ebrahim. "The Sacrificial Son – Ishmael or Isaac (Ismail or Ishaq)?" http://ebrahimsaifuddin.wordpress.com/2007/04/09/the-sacrificial-son-ishmael-or-isaac-ismail-or-ishaq/ (accessed on 20 June 2008).

Smith, Gordon E. "From New France to a 'Millennial Mall': Identity Paradigms in Istvan Anhalt's Operas." *American Music* 24/2 (2006): 172–93.

Thompson, Leslie. "The Inspiration of a Composer." *Music Magazine* 3/2 (March/April 1980): 24–26.

Wimsatt, William K. and Monroe C. Beardsley. "The Intentional Fallacy." In *The Verbal Icon: Studies in the Meaning of Poetry*. Lexington: University of Kentucky Press, 1954, 3–18.

SEVEN

Which Displacement? Tracing Exile in the Postwar Compositions of István Anhalt and Mátyás Seiber

Florian Scheding

EVER SINCE THE EGYPTIAN Danaïdes arrived in Argos—quite possibly the first "foreigners to emerge at the dawn of our civilisation"[1] according to Julia Kristeva—migration has captured the human imagination. Indeed, the very myth of the Danaïdes prompted Aeschylus for a dramatization in his epic *The Suppliants*. Few factors can impact as severely as displacement upon personal life, creative output, and the cultural lives of societies. It thus appears that exile and, maybe even more so, displacement are characteristics intrinsic not only to the human condition but also to artistic contemplation and creative expression; they are among the cornerstones of its Western history, at any rate.

Since the early twentieth century, however, forced displacement and migration have reached a scale hitherto unprecedented in human history. Of course, there had always been refugees. However, the nature of modern warfare, with its technical power to kill more people more easily than ever before, including civilians, together with the modern invention of the nation-state, organized and powerful enough to impose its laws more efficiently (and with a tendency to demand unanimity among its citizens), has helped generate larger numbers of refugees than ever before. During the First World War and its aftermath, when the Russian, Austro-Hungarian, and Ottoman empires collapsed and the national borders were rearranged all over Europe, one and a half million Russians fled several successive revolutions, more than half a million people fled from Ottoman territories, and countless others fled because they "suddenly found themselves in isolated minorities in one of the fiercely nationalist successor states" of the Austro-Hungarian empire.[2] If these were large numbers (and I am not even considering contemporaneous refugee waves outside Europe resulting from the rise and fall of European colonialism), they were but a fraction of those created just two decades later. The Second World War produced an approximate 27 million refugees (not counting those who were displaced in ghettos and concentration camps), and two decades ago, estimates placed the number of refugees in the twentieth century to have exceeded a staggering 60 million, with a constant number of 10 to 12 million since the late 1970s.[3]

Obvious as this may sound, it is important to remember that such imposing numbers sometimes consume the individuals that constitute them, and that the quantitative magnitude of refugee numbers conceals the almost ungraspable qualitative fact that the 27 million refugees of the Second World War tell 27 million diverse tales of personal fates. Inevitably, these realities of displacement in the age of extremes (to use Eric Hobsbawm's words) have also affected and impacted profoundly upon many of the foremost creative and intellectual forces of our time in one way or another, including the figures to which this volume is dedicated, István Anhalt and György Kurtág.

What exactly does such a statement mean? For surely, beyond the quantifiable fact of enforced border crossing (or non-border crossing) with all its direct and often brutal immediacy on the biography of those affected lies the more mediate qualitative factor of displacement's impact upon contemplation and creativity. How is the latter informed by the former, or vice versa? When Hannah Arendt, Theodor W. Adorno, Bertolt Brecht, Albert Camus, Jacques Derrida, and Edward Said (to name but six very prominent examples) contemplated displacement and alienation and discussed the causes and consequences of exile, to what extent was this done without reference to their own biographies, which were all marked by very diverse exile experiences? In other words, how do the biographical data and creative output of one person, let alone a generation, correlate and interact, even assuming for the sake of the argument the stability of the self?

Two Biographies Marked by Exile: A Comparison

The present volume provides several in-depth contributions on selected episodes of the lives of, and particular aspects of individual works by, Anhalt and Kurtág. Rather than adding to these fundamental insights, I aim to widen my scope somewhat and give room to some contemplation on the relation of the displaced self and its creative output, or, if you like, on the relation between biography and workography. In order to limit my focus to a feasible width, I intend to zoom out only to include a comparison with a contemporary of Anhalt's, namely Mátyás Seiber.

The life and work of István Anhalt are outlined and discussed by some of the other contributors in some detail and, unlike in Seiber's case, have been examined at book length elsewhere.[4] It does seem suitable, however, to sketch briefly some biographical cornerstones and artistic backgrounds of Mátyás Seiber. Seiber was born on 4 May 1905 into the melting pot of Budapest, and his musical formation mirrors the two-sided outlook of his birthplace. While he belonged to, and was conversant in, the Austro-German musical tradition, his education with Zoltán Kodály accounts for his affiliation to Hungary's national school of composition. Following Béla Bartók, Seiber's early work represents an attempt of combining traditional Western art music with a Hungarian colour while, at the same time, aiming to extend the boundaries of traditional tonality within the canonically established formal framework.

After the proto-fascist regime of Admiral Miklós Horthy seized power in 1920 in an atmosphere of growing anti-Semitism, Seiber, an assimilated Jew, left Budapest in 1925 to settle in Frankfurt, where, in 1927, he accepted a professorship and established a jazz class at the prestigious Hoch Konservatorium. Besides his foundation of the jazz class, which many contemporaries regarded as scandalous, Seiber's compositional development reveals a continuing interest in the avant-garde. Following a handful of compositions that can be assigned to the New Objectivity, such as the *Divertimento* for clarinet and string quartet (1926–28), Seiber's compositions increasingly employ the embryonic twelve-tone-technique.[5] As one of Europe's centres of musical avant-garde, Frankfurt proved to be a stimulating environment indeed.

Everything changed in early 1933, when Hitler emerged as Reichskanzler in the general elections on 30 January. Swiftly implementing the new regime's ideology, the so-called Gesetz zur Wiederherstellung des Berufsbeamtentums [Law for the Restitution of the Professional Civil Service], promulgated on 7 April 1933, banned all "non-Aryans" from official positions. A mere three days later, on 10 April, the Nazi administration dismissed Seiber and a long list of other teaching and administrative staff in a *Säuberungsverfahren*, an act of ethnic cleansing, and denied any right of access to the conservatory's premises.

Seiber left Frankfurt shortly afterwards, in autumn 1933, and, following an odyssey that saw him back in Hungary, migrated to London in

1935, where he remained until his premature death in 1960. The first years in exile were marked by the struggle for economic survival and a creative crisis. Instead of continuing with the composition of serious music, Seiber accepted commissions for film and radio scores as well as arrangements of light and popular music for accordion ensembles and salon orchestras. Conversely, the mid-1940s witnessed a sudden reappearance of serious compositions, all of which are serial in technique and markedly interwar-expressionist in style. Indeed, in Britain's postwar years, Seiber eventually established a reputation for himself as composer, conductor, and one of the country's most renowned composition teachers, exerting some significant influences on a younger generation of British composers. (Hugh Wood, Peter Racine Fricker, and Don Banks were among his pupils.)

Several similarities between Anhalt's biography and that of Seiber can be observed at a glance. Both Anhalt and Seiber were born Hungarian and were educated under the guidance of Kodály at the Ferenc Liszt Conservatory. Both were and are Jewish and both suffered persecution on account of this, leaving Hungary and Central Europe as a consequence. Once migrated, both enjoyed distinguished careers as composers and teachers in their new adopted homes.

Yet, they were not born into the same Budapest: Seiber was born into the fin-de-siècle Budapest of the Austro-Hungarian Empire, Anhalt into the capital of the independent, yet geographically crippled Hungarian state. The treaty of Trianon that led to a loss of two-thirds of Hungary's territory to Austria, (former) Czechoslovakia, (former) Yugoslavia, and Romania was signed one year after Anhalt's birth, in June 1920. Moreover, Seiber and Anhalt did not study together or simultaneously. Seiber, while only fourteen years Anhalt's senior, left Budapest before Anhalt became a student at the Liszt Conservatory. Nor did the anti-Semitic persecution, which affected them both profoundly, take the same form: Anhalt was interned in a forced labour camp for Jewish youths in 1942, whereas Seiber had been dismissed from his post and had gone into exile almost a decade earlier. And they did of course both migrate, but not to the same country nor at the same time: Seiber left the European continent for Britain in the early years of the Nazi regime and before the outbreak of the Second World War, while Anhalt endured the war and fascist persecution in Hungary and then, after a brief spell in Paris from 1946 until 1948, left postwar Europe for Canada. Lastly, while one may assume that they knew each other (or at least of each other),[6] there is, to my knowledge, no extant evidence that they ever communicated, collaborated, or absorbed each other's music more closely than any two contemporary composers connected neither by geographical proximity nor by the same social circles.

Two Workographies and Exile: Another Comparison

Beyond this abstract of similarities and dissimilarities in their biographies lies the sphere of their compositional output, which one might equally be tempted to compare. Anhalt's youthful output prior to the immediate postwar years is unknown; one can therefore only speculate that, like so many of his fellow Kodály pupils at the Ferenc Liszt Conservatory in Budapest, Anhalt would have been urged to acquire a knowledge as profound as possible in all styles and techniques of European art music and "to assimilate the rich heritage of Western European music, the best of each era."[7] Additionally, Anhalt would have been exposed to Hungarian folk music and encouraged to incorporate aspects of it into his early compositions. Seiber certainly did: the 1st String Quartet (1924), for example, is Mozartian in form but employs a characteristic feature from Hungarian folklore, namely the pentatonic scale. And while young Anhalt enjoyed the Hollywood films screened in 1930s Budapest with their distinctive musical scores,[8] Seiber was much engaged in experimenting with jazz, not only as a teacher but as a composer, too. The two *Jazzolettes* (1929 and 1933) for two saxophones, trumpet, trombone, piano, and percussion most obviously refer to jazz not only by name but also as the instrumentation strongly suggests a jazz combo—Americanism, or exoticism at any rate, on both sides, then.

Admittedly, these similarities might simply mark them as children of their time and not be particularly revealing of anything other than the zeitgeist in interwar Budapest and elsewhere in Europe. Nonetheless, things change somewhat from here on. First, there is the issue of silence: Anhalt was silenced in a labour camp and, after his escape, spent the last years of the war in hiding. Seiber did not compose any music that could be said to continue the line of his interwar avant-garde compositions for almost the entire first decade after his migration to London. (Considering the fact that 90 per cent of Hungary's half a million pre-war Jewish population was killed during the Second World War under Horthy and during the German occupation, it is nothing short of a miracle that Anhalt's and also Seiber's family survived the Holocaust.)[9]

Matters become more obvious in the mid- to late 1940s. The oeuvres of both Seiber and Anhalt reveals a very brief period of only a handful of works one might be tempted to label neo-baroque. In 1940 and 1942,

Seiber transcribed selections of pieces for lute from Jean-Baptiste Besard's *Thesaurus Harmonicus* of 1603 for orchestra and published them under the titles of *Besardo Suites* No. 1 and 2, respectively. In 1944 he collaborated with Walter Goehr, another London-based émigré, on an arrangement of J.S. Bach's *Kunst der Fuge* for orchestra. Around the same time, in 1946, Anhalt wrote a *Concerto (in stilo di Handel)* for orchestra.

The next similarity is one of relative absence, or, if you like, of non-conformity. Even though neoclassicism was the marked preference in the style of many native composers in both the UK and Canada in the 1950s, we find hardly any work of either Seiber or Anhalt after the Second World War that could be described as predominantly neoclassical. This point of absence is perhaps reinforced when considering the technique to which both composers turned their attention instead: dodecaphonism. Anhalt's *Fantasia* for piano of 1954, violin sonata of the same year, and symphony composed 1954–58 thus compare with Seiber's *Fantasia* for flute, horn, and string quartet of 1945, *Tre pezzi* for violoncello and orchestra of 1956, and Violin Sonata of 1960, for example.

Anhalt's and Seiber's education with Kodály, and Anhalt's studies with Nadia Boulanger, are not exactly the most obvious pretexts for a turn away from neoclassicism and towards the language of the Schoenberg School. Boulanger reportedly discouraged Anhalt from engaging with dodecaphony and the Kodály pupils who remained in Hungary certainly eschewed it. Like Seiber, "Anhalt never received any formal instruction in twelve-tone techniques," as Robin Elliott reports, and, instead, learned what he knew "by studying the scores for himself."[10] Moreover, this similarity (the relative, or qualitative, absence of neoclassicism and move to dodecaphony instead) seems even more remarkable in the context of both composers' adopted homes, especially considering that they had to be interested in acculturating themselves and integrating into the musical establishments.

Admittedly, Anhalt's *Fantasia* does show the odd neoclassical reference point, bearing witness to the composer's formative years in Paris and his studies with Nadia Boulanger and Soulima Stravinsky. Nonetheless, the work's beginning leaves little doubt about the technical preference of the composer, as the twelve-note series on which the work is based is presented right away, without any preparation, in the opening bar (see example 7-1). The predominant idiom is that of an "almost completely orthodox Schönbergian technician," to quote John Beckwith. An advocate of Anhalt's work, Beckwith also commented on the musical context (or lack thereof) at the time of the premiere of the *Fantasia*: "I feel that the bewilderment

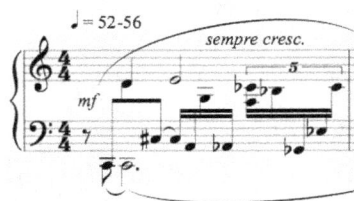

EXAMPLE 7-1 István Anhalt, *Fantasia* for piano (1954), m. 1, with kind permission of the composer.

caused by a recent performance of [Anhalt's] Piano Fantasia in Toronto was at least partly the result of a lack of acquaintance with his models [giving] unsuspecting listeners rather a shock ... It is indeed daring of him."[11] Less amiable critics commented on this in ever more harsh terms. Reporting from the first British concert with works exclusively by Seiber in the Wigmore Hall on 3 December 1945, the critic of the *London Times*, for instance, did not approve of the *Fantasia Concertante* for violin and string orchestra of 1944, and commented lukewarmly on the occasion of its premiere: "The actual novelties in this programme were a Fantasia Concertante for Solo violin (Mr. Max Rostal) and strings composed according to the twelve-tone formula of Schonberg [sic], and sounding like all the stuff so fabricated."[12] The choice of both Seiber and Anhalt to employ a compositional technique (serialism) and a musical idiom and texture closely linked to a relatively small circle of Central European interwar expressionists, then, can hardly have been born out of the aim of integration into the musical establishments of Canada and Britain respectively, especially given that this decision came at the expense of a predominant local trend (neoclassicism).

Paradoxically, the move towards dodecaphony seems unexpected not only in the context of contemporary Canada and Britain, but also in the context of postwar Europe. In the exclusive circles of the progressivist avant-garde obsessed with daily change and innovation on the European continent, Seiber's and Anhalt's music was too old to be taken seriously but too young to have already become canonical. In the historical context of Darmstadt and Donaueschingen, Boulez and Stockhausen, much of their music of the postwar years seems peculiarly conservative, even today. In 1950s Darmstadt it acquired, at best, nostalgic value. If Adorno could speak of the rapid aging of *postwar* avant-garde music,[13] Seiber's and Anhalt's postwar music, which owes so much to the expressionism of the *interwar* years, had to seem representative of an old world long gone.

The performance history of works by Anhalt in Darmstadt and Donaueschingen from 1946 until 1960 is quickly told: there is none. Seiber was performed on several occasions.[14] Nonetheless, he was regarded by the Darmstadt generation as a representative of the interwar period, a man who had been born into the Habsburg Empire, had been befriended by

Bartók, and had witnessed the birth of atonality. This meant respect for the past his works represented, but less so for his works of the present. Sarcastically put, Seiber was one of "the last survivors," administering the heritage of his generation (the musical expressionism of the interwar period) rather than participating in the creative processes and contemporaneous discourses of the postwar avant-garde. This was a paradoxical situation given that, born in 1905, Seiber was still a relatively young composer in the late 1940s and 1950s. Accordingly, Seiber's style has exclusively been described with attributes assignable to the interwar years. Writing in 1955, Gottfried Schweizer, for example, sweepingly described Seiber's oeuvre as "a synthesis of influences and stimuli from Bartók, Schönberg, and Berg" so that one could identify "the image of Mátyás Seiber" to be somewhere "between Bartók and Schönberg."[15] Other writers identified Hindemithian, Stravinskyian, and Kodályian stylistic proximities.[16] In a cynical turn of history, the compositions of the internationalist Seiber were thus not rendered cosmopolitan, but ex-territorialized as their geographical attachment was replaced by a historical, and indeed historicizing, connotation on the European continent.

Exile in the Row? Anhalt's *Fantasia* and Violin Sonata and Seiber's *Ulysses*

Beyond their preference for the dodecaphonic technique and similarities in instrumentation and titles, one also finds some remarkable similarities in compositional technique of the postwar music of Seiber and Anhalt. The works of both composers often employ dodecaphony in very flexible, yet similar ways. Permutations and repetitions of notes or tone groups, free manipulation of the row, fragmentation and transposition, feature more or less prominently in the works of both composers, for example in Anhalt's *Fantasia* for piano and Seiber's *Improvisation* for oboe and piano of 1957. Most obvious, maybe, is the very similar construction of the basic row.

For example, after the initial, strict deployment of the tone row in bar 1 (C, D, C sharp, E, A, G, A flat, C flat, F, B flat, G flat, E flat; see example 7-1), Anhalt's *Fantasia* is based upon a free manipulation of the tone row, including constant fragmentation and transposition. Frequent use is made of the outer sections of the row (C, D, C sharp, E and E flat, C), the amplitudes of both of which, C – E and E flat – C, outline the major and minor third. The tone row upon which Anhalt's Violin Sonata is based (E, F, E flat, G, B, G sharp, D flat, C, D, A sharp, F sharp, A; see example 7-2) is an exercise in symmetry. It emphasizes the minor and major second (and their inversion, the major and minor seventh) and the major and minor third (and their inversion, the minor and major sixth), and is thus symmetrical: the latter six notes are the inversion of the former half of the row. How similar Seiber. To mention but one example, all five movements of Seiber's cantata *Ulysses* of 1947 are based on dodecaphonic rows which are permutations of the same cell (E, G, G sharp and its variant E, A flat, G; see example 7-5, bass line). Like Anhalt's row, this cell consists, of course, of the major and minor third and the minor second. Like Anhalt's, too, all rows of *Ulysses* follow the principle of symmetry. For example, the second half of the basic row of the third movement of *Ulysses* (F, D, D flat, B flat, A, F sharp) is an inversion of the first (E, G, G sharp, B, C, E flat; see example 7-3). It is possible that these symmetries in the construction of the basic row, which are also present in other works such as Anhalt's Symphony (1954–58)[17] and Seiber's *Fantasia Concertante* and *Quartetto Lirico* for string quartet from 1951, for example, were inspired by Webern, as they parallel the architectural characteristics of several of his rows in the Symphony, Op. 21.

While Anhalt's *Fantasia* and Violin Sonata and Seiber's *Ulysses* widely employ serial techniques (see examples 7-1, 7-4, and 7-5), they do not completely abandon the boundaries of tonality. Major and minor thirds occur in all three rows and are used both directly and indirectly to elaborate and outline pitch structures. In so doing, these intervals contribute to the establishment of an implied tonal centre. In building almost the entire musical thematic material of *Ulysses* upon the same cell, E, G, G sharp and its variant E, A flat, G, E appears as the tonal centre, while in Anhalt's *Fantasia*, C is emphasized not only in the row, but throughout the work. The twelve horizontally organized notes of the rows in the mentioned works of both composers thus merge with the stereotypical third of tonality and, beyond that, with the principle of the rising and falling scale which is so basic to Western composition.[18]

EXAMPLE 7-2 István Anhalt, Sonata for Violin and Piano, basic tone row.

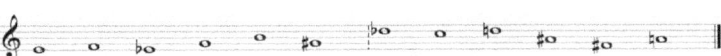

EXAMPLE 7-3 Mátyás Seiber, *Ulysses*, Movement 3, basic tone row.

EXAMPLE 7-4 István Anhalt, Sonata for Violin and Piano (1954), mm. 1–3, with kind permission of the composer.

EXAMPLE 7-5 Mátyás Seiber, *Ulysses*, Movement 1, mm. 1–10, with kind permission of Julia Seiber Boyd on behalf of the Mátyás Seiber Trust

Beyond these very technical compositional similarities, the overall architecture and sound world of Seiber's and Anhalt's compositions also reveal striking similarities. Both combine a Webernian architecture with Berg's tendency towards lyricism and tonal definition, as well as a subtlety and romantic(ist) warmth. The texture of much of Seiber's and Anhalt's music of the time is extremely active contrapuntally. Also, the term "stream-of-conscious expressionism," with which George Proctor has described

Anhalt's serial music, can almost as aptly be applied to Seiber's contemporaneous compositions.[19]

Dodecaphony in Exile

With Seiber's premature death in 1960, the comparison of these two composers and their oeuvres comes to a halt. What can be said until this point, however, is that in venturing towards an aesthetic very much associated with the Central European interwar avant-garde—and thus associated with the aesthetic program of a particular music in a particular place that had, by 1945, disappeared from the map—one discovers tensions between concrete compositional change and compositional meta-continuity in Anhalt's and Seiber's work. The employment of dodecaphony and the turn towards the musical idiom of the Viennese School post-1945, then, cannot be understood as a mere re-territorialization of an aesthetic continuum. Instead, it has to be interpreted as a very deliberate choice, a choice as unexpected (at least given Anhalt's biographical precedents) as it was risky in the context of the comparatively conservative cultural environments in Canada and Britain and the radically progressive musical circles on the European continent. Indeed, I would argue that the existential untranslatability of music's performative aspect (i.e., that there exist different geocultural circumstances and political, societal, and cultural contexts) implies that this turn to dodecaphonism is indicative of a process of a de-territorialized and displaced nostalgia, an expression of an exile's feeling of profound loss. "The achievements of exile," as Edward Said puts it, "are permanently undermined by the loss of something left behind forever."[20] This conscious altering (in Anhalt's case) and resuming (in Seiber's case) of the direction of their compositional pathways and developments represents a moment of memory of a geographical and historical cultural past, a past displaced. Compositional change can then be understood as an attempt at historical continuity.

The impact of immigration upon the Canadian and English musical landscapes remains to be told, but a suspicion lingers that music associated with, or openly referring to, the Schoenberg School was regarded as alien, at least in the first one and a half decades after the end of the Second World War.

Many expressions of open hostility to interwar expressionism, and the Schoenberg School in particular, by British critics and writers could be quoted here, but even a statement by Seiber pupil Peter Racine Fricker, himself an advocate of the compositional style of his teacher's avant-garde works, highlights this perceived alien element and foreign geographical attachment when he equates cosmopolitan music with music "from abroad" and constructs it as the Other to the English style: "What happens is that since the war we've become more aware that Europe exists. For one thing, a lot of people have come over to England—Matyas Seiber, my teacher, for one. But I can't say that I was consciously writing cosmopolitan music when my first works became known, though I did myself want to get away from the English traditional style. The attitude in this country is based on the fact that we don't know enough of contemporary music from abroad."[21] Similarly, John Beckwith in 1956 wrote: "Acquaintance with the music of Joachim and Kasemets suggests that perhaps the newcomers are the only composers in Canada applying 12-note procedures in anything like the strict fashion of Krenek, Webern, and middle-period Schoenberg. This impression is strengthened when one comes to consider the music of István Anhalt, Hungarian-born, Paris-trained composer now teaching at McGill."[22]

It would be absurd, of course, to overgeneralize the particular cases of Anhalt and Seiber and suggest that the employment of Schoenbergian dodecaphony after 1945 conclusively links to the factor of migration. Not all émigrés composed serially, and several composers who had not composed serially and turned to it in the 1950s and 1960s were not émigrés. And yet, the connection of serialism and the musical émigrés in the United Kingdom and Canada is striking. Regarding Canada, one can mention Otto Joachim and Udo Kasemets; regarding the United Kingdom, émigré composers such as Webern pupil Leopold Spinner and Schoenberg pupil Egon Wellesz, who all favoured stylistic elements from the Schoenberg school, spring to mind.[23] Notwithstanding notable exceptions such as Humphrey Searle (who had studied with Webern in Vienna in 1937–38) and Elisabeth Lutyens, the few British-born composers who turned to dodecaphony in the postwar years (Peter Racine Fricker, for example) could almost exclusively be traced back directly to émigrés acting as teachers, such as Seiber. Among the generation of Canadian composers who began to employ serial techniques from the 1950s onwards (Harry Somers, Norma Beecroft, and Bruce Mather, for example), many were pupils of John Weinzweig, a son of Polish immigrants and a pioneer of serial composition in the Canadian context.

In any case, it seems unquestionable that the numerous Central Europeans who migrated to Canada and the United Kingdom around the Second World War contributed greatly to the widening of the musical base, a base from which a rich variety of music ensued.[24] This is particularly true of the situation in Canada, which, like the United States, was and still is a nation of immigrants.[25]

Comparative Studies as a Tool for Tracing the Impact of Exile

Assuming a work can reveal traces of migration and displacement merely because its author migrated at the time of its creation (and consequently coming full circle by suggesting that the work confirms the author's status as a migrant) is problematic because it takes the outcome of analysis for the process of analysis. The presupposition that biographical experiences are the sole determinant of creative output is as absurd as suggesting that every minute experience faced by a creative artist is likely to shape his or her art. Admittedly, displacement is not a minute experience. Still, at every stage of his or her life a composer can keep composing the same way, or change his or her approach or style, or stop composing, or return to composing for any number of circumstantial reasons (financial, aesthetic, etc.) or without any evidently traceable reason. As Carl Dahlhaus put it: "The attempt to associate specific works with specific, biographically tangible elements of the life shows time and again that a connection that looks plausible as long as it is left to a vague suggestion proves to be dubious and fraught with more guesswork than is desirable as soon as any attempt is made to be precise about it."[26] The problem of linking too directly the personal situation of a composer with the factor of displacement within his or her musical output becomes particularly apparent in cases when the composer eventually integrates in his or her adopted country. Anhalt and Seiber are both a case in point. Integration and acculturation did not interrupt the hybrid fluidity of their creative processes and imply that, suddenly, compositional activity ceased to be affected by displacement, a conclusion based on the same misconception that would allege an all-encompassing theme of displacement prior to naturalization.

Even if it were a composer's intention to transmit traces of displacement, this intended meaning of the composer is not the principal factor in the analysis and understanding of art. In Jacques Derrida's words, an artist can always say "more, less, or something else than he [or she] would mean,"[27] or—even though we know about the intended meaning through sketches, letters, publications, personal notes, etc.—convey it unsuccessfully, or change his or her mind, or mean more or less than analysis can reveal or one can detect, or mean something that words cannot express, or mean something and not be aware of it, or not mean anything at all.

In other words, intentionality, that is, the (ontological) notion of the intention of the author, differs from meaningfulness, that is, the (phenomenological) notion of the meaning of the artwork. This does not, of course, render the intention of the composer irrelevant. Rather, the author's intentions, be they conscious, subconscious, or unconscious, are one aspect of the material that nurtures the artwork's ontological genesis—its coming into existence—but need not necessarily affect its actual phenomenological existence.

In a nutshell, while it is clear that both Seiber and Anhalt were affected by displacement, their biographies are not the starting points or bases from which to approach their works, even if displacement is the hallmark of their very biographies. For example, the occasional Hungarian accent in *Sparkskraps* is no justification to identify any Hungarian provenance or nostalgia and the engagement with the Holocaust in *Sonance•Resonance (Welche Töne?)* does not allow for a biographically based tracing of either geographical attachment or displacement, quite simply because Anhalt's biography is neither a necessary nor a sufficient condition for these compositions. "There is no formula for predictably defining how a man writes by using his geographical and family origins as firm and sole indicators," to use Isván Anhalt's words. "His birthplace and ancestry may be of great or little consequence, or they may appear to have no direct influence."[28] In the same way, Mátyás Seiber's *Elegy* for viola and orchestra does not suggest conclusively a composer of Hungarian birth resident in Britain, in spite of the very Hungarian melody with which the work opens. Albeit less eloquently than Anhalt, Seiber's self-assessment hinted in the same direction when he rejected any suggestion "that the use of such material [Hungarian folklore] has affected in any way the musical style of my ... more 'abstract' works."[29]

A comparative approach can remedy to some extent the dilemma such qualitative aesthetic assessments pose because it adds a moment of quantitative analysis. In highlighting similarities and differences in the works of composers with similar biographical backgrounds, patterns can be distilled and these patterns can then be applied to consider traces of displacement in an individual composer's oeuvre. Both Seiber and Anhalt share very similar, yet diverse, biographical backgrounds. Comparing them can reveal that their migration triggered moves towards the avant-garde, which both interpret in very similar ways. Even a brief perusal of a selection of Seiber's and Anhalt's postwar works can reveal certain similarities that might not easily be understood in isolation—but they do acquire some sense in a comparative context. The choice of Seiber and

Anhalt to compose serial music in the first one and a half decades after the Second World War, combined with similarities in their respective compositional techniques, is a case in point. Serialism as interpreted by Seiber and Anhalt thus does reveal traces of migration and acculturation and is itself part of a narrative of displacement.

Notes

1 Julia Kristeva, *Strangers to Ourselves*, trans. Leon Roudiez (New York: Columbia University Press, 1991), 42.
2 These are estimates by William Smyser, United Nations Deputy High Commissioner for Refugees from 1981 to 1986. See Smyser, *Refugees: Extended Exile* (New York: Praeger, 1987), 5.
3 Ibid., 3.
4 See particularly Robin Elliott and Gordon E. Smith, eds., *Istvan Anhalt: Pathways and Memory* (Montreal and Kingston: McGill-Queen's University Press, 2001).
5 It is possible that Seiber gained insight into the works of the Schoenberg School via Adorno, who was teaching at Frankfurt's Institut für Sozialforschung at the time and had been a pupil of Alban Berg in 1925.
6 Since they were both Kodály pupils, this assumption may be deemed reasonable. Also, elected 1st Vice-President of the ISCM in 1960, Seiber could well have been exposed to a composer like Anhalt, as much as Anhalt would presumably have been aware of Seiber given the latter's position.
7 "das reiche Erbe westeuropäischer Musik, das Beste aller Zeiten uns zu eigen zu machen." Zoltán Kodály, "Dreizehn junge Musiker," in *Wege zur Musik: Ausgewählte Schriften und Reden*, ed. Ferenc Bónis (Budapest: Corvina Kiadó, 1983), 255.
8 As reported by John Beckwith in his paper "István Anhalt: A Character Sketch," held at the University of Calgary, 23 January 2008, on the occasion of the conference on which this volume is based.
9 This number is taken from Paul Tabori, *The Anatomy of Exile* (London: Harrap, 1972), 252. Other authors have suggested different numbers. István Déak argues that by 1944, 95 per cent of the Jewish population were still alive ("Admiral and Regent Miklós Horthy," *Hungarian Quarterly* 37/143 [1996]: 85–86) while Iván Berend and György Ránki estimate that 500,000 people were murdered during the war (*East Central Europe in the 19th and 20th Centuries* [Budapest: Akademiai Kiadó, 1977]), an estimate David Cooper calls "conservative" (David Cooper, "Béla Bartók and the Question of Race Purity in Music," in *Musical Constructions of Nationalism: Essays on the History and Ideology of European Musical Culture 1800–1945*, ed. Harry White and Michael Murphy [Cork: Cork University Press, 2001], 30fn.13).
10 Robin Elliott, "The Instrumental Solo and Chamber Music," in *Istvan Anhalt: Pathways and Memory*, 100.
11 John Beckwith, "Composers in Toronto and Montreal," *University of Toronto Quarterly* 26/1 (1956): 61.

12 "Two Concerts of Modern Music: Machine-Made Counterpoint," *London Times*, December 5, 1945.
13 Theodor W. Adorno, "Das Altern der Neuen Musik," in *Dissonanzen: Musik in der verwalteten Welt*, 7th ed. (Göttingen: Vandenhoeck & Ruprecht, 1991), 136–59.
14 The *Elegy* for viola and orchestra (1953) was performed in Donaueschingen in 1954, the *Permutazioni a cinque* for wind quintet (1958) posthumously, in 1961. The cantata *Ulysses* (1947), the *3 Morgenstern Songs* for voice and clarinet (1927–29), and the *Fantasia Concertante* were included in programs at the International Summer Courses for New Music, Darmstadt, in 1951, 1953, and 1955, respectively.
15 See Gottfried Schweizer, "Komponistenportrait: Mátyás Seiber 50 Jahre," *Musica* 9/5 (1955): 233–34, and "Zwischen Bartók und Schönberg. Das Bild Mátyás Seibers," *Zeitschrift für Musik* 116/5 (1955): 269–72.
16 See, for example, Colin Mason, "The Musical Personality of Mátyás Seiber," *Listener* 57/1453: 205 and Hans Keller, "Mátyás Seiber and His Twelve Notes" *Listener* 51/1311 (1954): 669.
17 William Benjamin has analyzed the symmetries in the Symphony in some detail. See "Alternatives of Voice: Anhalt's Odyssey from Personalised Style to Symbolic Expression," in *Istvan Anhalt: Pathways and Memory*, 164–308.
18 This deliberate "tonal" and "scale" treatment is reminiscent of the scale-like row in Alban Berg's *Lyric Suite* and the row in Berg's Violin Concerto, with its alternating minor and major thirds and the four complementing whole tones.
19 George Proctor, *Canadian Music of the Twentieth Century* (Toronto: University of Toronto Press, 1980), 84.
20 Edward W. Said, "Reflections on Exile," in *Reflections on Exile and Other Essays*, 3rd ed. (Cambridge, MA: Harvard University Press, 2002), 173.
21 Peter Racine Fricker, quoted in "Composer's Integrity as an Artist," *London Times*, September 7, 1959.
22 John Beckwith, "Composers in Toronto and Montreal," 61.
23 The reception of the later works of Egon Wellesz presents a parallel case to Seiber's, as they were deemed too old-fashioned for the European avant-garde despite their atonality. Erich Itor Kahn's music was largely ignored in postwar Europe too, in spite of the efforts of René Leibowitz and Hans Rosbaud, who performed and promoted his music.
24 The considerable body of musicological exile studies has, so far, largely focused on Austro-German migration to the United States, with a marked preference on biographical case studies of elite individuals (see, for example, Reinhold Brinkmann and Christoph Wolff, eds., *Driven into Paradise: The Musical Migration from Nazi Germany to the United States* [Berkeley: University of California Press, 1999]). Significantly less emphasis has been placed on migration to the United Kingdom and Canada. With regards to the United Kingdom, Jutta Raab Hansen's monograph *NS-verfolgte Musiker in England* (Hamburg: von Bockel, 1996) is a valuable, if isolated, exception.
25 In fact, the cultural landscapes in the musical centres of Canada (especially in Toronto and anglophone Montreal) were long dominated by British expatriates, a situation Barbara Pentland, for example, complained about bitterly

(see "Canadian Music 1950," *Northern Review* 3 (February/March 1950): 43–46). Pentland's complaint highlights that Canada at the time was still a "dominion" of the disintegrating empire and only beginning to emerge from its British colonial past.

26 Carl Dahlhaus, *Ludwig van Beethoven: Approaches to His Music*, trans. Mary Whittall (Oxford: Clarendon Press, 1991), 10.
27 Jacques Derrida, *Of Grammatology*, rev. ed., trans. Gayatri Chakravorty Spivak (Baltimore: Johns Hopkins University Press, 1997), 158.
28 István Anhalt, "About One's Place and Voice," in *Identities: the Impact of Ethnicity on Canadian Society*, ed. Wsevolod Isajiw (Toronto: Peter Martin Associates, 1977), 45.
29 Mátyás Seiber, "Folk Music and the Contemporary Composer," *Recorded Folk Music* 2/4 (1959): 9.

Bibliography

"Composer's Integrity as an Artist." *London Times*, 7 September 1959.
"Two Concerts of Modern Music: Machine-Made Counterpoint." *London Times*, 5 December 1945.
Adorno, Theodor W. "Das Altern der Neuen Musik." In *Dissonanzen: Musik in der verwalteten Welt*, 7th ed., 136–59. Göttingen: Vandenhoeck & Ruprecht, 1991.
Anhalt, István. "About One's Place and Voice." In *Identities: The Impact of Ethnicity on Canadian Society*, edited by Wsevolod Isajiw, 39–45. Toronto: Peter Martin Associates, 1977.
Beckwith, John. "Composers in Toronto and Montreal." *University of Toronto Quarterly* 26/1 (1956): 47–69.
Berend, Iván, and György Ránki. *East Central Europe in the 19th and 20th Centuries*. Budapest: Akademiai Kiadó, 1977.
Brinkmann, Reinhold, and Christoph Wolff, eds. *Driven into Paradise: The Musical Migration from Nazi Germany to the United States*. Berkeley: University of California Press, 1999.
Cooper, David. "Béla Bartók and the Question of Race Purity in Music." In *Musical Constructions of Nationalism: Essays on the History and Ideology of European Musical Culture 1800–1945*, edited by Harry White and Michael Murphy, 16–32. Cork: Cork University Press, 2001.
Dahlhaus, Carl. *Ludwig van Beethoven: Approaches to His Music*. Translated by Mary Whittall. Oxford: Clarendon Press, 1991.
Deák, István. "Admiral and Regent Miklós Horthy." *Hungarian Quarterly* 37/143 (1996): 78–86.
Derrida, Jacques. *Of Grammatology*. Revised edition. Translated by Gayatri Chakravorty Spivak. Baltimore: Johns Hopkins University Press, 1997.
Elliott, Robin, and Gordon Smith, eds. *Istvan Anhalt: Pathways and Memory*. Montreal and Kingston: McGill-Queen's University Press, 2001.

Keller, Hans. "Mátyás Seiber and His Twelve Notes." *Listener* 51/1311 (1954): 669.
Kodály, Zoltán. "Dreizehn junge Musiker." In *Wege zur Musik: Ausgewählte Schriften und Reden*, edited by Ferenc Bónis, 255–59. Budapest: Corvina Kiadó, 1983.
Kristeva, Julia. *Strangers to Ourselves*. Translated by Leon Roudiez. New York: Columbia University Press, 1991.
Mason, Colin. "The Musical Personality of Mátyás Seiber." *Listener* 57/1453 (1957): 205.
Pentland, Barbara. "Canadian Music 1950." *Northern Review* 3 (February/March 1950): 43–46.
Proctor, George. *Canadian Music of the Twentieth Century*. Toronto: University of Toronto Press, 1980.
Raab Hansen, Jutta. *NS-verfolgte Musiker in England*. Hamburg: von Bockel, 1996.
Said, Edward W. "Reflections on Exile." In *Reflections on Exile and Other Essays*, 3rd ed., 173–86. Cambridge, MA: Harvard University Press, 2002.
Schweizer, Gottfried. "Komponistenportrait: Mátyás Seiber 50 Jahre." *Musica* 9/5 (1955): 233–34.
———. "Zwischen Bartók und Schönberg. Das Bild Mátyás Seibers." *Zeitschrift für Musik* 116/5 (1955): 269–72.
Seiber, Mátyás. "Folk Music and the Contemporary Composer." *Recorded Folk Music* 2/4 (1959): 6–9.
Smyser, William. *Refugees: Extended Exile*. New York: Praeger, 1987.
Tabori, Paul. *The Anatomy of Exile*. London: Harrap, 1972.

EIGHT

Letters to America

RACHEL BECKLES WILLSON

WHEN ASKED DURING THE 1980s whether he might consider leaving Switzerland and returning to the land of his birth, Sándor Veress replied in the negative, and explained himself by stating that he was a "member of the Hungarian emigration."[1] The claim is not unambiguous: on the one hand it suggests alienation from Hungarian soil, while on the other it reveals loyalty to a Hungarian identity. To a large extent we can understand it as an angry reaction to the Soviet occupation of Hungary and Veress's (consequently) fraught emigration in 1949. As he explained at other times in the 1980s, Switzerland provided a refuge at that difficult moment and had also offered a space in which to develop his work in the "wide European horizons" that he could suddenly sense.[2] It was an entirely different world from the Eastern Bloc that he had gratefully left behind.

We can be deceived by the singularity of his perspective in the 1980s, however. Here I relocate our point of gravity to the 1950s and swivel the lens around 180 degrees, thus using Veress's early émigré years to look forward. I make that move in order to examine the fact that while making Switzerland his home, Veress was simultaneously trying to move to the United States.[3] He was offered a university post, he made more than one visa application, and he even composed a seven-page autobiography for the American authorities to support his case.

That autobiography will provide my initial focus in the pages that follow. Given that it attempts to justify Veress's (by-then regretted) decision to join the Communist Party in 1945, however, I suggest that it should be understood less as an account of the past than as a wager on the future, as a forward-looking gesture toward yet another emigration and a new life beyond Europe. My second focus will be on Veress's *Sinfonia Minneapolitana* (1952–53), which I argue can be viewed in a related light. Although Andreas Traub has indicated that this work was a product of Eastern European influence, it was commissioned by the American Frederick Mann Foundation and first performed in Minneapolis in March 1954.[4] It offers us a musical parallel to the autobiographical statement, I suggest, because it makes another gesture from Europe toward an imaginary future in the United States. My reading of this work will enable us to rethink Veress's position in the 1950s, and also to understand "the Hungarian emigration" through a somewhat different lens.

Bern to Pittsburgh and Washington

The background to the autobiographical statement can be traced from Veress's correspondence with three Hungarians, who sought to help with his emigration in very practical ways. These were: ex-diplomat-turned-writer Stephen (István) Borsody (1911–2000), who was teaching Russian and East European history at the Pennsylvania College for Women in Pittsburgh (now Chatham University); Géza Soós (1912–53), a lawyer-turned-preacher who lived in Munich until 1952, when he relocated to the United States;[5] and the Washington-based István Csicsery-Rónay (b. 1917), who had been active in the Smallholders' Party in Hungary after the war and remained politically active in Hungarian interests.[6]

Borsody presumably arranged Veress's invitation to teach at the Pennsylvania College for Women from autumn 1948.[7] Unable to secure the visa that would allow him to enter and work in the United States, Veress never actually took this up, but in the years that followed first Soós, then Csicsery-Rónay, joined an ongoing discussion about his projected move to North America. With the benefit of hindsight, it seems unlikely that Veress could have gained entry at the time, and although Borsody was ready to set up another job for him in Pittsburgh, he was himself increasingly aware that American policy vis-à-vis communists and former communists rendered the legal obstacles almost insurmountable.[8] Nevertheless, Veress's other correspondents—both active within organizations striving to help émigrés and potential émigrés from Hungary—cherished hopes at certain moments, because exceptions did occur. Soós, for example, wrote to Veress on 1 March 1951 saying that there was now a precedent, and that Veress should fill out the relevant forms (which he enclosed with his letter). Veress may well have done this and presumably took Soós's hopes on board (Veress's own letters are missing, but Borsody's letter of 23 March 1951 reflects his optimism). However, a little over two weeks later, Soós wrote with consternation to say that he only now realized that Veress had left Hungary after 1 January 1949, which disqualified him automatically from the scheme he had sought to use.

Veress's own position was clearly divided. He was keen to go because he was anxious about another possible war in Europe and unhappy with his teaching responsibilities and financial situation. Nevertheless, he was uncertain whether conditions would be better in the United States, and sensed that initiating visa applications might damage his reputation in Bern.[9] Such anxiety may partially explain the lack of enthusiasm for emigration that is apparent at certain points in his letters. For instance, Csicsery-Rónay wrote with excitement at the end of 1953 to say that Veress could now get a visa within a week because his (English) spouse was a citizen of an "open quota" country, but Veress only responded to the news briefly in passing, remarking that it was "interesting" in his letter of some six weeks later.[10] Yet he did continue to seek advice on the matter, and his exchanges with Csicsery-Rónay proliferated as those with Borsody dwindled.[11] He became interested in shorter visits, and also had the idea of entering the country on a visitor visa on the basis of an invitation to the premiere of his *Sinfonia Minneapolitana*, but, as Csicsery-Rónay warned him, that was equally difficult to arrange.[12]

The autobiographical statement itself survives today as three typescripts. The first is corrected with ballpoint pen annotations, and these (essentially linguistic refinements) are incorporated into the second (see plate 8-3 in the appendix). This, labelled "first draft" (*Elsőfogalmazvány*), has further alterations made in ballpoint and, more significantly, major cuts marked with a red pencil; correspondence indicates that it dates from 1952.[13] The third and apparently final version incorporates most of these adjustments and was written in about 1955 (see plate 8-3 in the appendix).[14] Veress's re-engagement with the statement after a three-year gap may have been triggered by contact in Minneapolis, because in a letter dated 4 October 1955 he wrote to tell Csicsery-Rónay about an invitation to visit there that he had had to turn down because it required an instant response. We currently have no information as to whether he ever submitted the statement to the authorities, although on 10 July 1956 he wrote to Csicsery-Rónay saying that he had found a good contact at the US Embassy and had handed in a visa application, hoping to spend "3–4 months" at a North American university. Conceivably he attached a copy then.[15]

The only published interpretation of the statement so far uses it to furnish the argument that a clear distinction can be drawn between the ideals of the monolithic, communist state apparatus that consolidated in 1948, and Veress's original interest in the Communist Party in 1945.[16] From this perspective, we understand Veress as a victim of unanticipated social transformation and the invasion of the Soviet Union, as a liberal social democrat who was hoodwinked. I have demonstrated elsewhere, however, that Veress's act of joining the Communist Party has a complex prehistory, and even if he did see himself as a victim of the Soviet Union, it is likely not the only way he saw himself.[17] Addressing the contortions that his self-construction entailed may help us understand how he saw himself in other ways; in particular, with respect to his future.

The "victim" notion emerges somewhat heavy-handedly in the statement itself, which Veress rather disarmingly referred to as "my 'story'" at the end (p. 7/p. 5, quote marks original). Thus, in the family history with which he opened the statement, each of his ancestors appeared in a tragic mould: all worked for a noble national cause—whether independence, infrastructure, or intellectual advancement—and all but one suffered greatly from the actions of forces understood to be alien to Hungary. His maternal great-grandfather and his paternal grandfather served in the "War of Independence against Austria in 1848–49" (not the "revolution," we note!), the former imprisoned and the latter living outside Hungary thereafter (p. 1/p. 1); his father, a "well-known historian" was still living "in the greatest misery in Hungary" (p. 2) (in the later version of the statement he had "died with a broken heart" [p. 1]); his uncle was a professor and founder of the University of Economics in Budapest and was imprisoned in 1919 under Hungary's communist regime, escaping "execution only by sheere [sic] good luck" (p. 2/p. 2). As Veress wrote, "[t]hese family traditions decided the atmosphere in which I grew up" (p. 2/p. 2); or, we might say, these family stories were constructed by Veress through the lens of one of his self-visions at the time.

To complicate matters, however, it is clear from the correspondence that assigning Veress authorship of the text is problematic, because he did not write it alone. Rather, he wrote it on Borsody's instructions.[18] It is worth reading them so that we can more fully appreciate the point:

> I think this statement needs to be in three sections. Explain why you joined the party, make clear your anti-communist faith, and finally profess your pro-western, pro-democratic faith. You will write the last two parts easily I think. The first section has to be carefully framed with

regard to the situation here. It needs to be threaded through with the idea that your joining *was not an anti-American step in the context of the time*, and above all was not a pro-communist declaration! Emphasise that you were never a communist, that your becoming a party member was a mere formality, an expedient step that wasn't even immoral, because it served artistic and personal aims. There were no politics in it. You never did any party work. You can easily explain the artistic and personal aims. As a nominal party member, *you felt that you could promote the regeneration of Hungarian musical life—and in connection with this you also need to relate your disappointments* of course. In the personal aims, mention Enid's British citizenship, and the awful difficulties of mere survival. And finally, running throughout the statement should be your western essence, your permanent ties with western culture, to which your activities and actions at all times—including during your party membership—bear most eloquent proof. I ask you only to make an effort and consider that it's not an objective history of your case that is needed now, but a statement on the basis of which we can get the visa in this country, which is hysterically untrusting and suspicious of 'ex-communists.'[19]

The text in Veress's statement that follows on from his family background incorporates each of Borsody's instructions very precisely apart from two, and these are present by implication. First, although Veress did not say that he was never anti-American, he did say that he had followed American and British wartime radio broadcasts that led him to believe he should welcome the Soviets as heralds of democracy. Similarly, he did not say that he was never a communist, but he did say that he was not pro-communist, was in fact anti-communist, that his membership was nominal, and so on. His message was ultimately an elaboration of Borsody's advice; indeed, the statement's most obvious surface is a plethora of instances of "democratic" and "democracy"—precisely in line with Borsody's instruction. In the first draft they appear thirteen times (plus one "undemocratic"), incidentally reduced to twelve in the later version. And because "democracy" was double-edged—used rhetorically by both superpowers in the Cold War—Veress wrote a closing sentence stating "my convictions were always strongly democratic *in the western sense of the word*" (p. 7/p. 6, my italics). Reinforcing this point, in an addition to the first draft he said that communists had been "camouflaged behind a democratic façade" when he joined the party (p. 4/p. 3).

But Borsody's influence did not stop with his initial advice. Most of the alterations incorporated into the final version most probably stem from him too. In June 1952 Veress wrote to him to say—with ambivalence and hesitation—that he had composed a draft statement that he would like help with.[20] No response from Borsody has come to light.[21] However, in a letter written to Csicsery-Rónay on 8 April 1953, Veress stated that Borsody had made some observations about the statement indeed and had "thoroughly revised it."[22] It is more than likely, then, that at least some of the cuts stem from his recommendations. The annotations are partly of a different nature, but even these may have been noted in response to the (missing) letter with which Borsody enclosed the revised text.

All cuts made in red pencil alter Veress's relationship to the party.[23] In his first draft he had attempted to trivialize the decision he made by constructing the four main postwar parties as apparently working for the same "democratic" aims, and stating that either friendship or even the location of the nearest party office had often been the reason for selecting one or the other (p. 4). His section referring to US and UK broadcasts was also cut; perhaps that would have been too critical of the nation in which he sought a place. Another deletion removed Veress's statement that the Communist Party saved him several times from Russian arrest directly after the siege of Budapest. This was not only implicitly dissonant with a later claim that he never himself benefited from his position (did the benefits stop once he joined, one might ask?), but also might have triggered unhelpful speculation as to why he had been arrested in the first place.

The largest number of cuts, however, is of precisely the text that constructs Veress's individual and positive role within a political hierarchy that is otherwise a negative force. This is the case not only in the postwar era, but even earlier on, during the years when Hungary was allied with fascist Germany. The first version states that once appointed Professor of Composition in 1943, and being of Aryan origin, Veress could help people in need (p. 3). Five other instances construct him as a man who used the communist power for his own sense of good. He used his "artistic position to counteract ... certain destructive communist moves" (p. 1); he "made moves ... to help people, friends and young artists when they got into difficulties caused by communist politics" (p. 1); he wanted to protect his wife with his membership (pp. 4–5); he "helped many valuable people who were in difficulty merely on the grounds that they did not belong to the communist party" (p.5); and he had until 1948 a "unique and independent position *in the Communist party*" (only the section I have italicized here was cut, p. 6). All these reveal a figure who has his own sense of values and is fighting the values of the system of which he is nevertheless a part. And all were removed, even though Borsody had suggested in his first guidelines that they were appropriate.

This is peculiarly ironic because, when Veress first wrote the statement, he asserted his autonomy very firmly to Borsody. In his hesitant letter requesting editorial help, he claimed that he had written something rather against his own will, and with difficulty, but that he *wasn't* following Borsody's guidelines.[24] There was no point in assuming a democratic and anti-communist tone, he said, because anyone could do that. He found it preferable to submit a sort of curriculum vitae with the true facts, without any particular attempt to colour them in the interest of his future.

Having read his forcefully democracy-infused statement, which is so much at odds with these claims, we might ask whether he had a naive grasp of what he was doing, or whether he simply strove to deny it, drawing a firm line between Borsody and himself. Either way (and there may have been a combination of the two at play), the *letter* is a rhetorical performance of his individual autonomy.[25] The irony is that he made this gesture shortly before he erased it from the *statement*, shedding his political autonomy by editing out his individual position in both the Nazi and Communist periods. He presumably regarded this rhetorical self-annihilation as an investment in the ideals of the American regime under which he wished to build a future.[26] I explore the nature of the future he envisaged in the next two sections.

Bern to Minneapolis in Words

Antal Doráti wrote to Veress with an official commission for the work that became *Sinfonia Minneapolitana* on 17 July 1951. It is likely that the project had been under discussion for some time; indeed, Borsody had specifically recommended to Veress even in 1949 that he try to enter the United States with a commission and performance, and that he use Doráti and the latter's position as chief conductor in Minneapolis.[27] *Sinfonia Minneapolitana* is thus inseparable from Veress's long-term plans for the United States, figuring within Veress's thoughts of emigration well before it was composed. The symphony as a genre, moreover, has long been associated both with nationhood and with personal identity, and that the *Sinfonia* can be placed within this broader tendency is immediately apparent from two sources: press responses and Veress's own verbal commentaries.[28]

Press coverage, for instance, conforms to traditional tropes of symphonic reception by identifying the new work both with Veress's personality and with his national identity. One critic noted that "Veress, on the evidence of this work ... is a man of individuality and creative vitality, also wit and humor."[29] The same critic offered data pertaining to Veress's national allegiances too, constructing him as a "noted 47-year old Hungarian composer now living in Switzerland," and drawing on stereotypes of nation to characterize the new work: "Magyar fire, exotic color and rhythmic patterns ... one of those wild Hungarian finales beloved by both Bartók and Kodály—and probably most other Hungarians." A preview article implied an extra dimension to Veress's citizenship, stating that he was a "fellow countryman" of Doráti who "fled Communist Hungary under dramatic circumstances."[30]

Veress's own commentary on the work is in a different mould, distinctly opposed to such an overt statement of political self-construction or national allegiance. This is nothing if not striking, given that he had been regarded in Hungary as the leading musical light of the nation, and was a dedicated ethnomusicologist and essayist who had in earlier decades sought to promote the incorporation of folk music into art music.[31] Now silent on folk music and Hungary, he offered only some basic information about the piece's formal architecture. In the context of the unmistakably idiomatic second theme (Traub categorizes it neatly with reference to Bartók's and Veress's field collections),[32] this is particularly conspicuous. It is equally significant that the text he wrote avoids reference to his newly developing compositional practice, namely the use of twelve-tone rows. The *Sinfonia* is plainly a part of his gradual exploration of rows; indeed, both the first and second main themes are constructed therefrom.

Nevertheless, while avoiding these subjects, Veress necessarily invoked others of equal significance. First, although he used a formal language that for many decades had been understood as neutral, or purely musical (he referred to the evolution of themes, a "choral-like contrapuntal texture," "sonata form," "rondo form," "exposition," "development," and "thematic cohesion," for example), no language is neutral. As recent scholarship has demonstrated, this discourse, which developed around the eighteenth- and nineteenth-century symphony, is associated closely with the rise of German nationalism and the construction of the canon, and it gained a spuriously ethical edge once entangled in the rising stock of putatively "autonomous" music in the early twentieth century.[33] Veress thus positioned his own symphony firmly in a historically central canonical European sphere, ignoring the postwar avant-garde, and downplaying both his "exotic" and his "eastern" (socialist) identity. In fact, the chosen genre itself is a sign of his centring project, because neither of his national models—Bartók and Kodály—had written symphonies in maturity.[34] Indeed, Veress's second symphony comes in line with his first one in this respect, if we follow Traub's suggestion that the earlier one (1940) was written as a strategic career investment with a view to emigration.[35]

Second, the work's title can be similarly understood. It makes explicit Veress's view of the world beyond Hungary, specifically toward the town whence his commission came, and the country where he sought a new home.[36] And one local newspaper was pleased to point out the symphony's special significance in its preview article and review: it was to be the "first orchestral work of symphonic structure ever named for this city," and then "the first major concerthall [sic] work to bear the name of our town."[37] But this too is a product of a historically Germanic, canonizing project: *Sinfonia Minneapolitana* gestured to providing listeners in Minneapolis with a musical experience of their civic harmony, building on the model provided by symphonic performances in nineteenth-century Germany, which had enfolded listeners in experiences of their (national) social harmony.[38]

Third, the Italianate title is resonant with a particular strand of Hungarian thought about Europe. To be sure, it is conceivable that the Italian presentation of the title was simply intended to reference a less besmirched European musical nation than Germany symbolized at that time, or it might even have been connected to Veress's Italian publisher Zerboni. But the significance of Italy for many Hungarians was more broad than these factors alone, and reinforces—in quite specific ways—Veress's ambition to contribute to a particular strand of European culture. During the 1920s, political relations between Hungary and Italy had become very friendly. A Hungarian Institute (Collegium Hungaricum) was established in Rome, and an Italian school in Budapest, each of which facilitated cultural exchange. At the same time, Hungarian historiography came to view the regime of Matthias Corvinus Hunyadi (from 1458 until his death in 1490) as not only a moment of strong connections with the Italian courts, but also as a golden age of westward-looking intellectual advancement for Hungary.[39] This political situation influenced Veress directly. First, the research of his father (an antiquary, bibliographer, and editor of medieval documents) became concerned with Hungarian-Italian connections, and he published a documentary history of Hungarians who had studied in Italy from the thirteenth to the nineteenth centuries.[40] Second, Veress won a studentship at the Collegium Hungaricum in Rome, where he resided from February 1941 to November 1942. (His father's publication coincided with this.)[41] Third, another important figure for Veress, Zoltán Kodály, had constructed a connection between Hungary and Italy through a putative Latin-German opposition. Drawing on the duality in his essay "What Is Hungarian in Music?" of 1939, he had even proposed that the reason Hungarian music was receptive to the influence of Bach, Beethoven, Schütz, and Brahms was that those composers "followed the Latin culture of forms."[42] Veress's partially veiled reference to Italy, then, signals a strong thread within his identity as a Hungarian, but one that evades folksy nationalism in favour of "enlightened" connections with his fellow Europeans. As we will see, references within the *Sinfonia* itself, however, point in partially conflicting and partially congruent directions.

Bern to Minneapolis in Music

The three movements of *Sinfonia Minneapolitana* (*Pesante/Allegro, Andante tranquillo con moto, Allegro molto*) are linked by two themes, referred to here for convenience as themes 1 and 2. The more prevalent is theme 1, which appears in all three movements, even while rhythmically augmented in the central one to match the slower tempo (see examples 8-1, 8-2, and 8-3).[43] Its first presentation is angular and chromatic, thus exposing its twelve-tone nature explicitly.

EXAMPLE 8-1 Sándor Veress, *Sinfonia Minneapolitana*, Movement 1, mm. 19–23, Theme 1. © by Sugarmusic—Edizioni Suvini Zerboni (Milan, Italy).

EXAMPLE 8-2 Sándor Veress, *Sinfonia Minneapolitana*, Movement 2, mm. 191–97, version of Theme 1. © by Sugarmusic—Edizioni Suvini Zerboni (Milan, Italy).

EXAMPLE 8-3 Sándor Veress, *Sinfonia Minneapolitana*, Movement 3, mm. 278–91, version of Theme 1. © by Sugarmusic—Edizioni Suvini Zerboni (Milan, Italy).

EXAMPLE 8-4 Sándor Veress, *Sinfonia Minneapolitana*, Movement 1, mm. 101–8, Theme 2. © by Sugarmusic—Edizioni Suvini Zerboni (Milan, Italy).

In contrast, and as already mentioned, theme 2 points directly to Hungary itself because it is related to folk song in terms of rhythm, phrase structure, and contour. As Traub notes, it is a generic four-line strophe, with six syllables per line, and a "stretched" or accented fourth syllable on each line.[44] However, its shape and pitch repetitions cannot entirely mask the fact that it, too, is a twelve-tone construction (see example 8-4). Episodically prominent in the first movement, theme 2 is entirely absent in the second, returning only at the end of the third movement, in which it is interwoven with a new form of theme 1. This basic reading of the themes' interactions suggests a move away from Hungarian material, and then a synthesis between Hungarian and non-Hungarian material.

As such, it can be incorporated smoothly into the prevailing understanding of Veress's early émigré activity. According to Gerlich, Lanz, and Traub, his first Swiss years were primarily times of engaging with twelve-tone techniques, and in this context the folk-song style of theme 2 can be seen as a (partially shelved) component of his musical past.[45] We might even posit a narrative in which within movement 1 the "present" (twelve-tone) visits the "past" (folk song); in movement 2 the "present" banishes the "past" entirely; and then in movement 3 it allows it back inside, now in a new framework. It furnishes a narrative of an émigré acclimatization, and indeed the fact that theme 2 (folk song) is partly constructed from the first pitches of theme 1 (twelve-tone)—in other words, that folk song is already understood through the lens of dodecaphony—could support the interpretation.

However, reflecting on the symphony as a national construction, and scrutinizing the interaction between themes 1 and 2 more closely, offers more complex possibilities.[46] As we have seen, theme 2 (Hungarian) is only heard in a context provided by much else; namely, after an introduction, theme 1, and an interlude. Although a series of entries of theme 2 suggests a gradual process of building, and accumulation, its fifth appearance, *fortissimo* in full strings and brass sections, disintegrates into a beating effect (see plate 8-1). Thereafter it is lost completely, and movement 1

Plate 8-1 Sándor Veress, *Sinfonia Minneapolitana*, Movement 1, mm. 137–40, breaking up of theme 2. © by Sugarmusic—Edizioni Suvini Zerboni (Milan, Italy).

PLATE 8-1 (conclusion)

dissolves into movement 2—in which theme 2 is entirely absent. Read symbolically and in combination, movements 1 and 2 thus construct the process of a national self-immolation.

In the third movement, theme 2 re-enters after more than half the movement has passed by, and it draws it towards a close. The tiered entries again mount in intensity, beginning in a quiet, song-like manner, on solo bassoon ([82] + 2), joined by the first horn [83], and then by English horn, clarinets, and further horns [84]. A short interlude precedes the theme's grandest entry, which is in full strings, flutes, and piccolos, as if in amassed, jubilant voices. Apparently inverting the self-destruction of movement 1, it is as if the metaphorical nation had been amassed and, with the assistance of an insistent, rallying drum beat, reconstituted itself in a gathering of voices. Indeed by this stage of the work, although theme 1 is sometimes present and even coexistent, the force of theme 2 comes to dominate and ultimately displace it. Read as such, *Sinfonia Minneapolitana* is less about émigré acclimatization than about national triumph over non-nationals.

This reading can be sharpened by placing *Sinfonia Minneapolitana* in the context of two works by Bartók. The first, *Cantata profana*, tells of nine young men who set out from their homes in the forest to hunt stags, but who are transformed into stags themselves and never return. Its opening sections comprise a contrapuntal scalic introduction and the perfect-fourth-saturated hunt narrative, both of which can be traced in the way that the *Sinfonia*'s "scene" is set. Its own introduction consists of broken passages of scales moving in contrary motion, and interjections of pairs of notes in perfect fourths and tritones in both brass and timpani. The parallel becomes particularly persuasive once one examines another similarity: namely, the way in which both works' first movements dissolve into their second movements following a climactic passage, and through a low-register ostinato, which functions as an unstable pedal by vacillating from one note to another (see example 8-5 and plate 8-2). In *Cantata profana*, this is the moment where the boys pass over a bridge in the forest, turn into stags, and thus leave behind the world of the human; in *Sinfonia Minneapolitana* it marks the threshold into movement 2 point in which theme 2 (Hungary) gets lost.

The consequences of this moment of transformation are different in the two works. In *Cantata profana* there is a re-encountering of the hunt music (the father will set out from domesticity); in *Sinfonia Minneapolitana* it heralds a re-encountering of theme 1 (non-Hungarian), which will constitute the basis for movement 2. In *Cantata profana* the further conse-

EXAMPLE 8-5 Béla Bartók, *Cantata profana*, Movement 2, mm. 180–88, string parts. © 1934 by Boosey & Hawkes, Inc. Copyright renewed. Reprinted by permission of Boosey & Hawkes, Inc.

quence is a confrontation between the human and the animal world—the father attempts to bring his sons home to domesticity, but the stags are never to return. In *Sinfonia Minneapolitana*, as we have seen, there is no confrontation between themes, but rather a surreptitiously innocent, song-like entry of theme 2 (Hungary), and eventually its amassed occupation of the dominant position. Whereas *Cantata profana* is essentially about separation, *Sinfonia Minneapolitana* seems to be about reclaiming, and in its triumphal close it becomes an affirmative statement about recovery.[47]

One more comparison reaffirms this quality; namely one with Bartók's major American work, his Concerto for Orchestra. Like *Sinfonia Minneapolitana*, the second theme of the first movement of this work is a

Plate 8-2 Sándor Veress, *Sinfonia Minneapolitana*, Movement 1, mm. 179–90. © by Sugarmusic—Edizioni Suvini Zerboni (Milan, Italy).

PLATE 8-2 (continued)

PLATE 8-2 (continued)

PLATE 8-2 (conclusion)

synthetic folk song, an eight-syllable strophic type (compare Example 8-4 with Example 8-6). In each work this theme re-emerges in a later movement. However, once again, the works are divergent: Bartók reconnects with the "Hungarian" theme in the central movement of his work, but does not, unlike Veress, use it to construct a triumphal finale. Where Bartók composed sadness and doubt into the Hungarian components of his Concerto,[48] Veress projected hope. Indeed we might map a narrative onto *Sinfonia Minneapolitana* in which the self-immolation in movement 1 is part of the past (whether Hungarians' collaboration with Nazi Germany or with Soviet communists); the second movement is a statement about the present (occupation under the Soviet Union); and the third movement is the hoped-for future uprising (the nation sheds its shackles and shines in autonomous glory).

EXAMPLE 8-6 Béla Bartók, Concerto for Orchestra, Movement 1, mm. 39–50, trumpets. © 1946 by Hawkes & Son (London) Ltd. Copyright renewed. Reprinted by permission of Boosey & Hawkes, Inc.

Bringing this into contact with Veress's verbal statements, however, gains us a perspective that grasps the character of *Sinfonia Minneapolitana* as a pivot between Europe and America. To recap briefly: there is a trope of "self-annihilation as investment" (in America) running through Veress's texts of the time; but as we have also seen, the *Sinfonia*'s musical fabric is engaged with Europe, and aside from the gesture of its title, it contains no signs of interest in or knowledge of America. These rather particular qualities are highly significant, and a brief revisiting of correspondence will reveal why.

In letters to both Borsody and Csicsery-Rónay, Veress's expressed unhappiness not just about his professional and financial situation in Europe, but also about his sense that European culture as a whole was sunk. As he put it to Borsody in December 1951, he had believed in the continent in 1945, but that belief was now shaken. Thoroughly disheartened by what he saw as Europe's spiritual and moral collapse, he wrote that Europeans had lost their sense of responsibility toward European traditions: "the shells are still there, but they are merely exteriors: within minds and souls there is disturbance and chaos beyond measure."[49] He told Csicsery-Rónay that Europe had gone crazy [*meghibbant*], and would "fall into the clutches of either the renascent Nazi-Teutons or Muscovy's Asiatic steppe-barbarism."[50] The threat of war was pressing, and he felt that the relatively small (4 million) population of Switzerland (which he found otherwise congenial), would be powerless to defend itself.

Thus he strove to preserve what he understood to be of cultural value and to seek a home for it elsewhere. In this sense he was aligned with many other members of the "Hungarian emigration," whose primary interest was to continue developing what they understood as their culture in exile (partly in public protest about the Soviet Union's occupation). Csicsery-Rónay himself was extremely active in Hungarian literature and letters, and regularly attempted to persuade Veress to work more in this field.[51] Veress's own position was less focused on Hungary specifically than what he called "European culture" (which recalls his textual commentaries on *Sinfonia Minneapolitana*), but he was as pragmatic as Csicsery-Rónay: European culture had been "pushed to the periphery," he said, "which today means America."[52] And although he was unsure whether America would be sufficiently "fertile soil," he hoped that the necessary qualities were there to help European cultural recovery: "there are signs suggesting that ... Americans have a few more grains of idealism, coupled with sober reality, than on average the Europeans do."[53] If not, he said bitterly, it will be "the end of this civilization."[54]

If we read *Sinfonia Minneapolitana* through this lens, we gain one further émigré narrative, one that finally integrates it with Veress's westward view out of Switzerland. First, the work emerges not only as a construction of a nation's self-destruction and triumph, but a construction of the same on a continental level. Even more significantly, however, as we understand from Veress's letters, his vision was that the European triumph would be not on European soil, but in the United States. In this light, *Sinfonia Minneapolitana* is not only a projection of national recovery, a throwing off of occupation on home soil. It is a projected cultural colonization, which is a little-discussed—but surely frequently present—facet of the so-called "Hungarian emigration."

Appendix: Autobiographic Statements by Sándor Veress

The sources for the two facsimiles presented in this annex are located in the Correspondence section of the Sándor Veress Collection conserved in the Paul Sacher Foundation (Basel, Switzerland) in a file labelled "USA / Antrag zur Immigration (Brief mit Entwürfen) von Sándor Veress (1955)." The Veress correspondence constitutes a significant portion of the Veress manuscript collection and will no doubt prove to be a rich source of information. It was transferred to the Sacher Foundation between 1992 and 2006 and is currently being inventoried. At present, the correspondence section is estimated to contain at least 5000 pages of written material covering a period from ca. 1940 to 1991. As one would expect, the majority of the letters are written in Hungarian; however, one also finds documents in German, English, French, and Italian.[55]

PLATE 8-3 Sándor Veress, second autobiographic statement (7 pages), Sándor Veress Collection, Paul Sacher Foundation.

> *considered*
>
> This paper should be ~~taken~~ as an attempt to make the motives understandable which, after the German occupation of Hungary, and the siege of Budapest by the Russians, led me /together with many intellectuals/ to join the H.C.P.
>
> I have no intention of excusing myself because excuses are justified only when wrong or sinful things have been committed. Should the mere fact of joining the C.P. in May 1945 regarded as an act of ~~wrong~~ *wrong conduct*, then, naturally, there is every cause for *Vindication.* ~~I accuse myself. But as~~ My activity in Hungary, during the period from 1945 till my voluntary exodus in February 1949, had nothing in common with communist politics but rather bore the positive marks of using my artisitic position to counteract — as long as such actions were possible — certain destructive communist moves in the artistic field, [I do not think ~~that~~ there is any *for which* need for ~~an excuse~~ *an apology* on my part. *action*
>
> There is one more thing I should like to mention before going into detail of *this* ~~my~~ subject: when giving an account of my activities during those three years in Hungary it is inevitable that I should sometimes speak about certain moves I have undertaken in various cases to help people, friends, young artists when they got into difficulties caused by communist politics. All these ~~mentionings should be taken as mere~~ *is rather statements of* facts ~~only~~ *and desiring* ~~not as wanting~~ to win special sympath~~ies~~ for my case. *acted on* *just* I ~~did whatsux them out of~~ humanitarian principles ~~as~~ *as* I did ~~the same things~~ during the Nazi-times.
>
> I come from a strong democratic family background. On my fathers side there were, among my a*n*cestors, many Protestant priests. My grand father fought in the War of Independence against Austria in 1848-49 and after the defeat of Hungary *I graduated* by the Armies of the *T*zar, emigrated with Kossuth, and lived *at the University* all his life, except *for* a short period of one and a half years, *of London* outside Hungary. My great grand father on my mothers side fought — though of Austrian origin — in the same war as colonel

PLATE 8-3 (continued)

2

and was then imprisonned for seven years by an Austrian Military Court for his democratic convictions against Austrian Absolutism. My father is a well known historian. His field of studies concern the relationship of Hungary to Italy from the 13th century onward, and Hungarian-Rumanian affaires during the 16th & 17th centuries. He published some 42 volumes of great importance mounty on these subjects. My grand father on my mothers side was Director of the Hungarian State Railways. His son, (my Uncle) was an economist, secretary of state after the first World War, a great friend of the late Premier of Hungary Count Paul Teleki, and together with him one of the founders of the University of Economics where he was professor till his early death in 1923.

These family traditions decided the atmosphere in which I was brought up till I finished my studies at one of the Gymnasiums in Budapest and at the Royal Academy of Music where I was pupil of Béla Bartók and Z. Kodály. Besides being a composer, pianist, and teacher I was, since my early youth very much interested in Musical Folklore and, parallel with my studies of Folk Music, in Ethnography and Ethnology. I made numerous collections of Folk Music in Hungarian as well as Rumanian villages and these journeys and studies brought me very near to the social problems of the peasantry with the inevitable consequences that I got in close contact with those democratic youth movements in Hungary /generally called "the Village Explorers"/ who fought for the rights of the peasantry and for a land reform. By the end of 1938 I went to London to study music teaching in various English schools and, as I was by then already engaged to my present wife, Batih born E.B., I intended to settle down in England. But the outbreak of the Second World War changed my plans. As at that time the Premier of Hungary was the late Count Teleki and I was convinced that his democratic regime would prevail and feeling strongly that I was needed at home I returned, together with my fiancé, to Budapest in November 1939, where we later got married.

PLATE 8-3 (continued)

3

the Hungarian Scientific Academy, after my return, I resumed my post till his departure to the USA in 1941. During the war years, as the political tension, especially after the suicide of Count Telekei begun to grow ~~myxastawativnzxwith thexpxexWesternxxxwssvxatisxalsmentsxbecamewmerexanxxwerawelsss~~ we begun to organize our anti Nazi, pro Western political groups and our organizatory activities for the event of a German invasion became especially widespread after Soviet Russia became an ally of the Western Powers. This event ~~namely~~ brought all ~~of us~~, group of pro Western minded people, in close contact with members of the subversive Hungarian C.P. because our aims then were the same: the forming of a united front against the Nazis /both German and Hungarian/ along the side of the USA, Great Britain and Soviet Russia. When Hungary was occupied by the German forces in the night of March 19th 1944, we all went to action helping & when we could and from that time on I spent my time chiefly ~~at~~ hiding and helping people — jews and political refugees — to escape from the Nazi terror. As I was already in 1943 appointed ~~ordinary~~ professor at the R. Academy of Music, and because of my so called "arian" origin, I held ~~had~~ a favorable position and under this facade I could do, ~~together~~ together with the members of our subversive organizations, rather much for people who were in need ~~of~~ of help. And, also being greatly influenced by the American and British radios, we did everything to prepare the way for the Russians in the strong belief that their victory would mean the ~~they will bring the victory~~ triumph /of democratic ideals. ~~after the Nazis~~. So we lived through the horrors of the siege of Budapest and in our ignorance about the real Soviet Russia /in ~~with~~ which we were certainly not alone/ ~~thus~~/ we greeted the ~~the~~ first Russian soldiers as the beginning of a new western-type democratic era for humanity and for Hungary.

When, at the end of the siege of Budapest, we came out of the cellars and begun to organize our lives again on after caused by the terrible ruins ~~of the~~ war there was one sole aspect for all of us: the building up of a healthy, democratic new Hungary.

PLATE 8-3 (continued)

4

Very soon the political parties begun to organize themselves but there was little difference then between the four chief democratic parties /the Small-Land-Holders, the Peasant-Party, the Social Democrats and the Communists/ for there were the imminent and basic problems of starting with reconstruction. Consequently there was, in my ignorance, almost no difference in the question as to which party one should belong for every party preached the same democratic ideals and each one had the same aim: reconstruction at first. There was little time then for political or ideological discussions. One almost joined a party on the grounds that its office was nearest to ones home or that ones friends, with whom one was fighting together in the Nazi times, were already in the ranks of the other party. My friends were equally divided among the Peasant and Communist Parties and so, although I never had any special sympathy for Communism, nor was I member of any political party before, I joined the C.P. in May 1945 on the grounds that among my friends with whom I was together during the Nazi times there were many sympathizers and also a few active communists.

— But there were two other motives also which made me to take this step: the mere fact that after the siege I was picked up three times in the streets by the Russians and arrested and each time it was a letter given to me by the C.P. which saved me from being deported like so many civilian prisoners. I simply felt a sort of gratefulness to those who rescued my life. One could, of course, ask why the communists did this before I was even a member of their Party? The answer to this is that I was generally accepted in Hungary as the leading composer, folklorist and teacher after the generation of Bartók and, because I was a well known protagonist of democratic reforms dating back to the times of the "Village Explorers" movement. The other motive of joining the Party was a certain uneasy feeling because of my English wife whom I thought to be able to protect better with a membership in this party.

During the three years which followed I never took part in any political gatherings nor did I even visit

PLATE 8-3 (continued)

5

those so called Communist Seminars where newcomers were systematically indoctrinated and I had no political activities whatever. However, my musical prestige gave me a certain authority ~~uxenxinxcasesxoutsidexthexmusicalxfieldx~~ and till about the autumn of 1948 I was still able to give support to many good reforms often ~~when~~ opposed by the communists and I could help many valuable people who ~~got~~ were in difficult~~ies~~ merely ~~by~~ on the ground ~~that~~ that they did not belong to the C.P. As a member of the Hung. Arts Council and the Board of Directors of the Academy of Music I could, in several cases, hinder undemocratic motions and further constructive propositions against communist intentions. But already by the ~~spring~~ beginning of 1947 it was clear to me that the C.P. was really an instrument only in the hands of the Soviet leaders and that the politics of the Party were in sharp contrast to democracy and to the national interests of Hungary. So I knew that I had to reconsider my position very seriously and ~~when~~ came to the conclusion that I had to ~~try to settle~~ ~~xithxmyxwife~~ leave my country ~~in a foreign country with my wife~~. It would have been ~~senseless~~ myoneless to leave the Party while I ~~am~~ was in Hungary

— such [action] would have had bad [dangerous] consequences.

and go into open opposition for ~~with such false heroism I would not have gained but only lost everything~~. To my good luck I was just at that time invited by the British Council as a ~~guest~~ visitor to England and I went to London at the beginning of February 1947. I used my official visiting time also to get into contact with my friends in trying to secure

some kind of post

~~my position materially~~ before my invitation expire~~s~~d. Unluckily I did not succeed in getting something permanent but in spite of this, and to the great consternation of the British Council, I did not go back to Hungary when my invitation expired after six weeks. I stayed on in London and even managed to bring out after nine months of unsuccessful efforts my wife from Budapest and only ~~when nothing had materialized~~ but ~~were~~ we forced to return to Budapest by the end of October, but opportune moment, to with ~~t~~ the strong conviction that at the first ~~occasion~~ we

would you try to

~~shall~~ leave the country. However, this was not an easy decision to make. Whatever the political situation was like

PLATE 8-3 (continued)

6

in Hungary one still had hopes that the country would perhaps not fall thoroughly under communist rule, although such hopes were, after the events of summer 1947, in swift decline. But leaving my country meant the giving up everything one had worked for through half a life time, and the leaving behind /and certainly for ever/ friends, pupils and, above all, my old parents and my brother who were dependent on me in every respect. I saw, on the other hand, that with the rapid change in the political atmosphere I would not be able to secure my unique and independent position in the C.P. for long time. Humanitarian principles were always decisive in my actions and I saw myself before a terrible dilemma: either I stay on and try to help, as long as it was possible, people individually but then I have to be a traitor to my democratic principles as well as to my art and to the Hungarian nation because I could help individuals only if I would say "yes" to things which were in sharp contrast to my democratic convictions. Or I leave Hungary by sacrificing my humanitarian principles. I chose the latter but I would not wish anybody ever to solve a similar problem.

IN the summer 1948 I went again to England and in the autumn to Switzerland. All these journeys were in connection with musical activities. In England I was member of the jury of the Llangollen International Choir Festival and in Basel, Switzerland, I was lecturing at the Int. Folk Music Conference. For concerts and artistic engagements one was, by then, still able to get an exit permit from the Hung. authorities. In the autumn 1948 there was the Int. Bartók-Musical Competition held in Budapest and I, as one of the organizers and member of the jury, had to be present. So I returned from Switzerland again, but ohly for a few months. In February 1949 a Ballet of mine was performed at the Royal Opera of Stockholm and I left Hungary on the 6th of February with the intention of not returning for I knew that this was my last chance of being able to get out. From Stockholm I went to Rome where my Ballet

PLATE 8-3 (conclusion)

7

was also performed and from there — at the beginning of March — to Zürich where I met my wife who left Budapest after me. Then I returned to Rome and in Novembre 1949 we finally settled down in Bern where I was invited Guest Professor at the University and later was appointed Professor for composition and Music Theory at the Conservatory of Bern. ~~Since then I am holding this post.~~ *which post I still hold.*

This is my story and it may perhaps be evident from it that my membership in the H.C.P. was purely a nominal one for I never took part in any party-politics nor was I ever exposed politically except in such cases of art-policy where I always acted according to my democratic principles and often against the intentions of the communists. Till the autumn of 1948 my artistic prestige was strong enough and enabled me to act idependently in those artistic organizations where I had a leading voice. But I never benefited for myself from my position and even refused to accept the "Kossuth Prize" /the Hung. equivalence of the Stalin-Prize/ when, ~~just after my departure~~ in 1949, I was awarded with. Very special external circumstances and a certain constellation of events ~~brought with themselves that~~ *influenced my* I join*ing* the H.C.P. just after the war although my convictions were always strongly democratic in the western sense of the word.

PLATE 8-4 Sándor Veress, third autobiographic statement (7 pages), Sándor Veress Collection, Paul Sacher Foundation.*

Első fogalmazvány

This paper should be considered as an attempt to make the motives understandable which, after the German occupation of Hungary, and the siege of Budapest by the Russians, led me /together with many *hungarian* intellectuals/ to join the Hungarian Communist Party. I have no intention of excusing myself because excuses are ~~justified~~ *necessary* only when wrong or sinful things have been commited. Should the mere fact of joining the Communist Party in May 1945 regarded as an act of misconduct then, naturally, there is every cause for vindication. My activity in Hungary, during the period from 1945 till my voluntary exodus in February 1949, had nothing in common with communist politics but/~~rather~~ bore the positive marks of using my artistic position to counteract – as long as such actions were possible –, certain destructive communist moves in the artistic field for which actions I do not think there is any need for an apology on my part.

There is one more thing I should like to mention before going into detail on this subject; when giving an account of my activities during those three years in Hungary it is inevitable that I should sometimes speak about certain moves I have undertaken in various cases to help people, friends and young artists when they got into difficulties caused by communist politics. All this is mere statement of facts and not as desiring to win special sympathy for my case. I acted on humanitarian principles just as I did during the Nazi-times.

I come from a strong democratic family background. On my fathers side there were, among my ancestors, many Protestant priests. My grand father fought in the War of Independence against Austria in 1848-49 and, after the defeat of Hungary by the Armies of the Czar, emigrated with Kossuth, graduated at the University of London and lived all his life, except for a short period of one and a half years, outside Hungary. My great grand father on my mothers side fought – though of Austrian origin – in the same war as colonel *and* was then *on the Hungarians side*

---

* As stated below, in note 13, the differences between the two writing implements used by Veress to correct his third autobiographic statement make them clearly distinguishable from each other in the facsimiles that appear in this volume. Marks made with a ballpoint pen are thin and dark, whereas those made with a red pencil are broader and lighter.

PLATE 8-4 (continued)

2

imprisonned for seven years by an Austrian Military Court for
his democratic convictions against Austrian Absolutism. My
father is a well known historian. His field of studies chiefly
concern Hungarian-Italian relationship from the 13th century
onward and Hungarian-Rumanian affaires during the 16th & 17th
centuries. He published some 42 volumes of great importance mainly on these subjects. He is still living, together with my
mother and my brother, in the greatest misery in Hungary. My
grand father on my mothers side was Director of the Hungarian
State Railways. His son /my oncle/ was an economist, secretary of State after the first World War, a great friend of the
late Premier of Hungary Count Paul Teleki, and together with
him one of the founders of the University of Economics in Budapest where he was professor till his early death in 1923. During
the short communist reign in 1919 he was imprisonned by the
Rákosi-Kun regime and escaped execution only by sheere good
luck.

    These family traditions decided the atmosphere in
which I was brought up till I finished my studies at one of the
Gymnasiums in Budapest and at the Royal Academy of Music where
I was pupil of Béla Bartók and Zoltán Kodály. Besides being
a composer, pianist and teacher I was, since my early youth,
very much interested in Musical Folklore and, parallel with
my studies in Folk Music, in Ethnography and Ethnology. I made
numerous collections of Folk Music in Hungarian as well as
Rumanian villages and these journeys and studies brought me
very near to the social problems of the peasantry with the
inevitable consequences that I got in close contact with those
democratic youth movements in Hungary /generally called "the
Village Explorers"/ who fought for the rights of the peasantry
and for a land reform. By the end of 1938 I went to London to
study music teaching methods in various English schools and,
as I was by then already engaged to my present wife British
born Enid Mary Blake, I intended to settle down in England.
But the outbreak of the second World War changed my plans.
As at that time the Premier of Hungary was the late Count Teleki,

[Handwritten margin note: He died three years ago with a broken heart while my mother is still living together with my brother and his family in the university town of Pécs in Southern Hungary.]

PLATE 8-4 (continued)

3

and as I was convinced that his democratic regime would prevail and feeling strongly that I was needed at home, I returned, together with my fiancé, in November 1939 to Budapest where we later got married. Already for many years assistent to Béla Bartók at the Hungarian Scientific Academy, after my return I resumed my post till his departure to the USA in 1941. During the war years, as the political tension, especially after the suicide of Count Teleki begun to grow, we begun to organize our anti Nazi, pro Western political groups and our organizatory activities for the event of a German invasion became especially widespread after Soviet Russia became an ally of the Western Powers. This event brought all groups of pro Western minded people in close contact with members of the subversive Hungarian Communist Party because our aims then were the same: the forming of a united front against the Nazis /both German and Hungarian/ along the side of the USA, Great Britain and Soviet Russia. When Hungary was occupied by the German forces in the night of March 19th 1944, we all went into action helping where and when we could, and from that time on I spent my time chiefly hiding and helping people - jews and political refugees - to escape from the Nazi terror. As I was already in 1943 appointed Professor at the R. Academy of Music, and because of my so called "arian" origin, I held a favorable position and under this facade I could do, together with the members of our subversive organizations, rather much for people who were in need of help. And, also being greatly influenced by the American and British radios, we did everything to prepare the way for the Russians in the strong belief that their victory would mean the resurgence of democratic ideals. So we lived through the horrors of the siege of Budapest and in our ignorance about the real Soviet Russia /in which we were certainly not alone/ we greeted the first Russian soldiers as the beginning of a new Western-type democratic era for humanity and for Hungary.

When, at the end of the siege of Budapest, we came out of the cellars and begun to reorganize our lives again after the terrible ruins caused by war, there was one sole aspect

PLATE 8-4 (continued)

4

for all of us: the building up of a healthy, democratic new
Hungary. Very soon the political parties begun to organize
themselves but there was little difference _then_ between the
four chief democratic parties /the Small-Land-Holders, the
Peasant-Party, the Social Democrats and the Communists/ for
there were the imminent and basic problems of starting with
reconstruction. Consequently there was, in my ignorance, almost
no difference in the question as to which party one should
belong for every party preached the same democratic ideals and
each one had the same aims: reconstruction at first. There was
little time then for political or ideological discussions. One
almost joined a party on the grounds that, in a big city without
means of communication, its office was nearest to ones home
or that ones friends, with whom one was fighting together in
the Nazi times, were already in the ranks of one or the other
party. My friends were equally divided among the Peasant and
Communist Parties and so, although I never had any special
sympathy for Communism, nor was I member of any political party
before, I joined the Hungarian Communist Party in May 1945 on
the grounds that among my friends, with whom I was together
during the Nazi times, there were sympathizers and also a few
active communists. But there were two other motives also which
made me to take this step. The mere fact that after the siege
I was picked up three times in the streets and arrested by the
Russians and each time it was a letter given to me by the Communist Party which saved me from being deported like so many civilian prisoners. I simply felt a sort of gratefulness to those
who rescued my life. One could, of course, ask why the Communist
Party did this before I was even a member of their Party? The
answer to this is that I was generally accepted in Hungary
as the leading composer, folklorist and teacher after the generation of Bartók and, because I was a well known protagonist
of democratic reforms dating back to the times of the "Village
Explorers" movement. The other motive for joining the Party was
a certain uneasy feeling because of my English wife whom I

PLATE 8-4 (continued)

5

thought to be able to protect better with a membership in this party. During the three years which followed I never took part in any political gatherings nor did I even visit those so called Communist Seminars where newcomers were systematically indoctrinated and I had no political activities whatever. However, my musical prestige gave me a certain authority and till about the autumn of 1948 I was still able to give support to many good reforms often opposed by the communists, and I could help many valuable people who were in difficulty merely on the grounds that they did not belong to the Communist Party. As a member of the Hungarian Arts Council and the Board of Directors of the Academy of Music I could, in several cases, hinder undemocratic motions and further constructive propositions against communist intentions. But already by the beginning of 1947 it was clear to me that the Communist Party was really an instrument only in the hands of the Soviet leaders and that the politics of the Party were in sharp contrast to democracy and to the national interests of Hungary. So I knew that I had to reconsider my position very seriously and came to the conclusion that I had to leave my country. It would have been impossible to leave the Party while I was in Hungary and go into open opposition for such an action would have had dangerous consequences. To my good luck I was just at that time invited by the British Council as a visitor to England and I went to London at the beginning of February 1947. I used my official visiting time also to get into contact with my friends in trying to secure for myself some kind of post before my invitation expired. Unluckily I did not succeed in getting something permanent but in spite of this, (and to the great consternation of the British Council,) I did not go back to Hungary when my invitation expired after six weeks. I stayed on in London and even managed to bring out my wife from Budapest and only after eight months of unsuccessful effort was forced to return to Budapest was by the end of October, (1947) but with the strong convict-

PLATE 8-4 (continued)

6

ion that at the first opportune moment we would try again to leave the country. However, this was not an easy decision to make. Whatever the political situation was like in Hungary one still had hopes that the country ~~perhaps~~ would perhaps not fall thoroughly under communist rule, although such hopes were, after the events of summer 1947, in swift decline. But leaving my country meant the giving up of everything one had worked for through half a life time, and the leaving behind /and certainly for ever/ of friends, pupils and, above all, my old parents and my brother who were dependent on me in every respect. I saw, on the other hand, that with the rapid change in the political atmosphere I should be unable to secure my unique and independent position ~~in the Communist Party for a~~ *for a* long time. Humanitarian principles were always decisive in my actions and I saw myself before a terrible dilemma: either I stay on *and* try to help, as long as it was possible, ~~people individually~~ but then I had to be a traitor to my democratic principles as well as to my art *& artistic convictions* ~~and to the Hungarian nation because I could help individuals only if I would say "yes" to things which were in sharp contrast to my convictions.~~ Or I leave Hungary by sacrificing *and* ~~my humanitarian principles~~ *everything which was dear to me*. I chose the latter but I would not wish anybody ever to solve a similar problem.

In the summer 1948 I went again to England and in the autumn to Switzerland. All these journeys were in connections with musical activities. In England I was member of the jury of the Llangollen International Choir Gestival and in Basel, Switzerland, I was lecturing at the International Folk Music Conference. For concerts and artistic engagements one was, by then, still able to get an exit permit from the Hungarian authorities. In the autumn 1948 there was the International Bartók-Musical Competition held in Budapest and I, as one of the organizers and member of the jury, had to be present. So I returned from Switzerland again, but only for a few months. In February 1949 a Ballet of mine had its first per-

PLATE 8-4 (conclusion)

7

formance at the Royal Opera of Stockholm and I ~~faik~~ left Hungary on the 6th of February with the intention of not returning for I knew that this was my last chance of being able to get out. From Stockholm I went to Rome where my Ballet was also performed and from there - at the beginning of March - to Zürich where I met my wife who left Budapest after me. Then I returned again to Rome and in November 1949 we finally settled down in Bern where I was invited as ~~Guest~~ Visiting Professor at the University and later was appointed Professor for Composition and Theory of Music at the Conservatory of Bern which post I still hold.

This is my "story" and it may perhaps be evident from it that my membership in the Hungarian Communist Party was purely a nominal one for I never took part in any party-politics nor was I ever exposed politically except in such cases of art-policy where I always acted according to my democratic principles and often ~~against even~~ very against the intentions of the Communists. Till the autumn of 1948 my artistic prestige was strong enough and enabled me to act independently in those artistic organizations where I had a leading voice. But I never benefited for myself from my position and even refused to accept the "Kossuth-Prize" /the Hungarian equivalence of the Stalin-Prize/ when, at the beginning of 1949, I was awarded with. Very special external circumstances and a certain constellation of events influenced my joining the Hungarian Communist Party just after the war although my convictions were always strongly democratic in the western sense of the word.

Notes

1 In conversation with his son Claudio Veress, during the 1980s. Anecdote passed on to me in Bern, 2 February 2007.
2 Andreas Traub, "Sándor Veress, Lebensweg—Schaffensweg," in *Sándor Veress Festschrift zum 80. Geburtstag*, ed. Andreas Traub (Berlin: Verlag K. Haseloff, 1986), 30; Andreas Traub, "Zur Biographie—Zur *Sinfonia Minneapolitana*," in *Zwischen Volks- und Kunstmusik: Aspekte der ungarischen Musik*, ed. Stefan Fricke, Wolf Frobenius, Sigrid Konrad, and Theo Schmitt (Saarbrucken: Pfau Verlag, 1999), 147.
3 For the first published account of Veress's early émigré years, see: Thomas Gerlich, "Neuanfang in der 'Wahlheimat'? Zu Sándor Veress' *Hommage à Paul Klee*," in *"Entre Denges et Denezy ..." Dokumente zur Schweizer Musikgeschichte 1900–2000*, ed. Ulrich Mosch and Matthias Kassel (Mainz: Schott, 2000), 399–406. I complemented Gerlich's work with reference to further sources (see Rachel Beckles Willson, *Ligeti, Kurtág, and Hungarian Music during the Cold War* [Cambridge and New York: Cambridge University Press, 2007]), but, since undertaking that research, a great deal more material has become available. Thus, what I provide here is more detailed and in certain areas corrective.
4 The premiere was originally to have been in 1953. Veress's letters of the time indicate that he was swamped by work and was not keeping up with his commitments generally; to add to his problems, he developed carpal tunnel syndrome, which prevented him from working for five weeks. Apparently as a result, he delivered *Sinfonia Minneapolitana* two weeks late, which meant that its premiere was postponed by one year. See letter to Csicsery-Rónay, 8 April 1953. The earlier date also emerges from correspondence with Doráti (see below), and was also mentioned in concert reviews (see below). All correspondence cited is housed in the Sándor Veress Collection at the Paul Sacher Foundation. I am grateful to Evelyn Diendorf for her help in navigating within this collection.
5 Soós studied law in Budapest and worked as a judge before joining the Ministry of Internal Affairs 1940–44. Already much involved with the Hungarian reformed church, he trained as a preacher after his emigration in 1946. In 1950 he established a periodical called *Új Magyar Út* [New Hungarian Way] which appeared in Munich and Washington. He was also one of the founders of SZEMRE (Szórványban Élő Magyar Református Egyház [Reformed Church of the Hungarian Diaspora]), an organization dedicated to supporting and providing Hungarian-language church services for Hungarian Protestants outside Hungary. He relocated to Washington in May 1952. Gyula Borbándi, *Nyugati magyar irodalmi lexikon és bibliográfia* [Western Hungarian Literary Encyclopedia and Bibliography] (The Hague: Mikes International, 2006), 230, 269; and Gyula Borbándi, *A magyar emigráció életrajza 1945–1985* [Biography of the Hungarian Emigration 1945–1985] (The Hague: Mikes International, 2006), 14.
6 Csicsery-Rónay had worked in the department of external affairs in the Smallholders' Party in Hungary 1945–47, but following the communist takeover (and eight months' imprisonment) left Hungary, arriving in the United States in

1949. Living first in Washington, he studied librarianship at the Catholic University of America; he then moved to work in the library of the University of Maryland. He returned to Hungary after the communists lost power (Borbándi, *Nyugati magyar irodalmi*, 63). His primary contact for Veress was Ferenc Nagy (1903–79), who had been first secretary of the Smallholders' Party and then prime minister of Hungary from 4 February 1946 to 31 May 1947, when he was forced out of his position. He settled in the United States (Ignác Romsics, *Hungary in the Twentieth Century* [Budapest: Corvina, 1999], 231). Along with other exiled politicians he attempted to maintain a coalition government presence outside the country and to persuade governments in Washington and London to fight for the cause—all this unsuccessfully. He was closely involved with the Hungarian National Committee (Magyar Nemzeti Bizottmány), however, which had support from Washington and worked in the interests of the Hungarian community outside the country. See Borbándi, *A magyar emigráció*, 52–55, 58–63, for a detailed account of the Committee.

7 The basic contours of this offer and the university's failed attempt to secure a permit for Veress can be established from letters between Borsody, Veress, and Paul Anderson (president of the Pennsylvania College for Women), dating from 26 April through 21 June 1949.

8 Borsody to Veress, 8 October 1950 and 23 March 1951.

9 Veress to Borsody, 9 December 1951. Another example of this tendency is a letter to Csicsery-Rónay dated 3 March 1952, in which Veress invokes the police, and the possibility that a visa application elsewhere might threaten the extension of his residency permit and teaching position in Switzerland.

10 Csicsery-Rónay to Veress, 13 December 1953; Veress to Csicsery-Rónay, 2 February 1954. The whole matter seems to have gone very quiet at that point. Only Veress's letter to Csicsery-Rónay of 4 October 1955 reveals his interest being rekindled by an invitation to Minneapolis, after which he and Csicsery-Rónay corresponded about guest professorships, commissions, and so on. Veress wanted some time out from teaching (he mentioned "two years") in order to focus on composing.

11 Veress seems generally to have hoarded and filed his correspondence, but there is a gap in Borsody and Veress's exchanges between 26 June 1952 and 17 December 1954, when Borsody wrote. Borsody opened his letter with the statement "Once again it is a year since we have written to one another," which suggests they had lapsed into merely exchanging annual Christmas greetings at some point. Nevertheless, there are surely at least two letters missing. Soós died in a car accident in 1953.

12 Veress to Csicsery-Rónay, 29 September 1953; Csicsery-Rónay to Veress, 22 October 1953.

13 The facsimiles in this book are published in black and white. Nevertheless, the texture and shade of the marks left by the two writing utensils make them clearly distinguishable: marks made with a ballpoint pen are thin and dark, whereas those made with a red pencil are broader and lighter.

14 Veress's father died in November 1953, and the final version states that he "died two years ago" (p. 1).

15 When Veress was considering whether to write the statement at all, he asked to whom this "újabb meaculpázás" [new *mea culpa*] should be sent, which suggests that he had already submitted a formal statement in some form. Veress to Borsody, 3 March 1952.

16 Claudio Veress, "Komponieren in Zeichen skeptischer Parteilichkeit. Eine politisch-werkbiographische Skizze der letzen ungarischen Jahre Sándor Veress' unter besonderer Berücksichtigung des Films *Talpalatnyi föld—Um einen Fussbreith Erde* (1948)," in *Sándor Veress. Komponist—Lehrer—Forscher*, ed. Anselm Gerhard and Doris Lanz (Kassel: Bärenreiter, 2008), 36–76.

17 Rachel Beckles Willson, "Veress and the Steam Locomotive in 1948," in *Sándor Veress. Komponist—Lehrer—Forscher*, 20–35. It is clear that some of his activities in the years prior to 1945 would have made him appear compromised with regard to the new political situation. Even though he worked to help struggling Jewish people during the Nazi era, he also chose to spend over a year in Mussolini's Rome. In 1943 he published a work with Universal Edition (from which Bartók and Kodály had withdrawn on political grounds). He also accepted a Japanese prize for his first Symphony (1940), which was subtitled "Hungarian Greetings on the 2600th Anniversary of the Japanese Dynasty," and premiered in Tokyo two months after the Japanese dynasty had made an alliance with fascist Germany and Italy. He even represented the Hungarian nation at a major Mozart festival organized by the Nazi party in Vienna in 1941: see Baldur von Schirach, "Wir rufen die Jugend zum Krieg für ihre Kunst," *Völkischer Beobachter* (Vienna Edition), 29 November 1941, front page. Veress's name appears in a list of delegates.

18 Three years earlier Borsody had advised Veress never to mention that he was a communist; but presumably the fact that Veress was unable to enter the country in 1949 revealed that this was untenable. Borsody to Veress, 3 August 1949.

19 Letter to Veress from István Borsody in Pittsburgh, 7 April 1952. "Ez a nyilatkozat, azt hiszem, három részből kell álljon: magyarázza meg, mért léptél be a pártba—legyen benne egy antikommunista és végül egy pro-nyugati, pro-demokrata hitvallás. A két utolsó részt, úgy hiszem, könnyű megírnod. Az első részt kell gonddal megszerkeszteni és tekintettel az itteni helyzetre. Át kell szőni azzal a gondolattal, hogy belépésed nem volt az akkori viszonyok között Amerika-elleni lépés, és főleg nem volt pro-kommunista deklaráció! Azt hangsúlyozzad, hogy sohasem voltál kommunista, párttagságod puszta formalitás volt, hasznossági lépés, ami erkölcstelen sem volt, mert művészi és személyes célokat szolgált. Politikum nem volt benne. Pártmunkát soha nem végeztél. A művészi és személyes célokat könnyen megmagyarázhatod. Mint névleges párttag, úgy érezted, a magyar zenei élet újjáteremtését mozdíthatod elő—s ezzel kapcsolatban el kell mondanod csalódásaidat is természetesen. A személyes céloknál Enid angol állampolgári mivoltát említsd, a szörnyű megélhetési nehézségeket. És az egész nyilatkozaton vonuljon végig nyugati mivoltod, a nyugati kultúrához való elszakíthatatlan kapcsolatod, aminek mindenkori működésed—párttagságod tartama alatt is—mindennél ékesebb bizonyítéka. Csak arra kérlek, erőltesd meg magadat, és gondolj arra, hogy most nem a Te eseted objektív történetére van szükség, hanem egy olyan nyilatkozatra,

aminek az alapján a vízumot—a 'volt komunisták' ellen hiszterikus bizalmatlansággal és gyanúval viseltető országba—akarjuk megszerezni." Underlining in original.
20 Letter to Borsody, 22 June 1952.
21 See note 11.
22 Letter to Csicsery-Rónay, 8 April 1953. "... elküldöttöm Pistának, hogy tegye meg rá észrevételeit. Ez is megtörtént, ő alaposan átfésülte és most csak az hiányzik, hogy én az ő megjegyzései alapján átirjam."
23 One cut marked in ballpoint noted his father's death (see also note 13).
24 Veress to Borsody, 22 June 1952.
25 Perhaps the aim of it was to *document* both a firm line and his sense of independence for posterity, and lodge it within his by-then burgeoning collection of correspondence. And perhaps it is not by chance that correspondence with Borsody is so incomplete at precisely this moment.
26 It is by no means clear whether the endeavour was realistic at all. The encouragements seem to have come primarily from Csicsery-Rónay, who advised Borsody in April 1952 that there was a strong chance the application could be successful (Borsody to Veress, 7 April 1952). Csicsery-Rónay's own activites in the United States would warrant a separate study and might offer a more nuanced view on Veress's case. His work in the interest of Hungarians and Hungary is substantial, and his enthusiasm for incorporating Veress into his own project is unmistakable. In an early letter to Borsody he wrote that he would "do everything to enable such an outstanding figure in Hungarian culture to gain a visa" (Borsody cited this in a letter to Veress dated 26 November 1951), and once in touch with Veress directly he rarely ceased pressing him to write in the interest of propagating Hungarian music; indeed, his very first direct communication to Veress (25 July 1952) was to ask him to write for his journal.
27 Borsody to Veress, 3 August 1949. I have not been able to examine the complete correspondence about the commission between Doráti and Veress, as only letters from Doráti are housed at the Paul Sacher Foundation. The first relevant letter seems to be from Doráti to Veress, dated 17 July 1951, which announces that Mr. Frederick Mann would like to commission Veress to write a symphonic work for the Minneapolis Symphony Orchestra's 1952–53 season. A number of subsequent letters from Doráti are also available (1952: 26 July, 29 September, 26 October; 1953: 3 January, 21 February, 11 May), in which he provides further details relating to timing, commission, dedication and so on.
28 For recent work on these subjects see for instance Mark Evans Bonds, *Music as Thought: Listening to the Symphony in the Age of Beethoven* (Princeton, NJ: Princeton University Press, 2006); Peter Franklin, *Mahler: Symphony No. 3*, Cambridge Music Handbooks (New York: Cambridge University Press, 1991); and "Gustav Mahler" in *Grove Music Online* ed. L. Macy, http://www.grovemusic.com (accessed 25 March 2008).
29 John H. Harvey, "Symphony Review," *St. Paul Pioneer Press*, 13 March 1954. I am grateful to Steve Granger of the Anderson Library, University of Minnesota, for sending me reviews of the concert.

30 There is no author for the preview, "Symphony to Present Stern and Opus Named for City," *Minneapolis Star* (evening edition), 11 March 1954.
31 Beckles Willson, *Ligeti, Kurtág, and Hungarian Music*, 14–25, and Beckles Willson, "Veress and the Steam Locomotive in 1948."
32 Traub, "Zur Biographie," 149.
33 See Sanna Pederson, "On the Task of the Music Historian: The Myth of the Symphony after Beethoven," *Repercussions* 2/2 (1993): 5–30, and multiple essays in Jim Samson, ed., *The Cambridge History of Nineteenth-Century Music* (Cambridge and New York: Cambridge University Press, 2001).
34 Bartók had composed a symphony in 1904, but withdrew it; Kodály completed a symphony in 1961.
35 See Andreas Traub, "Verlust und Utopie. Bemerkungen zum Lebens- und Schaffensweg von Sándor Veress," in *Sándor Veress. Komponist—Lehrer—Forscher*, 77–87.
36 In fact, the title probably stems from Doráti's suggestion, but it was only one in a range of ideas he put forward. The final selection and precise form were apparently Veress's own choice. Veress planned to call the work "Tripartita" (Doráti to Veress, 26 October 1952), but, from a letter written by Doráti on 21 February 1953, it seems that Veress had asked him whether the title was appropriate: Doráti suggested that another one might not be bad, and that perhaps one could be found that "said a little more" [*kissé többet mond*] about the piece. He added that once he had got to know it, he would willingly assist in finding a title. By 11 May, when he wrote again, he had had the score for some time and he asked Veress to consider changing the title. Apparently in response to what Veress himself had written about an attempt to represent the "content" of the work, he agreed that "Metamorphoseon" [*sic*] really wouldn't do. It was clumsy [*nehézkes*] and aroused antipathy [*ellenszenvet keltő*]. But he suggested that a title drawing on the external circumstances of the work might be good, and that he himself liked "Minneapolis" Sinfonia. He advised Veress that in Italian it would be "Sinfonia da Minneapolis," but that it could easily be translated into French or English. He also suggested that "Symphony 1953" wouldn't be bad, or something that connected it to the place where Veress wrote it (possibly "Sinfonia Basilesa"—but this is illegible).
37 See previous footnote, and John K. Sherman, "Isaac Stern, 'Local' Work Featured by Symphony," *Minneapolis Star*, 13 March 1954.
38 See "Listening to the German State: Nationalism," in Bonds, *Music as Thought*, 79–103, especially 92ff.
39 Ignotus describes Matthias's reign with characteristic clarity: "His European outlook made him less interested in saving Europe from the Turks than in extending his control to regions westward ... Italian historians and Hungarian men of letters under his patronage wrote in Latin; and the *Corvina* books produced for his library were among the finest specimens of Renaissance craftsmanship ... Hungary became utterly cosmopolitan." Paul Ignotus, *Hungary* (London: Ernest Benn, 1972), 30.
40 Veress mentioned his father's interests in his statement for the US authorities: "my father ... was a well-known historian. His field of studies chiefly concerned Hungarian-Italian relationship [*sic*] from the 13th century onward

and Hungarian-Rumanian affaires [sic] during the 16th and 17th centuries." The book I refer to here is vast: a 160-page introduction precedes 700 pages of documents in Hungarian and Latin. See Endre Veress, *Olasz egyetemeken jart magyarorszagi tanulok anyakönyve es iratai, 1221–1864* [Matriculation Records and Other Documents Relating to Students from Hungary at Italian Universities, 1221–1864] (Budapest, 1941). It appeared as the third volume in a series entitled 'Olaszorszagi magyar emlekek' [Hungarian Records in Italian Archives] edited by the Római Magyar Történeti Intézet [Hungarian Institute of History in Rome].

41 The precise dates were provided for me by Claudio Veress, who reconstructed them from Veress's concert engagements, travel documents, and correspondence. Email communication, 29 July 2006.

42 This claim could also be understood as a gesture of separating Hungary from contemporary (Nazi) Germany. Anna Dalos further suggests that Kodály's formulation was reinforced by the work of art historian Heinrich Wölfflin, whose *Renaissance und Baroque* (1907) and *Kunstgeschichtliche Grundbegriffe* (1917) polarized Italian and German spirit and culture. Anna Dalos, *Forma, harmónia, ellenpont: Vázlatok Kodály Zoltán poétikájához* (Budapest: Akademiai kiadó, 2007), 307–12. The relevant chapter of this book is available in English; see Anna Dalos, "Zoltán Kodály's Art of Fugue: About the Neo-Classicism of the Concerto for Orchestra," in *Essays in Honor of László Somfai on His 70th Birthday: Studies in the Sources and the Interpretation of Music*, ed. László Vikárius and Vera Lampert, 331–47 (Lanham, MD: Scarecrow Press, 2005); Kodály's essay in English is published in Ferenc Bónis, ed., *The Selected Writings of Kodály*, trans. Fred McNicol (London: Boosey & Hawkes, 1974), 28–33.

43 Traub refers to the two themes as Hauptthema and Seitenthema, and prefers to consider the work in two movements, as the Andante follows the initial Allegro without pause.

44 Traub, "Zur Biographie," 149.

45 Gerlich, "Neuanfang in der 'Wahlheimat'?"; Traub, "Zur Biographie"; Lanz, "Es ist aber nur Mittel, nigh 'Ziel,'" in *Sándor Veress. Komponist—Lehrer—Forscher*.

46 Precisely this opposition was crucial to the way "Hungarian" was constructed in Veress's formative years. See Beckles Willson, *Ligeti, Kurtág, and Hungarian Music*, 13–25; and for Veress's own view, "[Komponisten-Selbstportrait]," in *Sándor Veress. Aufsätze, Vorträge Briefe*, ed. Andreas Traub (Hofheim: Wolke Verlag, 1998), 24–26.

47 It was long conventional to understand the stags' transformation as a regaining of nature and purity, but this does not tie in convincingly with the resignation of the ending. Indeed a recent article has argued that attention should be paid to the musical ambivalence of this close, and has suggested that there is in fact much nostalgia in the final cry for purity. Nicky Losseff, "Casting Beams of Darkness into Bartók's *Cantata profana*," *Twentieth-Century Music* 3/2 (2007): 221–54.

48 Its fourth movement, "Intermezzo interrotto," contains a theme that is in part a parody of Shostakovich's Seventh Symphony ("Leningrad"), and also a quotation of a popular song, "Szép vagy, gyönyörű vagy Magyarország"

["You are lovely, you are beautiful, Hungary"] by Zsigmond Vincze. This has triggered narrative readings of the Concerto that construct Bartók's putative contempt for Soviet aesthetics, and his homesickness.

49 Veress to Borsody, 9 December 1951. "A mai dimenziókban 'periféria' pedig Amerikát és a nem kommunista uralom alatt lévő csendestengeri vidékeket jelenti. Itt, a központban ez már csak igen keveseknek fogalom- és érzésvilágában valóság. Részben az európai ember rettenetes elanyagiasodása, részben a meg nem oldott szociális problémák akozta feszültség /mint Itáliában és Franciaországban/ megsemmisítette az európai ember felelősségtudatát azokkal a hagyományokkal szemben, amit az 'európaiság' jelent. A keretek még állanak, de ez immár csak külsőség, míg a fejekben és lelkekben mérhetetlen zavar és káosz van. ... Európa vagy az újjászülető náci-teutónok, vagy a steppeázsiai muszka barbarizmus igája alá fog kerülni."

50 Veress to Csicsery-Rónay, 26 November 1952. He mentioned war to Csicsery-Rónay in a letter dated 8 November 1953.

51 Throughout his years in the United States he worked to promote Hungarian matters, writing books, founding the journal *Hírünk a világban* [Our Renown in the Wider World] in 1951, establishing the publishing house Occidental Press in Washington in 1954, and contributing to numerous other publications and literary organizations (Borbándi, *Nyugati magyar irodalmi*, 111). He was one of many Hungarian émigrés who elected, out of loyalty to the Hungary in which they believed, to limit very carefully the extent to which they associated themselves with the country in which they settled (often not even applying for citizenship). On this subject see Borbándi, *A magyar emigráció*, 59. Csicsery-Rónay mentioned the subject to Veress himself, and he eventually returned to Hungary after the communists lost power (Csicsery-Rónay to Veress, 18 February 1953). Veress himself did apply for Swiss citizenship in the mid-1970s, but his stance against communism in Hungary was equally resolute and shaped his determination to remain an émigré until the regime changed. The arduous citizenship-acquisition process was completed only two months before he died in 1992. For a documentary account, see Doris Lanz, "Ein gewundener Weg zur Passhöhe. Dokumente zu Sándor Veress' Einbürgerung in die Schweiz," in *Sándor Veress. Komponist—Lehrer—Forscher*, 241–77.

52 Veress to Borsody, 9 December 1951.

53 Ibid. "A kérdés csak az, hogy a 'perifériák' elég frissek-e és táptalajuk megfelelő-e az innen menekülő és áramló kultúra továbbtenyésztésére? Avagy ott is ilyen-e a rothadás?" "De vannak jelek, melyek, ha nem is csalnak, mintha azt mutatnák, hogy idealizmusból, ha nem is kilók, de még mindig több gramm maradt az amerikánusokban, párosulva egy józan realitással, mint az európai ember átlagban."

54 Veress to Borsody, 9 December 1951. "... ami persze ennek a civilizációnak végét jelentené."

55 The author would like to thank Evelyne Diendorf, librarian at the Paul Sacher Foundation, for kindly providing us with this information.

Bibliography

Beckles Willson, Rachel. *Ligeti, Kurtág, and Hungarian Music during the Cold War*. Cambridge and New York: Cambridge University Press, 2007.

———. "Veress and the Steam Locomotive in 1948." In *Sándor Veress. Komponist—Lehrer—Forscher*, edited by Anselm Gerhard and Doris Lanz, 20–35. Kassel: Bärenreiter, 2008.

Bonds, Mark Evan. *Music as Thought: Listening to the Symphony in the Age of Beethoven*. Princeton, NJ: Princeton University Press, 2006.

Bónis, Ferenc, ed. *The Selected Writings of Kodály*. Translated by Fred McNicol. London: Boosey & Hawkes, 1974.

Borbándi, Gyula. *A magyar emigráció életrajza 1945–1985* [Biography of the Hungarian Emigration 1945–1985]. The Hague: Mikes International, 2006.

———. *Nyugati magyar irodalmi lexikon és bibliográfia* [Western Hungarian Literary Encyclopedia and Bibliography]. The Hague: Mikes International, 2006.

Cooper, David. *Bartók: Concerto for Orchestra*. Cambridge University Press, 1996.

Dalos, Anna. *Forma, harmónia, ellenpont: Vázlatok Kodály Zoltán poétikájához*. Budapest: Akademiai kiadó, 2007.

———. "Zoltán Kodály's Art of Fugue: About the Neo-Classicism of the Concerto for Orchestra." In *Essays in Honor of László Somfai on His 70th Birthday: Studies in the Sources and the Interpretation of Music*, edited by László Vikárius and Vera Lampert, 331–47. Lanham, MD: Scarecrow Press, 2005.

Franklin, Peter. "Gustav Mahler." In *Grove Music Online*, edited by L. Macy, http://www.grovemusic.com (accessed 25 March 2008).

———. *Mahler: Symphony No. 3*. Cambridge Music Handbooks. New York: Cambridge University Press, 1991.

Gerhard, Anslem and Doris Lanz, eds. *Sándor Veress. Komponist—Lehrer—Forscher*. Kassel: Bärenreiter, 2008.

Gerlich, Thomas. "Neuanfang in der 'Wahlheimat'? Zu Sándor Veress' Hommage à Paul Klee." In *"Entre Denges et Denezy..." Dokumente zur Schweizer Musikgeschichte 1900–2000*, edited by Ulrich Mosch and Matthias Kassel, 399–406. Kassel, Mainz: Schott, 2000.

Ignotus, Paul. *Hungary*. London: Ernest Benn, 1972.

Lanz, Doris. "Ein gewundener Weg zur Passhöhe. Dokumente zu Sándor Veress' Einbürgerung in die Schweiz." In *Sándor Veress. Komponist—Lehrer—Forscher*, 241–77.

———. "Es ist aber nur Mittel, nigh 'Ziel': Zur Rolle der Zwölftontechnik bei Sándor Veress und Wladimir Vogel um 1950." In *Sándor Veress. Komponist—Lehrer—Forscher*, 88–106.

Losseff, Nicky. "Casting Beams of Darkness into Bartók's *Cantata profana*." *Twentieth-Century Music* 3/2 (2007): 221–54.

Pederson, Sanna. "On the Task of the Music Historian: The Myth of the Symphony after Beethoven." *Repercussions* 2/2 (1993): 5–30.

Romsics, Ignác. *Hungary in the Twentieth Century*. Budapest: Corvina, 1999.
Samson Jim, ed. *The Cambridge History of Nineteenth-Century Music*. Cambridge and New York: Cambridge University Press, 2001.
Traub, Andreas, ed. *Sándor Veress. Aufsätze, Vorträge Briefe*. Hofheim: Wolke Verlag, 1998.
———. "Sándor Veress, Lebensweg—Schaffensweg." In *Sándor Veress Festschrift zum 80. Geburtstag*, edited by Andreas Traub, 22–97. Berlin: Verlag K. Haseloff, 1986.
———. "Verlust und Utopie. Bemerkungen zum Lebens- und Schaffensweg von Sándor Veress." In *Sándor Veress. Komponist—Lehrer—Forscher*, 77–87.
———. "Zur Biographie—Zur *Sinfonia Minneapolitana*." In *Zwischen Volks- und Kunstmusik: Aspekte der ungarischen Musik*, edited by Stefan Fricke, Wolf Frobenius, Sigrid Konrad, and Theo Schmitt, 146–54. Saarbrucken: Pfau Verlag, 1999.
Veress, Claudio. "Komponieren in Zeichen skeptischer Parteilichkeit. Eine politisch-werkbiographische Skizze der letzen ungarischen Jahre Sándor Veress' unter besonderer Berücksichtigung des Films *Talpalatnyi föld—Um einen Fussbreith Erde* (1948)." In *Sándor Veress. Komponist—Lehrer—Forscher*, 36–76.

NINE

Roots and Routes: Travel and Translation in István Anhalt's Operas[1]

Gordon E. Smith

> *One spends a lifetime acting and leaving "traces," leaving the question open: do all these comings & goings & doings "add up" ... to a "pattern," i.e., is a "tikkun" possible? This is the theme of the new piece.*
> —István Anhalt to George Rochberg, 3 March 1995

"CENTRES AND PERIPHERIES, ROOTS AND EXILE"—the themes of this conference on the music of István Anhalt and György Kurtág—evoke significant frameworks for understanding the music of István Anhalt, whose operas are the subject of this paper. I begin with Anhalt's words from another time:

"Father, I am a musician and haven't had the opportunity in months to play my instrument, the piano. Is there a piano in the house? Could I play it for a short while?" The monks were dumbfounded by this strange request, but they decided to allow him in, and directed Istvan to a room with a piano in it. With a monk watching him closely, Istvan played some piano pieces, which he had picked up previously as a student at the Budapest Academy of Music. Then, after a few minutes of playing, Istvan stopped and told the monk of his true identity, and that his life was in danger. "I wanted to avoid going to Austria and asked him if he could help me get to Budapest." Visibly shaken by Istvan's story, the monk took Istvan to the head of the monastery, who after asking him a few questions agreed to help him get to Budapest that same night. He also gave Istvan identity papers, issued in someone else's name, which stated that he was a member of paramilitary organization. Istvan was taken by a monk to a nearby railroad station. The monk bought him a ticket and stayed with him until the train arrived to make sure of his safety. To help pass the time Istvan asked him to relate the history of the Salesian Order. "I don't remember anything of what he said," Istvan related. "My thoughts must have been on other things."[2]

This narrative reads as a telling link to the conference themes of centres, peripheries, roots, exile, and to this paper, in which first I examine Anhalt's operas as a group, and then move to a more detailed discussion of *Traces (Tikkun)*, Anhalt's opera which most closely evokes parallels to his own life experience.

István Anhalt has composed four operas spanning a period of approximately thirty years: *La Tourangelle* (1970–75), *Winthrop* (1977–86), *Traces (Tikkun)* (1994–95), and *Millennial Mall (Lady Diotima's Walk)* (1999–2000).[3] Inspired by the conference theme of centres and peripheries, in example 9-1 I have situated the operas on the four corners—*peripheries*—and I have added a fifth work, the duo-drama for voice and piano, *Thisness* (1986), in the *centre*. In significant ways, *Thisness* is a pivotal piece in the context of Anhalt's four operas. A commission of the Vancouver New Music Society in 1986 for Phyllis Mailing and Richard Epp (piano), *Thisness*, subtitled "a duo-drama," is a ten-part dramatic work in which the singer and the pianist are required to wear costumes and act out roles. Anhalt wrote the text himself (nine poems and the description of a short pantomime). The narrative is a journey of retrospection that is played out on psychological, emotional, historical, and even physical levels.[4] *Thisness* represents an exploration of certain themes that pervade Anhalt's operas: the search for the past; the mysteries of childhood; personal identities; the root causes of cruelty; reason, unreason; dreaming and the absurd; performance of music as spectacle; beauty and peace.

As much as *Thisness* is untraditional in terms of conventional musical genres, Anhalt's four operas are *not* operas in the traditional sense of the opera genre—music, staging, drama, plot—but, as their respective subtitles suggest ("a musical tableau"; "a historical pageant"; "a pluri-drama"; "a voice-drama for the imagination"), they are, as Anhalt suggests, "mind operas" that do not depend principally on conventional operatic devices. As Anhalt has written to John Beckwith, "The full effectiveness of all of these four works is realizable *by sound only* … Without a visual complement *provided for the listener/viewer*, the latter has to *work* in creating this complement in his/her imagination. As such this person becomes an even

EXAMPLE 9-1 Istvan Anhalt's Operas.

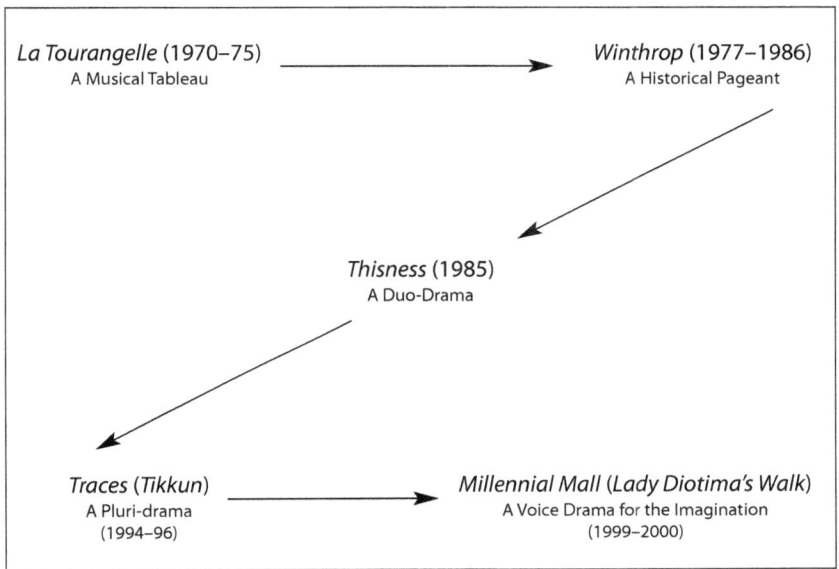

more engaged participant in a joint creative experience."[5] Thus, in their different explorations of relationships between inner and outer worlds, they don't require visual dimensions, but rely on music and words to induce the listener into imaginary worlds of memory, history, and contemporary society. Importantly, with respect to this conference's themes, they also engage themes of centre and periphery, immigration and exile, roots and routes, and travel and translation.

As a group, Anhalt's operas can be thought of as following intersecting pathways of personal, ethically searching, and creative dimensions. From other vantage points, Anhalt's operas also present themselves as multi-level voyages of discovery, which, in the composer's interpretation, resonate with Mikhail Bakhtin's "chronotope," that is, time-place concept.[6] Each opera has its own landscape, evocative of a particular time and place, subject to a recognizable moment of history, and shaped through action, experience, memory, and reflection. Moreover, I would suggest that they resonate with Anhalt's search for a fitting role and identity in North America, and specifically in Canada—his adopted country—not only for an identity as a composer, but even more broadly, for an identity as a human being.

The different periods and sites of the four operas—seventeenth-century France and New France (*La Tourangelle*), England and New England (*Winthrop*), a chain of locations that suggest sites in the life of an individual (*Traces [Tikkun]*), and finally, an imaginary public place—a Millennial Mall—around the year 2000 (*Millennial Mall [Lady Diotima's Walk]*)—with their respective focuses on religious creeds and value systems, further place these works as reflections of the pathway of Anhalt's gradually emergent Canadian, North American experience. Thus, the concepts of *place* and *displacement* in Anhalt's music are much more than geographic locations and physical movements; they also embody metaphorical ideas of being and dwelling, and ideas pertaining to danger, persecution, exile, adaptation, and the resultant imperative discovery of others and the emergent self—*all* recurring and crucial links that are indispensable for the understanding of Anhalt's music, and his operas in particular. Referring to *La Tourangelle*, *Winthrop*, and *Thisness* (see above), Anhalt comments that each of these pieces has "a common *locus* ... It is not a place, nor is it an area, but rather a 'state,' both in the physical and psychic sense: 'the state' of being 'in transit,' going from one place to another, propelled by some urge to 'move,' for one reason or another ... I may add ... it is rather the memory of being in transit,' that I was composing in these works."[7] As Doreen Massey has written with respect to the politics of place, it is perhaps more useful to think of places not necessarily as places on maps, but as "constantly shifting articulations of social relations through time."[8] And as James Clifford has argued with respect to aspects of travel and translation in the late twentieth century, in many, probably most, contemporary sites of artistic and ethnographic inquiry, dwelling and travel—or *roots* and *routes*—are not necessarily contested, separate processes, but are close to each other and are often connected.[9]

In what follows, I consider some of these ideas within the framework of Anhalt's opera *Traces (Tikkun)*, the opera which, as I have mentioned, is closest to aspects of Anhalt's life story. In this discussion, I would like to raise some questions related to the conference themes. For example, is there a *centre* in *Traces (Tikkun)* or might it be better to think of the piece in terms of *periphery* or a series of *peripheries*?

How are Clifford's notions of *roots* and *routes* and *travel* and *translation* played out in the work? How close are these ideas in the kinds of narratives Anhalt presents in *Traces (Tikkun)*? And perhaps most importantly, where and how does Anhalt's "voice" figure within the contexts of these questions? Example 9-2 is a graphic representation of some of these concepts. The circular shape is deliberate, as these ideas do not exist independ-

EXAMPLE 9-2 Intersecting Concepts and István Anhalt's Music.

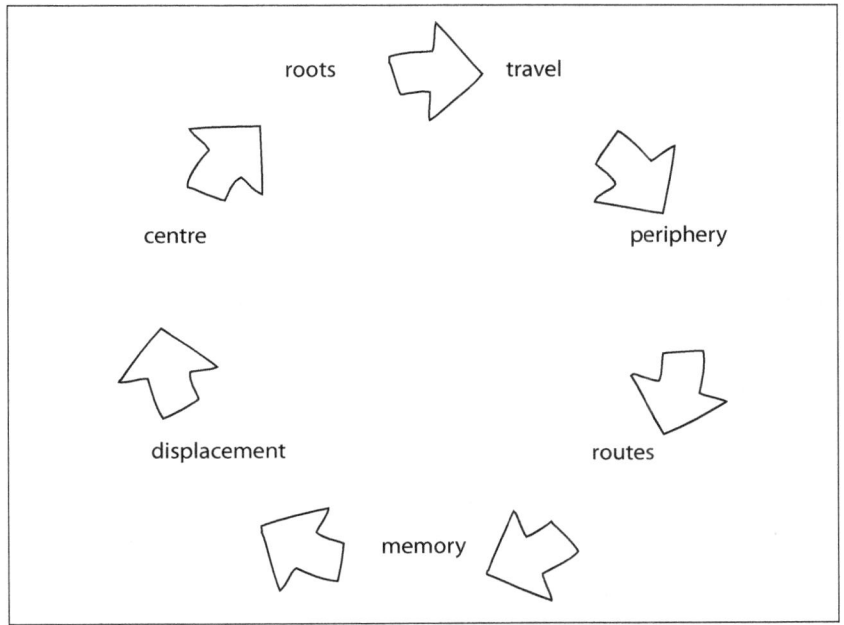

ently from each other, but rather, they can be regarded as flowing into and out of each other. Dualisms such as "centres" and "peripheries," and "roots" and "routes," for example, do not represent opposites as much they represent likenesses when we listen to Anhalt's words and his music. "Centres" can be, and indeed *are*, "peripheries," and "roots" and "routes" are much more than an engaging play on words.

As Clifford has observed, "roots always precede routes," but what would happen if "travel ... were untethered, seen as a complex and pervasive spectrum of human experiences? Practices of displacement might emerge as *constitutive* of cultural meanings rather than as their simple transfer or extension."[10] An important note with respect to example 9–2 is that the placement of *memory* alone, and at the base of the circle, is also deliberate. Memory is a pivotal theme in Anhalt's thought processes, his writings, and his music.

Before the discussion on *Traces (Tikkun)*, I provide here a brief background on my experience with Anhalt, as I, along with a number of others, regard our relationships with Anhalt as an integral part of knowing Anhalt and his music. Going a step further, I can honestly say that I would never have done as much work on Anhalt and his music as I have done if I had not had the experience of knowing him.

I first met Anhalt in 1990 when I was asked to write an essay on him for an issue of the *Queen's Quarterly*, commemorating the sesquicentennial of Queen's University (Kingston, Ontario) and celebrating the lives and work of ten distinguished Canadians.[11] My association with Anhalt continued through the 1990s when I was working with Robin Elliott on a book of essays dealing with Anhalt's life and work. Most recently, I wrote a text on Anhalt's operas, which was published in 2006 in *American Music* (see note 1). Over time, I have come to regard my ongoing interaction with Anhalt as a kind of fieldwork, which can be viewed as linking to ideas of reflexive ethnography, that is, fieldwork as human interaction and shared experience in which the composer is regarded as informant, revealing modalities of individual creativity and their relationships to specific life experiences.[12] Looking back, I didn't set out to do this research with ethnomusicological models in mind. Considering Anhalt as an informant emerged gradually as a result of our working together regularly over a period that is now close to twenty years. Initially, I made tapes of our conversations, consisting for the most part of my questions, and Anhalt's extensive responses, typically linking his life experiences to his creative work as a composer. As we got to know and trust each other, gradually the tape recorder was replaced by lengthy conversations in person or on the telephone. As other authors in this book will also know, Anhalt is a fascinating interlocutor who derives stimulation and inspiration from conversations with colleagues and friends. Much of the following discussion about his third opera, *Traces (Tikkun)*, is around various guises of Anhalt's "voice."

Traces (Tikkun)

In Anhalt's first two operas, *La Tourangelle* and *Winthrop*, the composer did extensive research into the religious backgrounds of the respective operas' protagonists, Marie de l'Incarnation (Roman Catholicism) and John Winthrop (Protestant Calvinism). This research was an essential part of Anhalt's "putting down roots" in his adopted country, Canada, and, in retrospect, he came to regard Marie de l'Incarnation and John Winthrop as "spiritual guides" in his learning about these two world religions. After depicting certain parts of Catholicism and Calvinism in his first two operas, both within North American historical and societal contexts, not surprisingly, Anhalt decided to look back at his own personal experiences. This exploration led him to the discovery of the world of Jewish mysticism through the writings of Gershom Scholem in the 1980s. Anhalt's gradual pursuit of knowledge about his religious roots included subtle allusions to Judaism, also in his three orchestral pieces of the late 1980s,[13] and was further grounded in the course of a trip to Israel in 1992. In 1991, it also led to his work on a projected opera libretto about the Jewish-American physicist J.R. Oppenheimer.[14]

Developing an understanding of what constitutes Judaism and being a Jew in relation to "being/remaining an individual" may be considered a motivation behind the Oppenheimer project, as it was behind *Traces (Tikkun)*, completed in 1995. The word "traces" in the title of the piece stands for some, or all, of the actions, steps, or decisions a person undertakes in his or her life. "Tikkun" denotes a concept borrowed from kabbalistic thought. It represents a "making into a whole" something that may have been a whole before, but subsequently has fallen apart. As Anhalt comments, the word may also suggest questions about freedom of choice, determinism, and the relationship between individuals and society. In one of four citations at the beginning of the score, Anhalt refers to the "tikkun" concept by way of an excerpt from Gershom Scholem's *Kabbalah*:

> Tikkun ... the restoration of the universe to its original design[15]
>
> The process of creation involves the departure of all from the One, and the crucial turning-point in this cycle takes place within man, at the moment he begins to develop an awareness of his own true essence and yearns to retrace the path from the multiplicity of his nature to the Oneness from which he originated.[16]

Embedded in these words are Scholem's ideas about creation, displacement, learning, searching for one's identity, ideas which Anhalt builds into a thematic framework and a libretto for the opera.

Traces (Tikkun) had its premiere performance at the Glenn Gould Studio (Canadian Broadcasting Corporation) in Toronto in May 1996, with Doug MacNaughton, baritone, and the Encounters Chamber Orchestra under the direction of Gary Kulesha. The work may be considered a continuation of the hermeneutic pathway on which Anhalt had embarked with *La Tourangelle* and *Winthrop*. Within this context,[17] the genesis of *Traces (Tikkun)* took place over a twenty-five-year period (from 1970), and in some respects may be understood as part of Anhalt's personal memory of the past, his recent public phase of his search for a sense of identity as an individual, and also as an individual who is a participant in the historical Jewish experience. Significantly, the dedication of *Traces (Tikkun)* is in memory of László Gyopár, István Székely, Ödön Taubner, and László Weiner, who were fellow students of Anhalt's at the Ferenc Liszt Hungarian Academy of Music in Budapest during 1937–40, and who lost their lives in forced labour camps for Jews run by the Hungarian Army in the Second World War.

Traces (Tikkun) is a series of dialogues with distant, and not so distant, voices, including, among numerous others, that of the composer.[18] Like Anhalt's two earlier operas, *Traces (Tikkun)* focuses on one protagonist. Anhalt explains that the single character in the opera is nameless:

> He [the protagonist-hero] is, probably, a much travelled Europe-born, Jew who settled in and let down roots in Canada after his experience in, and survival of, the years between, say 1920–1950, in Europe. While he is an eager learner of things North-American, he is also hanging onto his European memories, which slowly, ever-so-slowly, he begins to understand. In reality, he swings back and forth between an involvement in the late twentieth-century scene in Canada, and the rich storehouse of his memories. Slowly these two strands start making sense to him in relation to each other.[19]

My earlier comments on intersecting themes in Anhalt's work (see example 9-2 above), including expanded notions of *dwelling* and *travelling*, inspired by Clifford's comments (above), and Anhalt's ongoing focus on *memory*, also resonate here and through much of this discussion.

The dialogic aspect of *Traces (Tikkun)* is tied to Anhalt's expression "pluri-drama," which he uses as a subtitle to describe the work. The singer (protagonist), a lyric baritone, displays signs of diverse influences of different people, situations, and events from a long life. The role requires that the soloist portray in soliloquies and pseudo-dialogues, in a variety of singsong intonations, the minds and voices of about a dozen people. At the beginning of the score Anhalt explains:

> The Baritone Solo "gives voice" in this "pluri-drama" to a number of persons in implied situations. This may be taken as enacting the semblance of dialogues and other kinds of utterances, in addition to conveying monologues. Alternatively, one may take TRACES as if taking place in the *mind* of a *single* person, who absorbed into his memory the "traces" of such past exchanges. Another possibility remains; namely, to combine these two "hearings" and, thereby, to leave a remaining ambiguity unresolved, thus placing the piece at, yet, a farther horizon.

PLATE 9-1 István Anhalt, dedication page from the score of *Traces (Tikkun)* (1994), with kind permission of the composer.

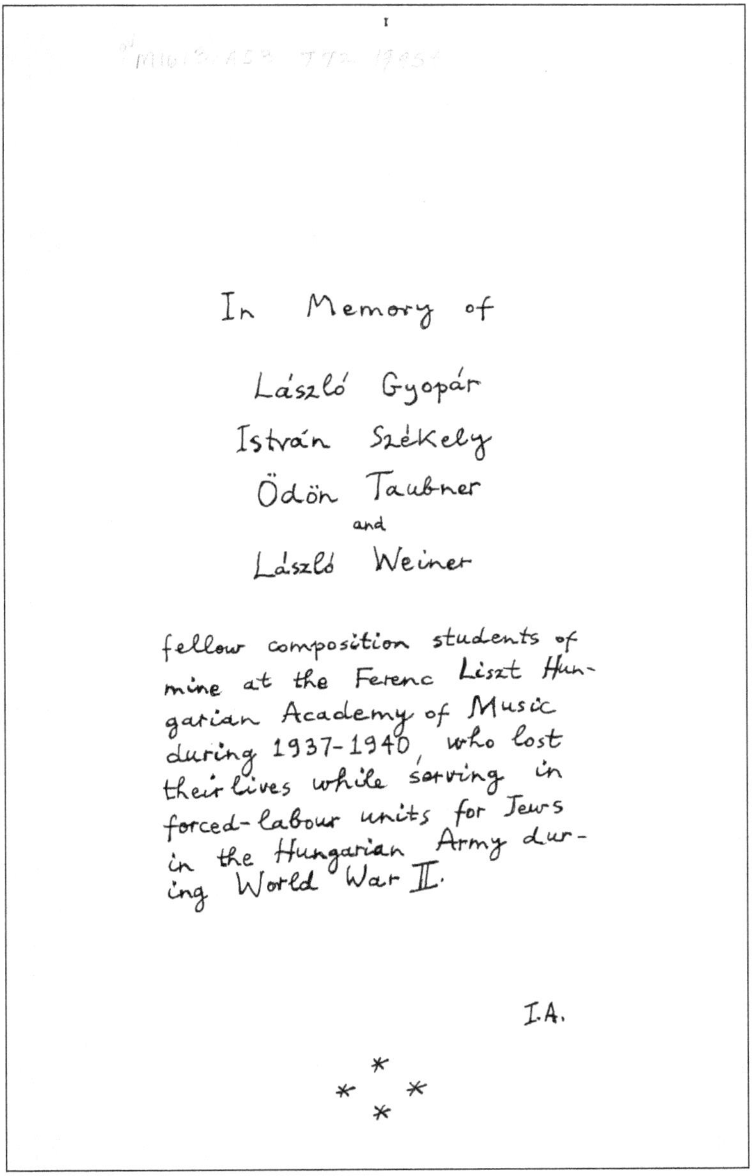

In Memory of

László Gyopár
István Székely
Ödön Taubner
and
László Weiner

fellow composition students of mine at the Ferenc Liszt Hungarian Academy of Music during 1937-1940, who lost their lives while serving in forced-labour units for Jews in the Hungarian Army during World War II.

I.A.

Unlike *La Tourangelle* and *Winthrop*, for which Anhalt compiled the librettos mostly from pre-existing texts, the libretto of *Traces (Tikkun)* was written by the composer, with allusions to diverse situations in which he was a participant, as well as from exposure to various types of expressions found in different sources—personal accounts of friends and others, and printed ones, including the daily newspapers. Themes of roots, displacement, and memory are pervasive. Again, in Anhalt's words:

> In the libretto ... one reads of some of the life experiences of an unnamed man, details of the kind I myself was personally familiar with, or could imagine, and which, I strongly felt, were also shared by many of those who, after certain experiences, were compelled to seek admittance into a new community where they hoped they could find conditions that would be conducive to a more peaceable existence than the one which was their lot before. Simply put, "Traces (Tikkun)" is, once again, the tale of immigrant-emigrant, like Marie de l'Incarnation and John Winthrop. It might be worth noting that the word "Jew" does not appear in this text, thus allowing for a greater generality, a greater amplitude of relevance based on the shared motive of displacement in the search for a new homeland.[20]

Traces (Tikkun) is about three-quarters of an hour in length and is conceived in ten sections, which proceed in an uninterrupted flow: 1 "Arrival"—2 "Questions"—3 "Labyrinth"—4 "Oasis"—5 "Desert Town"—6 "Metropolis"—7 "In the Highdome"—8 "After the Show"—9 "Visitors"—10 "The Answer." In a recent conversation with Anhalt about *Traces (Tikkun)*, he discussed the sections of the opera, highlighting certain personal perspectives, perspectives which link directly to his life story. In the following, I highlight some of these perspectives. For example, in the "Arrival" section with which the opera begins, Anhalt creates a kind of reversal of a dialogic situation. The opening words of the singer are in the form of a question—"Is someone here, speaking?"—to which he then replies—"I'm listening." In this way, the composer sets up a series of imaginary ongoing dialogues between the performer and the members of the audience, with the intent of drawing the audience into the work, making it a co-creative partner in the course of the performance. In the second section, "Questions," we hear— "anyone might get called up, everybody's on their own"—followed by the questions— "When? Where? Why? Who?"—which are central to this work overall and, one might argue, to much of Anhalt's creative work. Plate 9-2 is the opening page of the score, containing Section I ("Arrival") followed by the beginning of Section II ("Questions").

PLATE 9-2 István Anhalt, *Traces (Tikkun)* (1994), "Arrival" (I) and opening of "Questions" (II), mm. 1–7, score page 1, with kind permission of the composer.

In addition to the dialogic framework (noted above), this critical opening moment is reinforced musically by the baritone intoning the opening two lines a cappella in a "hesitant" and "groping" manner. The opening is followed by the series of the protagonist's "questions" accompanied at first by muted strings; as the section proceeds and the protagonist's questions become more persistent and urgent, the momentum of the music increases with added instruments (e.g., winds; percussion; piano arpeggiated figures interacting with the vocal line) and a general increased textural reinforcement to the voice.

Anhalt describes the third section, "Labryinth," in the following:

> The would-be answers [to the "Questions" in section II] turn into an account, developing into an enactment, of a series of nightmares, or recurring dreams. Terrible images follow in close, relentless succession: narrow, suffocating passageways, underground tunnels, foiled attempts at escaping, a sense of disorientation in the dark, threatening loud noises, surging water, the fear of drowning, etc. Then comes sudden relief: one awakens; there is light again and fresh air. This scene of fear stands for any and all threatening situation(s) a person might have encountered in life. It symbolizes extreme danger, as well as a sudden liberation from it.[21]

In relation to Anhalt's life experience, the "Labyrinth" section of *Traces (Tikkun)* can be interpreted as describing the "unreal existence" in the forced labour camp in the Second World War, followed by "bursting free" from that "underground hell to an 'Oasis'" (the quoted words are Anhalt's). The music adds to the desperateness of this situation, especially Anhalt's use of orchestration and musical texture. The section builds out of a warning ("Have no illusion ..."), declaimed by the protagonist, accompanied by the strings and the horns in a slow-moving, quiet tempo, creating a mysterious sense of anticipation; this proceeds to a powerfully protracted crescendo in which the musical texture expands gradually to the full orchestra and the use of pounding, syncopated rhythmic figures, made more powerful by dissonant sounds. Registral extremes and a range of instrumental playing techniques add to the dramatic tension, expressed in potent phrases such as "more and more turns ... countless loops ... boiling whirlpools ... torrents of foam." The voice lines dramatize the text in their undulating ("turning," "looping") contours, and gradually the voice part is submerged in the musical texture as the protagonist becomes more and more disoriented. Plate 9-3 shows the final page of the "Labryinth" and the opening page of "Oasis." The musical styles described here reach a climax with the fermata (*Sostenuto*) in measure 166, followed by the unaccompanied "bursting free" moment of this drama with the protagonist's high-pitched proclamation "into life" (these words are preceded by "until you burst free in the air ... into life"—not shown in plate 9-3). While the vocal line continues the exuberance of relief in the opening of "Oasis" (e.g., rising, joyful figures on "Light!" "Light!" "Life!" etc.), the musical style of this section is markedly different. Notably, there is a lighter, gentler approach to the orchestration, more delicate textural contrasts, and a general relaxing of the dramatic and musical tension which dominated the preceding section.

"Desert Town" (Section V) represents a situation in which there are two types of people on either side of a walled town, an interesting parallel to travel metaphors around centres and peripheries. What Anhalt is talking about here is gaining acceptance in a new-found, safe home. In "Desert Town," the composer exploits the dialogic idea, with the protagonist "speaking" for the "insiders" *and* the "outsiders," effecting a dramatic negotiation between the two groups involving words and music. "Desert Town" contains a large range of vocal techniques, from spoken text, to degrees of "sprechgesang," to singing, all emphasized by Anhalt's sensitive attention to the expressive potential of the text (i.e., articulation, dynamic ranges, vocal "lines," range, etc.).

In section 7, "In the Highdome," Anhalt composed a rock concert. Anhalt describes part of the genesis of this section in the following:

> In the passage "In the Highdome" a rock concert is in progress ... I felt I want to depict its legitimacy for the young, the overall legitimacy of Dionysus ... I composed the music "in stages": first it was a trio of instrumentals: an electronic guitar, a synthesizer and a drum-set, accompanying a *Sprechstimme* voice. Then came added glassy strings glides when "transport" sets in ... then the voice was turned into a 75% sung line, rather deep and angular in flow; then a few woodwind turns & tremolos were added ... some rap-like, machine gun-like, recitation of text (depicting angular prancing around) remained in the vocal line.[22]

As Anhalt explains, the rock music "scene" is enhanced with vivid orchestration, and added rock band instruments, amplification of the voice part, as well as pounding, syncopated rhythmic figures, often reinforced with block dissonant sound shapes (plate 9-4). In the following section, "After the Show," the protagonist takes on the role of a pop performer and the references to commercial aspects of show business are followed by allusions to dark personal stories which the promoter tells the protagonist

PLATE 9-3 István Anhalt, *Traces (Tikkun)* (1994), final page of the "Labyrinth" (III) and the opening page of "Oasis" (IV), mm. 165–73, score pages 46–47, with kind permission of the composer.

Plate 9-3 (conclusion)

190   PLACE AND DISPLACEMENT

PLATE 9-4   István Anhalt, *Traces (Tikkun)* (1994), "In the Highdome" (VII), mm. 428–31, score page 100, with kind permission of the composer.

to "keep ... to yourself." This section contrasts with the rock concert, implying a clash of younger and older generations, and of world view and values.

In the penultimate section of the opera, "The Visitors," Anhalt describes what he thought his ninety-year-old mother might have experienced in a Kingston (Ontario) hospital at the end of her life. Memories of a shut-in, in which a sense of time and purpose slip away, gradually give way to the voice of a young child: "I love you like infinity, a small child told me once, How did she know?" The child was his granddaughter, Astrid, who once said that beautiful line to him, "I love you like infinity" (mm. 595–97). And the visitor at the door (at the end of "The Visitors," mm. 599–600, p. 140), Anhalt relates, is death. The final section, "The Answer" tells a story of one walking on past life, and the body surrendering itself to nature. Here the *tikkun* concept is expressed in words and music. Anhalt describes this climactic point in the opera in the following:

> I have tried to say so much (in text and music) in this ca. 35–40 minute work, taking it even as far as the moment of a death, which I conceive here as being the reintegration of the self, reduced here to its most elementary particles in the universe ... What is certain is that the "human" gives way to a transformation which takes the procedural "form" of a merging ... we become dust, once again, awaiting perhaps in billions of years another cosmic miracle and some of our residue could, just might, once again be part of a "life" ... But human life? This is ridiculously too unrealistic (i.e., improbable) to expect to happen! The odds are astronomically against it.[23]

As Anhalt relates, in "The Answer" he was attempting to "compose" the puzzle of death, our final creative act as human beings. Through "The Answer," the tempo of the music gradually slows down, textures become thinner, the voice becomes fainter, and one senses the underlying message of this drama in a powerful way. The musical sounds are enhanced by the harmonics in the strings, creating an otherworldly atmosphere in which the human body gradually surrenders itself. Words (e.g., "I'm ready ... There is nothing, nothing else left to do ... I obey and move along feeling extremely light ... with things melting into a blur of grey") and sounds gradually diminish until the final page of the score, where the voice, accompanied only by claves (wooden blocks), gradually disappears following a series of detached utterances. The "voice" that wondered if anyone was there (see plate 9-2 – "Is someone here ... speaking? ... I'm listening") ceases to exist (see plate 9-5).

PLATE 9-5 István Anhalt, *Traces (Tikkun)* (1994), "The Answer" (X), mm. 648–54, score page 156, with kind permission of the composer.

As can be seen in the foregoing examples, Anhalt makes use of a multiplicity of musical styles in *Traces (Tikkun)*, including a wide orchestral palette of instrumental colour, a range of rhythms and tempi, tonal and tonal harmonic idioms, and enormous textural variety. Inevitably, these musical parameters are linked to each other and are inspired by the opera's narrative. In particular, Anhalt's use of the voice throughout *Traces (Tikkun)* is unique. Instead of drawing on some extended vocal techniques in the manner of composers such as Stockhausen or Trevor Wishart, his vocal discourse is actually more rooted in ideas and the diverse domains of prosody (intensity, rhythm, speed, intonation, inflection, etc.), which he had studied on a sabbatical leave (1976–77) while attending Professor J.L.M. Trimm's classes in articulatory phonetics and prosody at Cambridge University. At that time, he also visited Dr. John Laver of the University of Edinburgh, an expert on voice quality, and Dr. David Crystal of Reading University, an eminent authority on prosody, thereby expanding his growing interest in aspects of prosody and their deployment possibilities in a musical composition.[24] In *Traces (Tikkun)*, Anhalt builds on this background, creating a dramatic work that contains affective use of vocal and orchestral writing that serves well the elements of the opera's dramatic situations. As with *La Tourangelle* and *Winthrop*, and *Millennial Mall (Lady Diotima's Walk)*, the "performance" of *Traces (Tikkun)* invites the audience into an imaginary world of the protagonist's "voices," underlining Anhalt's predilection for exploring the expressive potential of the voice as a musical *and* dramatic instrument:

> In this single voice, a self and numerous others are made to co-exist, hence the appellation of the work as a "pluri-drama." Through this I aimed to portray the reciprocal interactions of two existential dimensions, those of a self and its "others," in a single mind, through a single voice. The compositional aim, which amounts also to a challenge to the audience, was to create a succession of implied scenes/situations that would endeavour to decipher the identity (or the "type") of the implied others, as well as the time and the place (the chronotope) of the action. Through this device of the "many in one" I aimed at placing an entire chain of events (the traces) in the mind of a single person (and in a single voice). From the angle of this objective the number of actual protagonist-singers had to be one. The textures of the orchestral layer aim at mirroring the multifaceted work of the mental process and the many features of the "situations."[25]

To return to Anhalt's four operas, there is what one could call an "ethical quest," which is connected to the selection of the operas' themes, the belief systems of their protagonists, and their respective societal contexts. Considering again Bakhtin's "chronotope" idea, we might say that Anhalt's various searches for the past are also searches for the present. Times and places are close to each other, and stories from the past are also stories about now. Different landscapes merge, and travel becomes more like a metaphor for knowing than a concept of movement across places and through time. Casting back to Clifford's dualism, *roots* and *routes* can, indeed, collapse into each other. In *Traces (Tikkun)*, travel and translation connect to Anhalt's life story in subtle, and at times not so subtle, ways. In this work, there are no defined historical or literary starting points or contexts, as in the other three operas. Centres and peripheries in *Traces (Tikkun)* are inspired by Anhalt's life story, and the work stands as a moving creative statement with respect to the representation of life experience.

In a talk preceding the 1996 premiere of *Traces (Tikkun)*, Anhalt made reference to the Austrian writer Robert Musil, who asked: "How did I come to be myself?" As much as one can interpret this question in personal, individualized ways, Anhalt's probe here also challenges us to respond to his music as a means to understanding identity processes as shared human experience. And it reminds us of the vital theme of displacement in Anhalt's work. Anhalt *came to be himself* as an artist—and as a human being—through processes of migration and displacement. As well, we may note the conflation of "centres" and "peripheries," "roots" and "routes," and the importance of *memory* (see example 9-2) as pivot points in this discussion. Finally, we have seen the critical importance of the listener in *Traces (Tikkun)*, an importance we can say extends to all of Anhalt's music. What stands out in *Traces (Tikkun)*, though, is that the audience is "invited in" to an imaginary world of life experiences at the very beginning of the opera. What also stands out is the importance of Anhalt's "voice" in and through the work. Considering that importance, I can't help but think that his opening line in *Traces (Tikkun)*, which Robin Elliott and I used as an epigram for *Pathways and Memory*—"Is someone here ... speaking? I'm listening"— positively assures us of an identity and a presence that is distinctively Anhalt. In a telling and moving way, these words also might be interpreted as paralleling Anhalt's question to the monk at the Salesian monastery in Esztergom in 1944, cited in the narrative at the opening of this paper: "Father, I am a musician and haven't had the opportunity in months to play my instrument, the piano. Is there a piano in the house? Could I play it for a short while?"

Notes

1. The title of this paper is a paraphrase of James Clifford's book title, *Routes: Travel and Translation in the Late Twentieth Century* (Cambridge, MA: Harvard University Press, 1997). Readers may also want to consult my article, "From New France to a 'Millennial Mall': Identity Paradigms in Istvan Anhalt's Operas," *American Music* 24/2 (2006): 172–93. Parts of that text are included in this paper with the permission of the editor of *American Music*. In this text, I have expanded the discussion in the *American Music* article based on further study and interactions with István Anhalt, specifically about his life experiences as they intersect with his opera *Traces (Tikkun)*. As always, I am sincerely grateful to István for sharing his moving life stories with me, and for allowing me to write about them in this way.
2. This excerpt is taken from Anhalt's recently published account on the pivotal role played by the Superior of the Salesian Order in Budapest, János Antal, in saving Anhalt's life following his escape from the forced labour camp of which he was a part in the Second World War. See Anhalt, "Antal, János" in *The Righteous among the Nations,"* ed. Mordecai Paldiel (Jerusalem: Jerusalem Publishing House and Yad Vashem, The Holocaust Martyrs' and Heroes' Remembrance Authority, Jerusalem, Israel, 2007), 15–17. For a revealing account of the Hungarian labour camp context in this period, see Judit Pihurk's article "Hungarian Soldiers and Jews on the Eastern Front, 1941–1943," *Yad Vashem Studies* 35 (2007): 71–102.
3. These dates include the periods Anhalt worked on the composition of each opera. The second date in each parenthesis is that of the first performance.
4. See Anhalt's article "*Thisness*: Marks and Remarks" in *Musical Canada: Words and Music Honouring Helmut Kallmann* (Toronto: University of Toronto Press, 1988), 211–31, for the libretto and the composer's commentary on the work.
5. Anhalt to Beckwith, unpublished letter, 2001. Anhalt Fonds, National Library.
6. This is an important concept in Anhalt's work, and one which he uses as a theme in his text, "A Continuing Thread ... Perhaps," in *Istvan Anhalt: Pathways and Memory*, ed. Robin Elliott and Gordon E. Smith (Montreal and Kingston: McGill-Queen's University Press, 2001), 433–44. (See note 14 below.) "Chronotope" means literally "time-space" with no priority to either dimension. As Bakhtin puts it: "In the literary artistic chronotope, spatial and temporal indicators are fused into one carefully thought-out concrete whole. Time, as it were, thickens, takes on flesh, becomes artistically visible; likewise space becomes charged and responsive to movements of time, plot and history" (Bakhtin, "Discourse in the Novel," in *The Dialogic Imagination*, ed. Michael Holquist [Austin: University of Texas Press, 1981], 84).
7. István Anhalt, "Music: Context, Text, Counter-text," *Contemporary Music Review* 5 (1989): 113.
8. Doreen Massey, "Places and Their Pasts," *History Workshop Journal* 39 (1995): 188.
9. See, for example, Clifford's article "Spatial Practices: Fieldwork, Travel, and the Disciplining of Ethnomusicology," in *Routes: Travel and Translation in the Late Twentieth Century*, 52–91.

10 Ibid., 3.
11 Gordon Smith, "Deep Themes Not So Hidden in the Music of István Anhalt," *Queen's Quarterly* 98/1 (1991): 99–119.
12 Ethnomusicological models with respect to fieldwork (i.e., interaction with human subjects) and reflexivity concepts come to mind here. See, for example, Tim Cooley's "Casting Shadows in the Field: An Introduction," 3–19, and Jeff Todd Titon's article, "Knowing Fieldwork," 87–100, both in *Shadows in the Field: New Perspectives for Fieldwork in Ethnomusicology*, ed. Gregory R. Barz and Timothy Cooley (New York: Oxford University Press, 1997). For updates and other fieldwork perspectives, readers may wish to consult the second edition of this collection (2008).
13 See Alan Gillmor's "Echoes of Time and the River," and William Benjamin's "Alternatives of Voice: Anhalt's Odyssey from Personalized Style to Symbolic Expression" in *Istvan Anhalt: Pathways and Memory*, 233–307, for probing discussions of the different ways the theme of Judaism is treated in Anhalt's orchestral pieces *Simulacrum* and *SparkskrapS*.
14 Pressured by a stringent time frame set by the Canadian Opera Company for the commission to compose the opera, this project was eventually abandoned for a series of reasons. The complete Oppenheimer libretto is in the Anhalt Fonds in the National Library in Ottawa. Parts of the correspondence between Anhalt and the COC are also in the Anhalt Fonds in the National Library.
15 Gershom Scholem, *Kabbalah* (New York: Quadrangle, 1974), 140.
16 Ibid., 152.
17 For links with Anhalt's earlier compositions, see his "A Continuing Thread … Perhaps" in *Istvan Anhalt: Pathways and Memory*, 433–44.
18 On a more pragmatic, but no less interesting, level is the ongoing dialogue between Anhalt and American composer George Rochberg. The two first met at the International Conference of Composers held in Stratford, Ontario, in 1960 and developed a deep friendship that has extended for over forty years. Their correspondence (in the Anhalt Fonds at the National Library of Canada in Ottawa) is the subject of a recent book by Alan M. Gillmor, *Eagle Minds: Selected Correspondence of Istvan Anhalt and George Rochberg 1961–2005* (Waterloo, ON: Wilfrid Laurier University Press, 2005). In addition to this source, Rochberg reflects on his long friendship with Anhalt and on other topics (links and differences in the two composers' respective backgrounds, politics, Jewish identity) in his essay "Reflections on a Colleague and a Friend" in *Istvan Anhalt: Pathways and Memory*, 355–63.
19 Istvan Anhalt, "An Operatic Triptych," in *Istvan Anhalt: Pathways and Memory*, 370–71.
20 Ibid., 370.
21 Ibid., 386.
22 Anhalt to Rochberg, 7 September 1995, in *Eagle Minds*, 297–98. Anhalt's correspondence with George Rochberg contains a number of informative discussions on *Traces (Tikkun)*, both in terms of its genesis and critical intellectual identities, and its place within the broader contexts of Anhalt's life and creative work. See *Eagle Minds*, 272–74, 277–78, 284–86, 297–98, 308–9, 322–25.
23 Anhalt to Rochberg, 7 September 1995, in *Eagle Minds*, 298.

24 Anhalt discusses aspects of vocal techniques in twentieth-century music in his book *Alternative Voices*; see also his article, "Composing with Speech," in *Proceedings of the Seventh International Congress of Phonetic Sciences* (Paris: Mouton, 1972), 447–51.
25 Anhalt, "An Operatic Triptych," 389. See also "On the Way to *Traces*: A Dialogue with the Self," in *Istvan Anhalt: Pathways and Memory*, 400–11, which is the text of a solo "dialogue" about *Traces (Tikkun)* presented by Anhalt before its premiere in 1996.

Bibliography

Anhalt, István. *Alternative Voices: Essays on Contemporary Vocal and Choral Composition*. Toronto: University of Toronto Press, 1984.
———. "Antal, János." In *The Righteous among the Nations*, edited by Mordcai Paldiel, 15–17. Jerusalem: Jerusalem Publishing House Ltd. and Yad Vashem, The Holocaust Martys' and Heroes' Remembrance Authority, Jerusalem, Israel, 2007.
———. "A Continuing Thread ... Perhaps." In *Istvan Anhalt: Pathways and Memory*, edited by Robin Elliott and Gordon E. Smith, 433–44. Montreal-Kingston: McGill-Queen's University Press, 2001.
———. "Music: Context, Text, Counter-text." *Contemporary Music Review* 5 (1989): 101–35.
———. "On the Way to *Traces*: A Dialogue with the Self." In *Istvan Anhalt: Pathways and Memory*, 400–11.
———. "An Operatic Triptych." In *Istvan Anhalt: Pathways and Memory*, 369–99.
———. "*Thisness*: Marks and Remarks." In *Musical Canada: Words and Music Honouring Helmut Kallmann*, edited by Frederick Hall and John Beckwith, 211–31. Toronto: University of Toronto Press, 1988.
Bahktin, Mikhail. "Discourse in the Novel." In *The Dialogic Imagination*, edited by Michael J. Holquist, 259–422. Austin: University of Texas Press, 1981.
Benjamin, William. "Alternatives of Voice: Anhalt's Odyssey from Personalized Style to Symbolic Expression." In *Istvan Anhalt: Pathways and Memory*, 164–307.
Clifford, James. *Routes: Travel and Translation in the Late Twentieth Century*. Cambridge, MA: Harvard University Press, 1997.
Cooley, Timothy J. "Casting Shadows in the Field: An Introduction." In *Shadows in the Field: New Perspectives for Fieldwork in Ethnomusicology*, edited by Gregory F. Barz and Timothy J. Cooley, 3–19. New York: Oxford University Press, 1997.
Gillmor, Alan M. *Eagle Minds: Selected Correspondence of Istvan Anhalt and George Rochberg 1961–2005*. Waterloo, ON: Wilfrid Laurier University Press, 2007.
———. "Echoes of Time and the River." In *Taking a Stand: Essays in Honour of John Beckwith*, edited by Timothy J. McGee, 15–44. Toronto: University of Toronto Press, 1995.

Massey, Doreen. "Places and Their Pasts." *History Workshop Journal* 39 (1995): 182–92.
Pihurik, Judit. "Hungarian Soldiers and Jews on the Eastern Front, 1941–1943." *Yad Vashem Studies* 35 (2007): 71–102.
Scholem, Gershom. *Kabbalah*. New York: Quadrangle, 1974.
Smith, Gordon E. "Deep Themes Not So Hidden in the Music of István Anhalt." *Queen's Quarterly* 98/1 (1991): 99–119.
———. "From New France to a 'Millennial Mall': Identity Paradigms in Istvan Anhalt's Operas." *American Music* 24/2 (2006): 172–93.
Titon, Jeff Todd. "Knowing Fieldwork." In *Shadows in the Field: New Perspectives for Fieldwork*, 87–100.

TEN

Le fonds István-Anhalt (MUS 164) à Bibliothèque et Archives Canada : auto-construction du compositeur et rôle du lieu dans son œuvre

RACHELLE CHIASSON-TAYLOR

LE FONDS ISTVÁN-ANHALT (MUS 164) conservé à Bibliothèque et Archives Canada (BAC) est une source primaire privilégiée pour l'étude des différentes facettes de la vie personnelle et professionnelle du compositeur, et il permet de suivre sa longue et productive carrière. Ce fonds figure parmi les plus importantes acquisitions de BAC dans le domaine de la musique classique canadienne contemporaine.

L'organisation conceptuelle du fonds a été revue entre 2001 et 2004. Le chercheur y découvrira de nombreux documents sur l'émergence de ce fondateur de la musique électronique au Canada, les étapes de la genèse de plusieurs de ses œuvres musicales, des écrits publiés et inédits, ainsi qu'une volumineuse correspondance avec le compositeur George Rochberg et plusieurs autres musiciens comme Glenn Gould, Jean Papineau-Couture, R. Murray Schafer, Milton Babbit, John Beckwith ou John Cage.

À ces témoignages d'intense activité créatrice s'ajoute la chronique émouvante d'un émigré-immigrant : ses racines hongroises et sa culture musicale d'origine, sa survie à la destruction engendrée par la Seconde Guerre mondiale, son départ vers le Canada et enfin sa grande implication dans la vie culturelle canadienne.

Dans cet essai, nous ferons d'abord un bref historique du fonds et un recensement des plus récents versements consentis par le compositeur, ce qui constituera une mise à jour du chapitre d'Hellmut Kallmann paru en 2001 dans l'ouvrage *Istvan Anhalt : Pathways and Memory*[1]. Dans un deuxième temps, nous présenterons quelques conceptions de la musicologie archivistique, puis nous exposerons les grandes lignes de ce qui nous semble émaner du fonds István-Anhalt.

Historique du fonds et recensement des versements après 2001

Les négociations entre le compositeur et la Division de la musique de l'ex-Bibliothèque nationale du Canada[2] ont débuté en 1984, année où Anhalt prit sa retraite de l'Université Queen's. Les premiers versements de documents sont effectués en mars 1985. Selon Hellmut Kallmann, directeur de la Division de la musique à l'époque, « L'acquisition originale fut suivie d'un bon nombre de versements ultérieurs, chacun comprenant une grande variété de matériel tel que de la correspondance, des partitions, des esquisses, des enregistrements sonores, des notes de cours, du matériel promotionnel, des photos, ainsi que des objets et documents relevant de diverses activités autres que celles que nous venons de mentionner »[3]. En 1988, le fonds s'enrichit de cinq compositions récentes, totalisant 1087 pages : *Winthrop, Thisness, Simulacrum, SparkskrapS* et *A Wedding Carol*. Un autre versement, transféré en 1993, inclut un abondant matériel ayant servi au projet de l'opéra *Oppenheimer*, dont Anhalt écrivit le livret (à l'époque du versement de 1993, le matériel musical d'*Oppenheimer* se limite à quelques esquisses). Les esquisses et manuscrits de l'opéra *Millenial Mall* sont ajoutés au fonds István-Anhalt au printemps 2000. Depuis, sept versements ont été enregistrés, dont des éléments importants de la correspondance, passionnante, entre Anhalt et le compositeur américain George Rochberg, correspondance qui a récemment fait l'objet d'un recueil publié sous la direction d'Alan Gillmor[4]. L'avant-dernier versement date d'août 2006 et contient, entre autres, les manuscrits de *The Tents of Abraham, ... the timber of those times ... (... a theogony ...)* et *Four Portraits from Memory*. Le plus récent versement date de 2009.

À l'heure actuelle, le fonds contient des archives datées des années 1890 à 2008 et comprend 14,47 mètres linéaires de documents textuels, 2 292 photographies, 112 diapositives, 51 négatifs, 211 bandes sonores, 15 cassettes sonores, 2 disques sonores, 8 disques compacts, 1 bande vidéo et 2 disquettes numériques. Depuis le dernier recensement fait par Helmut Kallmann en 2001, le cadre de classement et l'organisation conceptuelle du fonds ont été considérablement modifiés, passant de douze à neuf séries, ces dernières comprenant plusieurs sous-séries, sous-sous séries et dossiers[5]. En voici un bref tour d'horizon.

MUS 164/A : DOCUMENTS PERSONNELS ET BIOGRAPHIQUES. — 1927-[199-]. Notes biographiques, journaux intimes, passeports, certificats, calendriers annotés, bulletins scolaires, lettres de recommandation (Zoltán Kodály, Louis Fourestier, etc.). Les nombreux dossiers contenant des recherches généalogiques (correspondance, notes, arbres généalogiques, brochures, plans et cartes géographiques, ainsi que le manuscrit de l'essai *An Interim Account of My Search for Genealogical Information Pertaining to My Family's Background*, dédié aux membres de sa famille) démontrent l'intérêt du compositeur pour ses origines.

MUS 164/B : CORRESPONDANCE PERSONNELLE ET PROFESSIONNELLE. — 1923-2006. Le compositeur, comme l'a précisé Kallmann[6], a entretenu une correspondance avec plusieurs musiciens, dont Luciano Berio, György Ligeti, George Rochberg (env. 20 cm linéaires de documents textuels pour ce dernier), Nadia Boulanger, John Cage, Glenn Gould, Karlheinz Stockhausen, John Beckwith, Pierre Mercure, Jean Papineau-Couture, Clermont Pépin, R. Murray Schafer, John Weinzweig, Edgard Varèse, Gilles Tremblay, Bruce Mather et Per Nørgård. La série est composée des sous-séries MUS 164/B1 (Correspondance familiale); MUS 164/B2 (Dossiers alphabétiques); MUS 164/B3 (Correspondance générale) et MUS 164/B4 (Lettres de recommandation).

MUS 164/C : ENSEIGNEMENT ET ADMINISTRATION. — 1949-1988. Les nombreuses activités d'Anhalt en tant que pédagogue et administrateur, d'abord à l'Université McGill puis à l'Université Queen's, sont recensées dans cette série de documents. Quelques dossiers relatifs à son enseignement à l'Université d'État de New York à Buffalo s'y trouvent également. La série est formée des sous-séries MUS 164/C1 (Université McGill); MUS 164/C2 (Université Queen's); MUS 164/C3 (Université d'État de New York à Buffalo) et MUS 164/C4 (Varia).

MUS 164/D : ŒUVRES MUSICALES. — [194-]-2000. Cette série de documents témoigne des activités de composition d'István Anhalt ainsi que du cheminement de sa pensée musicale depuis ses premières œuvres, conçues au début des années 1940. Documents de recherche, notes, ébauches et enregistrements sonores présents en très grande quantité illustrent le processus de création du compositeur et offrent un accès privilégié à la genèse et aux transformations de ses œuvres. On y trouve aussi des copies manuscrites de *Missa* (László Gyopár) et d'une partie de l'ouverture d'*Obéron* de Carl Maria von Weber. La série comprend les sous-séries MUS 164/D1 (Musique de scène et multi-média); MUS 164/D2 (Orchestre); MUS 164/D3 (Musique de chambre); MUS 164/D4 (Piano); MUS 164/D5 (Chœur ou voix); MUS 164/D6 (Musique électroacoustique) et MUS 164/D7

(Varia). Le contenu de cette série et de ses sous-séries est organisé en ordre chronologique.

MUS 164/E : DOCUMENTS RELATIFS AUX ŒUVRES MUSICALES. — 1948-2000. Enrichissant le matériel musical originel, sont abondamment documentées les activités relatives à la réception des œuvres musicales (concerts, promotion, etc.), ce qui permet de retracer leur évolution. Cette série contient, entre autres, de la correspondance, des contrats, des rapports, des journaux intimes, des programmes de concerts, des notes de programmes, des horaires, des notes, des dessins, de la publicité, des périodiques et des coupures de presse.

MUS 164/F : ÉCRITS. — 1943-2000. István Anhalt a en outre écrit de la prose et de la poésie. Plus de vingt textes sont publiés, parmi lesquels l'ouvrage d'envergure *Alternative Voices: Essays on Contemporary Vocal and Choral Composition*[7] et l'essai *Music: Context, Text, Counter-Text*[8]. En 2001 paraît *István Anhalt: Pathways and Memory*, sous la direction de Robin Elliott et Gordon E. Smith, incluant quatre articles du compositeur[9]. Parmi les nombreux essais inédits citons l'impressionnant *A Weave of Life Lines*, comprenant 528 pages manuscrites, une description détaillée des expériences vécues par le compositeur depuis son enfance jusqu'aux années 1990[10], et l'émouvant et poétique *The Bridge : A Parable*[11]. La série est composée des sous-séries MUS 164/F1 (Écrits d'István Anhalt) et MUS 164/F2 (Écrits de collègues et d'amis).

MUS 164/G : AUTRES ACTIVITÉS ET INTÉRÊTS. — 1939-1999. Cette série illustre les multiples intérêts et activités d'István Anhalt : recherches sur la musique électronique et contemporaine, linguistique, sémiologie, techniques vocales et religion. Elle témoigne aussi de ses activités à la Ligue canadienne des compositeurs, à l'Association canadienne des écoles universitaires de musique, à la Société internationale pour l'éducation musicale et à l'Université Western Ontario. On y retrouve principalement de la correspondance, des procès-verbaux, des rapports, des notes, des textes, des listes de membres, des programmes de concerts, des dépliants et des coupures de presse.

MUS 164/H : PHOTOGRAPHIES. — [ca 1890]-2000. Le fonds István-Anhalt contient de très nombreuses photographies, représentant principalement le compositeur, des membres de sa famille et diverses personnes auxquelles il est lié personnellement ou professionnellement. Sont inclus de nombreux clichés de répétitions et de concerts. On y trouve également des photographies de spectrogrammes et d'appareils électroniques ayant servi à l'élaboration de ses œuvres électroacoustiques. La série est formée des sous-séries MUS 164/H1 (Famille); MUS 164/H2 (Autres personnes); MUS 164/H3 (Œuvres musicales) et MUS 164/H4 (Varia).

MUS 164/I : ENREGISTREMENTS SONORES. — [196-?]-1990. La série contient des enregistrements sonores archivistiques, c'est-à-dire non commerciaux, d'œuvres d'István Anhalt (*Electronic Composition*s, n° 2-4, *La Tourangelle, Winthrop*) ainsi que des œuvres d'autres compositeurs. La série est composée des sous-séries MUS 164/I1 (Œuvres musicales); MUS 164/I2 (Conférences et interviews) et MUS 164/I3 (Varia).

La musicologie archivistique : quelques réflexions

Dans l'essai qui sert d'introduction à son ouvrage sur la musicologie archivistique, le musicologue britannique Andrew Wathey écrit que plusieurs générations d'historiens ont défini la place des archives en rapport avec les philosophies qui leur ont servi de modèle pour leur compréhension de l'Histoire[12].

Par exemple, l'historien allemand Leopold von Ranke (1795-1886), réagissant à l'historicisme moralisateur de son époque, se donna comme mission de valoriser la preuve documentaire et d'élever le document archivistique au statut de texte presque sacré[13]. Sous son influence est née, dès les années 1850, une puissante école d'historicisme positiviste, encore vivante aujourd'hui malgré les sévères critiques dont elle a fait l'objet dans les années 1960 par l'historien britannique Edward Hallett Carr : « Le dix-neuvième siècle, obsédé par la preuve, s'appuyait sur les documents sources pour nourrir son obsession. Les documents archivistiques étaient devenus l'Arche de l'Alliance dans le temple des faits »[14].

Plusieurs musicologues semblent ignorer le cheminement critique auquel ont abouti les débats en histoire et en historiographie. Bien entendu, la conjugaison de l'esthétique et de l'histoire, caractéristique de l'étude des objets musicaux, ne saurait échapper à une pensée critique tenant compte de la nature de ces objets[15]; c'est sans doute pourquoi les musicologues préfèrent suivre à une distance respectueuse les débats soulevés par la critique littéraire[16]. Il n'en reste pas moins que les documents d'archives ne relèvent pas de simples « faits » : dans les disciplines historiques, on reconnaît l'importance du contexte, même si en 1983 un musicologue a pu affirmer haut et fort, dans la plus pure tradition rankéienne : « les documents d'archives [...] dès le départ, auront comme but premier d'enregistrer les faits de façon purement objective »[17]. Rien n'est à mon avis plus éloigné de la réalité : le document comme son contexte doivent absolument être considérés avec circonspection et exhaustivement pour être en mesure de participer à la construction d'un savoir. Le document ne recèle pas une réponse directe à la question posée par le chercheur, quoique plus la question soit complexe, plus le document d'archives soit en mesure de parler[18] !

Selon le musicologue Rob C. Wegman, l'attitude de Roger Bowers reflète la « pensée d'antiquaire » qui a dominé la musicologie archivistique britannique et anglo-saxonne durant une grande partie du XXe siècle[19]. Selon cette musicologie d'antiquaire (*musical antiquarianism*), l'information essentielle d'un document réside dans l'objet, dans le texte lui-même[20]. Le travail du musicologue consiste simplement à découvrir le texte, à le rendre accessible en le transcrivant et à laisser les faits parler d'eux-mêmes. Une découverte sensationnelle équivaut ainsi à un *document* sensationnel, et l'histoire de la musique est censée s'écrire sur la base d'une série de documents de ce type.

Selon Andrew Wathey, nous devons « repenser » les critères et méthodes de traitement et d'interprétation des documents d'archives, car une certaine tradition musicologique, qu'il qualifie de « monumentaliste », inspirée d'une approche canonique des sources musicales, a imposé des conditions restrictives à leur usage. Dans cette tradition, les sources musicales dont le taux de survie reste assez faible sont considérées comme de véritables reliques, ce qui nuit à la compréhension des cultures musicales antérieures[21].

L'histoire de la musique reste cependant fondée principalement sur l'histoire du *style musical*, ce qui est révélateur d'un désir de ne pas s'écarter du texte musical. Les archives ne sont alors que les outils d'un révisionnisme historique musical, non les témoins de nouvelles directions[22].

Les caractéristiques physiques d'un fonds d'archives peuvent impressionner l'imaginaire et la conscience du chercheur. Un grand fonds d'archives bien organisé et cohérent apparaîtra ainsi très attirant de prime abord, mais ces qualités superficielles peuvent cacher un manque de continuité historique. Par ailleurs, la présence dans un fonds de documents variés et bien classés peut conduire le chercheur à croire que les documents parlent d'eux-mêmes et ne requièrent aucune interprétation. Le Fonds Istvan-Anhalt pourrait offrir un danger de ce type.

Ces diverses considérations nous amènent à réfléchir à ce qui *émane* d'un fonds. Cette notion d'émanation relève-t-elle – à l'inverse des excès du positivisme archivistique dont nous venons de parler – de la fantaisie et de la pure invention ? Certes, elle semble loin de l'objectivité de la preuve documentaire. Nous savons par ailleurs, en tant qu'archivistes, historiens, musiciens et musicologues, qu'une multiplicité de facteurs et de conditions contribuent à la construction d'une historiographie, à la narration historique ou à l'échafaudage d'une personnalité réputée avoir influencé le cours de l'Histoire.

En fait, ce qui émane d'un fonds d'archives dépend avant tout de son créateur. Il n'existe pas une seule et unique façon, un seul « style » pourrait-on dire, de verser ses documents à une institution dont le mandat est de préserver la mémoire collective d'une nation. Certains ne se soucient guère de leur héritage documentaire, le laissant dans son intégralité au bon jugement de leur succession. D'autres, à l'inverse, éliminent presque toute trace de cheminement personnel, ne conservant que les éléments ayant déjà eu une influence sur le public par la publicité ou la littérature secondaire. D'autres enfin – nettement plus rares – veulent construire un fonds d'archives à leur image, afin qu'il reflète leurs idées et leurs orientations. C'est à cette dernière catégorie qu'appartient István Anhalt.

Anhalt et son œuvre : sentiers de la construction de soi

István Anhalt a livré à Bibliothèque et Archives Canada une documentation surprenante, permettant au chercheur de découvrir sa vie et son œuvre sur une matrice de déchirure et de quête identitaire. Cette quête – ainsi que son thème sous-jacent, la découverte des croyances et des traditions de l'autre – est échafaudée sur le désir de quelque chose d'on ne peut plus immatériel : la transcendance. Dans cette section, nous allons illustrer cette position grâce à quelques exemples.

Dans le fonds István-Anhalt, plusieurs documents sont accompagnés d'explications fournies par le compositeur : une organisation conceptuelle a présidé à leur versement. Anhalt a pris soin, par exemple, de dactylographier sur de petits cartons des descriptions très détaillées du contenu visuel ou textuel de ses documents. Affaire de narcissisme ? On ne saurait le lui reprocher. Fort désir d'être compris ? Sans doute. Mais ce qui émane avant tout de ce souci de précision de la part d'Anhalt, c'est une quête titanesque de sens et d'identité. En somme, son souci d'auto-construction est ici tout à fait palpable.

La rupture familiale (1925), l'expérience douloureuse de la Seconde Guerre mondiale, l'expatriation vers le Québec (1949), la construction d'une carrière de compositeur et de pédagogue (y compris son travail de pionnier de la musique électroacoustique dans un contexte institutionnel au départ récalcitrant), la fondation d'une famille, le spectre de la violence à Montréal lors de la crise d'Octobre 1970, le départ vers Kingston (1971), la quiétude retrouvée et la retraite sereine (1984) : tous ces jalons biographiques sont mis en relief dans le fonds. Il en émane une quête de sens, une sourde angoisse de l'expérience et une gratitude profonde, traces formant comme autant de sillons entrelacés.

Dans ce fonds, les œuvres musicales sont accompagnées d'une abondante correspondance et d'écrits personnels; leurs versions finales sont précédées de très nombreuses esquisses. Le chercheur peut ainsi en suivre de près la genèse et saisir le sens des interventions qui en limitent ou en élargissent la portée.

À titre d'exemple, prenons le solo n° 3 (pour baryton lyrique) de la première partie de *Tikkun (Traces)*, son « pluri-drame » achevé en 1995. Les esquisses musicales des figures 10-1, 10-2 et 10-3 sont contenues dans deux dossiers différents, de même que les esquisses textuelles des figures 10-4 et 10-5. Lues en lien avec la correspondance du compositeur – dont nous insérons des extraits entre les figures 10-1, 10-2 et 10-3 d'une part et les figures 10-4 et 10-5 d'autre part –, ces esquisses nous permettent de mieux saisir son cheminement intellectuel, artistique et symbolique. Sa musique vocale tardive, particulièrement cette œuvre profondément marquante pour lui qu'aura été *Tikkun*, a été échafaudée d'abord sur les textes. On voit très clairement qu'Anhalt les a mis en musique avant d'ajouter d'autres éléments comme l'accompagnement orchestral, qu'il les a rédigés avant de concevoir un schème musical dans lequel les insérer.

Dans une lettre à George Rochberg datée du 14 juillet 1993, Anhalt offre un bilan très précis des progrès de *Tikkun* : « Je terminerai cette ébauche dans une semaine. L'œuvre sera fortement condensée. Mon estimation est qu'elle sera réduite d'environ 35 % en coupant, sans égard pour le sang qui en coulera, tous ces mots que je considère comme "littérature" plutôt que "livret"[...]. Ainsi, à mon avis, la pièce durera approximativement 35 minutes lorsqu'elle sera exécutée »[23]. Voilà qui ne laisse au lecteur aucun doute sur les derniers moments de rédaction de l'œuvre, ce que confirme l'examen des esquisses précédant la version finale.

Voilà aussi qui nous amène à souligner que l'exactitude émane non pas d'un document pris individuellement, mais de l'ensemble du fonds, grâce à la concordance entre ce qui est dit et ce qui est fait : auto-construction et souci de véracité se rejoignent.

Dans sa correspondance, outre le rôle prépondérant de la mémoire, le compositeur parle en abondance du thème de la réconciliation. La révision du manuscrit inédit de *Bridge* (Le pont), par exemple, se veut un poignant plaidoyer, un « cri du cœur » comme Anhalt écrira à Rochberg, pour la réconciliation entre les différentes cultures[24].

Les relations du compositeur avec les institutions canadiennes sont documentées dans les séries de correspondance professionnelle et d'activités pédagogiques, et on décèle dans ces séries la très grande préoccupation d'Anhalt pour la justesse d'une représentation publique de sa

FIGURE 10-1 István Anhalt, *Traces (Tikkun)* (1994), esquisse (1992-93), Bibliothèque et Archives Canada, MUS164/D1,98. Reproduit avec l'aimable autorisation du compositeur et de Bibliothèque et Archives Canada.

FIGURE 10-2 István Anhalt, *Traces (Tikkun)* (1994), esquisse (1992-93), Bibliothèque et Archives Canada, MUS164/D1,98. Reproduit avec l'aimable autorisation du compositeur et de Bibliothèque et Archives Canada.

FIGURE 10-3 István Anhalt, *Traces (Tikkun)* (1994), esquisse subséquente du passage présenté dans les figures 10-1 et 10-2, Bibliothèque et Archives Canada, MUS 164/D1,99. Reproduit avec l'aimable autorisation du compositeur et de Bibliothèque et Archives Canada.

pensée. Cette question pourrait faire l'objet d'une étude à part entière sur la représentation et la réception publiques de l'artiste dans le contexte social canadien.

Le rôle du lieu dans l'œuvre musico-dramatique d'István Anhalt

Le rôle que joue le lieu dans l'œuvre d'Anhalt nous semble particulièrement important, et c'est sur cela que nous terminerons. Ce thème rejoint celui de l'auto-construction du compositeur comme émigré-immigrant ainsi que celui de la réconciliation.

Se sentant obligé de quitter le Québec après la crise d'Octobre 1970, Anhalt embrasse avec passion une vie nouvelle, mais aussi un *genre* nouveau dans sa production : l'opéra. Il se servira de ce type de composition pour explorer le sens profond des contextes culturels. Dans *La Tourangelle* (1975), Anhalt creusera l'héritage qu'aura laissé au Québec Marie de l'Incarnation, une ursuline mystique, figure fondatrice de la Nouvelle-France. Il réalisera un travail similaire avec un autre opéra, *Winthrop* (1983),

FIGURE 10-4 István Anhalt, *Traces (Tikkun)* (1994), manuscrit de la page couverture (18 juillet 1993), Bibliothèque et Archives Canada, MUS164/D1,100. Reproduit avec l'aimable autorisation du compositeur et de Bibliothèque et Archives Canada.

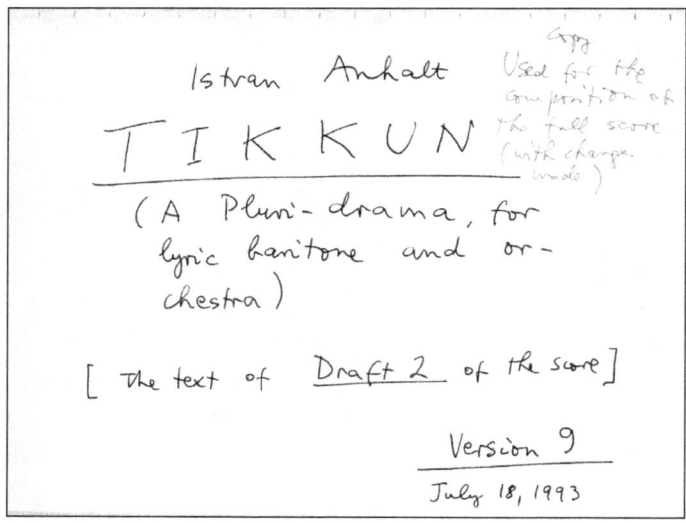

dont le livret est inspiré de la biographie d'une autre figure fondatrice, de la Nouvelle Angleterre cette fois, figure qu'Anhalt assimile à l'histoire canadienne-anglaise : le gouverneur anglais John Winthrop. Il continuera, infatigable, à creuser le souvenir de lieux et d'événements avec *Tikkun* (1995), qu'il dédiera aux victimes des violences du régime nazi et à ceux qui tentèrent de leur venir en aide. Il se rendra ensuite, toujours déterminé, aux confins du méta-lieu, voire de la méta-mémoire, avec les déambulations de Dame Diotima dans *Millenial Mall* (1999)[25].

Depuis son exil de Montréal en 1971, écho de son exil de Hongrie en 1949, Anhalt s'est occupé à défaire, fil par fil et au fil de ses œuvres musicodramatiques, toutes les pelotes qui formaient le nœud de son angoisse identitaire pré-kingstonienne. Le rôle du lieu et son importance chez le compositeur sont facilement analysables dans les éléments de correspondance et les écrits versés dans le fonds István-Anhalt. Kingston lui permet de « respirer intellectuellement », dit-il, de renouer avec son imaginaire historique, de retrouver en lui les mots pour dire l'importance de se retrouver là où il devrait être[26].

Figure 10-5 István Anhalt, *Traces (Tikkun)* (1994), corrections aux textes (version du 18 juillet 1993), correspondant aux passages musicaux des figures 10-1, 10-2 et 10-3, Bibliothèque et Archives Canada, MUS164/D1,101. Reproduit avec l'aimable autorisation du compositeur et de Bibliothèque et Archives Canada.

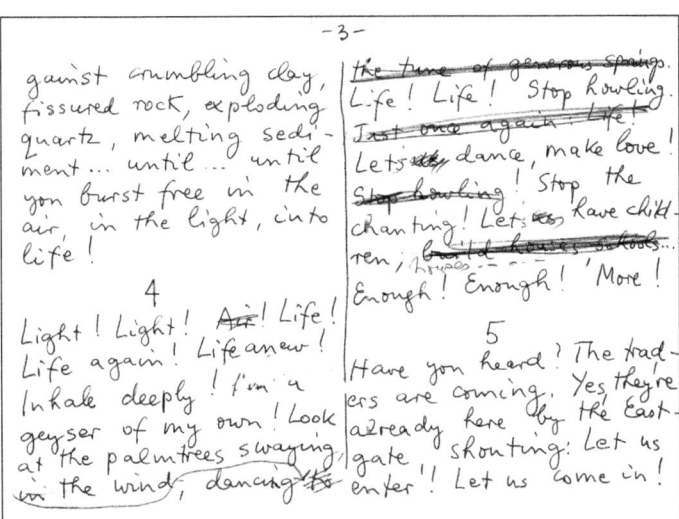

Notes

1. Hellmut Kallmann, « The Istvan Anhalt Fond », dans *Istvan Anhalt, Pathways and Memory*, sous la direction de Robin Elliott et Gordon E. Smith, Montreal & Ithaca, McGill-Queen's University Press, 2001, p. 342-354.
2. Le projet de loi canadien C-8, promulgué le 22 avril 2004, a conduit à la fusion de la Bibliothèque nationale du Canada et des Archives nationales du Canada. La Division de la musique de la Bibliothèque nationale du Canada, où se trouvaient les archives de compositeurs, a été relocalisée au sein de la nouvelle institution fusionnée, Bibliothèque et Archives Canada. Aujourd'hui, le fonds István-Anhalt relève de la Section de la Musique au sein de la Division des Collections spéciales et archives canadiennes de Bibliothèque et Archives Canada.
3. Hellmut Kallmann, *op. cit.*, p. 343.
4. Alan M. Gillmor (dir.), *Eagle Minds: Selected Correspondence of Istvan Anhalt and George Rochberg (1961-2005)*, Waterloo. ON, Wilfrid Laurier University Press, 2007.
5. On se référera, comme nous l'avons fait ici, à l'excellent instrument de recherche disponible sur le site Internet de Bibliothèque et Archives Canada, *Le Fonds István Anhalt* (consulté le 12 février 2009).
6. Hellmut Kallmann, *op. cit.*, p. 345-347.

7   István Anhalt, *Alternative Voices: Essays on Contemporary Vocal and Choral Composition*, Toronto, University of Toronto Press, 1984.
8   István Anhalt, « Music : Context, Text, Counter-Text », dans *Contemporary Music Review* 5, 1989, p. 101-135.
9   István Anhalt, « An Operatic Triptych in Multiple Texts »; « On the Way to *Traces*: A Dialogue with the Self »; « From "Mirage" to *Simulacrum* and "Afterthought" »; « Millennial Mall (Lady Diotima's Walk): A Voice-Drama for the Imagination », dans *István Anhalt: Pathways and Memory*, p. 369-445.
10 István Anhalt, texte manuscrit de *A Weave of Life Lines*, 1992-2000, Bibliothèque et Archives Canada, MUS164/F1,77 à F1,79.
11 István Anhalt, texte manuscrit de *The Bridge*, 1990-1991, Bibliothèque et Archives Canada, MUS164/F1, p. 76.
12 Andrew Wathey, « Musicology, Archives and Historiography », dans *Musicology and Archival Research: Colloquium Proceedings*, sous la direction de B. Haggh, F. Daelemans et A. Vanrie [Archief- en Bibliotheekwezen in België, extranummer 46], Bruxelles, Algemeen Rijksarchief, 1994, p.1-26.
13 Leopold von Ranke, *Geschichte der romanischen und germanischen Völker von 1494 bis 1514*, Leipzig, Duncker & Humblot, 1885. Dans ce premier ouvrage publié, Ranke affirme d'entrée de jeu que l'historien a le devoir de démontrer « wie es eigentlich gewesen » [ce qui s'est véritablement passé], en reléguant la littérature secondaire, aussi ancienne qu'elle soit, au deuxième rang, pour cibler plutôt les sources primaires. Ranke croyait que l'historien n'avait aucun mandat pour juger l'histoire, mais conférait quand même à ce dernier l'autorité d'en construire une narration qui refléterait l'ordre, et non le chaos, que Dieu voulait pour l'humanité. Cette narration devait être fondée sur l'examen des documents d'archives.
14 Edward H. Carr, *What Is History?*, New York, Knopf, 1962, p. 16.
15 Carl Dahlhaus, « The Significance of Art: Historical or Aesthetic? », dans *The Foundations of Music History*, traduit de l'allemand par J.B. Robinson, Cambridge University Press, 1997, p. 19-32. Je remercie le professeur Friedemann Sallis pour ses précieux conseils et pour cette proposition de référence.
16 L'exemple le plus frappant est la sémiologie musicale. Voir aussi diverses réflexions sur le nouvel historicisme littéraire en rapport avec la musicologie et les tendances en musicologie aux confins des XXe et XXIe siècles (incluant l'influence de Foucault) dans les ouvrages à essais tels *Disciplining Music: Musicology and its Canons*, sous la direction de Katherine Bergeron et Philip V. Bohlman, Chicago, University of Chicago Press, 1992, ou *Rethinking Music*, sous la direction de Nicholas Cook et Mark Everist, Oxford, New York, Oxford University Press, 1999.
17 Roger Bowers, « The Performing Ensemble for English Church Polyphony, c. 1320-c. 1390 », dans *Studies in the Performance of Late Mediaeval Music*, sous la direction de Stanley Boorman, Cambridge University Press, 1983, p. 164.
18 Le problème de la valeur du document archivistique en rapport avec l'histoire de la musique est débattu sous plusieurs formes et dans plusieurs contextes dans la littérature musicologique actuelle. Récemment, par exemple, Katharine Ellis a critiqué avec finesse un ouvrage portant sur des textes primaires journalistiques sur la musique au XIXe siècle; elle a affirmé que l'observation d'un matériau primaire volumineux n'exclut pas un point de vue com-

plètement déconnecté de son contexte. Voir Katharine Ellis, « L'écriture de la critique musicale au temps de Berlioz (review) », *Music and Letters* 88, n⁰ 2, 2007, p. 362-364. Un autre très bel exemple d'étude fondé sur des sources archivistiques porte sur la réception publique d'une créatrice de productions culturelles d'Annegret Fauser, « Creating Madame Landowska », dans *Women in Music : A Journal of Music and Culture* n⁰ 10, 2006, p. 1-23.

19 Rob C. Wegman, « Elaborating Themes : The Collaboration between Archivists and Historians », dans *Musicololgy and Archival Research : Colloquium Proceedings*, sous la direction de B. Haggh, F. Daelemans et A. Vanrie, p. 28.

20 Pour comprendre les origines plus lointaines de la « musicologie d'antiquaire » britannique, voir Mark Salber Phillips, « Reconsiderations on History and Antiquarianism: Arnaldo Momigliano and the Historiography of Eighteenth-Century Britain », *Journal of the History of Ideas* 57, n⁰ 2, 1996, p. 297-316. Cette orientation musicologique aurait incité par exemple Donald Tovey à affirmer, sur la base de sources primaires et avec la plus grande certitude : « Where Beethoven (or any other composer) could not make up his mind, the editor has no business to make it up for him ». Cité dans Edmund H. Fellowes, « Doubtful Readings », *The Musical Times* 72, n⁰ 1060, 1931, p. 536-537. Dans l'Europe francophone, la trace de cet héritage, qui a connu un véritable essor au XIXe siècle, particulièrement sous l'influence de Fétis, se retrouve dans la nomenclature de certains programmes universitaires en histoire de la musique, comme « Archéologie de la musique », et dans la spécialisation en archéologie musicale. Et, comme l'affirme Sophie Anne Leterrier, « Les termes de "musicologue" et de "musicologie" n'ont reçu droit de cité dans nos dictionnaires qu'à la fin du XIXe siècle et au début du XXe siècle. Pendant la majeure partie du XIXe siècle, on parlait plus volontiers de "science de la musique", "d'archéologie musicale", pour désigner la quête de la musique du passé *à travers ses vestiges* » (mes italiques). Voir Sophie Anne Leterrier, « L'archéologie musicale au XIXe siècle : constitution du lien entre musique et histoire », dans *Revue d'Histoire des Sciences Humaines* 14, n⁰ 1, 2006, p. 49-69.

21 Selon Andrew Wathey, la prédominance du manuscrit choral de Old Hall et du livre de chœur d'Eton, grands survivants parmi les textes musicaux de l'Angleterre pré-renaissante, a eu un effet pervers sur le reste de l'historiographie de la musique en Angleterre au XVe siècle. Voir Wathey, « Musicology, Archives and Historiography », dans *Musicology and Archival Research: Colloquium Proceedings*, p. 6.

22 *Ibid*.

23 Cité dans Allan Gillmor (dir.), *opus cité*, p. 273.

24 István Anhalt à George Rochberg, 3 octobre 1992, cité dans Allan Gillmor (dir.), *opus cité*, p. 263.

25 Néanmoins, l'avènement de productions culturelles de tous genres s'explique aussi concrètement, si l'on veut absolument se détacher de la psyché du créateur. Par exemple, ce fut une commande de la Société Radio-Canada, visant une œuvre centrée sur l'ordre et le sens qu'aura pu apporter la religion à la société canadienne dans l'imaginaire historique, qui aura fourni les conditions matérielles propices à la création de *La Tourangelle*.

26 Robin Elliott, « The Kingston Years, 1971–present », dans *István Anhalt : Pathways and Memory*, p. 66.

Bibliographie

Anhalt, István. *Alternative Voices: Essays on Contemporary Vocal and Choral Composition*. Toronto : University of Toronto Press, 1984.

———. « Music : Context, Text, Counter-Text », *Contemporary Music Review*, vol. 5 (1989), p. 101-135.

———. « An Operatic Triptych in Multiple Texts »; « On the Way to Traces: A Dialogue with the Self »; « From "Mirage" to Simulacrum and "Afterthought" »; « Millennial Mall (Lady Diotima's Walk): A Voice-Drama for the Imagination ». Dans *István Anhalt: Pathways and Memory*, sous la direction de Robin Elliott et Gordon E. Smith, Montréal & Kingston, McGill-Queen's University Press, 2001, p.369-445.

Bergeron, Katherine et Philip V. Bohlman, dir. *Disciplining Music: Musicology and its Canons*. Chicago : University of Chicago Press, 1992.

Bibliothèque et Archives Canada. Fonds István Anhalt (MUS164)/F1,77 à F1,79.

———. Fonds István Anhalt (MUS164)/F1,76.

———. *Le Fonds Istvan Anhalt* [en ligne]. Téléchargeable à partir du lien : http://www.collectionscanada.gc.ca/obj/028021/f2/01-f.pdf.

Bowers, Roger. « The Performing Ensemble for English Church Polyphony, c. 1320–c.1390 ». Dans *Studies in the Performance of Late Mediaeval Music*, sous la direction de Stanley Boorman, Cambridge University Press, 1983, p. 161-192.

Carr Edward Hallett. *What Is History?* New York : Knopf, 1962.

Cook, Nicholas et Mark Everist (dir.). *Rethinking Music*. Oxford ; New York : Oxford University Press, 1999.

Dahlhaus, Carl. « The Significance of Art: Historical or Aesthetic? ». Dans *The Foundations of Music History*, traduit par J. B. Robinson, Cambridge University Press, 1997, p. 19-32.

Ellis, Katharine. « L'écriture de la critique musicale au temps de Berlioz (review) ». *Music and Letters*, vol. 88, n°2 (2007), p. 362-364.

Fauser, Annegret. « Creating Madame Landowska ». *Women in Music: A Journal of Music and Culture*, vol. 10 (2006), p. 1-23.

Fellowes, Edmund H. « Doubtful Readings ». *The Musical Times*, vol. 72, n°1060 (1931), p. 536-537.

Gillmor, Alan M., dir. *Eagle Minds: Selected Correspondence of István Anhalt and George Rochberg (1961–2005)*. Waterloo, ON : Wilfrid Laurier University Press, 2007.

Gouvernement du Canada. Loi constituant Bibliothèque et Archives du Canada, modifiant la Loi sur le droit d'auteur et modifiant certaines lois en conséquence. Ottawa, 22 avril 2004.

Kallmann, Helmut. « The Istvan Anhalt Fond ». Dans *István Anhalt, Pathways and Memory*, sous la direction de Robin Elliott et Gordon E. Smith, Montréal & Kingston, McGill-Queen's University Press, 2001, p. 342-354.

Leterrier, Sophie Anne. « L'archéologie musicale au XIXe siècle : constitution du lien entre musique et histoire ». *Revue d'Histoire des Sciences Humaines*, vol. 14, n⁰ 1 (2006), p. 49-69.

Ranke, Leopold van. *Geschichte der romanischen und germanischen Völker von 1494 bis 1514*. Leipzig : Duncker & Humblot, 1885. Consultable en ligne à la page : http://www.archive.org/details/geschichtenderrooorankuoft.

Salber-Philips, Mark. « Reconsiderations on History and Antiquarianism: Arnaldo Momigliano and the Historiography of Eighteenth-Century Britain ». *Journal of the History of Ideas*, vol. 57, n⁰ 2 (1996), p. 297-316.

Smith, Gordon E. « The Kingston Years, 1971–Present ». Dans *István Anhalt : Pathways and Memory*, sous la direction de Robin Elliott et Gordon E. Smith, Montréal & Kingston : McGill-Queen's University Press, 2001, p. 65-91.

Wathey, Andrew. « Musicology, Archives and Historiography ». Dans *Musicology and Archival Research: Colloquium Proceedings*, sous la direction de B. Haggh, F. Daelemans et A. Vanrie [Archief- en Bibliotheekwezen in België, extranummer 46], Bruxelles, Algemeen Rijksarchief, 1994, p. 1-26.

Wegman, Rob C. « Elaborating Themes: The Collaboration Between Archivists and Historians ». Dans *Musicology and Archival Research: Colloquium Proceedings*, sous la direction de B. Haggh, F. Daelemans et A. Vanrie [Archief- en Bibliotheekwezen in België, extranummer 46], Algemeen Rijksarchief, Brussels, 1994, p. 27-35.

Perspectives on Reception, Analysis, and Interpretation

ELEVEN

Sewing Earth to Sky: István Anhalt and the Pedagogy of Transformation

Austin Clarkson

> *How delicately*
> *The silver threads of rain*
> *Sew sky to earth.*
> —Bashō[1]

As composer, author, scholar, and educator, István Anhalt has amply demonstrated how the creative and the receptive interflow in a continuous process of renewal. He is as concerned with the relationship between the artwork (the text) and the conditions under which it is presented (the context) as with the outcome of the aesthetic experience (the counter-text). His compositions and writings weave text, context, and counter-text into a fabric of music, and words about music, that radiates seamlessly from the core of personal experience to the periphery of communal response and back again. Art is often pictured as raining down from supernal realms upon the passive audience below, but sewing involves motion in several directions, and Bashō's rain threads upwards as well as down. Anhalt's aesthetic, which holds that responding to art is as creative an act as making it, thus presents an extraordinary challenge to educators. In place of showering students with theories, facts, and skills, Anhalt insists on sewing earth and sky together in what we may call the "pedagogy of transformation." His musical works unfold a boldly personal quest for knowledge of Self and Other, while his commentaries on them exemplify in remarkable depth how to conduct the creative process itself.

Anhalt expects the listener to be as fully engaged in the act of reception as the composer is in fashioning the artwork and the musician in performing it: "What matters here is the process that changes text and its context into a compound new text, which, in turn, is 'read' in one, or another, still broader context, and so on seemingly without end."[2] He provides many examples of the form that responses may take—another piece of music, a probing analysis, a memoir, a poem, a story. While drawing on a capacious library of philosophy, anthropology, sociology, and psychology, Anhalt grounds his hermeneutic doctrine in the tradition of the Kabbalah. He cites Isaac the Blind, the thirteenth-century author, on the three degrees of manifestation of the text: primordial Torah that resides in the mind of God; written Torah, the potential, incipient form; and oral Torah, the embodied, enacted form.[3] Meaning arises at the confluence of all three levels: archetypal images from the primordial past, memories and experience from the here and now, and intimations of the not-yet-known. By way of analogy, it is the moment of illumination that T.S. Eliot depicts in a mandala-like garden:

> There they were as our guests, accepted and accepting.
> So we moved, and they, in a formal pattern,
> Along the empty alley, into the box circle,
> To look down into the drained pool.
> Dry the pool, dry concrete, brown edged,
> And the pool was filled with water out of sunlight,
> And the lotos rose, quietly, quietly,
> The surface glittered out of heart of light,
> And they were behind us, reflected in the pool.
> Then a cloud passed, and the pool was empty.[4]

Archetypal meaning hovers among the guests reflected in the pool, incipient meaning flows in as the pool fills with water, and embodied meaning blossoms with the lotos. Citing Paul Ricoeur, Anhalt notes that multiple interpretations decontextualize a text sociologically and psychologically, and that a particular act of reading recontextualizes the text.[5] The vital link is "the one who listens and responds." The act of responding initiates a counter-text, which forms the basis for another response, and so on in a chain reaction of aesthetic experience. Interpretations accumulate from multiple readings. Asserting the validity of personal revelation, Anhalt cites Isaac Luria, the Kabbalist of Safed: "Every word of the Torah has six hundred thousand 'faces,' that is, layers of meaning or entrances, one for each of the children of Israel who stood at the foot of Mount Sinai. Each face is turned toward only one of them; he alone can see it and decipher it."[6] For Anhalt, aesthetic interpretation is not the prerogative of the author or the expert critic, but is distributed among the attentive faithful. Because each individual has equal access to the text, each has a responsibility to participate in the reception of the artwork, in the construction of its meaning, and in the interrogation of its truth values. Thus, Anhalt is in the line of the spiritually informed pragmatism of William James, C.G. Jung, and John Dewey. Dewey held that aesthetic experience is not mere contemplation, for the viewer and the artwork merge in a procreative act that "marks a new birth in the world."[7] This tradition lives on in the so-called "rabbinical hermeneutic" of Hélène Cixous, for whom reading is as creative an act as writing: "Writing and reading are not separate. Reading is a part of writing. A real reader is a writer. A real reader is already on the way to writing."[8]

The purpose of art in Anhalt's Orphic philosophy is to alleviate the ills and suffering of humankind, and music that employs the voice has a privileged role, for the voice is "the most intimate musical means for expression."[9] The composer's songs offer an ethical template for the nurture and well-being of the community. The role of language is tied so intimately to music that Anhalt composed both the text and the music of his dramatic works. *La Tourangelle*, *Winthrop*, and *Traces (Tikkun)* treat the stories of emigrants who seek a homeland in the New World. Their spirituality is grounded in the cultures with which he came in contact on his journey: French Catholicism, English Puritanism, and Central European Judaism, respectively.[10] The fourth opera of the series, *Millenial Mall (Lady Diotima's Walk)*, portrays the cults of consumerism, youth, and the body and the absence of Eros.[11] Based on situations set in the past and present of his native and adoptive homelands, these compositions mark a path that has both an inner- and outer-directed trajectory. That path culminated in *Twilight~Fire*, an orchestral work on the story of Philemon and Baucis from Ovid's *Metamorphoses* (the aged couple whose devotion to each other and to the highest ethical principles was honoured by the gods). In Anhalt's words, "In this tale the reward of the old couple is contrasted with the calamity visited on their heartless neighbours, the folk who decided to ignore the imperatives of a prevailing *ethos*, thereby forfeiting their right to a viable community, an *ethnos*!"[12] In these works—as in *The Tents of Abraham*, which addresses the primordial roots of the present-day conflict between Israelis and Palestinians—the tension between *ethos* and *ethnos* pervades Anhalt's work. These dramas of *ethos* and *ethnos* take place in a "memory space" that admits myth, legend, oral history, written history, literature, and "one's personal past."[13] He formulates the goals of personal individuation and social utopia in terms of "*Tikkun*," the Kabbalist notion of the restoration of the original perfection and unity of the universe. An epigraph at the head of the score of *Traces (Tikkun)* assigns to each individual a role in this task: "and the crucial turning-point in this cycle takes place within man, at the moment he begins to develop an awareness of his own true essence and yearns to retrace the path from the multiplicity of his nature to the Oneness from which he originated."[14] This is a ceaseless quest for transformation: "The essence here might not be looked for so much in the finding, but instead, in the frame of mind of never giving up searching for it, yearning after it."[15]

In commenting on *Tikkun*, Anhalt refers to Martin Buber's notion that the individuation process depends on acts of dialogue.[16] Indeed, Anhalt's aesthetic is remarkably consonant with Buber's humanistic Hassidism and the centrality of dialogue. The dramatic works are neither historical pageants nor veristic dramas, but moral parables in which spiritual dialogues (*I-Thou*) counterpoint with mundane dialogues (*I-It*). According to Buber, "mutuality is the door into our existence."[17] Failures of mutuality from which arise the suffering of persecution, exile, and loss of soul are redeemed when the *I* renews reciprocity with the *Thou*. The core theme of *Tikkun* is "the dialogical relationship between people, as distinct from, &/or complementary to, the monological one."[18] In *Millennial Mall*, the dialogue is between the inhabitants of the mall and Diotima, the avatar of Love. She posits "an alternate view of life, the self, the lines/bonds that bind 'selves' (like friends, for example) together and also suggests hints how to be at peace with the 'nearby' as well as with the 'great beyond.'"[19] Dialogue is the modality of individual redemption (dialogue within) and social renewal (dialogue without).

Fredric Jameson distinguishes two views of Utopia: the revolutionary that wants to change human nature from without, and the transformative that seeks to change human nature from within. The "radical transformation of subjectivity presupposed by most revolutions" imposes a "mutation in human nature and the emergence of whole new beings." On the other hand, the approach from within assumes that "the impulse to Utopia is already grounded in human nature." Jameson warns that neither strategy is sufficient. "Resolution in either direction would be fatal for Utopia itself"; the former would lead to totalitarianism, and the latter would draw too close to "current, everyday reality," for it would forfeit its "claim to any radical transformation of the system itself."[20] Anhalt would disagree with Jameson on the last point, for he claims that the endogenous capacity for individuation has the potential for transforming the individual and ultimately society. But where Buber insists on a transcendent deity as the ultimate *Thou*, Anhalt turns to Jung's concept of the Self as the totality of the human personality. The essay "Music: Context, Text, Counter-text" (the continuation of "Text, context, music") begins with a quote from Jung on psychological projection: "Projections change the world into the replica of one's unknown face ... What, then, is this projection-making factor? The East calls it the 'Spinning Woman'—Maya, who creates illusion by her dancing."[21] The "inward movement" of Arachné, the master-weaver of the imagination, leads Anhalt to the Prado Museum and the experience of viewing *Las Hilanderas (The Spinners)* by Velázquez. He weaves a richly allusive "counter-text" from the resonances between the local time-space of the here-and-now and the archetypal depths of the painting's symbolism. The essay continues with a typology of a vast repertoire of vocal works written after the Second World War. To the intricate web of categories, Anhalt affixes dozens of compositions from Berio and Birtwistle to Schafer and Stockhausen, including his own operas. It is a multi-focal, multi-dimensional network of interpretations that delineates the topography of his capacious mind.

Let us return to the web-spinning factor of projection. According to Jung, projection is the process by which an unconscious quality or content of the subject is thrown onto an outer object and perceived and reacted to by the subject as though that quality or content belongs to the object itself.[22] Through projection, the subject identifies with qualities in the object and, by so doing, bonds with it. Viewing an artwork that evokes projections constellates an inter-subjective space that is alive with images and feelings.[23] Standing in front of the Velázquez painting, Anhalt models how to let the creative imagination convey to consciousness sensations and feelings, memories and incipient portents. Reflecting on these projections enabled Anhalt to recognize some aspect of himself that he had not known before—his "unknown face." Such encounters widen the ego's horizon with intimations of what is not yet known of the totality of the psyche. It is an awesome experience that, for want of a better word, is often described as spiritual. For Anhalt it was the influx into consciousness of contents that seemed to come from beyond the ego, from some "not-I." In a further expansion of the web, Anhalt imagines a thread that links the interpretations of all those who have stood before that canvas during past centuries with all those to come. It is an ecstatic participation in the shared "currents of recognition, a sense of solidarity, empathy and, finally, understanding." The picture "metamorphosed into a symbolic mirror ...

showing in a sharp light a part of the topography of this painter's mind,"[24] and, Anhalt infers, of his own.

Jung referred to the channel that the creative imagination activates between the primary process of the unconscious and the secondary process of conscious ego-awareness as "the transcendent function."[25] He developed a therapeutic technique for enhancing the flow of images that he called "active imagination." He discovered that the spontaneous products of the activated imagination embody the highest expression of a person's individuality and "may even create that individuality by giving perfect expression to its unity."[26] Many artists, Anhalt among them, have found how to activate the imagination in service of the creative process. While composing *Tikkun*, he said that he had no "consciously thought-out purpose;" it was "just one more act of the sleepwalker."[27] During the terrifying scenes, he found himself in a heated argument between his "silent self and [his] characters." Conducting a dialogue between partial personalities is a basic technique for activating the imagination. Indeed, as Anhalt said, "That is how the opera grew."[28] Through documenting the creative process and commentaries on the resulting works, Anhalt leaves a rich record of the unfolding drama of individuation and provides a model for the pedagogy of transformation.

Activating the Imagination in the Classroom

The challenge for educators is to harness the transformative potential of the creative imagination in the regular classroom. During the 1970s, I became concerned by the widening division between critical and experiential approaches to the arts and proposed a course for fine arts majors on the deep structure of the creative process. Foundations of Creative Imagination was offered as a two-semester course for the first time in 1984 with a team of instructors that included specialists in visual art, expressive movement, music, voice and storytelling, and the psychology of Jung.[29] The class of 1994–95 decided to stay together.[30] An exercise for activating the imagination while viewing a work of visual art was adapted for an interpretive exhibit in a major art museum. During the years of operation (1993–2003), tens of thousands of visitors sat in a booth titled "Explore a Painting in Depth," put on a headset, and listened to a twelve-minute exercise while viewing *The Beaver Dam*—a wilderness landscape by the Canadian painter J.E.H. MacDonald. The approval rating was overwhelmingly positive. Fifteen hundred visitors, representing dozens of nationalities, many professions, and all ages and educational backgrounds, left

Share Your Reaction Cards that described their experiences in words and drawings.[31] Visitors, who normally would spend a few seconds in front of a picture in a room full of artworks, discovered that twelve minutes of focused viewing greatly intensified the experience. Many reported that the canvas, which at first seemed dull and boring, came alive. The projection-making factor filled the "inter-subjective" zone between the viewer and the painting with intense images, felt meanings, and an experience of bonding with the artwork. One visitor wrote that the painting "became a part of me and I a part of it." Another: "Art is also the EXPERIENCE, giving a whole new dimension to it." Many said that the exercise had a spiritual effect: "There is power and spirit in this painting that I never even glimpsed before sitting down. Communion." Another: "Est une oeuvre spirituelle—une prière pour la nature." Another: "Listening to the choir of nature & dancing with my spiritual self. THIS IS FREEDOM."[32] Some wrote that they had forgotten that they had an imagination, or didn't know they had one. When aesthetic experience engages the mind, body, and spirit, we know that the transcendent function has become a conduit for a dialogue in images and feelings between the ego-system and the Self-system. The disparate parts of the personality seem to unite with past memories and future portents in a state of plenitude and wholeness. The exhibit in the art gallery provided proof of Anhalt's contention that aesthetic experience is an opportunity for a transformative dialogue between the ego and the Self, and that the counter-texts of words and/or drawings contribute to the reception history of the artwork.

Activating the Imagination with Sound

The pedagogy of transformation calls for engaging the deep structure of the creative process in various aesthetic media. A program for activating the imagination through music was conducted during the fall of 1996 with four graduate students. The seven weekly three-hour sessions consisted of exercises in performing and listening to music and other exercises that were conducted mainly in silence. The sessions were tape-recorded and the discussions were transcribed. The participants were interviewed on the overall effects of the program four to six weeks after it ended. Participant A was a Canada-born master's candidate in holistic education with no musical training. Participant B was a US-born master's candidate in women's studies and music and was a trained singer. Participant C was a Hong Kong-born PhD candidate in musicology who played the zheng. Participant D was a Canada-born PhD candidate in musicology who was also a professional pianist. All were female. I shall discuss three of the exercises.

Exercise 1: Fantasy Journey[33]

The instructor gives a brief relaxation, and then guides the participants on an imaginary journey to leave the classroom and go to some place in the country. After they arrive, they look around, then sit on the ground. They put an ear to the ground and listen for sounds coming from the earth. After a while they get up and imagine a hill or mountain in the distance from which comes a beautiful sound. They go to find its source. The exercise lasts about fifteen minutes and concludes with a pre-arranged signal. The participants record the experience using crayons and paper, and share the results with the group.

Exercise 2: Silent Solo-Silent Duet[34]

Silent Solo: Participants sit in pairs face to face, knees almost touching. They are asked to imagine a musical solo. After about six minutes they record the experience with crayons and paper, then exchange with the partner. Silent Duet: The pairs resume sitting face to face and are asked to imagine a musical duet with the partner. After about six minutes, they record the experience using crayons and paper, and then share with the group.[35]

Exercise 3: Phoneme Fantasy

(1) Vocalizing: Participants voice vowels and consonants while moving about, letting the sounds shape their postures and gestures. (2) Group improvisation: Participants improvise a melody using any and all phonemes. The improvisation comes to an end of its own accord. (3) Phoneme Fantasy: The participants select a letter. After a brief relaxation, they imagine that the letter is entering the body and transforming. The exercise concludes after about fifteen minutes with a pre-arranged signal. They record the experience using crayons and paper and share with the group.

Results

The following gives the responses of the four participants to Exercise 1; of Participants B and C to Exercise 2; and Participants A and D to Exercise 3.

Exercise 1: Fantasy Journey

A imagines going to a place that she has visited—Galliano Island off the west coast of Canada. She smells the evergreens in the forest and walks to the beach, where there are big rounded rocks. She sits on a grassy spot overlooking the ocean and feels the warmth of the sun. When she puts her ear to the earth, she hears a deep hum, solid, comforting, and sustaining. She then hears powerful, contrasting sounds of the wind blowing and waves crashing against the rocks. She notices the difference between the vastness and power of the water and the solidity and restfulness of the earth. When she goes to the mountain, she feels a sound energy like a tuning fork, or a bell with one sustained clap. The mountain reaches to the sky, and she feels like moving in the same way—digging into the ground and reaching up, spiralling down and up. She notes the contrast between the spiralling energy and the energies of the earth, wind, and water. When she hears the signal to return, she lingers, wanting to bring back a sense of the seawater and the smells of the forest. She leaves the lower right of the picture blank for something new, a sense of discovery.

Initially B thinks of going to a known place by the sea, but then decides not to and finds herself in a flat hayfield with a single tree. It is sunny with a few clouds in the sky. She sits down under the tree. The shade is welcome, because the day is very warm. She puts her ear to the ground and hears sounds like wind chimes, but much richer. There is no mountain to be seen, because the land is so flat, so she turns to face the tree and listens. The sound of the tree comes from far below and is much deeper than the sound from the ground. She feels as though her body is expanding. She steps into the tree and is surrounded by the bark, senses the roots of the tree and where the grass has been worn away. When she hears the signal to conclude, she does not want to leave. When she starts to return, she goes part way while remaining inside the tree. She drew the scene within a white circle to approximate the form of a mandala.

C goes to a place that recalls her Chinese heritage. It is a dry riverbed surrounded by high cliffs. The river once had a lot of water, but there is a drought. The day is cold and cloudy, but not windy. A larger-than-life-size statue of the Buddha is carved into the cliff, and there are trees with lateral branches and leaves as in a Chinese painting. She walks on the riverbed. When she puts her ear to the ground, she hears the tinkling of tiny droplets of water that quickly become a flood gushing towards her with a deafening roar so loud that she can't bear it. She looks for a hill, sees a sand dune, and hears a loud resonance like a thousand horses racing and people fighting. She climbs to the top of the dune and sees a crescent-shaped lake with water that is turquoise and murky. Suddenly she hears a voice loudly reciting a poem that she had learned as a child: "Nice grapes, nice wine in a jade bowl, which is so translucent you can see through it. And I want to drink from it while sitting on a horse playing the pi-pa. And then if you see someone lying down and sleeping in a battlefield all filled with sand, don't laugh. Ask yourself a question: How many of these people in historic times will return after the battle?" When she hears the signal to return, she does not want to leave. She lingers, walking backwards so that she can continue looking at the scene. Eventually she realizes that she has to walk forward, so she turns around and comes back.

D goes to a rural scene near her childhood home. She sits on her favourite rock in a forested area with a brook and swampy ground. She puts her ear to the earth and hears a very low rumbling sound that she thinks must be water flowing deep underground. It has a low kind of hum, a comforting "mmm-aahhh" sound. From the hill in the distance she hears the sound of a bell. The meandering path to the sound is difficult and winds through trees, past a meadow and a pond. She arrives to find an old wooden chapel and an old man pulling the rope of the bell. The sound of the bell echoes in the distance and draws animals—squirrels, foxes, deer—from all over the place to come and meet there too. The scene is so wonderful and smells so good—the wood, the trees, the grass—that she does not want to leave. She returns very quickly without looking back.

Exercise 2: Silent Solo-Silent Duet

The participants did the exercise with different partners at three meetings. On the third occasion B was partnered with C, and A with D. C's solo was as follows: She is sitting in meditation on a beach while watching the sun giving out its last radiance. She hears low sounds from water flowing and splashing on the sand and from the moving air. The sounds are very rhythmic, in a regular metre. A row of wristwatches suggests the passage of time, and a series of picture frames represent scenes of her life from the past to the present. She feels very content and at peace, as there is nothing that she wants to go back and redo in her life. B described her solo as follows: She first imagines a very high sound, like the sound of Tibetan bells, but it is from her own voice; then she hears very low, grounded sounds, like Tibetan monks chanting. The sounds, which were very far above and below, now are centred in her body. The sounds are shooting out from every pore of her skin in the form of lights of different colours. The sound is more like a vibration than music as such.

After exchanging their accounts of the Silent Solo, B and C proceed with the Silent Duet. Knowing that B is a vocalist, C imagines high-pitched, legato strings playing an accompaniment. She imagines that B responds by singing melodious phrases, which C accompanies heterophonically. To add interest, she changes the harmony while B continues to sing. The duet continues pleasantly, until it is suddenly interrupted by several bolts of lightning and thunder. The earth flips inside out, the red magma from inside the earth flowing out and the oceans flowing in to fill the empty sphere. The continents hang on the inside walls of the sphere. The shock of this vision stops her imagining the duet. After she collects herself, C hears fearful, dissonant sounds, including shrieks from wild animals. She is glad when the exercise ends, as she did not like being so out of control. Meanwhile, B imagines an ostinato, "dum-di-daya," that continues during the whole exercise. She feels the ostinato in her body as a kind of rocking motion. She hears a different rhythm from her partner that disappears. She feels very rooted in her ostinato, which is constantly transforming. She is then playing in an orchestra, remaining centred in her ostinato while accompanying her partner, who is sounding the rest of the orchestra.

Exercise 3: Phoneme Fantasy

Participant A chose the letter *A*: The sound at first is a sigh of pleasure, "aaahh," on getting into a bath. But then a bolt of lightning blows everything into fragments, cracks things open, shakes things up. She shrieks, "AAAAHHH!" The *A* transforms once more into the "aha!" of a new idea, as if turning on a light bulb. The fantasy ends with the image of screwing a light bulb into the earth, which brings the pleasant feeling that warring, disparate things are now working harmoniously together. Participant D chose the letter *O*: The shape of the letter brings memories of childhood games with a beach ball and of rolling downhill inside a tire. The *O*s become very small and enter her body through her ears and mouth. The *O*s flow through her body in tiny droplets of sound energy, like blood running through her veins. She recognizes that many parts of her body are in the shape of *O* (eyes, mouth, head, etc.). The fantasy concludes with her whole body enclosed in the *O* while she gives birth to the *O*.

These narratives display a remarkable combination of uniquely personal imagery with archetypal motifs. In general they have a basic dramatic form: the initial condition is answered by an opposing condition (the reversal or *peripeteia*), and the working out (the contest or *agon*) resolves the opposing factors in a new condition (the denouement or *lysis*). In A's Phoneme Fantasy the "aahh" of getting into the bath and the shriek of alarm at the lightning strike are opposed aspects of the phoneme *A*. The contest, which A described as a "duel to the death," resolves into the "aha!" of a new idea, an image of harmony between light (the bulb) and darkness (the earth). The resolution for A was the discovery that opposed feeling states can coexist, which is OK. Participant B's Fantasy Journey took place in a hayfield beside a solitary tree, where the opposing elements were the sounds from the earth and from the tree. The working out resulted in her body merging with the tree, while the denouement was an ecstatic state of being the tree. The experience was so awesome that she did not want to return. Participant C's Fantasy Journey began in a dry riverbed, where she heard tinkling sounds of tiny droplets of water. The reversal was a terrifyingly loud flood of water. The water motif resolved in the calm of the turquoise lake, while the turbulent sounds of the flood continued in the sounds of battle and horses' hooves. The resolution came in a voice declaiming a poem from childhood that brought opposing factors into a new equilibrium: drinking wine, playing music, and riding a horse while recalling the outcome of a battle. Participant D's Fantasy Journey began with a scene remembered from childhood. The opposing sound elements were the low, comforting hum of the earth and the tolling bell from the mountain. The working-out was the long, difficult trek to the chapel, while the resolution was the discovery of a place of spiritual peace and harmony where animals were also gathering. C's Silent Duet narrative did not achieve resolution. The harmonious duet she imagined with her partner was interrupted by a terrifying image of the earth turning inside out accompanied by dissonant sounds. The *agon* did not resolve, and C was glad when the exercise ended. A resolution might have occurred had the exercise lasted longer than six minutes.

With the exception of the Silent-Duet of C, the exercises left the participants with feelings of peace, fulfilment, and even awe. As with the other active-imagination exercises, synesthesias are commonplace, such as when sounds are imagined as streams or fountains of coloured lights emanating from the body. As in the reports of the Silent Solo-Silent Duet exercise, sense modalities merge in remarkable and novel combinations. Sounds combine with visual, tactile, and proprioceptive sensations in reports of the weather, lighting conditions, colours, odours, textures, and physical postures and gestures. The feeling tone of the images ranges from joy and happiness to anxiety and fear, but with few exceptions the narratives conclude with feelings of wonder and awe such that participants wish the experience would not end. While the narratives share common features, the details are always uniquely personal.

The Phoneme Exercise contacts the sounds of language at a pre-verbal level. The phoneme *A* manifested as a series of exclamations: the sigh of pleasure, "aahh," the shriek of alarm, "AAAHHH!" and the "aha!" of a new idea. The letter *O* began as fun-filled play with a beach ball and rolling down a hill inside a tire, then transformed into tiny particles of sound energy that travelled through the body. The resolution was being enclosed in the *O* while giving birth to the *O*, a conjoining of opposites in an overarching unity. The participant was left with the feeling that she was both possessed by and worshipping the essence of the letter *O*.

During the debriefing sessions each participant concluded that the program had been transformative. A said that the most important outcome of the program was the discovery of the transpersonal dimension of communication, and that this brought her a new understanding of community. B remarked that the Fantasy Journey exercise in particular had been transformative: "It's not like I could just step out of that experience and come back as I was before. I came back transformed by it."[36] The program in general taught her to let go of her fear of facing the blank sheet of paper and responding to the impulse of the moment. She learned how to go with "the lack of intent" and to trust "an emptiness inside from which something comes." She experienced the transpersonal as "something bigger than me that includes me." She also remarked on the spiritual aspect of the program, which had renewed the importance of going into the unknown, and of "the non-judgmental waiting for things to arise."[37] During the debriefing, D recalled the Phoneme Fantasy with the letter *O*:

> It was a primal feeling of oneness. The circuitry of it makes me think of connections with the earth, the sun, time, the cycle of the seasons that keeps returning. You know what, it was almost like a mode of worship. I know that sounds bizarre. It was like a ritual to the god 'O,' an acknowledgment that that essence exists. You know, like a shaman will take on the personality of an animal. In a sense, I felt it was a ritual in which I took on that 'O,' and I think that's why I can't identify it as a specific emotion. It was more an experience.[38]

D said that she would have liked to do the exercise again with other letter sounds: "It would be that aha! feeling that I knew it was in me all the time, but I never acknowledged it, or had words for it." She trusted that such images existed in the unconscious and could be contacted by activating the imagination. Most important, the program had reconnected D with music, from which she had become alienated during her doctoral studies:

> I guess that what I can really say in summary is that I felt it was within me and music was a part of who I was, who I am. And that the decision wasn't such a hard one, in a sense that it wasn't a decision I needed to make outside myself. The music was already there, and it was a question of just letting go, and relaxing, and letting it happen. And it didn't seem to matter then whether it was academic, or whether it was performing, or studying it through symbols, or whatever.[39]

The program for activating the creative imagination had transformative effects, which confirms Buber's idea of "the presentness and immediacy of the *I-Thou* relationship." Buber regarded art as one of the forms of the *I-Thou* relationship: art exists as art only when the created form is taken up into the meeting of I and Thou and not only when it is left as a detached object of observation and analysis.[40] The artwork is bodied forth "into the world of *It* ... able to be experienced and described as a sum of qualities." When the creative imagination of the listener is activated, "it can face the receptive beholder in its whole embodied form."[41] Or as Anhalt stated by way of explaining "Tikkun": "It represents 'a making into a whole' from fragments something that may have been a whole before, but subsequently has fallen apart."[42]

In the Silent Solo-Silent Duet exercise, the playful invention of musical actions brought feelings of intense mutuality and reciprocity. Because A was not musically trained, she found that imagining a duet with another person was difficult at first. As she became more familiar with the exercise, she was deeply affected by the communication that transpired with successive partners:

> It was like something inside me kind of shifted so that I was able to still have that part of myself and send it to the other person, but also be able to receive from that other person in my imagination. But just the awareness of doing a duet with somebody changed the whole communication process, because rather than my idea coming out, and then their idea coming over to me, instead of having two separate things, it became a third thing, and also just one thing.[43]

It was not a simple two-way exchange of information, but took place within a larger transpersonal container for the *I-Thou* experience. For A, this was the discovery of a new concept of how to relate to another person and to the community. It "creates a kind of sacredness about life or about the connection between people ... a whole other stance of what community is. And it is totally the unseen world."[44] Restoring the inner dialogue between the ego and the Self transformed the outer relationship between Participant A and her community.

The Pedagogy of Transformation

Beneath Anhalt's accounts of his creative process, commentaries on his works, and the works themselves flows an urgent critique of the place of the arts in the culture at large.[45] His Orphic aesthetic is directed to restoring through art the dialogue between the ego and the Self and between the Self and Others. In remarks on *Traces (Tikkun)* he notes the reciprocity that links the knowledge of oneself and the knowledge of others: "There might also be a causal connection between the two: the better I understand myself, the greater is the likelihood that I will understand others." Achieving such understanding is the goal of an education directed to the lifelong task of individuation: "This process, from the self to the other, or in the reverse order, is being played out as long as the thinking person lives. This knowledge, acquisition, retention, erosion, mutation, and so on, persists to the end of one's life."[46] The role of the creative process is to reveal this "process of self-discovery" through a sustained dialogue between the ego and the Self. The work "serves as a mirror, image, an echo, telling the maker about the appositeness of a preceding act." The work mirrors the unknown face of the maker: "The writer interacts with the reflections that the work in the making sends back, as a sort of mirror."[47] The work and its maker become "their own reflected 'other.' This reflected (and re-reflected) other is the *simulacrum* that helps writers to make a new 'trace'—a new work, a new phase in their ongoing *carmen perpetuum*."[48] The fundamental idea of *Traces (Tikkun)* is of an individual in dialogue with his component personalities: "the reciprocal interactions of two existential dimensions, those of a self and its 'others,' in a single mind, through a single voice."[49] Anhalt looks on his successive compositions as tracings of the ever-unfolding "perpetual poem" of his life. And with that image he lays out a template for a pedagogy of transformation that begins with discovering the interrelationship between the *I-Thou* within and the *I-Thou* without.

The task of striving for *Tikkun* that underlies Anhalt's life's work finds an antecedent in Buber's program of transformative education. Buber draws a distinction between teachers who impose themselves on someone, and those who help someone to unfold. His educator lives in a world of individuals, each of whom is "in a position to become a unique, single person, and thus the bearer of a special task of existence which can be fulfilled through him and through him alone." Each person is engaged in a process of actualization that is a constant struggle with countervailing forces. The educator does not impose himself, for he believes that the actualizing forces must work themselves out, for "in every man what is right is established in a single and uniquely personal way."[50] The theory and practice of transformative pedagogy have won many advocates during the last two decades.[51] They challenge the school of Jean Piaget, who regarded the "magical thinking" of children as a phase that leads to cognitive processes that are relatively free of symbolic representations.[52] Similarly they oppose cognitive psychologists, who are interested in the re-creative and reproductive functions of the child's imagination but not its creative and productive capacities.[53] Cognitivists regard creativity as a product-oriented, outer-directed, and expert-assessed activity. They think that art is the rational rearrangement of known contents, and believe that artworks have explicit, discursive meanings established by authors and critics. The cognitive view of art pays little attention to the transformative power of aesthetic experience.

Anhalt models a pedagogy that is based on activating the creative imagination and engaging the deep structure of the creative process and, by doing so, mobilizing the dialogue between the ego and the Self. At first we experience the "I" as fixed, self-consistent, unified, and identical with itself.[54] Activating the creative imagination throws up images and feelings that the "I" experiences as coming from some "not-I." And yet the "I" is in no doubt as to the authenticity of these expressions. After formulating the images and feelings in some expressive medium, the "I" reflects on the meaning of these metaphors from the "not-I." As the "I" discerns their import, it acknowledges the value of maintaining an open channel to the "not-I." The "I" and "not-I" are then subsumed in a more inclusive, resilient, and differentiated conscious standpoint. According to Wolfgang Giegerich, the conscious dialectic between the ego and the Self is not a static structure, but a fluid process and performance. The dialectic between the "I" and the "not-I" leads to the awareness of a larger entity within which the dialectic is taking place. This is the "third thing" of which Participant A spoke after the Silent Duet, and of which Participant B said after the

Fantasy Journey that she felt "something bigger than me that includes me." The "third thing" is the ambience of the transcendent function, within which relationship to the Other within and the Other without is achieved and individuation proceeds. Anhalt attests that the interplay between inner reality and outer reality is a crucial factor in his creative process: "What was yesterday an 'exteriority,' through absorption becomes an 'interiority' a (shorter/longer) while later." A new text emerges from a dialogue with himself, and when the work is completed he feels transformed: "I feel I am no longer the same person as the one who pencilled in an early draft."[55]

I conclude with a set of concepts that form the basis for a program of transformative teaching and learning: (1) creativeness is a drive directed to the realization of the innate potential of the individual; (2) activating the creative imagination in various expressive media bridges the primary process of the unconscious and the secondary process of conscious ego awareness in the tertiary process, the so-called transcendent function; (3) the images, feelings, thoughts, sensations, memories, and portents evoked by the activated creative imagination are adaptive and homeodynamic and further the individuation process; (4) discovering correspondences between emergent personal symbols and symbol systems of cultures past and present develops a symbolic attitude, thus bringing inner, personal reality into relation with outer, consensual reality; (5) developing the *I-Thou* dialogue within furthers the *I-Thou* dialogue without. Engaging in the creative process generates mutual understanding and reciprocity in the community.

István Anhalt has lived his career according to the imperative that the individual has a responsibility to maintain a continual communion between the ego and the aesthetic Self in order to strive for *Tikkun* in the individual and in society at large. I close with the hope that this essay will lead to a fresh appreciation of Anhalt's *carmen perpetuum* and the principles of transformative teaching and learning that he so richly and valuably exemplifies.

Notes

1   Quoted in R.H. Blyth, *Haiku*, vol. 3 (Tokyo: Hokuseido Press, 1981), 722. This haiku appeared also as the epigraph to "Between the Keys: Istvan Anhalt Writing on Music," my contribution to *Istvan Anhalt: Pathways and Memory*, ed. Robin Elliott and Gordon E. Smith (Montreal & Kingston: McGill-Queen's University Press, 2001), 324. There, it provided an image for the special relationship in Anhalt's oeuvre between speech, speech about music, and music itself.

2 Anhalt, "Text, Context, Music," *Canadian University Music Review* 9/2 (1989): 11.
3 Ibid., 5.
4 T.S. Eliot, "Burnt Norton," *The Complete Poems and Plays 1909–1950* (New York: Harcourt, Brace, 1952), 118.
5 Anhalt, "Text, Context, Music," 14.
6 Ibid., 18.
7 John Dewey, *Art as Experience* (New York: Minton, Balch, 1934; repr. New York: Capricorn Books, 1958), 267.
8 Hélène Cixous, *Three Steps on the Ladder of Writing*, trans. S. Cornell and S. Sellers (New York: Columbia University Press, 1993), 20.
9 Anhalt, *Alternative Voices: Essays on Contemporary Vocal and Choral Composition* (Toronto: University of Toronto Press, 1984), 267.
10 Anhalt, "An Operatic Triptych in Multiple Texts," in *Istvan Anhalt: Pathways and Memory*, 370.
11 Anhalt, "Millennial Mall (Lady Diotima's Walk): A Voice-Drama for the Imagination," in ibid., 457–64.
12 Anhalt, "Twilight~Fire (Baucis' and Philemon's Feast)," address to the Eastern Ontario Regional Seminar, 2008, of the Academies of Arts, Humanities and Sciences of Canada at Queen's University, 5 April 2008. With thanks to Prof. Anhalt for a copy of the address.
13 Anhalt, "On the Way to *Traces*: A Dialogue with the Self," in *Istvan Anhalt: Pathways and Memory*, 403, 410.
14 One of the epigraphs at the head of the score of *Tikkun*. Quoted in G. Scholem, *Kabbalah* (New York: Quadrangle, 1974), 152.
15 Anhalt, "On the Way to *Traces*," 411.
16 Ibid., 401.
17 Martin Buber, "Postscript" to *I and Thou* (New York: Scribner, 1958), 131.
18 Anhalt, "Letter to George Rochberg (20 January 1994)." In *Eagle Minds: Selected Correspondence of Istvan Anhalt and George Rochberg*, ed. Alan Gillmor (Waterloo, ON: Wilfrid Laurier University Press, 2007), 277.
19 Anhalt, "Letter to George Rochberg (15 June 1998)," in ibid., 344.
20 Frederic Jameson, *Archaeologies of the Future: The Desire Called Utopia and Other Science Fictions* (London: Verso, 2005), 168.
21 Anhalt, "Music: Context, Text, Counter-text," *Contemporary Music Review* 5 (1989): 101.
22 Andrew Samuels, Bani Shorter, and Fred Plaut, *A Critical Dictionary of Jungian Analysis* (London: Routledge and Kegan Paul, 1986), 113–14.
23 Buber founded his philosophical anthropology of dialogue on the notion of the "inter-human" and of "meeting." See the essays "Distance and Relation" and "Elements of the Interhuman" in Martin Buber, *The Knowledge of Man* (New York: Harper and Row, 1965).
24 Anhalt, "Music," 103.
25 C.G. Jung, "The Transcendent Function," in *Collected Works of C.G. Jung*, vol. 8 (Princeton, NJ: Princeton University Press), 67–91.
26 Jung, *Psychological Types*, in *The Collected Works*, vol. 6 (Princeton University Press, 1971), para. 720; Jung, *The Spirit in Man, Art, and Literature*, in *The Collected Works*, vol. 15 (Princeton, NJ: Princeton University Press, 1966), para. 714.

27 Anhalt, "On the Way to *Traces*," 409.
28 Ibid., 407.
29 See A. Clarkson, "A Curriculum for the Creative Imagination," in *Creativity and Music Education*, ed. T. Sullivan and L. Willingham (Toronto: Canadian Music Educators' Association, 2003), 52–76; "Educating the Creative Imagination: A Course Design and Its Consequences," *Jung: The e-Journal of the Jungian Society for Scholarly Studies* 1 (2005): n.p., http://www.the jungiansociety.org; "Structures of Fantasy and Fantasies of Structures: Engaging the Aesthetic Self," *Current Musicology* 79–80 (2005): 67–94, 301.
30 Between 2002 and 2010, the artist-teachers of the group have provided a program on the creative imagination to some 4000 schoolchildren. See A. Clarkson, "The Dialectical Mind: On Educating the Creative Imagination in Elementary School," in *Education and Imagination: Post-Jungian Perspectives*, ed. R. Jones, A. Clarkson, S. Congram, and N. Stratton (London: Routledge, 2008), 118–41.
31 See A. Clarkson and D. Worts, "The Animated Muse: An Interpretive Program for Creative Viewing," *Curator: The Museum Journal* 48 (2005): 257–80.
32 Ibid., 271–72.
33 This fantasy journey exercise was adapted from a sonic meditation given by Pauline Oliveros at York University in the summer of 1974. It is not included in her *Sonic Meditations* (Baltimore: Smith Publications, 1971), and, in fact, she later said that she did not recall this particular exercise.
34 The Silent Solo-Silent Duet exercise was adapted from a program in transpersonal communication developed by the psychologist Henry Reed. See "Close Encounters in the Liminal Zone: Experiments in Imaginal Communication," *Journal of Analytical Psychology* 41/1 (1995): 81–116; 41/2 (1995): 203–6.
35 When participants are musicians and have instruments with them, they may go to practice rooms and prepare a two-minute improvisation based on what they imagined during the Silent Duet. They return after thirty minutes or so and perform the improvisations for the group. The performances are recorded (audio or video), played back, and discussed.
36 Transcript of debriefing session with B, 29 January 1997.
37 Ibid.
38 Transcript of debriefing session with D, 1 April 1997.
39 Ibid.
40 Maurice Freedman, "Introductory Essay," in Buber, *The Knowledge of Man* (New York: Harper and Row, 1965), 52.
41 Buber, *I and Thou*, 10, as quoted by Freedman, ibid., 52.
42 Anhalt, "An Operatic Triptych," 385.
43 Transcript of debriefing session with A, 27 January 1997.
44 Ibid.
45 For a diatribe on this topic, see Anhalt, "Letter to George Rochberg (27 November 1996)," *Eagle Minds*, 314–18. He laments "the demise of serious music from the cultural landscape" and the effects of political/economic policies that subject cultural institutions to massive budgetary cuts that affect the entire educational sector (314).
46 Anhalt, "An Operatic Triptych," 388.

47 Ibid., 389.
48 Ibid.
49 Ibid.
50 Buber, *Knowledge of Man*, 83.
51 K. Egan, *Imagination in Teaching and Learning: The Middle School Years* (University of Chicago Press, 1992); M. Greene, *Releasing the Imagination: Essays on Education, the Arts and Social Change* (San Francisco: Jossey-Bass, 1995); J. Miller, *The Holistic Curriculum* (revised edition) (Toronto: OISE Press, 2001); A.D. Efland, *Art and Cognition: Integrating the Visual Arts in the Curriculum* (New York: Teachers College Press, 2002); E. Eisner, *The Arts and the Creation of Mind* (New Haven, CT: Yale University Press, 2002); C. Mayes, *Jung and Education: Elements of an Archetypal Pedagogy* (Lanham, MD: Rowman and Littlefield, 2005); B. Neville, *Educating Psyche: Emotion, Imagination and the Unconscious in Learning*, 2nd ed. (Greensborough, Australia: Flat Chat Press, 2005); P. Cranton, *Understanding and Promoting Transformative Learning* (San Francisco: Jossey-Bass, 2006); D. Dobson, *Transformative Teaching: Promoting Transformation through Literature, the Arts and Jungian Psychology* (Rotterdam: Sense Publishers, 2008). The Imaginative Education Research Group at Simon Fraser University, directed by Kieran Egan, has developed curriculum guidelines, teacher training programs, lesson plans, and research studies that promote learning in many subject areas. See www.ierg.net.
52 Jean Piaget, *Play, Dreams, and Imitation in Childhood* (New York: Norton, 1962), 289.
53 See Paul L. Harris, *The Work of the Imagination* (Oxford: Blackwell, 2000); G. Currie and I. Ravenscroft, *Imagination in Philosophy and Psychology* (Oxford: Clarendon Press, 2002).
54 See Wolfgang Giegerich, "Jung's Thought of the Self in the Light of Its Underlying Experience," in *The Neurosis of Psychology: Primary Papers towards a Critical Psychology*, vol. 1, ed. Greg Mogenson (New Orleans: Spring Journal Books, 2005), 183.
55 Anhalt, "Letter to George Rochberg (6 October 1997)," in *Eagle Minds*, 331.

Bibliography

Anhalt, Istvan. *Alternative Voices: Essays on Contemporary Vocal and Choral Composition*. Toronto: University of Toronto Press, 1984.

———. "Music: Context, Text, Counter-text." *Contemporary Music Review* 5 (1989): 101–35.

———. "Text, Context, Music." *Canadian University Music Review* 9/2 (1989): 1–21.

———. "Twilight~Fire (Baucis' and Philemon's Feast)." Address to the Eastern Ontario Regional Seminar, 2008, of the Academies of Arts, Humanities and Sciences of Canada at Queen's University, 5 April 2008.

Blyth, R.H. *Haiku*. Vol. 3. Tokyo: Hokuseido Press, 1981.

Buber, Martin. *I and Thou*. New York: Scribner, 1958.

———. *The Knowledge of Man*. New York: Harper and Row, 1965.

Cixous, Hélène. *Three Steps on the Ladder of Writing*. Translated by S. Cornell and S. Sellers. New York: Columbia University Press, 1993.

Clarkson, A. "Between the Keys: Istvan Anhalt Writing on Music." In *Istvan Anhalt: Pathways and Memory*, edited by R. Elliott and G.E. Smith, 324–41. Montreal and Kingston: McGill-Queen's University Press, 2001.

———. "A Curriculum for the Creative Imagination." In *Creativity and Music Education*, edited by T. Sullivan and L. Willingham, 52–76. Toronto: Canadian Music Educators' Association, 2003.

———. "The Dialectical Mind: On Educating the Creative Imagination in Elementary School." In *Education and Imagination: Post-Jungian Perspectives*, edited by R. Jones, A. Clarkson, S. Congram, and N. Stratton, 118–41. London: Routledge, 2008.

———. "Educating the Creative Imagination: A Course Design and Its Consequences." *Jung: The e-Journal of the Jungian Society for Scholarly Studies* 1 (2005): n.p. http://www.thejungiansociety.org.

———. "Structures of Fantasy and Fantasies of Structures: Engaging the Aesthetic Self." *Current Musicology* 79–80 (2005): 67–94, 301.

Clarkson, A. and D. Worts. "The Animated Muse: An Interpretive Program for Creative Viewing." *Curator: The Museum Journal* 48 (2005): 257–80.

Cranton, P. *Understanding and Promoting Transformative Learning*. San Francisco: Jossey-Bass, 2006.

Currie, G. and I. Ravenscroft. *Imagination in Philosophy and Psychology*. Oxford: Clarendon Press, 2002.

Dewey, John. *Art as Experience*. New York: Minton, Balch, 1934. Reprint, New York: Capricorn Books, 1958.

Dobson, D. *Transformative Teaching: Promoting Transformation through Literature, the Arts and Jungian Psychology*. Rotterdam: Sense Publishers, 2008.

Efland, A.D. *Art and Cognition: Integrating the Visual Arts in the Curriculum*. New York: Teachers College Press, 2002.

Egan, K. *Imagination in Teaching and Learning: The Middle School Years*. Chicago: University of Chicago Press, 1992.

Eisner, E. *The Arts and the Creation of Mind*. New Haven, CT: Yale University Press, 2002.

Eliot, T.S. *The Complete Poems and Plays 1909–1950*. New York: Harcourt, Brace, 1952.

Giegerich, Wolfgang. "Jung's Thought of the Self in the Light of Its Underlying Experience." In *The Neurosis of Psychology: Primary Papers towards a Critical Psychology*, edited by Greg Mogenson, 1: 171–89. New Orleans: Spring Journal Books, 2005.

Gillmor, Alan, ed. *Eagle Minds: Selected Correspondence of Istvan Anhalt and George Rochberg 1961–2005*. Waterloo, ON: Wilfrid Laurier University Press, 2007.

Greene, M. *Releasing the Imagination: Essays on Education, the Arts and Social Change*. San Francisco: Jossey-Bass, 1995.

Harris, Paul L. *The Work of the Imagination*. Oxford: Blackwell, 2000.
Jameson, Frederic. *Archaeologies of the Future: The Desire Called Utopia and Other Science Fictions*. London: Verso, 2005.
Jung, C.G. *Psychological Types*. In *The Collected Works of C.G. Jung*, vol. 6. Princeton University Press, 1971.
———. *The Spirit in Man, Art, and Literature*. In *The Collected Works of C.G. Jung*, vol. 15. Princeton, NJ: Princeton University Press, 1966.
———. "The Transcendent Function." In *The Structure and Dynamics of the Psyche*, edited by William McGuire, 67–91. *Collected Works of C.G. Jung*, vol. 8. Princeton, NJ: Princeton University Press, 1981.
Mayes, C. *Jung and Education: Elements of an Archetypal Pedagogy*. Lanham, MD: Rowman and Littlefield, 2005.
Miller, J. *The Holistic Curriculum*. Revised edition. Toronto: OISE Press, 2001.
Neville, B. *Educating Psyche: Emotion, Imagination and the Unconscious in Learning*. 2nd ed. Greensborough, Australia: Flat Chat Press, 2005.
Oliveros, Pauline. *Sonic Meditations*. Baltimore: Smith Publications, 1971.
Piaget, Jean. *Play, Dreams, and Imitation in Childhood*. New York: Norton, 1962.
Reed, Henry. "Close Encounters in the Liminal Zone: Experiments in Imaginal Communication." *Journal of Analytical Psychology* 41/1 (1995): 81–116; 41/2 (1995): 203–6.
Samuels, Frederic, Bani Shorter, and Fred Plaut. *A Critical Dictionary of Jungian Analysis*. London: Routledge and Kegan Paul, 1986.
Scholem, G. *Kabbalah*. New York: Quadrangle, 1974.

TWELVE

György Kurtág's *Játékok*: A "Voyage" into the Child's Musical Mind

Stefano Melis

The title of this chapter[1] refers to the fascinating metaphor of a "voyage of discovery" that György Kurtág used to describe the pedagogical and aesthetic essence of his *Játékok*.[2] For Kurtág, the writing of these piano compositions was tantamount to going "on a pilgrimage to his childhood," a project that enabled him to investigate the complex nature of a child's musical mind and the close proximity between music and childhood play.

This essay will focus on the nature of the creative processes employed by Kurtág in selected compositions, considered in relation to various approaches to musical comprehension that can come into play in a child's musical mind.[3] First, I will examine the specific modality of how form is comprehended in children and its relationship to physical gesture.[4] For a child, understanding form means the ability to relate the iconic-spatial logic of a composition to the sensory-motor logic which lies at the foundation of the planning and realization of the performance gesture. A second modality of musical comprehension involves expressive and symbolic communication. A child learns to find meaning through the various types of associations between musical materials and structures on the one hand, and the images and contents of his or her background experience on the other.[5]

Sound Exploration and Creation of Musical Images

Our voyage into the child's musical mind, heard through the music of *Játékok*, begins with an analysis of *Totyogós* (Toddling) (see example 12-1). Designed for very young children who are unable to use the entire keyboard while sitting on the piano stool, Kurtág recommends it be performed, even by adults, "standing, walking—in a silly, joking manner."[6] It is built around highly diverse sound elements: clusters with the palm and the forearm, single notes and silences. Equally diverse is the manner of playing the sound elements with regards to the dynamic intensity, the quality of the timbre, the manner of the attack, and the articulation of measures of time. Moreover, the notation, giving only approximate performance details, leaves much room for the player's creative freedom. As such, it may be deduced that one of the primary pedagogical goals of *Játékok* is to orient the child along a path of sound discovery and a way of searching for and practising a specific personal style in performance techniques. This perspective also opens cognitive and experiential horizons that are generally neglected during the first stages of learning an instrument. In discussing the sound elements of Kurtág's music, this paper will show that they are complex phenomena that must be analyzed and reconstructed. As well as pitch and duration, we will also be examining other parameters such as attack, core, decay, and silence. In other words, the "voyage of discovery," from the first steps in learning an instrument onwards, should be understood above all as a voyage along which the player "constructs" sound objects according to his or her expressive intentions,[7] as an interactive path of the adaptive structuring of the musical mind in relation to the world of sound that the piano can potentially offer.[8]

An initial overview of the score shows that the child, while learning the piece, is stimulated to mentally represent a dynamic succession of nine musical figures, through which the flow of sound elements creates a meaningful environment that must be configured by the performer. Each figure is coherent and internally homogeneous,[9] but it can be clearly distinguished from those that are contiguous because of at least one of the following aspects: the positioning in different registers of the keyboard, the different number and duration of the constituent elements, the contrasts of the sound dynamics, and the quality of the timbre in relation to the attack modality of the sound. The dominant compositional principle is therefore the contrastive transition, applied in all the parametric dimensions, which enables even a very young child to perceive each figure (or group of figures) in a piece as a distinct, separate unit.

EXAMPLE 12-1 György Kurtág, *Játékok* I [Games I] (1973–78), "Totyogós" ["Toddling"], with clusters delineated and numbered. © Editio Musica Budapest.

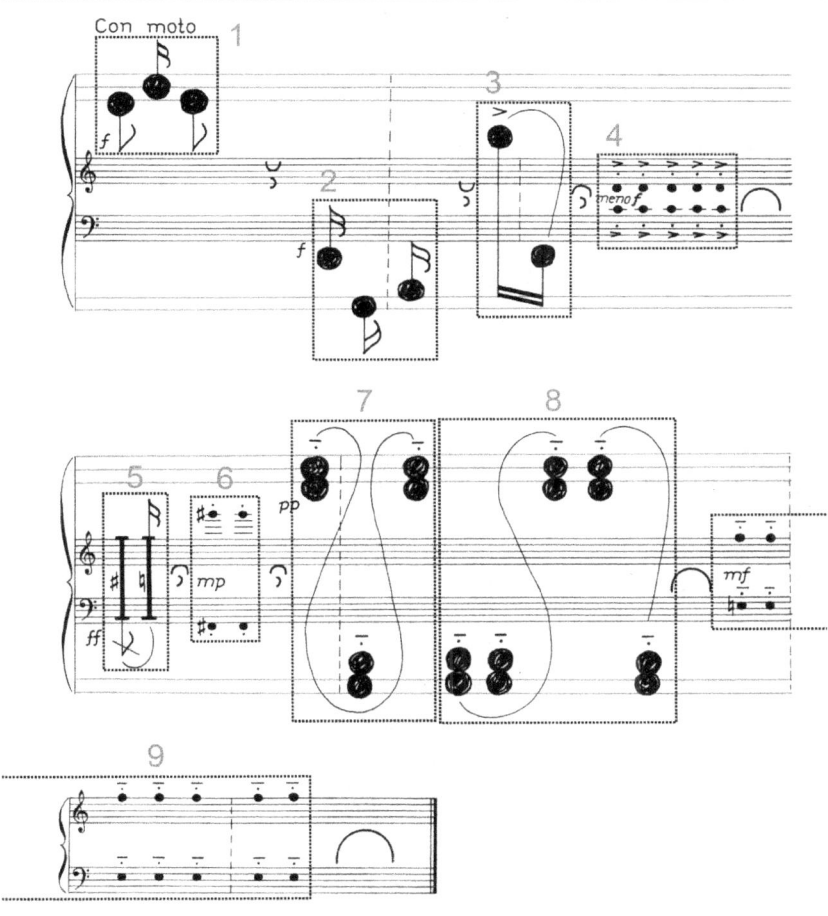

Among the factors determining what we might call the perceptive potency of the musical figures, the rhythm and the dynamic of performance gestures are most prominent. Indeed, it is clear that it is motor continuity, the merging of successive individual arm movements into a single, fluid overall gesture, that confers a sense of organic unity on the rhythmic patterns corresponding to each configuration.[10] This would imply that the figural units of the musical structure coincide with the motor units of the performance gesture, thereby facilitating an understanding of the musical meaning.

The separation created by the pauses that are placed between one figure and the next contributes to the reinforcing of the pregnancy of each segment's rhythmic form.[11] The silences have varying durations, which the child codifies in his or her mind by a qualitative, and not quantitative, measurement of the breve/long ratio. During these silences the child moves his or her body in relation to the position of sound events in the high, medium, and low registers of the keyboard, but he or she also thinks and mentally anticipates the pattern of the next performance gesture and the corresponding sound image.[12] Considering their particularly dynamic and perceptive nature, it could be assumed that these rests take on a role of not only distinguishing but also of linking individual rhythmic groups, and as such they are not dead time or mere background to the figure. It is more appropriate to describe the series of rhythmic groups as a "chain of forms," or, better still, as a "conjunction of forms."[13]

Each rhythmic group is made up of a varying number of elements, from two to a maximum of seven, respecting the limitations inherent in the child's "psychological present," that is to say, his or her short-term memory capacity. Sometimes, when the number of elements exceeds three, the notational symbols (distinct curvilinear arcs or vertical broken lines) indicate the presence of subsets, which enable a better perceptive organization of the elements within the rhythmical unity.[14] This is the case for the figures eight and nine, which are organized in 3+2 and 2+3+2 formations respectively. In general, this way of structuring rhythmic groups should be seen in conjunction with the child's ability to hierarchically codify rhythmic sequences over two different levels: groups and subgroups.[15] Rhythmic perception is also influenced by variations in sound intensity that bring out certain sound objects compared with others within the same sequence. Indeed, especially in the structuring of the more numerous groups, it is important to emphasize the presence of those accentuating aspects that promote a more efficient perceptive organization, and which help to retain and reproduce the same sequence in a better way. In the last musical figure, for example, the intensifying accent, positioned in the first element after both broken vertical lines, plays a determining role, providing dynamic direction and unity to the group, even identifying the aforementioned subgroups.

These initial analytical comments lead us to observe that musical thought, in compositions like *Toddling*, is primarily expressed in the form of sensory-motor dynamisms that place the flow of events in significant sound forms. The imaginative process that is at the origin of the mental representation of musical figures is not, however, limited to solely sensory-motor images. Through the dense synesthetic network of intersensory connections that forms the foundation of the entire perceptive system, it is possible that the activation of any representational modality may trigger configurative processes that refer to other channels of sensory information.[16] Thus, musical images are situated in an overall *habitat*, in which they are present and define themselves, involving the player's entire body in the interpretative task.[17]

The holistic nature of musical thinking takes on great importance in understanding the compositions of *Játékok*. I refer here to figures seven and eight of *Toddling*. The same sound object (two paired clusters played with the palms of both hands) must be played at opposite ends of the piano's registers. These musical figures, despite the increased spatial and temporal distance between constitutive events, still acquire a sense of organic unity and compactness. This is achieved by concentrating the mind's eye on the interaction between the choreographic aspects of this music and the graphic images of the notation. These iconic images inform the preparation and presentation of the performance gestures. This explains how the sight of the large curvilinear arcs of figures seven and eight could physically guide the parallel movement of the arms and the whole body along the keyboard, a movement that, due to the *pianissimo* dynamics, should be slow and fluidly continuous. But it also explains how a graphic image can create a corresponding acoustic image in the mind, which the act of performance should seek to reproduce, thus conditioning the creation of the corresponding sensory-motor image.

According to Kurtág, it is essential that musical images also be imprinted on the player's mind as a tactile representation. Indeed, he emphatically recommends that the performers be always "within the keyboard" in their perceptive control of sounds, especially in situations in which the performance gesture must link sound objects that are fairly distant in the diastematic space. In such cases, the performers must imagine that they continue to feel contact with the sound element they have just played in order to prefigure the sensation of the following element and anticipate its corresponding tactile image.[18]

From the concept of contact motion (described above) the composer moves on, through a synesthetic analogy, to the concept of contact hearing: "By the way, I have the impression that I do not necessarily hear with my ears and see with my eyes … I found this to be the case in my encounter with cathedrals … I had the feeling that I was sensing the space with my

EXAMPLE 12-2 The mental representation of musical images.

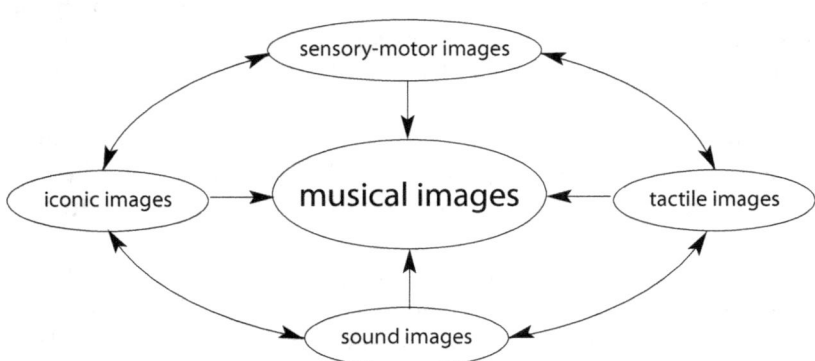

skin, with my back, when I was not looking ... For me the same thing occurs with music. In a mysterious way, it seems to pass from one sensibility to another. I hear things without actually hearing them."[19] Therefore, the mental shape of musical images is, for Kurtág, the result of a complex relational network that involves a multitude of sensory codes in the imaginative process (see example 12-2). Every mode of mental representation reverberates against the others through reciprocal conditioning and a continual interchange in devising and controlling the interpretative act.[20] In other words, the child finds his or her own personal way of hearing the cohesive tension within each musical image when he or she learns to listen with his or her whole body, when his or her hands develop an ability to see, listen, and think, and when his or her hearing can function as remote touch.

Performance Experience and Interiorization of the Overall Form of the Piece

Let me return to *Toddling* and consider its structure as a whole. To the ear the piece presents itself as a collection of unconnected sound events. As Kurtág states, it may seem as though everything can be performed carelessly, as though by accident, but in fact this music provides the performer an opportunity to reflect on how the physical sensations of performance are related in musical terms to the sounding events.[21] The child is invited to exercise his or her natural tendency to create groups, activating broader connections on the basis of recognition of repetitions, analogies, and similarities

EXAMPLE 12-3 György Kurtág, *Játékok* I [Games I] (1973–78), "Totyogós" ["Toddling"], clusters 1, 2, 7, and 8. © Editio Musica Budapest.

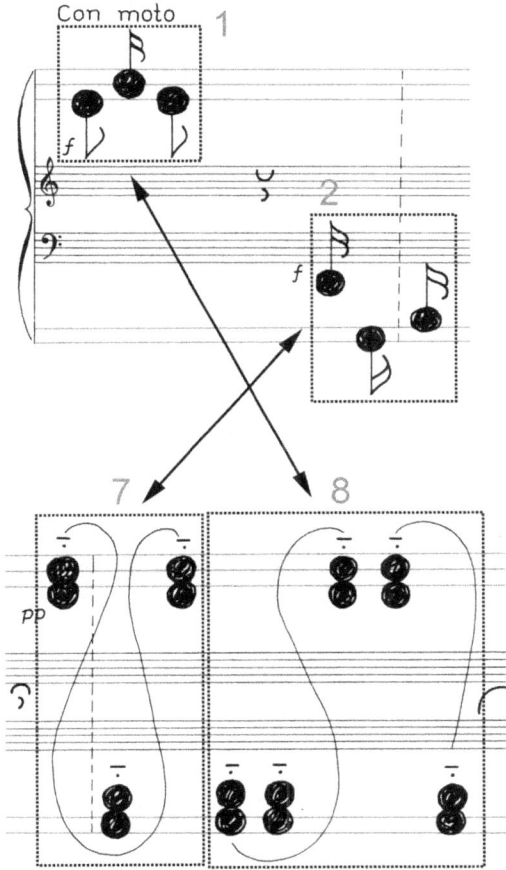

between even non-contiguous musical figures. Thus, he or she feels the strong link of similarity connecting the first two figures to each other, from both a rhythmic, sensory-motor, and iconic point of view; in fact, the second figure is in perfect symmetry with the first. At the same time, the child tests the fairly pronounced contrast, caused by the opposition of extreme registers, on the level of sound perception. But recognition of the analogy can go beyond perceptive immediacy: in figures seven and eight, for example, a reiteration in a varied form of the first two is presented. The iconic-motor passage, despite being highly distant in both space and time, is in fact the same (see example 12-3). More subtle, however, is the similarity—

noticeable mainly on the level of sensory-motor impression—that connects figure three with figure six (both require the same opening of arms and the same diastematic positioning) and figure four with figure five (both are produced with the arms close together at the centre of the keyboard).

Thus, even if the child uses relations restricted within a limited temporal sphere, this should not render him or her incapable of operating certain time actions within his or her perception of the overall structure. The perceptive act is capable of broadening the focal point from the prehensile immediacy of single musical figures to the full syntactical-propositional dimension of the formal structure. In this piece, the principle of repetition creates references, imposes links across distances, stimulates perception to group objects in ever-wider spans, and creates links between sections.[22] It therefore generates an incipient level of hierarchical organization of musical form, forcing the child to work from memory. But as we have observed, nothing in *Toddling* is exactly repeated. Everything changes in a continual flow of mnemonic references to roughly similar figurative articulations, creating a perfect balance between tension and recognition, analogy, and a tendency towards surprise. Beyond the changing perceptive physiognomy of musical figures, the child can experience, for example, the different emotional impacts that the application of the same syntactical principle can create in different expressive contexts: I refer to the reciprocal relation of question/answer that we find in each figure couple 1-2, 3-4, 5-6, and 7-8.[23]

Examining the structure of *Toddling* in greater depth, one can observe that previously noticed relationships of similarity arrange the flow of musical events according to a cross pattern that connects figure one to figure eight, figure two to figure seven, figure three to figure six, and figure four to figure five. The result is a *chiasmo* arrangement, which leads to the succession of two symmetrical sequences of four elements followed by a single figure that works as a coda (see example 12-4). Furthermore, the perception of this structural symmetry is even reinforced on the level of iconic representation. The diastematic layout of sound events draws a single large X shape across the score, beginning and ending with the broad openings at opposite registers of the piano and crossing over in the centre of the composition, which is also the centre of the keyboard.

The overall figurative route can be imprinted on the child's conscience as a "mental map," but it is in the act of playing and listening that the musical form assumes its true dynamic essence of "geometry of movement" and "architecture of time."[24] It is in the here and now of the sub-

EXAMPLE 12-4 György Kurtág, *Játékok* I [*Games* I] (1973–78), "Totyogós" ["Toddling"], structural diagram showing the chiastic arrangement.

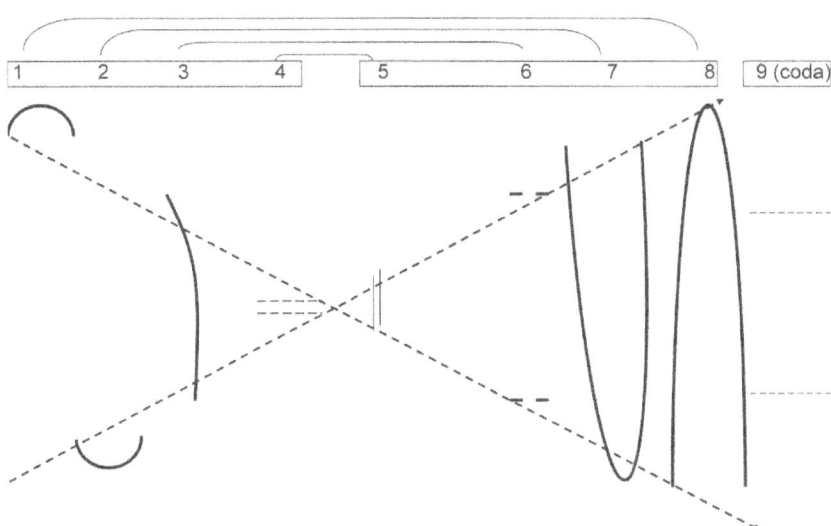

jective experience, lived directly, that the parts come together to form a whole. The performing extemporaneousness that gives shape to individual events interacts with the mnemonic route of a before and an after, determining a performing context where what counts most is the overall direction of the process, the fluidity and the continuity of the course of development whose details can be carried out in a different way every time. The pedagogical goal of understanding the structure of the musical event as a *fluens* form is thus associated with that of the creative liberty of the young performer, to which Kurtág makes specific reference in his Foreword.[25]

Symbolic Projections and Expressive Communication in Practising the Piano

I now shift my focus to another aspect of the child's experiential horizon in his or her voyage of musical discovery through *Játékok*; namely, the use of a specific type of imaginative thought through which it is possible to invest symbolic values in musical language structures, and which confers on the act of instrumental practice a power that is in some way representative—that refers to something other than itself. In this respect, the pedagogical goal is to project an understanding of the musical event into the widest dimension of the child's playful-symbolic experience, where playing an instrument can become a way of symbolically expressing and communicating his or her own experiences and personality.

A useful starting point from which to orientate our observations in this sphere of a child's musical thought comes from Roger Caillois, a French academic and the author of an important study on the phenomenological characteristics of playing. In his taxonomical classification, Caillois describes four main categories of playing, respectively called *agon, alea, mimicry*, and *ilinx*.[26] I will follow, therefore, the typologies listed in the taxonomy to identify, one by one, the similarities that can be compared with certain aspects of the compositions of *Játékok*.

The first playful feature, the *agon*, refers to all games that have competitive features, in which can be discerned impulses characterized by the achievement of speed, resistance, strength, memory, ability, or ingenuity. "Practise of *agon* presupposes constant attention, appropriate training, assiduous efforts and a will to win. It involves discipline and perseverance."[27] This all comes back to a desire to master and ensure the success of one's own performance intentions. Browsing the list of pieces within *Játékok*, one realizes to what extent *agon* is one of the most recognizable playful features of the work. Take, for example, the explicit references to competition in pieces such as *Veszekedés* 1 (Quarrels) in which *agon*, considered even in its physical brutality, becomes musical in the form of accentuated contrasts in figures and gestures. The game of competition assumes the meaning of the effort of conquest in compositions such as *Hommage à Csajkovskij* and *Hommage à Paganini*, which stimulate the young player to discover immediately the pleasure of testing himself against the most difficult tasks, to break through his or her own limitations in the *prestissimo possibile* or as *il più forte possibile* (see example 12-5).

The second playful category of Caillois's taxonomy, the *alea*, concerns the group of games characterized by the uncertainty of achieving one's own performing intentions. This aspect is very present in *Játékok*. First, it refers to the improvised component that represents the extemporaneity of the performance, especially when it is driven into the *paidia* of a frenetic exaltation of what does or can go out of control. This dimension of unbridled virtuosity has always been the pendant of the rigorous execution of carefully notated texts. Kurtág alludes to this in titles such as *Wrong notes allowed* and states it directly in the Foreword to *Játékok*: "Let us tackle bravely even the most difficult task without being afraid of making mistakes."[28]

EXAMPLE 12-5 György Kurtág, *Játékok* I [Games I] (1973–78), "Hommage à Paganini." © Editio Musica Budapest.

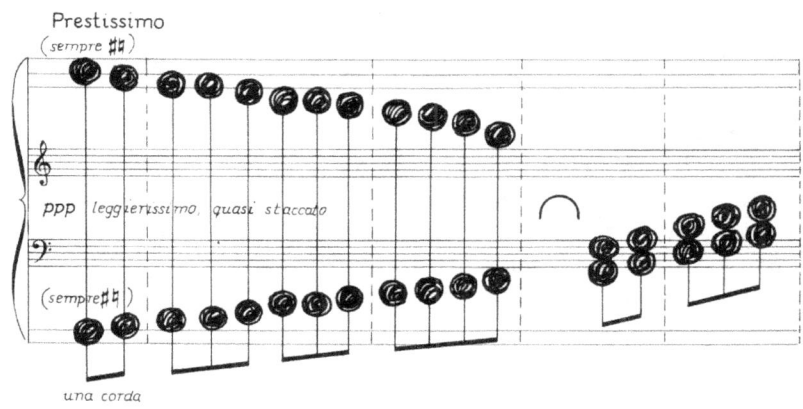

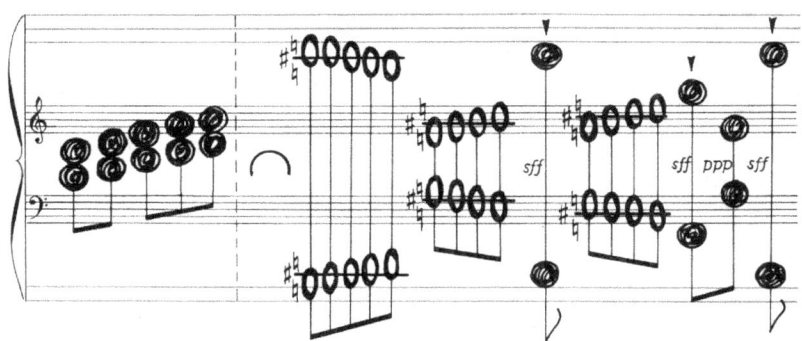

For the purposes of this inquiry, the playful features of *mimicry* deserve particular attention. Caillois described the concept of *mimicry* as being based on

> the fact that the subject plays at believing, in making himself and others believe that he is another. He denies, alters, and temporarily abandons his own personality to claim another. Clearly, theatrical representation and dramatic performance come fully under this group ... Except for one, mimicry has all the features of playing: freedom, convention, suspension of reality, delimited space and time. However, there is no continuous subjecting to imperative, precise rules: they are replaced by ... [the]

concealment of reality, the simulation of another reality. Mimicry is continuous invention.[29]

We can become aware of the importance of *mimicry* in Kurtág's pedagogical thought by examining the composition entitled *Unottan* (Bored), which is also targeted at very young children who are unable to reach the entire keyboard while seated on the stool (see example 12-6). Overall, the score assumes a semblance of a real script to be performed, involving numerous expressive codes that interact.[30] The directions are, however, only a starting point that should trigger the interpretative process, a sort of semantic canvas based on the concept of binary opposition. Formally, the contrast corresponds, in terms of symbolic investment, to the clear juxtaposition of the images of indolence and abandon, with the feeling of boredom and the angry and sudden reaction that enables the player to unleash all of the emotional tension that has built up.

As regards the articulation of sound events, any analysis of this must include the profound correlative relationship that links the expressive performing gesture—and more generally the postural pose of the entire body—to the features of the musical journey. At times, though, the expressiveness of body language manages to overshadow the aesthetic autonomy of the work through actions that are not solely for producing sound. This is the case in the sequence suggested by the composer to be carried out at the topical point of the whole project, where the performer must "walk beyond the keyboard absentmindedly, then return suddenly with rage."

Over the arc of the first formal section (delimited by the long fermata), the four micro-units (distinguished in the score by the vertical broken lines) are perceived by the child as a coherent *gestalt* because it is made up of similar acoustic-gestural configurations. The piece begins with sounds whose pitches are given only approximately. Then, we notice a varied typology of *glissandi* on black and white keys. These *glissandi* are subjected to a gradual process of transformation with regard to their gestural expressiveness. The transformation is characterized throughout by a slow rhythm and a low level of intensity. In particular, in the second structural microunit, the "mute" variation of the *glissando* should be noted, over which three individual sounds are layered. Within each of the four micro-units, sound elements are arranged neatly along the keyboard with the same duration, giving rise to sound profiles that have the same rectilinear direction and extension into the acoustic space, although they alternate between low and high sounds.

EXAMPLE 12-6 György Kurtág, *Játékok* I [Games I] (1973–78), "Unottan" ["Bored"]. © Editio Musica Budapest.

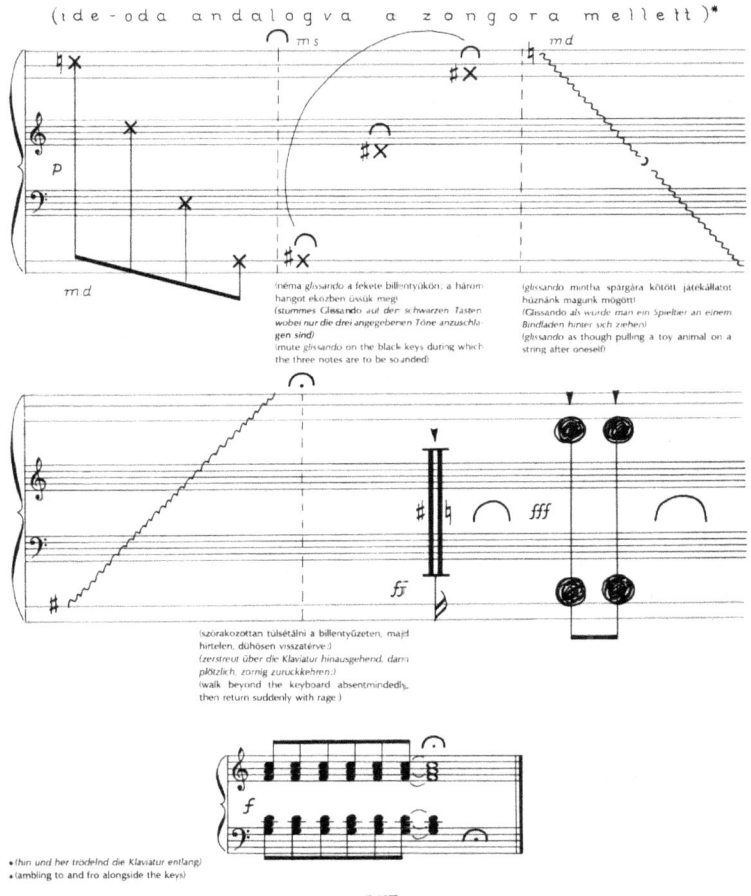

Overall, the formal and articulatory characteristics of the performing gestures, intrinsically linked to the acoustic quality of the sound materials produced, are put into a metaphorical relationship with properties, actions, and emotional states that refer to an analogous perceptive configuration. Continuity, graduality, regularity, linearity, periodicity, and predictability make up the procedural indicators of the sound-motor experience in the first part of the piece. These perceptive stresses can also be linked, depending on the child's cognitive and emotional style, to symbolic images relating to balance, calm, and serenity but also depressing passivity or being sweetly rocked in the languorous arms of boredom, as the piece's title suggests (see example 12-7).

There is another aspect that should not be neglected. It is the concomitance of factors that tend to generate a process of a regressive nature: the duration of sound elements, from one micro-unit to another, gradually increases in length; contact with the keyboard, when moving from single sounds to *glissandi*, becomes ever closer and more continuous; and, presumably, performance gestures become increasingly slower. Moreover, the number of sound elements in the micro-unit sequence decreases from four to one, so the child has to control, together with the other mentioned factors, this regressive numeric sequence during his or her performance.

This subsidence in the keyboard, this regression in which movements slow to immobility, can refer analogically to manifestations of the organism, such as the act of falling asleep, or psycho-motor patterns such as fainting and dissolving. But also, at the opposite extreme, it refers to patterns of a tactile-kinesthetic nature, referring, for example, to the heavy-light polarity suggested by Kurtág's image of walking up and down next to the piano "as though pulling a toy animal on a string after oneself." The game proposed could, indeed, assume the characteristics of an increasingly tiresome action, due to the resistance of the imaginary animal, which could display its reluctance to being dragged to such a point that it seems to struggle with its young owner.

EXAMPLE 12-7 György Kurtág, *Játékok* I [*Games* I] (1973–78), "Unottan" ["Bored"], diagram of the first formal section.

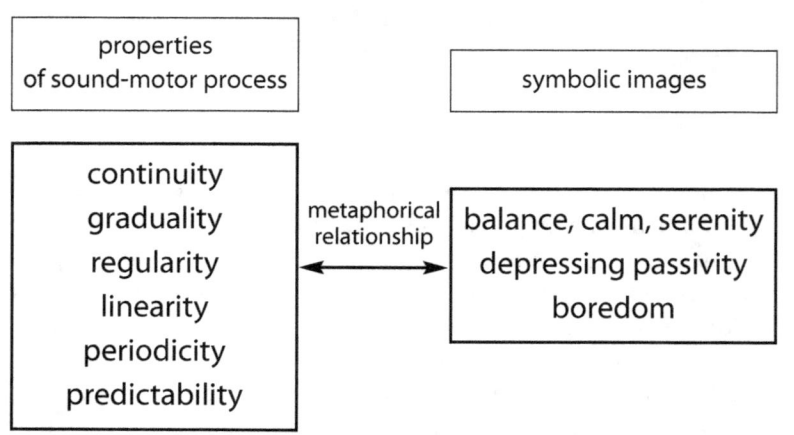

Another possible comparison, this time referring to topological relations, can be generated by alternating the movement alongside the keyboard, which, due to the visual transposition mediated by the graphical sign on the score, is comparable to a walk where downward slopes alternate with ascents. (This is the reason for the composer's expression "ambling to and fro alongside the keys.") This experience is very important for the child, who is learning to dominate the concept of the directionality of a sound profile in a diastemic space, associating it to the high/low polarity.

A useful idea in guiding our symbolic understanding of the second part of the piece comes in the last feature of childish playfulness suggested in the taxonomy of Caillois. This is *ilinx*, or the "search for dizziness," or even "an attempts to destroy momentarily the stability of perception and bring one's consciousness to a kind of voluptuous panic." Caillois than goes on to comment:

> Every child knows well that, by spinning around on the spot, he can achieve a centrifugal state of dispersion and disorientation in which his body has difficulty regaining balance and his perception its normal state ... This dizziness is often accompanied with the usually repressed desire for disorder and destruction, which betrays coarse, brutal forms of affirming the personality.

The ilinx:

> is at play in any display of joyous exuberance expressed by an immediate and chaotic agitation, a state of amusement and free and spontaneous relaxation that is often excessive, whose improvised and anarchic nature remains the main, if not the only reason for being ... This elementary need for noise and agitation initially appears as an impulse to touch everything, grab things, try them, smell them and then drop any accessible objects. This frequently becomes a taste for breaking things, a pleasure in destruction.[31]

One can notice the phenomenological feature of *ilinx* in many compositions of *Játékok*: in their taste for surprise, for the unpredictable, and for the unexpected event that bursts in and interrupts processes whose course is drawn in such a way as to foresee future events. This aspect is present in an exemplary way in the second part of *Bored* as well, in which we find the sense of destruction and a loss of order and control that stands out against the first section of the piece. In fact, in the second part, the child experiences a different kind of performing gesture: one which is no longer longitudinal and horizontal but vertical in relation to the keyboard (*clusters* with forearms and the palms of the hands, chords with six sounds). The performance of these sound elements is set out in a way that increases the distance between the body and the piano, freeing up the breadth and the speed of the gesture until it reaches the furthest limits of physical ability, both in the energy required and the span of the limbs. The method for measuring distances and the orientation of the body also changes: one no longer moves in one direction and then another along the keyboard; instead one is placed firmly at the centre of a topological relationship of symmetry, using both arms at the same time. Finally, one can observe that the formal and temporal discontinuity of the composition's epilogue is generated by the convulsive succession of changes in the way the player touches the keyboard and by the particularly significant role that silences assume. In particular, the second pause, longer than the previous one, tends to acquire an increased sense of breaking and wrong footing due to the unexpected euphony of the final chords after the increased aggressiveness of the previous clusters (see example 12-8).

EXAMPLE 12-8 György Kurtág, *Játékok* I [*Games* I] (1973–78), "Unottan" ["Bored"], diagram of the second formal section.

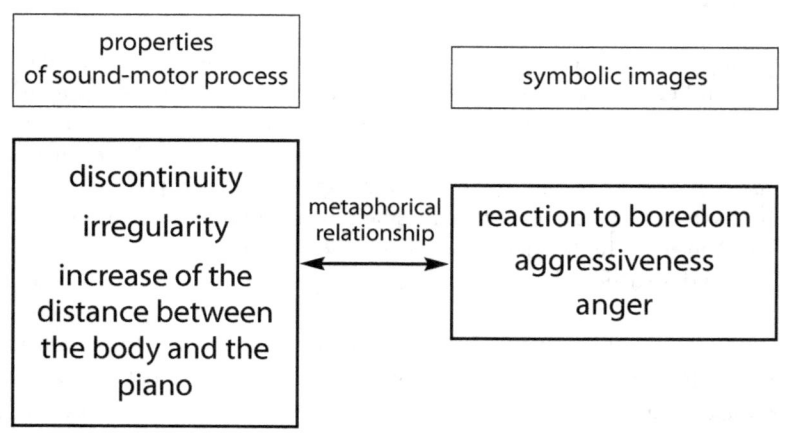

Conclusion

This analysis of selected compositions has highlighted some essential aspects about Kurtág's pedagogic thought, which require some final remarks. First, *Játékok* must be understood not only as a possible way to learn how to play the piano but also, and especially, as a way to guide the forming of a child's musical mind as a whole. This implies that instrumental training and general music education overlap, sharing a common pedagogic goal; namely, the development of musical intelligence in all possible dimensions. According to Kurtág, knowing and doing, thinking and playing, understanding the musical structures, and knowing how to communicate them by a conscious performing act are all aspects that require a reciprocal integration into the learning of a musical instrument. Moreover, the analytical remarks in the third part of this essay underline the necessity of knowing oneself through the musical experience and of playing to express the richness of one's own interiority. Here one can better appreciate the role of these pedagogical aspects in motivating both the child's learning and the educational action. Finally, one can observe that the musical structures of *Játékok* may be deeply interiorized by the child, and that they may have a role to play in shaping the child's mind (a role that Vygotsky calls "instrument stimulus"). In other words, understanding and performing the compositions of *Játékok* can act as a gateway to future cognitive and musical accomplishments. The work becomes a medium through which children transform their own psychic processes, interiorize new thought mechanisms, and develop new ways of controlling their own behaviour in their musical experiences.[32]

Notes

1. To my friend István Balász, for having passed on to me the passion for Kurtág's music. I would like to thank Friedemann Sallis, Kenneth DeLong, and Aaron Dalton for their kind suggestions regarding this text.
2. In one of his rare papers, György Kurtág declared: "Je pense que l'idée d'exploration et de voyage contenue dans cette oeuvre *(Játékok)* est très importante: peut-être un voyage autobiographique, ou le voyage biographique de chacun de nous." ("Játékok: Une leçon de György Kurtág," in *György Kurtág: Entretiens, textes, écrits sur son oeuvres*, ed. Philippe Albèra [Genève: Éditions Contrechamps, 1995], 21.)
3. On the concepts of "musical mind" and "mental representation" of musical structures, see John A. Sloboda, *The Musical Mind: The Cognitive Psychology of Music* (Oxford and New York: Oxford University Press, 1985).
4. Research that establishes that children five to seven years old possess a beginning skill in the comprehension of musical form can be found in: Coral Davies,

"'Listen to my song': A Study of Songs Invented by Children Aged 5 to 7 Years," *British Journal of Music Education* 9/1 (1992): 19–48. Davies asserts that spontaneous children's songs can be seen as "structurally organized units" which are due to the child's capacity of understanding all the structural rules of songs. It seems that, during the autonomous song productions, the child acquires these structural rules at an unconscious level.

5 For a more in-depth explanation on this subject, see Stefano Melis, "'Játékok' di György Kurtág. Il primo apprendimento strumentale tra esplorazione, gioco e comprensione musicale," *Il Saggiatore Musicale* 12/1 (2005): 147–69.

6 For Kurtág, this piece belongs to "une catégorie de pièces dans *Játékok* que j'ai pu expérimenter après quelques mois avec les enfants: j'ai constaté que dans certains cas, mon idée de 'prise de possession totale' du clavier n'était pas réalisable, parce que les enfants étaient trop petits et l'ouverture des bras insuffisante. Je n'ai pas voulu renoncer à mon idée: j'ai pensé qu'en se promenant autour du piano, on pourrait tout jouer; et qu'en même temps, la distance parcourue pour rejoindre les deux extrémités du clavier pourrait être une expérience physique pour l'enfant" (Kurtág, "Játékok: Une leçon," 25).

7 Kurtág defines "basic elements" as the sonorous objects which arise from the exploration of the piano keyboard. On the concept of "sonorous element," understood as a perceptive unitary form, see Abraham Moles, *Théorie de l'information et perception esthétique* (Paris: Flammarion, 1958) and Pierre Schaeffer, *Traité des objets musicaux* (Paris: Seuil, 1966).

8 In his Foreword to *Játékok*, Kurtág writes: "The idea of composing *Játékok* was suggested by children playing spontaneously, children for whom the piano still means a toy. They experiment with it, caress it, attack it and run their fingers over it. They pile up seemingly disconnected sounds, and if this happens to arouse their musical instinct they look consciously for some of the harmonies found by chance and keep repeating them" (Budapest: Editio Musica, 1979). Therefore, this approach to playing piano is not a preordinate learning of notes, as happens in most piano methods, but on the contrary it is a subjective construction of "sonorous objects" within the concrete subjective experience of the production, sensory-motor perception, and mental representation of sound. In order to understand better the sense of this pedagogical attitude, it is useful to recall the Piagetian concept of "construction of reality," referring to the beginning phase of human development. One can assume an analogical relation between the task described here—that of the child who takes the first steps towards the mental construction of the sonorous objects—and the baby behaviour when he or she lives his or her first moments of relationship with reality. As described by Kurtág, the child—who is in front of the piano for the first time—behaves in an analogous way to the baby, newly immersed in reality, who does not distinguish between himself and the world. Through the motor actions, he or she knows a reality that is different from himself, interiorizing the laws which structure this interaction (Jean Piaget, *La costruzione del reale nel bambino* (1937) [Firenze: La Nuova Italia, 1973]).

9 The sonorous elements within each figure are linked together by the gestaltic rule of similarity. On the principles of similarity and contrast in relation to

structural perception and comprehension of music, see Irène Deliège, "A Perceptual Approach to Contemporary Musical Forms," in *Music and the Cognitive Sciences: Proceedings from the Symposium Paris, 14–18 March 1988,* ed. Simon McAdams and Irène Deliège, *Contemporary Music Review* 4 (1989): 213–30, and Irène Deliège, "Similarity Perception ↔ Categorization ↔ Cue Abstraction," *Music Perception* 19 (2001): 233–43.

10 On the theories which explain the tendency of perception to distinguish rhythmic patterns by the unity of a corresponding kinesthetic reaction, see Paul Fraisse, *Psicologia del ritmo* (1974) (Roma: Armando Editore, 1979), 61.

11 In this context, one can notice the effect of the law of "temporal proximity," which orients the perception to recognize a border between two sound events that are separated either by a remarkable interval of pause or by a long temporal distance between the respective attack points. On the gestaltic law of "temporal proximity," see Fraisse, *Psicologia del ritmo,* 59.

12 The child who plays *Toddling* can experience, as Kurtág asserts, "le transport à distance d'un événement musical déterminé." The Hungarian composer then goes on to comment: "Un des précurseurs du solfège de Kodaly, peut-être même l'inventeur du système, était Jenő Ádám, qui a travaillé avec les enfants de l'école primaire; l'une des expériences qu'il confiait à ses enfants était justement: 'Prends ce son, cours autour de la maison et ramène-le moi.' Ce travail est important pour moi" (Kurtág, "Játékok: Une leçon," 25).

13 Fraisse, *Psicologia del ritmo,* 64.

14 Ibid., 63.

15 On the child's ability to hierarchically organize rhythmic patterns, see Claire Gérard and Catherine Auxiette, "The Role of Melodic and Verbal Organization in the Reproduction of Rhythmic Groups by Children," *Music Perception* 6/2 (1988): 173–92.

16 The term "synesthesia" indicates the phenomenon of perception where two distinct senses are activated by a stimulation which regards only one of them. On the concept of synesthesia as a pedagogical perspective, especially on the capacity of using all representational systems as resources in learning and performing, see Robert Dilts et al., *Neurolinguistic Programming: The Study of the Structure of Subjective Experience* (Cupertino: Meta, 1980). On the phenomenon of synesthesia, see also Vilayanur S. Ramachandran and Edward M. Hubbard, "Psychophysical Investigations into the Neural Basis of Synaesthesia," *Proceedings of the Royal Society of London* 1470 (2001): 979–83; Vilayanur S. Ramachandran and Edward M. Hubbard, "The Phenomenology of Synaesthesia," *Journal of Consciousness Studies* 10/8 (August 2003): 49–57; Simon Baron-Cohen and John E. Harrison, eds., *Synaesthesia: Classical and Contemporary Readings* (Oxford: Blackwell, 1997); Fernando Dogana, *Suono e senso* (Milano: Franco Angeli, 1983), 171–226. For more on synesthesia in music, see Cristina Cano, *La musica nel cinema: Musica, immagine, racconto* (Roma: Gremese, 2002), 40–67.

17 On the concept of "musical image," see Marco De Natale, *La Musica come gioco: Il dentro e il fuori della teoria* (Bern: Peter Lang, 2004).

18 In this respect, Kurtág declares: "Ce qui m'intéressait, c'était … qu'il y ait une sorte de contact physique avec le clavier—et pas uniquement au travers des

deux mains. L'aspect tactile est très important chez l'enfant, il est à développer. L'instrument ne doit pas être perçu comme 'étranger'; Matisse a écrit que le crayon doit être la continuation de la main, et nous pouvons nous approprier cette affirmation. Je cherchais à faire en sorte que l'approche fût vraiment vivante, de chair et de sang" (Kurtág, "Játékok: Une leçon," 24).

19 "J'ai d'ailleurs l'impression que ce n'est pas forcément avec les oreilles que j'entends et avec les yeux que je vois ... J'ai retrouvé cette impression dans mes rencontres avec les cathédrales ... et j'y ai eu l'impression de sentir l'espace avec ma peau, avec mon dos, lorsque je ne regardais pas ... Pour moi, il en va fréquemment de même pour la musique. Elle passe d'une façon mystérieuse d'une sensibilité à l'autre, j'entends les choses sans les entendre." Bálint A. Varga, "Entretien avec György Kurtág," in *György Kurtág: Entretiens, textes, écrits sur son oeuvres*, ed. Philippe Albèra (Genève: Éditions Contrechamps, 1995), 16–17.

20 The interactive modality of the imagining thought in musical performance can be explained by referring to the concept of "physiognomic knowledge," a phrase coined by the philosopher Michael Polanyi. According to this point of view, the semiotic process of the musical imagining thought would work in a way which lets us pass from "proximal" knowledge (sensory-motor and tactile images) to "distant" or "focal" knowledge, to which we owe the formation of the musical images in different forms (iconic, acoustic, and symbolic images). Michael Polanyi, *La conoscenza inespressa* (1968) (Roma: Armando Editore, 1979), 28–29.

21 "Tout peut paraître joué avec insouciance et comme au hasard, mais où nous pouvons combiner sensation physique et réflexion sur ce qui ce passe en termes musicaux." Kurtág, "Játékok: une leçon," 25.

22 On repetition as a fundamental genetic principle of music construction, see De Natale, *La musica come gioco*, 187ff.

23 This micro-structural logic is widespread in *Játékok*. The author describes it as it follows: "Pour commencer, mon idée fut d'abord de trouver, pour l'enfant, la possibilité ... de quelque chose qui soit un 'rythme organique' (ce n'est pas une définition mais pour moi, c'est important): d'avoir beaucoup de silence, c'est-à-dire des actions acoustico-organiques qui stimulent des réponses, des conséquences: quelque chose, en somme, de très primitif ... Ce qui advient après une proposition, c'est une conséquence organique de celle-ci" (Kurtág, "Játékok: Une leçon," 22).

24 For more on the concept of musical form as "geometry of movement" and "architecture of time," see De Natale, *La musica come gioco*, 179–216.

25 "Playing is just playing. It requires a great deal of freedom and initiative from the performer. On no account should the written image be taken seriously but the written image must be taken extremely seriously as regards the musical process, the quality of sound and silence" (Kurtág, Foreword to *Játékok* I).

26 Roger Caillois, *I giochi e gli uomini. La maschera e la vertigine* (1964) (Milano: Bompiani, 1981), 28.

27 "La pratica dell'*agon* presuppone un'attenzione costante, un allenamento appropriato, degli sforzi assidui e la volontà di vincere. Implica disciplina e perseveranza" (Ibid., 31).

28 Numerous pieces related to the concept of *alea* are contained into the first book of *Játékok*.
29 Caillois's concept of *mimicry* is based "sul fatto che il soggetto gioca a credere, a farsi credere o a far credere agli altri di essere un altro. Egli nega, altera, abbandona temporaneamente la propria personalità per fingerne un'altra … È evidente che la rappresentazione teatrale e l'interpretazione drammatica entrano a pieno diritto in questo gruppo … Ad eccezione di una, la *mimicry* presenta tutte le caratteristiche del gioco: libertà, convenzione, sospensione del reale, spazio e tempo delimitati. Non vi si trova, tuttavia, assoggettamento continuo a regole imperative e precise: lo sostituiscono … la dissimulazione della realtà, la simulazione di un'altra realtà. La *mimicry* è invenzione continua" (Caillois, *I giochi*, 36–40).
30 For more on the concept of script, see Nicholas Cook, "Music as Performance," in *The Cultural Study of Music: A Critical Introduction*, ed. Martin Clayton, Trevor Herbert, and Richard Middleton (New York: Routledge, 2003), 206–7.
31 This is *ilinx*, or the "search for dizziness," or even "un tentativo di distruggere per un attimo la stabilità della percezione e a far subire alla coscienza una sorta di voluttuoso panico." Caillois than goes on to comment: "Ogni bambino conosce altrettanto bene, girando vorticosamente su se stesso, il modo di accedere a uno stato centrifugo di dispersione e sbandamento in cui il corpo non ritrova che a fatica il suo equilibrio e la percezione della sua naturalezza … Questa vertigine si accompagna spesso con il gusto normalmente represso del disordine e della distruzione che tradisce forme rozze e brutali di affermazione della personalità." The *ilinx* "interviene in ogni manifestazione di gioiosa esuberanza espressa da un'agitazione immediata e caotica, da uno stato di svago e distensione libera e spontanea, spesso eccessiva, il cui carattere improvvisato ed anarchico resta l'essenziale, se non l'unica ragion d'essere … Questo bisogno elementare di chiasso e di agitazione appare inizialmente come impulso a toccare tutto, ad afferrare, assaggiare, annusare e poi lasciar cadere ogni oggetto accessibile. Diventa spesso piacere di fare a pezzi, gusto della distruzione" (Caillois, *I giochi*, 40–45).
32 Lev S. Vygotsky, *Pensiero e linguaggio* (1934) (Bari: Laterza, 1990). These considerations let us better appreciate the educational significance of Kurtág's words: "Beaucoup de pièces peuvent être une stimulation pour l'improvisation. J'ai une façon très primitive de penser la musique: comme recherche continue. C'est une façon d'approcher la musique qui, dans les premières années d'étude, doit cohabiter avec toute la littérature traditionnelle. Certains procédés suggérés par *Játékok* peuvent être appliqués à ces oeuvres traditionnelles. Même si ce n'est pas une méthode rigide, elle peut devenir un modèle de lecture ou d'analyse d'autres pièces" (Kurtág, "Játékok: Une leçon," 30).

Bibliography

Baron-Cohen, Simon and John E. Harrison, eds. *Synaesthesia: Classical and Contemporary Readings*. Oxford: Blackwell, 1997.

Caillois, Roger. *I giochi e gli uomini: La maschera e la vertigine* (1964). Milano: Bompiani, 1981.

Cano, Cristina. *La musica nel cinema: Musica, immagine, racconto*. Roma: Gremese, 2002.

Cook, Nicholas. "Music as Performance." In *The Cultural Study of Music: A Critical Introduction*, edited by Martin Clayton, Trevor Herbert, and Richard Middleton, 204–14. New York: Routledge, 2003.

Davies, Coral. "'Listen to my song': A Study of Songs Invented by Children Aged 5 to 7 Years." *British Journal of Music Education* 9/1 (1992): 19–48.

Deliège, Irène. "A Perceptual Approach to Contemporary Musical Forms." In *Music and the Cognitive Sciences: Proceedings from the Symposium Paris, 14–18 March 1988*, edited by Simon McAdams and Irène Deliège. *Contemporary Music Review* 4 (1989): 213–30.

———. "Similarity Perception ↔ Categorization ↔ Cue Abstraction." *Music Perception* 19 (2001): 233–43.

De Natale, Marco. *La musica come gioco: Il dentro e il fuori della teoria*. Bern: Peter Lang, 2004.

Dilts, Robert, John Grinder, Richard Bandler, Leslie C. Bandler, and Judith DeLozier. *Neurolinguistic Programming: The Study of the Structure of Subjective Experience*. Cupertino, CA: Meta, 1980.

Dogana, Fernando. *Suono e senso*. Milano: Franco Angeli, 1983.

Fraisse, Paul. *Psicologia del ritmo* (1974). Roma: Armando Editore, 1979.

Gérard, Claire and Catherine Auxiette. "The Role of Melodic and Verbal Organization in the Reproduction of Rhythmic Groups by Children." *Music Perception* 6/2 (1988): 173–92.

Kurtág, György. *Játékok* I. Budapest: Editio Musica, 1979.

———. "Játékok: Une leçon de György Kurtág." In *György Kurtág: Entretiens, textes, écrits sur son oeuvres*, edited by Philippe Albèra, 21–31. Genève: Éditions Contrechamps, 1995.

Melis, Stefano. "'Játékok' di György Kurtág. Il primo apprendimento strumentale tra esplorazione, gioco e comprensione musicale." *Il Saggiatore Musicale* 12/1 (2005): 147–69.

Moles, Abraham. *Théorie de l'information et perception esthétique*. Paris: Flammarion, 1958.

Piaget, Jean. *La costruzione del reale nel bambino* (1937). Firenze: La Nuova Italia, 1973.

Polanyi, Michael. *La conoscenza inespressa* (1968). Roma: Armando Editore, 1979.

Ramachandran, Vilayanur S. and Edward M. Hubbard. "The Phenomenology of Synaesthesia." *Journal of Consciousness Studies* 10/8 (August 2003): 49–57.

———. "Psychophysical Investigations into the Neural Basis of Synaesthesia." *Proceedings of the Royal Society of London* 1470 (2001): 979–83.
Schaeffer, Pierre. *Traité des objets musicaux*. Paris: Seuil, 1966.
Sloboda, John A. *The Musical Mind: The Cognitive Psychology of Music*. Oxford and New York: Oxford University Press, 1985.
Varga, Bálint A. "Entretien avec György Kurtág." In *György Kurtág: Entretiens, textes, écrits sur son oeuvres*, 11–20.
Vygotsky, Lev S. *Pensiero e linguaggio* (1934). Bari: Laterza, 1990.

THIRTEEN

Arracher la figure au figuratif : la musique vocale de György Kurtág

Alvaro Oviedo

György Kurtág excelle dans la création d'images musicales dans son œuvre vocale. Nombreux sont les traits de son écriture qui permettent un tel jaillissement d'images : le caractère aphoristique d'une grande partie de ses pièces, la spécificité du matériau musical utilisé, la force extraordinaire du geste. À chaque fois, la question est posée : comment tisser des liens entre musique et texte à partir de figures musicales caractérisées sans tomber dans l'illustration, dans un rapport figé entre sens musical et sens langagier ? Commençons par quelques considérations générales sur le rapport entre musique et texte.

Il s'agit tout d'abord de penser musique et langage comme deux couches de natures hétérogènes qui coexistent dans l'œuvre vocale, deux niveaux qui sont en constant glissement et, l'un vis-à-vis de l'autre, en constant décalage. L'une des caractéristiques fondamentales de l'art musical est justement cette fluidité, ce caractère insaisissable dû à sa nature temporelle, qui empêche ou rend pour le moins instable une correspondance figée entre l'un de ses moments et un texte ou une quelconque signification.

Or, si texte et musique ne se confondent pas dans un ensemble homogène, ils ne sont pas pour autant deux éléments irréconciliables au sein de l'œuvre vocale. Entre les deux peuvent se produire des effets de croisement, de jonction, en conséquence notamment du caractère historique du matériau musical et des connotations que celui-ci véhicule. Le temps d'un instant, ils peuvent se rapporter l'un à l'autre, mais pour revenir ensuite au décalage et à l'instabilité qui caractérisent leur rapport. Ni homogènes, ni irréconciliables, texte et musique apparaissent comme deux niveaux de sens, de part et d'autre d'une frontière qui les sépare mais qui est, en même temps, le lieu où ils entrent en contact, lieu de possibles mélanges. C'est à cette frontière qui différencie et articule que se produit le sens, dans le rapport entre musique et texte.

Nous étudierons le rapport particulier que Kurtág tisse entre musique et texte à partir notamment de l'opus 24, *Kafka-Fragmente*. L'œuvre fut composée entre 1985 et 1987 pour violon et voix de soprano; le texte est issu de divers extraits du journal et de la correspondance de Franz Kafka, ainsi que de ses aphorismes. À partir d'un matériau souvent extrêmement réduit, Kurtág compose ici son cycle de miniatures le plus étendu : ce sont quarante pièces, dont la plupart ne dépassent pas les deux minutes, réparties en quatre sections. Ici, comme dans toute son œuvre vocale, l'écriture cherche de manière soutenue le croisement du texte et de la musique, l'arrêt de leur glissement dans la cristallisation d'une multitude d'images musicales qui se rapportent de manière explicite au texte. Kurtág déploie pour cela un grand nombre de processus dans plusieurs dimensions, mettant en résonance les mots de Kafka avec le matériau musical, la forme, les gestes des interprètes, allant du niveau le plus direct, pragmatique et littéral au niveau le plus symbolique et abstrait. Par la mise en relation de ces dimensions, la simple illustration du texte est déjà dépassée. De manière constante, si des rapports de représentation se créent entre une figure musicale et le texte, l'écriture de Kurtág tend à les déborder, à les attirer vers autre chose.

À partir de *Kafka-Fragmente* – mais on citera aussi les pièces pour piano qui constituent *Játékok* – on développera ici une série de traits particuliers de l'écriture de Kurtág, de manière à mettre en évidence dans un premier temps la cristallisation de l'image musicale, son côté figé et figuratif vis-à-vis du texte. Dans un deuxième temps, d'autres caractéristiques de l'œuvre viendront souligner l'autre face fondamentale de l'image chez Kurtág : l'aspect intensif, énergétique et dynamique qui complète et en même temps déjoue l'élément figuratif et figé. Traitées ici les unes après les autres pour rendre plus claires leurs interactions, les perspectives figuratives et énergétiques constituent en réalité les faces d'un même geste complexe, un mouvement qui instaure et en même temps défigure l'élément figuratif. Ce serait cela l'image musicale chez Kurtág : un mouvement saisi dans le cours de son accomplissement, celui de l'action des forces énergétiques sur les représentations figuratives.

Fixation de l'image

Le premier trait de cette écriture, propre à éclairer l'établissement des images, concerne la brièveté des pièces. Presque tout le catalogue du compositeur se caractérise par une recherche quasiment obsessionnelle de la concision. Ce travail de réduction de la forme et de condensation du matériau, Kurtág le décèle, pour se l'approprier ensuite, chez certains compositeurs romantiques, chez Béla Bartók et surtout chez Anton Webern, dont il copia, lors de son séjour à Paris, de nombreuses partitions. Dès son opus 1, cette brièveté favorise la cristallisation de l'image musicale : elle permet une saisie synthétique de la pièce, réunissant dans l'instant tous les éléments, par ailleurs hétérogènes, qui la constituent. Par ailleurs, par leur concision, ces pièces s'insurgent contre une qualité que l'on peut considérer comme inhérente à la musique, c'est-à-dire le temps, la durée, qualité qui contribue à la précarité de toute signification assignée à la musique.

D'autres éléments de l'écriture viennent intensifier l'unité et la clôture de certaines pièces, favorisant en même temps un rapport étroit entre le moment musical et le texte. L'un des moteurs de l'écriture de Kurtág est le contraste. Les pièces sont souvent regroupées en cycles et leur succession se fait généralement sur la base d'une différenciation de moments caractérisés. Renforçant leur démarcation, l'utilisation fréquente de parenthèses formelles – l'apparition d'un même élément au début et à la fin – closent les pièces sur elles-mêmes en les détachant de ce qui les entoure. Finalement, à chaque arrêt, le silence entre les pièces interrompt le flux musical et marque une claire articulation, coupant l'instant de ce qui précède et de ce qui suit, unifiant texte et musique presque comme dans un emblème où image et légende se complètent.

Un deuxième trait est le caractère spécifique du matériau musical utilisé par Kurtág. On a parlé du contraste entre les différents fragments; or l'opposition d'éléments caractérisés ne concerne pas seulement l'articulation des pièces dans le recueil, mais aussi celle des matériaux à l'intérieur de certains fragments. Ceci est évident à la lumière des textes de Kafka choisis par Kurtág dans *Kafka-Fragmente*. Les aphorismes et les extraits du journal de l'écrivain tchèque sont souvent construits à partir de la comparaison ou de l'opposition de deux propositions. La structure binaire des textes est alors souvent reprise par la musique selon un procédé très simple qui consiste à organiser la pièce à partir d'éléments contrastants, sur la base par exemple de deux champs harmoniques ou de deux caractères rythmiques. Ces matériaux sont fréquemment juxtaposés, par exemple dans l'alternance de consonances jouées pianissimo et de dissonances jouées fortissimo qui accompagnent, dans le onzième fragment de la première partie, la succession des mots « endormi, réveillé » (exemple 13-1). Les matériaux contradictoires peuvent être aussi superposés, comme dans le premier fragment de l'œuvre, qui comporte un ostinato au violon et un déploiement libre, presque chaotique, de la partie vocale : c'est ainsi qu'est reprise l'opposition entre « les bons » qui « marchent du même pas » et « les autres » qui « dansent autour d'eux la danse du temps » à laquelle fait référence le texte de Kafka (exemple 13-2).

Mais il existe une spécificité encore plus notoire de ce matériau musical : le contraste de moments caractérisés n'est possible ici que grâce à la qualité historique de ces matériaux. Collectionneur d'« *objets* volés » et « *objets* trouvés », Kurtág utilise dans son œuvre des vestiges figés des langages musicaux du passé. Restes de la tonalité, bribes de danses, figuralismes : il s'agit là d'un matériau hautement sédimenté, un matériau autour duquel se sont solidifiées des connotations particulières, qui véhicule une mémoire et déploie, au-delà de lui-même, c'est-à-dire du purement sonore, des images qui lui sont associées.

Citons par exemple les apparitions fantomatiques de la tonalité dans *Kafka-Fragmente*. Comme de fugaces souvenirs, les restes du système tonal

EXEMPLE 13-1 György Kurtág, *Kafka-Fragmente*, Op. 24 (1985-87), pour soprano et violon, « Sonntag, den 19. Juli 1910 (Berceuse II) », début du fragment I-11. © Editio Musica Budapest.

EXEMPLE 13-2 György Kurtág, *Kafka-Fragmente*, Op. 24 (1985-87), pour soprano et violon, « Die Guten gehen im gleichen Schritt », début du fragment I-1. © Editio Musica Budapest.

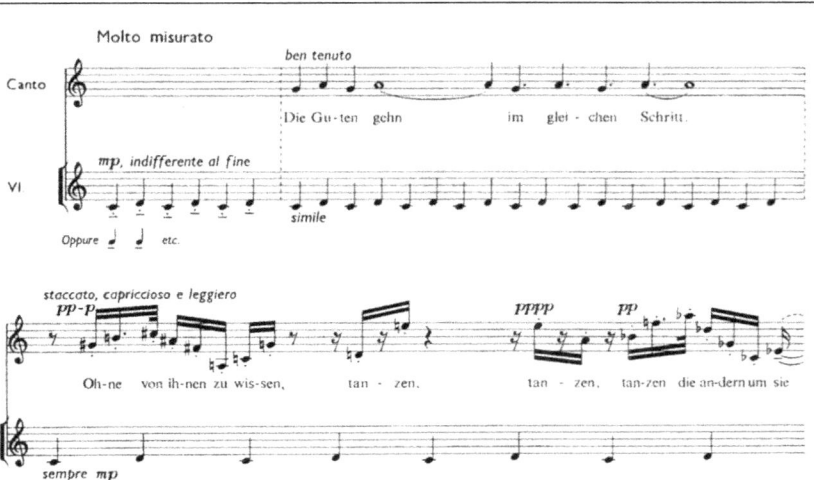

surgissent dans une écriture qui correspond plutôt à un travail modal. Toujours évanescent, le système tonal n'organise pas l'écriture de Kurtág, mais des bribes en apparaissent – des accords, une cadence, des bouts de gamme, des oppositions entre consonance et dissonance –, renvoyant un instant à cette tradition musicale et à ce qu'elle véhicule comme sens. Dans le rapport avec le texte, ces moments sont par exemple associés au mot « pur » dans le fragment III-6 « Der begrenzte Kreis » [Le cercle limité] ou ironiquement aux mots « la plus belle expérience » dans le texte du fragment I-13 (« Un jour je me suis cassé la jambe, ce fut la plus belle expérience de ma vie ») (exemples 13-3 et 13-4). Au-delà des références à la tonalité, d'autres éléments très caractérisés apparaissent, souvent en tant que figuralismes qui renvoient au texte : un ostinato dans la première pièce, des lignes descendantes contrastant avec des sonorités aiguës et aériennes dans le fragment III-4, une longue vocalise sur le mot *Musik* dans le fragment sur la danseuse Eduardowa.

Ce sont des matériaux qui ont perdu leur fluidité originelle, ils se sont solidifiés, figés et, dans leur rapport au texte, relèvent du cliché, du code et de la convention. Ce sont ces formules utilisées par Kurtág, souvent contrastées et donnant forme à une miniature, qui nous permettent de parler d'images musicales dans le sens le plus élémentaire, c'est-à-dire dans leur fonction illustrative, dans leur dimension figurative vis-à-vis du texte.

Exemple 13-3 György Kurtág, *Kafka-Fragmente*, Op. 24 (1985-87), pour soprano et violon, « Der begrenzte Kreis », fragment III-6. © Editio Musica Budapest.

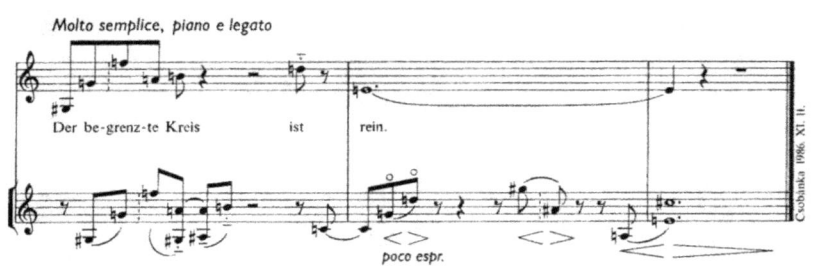

Exemple 13-4 György Kurtág, *Kafka-Fragmente*, Op. 24 (1985-87), pour soprano et violon, « Einmal brach ich mir das Bein », début du fragment I-13. © Editio Musica Budapest.

La possibilité d'associer le sens musical au sens verbal, c'est-à-dire le caractère langagier de la musique, est étroitement lié à cet aspect du matériau musical. Carl Dahlhaus écrit que le matériau musical, dans le sens que Theodor W. Adorno attribue à ce concept, n'est pas à considérer en tant que pure matière, mais comme « la somme des relations sonores préformées et déterminées par l'histoire »[1]. En tant que lieu où s'est sédimentée l'expérience passée, le matériau ressemble « à un langage aux formules usées » mais, poursuit le musicologue, et l'on verra comment cela se passe dans le cas de Kurtág, s'ouvre « également aux possibilités d'expression nouvelles »[2].

Dynamisation de l'image

Nous avons jusqu'à présent, avec ces considérations concernant les formes brèves et les particularités du matériau musical, fait référence à l'aspect « fixe » de l'image musicale. Or, l'image chez Kurtág comporte une double face et dépasse la simple illustration du texte. Car l'image musicale est dynamique, dans le sens où elle possède une force propre, celle de sa nature intrinsèque. Celle-ci est de l'ordre de la manifestation, de l'objectivité sonore et ne se réduit pas à la transposition d'un texte ou à une métaphore visuelle.[3] Plusieurs traits de l'écriture de Kurtág vont dans cette direction : ils constituent une deuxième série d'aspects orientés vers une ouverture du sens, manifestant le caractère intensif, énergétique et dynamique de l'image musicale.

Si, comme nous l'avons vu, la brièveté de la forme permet une saisie synthétique des pièces, elle est aussi l'un des facteurs qui multiplie leur intensité. Loin d'une quelconque pauvreté et d'un rapport simple vis-à-vis du texte, dans cette réduction à l'essentiel du matériau, chaque note devient un monde, débordant le cadre restreint de la miniature et le rapport univoque vis-à-vis des mots. Chaque instant se charge d'une force rare car il recèle, sous une apparente austérité, la charge sédimentée du matériau, une densité qui persiste en tant que soubassement latent. L'aphorisme musical paraît ainsi coïncider avec la forme brève littéraire, forme privilégiée du texte vocal chez Kurtág, caractérisé par une abondance de sens en peu d'éléments.

Par ailleurs, pareil en cela au fragment littéraire, le fragment musical acquiert un double caractère à l'intérieur du recueil : fermé sur lui-même, comme on a pu le voir plus haut, il est en même temps ouvert sur le reste du cycle. En effet, le fragment musical est à considérer concurremment de deux manières, « comme parole absolue, indépendante et se suffisant à elle-même, mais aussi comme élément d'une série dans laquelle elle est prise et dans laquelle elle est susceptible de faire entendre un autre sens ».[4] Le recueil de pièces brèves se donne alors comme une forme ouverte, où une multiplicité de liens se tissent entre tous les éléments du cycle. En ce sens, dans *Kafka-Fragmente*, les pièces « doubles », pièces qui sont reprises à distance, constituent le rapport le plus évident entre certains fragments. D'autres liens se manifestent à travers les titres dont Kurtág a pourvu les pièces, par exemple entre les berceuses, les « scènes » dans le tramway et dans la gare, les *in memoriam*, etc. Enfin, de manière latente ou tout aussi manifeste que dans les fragments « doubles », la reprise d'une technique particulière, d'un matériau, d'un motif, d'une sonorité spécifique, produit à chaque fois de nouveaux effets de sens.

La structure de l'œuvre comme recueil de fragments fait que le sens d'une figure musicale peut être modifié selon sa position dans le recueil et sa relation avec d'autres éléments. Ceci a pour conséquence de dynamiser le moment musical qui se rapporte au texte, de manière à ce qu'on ne puisse pas lui attribuer une assignation fixe. Le procédé employé est la circulation des éléments dans le cycle, toujours changeants et jamais associés de manière définitive à une signification précise. Dans l'œuvre de Kurtág existe une forte mobilité des matériaux, des techniques et des motifs qui, s'ils peuvent correspondre dans un premier moment à une idée particulière du texte, se transforment par la suite, devenant des entités plurivoques.

Arrêtons-nous à présent sur ce qui constitue certainement la plus forte possibilité de dépasser le caractère illustratif d'un matériau réifié en relation au texte dans la musique de Kurtág : la force du geste. Qu'il s'agisse de composition, de pédagogie ou d'interprétation, l'importance du geste est une constante chez Kurtág et c'est peut-être dans *Játékok*, point de croisement de ces trois activités, que cette dimension apparaît le plus clairement. *Játékok*, sorte de laboratoire d'où sortent, et où reviennent parfois, plusieurs de ses idées, est un ensemble de pièces brèves pour piano que Kurtág commence à composer dans les années 1970 et qui ont été conçues d'abord pour accompagner l'enfant dans sa première approche du piano. Ce but pédagogique va, avec les cahiers successifs, laisser la place à une sorte de carnet de bord, journal intime musical dont le teint autobiographique est, par ailleurs, présent dans toute l'œuvre du compositeur.

Dans la préface du recueil, Kurtág encourage l'élève à « circuler sans peur, avec rapidité sur tout l'espace du clavier, dès le début de l'apprentissage, au lieu de chercher la note avec circonspection, au lieu de compter les rythmes »[5]. En effet, dans une partie des pièces du premier volume, et pour rendre plus vivante l'approche de l'enfant avec l'instrument, « la note importe peu, ce sont le geste et le registre approximatif qui comptent »[6]. Il s'agit de penser la musique en termes presque physiologiques car, selon la déclaration de Kurtág dans une conférence dédiée à cette œuvre, il s'agit dans l'interprétation de « combiner sensation physique et réflexion sur ce qui se passe en termes musicaux »[7]. L'importance accordée au geste musical commence par une attention particulière au rapport du musicien avec son instrument. Le piano ne doit pas être perçu par l'enfant comme un corps étranger. Le contact physique avec l'instrument doit se faire de manière vivante, l'approche doit être de « chair et de sang »[8].

Au-delà du pédagogique et de l'interprétation, le soin du geste est un élément déterminant directement l'écriture de Kurtág. Sa conception rythmique découle de cette préoccupation. Il s'agit d'un système conçu à partir de valeurs longues et brèves en lien avec le tempo choisi, plutôt commandé par le geste que par la soumission à l'exactitude d'un débit régulier. En concordance avec ce principe, Kurtág tend, dans sa musique, à se rapprocher de la diction du langage parlé, d'un caractère *parlando*, qui témoigne de l'abandon de la rigueur de la mesure pour s'accorder à une rythmique plus souple, celle de la musique folklorique, marquée par le débit naturel de la parole.

Soulignant l'aspect corporel et gestuel de sa musique, de nombreuses formes de danses surgissent dans l'œuvre de Kurtág. Dans *Kafka-Fragmente*, par exemple, valses, marches, csárdás, « danses hassidiques », reviennent à plusieurs reprises en tant que gestes figés dont il s'agirait peut-être de retrouver et réactiver l'origine corporelle. Pourtant loin du théâtre musical, le compositeur hongrois demande à l'interprète de son œuvre d'être attentif à toute une série d'indications concernant des postures (*se figer*), des attitudes (*avec élan, indifferente al fine*), et des gestes particuliers qui peuvent avoir ou non des résultats effectifs sur la sonorité. C'est le cas dans le fragment I-4 de *Kafka-Fragmente*, pièce-pantomime où la cantatrice doit mimer les gestes du violoniste. Dans la partition, on lit : « la pièce doit être une sorte de pantomime. La cantatrice doit suivre les acrobaties et la rage du violoniste avec une tension montante, avec excitation et même avec peur, jusqu'à ce que la voix tombe aussi à la fin »[9]. Pour clore la pièce, la soprano, avec la charge des mouvements physiques qu'elle vient de réaliser, doit exposer (en Sprechstimme) encore une fois le seul mot qui constitue le texte de ce fragment, *Ruhelos* [sans répit] (exemple 13-5). Les gestes imitant le violoniste marquant de leur empreinte le chant, la cantatrice ne peut prononcer le mot que *senza voce*, comme l'indique la partition. Cette expérience physique – l'empreinte du geste dans le résultat

EXEMPLE 13-5 György Kurtág, *Kafka-Fragmente*, Op. 24 (1985-87), pour soprano et violon, « Ruhelos », fragment I-4. © Editio Musica Budapest.

1 Das Stück soll eine Art Pantomime sein. Die Sängerin folgt den Akrobatien und dem Wüten des Geigers mit wachsender Spannung, Erregung, sogar Angst, bis ihr am Ende wirklich auch die Stimme versagt.

The piece should be a kind of pantomime. The singer follows the acrobatics and the rage of the violinist with increasing tension, excitement, moreover fear, until her voice also fails in the end.

A darab egyfajta pantomim legyen. Az énekesnő növekvő feszültséggel, izgalommal, sőt félelemmel követi a hegedűs akrobatikáit és dühöngését, mig a végén a hangja is felmondja a szolgálatot.

2 Mit grellem, gepreßtem Ton – die Sekundenreibungen sirenenartig, aber auch die Oktaven und Unisoni unangenehm falsch

With a strident, choked sound–the second clashes screaming, but even the octaves and unison unpleasantly out of key.

Fülsértő, préselt hangon – a szekund-súrlódásokat szirénázva, de az oktávokat és uniszónókat is kellemetlenül hamisan.

sonore, cette trace qui demeure, devient audible et participe au sens de la musique – est fondamentale dans l'œuvre du compositeur hongrois.

Le balbutiement dans le fragment IV-2, la voix entrecoupée dans le fragment IV-6 ou les cris du fragment I-19 placent le musical au plus proche du physiologique. Kurtág conçoit des gestes expressifs qui, ayant une origine corporelle, deviennent autant de manières de créer une tension singulière dans le discours musical, et de réactiver ainsi un matériau qui avait perdu tout dynamisme. Avec cette présence du corps, le caractère de langage du matériau musical, les significations qu'il véhicule de par son caractère objectif, est déjoué. La force du geste apparaît comme l'élément qui réactive les formules figées et dynamise les images musicales, désarmant le rapport de représentation vis-à-vis du texte.

La sensation

On a décrit les deux faces de l'image musicale chez Kurtág, l'une plus statique, l'autre dynamique et la manière dont elles se complètent pour détourner le caractère figuratif que certains gestes musicaux pourraient prendre en relation avec le texte. Cette manière de partir d'un élément figuratif pour l'attirer vers autre chose fait penser à certains peintres qui travaillent au XXe siècle à partir de la figuration et qui déploient, tout en gardant l'élément illustratif, toute une série de dispositifs pour le transformer. Nous faisons ici référence à l'œuvre de Francis Bacon et à l'interprétation que nous en livre Gilles Deleuze[10].

La peinture figurative implique l'existence d'un rapport entre une image et un objet qu'elle est censée représenter. De même que l'on parle de figuration en peinture, on pose ici l'hypothèse que, dans l'œuvre de Kurtág, un rapport similaire de représentation s'établit entre le matériau musical et le sens du texte. Si le figuralisme musical, dont Kurtág fait grand usage, est défini justement en tant que représentation du texte mis en musique, comme matérialisation sonore du référent du mot, on peut alors parler d'un caractère figuratif dans cette musique, car l'art figuratif « ne présente pas seulement une disposition de formes, masses, couleurs à considérer en elle-même, mais en plus il représente une autre chose […]. L'œuvre pose, à travers elle-même, autre chose qu'elle même »[11].

Or, selon Deleuze, au-delà de toute hiérarchie, différence ou autonomie, un problème est commun à tous les arts : « en peinture comme en musique, il ne s'agit pas de reproduire ou d'inventer des formes, mais de capter des forces. C'est même par là qu'aucun art n'est figuratif »[12]. Pourtant, dans les tableaux de Bacon il y a toujours un élément figuratif qui subsiste : un Pape, un homme qui crie sous un parapluie. Cependant, si Bacon tient à la figure, ce n'est que pour l'arracher au figuratif. De même, Kurtág ne renonce en rien à la figure musicale représentant un moment du texte ; pourtant son écriture travaille sans cesse à son dépassement. Le fait de placer la figure au centre de leur création tout en la déjouant semble caractériser l'œuvre de Kurtág comme celle de Bacon. La deuxième série d'éléments auxquels on a précédemment fait allusion nous permet de soutenir la comparaison.

La fragmentation, la circulation des motifs dans le cycle iraient dans le sens d'une libération de la figure qui n'est plus attachée de manière définitive à un sens précis. Sans renoncer à la figure locale qui peut s'attacher au mot, Kurtág, conscient du caractère plurivoque du phénomène musical, élargit la sphère des relations au texte, une sphère qu'il dynamise en multipliant les décalages, la rendant instable.

Mais ce premier type de processus n'acquiert toute sa puissance que par la présence de l'incroyable intensité du geste. Ainsi, à partir d'un matériau hautement sédimenté, avec sa charge historique et son rapport conventionnel avec le texte, le compositeur est capable de capter les forces de la sensation, de ce qui, d'après Paul Valéry, « se transmet directement, en évitant le détour ou l'ennui d'une histoire à raconter »[13]. Selon Deleuze, c'est bien en cela que consiste la tâche de l'artiste.

Ce qui prime dans la musique vocale de Kurtág, ce n'est pas la représentation musicale du sens du texte, mais ce qu'il fait subir à cette représentation, la manière dont il dépasse et excède le figuralisme. Ce que donnent à entendre ses images est un travail de déformation de l'élément figuratif, un mouvement toujours en train de s'accomplir qui dévoile ou renouvelle le flux et le grouillement oubliés dans l'élément réifié du langage musical. Fragmentation et puissance du geste libèrent de la simple illustration le lien entre musique et texte, et le font entrer dans l'ordre de la sensation, présence qui agit directement sur le système nerveux.

Notes

1 Carl Dahlhaus, « Sens et non-sens dans la musique », dans *Essais sur la nouvelle musique*, Genève, Contrechamps, 2004, p. 170.
2 *Ibid.*
3 « "Enargétique" dans le sens de "enargeia", expression utilisée par Homère dans le livre XIV de l'Odyssée (161) au moment où Eumée s'en va et apparaît sous les traits d'une jeune femme très belle. Ce qui apparaît à Ulysse est la déesse, mais son fils Télémaque ne la voit pas, et Homère dit : "Car ce n'est pas à tous que les dieux apparaissent 'enargeis'". Normalement on traduit le mot "enargeis" par "visible", mais "argos" veut dire "étincelant, ce qui brille de soi même". [Martin] Heidegger, qui cite ce passage dans un court texte, *Zur Frage nach der Bestimmung der Sache des Denkens*, un discours prononcé en 1965 en honneur de [Ludwig] Binswanger, réfléchissant sur le mot utilisé par les latins pour traduire "enargeia", "evidentia" ("évidence", dans le sens de "devenir visible") met en relief la responsabilité des latins dans le passage

d'une "vision rayonnante", archaïque, fondée sur la force propre de la nature intrinsèque de l'objet, sur son énergie profonde, à une vision basée sur la signification donnée à la chose par le sujet qui regarde. Le propre de l'image musicale est sa nature rayonnante, sa nature "énargétique" qui dérive de son énergie intrinsèque. Mais le "paradigme rétinien", dominant dans la civilisation occidentale, a tout fait pour étouffer l'"enargeia" sous des métaphores poétiques fondées sur les relations mimétiques de l'image visuelle ». Gianfranco Vinay, « Post-scriptum philologique sur l'interprétation, l'exécution et l'analyse », *Musimédiane*, n°2, 2006, note 9.
4 Bernard Roukhomovsky, *Lire les formes brèves*, Paris, Nathan, 2001, p. 8.
5 György Kurtág, « Préface à *Játékok* », dans *György Kurtág. Entretiens, textes, écrits sur son œuvre*, sous la direction de Philippe Albèra, Genève, Contrechamps, 1995, p. 33.
6 György Kurtág, « *Játékok* : une leçon de György Kurtág », dans *György Kurtág. Entretiens, textes, écrits sur son œuvre*, p. 26.
7 *Ibid.*, p. 25.
8 *Ibid.*, p. 24.
9 György Kurtág, *Kafka-Fragmente* (partition), Budapest, Edito musica, 1992, p. 4.
10 Gilles Deleuze, *Francis Bacon. Logique de la sensation*, Paris, Seuil, 2002.
11 Etienne Souriau, *Vocabulaire d'esthétique*, Paris, Presses Universitaires de France, 1999, p. 743.
12 Gilles Deleuze, *op. cit.*, p. 57.
13 Cité par Gilles Deleuze, *op. cit.*, p. 40-41.

Bibliographie

Adorno, Theodor W. *Mahler, une physionomie musicale*. Traduit par Jean-Louis Leleu et Théo Leydenbach. Paris : Minuit, 1976.
———. *Théorie esthétique*. Traduit par Marc Jimenez et Eliane Kaufholz. Paris : Klincksieck, 1995.
Albèra, Philippe (dir.). *György Kurtág. Entretiens, textes, écrits sur son œuvre*. Genève : Contrechamps, 1995.
Dahlhaus, Carl. *Essais sur la nouvelle musique*. Traduit par Hans Hildenbrand. Genève : Contrechamps, 2004.
Deleuze, Gilles. *Francis Bacon. Logique de la sensation*. Paris : Seuil, 2002.
———. *Logique du sens*. Paris : Minuit, 1969.
Kurtág, György. *Kafka-Fragmente* (partition). Budapest : Edito Musica, 1992.
Roukhomovsky, Bernard. *Lire les formes brèves*. Paris : Nathan, 2001.
Souriau, Etienne. *Vocabulaire d'esthétique*. Paris : Presses Universitaires de France, 1999.
Vinay, Gianfranco. « Post-scriptum philologique sur l'interprétation, l'exécution et l'analyse ». *Musimédiane*, *n^o* 2, 2006. Disponible en ligne à l'adresse : http://www.musimediane.com/spip.php?article53.

FOURTEEN

Dirges and Ditties: György Kurtág's Latest Settings of Poetry by Anna Akhmatova

JULIA GALIEVA-SZOKOLAY

GYÖRGY KURTÁG'S INTEREST IN languages is evident in the wide array of verbal sources he has used in his work. Texts, titles, and mottoes in Hungarian, German, French, English, Italian, Russian, ancient Greek, and, more recently, Romanian appear in his compositions of the past few decades.[1] This impressive polyglossia possibly reflects Kurtág's relentless desire to obtain a fresh look at himself, for an immersion into a foreign language and literature can be an exhilarating experience which can have a profound impact on an individual's sense of identity, especially in the case of artists.[2] Perhaps the composer's interest in exploring different linguistic realities was nurtured by memories of the polyethnic environment of Lugos, Bánát, where he spent his formative years.[3] It is remarkable that *Messages of the Late Miss R.V. Troussova*, Op. 17, commissioned and premiered in France by the Ensemble Intercontemporain, which launched Kurtág's international recognition in the early 1980s, was a setting of poetry by a Russian author, Rimma Dalos, who resided in Hungary. The choice of the Russian language, somewhat "peripheral" to Western European artistic discourse and rather unpopular among the Hungarian intellectual elite during the period of Soviet rule, proved effective in stimulating the composer's creative development. The sheer quantity of Kurtág's Russian vocal scores, which have emerged periodically since the mid-1970s, suggests that this venture was gratifying and necessary for him, providing an important outlet for his artistic impulses. The list shown in table 14-1 demonstrates that the musical realization of Russian material has become, over the years, an indispensable component of Kurtág's self-fashioning.[4]

TABLE 14-1 György Kurtág, Russian works written between 1976 and 2008.

1976	*Музыка для голоса и камешек* [*Music for voice and pebbles*] to the composer's text;
1976	*И снова дождь* [*It rains again*] for voice, oboe, clarinet in B flat, cimbalom, harp and celesta to poem by Matsukura Ranran in Russian translation of Vera Markova (version for voice and piano);
1976–1980	*Послания покойной Р.В.Трусовой* **op. 17** [*Messages of the Late Miss R.V.Troussova*] for soprano and chamber ensemble to twenty-one poems by Rimma Dalos;
1979	*Omaggio a Luigi Nono* **op. 16**, six choruses for mixed choir to poems by Anna Akhmatova and Rimma Dalos;
1979–1980	*Пословица* [*Proverb*] for voice and stones to folk text;
1979–1981	*Примус X* [*Primus X*] for four–five children's voices, violin, trumpet or clarinet or viola and trombone to poem by Osip Mandelstam (part of *Háromgyerekdal* [*Three children's songs*, 1971–1981] on Russian and Hungarian texts by Osip Mandelstam and Júlia Vámos);
1979–1982	*Сцены из романа* **op. 19** [*Scenes from a Novel*] for soprano, violin, double bass and cimbalom, fifteen songs to poems by Rimma Dalos;
1980–1994	*Песни уныния и печали* **op. 18** [*Songs of Despair and Sorrow*], six choruses for double choir and instruments to poems by Mikhail Lermontov, Aleksandr Blok, Sergei Esenin, Osip Mandelstam, Anna Akhmatova, and Marina Tsvetaeva;
1982	*Разбилась любовь ...* [*Broken love*] for voice and piano to poem by Rimma Dalos;
1982–1987	*Реквием по другу* **op. 26** [*Requiem for the Beloved*] for voice and piano to poems by Rimma Dalos;
1983	*Как сердечко твое ...* [*And how thy heart*] for solo voice to poem by Rimma Dalos;
1983–1985	*За колос ячменя* [*A spike of barley*] for voice and piano to poem by Matsuo Bashō in Russian translation of Vera Markova;
1989–in progress	*Письмо Модеста Арсению* [*A letter from Modest to Arseny*] for male voice and piano to text by M. Musorgsky;
1996	*Встреча* [*A meeting*] for solo voice to text by Daniil Kharms;
1996	*Как же странно мне было ...* [*I felt strange*] for solo voice to poem by Aleksandr Galich (version for voice and two trumpets *ad libitum*);
1997–1998	*До свиданья, друг мой ...* [*Farewell, my friend*] for solo voice to poem by Sergei Esenin;
1997–2008	*Four Songs to Poems by Anna Akhmatova* **op. 41** for soprano and ensemble;
2000	*Olyan, Amilyen ...* [*This is how I am*] for solo voice to poem by Anna Akhmatova (fragment) in Hungarian translation of Zsuzsa Rab.

This collection displays a notable diversity of literary sources, unmatched by works in any other language used by the composer, except, perhaps, his maternal Hungarian. At the same time, it highlights an inclination towards writings which offer a psychological inquiry into human nature by contemplating the traumatic experience of cultural, social, and personal isolation. The testimony of emigration, exile, and alienation unifies the vivid thematic palette of Kurtág's Russian scores. This tendency was first established in the musical responses to the opuses of the amateur émigré poet Rimma Dalos (b.1944), whose artistic alter ego—the mysterious "Late Miss R.V. Troussova"—exposed the author's profound personal crisis accompanied by her painful search for identity and questioning of her national heritage.[5] Since then, the focus on works of literature which convey the drama of self-definition remained, for Kurtág, a guideline for scripting his "Russian saga," inhabited by memorable characters from the Holy Fool (*юродивый*) to poet-prophet, and decorated by meaningful cultural symbols from the ditty (*частушка*) to the lament (*плач*). Various aspects of Russian culture and its traditions illuminate Kurtág's scores of the 1970s and '80s, reaching areas beyond the setting of Russian poetry; the works of the following decade expose an even tighter embrace of the world of Russian history, literature, and music.[6] In his approach to this repertoire, Kurtág appears to rely on what Richard Taruskin calls an idea of "otherness" exemplified in cultural images of Russia which represent it as intimately related, yet dramatically distinct from "Europe proper."[7] Taruskin suggests that territorial remoteness, ingenuity, "barbarism," innate spirituality, openness, hermetism, untamed emotionalism, suppressed sensuality, and so forth have been traditionally recognized as qualities which define Russian culture in a larger European context. The composer seems to forge this amalgam of cultural beliefs into a stable point of reference that helps determine his own place on both the national and international cultural platforms. For Hungarian audiences, and particularly for the domestic dissident circles Kurtág had been close to, the extent of his involvement with the Russian material revealed a personality unaffected by the rise and fall of the political tide, and strengthened the sense of alterity which had formed the core of Kurtág's artistic reputation from the beginning of the 1960s.[8] And for the public outside Hungary, mainly unfamiliar with the peculiarities of the local Hungarian political agenda, the association of Kurtág with the traditional idea of Russia as representing the Eastern frontier of the European cultural terrain emerged as an attractive factor that reinforced the astounding expressiveness of his lapidary style. Set against the "centrality" of Western

European artistic practices, Kurtág's move towards the "marginal" territory of Russian literature and poetry articulated his uniqueness and secured unwavering attention to his musical stance in the plurality of the postmodernist discourse. After the successful exposition of the Russian subject in the Rimma Dalos cycles, the composer has repeatedly reproduced the thematic constellations which accentuate the enticing otherness of Eastern European culture, having used both his mother tongue and Russian. Kurtág's "Russian explorations" of the late 1990s will be the main focus of the present overview.

Kurtág's Russian compositions of the past fifteen years contain a group of vocal miniatures based on the stylistically diverse texts of several twentieth-century authors, such as the acmeist Anna Akhmatova (1889–1966),[9] the "imaginist" and "village poet" Sergei Esenin (1895–1925), the absurdist writer Daniil Kharms (1905–42), and the dissident bard Aleksandr Galich (1918–77). These authors demonstrate Kurtág's fidelity to earlier poetic choices, with Akhmatova and Esenin being his long-term poetic associates.[10] The basic pattern of meaning and emotion also has much in common with ideas found in other Russian works by Kurtág, which embrace the themes of death and mourning, ethics and judgment, freedom and artistic integrity, self-examination and self-reproach. One essential aspect, however, makes this collection stand out; namely, its concern with the "poet's fate"—a particularly dense cluster of Russian cultural myths about the appropriate life and death for poets. The notion of the "poet's fate" is a curious blend of the Romantic concept of national genius and of Russian patriotic civic tradition. It envisions the poet as "more than a poet"[11]— as a "conscience of the nation" and a model to which society as a whole should attend.[12] Over the course of the nineteenth century, the poet's image acquired the aura of a victim of despotic oppression. This archetype survived well into the modern period, granting the poet a "mark of importance gratified by an extraordinary level of relevance" for Russian literature and society.[13] Anna Akhmatova, who navigated the arduous journey of her life in both Imperial Russia and the proletarian State of the Soviet Republics, assessed the martyrdom of Osip Mandelstam in the 1930s as an ideal poetic destiny and remarked on Joseph Brodsky's political trial in 1964: "What a biography is being made for our red-head! As if he had hired someone."[14] The thematic tendency of Kurtág's latest Russian settings corresponds with this cultural tradition which extols literary martyrs and political exiles: the Esenin song is a musical rendition of his suicide note; the Galich piece is an arrangement of a nostalgic ditty about forced emigration; and the Akhmatova collection elucidates her dramatic fate as a poet who lived "to accumulate, inherit, and stand for the literary legacy of an entire era."[15] These works are focused on various thematic elements of the collective Russian myth of the poet, which is by no means an organized entity, but a complex of overlapping concepts reflecting the historical circumstances of life in that country. Themes woven into the fabric of this myth range from general cultural and socio-political debates to specific issues of style and poetics, and often invoke discussions of national identity, artistic creativity, poetic craft, and poets' relations with the ruling class.

I would like to discuss Kurtág's interpretation of the Russian myth of the poet using his selection of verses by Anna Akhmatova, who contributed to this myth, not only by commemorating perished poets of her generation (Blok, Gumilev, Esenin, Mayakovsky, Mandelstam, Tsvetaeva, and others), but also by actively shaping her own life as this myth's supreme illustration.[16] Akhmatova appears in Kurtág's Op. 41 in relation to three other major national poets: Pushkin, Blok, and Mandelstam. By bringing them together, Kurtág combines several contrasting approaches and various presentation strategies. As we will see, the images of poetry unfold in the music in constantly shifting perspectives, at times resulting in what seems to be unexpected and paradoxical interpretations. Inspired by the current studies in Slavistics, my work will focus on Kurtág's response to the poetry, understood as an act of self-reflection, a search for aesthetic legitimacy, and a matter of imprinting a personal vision on some of the best-known excerpts in the Russian poetic tradition.

Four Songs to Poems by Anna Akhmatova, Op. 41: Poetic Sources

Four Songs to Poems by Anna Akhmatova, Op. 41, for soprano and instrumental ensemble is based on poems from different periods of Akhmatova's career (see table 14-2). The first "Pushkin: Who Knows What Such Fame Is Like" was written in 1943 during Akhmatova's short return from obscurity after more than two decades of state-imposed silence. The second, "I visited the poet," created in 1914, belongs to Akhmatova's early period and describes the visit she paid to Aleksandr Blok. The last two poems in the cycle respond to grim events: "Today Is the Nameday" to Blok's funeral in Petrograd in August of 1921, and "Voronezh: And the Whole Town" to Akhmatova's 1936 meeting in Voronezh with exiled Osip Mandelstam, before he was sent to die in a Siberian labour camp. At the time my text was written, the first three pieces of the cycle had been

Table 14-2 Anna Akhmatova, original and translated texts in György Kurtág's Opus 41.

Пушкин Кто знает, что такое слава! Какой ценой купил он право, Возможность или благодать Над всем так мудро и лукаво Шутить, таинственно молчать И ногу ножкой называть? ...	**Pushkin** Who knows what such fame is like! At what price did he buy the right, The possibility or the paradise To joke about it all so wisely and cunningly To be mysteriously silent, And to call a foot a "footsie"? <div align="right">March 7, 1943</div>
Александру Блоку Я пришла к поэту в гости, Ровно полдень. Воскресенье. Тихо в комнате просторной, А за окнами мороз. И малиновое солнце Над лохматым сизым дымом ... Как хозяин молчаливый Ясно смотрит на меня! У него глаза такие, Что запомнить каждый должен, Мне же лучше, осторожной, В них и вовсе не глядеть. Но запомнится беседа, Дымный полдень, воскресенье В доме сером и высоком У морских ворот Невы.	**To Alexander Blok** I visited the poet. Precisely at noon. Sunday. It was quiet in the spacious room, And beyond the windows, intense cold And a raspberry sun Above shaggy, bluish smoke ... How keenly my taciturn host Regarded me! He had the kind of eyes That everyone must recall, It was better for me to be careful, And not look at them at all. But I will recall the conversation, The smoky noon, Sunday In the tall, grey house By the sea gates of the Neva. <div align="right">January 1914</div>
*** А Смоленская нынче именинница, Синий ладан над травою стелется И струится пенье панихидное, Не печальное нынче, а светлое. И приводят румяные вдовушки На кладбище мальчиков и девочек Поглядеть на могилы отцовские, А кладбище – роща соловьиная, От сиянья солнечного замерло. Принесли мы Смоленской Заступнице, Принесли Пресвятой Богородице На руках во гробе серебряном Наше солнце, в муке погасшее – Александра, лебедя чистого.	*** Today is the nameday of Our Lady of Smolensk, Dark blue incense drifts over the grass, And the flowing of the Requiem Is no longer sorrowful, but radiant. And the rosy little widows lead Their boys and girls to the cemetery To visit father's grave. But the graveyard – a grove of nightingales, Grows silent from the sun's bright blaze. We have brought to the Intercessor of Smolensk, We have brought to the Holy Mother of God, In our hands in a silver coffin Our sun, extinguished in torment – Alexander, pure swan. <div align="right">August 1921</div>

Воронеж	**Voronezh**
O.M.	O.M.
И город весь стоит оледенелый.	And the whole town is encased in ice,
Как под стеклом деревья, стены, снег.	Trees, walls, snow, as if under glass.
По хрусталям я прохожу несмело.	Timidly, I walk on crystals,
Узорных санок так неверен бег.	Gaily painted sleds skid.
А над Петром воронежским – вороны,	And over the Péter of Voronezh – crows,
Да тополя, и свод светло-зелёный,	Poplar trees, and the dome, light green,
Размытый, мутный, в солнечной пыли,	Faded, dulled, in sunny haze,
И Куликовской битвой веют склоны	And the battle of Kulikovo blows from the slopes
Могучей, победительной земли.	Of the mighty, victorious land.
И тополя, как сдвинутые чаши,	And the poplars, like cups clashed together,
Над нами сразу зазвенят сильней,	Roar over us, stronger and stronger,
Как будто пьют за ликованье наше	As if our joy were toasted by
На брачном пире тысячи гостей.	A thousand guests at a wedding feast.
А в комнате опального поэта	But in the room of the poet in disgrace,
Дежурят страх и муза в свой черёд.	Fear and the Muse keep watch by turns.
И ночь идет,	And the night comes on
Которая не ведает рассвета.	That knows no dawn.
	March 4, 1936

"Pushkin," "I visited the poet," "Today is the nameday of our Lady of Smolensk," and "Voronezh" from *The Complete Poems of Anna Akhmatova*, translated by Judith Hemschemeyer, edited and introduced by Roberta Reeder. Copyright © 1989, 1992, 1997 by Judith Hemschemeyer. Reprinted by permission of Zephyr Press (www.zephyrpress.org). "Пушкин," "Александру Блоку," "А Смоленская нынче именинница," "Воронеж," reprinted by permission of FTM Agency Ltd. (litagent@ftm.ru), Russian Federation.

---

published by Editio Musica Budapest; the last remained unfinished until December 2008.[17] The complete cycle, consisting of the revised "Pushkin," "To Alexander Blok," "Today Is the Nameday," and the recently finished "Voronezh," premiered on 31 January 2009 in New York City (Natalia Zagorinskaya, soprano, UMZE Ensemble conducted by Peter Eötvös). My essay considers the first three songs of the cycle in the 1997 version.

"Пушкин" ["Pushkin"][18]

Kurtág placed "Pushkin," the poem written last, at the beginning of the work, establishing a historical framework of about one hundred years for the four poems of the cycle: from Pushkin (1799–1837) at the beginning to Mandelstam (1891–1938) at the end. Commencing with "Pushkin" may be a reference to the composer's entry into the world of Russian literature, as well as a tribute to that country's foremost poet.[19] Given the composer's literature-centred approach to Russian culture, Pushkin's predominance in every aspect of national art and literature was, for him, an indisputable axiom corroborated by every literary figure whose works he considered as material for his compositions: Lermontov, Blok, Dostoevsky, Mandelstam, and so on.[20] Akhmatova is no exception: her response to Pushkin in twenty-seven poems and in a volume of scholarly essays belongs among the most significant contributions to twentieth-century Russian literature. As Stephanie Sandler has demonstrated, Akhmatova used Pushkinian material to work out contemporary issues, pondering his image as a harbinger of her personal literary challenges. Akhmatova returned to Pushkin as model and solace and "sought an image of how Pushkin modelled his career ... Her Pushkin was a lonely victim of intrigue who risked his life, a Protean genius who absorbed literary lessons from other cultures, a noble poet who recorded the deaths of friends."[21] Kurtág's reading of "Pushkin" bears the imprint of Akhmatova's dialogue with her great predecessor. Consequently, we must begin with an analysis of the Akhmatova-Pushkin relationship, as presented in the poem.

Pushkin's legacy occupied a central place in Akhmatova's poetics, providing a backdrop against which she questioned her fate as a lyric poet and developed an effective strategy of survival in the context of a totalitarian regime that vilified her. In the 1930s, at the peak of the life-threatening purges, Akhmatova undertook an archival research of Pushkin's biography, applying the extracted knowledge to her own tragedy—a protracted unofficial ban on her poetry and persecution of her loved ones. In "Pushkin," written in 1943 during a war-forced evacuation from besieged Leningrad, she contemplates the poet's lesson of civic resistance and turns it into a measure for assessing the moral cost of her sudden official recognition during one of the most dramatic periods of her country's history. The "Pushkin" poem is an illustrative example of Akhmatova's masterful self-presentation by means of implied spiritual connection with the great predecessor: she speaks about *his* art, adopts one of Pushkin's most common metric patterns (iambic tetrameter), and employs easily recognizable allusions and quotations,[22] but her discourse is also self-referential. Pushkin, the *he* in the poem, is a *poet* like her, and the one who, like herself, knows the "price" of creating art. Akhmatova replicates Pushkin's manner of writing by using precise and highly picturesque imagery ("to joke," "to be mysteriously silent," "to call a foot a 'footsie'"). The swift movement from one image to another creates an atmosphere of lightness and wit, but the rhetorical tension contained in the above-mentioned verbal construction indicates that Akhmatova recognizes that Pushkin's style is many-layered and complex. Putting aside the humorous recall of a ballerina's feet Pushkin wrote about in the first chapter of *Eugene Onegin* (illustrated in the music by wide "skipping" figures), Akhmatova's representation of the national genius reveals her concern with the role of a poet who lives in a time of bereavement—like her own time of war, occupation, destruction, famine, and internal oppression.

By setting "Pushkin" for unaccompanied soprano, Kurtág gave maximum exposure to the text.[23] The preoccupation with the meaning projected over the immediate lexical content resulted in detailed performance instructions which emphasize the intensity and intimacy of the message and impart an individual character to every phrase: the opening note (*Non strascinato, con moto, tranquillo. Intenso, con intimissima sonorita*) is followed by the plethora of expression marks that specify the details of the message (*Piu intenso* at bar 4, *sempre dolce* and *pesante* at bar 8, *leggiero grazioso* at bar 12, *misterioso* at bar 13, *eco* and *leggierissimo* at bar 16). The composer carefully responded to the poem's syntactic and metrical organization and made only one textual modification near the end. The tendency towards naturalistic declamation is conveyed through the balanced melodic and rhythmic contour of the vocal part which recalls the stately style of Akhmatova's recitation of her poetry. The composer has claimed that he listened to the authentic recording of this poem; his vocal melody reflects the patterns of the poet's theatrical speech captured on that soundtrack.[24] At the same time, Kurtág stressed the poem's intimate tone by using a low dynamic level (ranging from *p* to *pppp*, with brief occasional *poco f*) and created a symmetrically sculpted melodic profile. His long-drawn slurs emulate the ascent and descent of the melody, giving a sense of the unhurried expanse which never loses inner tension. (See example 14-1.)

This careful musical rendition of the verbal text highlights the main idea of Kurtág's interpretation of the poem: decisions and sacrifices the artist makes along his chosen path. To a certain extent, Kurtág's own artistic credo is similar to that of Akhmatova's. Like the Russian poet, he remained detached from political activity, withheld aesthetic comments in public, and avoided official involvement with the reigning establishment. Like Akhmatova, he relentlessly raised ethical questions through art, and in so doing acquired a high moral authority in his country. For him, the need for public recognition did not outweigh the importance of preserving personal integrity; this is why the rhetorical questions "at what price" and "what such fame is," as well as the evocation of "mysterious silence," may be understood as references to his own public behaviour. Indeed, Kurtág's choice of text may well imply a hidden allegory to his own mode of conduct, indirectly identifying him with the poetic subject of Akhmatova's verses.

EXAMPLE 14-1 György Kurtág, *Four Songs to Poems by Anna Akhmatova*, Op. 41 (1997–2008), version of 1997, "Пушкин" ["Pushkin"], mm. 1–10. © Editio Musica Budapest.

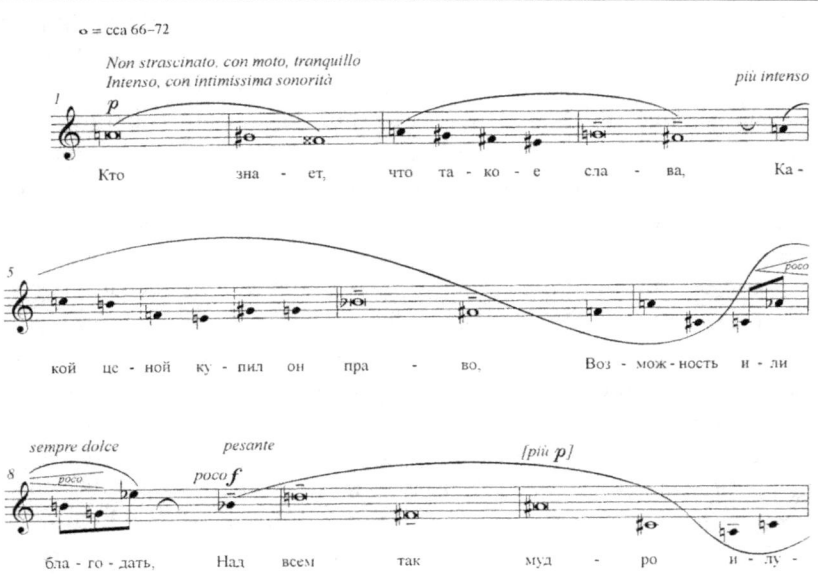

"Александру Блоку" ["To Alexander Blok"][25]

The second poem, "To Alexander Blok,"[26] is Akhmatova's earliest in the cycle. It is also the first of five poems she dedicated to Blok at different times of her life, and the beginning of a dialogue with Blok's work which infused her poetry with his all-encompassing presence.[27] The association with Blok governs many levels of Akhmatova's writing, overflowing generic borders and providing clues to some of her most enigmatic writing.[28] Kurtág's attentiveness to the Akhmatova-Blok poetic connection leaves an imprint on his selection of textual sources for two of his major Russian-language works: *The Messages of the Late Miss R.V. Troussova*, Op. 17, and *Songs of Despair and Sorrow*, Op. 18, which both contain texts by each poet.[29] The Op. 41 cycle includes Akhmatova's poetic responses to biographical events associated with Blok; namely, her 1913 visit with Blok and her reaction to his death in 1921.

The 1913 poem was conceived as a response to Blok's "madrigal" "Красота страшна, вам скажут" ["Beauty's Terrible, They'll Tell You," 1913], addressed and presented to Akhmatova during her visit. Blok's text portrayed her in a romantic, even operatic manner, wearing a Spanish shawl and a rose in her hair. Akhmatova's reply, which replicates the structural design of Blok's original (four unrhymed four-foot trochaic stanzas with three feminine and one masculine ending, the so-called Spanish *romansero*), is, by contrast, markedly non-romantic, and focuses on the poets' intellectual interaction. Akhmatova describes the meeting as a significant yet casual event, placing the main focus on its "staging" and depicting the surroundings in a greater detail than the portrayed individual—her host. This position may be understood in the context of Akhmatova's early style. Since her poetic debut in 1911, her work relates the story of unhappy love and transmits the image of a woman abandoned by a man: seduced, abused, and ignored.[30] Akhmatova made her entrance into the world of poetry as a woman-poet, a new species and a new voice which defined her identity but, by the same token, made her vulnerable to public judgment in two ways. First, numerous critical attempts to identify her with the lyric subject of her poems reinforced the tendency to regard them as purely autobiographical.[31] Therefore, Akhmatova must have been aware that any account of her encounter with Blok, the most famous and most influential poet of the pre-Revolutionary era, and a hero of countless amorous affairs, would be interpreted as yet another love story; and it seems that she made a tremendous effort to rule out such a reading by employing a highly reverent tone, ordinary vocabulary, and a simple setting. Second, the frequent critical accusations that she was merely writing a feminine lyrical diary damaged Akhmatova's reputation as a serious poet, for, according to Mandelstam, in the early decades of the twentieth century the feminine poetry was distorted by extensive lyrical exaltation, abusive use of metaphor, and the lack of a sense of history or historical responsibility.[32] Blok expressed even harsher views: he claimed that for a woman to be a poet is not simply absurd, but also obscene.[33] Thus, opposing the embarrassingly gendered title of *poetess*, Akhmatova positioned herself in the poem dedicated to Blok as a *poet* equal to her famous host.

Akhmatova's feminine lyricism was, without a doubt, a major innovative contribution to Russian poetry of the early twentieth century, and Kurtág responded to this in his setting of the text. His interpretation of the poem heightens the femininity of Akhmatova's writing and amplifies the poem's expressive potency: if, as Blok suggests, to be a poetess is obscene, and if to be obscene is to be "offensive to accepted standards of decency or modesty," then "the poetess's distorted voice … her mannerisms and emotionalism" confront the conventionalism of the ordinary.[34]

The notion of the excessive affect, attributed to the poetess, is used in the musical setting of the poem as a crucial expressive element. Kurtág employs a variety of devices easily qualified as mannerisms, such as the "bent pitch" and the assortment of acciaccaturas[35] in combination with the invariably syllabic declamation, the steady trochaic meter, and the monotony of dyadic pitch grouping. (See example 14-2.)

This type of vocalization is commonly associated in Kurtág's oeuvre with the obsessive affection of the lyric persona, the quality which relates the *me* of this song to the female protagonist of the Rimma Dalos cycles,

EXAMPLE 14-2 György Kurtág, *Four Songs to Poems by Anna Akhmatova*, Op. 41 (1997–2008), version of 1997, "Александру Блоку" ["To Alexander Blok"], mm. 1–5. © Editio Musica Budapest.

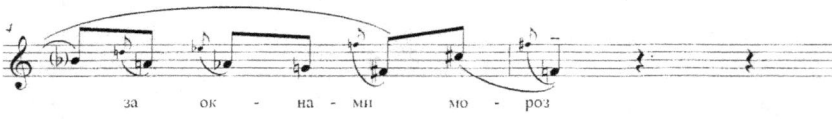

particularly to the title character of the *Messages of the Late Miss R.V. Troussova*.[36] Stephen Walsh recognized the exposed gender of the narrator in the *Troussova* as a significant characteristic of this modern *Frauenliebe und -Leben*.[37] The fixation on passionate excess, historically codified as one of the traits of feminine writing, liberates the poet-heroine of the *Messages of the Late Miss R.V. Troussova* from the limitations of the acceptable, allowing the composer to convey in the music "the astonishing sensual energy and candour" of the text.[38] In the setting of the Akhmatova poem, the above-mentioned expressive vocalization seems to allude to a similar meaning; namely, to a possibility of the amorous subtext of the poem, which is not dismissed by Akhmatova's biographers.[39] It appears that Kurtág's reading of the text resonates with the critics' assumption of the hidden romantic interest which connects the author of the poem with its addressee. The composer approaches the manifestly casual tone of the poem in an expressive mode which transmits the inner tension of the text, and transforms the humble utterance of the poet into a passionate monologue filled with drama and excitement. This transformation discloses Kurtág's interest in discerning the deeper layers of meaning which he bases on the present-day knowledge of Akhmatova's practices of self-mythologizing.[40] The composer absorbs Akhmatova's unwavering concern with the "malleability of the biographical text" and uses it as the starting point of his hypothetical investigation into the psychological content of the poem. Kurtág appears to have been particularly impressed with the idea that the historical context of Akhmatova's work can provide a sufficient ground for an artistic inquiry into its subtext, and that the consideration of the cultural norms of the early decades of the last century can give an impulse for changing the description of an unremarkable biographical episode into a sophisticated personal mythology, revealing the "uncanny 'literariness' of life and the transgressive vitality" of poetry.[41]

The performance instructions in the score support this idea. As he did in the first song, Kurtág placed a long remark concerning the tone with which the singer should approach the song at the beginning. The most striking part of this, given in Russian, reads *with humour and tenderness, at times even impertinently*. The word *impertinently*, or *impudently*, appears to strikingly contrast the attitude of respectful offering to the older colleague and mentor with which Akhmatova had fashioned the text, and the combination of *humour* and *tenderness* adds other remarkable details to the composer's interpretation of the poem.[42] But what may seem perplexing, or even incongruous, actually intensifies the song's subtext: *humour* appears to refer to Akhmatova's awareness of the public expectations, *tenderness* underlines the poem's tone of emotional persuasion, and *impudence* suggests that the poet is challenging the one-dimensional connection between a literary subject, a biographical person, and a cultural personage.

To underline this, the composer has chosen a type of declamation which remains rhythmically steady, with each line of the poem being placed in four sets of mono-rhythmic dyads almost throughout the entire song. Kurtág breaks the rhythmic monotony by shifting metric accents (see the end of bar 3) and by using embellishments as well as different kinds of attack, ranging from single accented and non-accented acciaccaturas to pairs or groups of grace notes. These differences correspond to shifts in emotion. Phrases marked by a higher concentration of ornaments alternate with passages of ordinary vocalization, reflecting the changing degree of anxiety on the part of the lyric persona. The tonal profile of the song also appears semantically charged as areas of tonal stability, marked by diatonic motifs and consonant intervals, interchange with sections of overlapping chromatic constellations. The fanciful ornamentations enrich the melody like chromatic figurations, creating a more complex harmonic field. The distinction between the different types of vocalization and the contrast between the diatonic and chromatic tonal organization serve to musically delineate various emotional states in the poem, from seriousness to flirtation, and from sincerity to sarcasm.

The ending of the "Blok" song employs an element of acting: the singer is expected to recite silently the final words with "tenderness and a sense of deep regret." The Russian *увы!* [*alas!*], which the singer has to say "deeply inside," has grown out of the phonetic merging of the first and the last syllables of the poem's concluding line. This last ironic gesture, which may also seem unrelated to the poem's content, in fact contributes to the interplay of solemnity and playfulness, self-mythologizing and earnest confession manifested throughout the song.

"Плач-причитание" ["The Wailing Lament"][43]

The third poem of the cycle, "Today Is the Nameday," presents a different side of Akhmatova: the mourner, whose poignant grief preserves her sense of self in the context of the enormous pressure exerted on individuals by a totalitarian regime. Akhmatova, the "Muse of Weeping,"[44] accepted the role of a chronicler whose annals reflect the discordant intensity of life in opposition to the reigning power. Blok's death was among the first in a sequence of devastating events which marked the bleak reality of the 1920s and 1930s. His funeral coincided with the tragic news of the arrest of Akhmatova's ex-husband, the outstanding poet Nikolai Gumilev, who was sentenced to death on unproven accusation of anti-Bolshevik conspiracy. For Akhmatova, both losses fused into one, creating an apocalyptic framework within which Blok's physical suffering becomes a symbol of the suffering of his contemporaries.[45] Rather symbolically, Blok's funeral fell on the day associated in the Orthodox canon with the Smolenskaya Icon of the Mother of God, venerated for the saintly capacity of comforting the sufferers. This is why the poem moves across two semantic clusters, the sorrowful lamenting and the observation of a majestic religious celebration. Kurtág's success as a composer resides in his ability to convincingly blend inconsolable grief with festive exaltation, which pervades the song from the first note to the last.

The title of this song, "Плач-причитание" ["The Wailing Lament"],[46] replicates the intensifying repetitiveness of archetypal Russian idioms[47] and is analogous to the Hungarian *sirató* [dirge] that Kurtág has frequently employed in his work. The genre of folk lament is often used by Russian intellectuals as a cultural symbol when commenting on the county's history of loss and destruction. It also paraphrases the title of a well-known work for soprano, piano, and three percussionists by the Russian composer Edison Denisov, *Плачи* [Lamentations] (1966). According to Kurtág, this work was one of the primary impulses for awakening his interest in Russian folklore and Russian culture.[48]

"The Wailing Lament" is the largest song in the cycle, both in length and in performing forces.[49] Kurtág highlighted the narrative sequence by gradually expanding the orchestration and vocal range. The scope of the textural, harmonic, and dynamic changes throughout the song contribute to a sense of irreversible progression. Yet, all three stanzas are unified by the same type of vocalization, growing out of a syllabic rendition of the text. (See example 14-3.)

The peculiar folk-like meter (the so-called *dolnik*, with a variable quantity of unstressed syllables placed between a fixed number of stressed ones, creating an unpredictable series of syllabic grouping) is fully realized by Kurtág in the process of forming the melody. The vocal line originates from narrow, descending melodic cells which replicate the style of the folk lament. The interplay of motives generates an improvisational quality, while the regularly located metrical accents (the first and the last stress in each line of the poem remain stable throughout) secure a consistency of the continuous mono-rhythmic flow.

To heighten the sense of anxiety and horror, Kurtág has chosen an incredibly fast tempo (eighth note = 352).[50] This feverish tempo transfigures

EXAMPLE 14-3 György Kurtág, *Four Songs to Poems by Anna Akhmatova*, Op. 41 (1997–2008), version of 1997, "Плач-причитание" ["The Wailing Lament"], mm. 1–20. © Editio Musica Budapest.

the funeral lament into a powerful outcry which transcends personal tragedy and seems to signal the eruption of an eschatological era in Russian history. Like Akhmatova, Kurtág emphasizes the poet's death as a representation of "cultural eclipse" that predicts national tragedy, as indicated by the metaphor of the extinguished sun.[51] Thus the mourning of the poet's death extends beyond private tragedy and transforms into apocalyptic rhetoric, linking this song with Kurtág's monumental *Songs of Despair and Sorrow*. This work also thrives on the theme of the poet's fate and constitutes a strong statement on the composer's sense of mission, rooted in the concept of artistic creation as a sacred calling: as a sacrificial, purifying, life-transforming struggle with the self.

"The Wailing Lament" is clearly the climax of Kurtág's Akhmatova cycle in its first version and casts a dark shadow over the preceding songs. Contemplating the poet's fate from a position of sadness is emblematic of the Russian myth of the poet, which was consistently explored by the composer in the first three songs of the cycle. Kurtág's decision to conclude the work with a song dedicated to Osip Mandelstam, another poet-martyr, is perfectly consistent with this idea.[52] The final shape of the composition has certainly changed upon the completion of the fourth song, but even in its incomplete version, the *Four Songs to Poems by Anna Akhmatova*, Op. 41, presents a compelling artistic statement. It illustrates Kurtág's sensitivity to a cultural tradition that he became part of as an outsider: a sensitivity that required a constant redefining of his own identity as a creative artist. Composition involving foreign poetry seems to have a self-assessing function for Kurtág: crossing the linguistic and cultural borders enables him to avoid complacency and forces him to reconsider his world view. The remarkable density and intensity of Kurtág's music is at least partially explained by his extraordinary ability to capture the subtle details of what was initially for him a foreign cultural discourse.

Notes

1. Among the titles of Kurtág's published works, one finds a similar multitude of linguistic sources—Hungarian, Russian (using the Cyrillic alphabet), German, Italian, French, English, Latin, etc., which, in some cases, are combined in the same composition. For example, Kurtág used English for the work title of Op. 41, *Four Songs to Poems by Anna Akhmatova*, and Russian (in Cyrillic script) for the movement titles. For the purposes of this essay, I have consistently referred to the title presented on the main page of the 1997 version of this work, which was incomplete at that time, but was nevertheless published and kindly made available to me by Editio Musica Budapest. Characteristically, upon completion of the cycle in December 2008, the composer changed the title of the work to *Анна Ахматова. Четыре стихотворения* [*Anna Akhmatova. Four Poems*]. In the body of my text, titles of Kurtág's works are given in English, and Russian terms and words are translated into English. In the Bibliography, all Russian titles are transliterated to the Latin alphabet, followed by the original language in Cyrillic in square brackets.

2. An illustration of this may be found in the works of the Russian émigré author Vladimir Nabokov, whose transition to writing in English, as demonstrated by Margarit Tadevosyan Ordukhanyan, reshaped his interaction with the external

world and determined his theoretical and practical conception of the text. See: Margarit Tadevosyan Ordukhanyan, "Strangers in Stranger Tongues: Vladimir Nabokov and the Writing of Exile, with Reference to Joseph Conrad, Hakob Asadourian, and Roman Jakobson" (PhD diss., Boston College, 2006).

3   *Bánát* (Rom. *Banat*, Hung. also *Bánság*)—a distant territory governed by a *ban* (local land administrator). When the word *Bánát* is used without any other qualification, it indicates the Temesvár banat, a Central European region incorporated into the Austrian Habsburg Monarchy and historically divided between Romania, Serbia, and Hungary. In 1919 most of the Bánát became a part of Romania. *Lugos* (Rom. *Lugoj*) is a town in Bánát, situated in the county of Krasso-Szoreny. During Kurtág's adolescent years, in the 1920s and 1930s, the Bánát was populated by Romanians, Germans, Hungarians, Serbs, Roma, and other national minorities.

4   This list contains both published (identified by an opus number) and unpublished (without an opus number) compositions by Kurtág. Some of the unpublished material exists in the form of sketches and drafts. The information on Kurtág's unpublished works was provided by the composer himself, as well as by the artistic director of the Hungarian publishing house Editio Musica Budapest, János Demény, and the musicologists Friedemann Sallis and Dina Lentsner; I would like to express my warmest thanks to them. The composer's manuscripts are conserved in the György Kurtág Collection of the Paul Sacher Foundation in Basel, Switzerland.

5   In the 1993 interview, Rimma Dalos explained that her poetry of the 1970s reflected the emotional difficulty of her cultural assimilation in Hungary. Philippe Albèra, "Entretien avec Rimma Dalos," in *György Kurtág: Entretiens, textes, écrits sur son oeuvre*, ed. Philippe Albèra (Genève: Contrechamps, 1995), 71.

6   During this period, references to Russian culture and traditions may also be found in several works which are not based on Russian texts. These works include the *Four Songs to Poems by János Pilinsky*, Op. 11 (1975), for baritone or bass and chamber ensemble, *The Little Predicament*, Op. 15b (1978), for piccolo, trombone, and guitar, and *Games* for piano (1975–79). The 1990s works based on Russian texts, and especially the monumental *Songs of Despair and Sorrow*, Op. 18, display a larger selection of authors, a wider circle of themes, and a deeper penetration into the historical context of the Russian poetry.

7   Richard Taruskin, "Others: A Mythology and a Demurrer," in *Defining Russia Musically: Historical and Hermeneutical Essays* (Princeton, NJ: Princeton University Press, 1997), xiv.

8   Kurtág's distinctive place in the musical life of Hungary from the 1950s to the 1980s and the political component of the Hungarian critical reception of Kurtág's Russian opuses in the 1980s are discussed in Rachel Beckles Willson, *Ligeti, Kurtág, and Hungarian Music during the Cold War* (Cambridge and New York: Cambridge University Press, 2007).

9   Acmeism (from the Greek *acme*: highest point or culmination) is a poetic movement of the early decades of the twentieth century which emerged as a reaction to the symbolist aesthetic; it expressed the neoclassical principle of

clarity and worshipped "poetic craft and cultural continuity." The group of acmeist poets in Russia included N. Gumilev, A. Akhmatova, O. Mandelstam, S. Gorodetsky, V. Narbut, and M. Zenkevich. For more detailed information, please see Justin Doherty, *The Acmeist Movement in Russian Poetry* (Oxford: Clarendon Press, 1994).

10 Between 1976 and 2000, Kurtág used eight poems of Anna Akhmatova (one of them in Hungarian translation; another as poetic epigraph, divided into two fragments) and two poems of Sergei Esenin, as follows: *Omaggio a Luigi Nono*, Op. 16—Anna Akhmatova, "Разрыв: Не недели" ["Parting: Not Weeks"] (1940), from the volume *Тростник* [*Reed*]; *Послания покойной Р.В. Трусовой* [*Messages of the Late Miss R.V. Troussova*], Op. 17—Anna Akhmatova, "Я улыбаться перестала" ["I No Longer Smile"] (1915), from the volume *Белая стая* [*White Flock*], part one; *Песни уныния и печали* [*Songs of Despair and Sorrow*], Op. 18—Sergei Esenin, "Вечером синим" ["Blue Evening"] (1925), Anna Akhmatova, "Распятие" ["Crucifixion"] (1943), from the cycle *Реквием* [*Requiem*], part X, 2; *Four Songs to Poems by Anna Akhmatova*, Op. 41—Anna Akhmatova, "Пушкин" ["Pushkin"] (1943), from the volume *Седьмая книга* [*Seventh Book*], "Александру Блоку" ["To Alexander Blok"] (1914), from the volume *Четки* [*Rosary*], part four; "А Смоленская нынче именинница" ["Today Is the Nameday of our Lady of Smolensk"] (1921), from the volume *Anno Domini* MCMXXI, "Воронеж" ["Voronezh"] (1936), from the volume *Тростник* [*Reed*]; "До свиданья, друг мой ..."—Sergei Esenin, "До свиданья, друг мой ..." ["Farewell, My Friend"] (1925); "Olyan, Amilyen"—Anna Akhmatova, "Какая есть" ["This Is How I Am"], fragment (1942), from the volume *Поэмы* [*Poems*] in Hungarian translation of Zsuzsa Rab.

11 This concept, expressed in a verse by the prominent Soviet poet Evgeny Evtushenko (b. 1933), is discussed by Andrew Baruch Wachtel in *Remaining Relevant after Communism: The Role of the Writer in Eastern Europe* (University of Chicago Press, 2006). See also Wachtel, ed., *Intersections and Transpositions: Russian Music, Literature, and Society* (Evanston: Northwestern University Press, 1998).

12 Svetlana Boym, *Death in Quotation Marks: Cultural Myth of the Modern Poet* (Cambridge and New York: Cambridge University Press, 1991), 10.

13 Wachtel, *Remaining Relevant*, 6.

14 Anna Akhmatova, as cited in Anatoly Naiman, "The End of the First Half of the Twentieth Century (an excerpt)," trans. Irena C. Katz, in *The Complete Poems of Anna Akhmatova*, vol. 2 (Somerville: Zephyr Press, 1990), 52.

15 Aleksandr Zholkovsky, "The Obverse of Stalinism: Akhmatova's Self-Serving Charisma of Selflessness," in *Self and Story in Russian History*, ed. Laura Engelstein and Stephanie Sandler (Ithaca: Cornell University Press, 2000), 64.

16 As heir to the Silver Age masters of жизнетворчество [self-creation, or life's art], Akhmatova practised an "imposition of an idealized grid upon everyday behavior in an attempt to achieve a perfect aesthetic organization of life." Boym, *Death in Quotation Marks*, 5.

17 Kurtág György, *Анна Ахматова. Четыре стихотворения*. 1. "Пушкин"—2. "Александру Блоку"—3. "Плач-Причитание"—4. "Воронеж," Op. 41 (1997–2008). EMB Z14212. The cycle is dedicated to Russian soprano Natalia Zagorinskaya.

18 The song was written in 1997 in Marlboro, USA, and revised in 2008 in St. André de Cubzac, France. "Pushkin" is dedicated to Russian literary critic Natalia Melnikova.
19 According to Zinaida Brájer, with whom I communicated in Februrary 2006 and who taught Russian language at the Franz Liszt Music Academy in Budapest and assisted Kurtág's Russian studies during the 1970s and 1980s, the composer memorized numerous strophes from Pushkin's novel *Eugene Onegin*. Kurtág dedicated several compositions to her: "Parting" from *Omaggio a Luigi Nono*, Op. 16, "A Spike of Barley," as well as *Songs of Despair and Sorrow*, Op. 18, and "To Alexander Blok" from *Four Songs to Poems by Anna Akhmatova*, Op. 41.
20 Most Pushkin-related images in Kurtág's scores, such as the reference to юродивый [Holy Fool] in *Scenes from a Novel*, Op. 19, and the use of expressions such as анафема [Excommunication] in *Kafka-Fragmente*, Op. 24, and говорком [parlando] in *Songs of Despair and Sorrow*, Op. 18, may be traced to a single source: Modest Mussorgsky's opera *Boris Godunov*, based on Pushkin's 1825 historical drama.
21 Stephanie Sandler, "Anna Akhmatova's Pushkin: Allegories, Ethics, Grieving for the Dead," in *Commemorating Pushkin: Russia's Myth of a National Poet* (Palo Alto: Stanford University Press, 2004), 175–76.
22 These allusions and quotations are the evocative epithets мудро и лукаво [wisely and cunningly], the exclamation *at what price* and the reference to a woman's feet at the end of the poem.
23 In the 2008 version of "Pushkin," the soprano is accompanied by flute, clarinet, violin, cimbalom (hammered dulcimer), harp, celesta, piano (the score requires *pianino con supersordino*—an upright piano with mute pedal), vibraphone, cymbals, triangle, bass drum, and maracas. Nevertheless, the contour of the vocal line, and the interpretative approach to the poetic text in this version, remain essentially the same as in the version of 1997.
24 In a private telephone conversation in March 2007. The authentic audio recording of "Pushkin" read by Akhmatova is available at: http://anna.ahmatova.com/audio.htm
25 "To Alexander Blok" was written in November 1997 in Amsterdam and revised in November 2008 in St. André de Cubzac, France. In the revised version, the soprano is accompanied by flute, clarinet, violin, double bass, cimbalom, harp, celesta, piano, bells, cymbals, maracas, bass drum, and snare drum. The song is dedicated to Zinaida Brájer (Зина).
26 In the manuscript and first publication of the poem, Blok's name was used as the title of the poem, but in the volume *Rosary* (1914) and in the later editions it became the dedication. See: N.G. Prozorova, "Opyt sravnitel'nogo analiza dvukh stikhotvorenii (Aleksandr Blok 'Krasota strashna, vam skazhut,' Anna Akhmatova 'Ia prishla k poetu v gosti')." In *'Tsarstvennoe slovo.' Akhmatovskie chteniia*, Vypusk 1 (Moscow: Nasledie, 1992), 141–49.
27 See V.N. Toporov, *Akhmatova i Blok: k probleme postroeniia poeticheskogo dialoga: "blokovskii" tekst Akhmatovoi* (Berkeley: Slavic Specialties, 1981).
28 See V.M. Zhirmunskii, "Anna Akhmatova i Aleksandr Blok." In *Teoriia literatury, Poetika. Stilistika*, edited by V.M. Zhirmunskii (Leningrad: Nauka, 1977), 323–54.

29 The epigraphs placed at the beginning of each of the sections of *Messages of the Late Miss R.V. Troussova*, Op. 17, are taken from the two parts of Akhmatova's poem "I No Longer Smile" (1940) and from fragments of two poems by Blok ("To the Muse," 1912, and "Grey Morning," 1913). Among the texts of *Songs of Despair and Sorrow*, Op. 18, we find poems of numerous authors, including Blok's "Night, an Empty Street …" (1912) and Akhmatova's "Crucifixion" (1943).
30 Stephanie Sandler, *Anna Akhmatova's Pushkin*, 205.
31 This tendency is exemplified by Leonid Kannegisser (1896–1918), whose 1914 critical response to Akhmatova's poetry stressed the direct relation between the events of the poet's life and the subjects of her poems. See L. Kannegisser, "Anna Akhmatova: Chetki." In *Anna Akhmatova: Pro et Contra* (Sankt-Peterburg: RKHGI, 2001), 92–93. In 1918 Kannegisser assassinated the chief of the Bolshevik secret police, Moisei Uritsky, which marked the beginning of the "Red Terror." A more objective view on Akhmatova's early poetry is found in the 1914 essay of Nikolai Nedobrovo (1882–1919), Akhmatova's close friend and mentor. Akhmatova considered this essay the "best written about her." See Vilenkin, K. *Vospominaniia s kommentariiami* (Moscow: Iskusstvo, 1982), 429. The essay of Nedobrovo is available at: http://www.akhmatova.org/articles/nedobrovo.htm. For a recent discussion of the biographical aspect of Akhmatova's early poetry, see G. Temnenko, "Liricheskii geroi i mif o poete (na materiale rannei liriki Akhmatovoi). In *Anna Akhmatova: epokha, sud'ba, tvorchestvo*, Krymskii Akhmatovskii nauchnyi sbornik, Vypusk 3 (Simferopol': Krymskii Arkhiv, 2005), 127–52.
32 Svetlana Boym, *Death in Quotation Marks*, 192.
33 Ibid., 197.
34 Ibid., 197, 199.
35 The composer calls them *appoggiaturas*.
36 Vocalization with acciaccaturas may be found in several sections of the *Messages of the Late Miss R.V. Troussova*, Op. 17. See "Why Should I Not Squeal Like a Pig" (II-3), "Pebbles" (III-3), "A Slender Needle" (III-4), "In You I Seek My Salvation" (III-7), "In the Cloudburst of Lustful Looks" (III-14).
37 Kurtág's original title of the *Messages of the Late Miss R.V. Troussova* was *Frauenleben und –schicksal*. See Stephen Walsh, "Messages from Budapest: Some New Works from Hungary," *Musical Times* (February 1981): 99. See also his "György Kurtág: An Outline Study (II)," *Tempo* 140 (1982): 10–19, as well as "Kurtág in Berlin," *Tempo* 168 (1989): 43–44.
38 Stephen Walsh, "Kurtág's Russian Settings: The Word Made Flesh," *Contemporary Music Review* 20/2,3 (2001): 78.
39 This subject is discussed in A. Marchenko, "'S nei ukhodil ia v more …' Anna Akhmatova i Aleksandr Blok: opyt rassledovaniia." *Novyi Mir* (1998) 8: 201–14, 9: 179–96.
40 Akhmatova's habits of self-presentation are discussed by Alexander Zholkovsky in "The Obverse of Stalinism: Akhmatova's Self-Serving Charisma of Selflessness," in *Self and Story in Russian History*, ed. Laura Engelstein and Stephanie Sandler (Ithaca: Cornell University Press, 2000), 46–68, and "Anna Akhmatova: Scripts, Not Scriptures," *Slavic and East European Journal* 40/1 (1996): 135–41.

41 Svetlana Boym, *Death in Quotation Marks*, 13.
42 A similar term, *insolente*, is used in "Counting-Out Rhyme" from *Scenes from a Novel*, Op. 19.
43 "The Wailing Lament" was written between March and December 1997 in Amsterdam and revised in December 2008 in St. André de Cubzac, France. The song is dedicated to Hungarian musicologist Márta Papp.
44 "О Муза Плача" ["Oh, Keening Muse"] is the title of the first poem from the 1916 poetic cycle by Marina Tsvetaeva, dedicated to Akhmatova.
45 The public response to Blok's death is discussed in: "The Voices of Silence: The Funeral of Aleksandr Blok. 'That which is already not Blok'. The Services for the Dead on Ofitserskaya Street." See University of California, Berkeley. *Mapping St. Petersburg* Project. http://stpetersburg.berkeley.edu/victoria/vic_1_1.html.
46 The English translation of the title is mine.
47 Examples of archetypal Russian idioms are *грусть-тоска* [sadness-longing], *печаль-скука* [sorrow-boredom], *горе-злосчастие* [woe-ill fate], etc.
48 The work on "The Wailing Lament" was begun in March 1997, soon after Denisov's death in Paris in November 1996. Kurtág considers it a commemoration of the Russian master. Private telephone conversation with the composer in spring 2006.
49 The instrumental ensemble of this 132-measure movement consists of cimbalom, violin, double bass, harp, piano (*pianino con supersordino*), celesta, and a group of percussion instruments consisting of bells, gongs, triangle, cymbals, tam-tam, vibraphone, and marimba. This ensemble demonstrates some of his favourite timbre combinations, such as the cimbalom–violin–double-bass trio featured, for example, in *Scenes from a Novel*, Op. 19, and associated with emotional unrest. The profusion of percussion instruments has a rich semantic history in Kurtág's music, too, the most relevant exponent being Tsvetaeva's "It's Time" from *Songs of Despair and Sorrow*, Op. 18, which also deals with the theme of mortality.
50 This metronome marking seems to represent an indication of intention rather than a real tempo; in the 2008 version of the song, the tempo has been changed to a dotted half note set at a rate of 116–120.
51 As observed by Boris Gasparov, Russian modernists often alluded to holy sacrifice when recounting the story of a poet's death. See Boris Gasparov, "The 'Golden Age' and Its Role in the Cultural Mythology of Russian Modernism," in *Cultural Mythologies of Russian Modernism: From the Golden Age to the Silver Age*, ed. Boris Gasparov, Robert P. Hughes, and Irina Paperno (Berkeley: University of California Press, 1991), 13–14.
52 The final song of the cycle, "Voronezh" (1997—14 December 2008), is written for soprano, flute, oboe, 2 clarinets, cimbalom, violin, double bass, 2 horns, 2 trumpets, 2 trombones, harp, celesta, piano, vibraphone, cymbals, gongs, bells, maracas, tam-tam, tom-tom, whip, wind machine, 2 sirens, bass drum, and piccolo snare drum. "Voronezh" is dedicated to the poet Rimma Dalos (*Римма*).

Bibliography

Akhmatova, Anna. *The Complete Poems of Anna Akhmatova*. Edited and introduced by Roberta Reeder. Translated by Judith Hemschemeyer. Brookline, MA: Zephyr Press, 1997.
Albèra, Philippe. "Entretien avec Rimma Dalos." In *György Kurtág: Entretiens, textes, écrits sur son oeuvre*, edited by Philippe Albèra, 71–74. Genève: Contrechamps, 1995.
Audiozapisi Anny Akhmatovoi. *Anna Akhmatova chitaet svoi stikhi*. "Pushkin." [Аудиозаписи Анны Ахматовой. *Анна Ахматова читает свои стихи*. "Пушкин."] http://anna.ahmatova.com/audio.htm (accessed 27 December 2008).
Beckles Willson, Rachel. *Ligeti, Kurtág, and Hungarian Music during the Cold War*. Cambridge and New York: Cambridge University Press, 2007.
Boym, Svetlana. *Death in Quotation Marks: Cultural Myth of the Modern Poet*. Cambridge and New York: Cambridge University Press, 1991.
Doherty, Justin. *The Acmeist Movement in Russian Poetry*. Oxford: Clarendon Press, 1994.
Gasparov, Boris. "The 'Golden Age' and Its Role in the Cultural Mythology of Russian Modernism." In *Cultural Mythologies of Russian Modernism: From the Golden Age to the Silver Age*, edited by Boris Gasparov, Robert P. Hughes, and Irina Paperno, 1–16. Berkeley: University of California Press, 1991.
Kannegisser, L. "Anna Akhmatova: Chetki." [Каннегиссер, Леонид. "Анна Ахматова: Четки."] In *Anna Akhmatova: Pro et Contra*, 92–93. Sankt-Peterburg: RKHGI, 2001.
Marchenko, A. "'S nei ukhodil ia v more …' Anna Akhmatova i Aleksandr Blok: opyt rassledovaniia." [Марченко, Алла. "'С ней уходил я в море …' Анна Ахматова и Александр Блок: опыт расследования."] *Novyi Mir* 8: 201–14, 9: 179–96 (1998).
Naiman, Anatoly. "The End of the First Half of the Twentieth Century (an excerpt)." Translated by Irena C. Katz. In *The Complete Poems of Anna Akhmatova*, 2: 47–52. Somerville: Zephyr Press, 1990.
Nedobrovo, N.V. "Anna Akhmatova. 'Ty vydumal menia …'" [Недоброво, Н.В. "Анна Ахматова. 'Ты выдумал меня …'"] In *Anna Akhmatova. Stat'i*. Edited by N. Degtiariova and L. Guller. http://www.akhmatova.org/articles/nedobrovo.htm (accessed 27 December 2008).
Ordukhanyan, Margarit Tadevosyan. "Strangers in Stranger Tongues: Vladimir Nabokov and the Writing of Exile, with Reference to Joseph Conrad, Hakob Asadourian, and Roman Jakobson." PhD diss., Boston College, 2006.
Prozorova, N.G. "Opyt sravnitel'nogo analiza dvukh stikhotvorenii (Aleksandr Blok 'Krasota strashna, vam skazhut,' Anna Akhmatova 'Ia prishla k poetu v gosti')." [Прозорова, Н.Г. "Опыт сравнительного анализа двух стихотворений (Александр Блок 'Красота страшна, вам скажут,' Анна Ахматова 'Я пришла

к поэту в гости').''] In *'Tsarstvennoe slovo.' Akhmatovskie chteniia*, Vypusk 1, 141–49. Moscow: Nasledie, 1992.

Sandler, Stephanie. "Anna Akhmatova's Pushkin: Allegories, Ethics, Grieving for the Dead." In *Commemorating Pushkin: Russia's Myth of a National Poet*, 175–213. Palo Alto, CA: Stanford University Press, 2004.

Taruskin, Richard. *Defining Russia Musically: Historical and Hermeneutical Essays*. Princeton, NJ: Princeton University Press, 1997.

Temnenko, G. "Liricheskii geroi i mif o poete (na materiale rannei liriki Akhmatovoi). [Темненко, Г. "Лирический герой и миф о поэте (на материале ранней лирики Ахматовой)."] In *Anna Akhmatova: epokha, sud'ba, tvorchestvo*, Krymskii Akhmatovskii nauchnyi sbornik, Vypusk 3, 127–52. Simferopol': Krymskii Arkhiv, 2005.

Toporov, V.N. *Akhmatova i Blok: k probleme postroeniia poeticheskogo dialoga: "blokovskii" tekst Akhmatovoi*. [Топоров, В.Н. *Ахматова и Блок: к проблеме построения поэтического диалога: "блоковский" текст Ахматовой*.] Berkeley: Slavic Specialties, 1981.

University of California, Berkeley. *Mapping St. Petersburg* Project. "The Voices of Silence: The Funeral of Aleksandr Blok." http://stpetersburg.berkeley.edu/victoria/vic_1_1.html (accessed 23 December 2008).

Vilenkin, K. *Vospominaniia s kommentariiami*. [Виленкин, К. *Воспоминания с комментариями*.] Moscow: Iskusstvo, 1982.

Wachtel, Andrew Baruch, ed. *Intersections and Transpositions: Russian Music, Literature, and Society*. Evanston, IL: Northwestern University Press, 1998.

———. *Remaining Relevant after Communism: The Role of the Writer in Eastern Europe*. Chicago: University of Chicago Press, 2006.

Walsh, Stephen. "György Kurtág: An Outline Study (II)." *Tempo* 140 (1982): 11–21.

———. "Kurtág in Berlin." *Tempo* 168 (1989): 43–45.

———. "Kurtág's Russian Settings: The Word Made Flesh." *Contemporary Music Review* 20/2,3 (2001): 71–88.

———. "Messages from Budapest: Some New Works from Hungary." *Musical Times* 122/1656 (1981): 97–100.

Zhirmunskii, V.M. "Anna Akhmatova i Aleksandr Blok." [Жирмунский, В.М. "Анна Ахматова и Александр Блок."] In *Teoriia literatury, Poetika. Stilistika*, edited by V.M. Zhirmunskii, 323–54. Leningrad: Nauka, 1977.

Zholkovsky, Aleksandr. "Anna Akhmatova: Scripts, Not Scriptures," *Slavic and East European Journal* 40/1 (1996): 135–41.

———. "The Obverse of Stalinism: Akhmatova's Self-Serving Charisma of Selflessness." In *Self and Story in Russian History*, edited by Laura Engelstein and Stephanie Sandler, 46–68. Ithaca, NY: Cornell University Press, 2000.

FIFTEEN

Interpreting György Kurtág and George Crumb: Through the Looking Glass

Dina Lentsner

THIS ESSAY IS INTERPRETIVE in its essence. Even its first sentence, if hypothetically considered a poetic work, may be structurally interpreted: the two outer words, "essay" and "essence" are at the periphery of the sentence's construction, creating a symmetrical phonic arch "essay"–"essence," and there is a keyword "interpretive" in its centre. In the following pages, the notion of the centre and periphery will be used in the terms of musical analysis. "Globalization entails a shift from two-dimensional Euclidian space with its centres and peripheries and sharp boundaries, to a multidimensional global space with unbounded, often discontinuous and interpenetrating sub-spaces," writes anthropologist Michael Kearney.[1] Music has now become a global, multi-dimensional space, in which I (the Russian-born American author) am writing an essay on four unique (but also interrelated) artistic and cultural identities:

- György Kurtág (1926–): Romanian-born Hungarian composer (currently residing in France) who wrote music to numerous texts by Rimma Dalos;
- Rimma Dalos (1944–): Russian poet (residing in Budapest since 1970);
- George Crumb (1929–): American composer who wrote music to numerous texts by Federico García Lorca;
- Federico García Lorca (1889–1936): Spanish/Andalusian poet murdered by the Fascists at the beginning of the Spanish Civil War.

This true multi-dimensional creative space is filled with the "interpenetrating sub-spaces": there is Kurtág's interpretation of Dalos's poem, as well as Lorca's poetic fragment and Crumb's musical realization of it, and finally my own reinterpretation of both composers' interpretations of the text. In this essay I choose to dissolve the boundaries between music and poetry in order to find and interpret the true essence, the *centre*, of the two composers' art. By using the term periphery in the sense of a trajectory that circumscribes a centre, I will be following this perimeter as a path along which I will recreate Kurtág's and Crumb's compositional process. In so doing, I intend to re-peripherize their structural and semantic whole according to my own conceptual blueprint.

György Kurtág is one of the most literary composers of our time. His interest in world literature and his remarkable ability to get into the depths of language are phenomenal. Kurtág's creative output includes solo, vocal-instrumental, and choral settings of Hungarian, German, Russian, French, English, Romanian, and ancient Greek texts. My fascination with Kurtág's Russian vocal works is the fascination of a native speaker who listens to Kurtág's settings to hear poetry—poetry internalized by the composer and interpreted through his music. Kurtág directs me, the listener, back to the poetry, to its deepest structural/semantic layers. This extreme sensitivity to the poetic text, I feel, is also characteristic of George Crumb, whose admiration for Lorca's poetry led to the extensive use of the poet's texts in the 1960s. Crumb's four books of madrigals strike me as having the same qualities that I find in Kurtág's Russian music: a high concentration of compositional ideas found in a context that is not necessarily technically sophisticated or technique driven. For both composers, the ultimate compositional goal is the creation of true music-text symbiosis, accomplished through compositional technique that is the result of their unique interpretation of the text.

My approach to Kurtág's and Crumb's vocal music originates in Yuri Lotman's structuralist method of poetic analysis. According to Lotman, poetry is the most semantically charged of all means of verbal communication. Lotman states: "Once we approach a text as a literary one, then in principle any element, right down to misprints, as E.T.A. Hoffmann perceptively remarked in the foreword to *Lebensanshichten des Katers Murr*, may turn out to be significant ... we are faced in one and the same text with the most varied sets of significant elements and, consequently, a complicated hierarchy of strata of meanings."[2] My approach to the poetic text, which follows Lotman's structuralist principles outlined in his work *Analiz poeticheskogo teksta (Analysis of the Poetic Text)*,[3] considers multiple levels of the poetic structure; namely, the lexical (word content), phonological (sound content), prosodic (metric organization), graphic (visual presentation), and grammatical. In each poetic work one or several structural levels may dominate over others.[4] This method for studying the text-music relationship in a vocal-instrumental composition does not discriminate between music and poetry: both arts are viewed as partners in the structural-semantic design. Structure is semantics, and, likewise the reverse, semantics is structure. Thus, in my view (as it follows Lotman's ideas on poetry), all inquiry into semantic meaning is necessarily an inquiry into structure.

The process of musico-poetic analysis contains three stages. The first one is a structural-semantic analysis of the poetic text as an independent unit. The second step is a structural-semantic analysis of musical counterpart as an independent unit, where I minimize the references to the text to the most obvious observations, such as word painting. The last stage involves a comparative structural-semantic analysis of both music and text, a musico-poetic analysis per se. This third step allows one to uncover and interpret that special layer of the text-music interaction in a vocal composition—its true *centre*—that may not be obvious, even for the composer himself.

For this essay I have chosen two pieces. The first is "Dream," a fragment from *Scenes from a Novel*, Op. 19, No. 6, composed in 1979–82, to the poems by Rimma Dalos. The second is *Madrigal* No. 2 from George Crumb's *Madrigals, Book III*, composed in 1969 to texts by García Lorca. Both texts concern the theme of dreaming.

György Kurtág, Сцены из Романа. *15 Песен на Стихи Риммы Далош* [Scenes from a Novel. 15 Songs to Poems by Rimma Dalos], Op. 19, "6. Сон" [Dream], for soprano, violin, and cimbalom[5]

Poetic Analysis of the Poem by Rimma Dalos

Table 15-1 shows the transliterated Russian text and its English translation by Sherwood and Howath published with the score of *Scenes from a Novel*. If written on one line, this poem becomes a prose piece—a diary entry that records a dream. Nevertheless, the second line of the Dalos poem is not completely in the style of prose because of the inversion of the natural word order ("blizosti tvoei" as opposed to the prose-like "tvoei blizosti"). "Blizosti tvoei proshu" should translate into English as "I beg for

TABLE 15-1 Rimma Dalos, "Сон" ["Dream"], transliterated and translated text

Snitsia odin i tot zhe son:	Every night the same dream:
blizosti tvoei proshu	I beg [for] you to come near,
Ty priblizhaesh'sia	You approach
ia ottalkivaiu tebia	I push you away.

you to come near" rather than "I beg you to come near," as given in the Sherwood/Howarth translation. The version "I beg for you to come near" is equivocal: it is not clear if the heroine is asking the beloved to come near (as intimated by the Sherwod/Howarth translation), or if she is begging in the sense of praying.

In the first three lines of the poem there is an extensive use of sibilants in the words "**sn**it**s**ia," "**s**on," "bli**z**o**s**ti," "pribli**zh**ae**sh'**ia." As example 15-1 demonstrates, these four words constitute two same-root pairs, snitsia/son and blizosti/priblizhaesh'sia. The first pair originates in the word "son" ("dream"), and the second one in the word "blizko" ("near"). Both of them belong to the semantic field "inside, inner, near."[6] The two sentences of the poem are connected through **pro-/ pri-** alliteration in the words "**pro**shu" and "**pri**blizhaesh'sia," as illustrated in example 15-2. Therefore, there are numerous phonological and semantic interconnections between the first three lines of the poem, whereas the last line, "ia ottalkivaiu tebia" ("I push you away") stands apart. Unlike the rest of the poem, the fourth line begins and ends with the same vowel "**ia**": "**ia** ottalkivaiu teb**ia**" (as shown in example 15-3).

EXAMPLE 15-1 Rimma Dalos, "Сон" ["Dream"], concentration of sibilants in the semantic field "inside, inner, near."

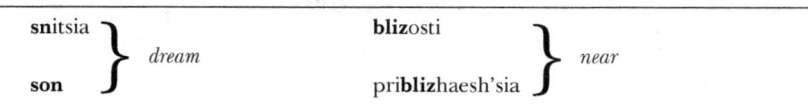

EXAMPLE 15-2 Rimma Dalos, "Сон" ["Dream"], pro-/pri- alliteration in the text.

Snitsia odin i tot zhe son:
blizosti tvoei **pro**shu
Ty **pri**blizhaesh'sia

EXAMPLE 15-3 Rimma Dalos, "Сон" ["Dream"], the sound bridge between the beginning and the end of the last line.

ia ottalkivaiu teb**ia**

The word "ottalkivaiu" ("push away") attracts attention because of its role on both the semantic and phonological levels of structure in this poem. It initiates a conflict between the words of the group "inside, inner, near" and itself, since "to push away" means "to distance." "Ottalkivaiu" is a word with natural iconicism: it sounds harsh because of its plosive double "t," and it is also "hard" because of its semantic meaning. "Pushing away" makes an illogical completion to the sequence of events described in the poem, but we accept it as dream logic and as an event that is happening over and over again. Besides, both the first and the last lines consist of eight syllables each, which add prosodic coherence to the overall structure of the poem.

To summarize, there are several phonological interconnections within the first three lines: a prosodic arch between lines one and four, and a phonological-lexical-semantic conflict between the first three and the last line. Moreover, since it is a recurring dream, there is a circularity implied in the semantics of the poem, where the first line also serves as the introduction or prelude to the dream. Graphically the sequence of events in this fragment may be represented as shown in example 15-4.

EXAMPLE 15-4 Rimma Dalos, "Сон" ["Dream"], graphic representation of the sequence of the events in the poem.

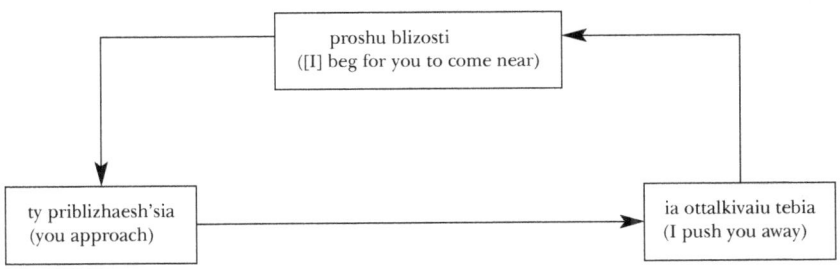

Music Analysis

In the musical counterpart of "Dream," the opposing ideas of stasis and separation are amalgamated. There is a two-layered structure in the voice line, where we find both word-painting (as in m. 10) and musical expression of the poetic subtext. The voice part in this piece is the carrier of its most important structural features. Following the four-line layout of the text, the voice line may be divided into four phrases: mm. 1–3, 4–7, m. 8, and mm. 10–11 (see example 15-5).

Wide-range intervals are a notable feature of the first two phrases. Phrase B is a variant of phrase A. E flat$_5$ is a point of reference for both phrases, as both A and B start with this pitch, and it is heard in the middle of phrase A. Moreover, in phrase B, E flat$_5$ has the longest duration of the whole fragment. Thus, the vocal line in the first two phrases shares two elements: the static E-flat$_5$ pedal and a wide, free-flowing melody.

In phrase C we hear a repeated E natural$_5$, which functions as the upper voice of the compound melody. There is a gradual expansion of the musical space, with the static E$_5$ in the upper part and the descending chromatic line D$_5$-C sharp$_5$-C natural$_5$ in the lower part of the compound line, coinciding with the phraseological unit "ty priblizhaesh'sia" ("you come near") in the text. Thus, the separation between the upper and lower parts of the melody in the setting contradicts the meaning of the words. The lower part of the compound melody (the chromatic descent) is emphasized by its metrical placement on the strong part of each beat in the measure.

Phrase D synthesizes the musical features from the previous three phrases. There is a compound melody with G sharp$_5$ as its upper part on

EXAMPLE 15-5 György Kurtág, Сцены из Романа. 15 Песен на Стихи Риммы Далош [Scenes from a Novel. 15 Songs to Poems by Rimma Dalos], Op. 19, "Сон" ["Dream"], the division of the vocal line into four phrases.

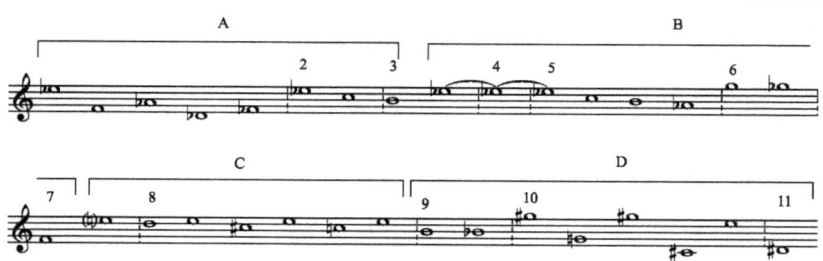

the word "[ia] ottalkivaiu" ("[I] push you away"). In this case, unlike in phrase C, the pedal G sharp$_5$ occupies the strong part of the first and the second beat of the measure, metrically accentuating the same pitch, which is also the highest of the fragment. Unlike the contradiction between the text and the music in phrase C, the fourth phrase is an example of Kurtág's word-painting: the static upper section of the melody is associated with the "I" image, whereas the lower section, falling farther and farther from G sharp$_5$ by two large gaps (m. 10), conveys the image of the "you" being "pushed away." The last word of the text, "tebia" ("you"), is assigned to pitches E$_5$ and D sharp$_4$. The latter represents the central pitch from the first two phrases (enharmonically respelled E flat), and the former represents the upper voice of the compound melody in the third phrase. Thus, the appearance of these two pitches at the end of the voice line summarizes the main semantic idea of this fragment—motion equals stasis—by concluding the musical motion of the fragment with its starting point.

As a result, the large-scale construction of the voice line consists of two layers. One of the two, shown with open note heads in example 15-6, links E flat$_5$, E natural$_5$, and D sharp$_4$ and represents stasis. The other layer of the melody, shown with the filled note heads, consistently creates distance between itself and the upper voice. Therefore, the large-scale opposition of stasis and separation echoes the contradiction between text and music found in the third phrase.

Since in this fragment the voice carries the main structural characteristics, I will not discuss the instrumental parts in detail; however, the content of the vocal line originates in the music heard in the instrumental

EXAMPLE 15-6 György Kurtág, *Сцены из Романа. 15 Песен на Стихи Риммы Далош* [Scenes from a Novel. 15 Songs to Poems by Rimma Dalos], Op. 19, "Сон" ["Dream"], the two-layered construction of the soprano part.

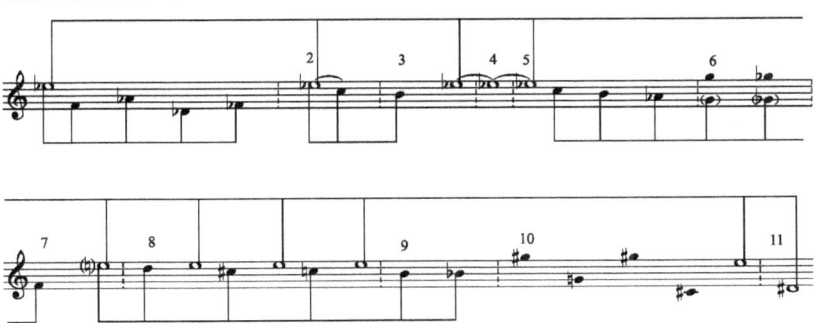

parts. The vocal part's compound melody in phrase C is an imitation of previously heard instrumental material. The cimbalom and violin play a significant role in creating a large-scale static effect. The E ostinato in the violin part, heard in the beginning of the fragment (mm. 1–3), corresponds to phrase A in the voice. We also find E flat$_5$ in the cimbalom on the strong part of each beat in mm. 7–8, coinciding with the phrase C in the voice line. There are both melodic and harmonic representations of the E-D sharp dyad that correspond to the last two pitches of the voice line in mm. 10–11. Thus, considering the instrumental parts and therefore the vertical aspect of the piece, the upper part of the large-scale compound melody does not move at all (as shown in example 15-6).

Musico-Poetic Analysis

In "Dream" as a whole, the two-layered (or macro compound) soprano part is structured as a system of the three levels of interrelationship between its four constituent phrases, as shown in example 15-7. There are several levels of formal links between these phrases: the "leaps" link (phrases A, B, and D), the "descending motion" link (phrases B and C), and the "micro-compound melody" link (phrases C and D). The descending motion becomes more organized intervallically as the melody progresses from phrase B to phrase C. Also, the strong-time pedal part of the compound melody in phrase D is, in a sense, a metrical inversion of the weak-time pedal in phrase C.

The interrelationships between phrases A, B, C, and D have an impact on the musico-poetic semantics of the fragment. On one hand, the story is quite simple: the heroine experiences a recurring dream in which she wants the beloved to come near her, but when he approaches, she pushes him away. On other hand, the idiosyncrasy of the musical structure offers, in a sense, a semantic context for what happens in the dream.

Dreaming is a static phenomenon; all events taking place in a dream are really non-events. Still, being a play of one's subconscious, a dream is the manifestation of one's feelings, senses, emotions, and intellect. "Dreaming transcends space and time in just the same way that waking thought does, simply because it is no more that a form of thought ... The dream is capable of continuing the intellectual work of the day and bringing it to a conclusion which had not then been reached," writes Sigmund Freud in his *Interpretation of Dreams*, discussing nineteenth-century scientific literature.[7] In Dalos's poem, the heroine experiences a recurring dream every night, which is already evidence of her preoccupation with one par-

EXAMPLE 15-7 György Kurtág, *Сцены из Романа. 15 Песен на Стихи Риммы Далош* [Scenes from a Novel. 15 Songs to Poems by Rimma Dalos], Op. 19, "Сон" ["Dream"], the interrelationship between four melodic phrases.

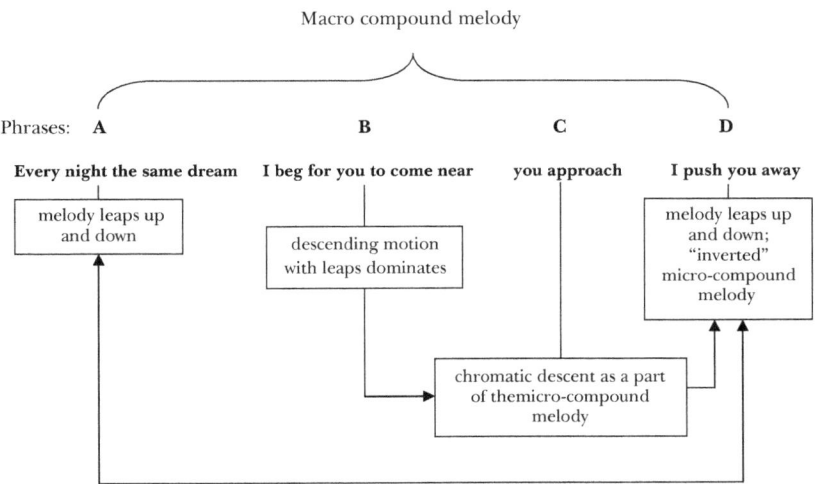

ticular thought, image, or feeling. The two-layered structure of the voice part represents the duality of the concept of dreaming itself—a phenomenon where stasis and motion coincide. Phrase A of Kurtág's setting, corresponding to the first line of the text, "Snitsia odin i tot zhe son" ("Every night the same dream"), is the introduction to the story. The story itself (the dream) is told in the next three lines of the poem, coinciding with the next three phrases of the fragment. Simultaneously, each new phrase contributes to the unveiling of the story's subtext.

Phrase D of the setting, corresponding to the last line of the text, "ia ottalkivaiu tebia" ("I push you away"), mm. 10–11, comprises a compound melody with a "jumpy" lower part "pushing away" from the pedal G^5, and expresses the meaning of the words as an explicit word-painting. In phrase C, with the text "ty priblizhaesh'sia" ("you approach"), the process of pitch separation resulting from the interaction between the two levels of the compound melody contradicts the notion of the nearness intimated by the text. In phrase B, corresponding to Dalos's second line "blizosti tvoei prochu" ("I beg for you to come near"), mm. 6–7, we find the two largest leaps in the fragment, A $flat_4$-G_5 and G $flat_5$-F_4. This creates a conflict between meaning of the words and its musical execution; more importantly, it excludes the notion of nearness and togetherness from the

EXAMPLE 15-8 György Kurtág's interpretation of Rimma Dalos's poem, as revealed though a backward reading.

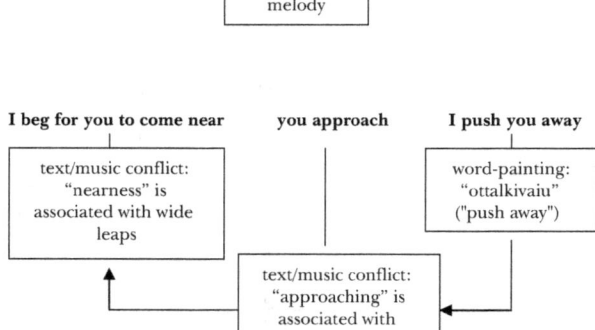

semantics of the fragment. The only unequivocal text-music consonance is found in the word-painting in phrase D, which was discussed above. Thus, Kurtág's interpretation of Dalos's poem reveals itself retrospectively, when the text is read backward (see example 15-8).

In Kurtág's setting, the distance between the two people is so great, so insurmountable, that even in the dream togetherness is impossible. There are two semantic fields found in Dalos's poem, those of "inside, inner, near" and "distance, separation." The latter is intimated in Dalos's text by just one word, "ottalkivaiu" ("push away"), found in the last line. Kurtág, however, makes the latter the focus, the essence of his "poem," but expresses it explicitly only in the last phrase. The musical construction of this fragment is progressive, as evidenced by the large-scale arch-like link between phrases A and D, and the two pairs of the micro-links between phrases B and C, and C and D, shown in example 15-8. Conversely, the musico-poetic structure of "Dream" is regressive, manifesting Kurtág's interpretation of Dalos's poem.

George Crumb, *Madrigals, Book III*, No. 2, "Gacela de la muerto oscura," ["Gacela of the Dark Death"], for Soprano, Harp, and Percussion

Poetic Analysis of an Excerpt from Federico García Lorca, "Gacela de la muerto oscura" ["Gacela of the Dark Death"]

In this madrigal, Crumb uses the first two lines of the last quatrain of Lorca's "Gacela of the Dark Death" (in original Spanish), which is the part of the collection called *Diván del tamarit*, written by Lorca in early 1930s. Crumb also provides the English translation by Gili, which I will use in this essay with one exception: I choose to translate "el sueño" as "the sleep" instead of "the dream" to avoid "to dream the dream" (word redundancy in the translation) and to separate the concepts of sleeping and dreaming. Also, since the sound content of the poem is a basis for phonological analysis, the transliteration into the working language—English—is essential. Thus, I will use the transliteration in the text and in all following examples. In table 15-2, I offer a transliteration and English translation of the original text.

The most striking and puzzling image of the excerpt—sleeping apples—is both beautifully poetic and complex. How do apples sleep? Does the image imply apples hanging on the trees and dreaming at night, or apples fallen down and lying on the ground, ripe, and ready to become a part of the "earth" (in the sense "soil")? If the dream of apples is the eternal dream of death, then the apple image may also carry the implication of death, their picking as being the very climax of one's life. Taking into consideration Lorca's preoccupation with death throughout his career, the second interpretation appears plausible. Still, according to Lotman, in order to infer the meaning from the text, it is necessary to consider all other levels of its structure besides its lexical content.

The apparent detail of the large-scale construction of the excerpt is the sound arch **k'ero-tierra,** the alliteration connecting the fragment's beginning and end. The roundness of the structure implies a semantic link

TABLE 15-2 Federico García Lorca, excerpt from "Gacela de la muerta oscura" ["Gacela of the Dark Death"], transliterated and translated text.

... k'ero dormir el' swen'yo de las manthanas	I want to sleep the dream of apples,
para aprender un ianto k'e me limp'e de tierra	to learn a lament that will cleanse me of earth

EXAMPLE 15-9 Federico García Lorca, "Gacela de la muerta oscura" ["Gacela of the Dark Death"], symmetrical structure of the text.

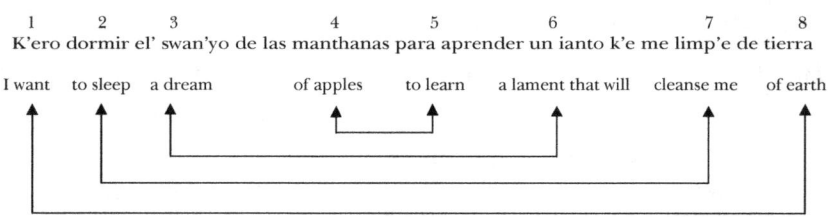

EXAMPLE 15-10 Federico García Lorca, "Gacela de la muerta oscura" ["Gacela of the Dark Death"], corresponding pairs of the words within symmetrical structure.

> to learn – apples (4/5)
> dream – a lament (3/6)
> to sleep – will cleanse [me] (4/7)
> I want – earth (1/8)

between the two words "[I] want" and "earth," which, if "earth" signifies "death," would imply, "I want death." This connection also suggests the overall symmetry of the structure. Examples 15-9 and 15-10 show the four pairs of corresponding words/concepts.

Considering the ambiguity of the apple image, the pairing of "manthanas" ("apples") with "para aprender" ("to learn") is semantically fundamental. Moreover, syntactically and graphically, the two words serve as the link between the two phrases and the two lines of the text. Both 4/5 and 1/8 pairs introduce something that may be considered as the subtext of Lorca's excerpt ("apples/to learn" and "I want/earth," respectively): each of the two pairs joins two dissimilar words/concepts in a paradoxical unit. By contrast, both middle pairs, 3/6 and 4/7, belong to one semantic field "dream/pure." Thus, the inherent symmetry of the text's structure allows for its synchronic reading, if we disregard the poem's temporal unfolding. Conversely, there are certain structural processes found in the diachronic dimension of the text, such as a progression involving the *r* sound that begins with the softer *r* in "k'ero dormir" ("I want to sleep") and continues in "para aprender" ("to learn"). Finally, this phonic sequence resolves in a single, but strong, rolled double *r* of "tierra" ("earth"), the last word of the text, as if the previous *r*'s generated and accumulated this new sound through repetition (example 15-11).

EXAMPLE 15-11 Federico García Lorca, "Gacela de la muerta oscura" ["Gacela of the Dark Death"], the diachronic *r*-sound progression.

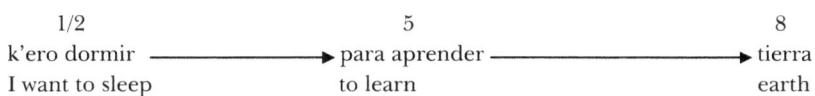

Thus, "I want to sleep to learn earth" is another subtext of the poetic excerpt, where the three units of the linear sequence mark structurally important stages of the text: its beginning, middle, and end.

The synchronic and diachronic readings of Lorca's text do not contradict but complement each other. Both aspects interpret text as a dream, but in the synchronic scheme of the excerpt the semantic field "dream/pure" occupies the peripheral positions in between outer sides and the centre of the construction. In the linear representation of the structure, the dream imagery is established from the beginning of the excerpt. Both synchronic and diachronic structures are shown in example 15-12.

The poetry unfolds in time, but when the process is complete, we, as readers, are able to seize the poetic moment and interpret the poet's words in our own way. In Lewis Carroll's *Alice's Adventures in Wonderland* and *Through the Looking-Glass*, Humpty Dumpty scornfully tells Alice, "When I choose a word ... it means just what I choose it to mean—neither more nor less," and Alice replies, "The question is ... whether you *can* make

EXAMPLE 15-12 Federico García Lorca, "Gacela de la muerta oscura" ["Gacela of the Dark Death"], superimposed synchronic and diachronic aspects of the text.

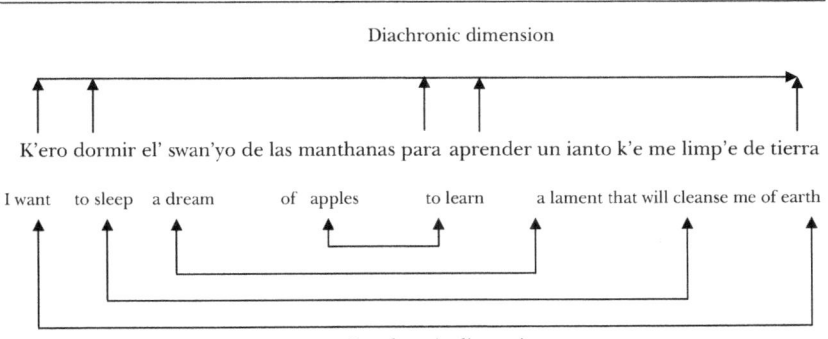

words mean so many different things."[8] Years after the publication of the *Alice* books, Charles Dodgson (a.k.a. Lewis Carroll) himself commented that "words mean more than we mean to express when we use them."[9] In my opinion, the beauty of Lorca's poetry lies not only in its striking imagery and overwhelming emotion, but also in the poet's ability, using Alice's words, to "make words to mean so many different things"—to invite a reader to construct his or her own system of textual interrelationship and meaning.

Music Analysis

The semantics of the musical counterpart of this madrigal are somewhat easier to discern, in comparison with the complexity of Lorca's text. In his music Crumb clearly foregrounds the semantic field of "dream/pure" found in the poetic fragment. The composer achieves this through both diachronic and synchronic structural musical processes. He simultaneously links and separates the concepts of the dreaming and lamenting by means of the melodic, rhythmic, and textural shift, as I will show below.

The most apparent sign of Crumb's semantic focus is his slight alteration of Lorca's text. The composer repeats the word "el' swan'yo" ("a dream") within the first phrase, and then repeats the whole phrase again, as shown in table 15-3.

In Crumb's musical reading of Lorca's text, there are three phrases with a distinctive structural interrelationship. The soprano line in the second phrase is a mirror inversion of the melody in the first phrase. Accompanied by the soft, sustained bass of the harp, in slow trancelike motion, both the original and the mirror versions bring out the image of a deep dream. In the score, Crumb specifies the character of the short instrumental interlude between the soprano's first two phrases as "dreamlike, gently undulating." The first musical gesture, corresponding to the words "K'ero dormir el' swan'yo" ("I want to sleep a dream"), mm. 1–2, predominantly ascends and comprises melodic thirds and seconds, with the descending turn at the end of the gesture. The repetition of the word "el'

TABLE 15-3 George Crumb's version of Federico García Lorca's text with the word repetition.

K'ero dormir el' swan'yo, el' swan'yo de las manthanas
K'ero dormir el' swan'yo, el' swan'yo de las manthanas
para aprender un ianto k'e me limp'e de tierra.

swan'yo" ("dream") in m. 3 is realized as a wider-range variant of the original motive. The ascending/descending motion formula is also characteristic of the musical gesture corresponding to the word "manthanas" ("apples") and has an even more enlarged range. Consequently, the mirror inversion in the second phrase of the madrigal possesses the same characteristics as the original melody, only in the opposite direction. Especially notable is the fragment's *ppp* climax on the second appearance of the word "manthanas" ("apples"), where the melody leaps upward a minor ninth (m. 9). The instrumental interlude heard between the first two phrases (m. 5) differs from them texturally and rhythmically and is too short to be considered as an independent formal unit. However, the interlude possesses a certain structural/semantic significance to the large-scale structure of the piece: it functions as anticipation, or prelude, to the third phrase.

The third phrase of the madrigal (m. 10) contrasts with the previous material in every aspect. The dreamlike character of the first two phrases is replaced by the lamenting gesture realized by the sequencing descending minor thirds. Instead of the slow, trancelike motion, we hear a soft but broken lament in all three parts, where vibraphone, harp, and soprano canonically imitate each other. The leading role, given to soprano in the first two phrases, is now played by the harp and vibraphone, which initially introduce the lament-gesture C_4-A_4, B_4-G sharp$_4$. Polyphonic texture and disjoint rhythmic patterns of the third phrase relate it to the instrumental interlude. Graphically, Crumb emphasizes an unrestrained flow of lamenting by containing the instrumental interlude and the third phrase each into one undivided measure. The structural link between the interlude and the last phrase imposes an alternative formal organization on the basic three-phrase construction of the piece (example 15-13).

As example 15-13 illustrates, the musical structure of the madrigal is both synchronic and diachronic, just like its poetic counterpart. The first two melodic phrases are mirror inversions of each other and, therefore, structurally synchronic. Conversely, the instrumental interlude and the lamenting phrase are structurally unequal and could not be reversed temporally; therefore, they are diachronic. Being the centre of symmetry for the mirror construction, the interlude serves as the structural bridge between the two coexisting dimensions of the piece.

As shown in example 15-14 below, the harmonic structure of the madrigal is functional in a traditional sense: its tertian foundation is implied by the horizontal dimension in the instrumental parts and the apparent

EXAMPLE 15-13 George Crumb, *Madrigals, Book III*, No. 2, "Gacela de la muerto oscura" ["Gacela of the Dark Death"], the links between sections in the setting.

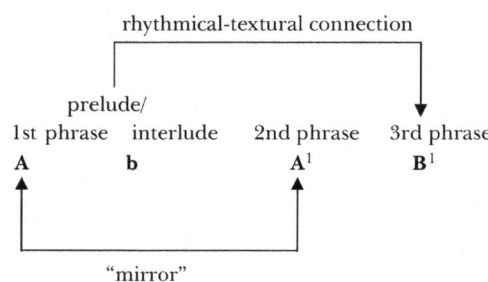

EXAMPLE 15-14 George Crumb, *Madrigals, Book III*, No. 2, "Gacela de la muerto oscura" ["Gacela of the Dark Death"], vertical/horizontal scheme of the madrigal with the resulting harmonic structure.

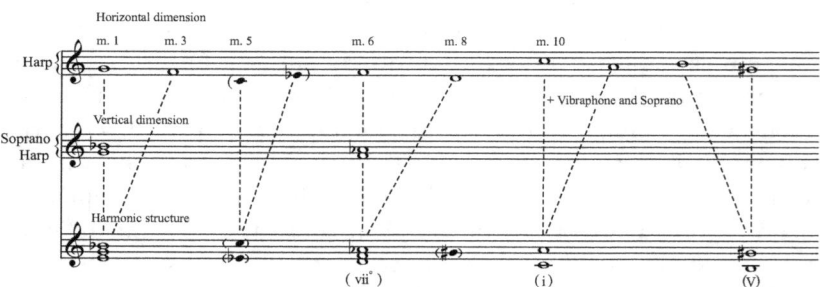

bass-plus-soprano texture in the first two phrases. In the resulting vertical-horizontal totality, there is a succession of the two diminished triads in the first two phrases, followed by the clearly tonic-dominant relationship of the C-A and B-G sharp dyads. The diminished triad succession, with its tonal ambiguity, leads to a sense of dreamlike, wondrous non-belonging. In the third, "lamenting," phrase, the implied tonic-dominant dyads alternate, recurring melodically multiple times in each line of the score, as if following a pattern of tension and release—a pattern that is also essential to the act of crying. Moreover, the lamenting motive, constructed of the minor thirds, is inherent in both horizontal and vertical dimensions of the whole piece.

EXAMPLE 15-15 George Crumb, *Madrigals, Book III*, No. 2, "Gacela de la muerto oscura" ["Gacela of the Dark Death"], overlapping synchronic and diachronic compositional processes in the madrigal.

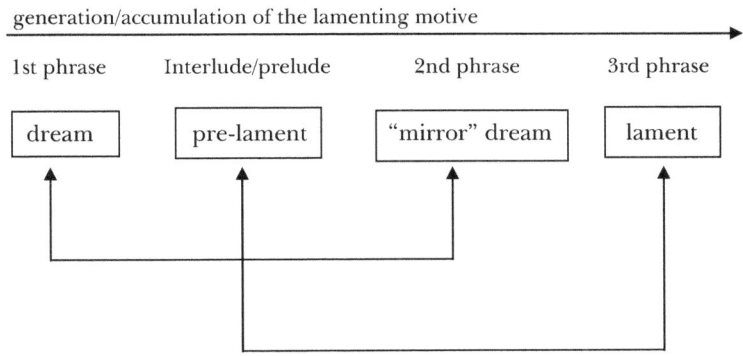

In retrospect, the reoccurrence of the melodic thirds in the first two phrases and in the instrumental interlude may be viewed as an integral part of the process that generates the lamenting gesture. This link and the overall tertian harmonic structure of the madrigal relate the two concepts of the dreaming and lamenting, and, simultaneously, the two dimensions of the piece—synchronic and diachronic (example 15-15).

Musico-Poetic Analysis

As seen from the musical analysis of the piece, Crumb concentrates on the two words/concepts found in Lorca's excerpt: those of dreaming and lamenting. In the text, these two notions occupy the peripheral position in the symmetrical synchronic structure. Moreover, they constitute one structural unit (3/6) belonging to the semantic field of the "dream/pure." The composer emphasizes the idea of dreaming by not only repeating the word "el' swanyo" ("dream") in the first phrase, but also repeating the whole phrase in the mirror inversion. The mirror image construct is both a compositional and a semantic device. Donald Rackin, the author of a study of Lewis Carroll's *Alice's Adventures in Wonderland* and *Through the Looking Glass*, wrote: "What we typically see in a mirror, besides our own image, is what lies behind us—in a sense, not where we are going, but where we have been ... In Carroll's formulation the mirror is ... simultaneously a snare and a means of escape: it all depends on what one makes of the seemingly innocuous preposition *through*."[10] The dream too may be both "a snare and a means of escape." In Lorca's text the dreaming is asserted by the tautological syntagma "dormir el' swan'yo" ("to sleep a dream") and by the image of sleeping apples that itself is a dream-fantasy. In his madrigal, Crumb intensifies the semantics of dreaming further by introducing the idea of the dream-mirror. Thus, the composer not only follows, selectively, the diachronic design of Lorca's text, but also signifies its symmetrical foundation through the use of a simple and effective compositional device—namely, inversion.

Another outcome of the mirror construction is the semantic weight put on the word "manthanas" ("apples"). As the last word of the first phrase and the first line in Lorca's text, "manthanas" contains an automatic emphasis. The ambiguity of the sleeping-apples image is semantically intense. Crumb amplifies the complexity of this image further by means of melodic pitch separation. The melodic gesture corresponding to the word "manthanas" ("apples") in the first phrase mimics the ascending/descending contour of the melodic line (in more dramatic form) with the rapid drop of a minor ninth at the end (mm. 3–4). Consequently, in the second phrase the direction of the pitches is reversed: now we hear the word "manthanas" in the higher register, leaping upward a minor ninth to the F sharp$_5$ (mm. 8–9). In a sense, Crumb's repetition of Lorca's first phrase, the mirror inversion used in the second musical phrase, and the pitch content and the double directionality of the "manthanas"-gesture all may be viewed as the composer's way of expressing the ambiguity of this poetic image.

Crumb's diachronic dimension of the piece is modelled after the diachronic aspect of the text. As previously discussed, in the text, the r-sound builds in intensity throughout the excerpt, and the r-tension reaches its culmination in the last word of the excerpt, "tierra" ("earth"). By the same token, the cumulative presence of the lamenting minor-third motive in Crumb's setting is underscored in the third phrase. As noted above, just as in Lorca's text, the intervallic content of the gesture couples the two concepts, "dreaming" and "lamenting," into one semantic field.

Conclusion

Crumb intensifies the two-dimensional design of the poetic excerpt by expanding its diachronic aspect (the generation of the lamenting motive) and musically focusing its synchronic aspect on one semantic field, "dream/pure." For him, "dream" and "lament" are the two keywords to Lorca's text, its semantic core. One the other hand, in the setting of Dalos's poem, Kurtág musically expresses the intensity inherent in the poem's subtext rather than in the poetic words per se, through the tension between progressive music structure and regressive musico-poetic construction. Figuratively speaking, in approaching the poetic text, Kurtág "digs in" whereas Crumb "digs out." Still, both Kurtág and Crumb are composers who approach the text as creative readers and interpreters, foregrounding textual elements that they consider the semantic centre. "Between center and periphery, and periphery and center, there is always an itinerary, a route," writes Gian-Paolo Biasin in his essay on literary criticism.[11] In the two pieces discussed above, Kurtág and Crumb might have followed different itineraries, but without a doubt, for both composers the conceptual centre of their vocal music lies in the depths of the poetic work. Ultimately, as a reader and listener, I created my own itinerary, my own web of interpenetrating subspaces in this complex, multi-dimensional, unbound musico-poetic space.

I would like to conclude by reinterpreting a quote from feminist literary scholar Hélène Cixous to apply to György Kurtág and George Crumb:

> I choose to work on the texts that "touch" me. I use the word deliberately because I believe there is a bodily relationship between reader and text. We work very close to the text, as close to the body of the text as possible; we work phonically, listening to the text, as well as graphically and typographically ... I like to work like an ant, crawling the entire length of a text and examining all its details, as well as like a bird that flies over it, or like one in Tsvetaeva immense ears, listening to its music.[12]

Let's keep listening.

Notes

1. Michael Kearney, "The Local and the Global: The Anthropology of Globalization and Transnationalism," *Annual Review of Anthropology* 24 (1995): 549.
2. Yuri Lotman, "The Content and Structure of the Concept of 'Literature,'" in *Twentieth-Century Literary Theory: A Reader*, 2nd ed., ed. K.M. Newton (New York: St. Martin's Press, 1997), 103.
3. Yuri Lotman, *Analiz poeticheskogo teksta: Struktura stikha* (Leningrad: Prosveshchenie, 1972) and *Analysis of the Poetic Text*, ed. and trans. D. Barton Johnson (Ann Arbor: Ardis, 1976).
4. This postulate relates Lotman's ideas back to Roman Jakobson's concept of the dominant: "Verse is a system of values; as with any value system, it possesses its own hierarchy of superior and inferior values and one leading value, the dominant." From Roman Jacobson, "The Dominant," in *Twentieth-Century Literary Theory: A Reader*, 6.

5 This piece has been previously discussed in Diana ("Dina") Lentsner, "Playing with Circles: A Musico-Poetic Study of György Kurtág's *Scenes from a Novel*, Op. 19 (1979–1982)" (PhD diss., Ohio State University, 2002).
6 I use the terms "semantic group" and "semantic field" interchangeably. The linguistic notion of the semantic field, according to Eva Kittay, is based on the idea "that both lexical items and the concepts associated with them come not singly but in groupings defined by specifiable relations of contrast and affinity." See Eva F. Kittay, "Semantic Fields and the Individuation of Content," in *Frames, Fields, and Contrasts: New Essays on Semantic and Lexical Organization*, ed. Adrienne Lehrer and Eva Kittay (Hillsdale, NJ: Lawrence Erlbaum Associates, 1992), 229. Thus, we place a word-pair "snitsia" and "son" (translated as "to dream" and "a dream," respectively), and also a word-pair "blizosti" and "priblizhaesh'sia" (literally, "closeness" and "to come close," respectively), into one semantic field or group.
7 Sigmund Freud, *The Interpretation of Dreams*, trans. Joyce Crick (New York: Oxford University Press, 1999), 55–56.
8 Donald Rackin, *Alice's Adventures in Wonderland and Through the Looking-Glass: Nonsense, Sense, and Meaning* (New York: Twain, 1991), 17–18.
9 Ibid., 18.
10 Ibid., 72.
11 Gian-Paolo Biasin, "The Periphery of Literature," *Modern Language Notes* 111/5 (1996): 982.
12 Hélène Cixous, "Conversations," in *Twentieth-Century Literary Theory: A Reader*, 228.

Bibliography

Biasin, Gian-Paolo. "The Periphery of Literature." *Modern Language Notes* 111/5 (1996): 976–89.
Cixous, Hélène. "Conversations." In *Twentieth-Century Literary Theory: A Reader*, 2nd ed., edited by K.M. Newton, 225–33. New York: St. Martin's Press, 1997.
Freud, Sigmund. *The Interpretation of Dreams*. Translated by Joyce Crick. New York: Oxford University Press, 1999.
Jacobson, Roman. "The Dominant." In *Twentieth-Century Literary Theory: A Reader*, 6–9.
Kearney, Michael. "The Local and the Global: The Anthropology of Globalization and Transnationalism." *Annual Review of Anthropology* 24 (1995): 549.
Kittay, Eva F. "Semantic Fields and the Individuation of Content." In *Frames, Fields, and Contrasts: New Essays on Semantic and Lexical Organization*, edited by Adrienne Lehrer and Eva Kittay, 229–52. Hillsdale, NJ: Lawrence Erlbaum Associates, 1992.
Lentsner, Diana ("Dina"). "Playing with Circles: A Musico-Poetic Study of György Kurtág's *Scenes from a Novel*, Op. 19 (1979–1982)." PhD diss., Ohio State University, 2002.

Lotman, Yuri. *Analiz poeticheskogo teksta: Struktura stikha*. Leningrad: Prosveshchenie, 1972.

———. *Analysis of the Poetic Text*. Edited and translated by D. Barton Johnson. Ann Arbor, MI: Ardis, 1976.

———. "The Content and Structure of the Concept of 'Literature.'" In *Twentieth-Century Literary Theory: A Reader*, 102–5.

Rackin, Donald. *Alice's Adventures in Wonderland and Through the Looking-Glass: Nonsense, Sense, and Meaning*. New York: Twain, 1991.

The Presence of the Past and Memory in Contemporary Music

SIXTEEN

György Kurtág et Walter Benjamin : considérations sur l'aura dans la musique

JEAN-PAUL OLIVE

Comment continuer?

Dans *Le style et l'idée*, au cours d'un texte traitant de théorie et de composition musicales, Schoenberg en arrive à se poser une question qui, sous sa naïveté apparente, soulève pourtant une infinité de problèmes : « Qu'est-ce qui permet qu'un son puisse succéder à un autre, à un son initial ? Comment est-ce logiquement possible? » se demande-t-il avant de continuer et d'insister encore : « Tous les problèmes imaginables et les plus tirés par les cheveux ont été étudiés, mais personne ne s'est jamais demandé : "Comment, après tout, puis-je relier deux sons l'un à l'autre?" »[1]. Avec une acuité plus ou moins grande et selon des sensibilités diverses, toutes les écritures importantes du début du XXe siècle ont, de fait, posé une question similaire; en intégrant le constat qu'elles ne disposaient plus de la tonalité comme d'un langage commun immédiat, ces musiques ont transcrit, à des degrés différents et en apportant des réponses singulières, la coupure d'avec la tradition. Elles témoignèrent avec force d'un rapport au passé qui ne pouvait plus guère persister selon une relation de continuité. Elles exprimèrent l'état moderne de l'expérience qui a subi l'effet du choc, ce choc que Walter Benjamin décryptait déjà dans la poésie de Charles Baudelaire et que György Ligeti décrit techniquement dans un texte où il associe des musiques aussi contrastées que celles de Debussy et de Webern : « Ce qui les rapproche aussi, écrit-il, c'est un langage musical ne connaissant que la juxtaposition d'égal à égal plutôt que la hiérarchie et la subordination. Une fois la sensible évincée, il devient impossible d'établir un réseau étroit de liens entre les éléments musicaux; ils s'agencent comme des pierres sans mortier dans la muraille de la forme »[2].

C'est probablement chez Webern que l'interrogation à propos du langage continue de nous marquer le plus par sa radicalité, et les courtes pièces que le compositeur écrivit durant les années 1910 présentent au moins trois caractéristiques révélatrices d'une telle position. La première semble spécifique de la position de l'École de Vienne et de son expressionnisme atonal et peut se définir par le refus d'employer toute formation sonore préexistante, tout élément préformé, tout idiome directement hérité de la tonalité. La deuxième caractéristique est le souci extrême d'une articulation de détail qui conserve, presque comme en creux dans la composition, les catégories historiquement constituées de la forme musicale; thème, antécédent, conséquent, pont, figure d'accompagnement demeurent, rétractés dans l'infiniment petit, les unités grâce auxquelles le compositeur structure ses aphorismes inouïs à partir de ce qui, pourtant, découpait, reliait et caractérisait le discours musical. Il semble bien que si Webern en était arrivé à rejeter les éléments constitués eux-mêmes, soupçonnés d'être frappés d'inertie par un processus de réification, ce soit pour mieux tenter de sauver une autre dimension du langage à travers les modes de relations sédimentés à partir de quoi s'élaborait le processus musical. La troisième caractéristique – une conséquence, en fait, des deux précédentes – est l'intensification du discours : si chaque élément, dans ces pièces, est d'une extrême brièveté, ce n'est pas par défaut, mais au contraire parce qu'il concentre une énergie et une expressivité qui ne supporteraient pas la dilution dans le temps. C'est ce qu'a très justement fait remarquer Schoenberg au sujet des *Bagatelles pour quatuor à cordes opus 9* dans le texte d'introduction qu'il leur a consacré : « Mais avoir su enfermer tout un roman dans un simple geste, exprimer tout son bonheur dans une seule exhalaison de souffle, voilà qui implique une concentration d'esprit ignorée de ceux qui se complaisent à épancher leurs émotions »[3]. Une écriture débarrassée des idiomes qui rapprochaient la musique de la communication, un sens aigu de l'articulation hérité de la tradition mais transféré dans une dimension nouvelle, l'intensification de chaque détail et de chaque relation entre les détails : ces trois caractéristiques de l'écriture ont ainsi entraîné l'œuvre de Webern dans un questionnement et un renouvellement de la catégorie d'expression.

György Kurtág a exprimé à plusieurs reprises ce qu'il devait à l'influence de Webern dont il a analysé en détail les pièces; il a aussi évoqué de quelle manière, à une époque précise de sa vie, il s'était posé au plus intime de lui-même, comme un drame personnel, la question de Schoenberg « Qu'est-ce qui permet qu'un son puisse succéder à un autre, à un son initial ? » Alors qu'il séjournait à Paris, lors d'une véritable crise existentielle, c'est semble-t-il à partir de cette question que le compositeur réussit à reprendre lentement le chemin de l'écriture, une écriture qui, par bien des aspects, se rapproche de celle de Webern : une forte tendance aux formes aphoristiques, un souci extrême du détail expressif, une densité particulièrement dramatique des relations entre les unités qui constituent les pièces. Cependant, si deux des caractéristiques rencontrées chez Webern – la structuration du discours et l'intensification – sont ici présentes, la première – l'absence de tout élément préformé – ne semble pas correspondre à l'écriture de Kurtág; chez lui, en effet, aucun tabou ne vient interdire l'usage de matériaux hérités du passé, aucune frontière autoritairement hermétique ne vient empêcher la remontée d'objets identifiés, seulement vaguement connus ou à demi oubliés.

Bien au contraire, il semble plutôt que, chez Kurtág, les éléments de la composition, dont la plupart sont tout aussi minuscules que chez Webern, soient souvent précisément choisis pour leur « potentialité d'évocation », une charge émotionnelle assumée à partir de laquelle s'édifie le geste musical. Celui-ci possède sa propre complexité technique, mais, grâce à ce qui demeure enfoui dans le matériau, se présente comme traversé par une immédiateté dramatique rare. Un son, un accord, un mouvement cadentiel, un motif sont présents avec leurs connotations, non pas comme simples éléments neutres de la construction, mais comme une matière déjà chargée d'esprit sédimenté, une matière historiquement spiritualisée.

Une telle attitude compositionnelle est fortement déterminée par la relation qu'entretient le sujet avec la mémoire, autant individuelle que collective; une telle démarche n'est pas sans rappeler ce bel aphorisme d'Elias Canetti, dans *Le cœur secret de l'horloge* : « À quoi bon te souvenir ? Vis le présent ! Vis le présent ! Mais c'est pour vivre le présent que je me souviens »[4]. En effet, la catégorie de la mémoire investit l'écriture de Kurtág dans toutes ses dimensions, de l'élément le plus isolé à la pièce entière, contribuant par l'existence de strates à demi recouvertes à la puissante densité expressive de cette musique. Elle peut concerner un objet simple, comme un accord parfait transfiguré par ses multiples dispositions. Mais il peut tout aussi bien s'agir d'une série ou d'un enchaînement que Kurtág manipule à sa manière, entraînant parfois l'objet trouvé (ou volé, c'est selon, comme l'explique le compositeur) dans une dérive au bord de l'absurde. On peut également rencontrer des éléments plus complexes : des mouvements de danse, des complaintes populaires, des lamentations funèbres, ou encore des réminiscences de formes du classicisme et bien sûr d'auteurs romantiques. Parfois, plus qu'à un objet, c'est à un processus qu'il est fait référence : un mouvement cadentiel, un style d'écriture en ostinato, un canon ou un *fugato*, voire un style ancien comme le style *concitato* du début du baroque. Une telle pratique s'étend régulièrement à la citation – exacte, approximative ou vague – de matériau, de forme ou de style.

Néanmoins, cette sorte de confiance dans la musique et dans son histoire, qui se manifeste dans l'usage des références et de la citation (une caractéristique qui rapproche l'écriture de Kurtág de celle de Walter Benjamin) ne se confond jamais ici avec la simple acceptation des conventions, avec la réception passive de ce qui s'est un jour pétrifié; le langage, en tant qu'héritage, n'est là que pour servir le présent, il n'apparaît qu'en étant immédiatement mis en question par un traitement qui réinjecte dans les éléments une nouvelle vitalité, mais aussi parfois une distance qui en accentue le caractère tragique. La brièveté des pièces, leur structuration et leur caractère fragmentaire, tout en consolidant l'élaboration du geste expressif, empêchent le langage de se refermer sur une attitude affirmative et évitent toute retombée dans un procédé discursif.

Peut-être en partie parce que la tradition musicale à laquelle appartient le compositeur hongrois n'a pas été complètement interrompue, sans doute aussi parce que son expérience et son rapport à la mémoire sont singuliers, Kurtág a répondu d'une manière particulière à la question de Schoenberg « Comment continuer à partir d'un son? ». À ces deux dimensions wéberniennes que sont l'extrême exigence de structuration et l'intensité expressive, Kurtág associe une troisième dimension qui fait intervenir de manière décisive la mémoire : cette caractéristique n'est autre que la présence de la dimension auratique, et, pour être plus précis, de l'aura telle qu'elle persiste dans la modernité, c'est-à-dire telle que Walter Benjamin l'avait analysée chez Baudelaire, dans son déclin.

Le proche et le lointain

La catégorie de l'aura occupe une place centrale dans la dernière période des écrits de Walter Benjamin; elle intervient de manière importante pour la compréhension et la critique de l'œuvre d'art, considérée aussi bien du point de vue de la production que du point de vue de la réception. Cependant, une telle notion n'est pas définie par Benjamin de manière simple et univoque; on a plutôt affaire, ici, à un concept mouvant, une constellation dont la définition évolue au fur et à mesure des écrits tardifs. Le concept d'aura apparaît à la fin de la deuxième période de la production benjaminienne, une période que l'on serait tenté de qualifier de militante : dans un contexte de rapports de forces historiques difficiles et menaçants, Benjamin cherche en effet, à la fin des années 1920, à se rapprocher d'une conception proche du marxisme dont la figure idéale, à ses yeux, semble bien à ce moment-là s'être identifiée à la personne de Bertolt Brecht. Mais la réflexion sur la question de l'aura se poursuivra durant les années qui suivent, notamment à travers les travaux sur « Paris, capitale du XIXe siècle » et l'étude de la poésie de Baudelaire. La catégorie d'aura, sans forcément présenter alors un visage contradictoire avec les définitions précédentes, est cependant pour le moins infléchie vers une autre direction. La nécessité de sa destruction, vers quoi tendaient les premiers textes sur l'aura, laisse place à la fin des années 1930 à une réflexion sur la persistance et le déclin de l'aura.

Aussi, si l'on veut saisir la teneur et les incidences de la catégorie d'aura chez Benjamin, s'avère-t-il nécessaire de conserver à l'esprit les définitions successives que l'auteur en a données. La première, peut-être la plus célèbre, apparaît dès 1933 dans l'article « La petite histoire de la photographie » et sera presque reprise à l'identique dans le non moins célèbre texte « L'œuvre d'art à l'ère de sa reproductibilité technique »; à la question « Qu'est-ce au juste que l'aura ? », Benjamin donne alors cette réponse : « Une trame singulière d'espace et de temps : l'unique apparition d'un lointain, si proche soit-il. Un jour d'été, en plein midi, suivre du regard la ligne d'une chaîne de montagnes à l'horizon ou d'une branche qui jette son ombre sur le spectateur, jusqu'à ce que l'instant ou l'heure ait part à leur manifestation – c'est respirer l'aura de ces montagnes, de cette branche »[5].

Cette première définition comporte déjà plusieurs éléments remarquables, dont le premier, peut-être le plus évident, est le recours décisif à l'expérience contemplative du beau naturel, celle-ci étant présentée en quelque sorte comme le modèle de ce que peut être l'expérience face à l'œuvre d'art. Cette relation au beau naturel, cependant, est un rapport proprement humain, fait sur lequel Benjamin avait mis l'accent dans un texte non édité, un manuscrit retrouvé à la Bibliothèque Nationale : « L'expérience de l'aura repose sur la traduction de la manière, jadis habituelle dans la société humaine, de réagir au rapport de la nature à l'homme. Celui qui est regardé – ou qui se croit regardé – lève son regard, répond par un regard. Faire l'expérience de l'aura d'une apparition ou d'un être, c'est se rendre compte de sa capacité à lever les yeux, ou de répondre par un regard. Cette capacité est pleine de poésie »[6]. Cette note manuscrite permet de mieux comprendre le sens d'une deuxième caractéristique donnée dans la définition de l'aura, lorsque Benjamin dit qu'elle est « une trame singulière d'espace et de temps ». Le manuscrit de Benjamin met l'accent sur le fait que cette trame particulière, unique, qui n'est autre que la contexture de l'œuvre, est « fabriquée » par l'homme, par l'artiste, et que la distance, « l'espacement »[7] liés à cette trame en sont partie intégrante au niveau de la production. Par ailleurs, Benjamin insiste fortement dans cette note sur la relation qui se noue entre le regardant et le regardé, une relation dont on peut légitimement penser qu'elle est directement liée à cet espacement. C'est précisément cette distance, constitutive de l'aura, qui est mise en avant dans l'expression « unique apparition d'un lointain, si proche soit-il », en évoquant dans l'œuvre une coexistence de deux plans, voire leur coagulation, qui les rend inséparables : le premier, pour ainsi dire immédiat, à portée de main à la surface de la chose contemplée; le second, éloigné au point qu'il semble inatteignable, transparaissant au travers de lui. Beaucoup d'éléments conduisent à penser que cette qualité particulière et complexe, qui apparaît énigmatiquement dans les œuvres, est intimement liée à la dimension du passé. C'est sur un tel phénomène qu'insistera ultérieurement Benjamin.

En effet, dans un grand article de 1939 consacré à la poésie de Baudelaire et intitulé « Sur quelques thèmes baudelairiens », si Benjamin revient à la question de l'aura, c'est maintenant pour en proposer une nouvelle définition qui porte au premier plan le rôle de la mémoire : « Si l'on entend par aura d'un objet offert à l'intuition l'ensemble des images qui, surgies de la mémoire involontaire, tendent à se grouper autour de lui, l'aura correspond, en cette sorte d'objet, à l'expérience même que l'exercice sédimente autour d'un objet d'usage »[8]. Dans le contexte de l'expérience moderne, au sens que lui donne Benjamin en employant le terme d' « expérience vécue » (*Erlebnis*) qu'il oppose à l'expérience telle qu'elle se présentait traditionnellement (*Erfahrung*), la catégorie de « mémoire involontaire » acquiert une fonction centrale. Si l'expérience vécue se caractérise par le phénomène du choc sous l'impact duquel elle se fragmente et se dissocie en instants discontinus que la conscience ne peut plus guère synthétiser, si cette expérience moderne ne peut donc plus s'insérer dans le tissu de la durée traditionnelle, alors la mémoire involontaire, de même que la remémoration et les correspondances baudelairiennes, constituent la manifestation de la remontée possible du passé, coupé du présent et de la conscience, un passé qui apparaît non sans une certaine qualité d'étrangeté.

Alors que, dans la période précédente, notamment dans l'article sur « L'œuvre d'art à l'ère de sa reproductibilité technique », Benjamin critiquait (non sans raison) la dimension cultuelle liée à l'aura et semblait prendre acte de la destruction nécessaire d'un tel phénomène, jusque même en décliner les avantages possibles dans le champ politique, il semble tout aussi clair qu'à cette nouvelle étape de sa réflexion, il est amené à reconsidérer les données du problème. L'intérêt qu'il porte à des auteurs tels que Proust et Baudelaire, mais aussi au surréalisme, le conduisent maintenant à de nouvelles formulations. Il n'est plus ici question de la destruction de l'aura mais, concernant l'expérience moderne d'un sujet qui se voit déconnecté du passé et de la tradition, il importe plutôt de saisir les mécanismes grâce auxquels ce sujet est à même de ressentir à nouveau une dimension de l'expérience qui, sans cela, se verrait menacée de mutilation, si ce n'est de disparition. Ce qui est alors ici en jeu n'est autre que la fonction du langage, de la poésie, de l'art; Benjamin en a plus qu'une intuition et c'est ce qu'indique l'expression « déclin de l'aura ». Si, dans cette nouvelle approche, l'aura persiste bien, ce n'est plus sous la forme unie héritée des cultes anciens, ce n'est plus en tant que pouvoir magique et religieux dont il faudrait absolument se défaire. C'est maintenant sur un mode interrogatif qu'elle opère sa puissance, et, par là, libère une forte potentialité critique. C'est alors qu'apparaît clairement dans le texte sur Baudelaire en quoi réside le pouvoir de l'aura, une dimension profondément humaine qui semble maintenant irremplaçable. Cette dimension est intimement liée au regard. Benjamin écrit[9]:

> Or le regard est habité par l'attente d'une réponse de celui auquel il s'offre. Que cette attente reçoive une réponse (dans la pensée, elle peut s'attacher au regard intentionnel de l'attention aussi bien qu'à un regard au sens littéral du terme), l'expérience de l'aura connaît alors sa plénitude. "La perceptibilité, considère Novalis, est une attention". La perceptibilité dont il parle ainsi n'est autre que celle de l'aura. L'expérience de l'aura repose donc sur le transfert, au niveau des rapports entre l'inanimé – ou la nature – et l'homme, d'une forme de réaction courante dans la société humaine. Dès qu'on est – ou se croit – regardé, on lève les yeux. Sentir l'aura d'un phénomène, c'est lui conférer le pouvoir de lever les yeux. Les trouvailles de la mémoire involontaire ont ce caractère.

Enfin, pour conclure sur cette question, une dernière définition de l'aura doit encore être évoquée ici : elle est de Th. W. Adorno et nous ramène au plus près de la musique. Adorno, qui avait bien compris l'importance de la catégorie d'aura ainsi que de son déclin pour la compréhension de l'art moderne, s'est efforcé de transférer celle-ci dans le champ musical. Dans la *Théorie esthétique* se rencontre une réflexion qui, sans trahir les définitions de Benjamin, s'en éloigne cependant dans la mesure où elle tente de cerner l'aura par son caractère technique : « Ce qu'on appelle aura est familier à l'expérience artistique sous le nom d'atmosphère de l'œuvre d'art dans la mesure où le rapport entre ses éléments renvoie au-delà de ceux-ci et permet à chacun des éléments particuliers de se dépasser »[10]. Pour Adorno, ce dépassement des éléments constitutifs des œuvres au-delà d'eux-mêmes constitue précisément le trait qui fait que les œuvres ne sont pas des choses prosaïques du monde; là réside ce « plus » qui fait de l'art un domaine singulier, une des dimensions de sa spiritualisation. Déjà, dans un article de 1959 sur le compositeur Ernst Krenek, Adorno avait fait référence à la notion d'aura dans des termes semblables; la définition qu'il en donnait alors était encore plus éclairante pour ce qui concerne la musique :

> Or la musique est sans doute l'art auratique par excellence, ce qui fait de nos jours sa difficulté spécifique : une cohérence musicale se réalise à la seule condition que ce qui apparaît isolément soit davantage que lui-même, qu'il soit transcendé vers une non-présence, un éloignement, et cette relation significative, médium de toute logique musicale, produit sans doute immanquablement quelque chose comme une atmosphère qui enveloppe la musique[11].

Si bien des éléments appartenant aux définitions de Benjamin sont ici présents, ils revêtent cependant une tonalité particulière du fait de leur importation dans le domaine de l'art des sons : ce sur quoi insiste Adorno en présentant la musique comme le plus auratique des arts, c'est cette qualité spécifique qui la caractérise (une nécessité, pourrait-on aller jusqu'à dire), qui n'est autre que le fait de se constituer dans une unité se situant en elle-même. Bien sûr, pour atteindre cette unité, un certain nombre de composantes techniques, inhérentes au musical, existent et participent à la composition, mais sans pourtant être suffisantes en elles-mêmes pour atteindre un véritable contexte de sens. Pour ne pas risquer de sombrer dans une absurdité technique ou dans la platitude mutique d'un objet inerte, il semble bien qu'une autre dimension soit nécessaire, une dimension qui travaille le temps, aussi bien le temps historique que celui de l'agencement des éléments dans l'œuvre. Cette dimension, qui a beaucoup à voir avec l'aura, n'est pas étrangère à la capacité de la musique à agencer les sons en constellations sonores dynamiques. En retour, grâce à cette action, la musique détient le puissant et évanescent pouvoir de l'évocation, la capacité éminemment auratique de réveiller le passé au sein du présent. Cependant, une observation s'impose ici car, dans ce processus, rien ne semble gagné d'avance, rien n'est automatique, rien n'est mécanique; tout dépend de la manière dont le compositeur s'y prend pour atteindre la puissance de l'évocation et pour que celle-ci, non pas matière morte mais agent actif, œuvre dans la trame du présent. Il ne s'agit pas ici d'un quelconque avatar du néo-classicisme ou d'une forme neutralisée comme dans les postures post-modernes. Il s'agit de la conscience aiguë d'une expérience moderne confrontée, par-delà le choc, au temps, à la tradition, à la question du sens. György Kurtág est passé maître dans cet art; son écriture, patiemment élaborée en absorbant l'histoire des œuvres musicales, une écriture à bien des égards proche de celle de Benjamin, détient au plus haut degré la capacité de réveiller l'aura, de nous faire percevoir son déclin, de nous faire sentir le pouvoir de l'aura dans son déclin.

Douze microludes ...

Composés en hommage au compositeur et chef d'orchestre András Mihály, les *Douze microludes pour quatuor à cordes* se présentent comme une série de brèves pièces musicales. Chacun de ces aphorismes possède son caractère propre, extrêmement marqué, mais la forme générale est structurée par une lente montée en demi-tons à partir du do, chaque microlude adoptant successivement pour centre une note polaire dont la place, la fonction, se trouvent chaque fois variées; à la fin de ce trajet, le microlude conclusif se polarise autour de la note si, douzième et dernier degré de la gamme chromatique. Au-delà de la référence explicite à András Mihály, un deuxième hommage est ici esquissé, latent, par l'évocation de l'organisation du *Clavier bien tempéré* de Jean-Sébastien Bach.

Comme on l'a remarqué dans la première partie de ce texte, il est aisé de constater que ces douze pièces recueillent une part de l'héritage webernien, particulièrement du Webern de la période atonale : la brièveté saisissante de la plupart des aphorismes, l'extrême structuration du matériau chromatique, l'articulation en unités bien définies qui conserve, en filigrane, le souvenir de certaines fonctions traditionnelles, l'expressivité des brefs éléments mis en contact. Cependant, comme on l'a aussi évoqué plus haut, une autre caractéristique s'impose au regard, qui n'est autre que la présence de matériaux connus – accords, rythmes, figures, fragments mélodiques, types –, ces matériaux ayant tous une valeur d'évocation très forte du fait de leur appartenance à un fond commun, à la tradition. Ces éléments, détenteurs d'une charge historique, sont évidemment largement responsables de la potentialité auratique des microludes; et s'il faut entendre ici qu'il s'agit de l'aura dans son déclin, ce n'est certes pas que son pouvoir en est diminué, mais que le compositeur, loin d'utiliser ces éléments avec l'évidence solide dont ils sont encore parfois porteurs, les réfléchit et les recompose selon de nouvelles constellations qui les interrogent. Un tel questionnement, inséparablement posé à même la présence de ces éléments, vient frapper de plein fouet notre perception et, ce faisant, nous fait nous interroger. Les modalités de ce questionnement sont cependant diverses, conduisant à un certain nombre de différenciations.

Un premier cas de figure repose sur l'évocation de caractères très reconnaissables, inscrits depuis longtemps dans les habitus musicaux : les huitième et neuvième microludes laissent ainsi transparaître dans leur texture le caractère d'une marche, soit par le rythme vigoureux des accords attaqués (dans le huitième), soit par la présence d'une étrange basse constituant un plan presque continu de l'écriture (dans le neuvième). La marche, dans l'imaginaire sonore, est fortement liée à l'idée d'un mouvement collectif, d'une avancée dynamique, parfois jusqu'à l'inexorable; la force du mouvement corporel qu'elle induit traverse tout tissu musical qui en adopte un certain nombre de traits. Cependant, dans les microludes, ces pièces à la fois sont des marches et n'en sont pas : les interruptions du rythme dans le huitième, la présence d'autres plans qui interfèrent avec celui de la basse dans le neuvième insèrent une distance pour l'auditeur à travers les torsions qui déforment le modèle, entraînant l'oreille vers un tout autre espace intérieur (il suffit de prêter attention aux si fantasques harmoniques du violon dans la neuvième pièce). Il s'agit précisément ici de la distance qui permet de sentir à la fois l'aura provenant de l'évocation et, en même temps, la coupure qui altère celle-ci.

Un deuxième cas de figure concerne l'emploi qui est fait d'éléments ou processus directement issus du langage tonal et qui conduisent, dans cette œuvre, à une posture très particulière : en effet, dans les microludes, si le langage tonal n'est pas résolument rejeté, il n'est pas non plus aveuglément adopté. Il y est en quelque sorte réfléchi à partir de ce qui, en lui, continue de nous toucher, par le jeu d'une expérimentation sensible prenant des formes chaque fois différentes. Si on emploie ici le terme d'expérimentation, c'est au sens fort du terme, car ce qui est mis en mouvement dans les trois exemples qui vont suivre n'est pas de l'ordre de l'action sur des objets neutralisés que l'on pourrait utiliser comme s'ils étaient des choses inertes. Il s'agit bien plutôt chaque fois de processus liés à la musique tonale, de processus dynamiques car il est ici question d'énergie engrangée dans le langage, de ce grâce à quoi le langage, dès lors qu'est refusée sa chute dans la simple communication, demeure poétiquement actif.

Le septième microlude est ainsi structuré autour de la note fa dièse, que l'ensemble des instruments atteignent à la fin de la première mesure grâce à un trait rapide qui donne à cette introduction son caractère fulgurant; ce fa dièse demeurera constamment tenu par le second violon, tandis que le violoncelle égrène, soutenu par d'étranges doublures aux autres instruments, une simple gamme de sol conduisant à la conclusion mystérieuse de la pièce. La confrontation qui se manifeste ici est l'une des plus fortes du langage tonal : la sensible (fa dièse) se trouve superposée à la gamme de sol, qui est elle énoncée sans sensible, avec un fa bécarre, comme si toute l'énergie de ce mécanisme fondateur de la tonalité se trouvait ramassé en une image dynamique.

Le premier des microludes, lui, donne à entendre un mécanisme tout aussi fondateur de la tonalité : la première partie de l'aphorisme repose sur un do grave de la basse, la deuxième partie, quant à elle, évolue sur une quinte sol-ré, qui n'est autre que le cinquième degré, la dominante du do initial. Les autres instruments, dans une atmosphère d'extrême douceur, font entrer à partir d'un « cluster diatonique » tous les degrés de remplissage de la gamme, conduisant le tissu sonore à une évolution harmonique progressive. La coda de la pièce, après une respiration, superpose les deux pôles fondamentaux du trajet de la pièce, « tonique » et « dominante ». Le microlude rétracte ainsi en quelques instants, en un raccourci saisissant, le parcours dynamique historique du langage tonal, parcours harmonique dont la résolution n'est plus univoque, comme elle l'était dans la tonalité, mais reste en suspens dans la coda, par la superposition sensible et réflexive des tensions retenues entre premier et cinquième degrés (exemple 16-1).

C'est encore une image de la tonalité qui nous est donnée à entendre dans le sixième microlude, une image dynamique par la distance qui œuvre en elle, par le traitement qui fait d'elle un objet à la fois proche et lointain. Cet aphorisme semble être tout entier consacré à l'accord de fa majeur, objet sonore dont la luminosité se transforme par le jeu des dispositions entre les deux violons qui le jouent. Autour de cet objet immobile bien que changeant viennent frotter, en brefs éclats à l'alto et au violoncelle, les rapports de tension, les dissonances, que recelait la tonalité, mais qui se superposent ici à l'accord, comme si le temps de la tonalité était à la fois bouleversé, concentré et suspendu; la pièce est aussi prenante qu'une miniature expressionniste, mais, dans ses tensions contenues, la

EXEMPLE 16-1 György Kurtág, *Hommage à Mihály András*, Op. 13 (1977-78), « 12 Microludes pour quatuors à cordes », n° 1. © Editio Musica Budapest.

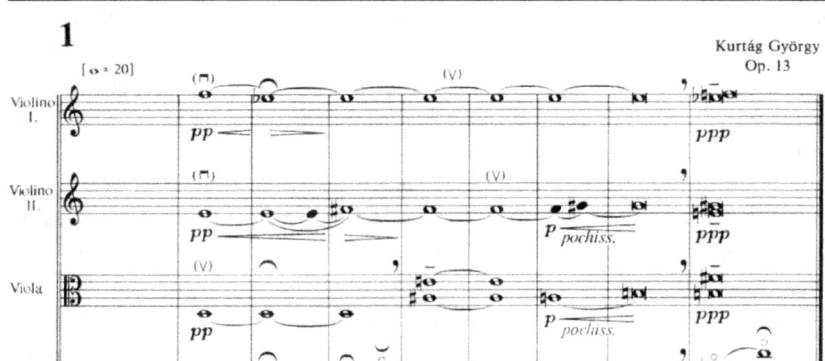

musique semble évoluer autour de l'apparition d'un objet connu qu'elle se remémore; en approchant du centre de la pièce, le plan de l'accord se déforme de plus en plus vers la dissonance; l'autre couple d'instruments dialogue toujours en brèves interventions dramatiques. Puis l'accord se détend à nouveau jusqu'à ce qu'on retrouve la sonorité de fa majeur, transférée aux instruments graves ; ce sont maintenant les violons qui posent tendrement les notes sensibles sur cette lumière adoucie. Le temps potentiel de la tonalité, celui-là même qui, condensé dans les rapports de la gamme tonale, se déroulait jadis si dynamiquement en produisant un temps extensif et directionnel, est ici concentré à l'extrême, métamorphosé en jeu de lumières et de transparences, en un filigrane des tensions tressées entre les deux strates superposées (exemple 16-2).

Enfin, le cinquième des microludes propose un cas de figure particulier dans la mesure où son matériau principal présente le caractère d'une citation : cette pièce, en effet, met délicatement en tension les fragments d'une tendre mélodie aux accents populaires, joués aux violons, avec une texture de sons harmoniques interprétée à l'alto et au violoncelle. Cette texture statique nous parvient comme de loin, son climat atonal contraste avec la mélodie diatonique; les deux espaces sont coexistants, ils interfèrent dialectiquement. La tendre et calme mélodie du passé s'interrompt et semble comme perdue dès qu'elle entre en contact avec la couche des sons harmoniques dissonants, et un tel processus devient encore plus

EXEMPLE 16-2 György Kurtág, *Hommage à Mihály András*, Op. 13 (1977-78), « 12 Microludes pour quatuors à cordes », n° 6. © Editio Musica Budapest.

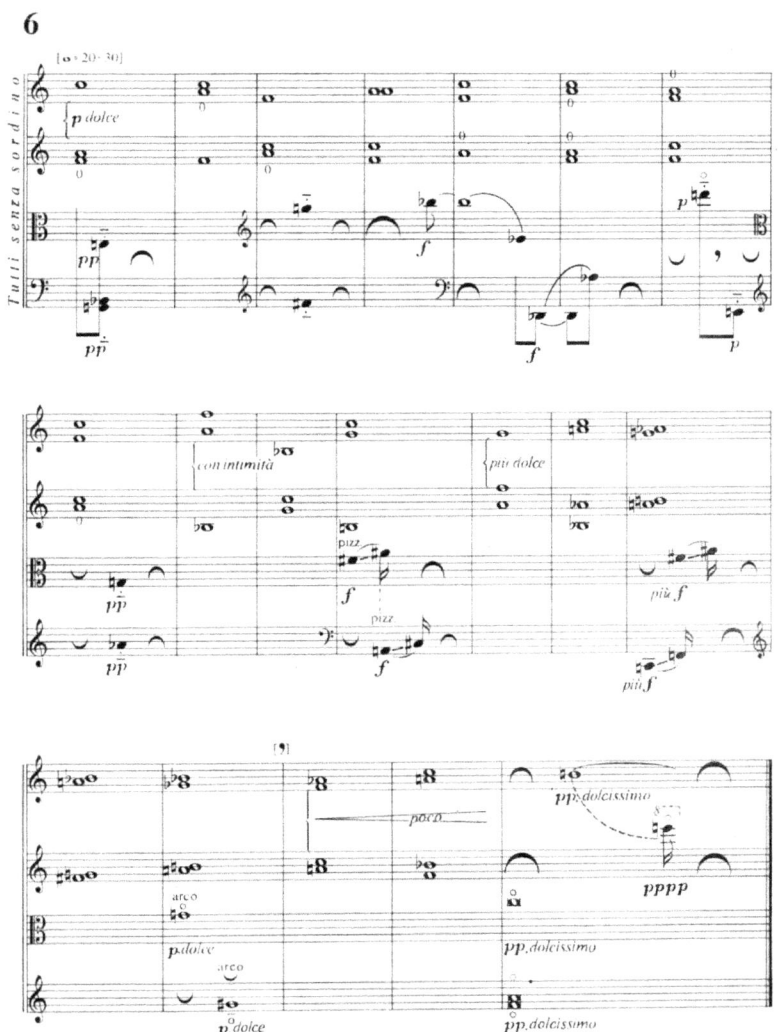

poignant à la fin de la pièce, lorsque les deux strates finissent par se fondre dans une même note qui persiste longuement (exemple 16-3).

Dans *Quasi una fantasia*, pièce pour piano et orchestre qui joue sur l'éclatement des instruments dans l'espace, Kurtág reprend ce microlude : il l'enrichit sur le plan du timbre, en complexifiant les deux plans par des

EXEMPLE 16-3 György Kurtág, *Hommage à Mihály András*, Op. 13 (1977-78), « 12 Microludes pour quatuors à cordes », n° 5. © Editio Musica Budapest.

sonorités troubles et mystérieuses, mais il l'étend, aussi, sur le plan de la durée, puisque les segments sont répétés comme autant de couches se superposant ou se répondant, légèrement décalées, nous parvenant de plusieurs points de l'espace au gré de la distribution des instruments soigneusement décrite au début de la partition. Les segments de la mélodie nous arrivent lentement et le temps s'étire en flux et reflux, en nappes distinctes et cependant entremêlées. C'est comme une expérimentation intérieure : l'irréversibilité du temps se constitue en paradoxe dès qu'apparaissent plusieurs couches, dès que les éléments reviennent, différents et pourtant semblables dans leurs silhouettes; comme des bois flottés dont les contours nous rappellent des objets connus et oubliés, les fragments apparaissent et disparaissent, se décalent et Kurtág, en épigraphe de la pièce, a choisi une strophe d'*Andenken*, « Ressouvenir », un poème de Hölderlin : « [...] Mais elle ôte / Et rend la mémoire, la mer, / Et l'amour aussi fixe attentivement des yeux, / Mais ce qui demeure, [...] ». Le dernier segment de la strophe est omis dans l'épigraphe; sans doute n'est-il pas à lire mais à percevoir dans le sensible en écoutant la pièce : « les poètes le fondent ».

Dans son livre sur Walter Benjamin, Hannah Arendt montre à quel point les moindres idées de celui-ci prirent leur source dans une conception radicale du langage; elle met aussi à juste titre l'accent sur le fait que Benjamin était un collectionneur de livres et sur l'importance que revêtait pour lui la citation. Si Benjamin collectionnait les livres, il collectionnait aussi les citations par centaines; selon Hannah Arendt, « le collectionneur détruit le contexte où son objet a jadis été seulement partie d'un tout vivant plus grand, et comme pour lui compte seulement l'unicité de l'authentique, il doit purifier l'objet choisi de tout ce qui est typique en lui »[12]. Une même exigence du langage et un usage comparable de la citation rassemblent Walter Benjamin et György Kurtág, mais, chez l'un comme chez l'autre, tout dépend en définitive de comment est traitée la citation, de ce qui en est fait. De ce point de vue, ce qui importe n'est pas seulement ce qui est cité – ce peut être une phrase précise, un accord, une échelle, un rythme – mais aussi, peut-être surtout, la manière dont on cite, c'est-à-dire la conservation de l'énergie cristallisée dans l'élément importé et la poursuite de son mouvement dans le présent. Pour définir cet usage radical du langage, Arendt a trouvé là encore, au sujet de Benjamin, des mots évocateurs qu'il nous faut méditer :

> Comme le pêcheur de perles qui va au fond de la mer, non pour l'excaver et l'amener à la lumière du jour, mais pour arracher dans la profondeur le riche et l'étrange, perles et coraux, et les porter comme fragments, à la surface du jour, il plonge dans les profondeurs du passé, mais non pour le ranimer tel qu'il fut et contribuer au renouvellement d'époques mortes. Ce qui guide ce penser est la conviction que s'il est bien vrai que le vivant succombe aux ravages du temps, le processus de décomposition est simultanément processus de cristallisation[13].

EXEMPLE 16-4 György Kurtág, *Hommage à Mihály András*, Op. 13 (1977-78), « 12 Microludes pour quatuors à cordes », n° 12. © Editio Musica Budapest.

Par le délicat travail de la jointure entre le passé et le présent se déploie dans les œuvres l'intense et problématique présence de la dimension auratique; plus précisément, à travers le déclin de l'aura qui octroie à cette musique sa force d'évocation et de remémoration, l'écriture de Kurtág nous donne à sentir l'exil de l'homme vis-à-vis du langage, et simultanément la tentative répétée de l'art pour renouer avec lui. C'est un langage qui, à travers son extrême élaboration, vise à une réconciliation avec la Nature que ces pièces, souvent fragmentaires, approchent énigmatiquement. Ce n'est pas sans raison que la fin des *Kafka-Fragmente* fait dériver la voix et le violon vers un univers où les oiseaux se mettent à parler. Là, à nouveau, une singulière proximité avec Webern se révèle, qui trouve son propre chemin dans cette dimension qu'avait relevée Adorno en évoquant, au sujet de l'auteur des *Six bagatelles pour quatuor à cordes*, la figure kafkaïenne d'Odradek. Le douzième aphorisme qui conclut les *Microludes* nous amène lui aussi au seuil d'un tel monde. Sur le diaphane éventail aux teintes chromatiques se posent les délicates et nerveuses phrases de l'alto; le papillon lève sur nous son regard d'énigme, qui sait sans savoir combien fragile et éphémère est la vie (exemple 16-4).

Notes

1 Arnold Schoenberg, *Le style et l'idée*, Paris, Buchet Chastel, 1977, p. 209.
2 György Ligeti, « Aspects du langage musical de Webern », dans *Neuf essais sur la musique*, Genève, Contrechamps, 2001, p. 40.
3 Arnold Schoenberg, *op. cit.*, p. 381.
4 Elias Canetti, « Le cœur secret de l'horloge », dans *La conscience des mots*, Paris, Le livre de poche, 1989, p. 129.
5 Walter Benjamin, « Petite histoire de la photographie », dans *Œuvres II*, Folio, Paris, 2000, p. 310.
6 Walter Benjamin, texte cité par Bruno Tackels, *L'œuvre d'art à l'époque de W. Benjamin*, Paris, L'Harmattan, 1999, p. 149.
7 Voir Georges Didi-Huberman, *Ce que nous voyons, ce qui nous regarde*, Paris : Minuit, 1992, p. 103-123.
8 Walter Benjamin, « Sur quelques thèmes baudelairiens », dans *Œuvres III*, Paris, Folio, 2000, p. 329.
9 *Ibid.*, p. 381.
10 Theodor W. Adorno, *Théorie esthétique*, Paris, Klincksieck, 1995, p. 379.
11 Theodor W. Adorno, « À propos de la figure de Krenek », dans *Moments musicaux*, Genève, Contrechamps, 2003, p. 99.
12 Hannah Arendt, *Walter Benjamin*, Paris, Allia, 2007, p. 99.
13 *Ibid.*, p. 111.

Bibliographie

Adorno, Theodor W. « À propos de la figure de Krenek ». *Moments musicaux*. Genève : Contrechamps, 2003.
———. *Théorie esthétique*. Paris : Klincksieck, 1995.
Arendt, Hannah. *Walter Benjamin*. Paris : Allia, 2007.

Benjamin, Walter. « Petite histoire de la photographie ». Dans *Œuvres II*. Paris : Folio, 2000.

———. « Sur quelques thèmes baudelairiens ». Dans *Œuvres III*. Paris : Folio, 2000.

Canetti, Elias. « Le cœur secret de l'horloge ». Dans *La Conscience des mots*. Paris : Le livre de poche, 1989.

Didi-Huberman, Georges. *Ce que nous voyons, ce qui nous regarde*. Paris : Minuit, 1992.

Ligeti, György. « Aspects du langage musical de Webern ». Dans *Neuf essais sur la musique*. Genève : Contrechamps, 2001.

Schoenberg, Arnold. *Le style et l'idée*. Paris : Buchet Chastel, 1977.

Tackels, Bruno. *L'œuvre d'art à l'époque de W. Benjamin*. Paris : L'Harmattan, 1999.

What Presence of the Past? Artistic Autobiography in György Kurtág's Music

Ulrich Mosch

Kurtág's compositions, as is well known, are noteworthy for their many intertextual relationships, both within his own works and between his many pieces based on music by other composers. To varying degrees, and in different ways, many of them are pervaded by assimilated "outside material" or by residues of his own past. Consequently, it often happens that different "temporal layers" are present in one and the same work.

In this article I will pursue two questions: First, in what form is the past present in Kurtág's music? And second, to what extent are the various forms of the present linked to Kurtág's artistic evolution and his dual capacities as a composer and pianist? Finally, I will place my findings in a larger context by means of a brief comparison with Bernd Alois Zimmermann, Helmut Lachenmann, and Wolfgang Rihm.

Digression: The Concept of Presence

Before I turn to the actual subject of my article, let me first present a few general theoretical considerations on the following question: What can presence of the past mean in music? Unlike the visual arts or architecture, where pictures, buildings, or pieces of sculpture have survived to our own day as relics of the past, and are thus physically present as real objects, music shares this character only in written form (as a handwritten or printed score) or in the form of a sound recording (as a gramophone disc, magnetic tape, compact disc, or DVD). In contrast, the moment we, as people of today, perform written music, form a mental image while reading it, or play a recording of it, it automatically partakes of the present. Early sheet music, whether handwritten or printed, bears witness to the past: it has old paper, antiquated scripts, unusual forms of printing, signs of wear and tear, and so forth. The same applies to early sound recordings. This is only partly the case, however, with the music itself, since—as the phenomenologist Roman Ingarden once put it—music, being notated and thus codified in writing, is an "intentional object" that only assumes actual shape in the moment of its performance, whether in physical reality or in the "mind's ear."[1] Only then does it become a real, temporal object. Performers of our own time must perforce use today's instruments to realize these objects as music, employing modern strings, contemporary performance techniques, and so forth.[2] Above all else, they cannot avoid using experiences and notions of sound and timbral relations that are marked by the existing music of our own age. This is true even when performers try to reconstruct the notions of previous eras and to approach their concept of sound. In short, viewed from the perspective of aesthetics, the music of the past, when performed today, is present in an eminent sense of the term: it becomes the *present-day* realization of a score from the past, or what we might call the past made present. True, the performers may be playing Machaut or Schumann, or even early Kurtág, but it is ineluctably *today's* Machaut, *today's* Schumann, or, though it may not immediately strike the ear as such, *today's* Kurtág. Even when musicians of our own day make an effort to play as in the seventeenth, eighteenth, or early nineteenth century, or as in the 1960s, it will always remain a matter of wish fulfillment from a present-day perspective, which none of them can hope to escape.

In this light, the strangeness we sense when listening to an early-twentieth-century recording of Camille Saint-Saëns or Ferruccio Busoni is due not only to the distinctive artistic personas of these two musicians, and to the performance traditions in which they stood, but at least equally to the discrepancy between then and now in our view and concept of music. Sound recordings capture the "real object" of a performance at a particular moment of history, thereby making the past accessible to us in the present, though it goes without saying, of course, that we hear this document with today's ears, just as we see old photographs with today's eyes. Thus, a basic distinction must be made between the presence of the past in the form of an aural recording, which reproduces a real object from the past (namely, the historically distant performance of a work of music), and the presence of an intentional object brought to life in performance or imagination. In the first case, the documented, historically real object differs fundamentally from its present-day counterpart, whereas the object from the past, in its modernizing musical re-enactment, does not differ fundamentally from the object created only recently: both belong to the same class of objects; that is, both are intentional objects and not real or ideal ones. Moreover, both are realized in the present day, and thus in the same cultural-historical context and out of the same state of awareness.[3]

According to Ingarden, the intentional object represented by a piece of music codified in writing has a "quasi-temporal structure" with precisely defined contours.[4] This very fact enables us, notwithstanding music's transitory nature, to treat it as an object with largely fixed and recognizable characteristics: to imitate and arrange it, or to extract parts from it and reassemble or integrate them into new contexts in altered form. The old and the new—or one's own music and that of other composers—differ merely in their compositional fabric, as can be recognized in changes of texture or lines of fracture. In performance, however, the contrasting passages are subject to the same conditions by virtue of their musical re-enactment. This is no less true of an entire concert consisting of works of different historical provenance than it is of quotations or allusions inserted into new contexts.

Putting aside sound recordings or audio-visual documents, the presence of residues from the past is possible, first and foremost, in the form of modified or transformed intentional objects in their entirety, as in the case of arrangements or transcriptions of entire works or movements. But it is no less possible in the form of fragments, as in the case of quotations. As far as their relation to the original is concerned, both reveal a (partial) identity of substance, structure, or shape,[5] with wide latitude accorded to the degree of congruence.[6] Much the same applies when reference is made to historical models not associated with a single author, such as musical forms, species of texture, dance types, or generic conventions (i.e., combinations of various features).

But presence is even conceivable where there is no longer any (partial) identity relation but only a relation of equivalence or analogy, where residues of the past appear only indirectly, so to speak, in the reflection of one's own art, as in the case of allusion or, more generally, definite negation. Yet the greater the distance from the point of reference, and the more abstract the relation, the more difficult it becomes to detect and perceive the presence of residues of the past at all. The limits dividing quotation from allusion, and vice versa, are no less blurred than those dividing arrangement and quotation.

Residues of the past in present-day music can be distinguished by authorship (that is, whether they were created by oneself or someone else), by intention (whether or not the reference is conscious and deliberate), and, in the case of deliberate references, whether they are stated or not. Whereas stylistic copies, arrangements, quotations, allusions, and references to generic conventions or movement types are by definition conscious, and thus intentional acts of reference (it is the composer who copies, arranges, quotes, alludes to, or implements something), echoes of one's own or someone else's music may be nothing more than side effects of the act of composition. Every composer stands in a nexus of traditions, whether he wants to or not, and thus prolongs the past in his use of compositional devices and procedures or forms, in his concept of music (whatever alterations it may have undergone), in his notion of sound, and so forth. As a result, such echoes happen without his being aware of it and without effort on his part. Whereas "not intended" automatically implies "not stated," both options are open in the case of intended references: to state them, thereby making them plain to everyone, or not to state them. In the latter case, composing becomes a game with the listener's previous knowledge, which is highly heterogeneous in its preconditions. When it is not stated in an epitext (a title, dedication, or label), a broad spectrum of possibilities opens up between the patently obvious and easily recognized quotation on the one hand, and a barely discernible allusion or hidden message for a few cognoscenti on the other. All the same, the referential character of quotations and allusions can only unfold to full aesthetic effect if the listener recognizes the reference.

Presence of the Past in Kurtág's Music—A Brief Phenomenology

The following discussion is not intended to pursue the subject of the "presence of the past in Kurtág's music" in general, but only those forms of presence that owe their existence to an active and deliberate reference to the music of another composer or to his own earlier music; namely, arrangement, quotation, recourse to models, allusion, and, as a special instance, the homage. Presence arising from unspecified forms of reference, such as the use of particular compositional devices or musical resources, is therefore disregarded. In Kurtág's case, the objects of reference are usually intentional objects in written form (i.e., works set down in writing), but sometimes they may also be the aforementioned models codified by musical and compositional practice.

Setting aside Kurtág's many relevant studies or *pièces d'occasion* from his early career and a few unpublished arrangements of a later date,[7] we find ourselves confronted in particular, as far as his arrangement of music by other composers is concerned, with a long series of pieces for piano (duet and six hands) and for two pianos that make up the collection *Átiratok Machaut-tól J.S. Bachig* [Transcriptions from Machaut to J.S. Bach] (1973–91), published in 1991. A comparison with the original models reveals that these pieces are, for the most part, transcriptions for modern instruments that largely preserve the register of the originals and generally leave intact the formal design and "quasi-temporal" structure, apart from a few sporadic and mostly insubstantial departures. At times, however, the choice of register was considerably altered to heighten the piece's dramatic structure and diversity. These alterations range from insubstantial interventions, as in the "Sonatina" from Johann Sebastian Bach's cantata *Actus tragicus* (BWV 106),[8] where the recorder parts have been partially split an octave apart, obviously for the sake of the timbre, to Henry Purcell's *Fantasia upon One Note*, where the tonal compass has been expanded an octave on both ends, and the outside parts are highlighted by octave doubling for long stretches at a time. Kurtág's assimilation of these pieces, each expressly identified as an arrangement, relates solely to the written notation and is thus oriented essentially on structure. In the process of his productive assimilation, things not conveyed in notation (i.e., everything considered self-evident by performers at the time of the work's creation) play a role in his handling of repeats (where *varietas* was evidently his guiding principle), but not in his handling of sound.

Kurtág's arrangement of the sixth movement from Anton Webern's *Second Cantata*, Op. 31 (1941–43), which entered his string quartet *Officium breve in memoriam Andreae Szervánszky*, Op. 28 (1984–89), belongs in this same context. It does not differ fundamentally from the arrangements just described above. This movement, too, is a transcription of a four-voice texture that retains the original registers and is fixed in a tonal space immutably plotted out with absolute pitch levels. Kurtág even adopted the words, although they are meant at best to be kept in mind during the performance and not spoken aloud. Further, the original piece is left intact both in its length and its quasi-temporal structure. That said, unlike the independent arrangements discussed above, this one is functionally integrated into a larger formal context, where it functions as a quotation with a referential character.[9] The quotation draws its specific meaning from the context in which the composer has placed it, at once in contrast and in assimilation. It makes no difference whether we are dealing with a self-contained whole from a work by another composer, as in this case, or a fragment, as in the excerpt from the *String Serenade* (1947–48) by the work's dedicatee Endre Szervánszky, with which the piece comes to an abrupt end.

Quotations are usually associated with an arrangement, where every degree of distortion, even those verging on unrecognizability, is conceivable. To remain with Kurtág's Op. 28, examples include his subsequent versions of the Webern arrangement (such as the added movement "Xa," in which the four-voice canon appears compressed into a two-voice canon doubled at a major third), or the fantasy on the harmonies of Webern's canon (movement V).[10] In these movements, Kurtág intervenes only marginally in the tonal space marked out by the registral fixation of pitch levels in the original. In contrast, he alters the temporal structure, even going so far in movement V that there is no longer a readily detectable connection with the original. However, since the quotations are labelled throughout the score, they are capable of fulfilling their aesthetic function for the listener.

If particular works of music form the points of reference in arrangements and quotations, then the point of reference in the case of models is usually a musical (and hence social) practice specific to a particular age—a practice within which the models emerged and were codified. Examples of the use of such models abound in Kurtág's music. In *Játékok I*, for instance, the second piece is a waltz prefaced with a prelude, and one of the final pieces in the same volume is a "Hoquetus," harking back to the medieval hocket. Among the other models Kurtág employed in the same work are chorale, sarabande, *csárdás*, and rondo. The various pieces entitled "Sirató" in *Játékok III* and *V* are special cases and are patterned after the like-named Hungarian folk dirge. They refer not only to the original model, but to a tradition of assimilation by Hungarian twentieth-century composers, beginning with Béla Bartók and Zoltán Kodály and extending to Sándor Szokolay and Csaba Szabó. A *sirató* is not a clearly defined form or compositional pattern but a conglomeration of features that distinguish this dirge as a form of folk-music practice.[11]

In the forms of presence discussed up to this point, the partial or far-reaching identity with the original model or object of reference allows us to make clear judgments as to the composer's intentions, even in those cases where the reference is left unstated. Things are more complicated in the case of allusions, which are normally left unstated. If the composer has said nothing about his intentions, we must operate with hypotheses, since the relations are ones of equivalence or analogy. These hypotheses may draw, for example, on the context of the work's genesis or the composer's life, and they help us to answer the aesthetically important question of whether we are indeed dealing with an allusion or perhaps only an involuntary echo.

These problems are exemplified by Kurtág's String Quartet, Op. 1, which has already been variously elucidated in the secondary literature from the standpoint of its relation to Webern, most recently in a detailed discussion by Tobias Bleek.[12] The relation between this piece and Anton Webern's compositions for string quartet is plain to hear. Equally obvious is the fact that we are not dealing with a quotation, for there is no immediately recognizable or even partial relation of identity to a particular model. Proceeding from a critique of the various hypotheses advanced for the Webern reference, Bleek nonetheless argues in favour of a specific reference to Webern's *Five Movements for String Quartet*, Op. 5. True, there is no denying a plausible relation between the two pieces, as can be seen by comparing their openings. Still, whether this is an actual allusion is, it seems to me, open to question. Whether we recognize this as a deliberate reference (a necessary prerequisite for the term allusion)[13] that must express itself in relations of equivalence or analogy (i.e., in a similar combination of features) depends on how much value we attach to the characteristics listed by Bleek as being common to both works; namely, the string quartet genre, the fact that both composers chose their respective work to be their first string quartet with an opus number, the large number of comparatively short movements (five in Webern's case, six in Kurtág's), the similar tempo indications ("Heftig bewegt," quarter note = 100, and "Poco agitato," quarter note = 100–96, respectively), and the importance of articulation, dynamics, timbre, and overall gesture. But is this combination of shared features, in the absence of such strong parameters as pitch or duration (rhythm), sufficient to warrant the term allusion?[14] Bleek's thesis is convincing only if we assume that the old hierarchy of compositional features has been levelled by attaching greater significance to timbre, articulation, and dynamics—an assumption not immune to criticism from perception psychologists. Moreover, whether we are actually dealing with equivalence or analogy is open to question from the listener's standpoint. Perhaps it would be better, and safer, to speak of traces of the deep study of Webern that Kurtág had just undertaken during his Paris stay of 1957–58, notably of his Opp. 5, 9, and 28 for string quartet. Whatever the case, the assumption that we are dealing with an allusion remains nothing more than a hypothesis, however plausible it might seem, until we can present documents proving that the reference was intended, and thus conscious and deliberate. Still, even if it is not an allusion, echoes of Webern are plain to hear.

Besides references to music by other composers, Kurtág's oeuvre contains a good many arrangements of his own music. Basically, they do not differ from references to music by other composers. The early works with opus numbers—especially the String Quartet, Op. 1, the Wind Quintet, Op. 2 (1959), and the Eight Piano Pieces, Op. 3 (1960–61)—already reveal many genetic relations to the piano pieces he had written a short while previously.[15] Later, too, Kurtág frequently returned to his earlier compositions. Some of these borrowings cover great spans of time, as in, to name only a few, *Hommage à R. Sch.*, Op. 15d (1979/1990),[16] *Officium breve*, Op. 28 (where arrangements from Webern's *Second Cantata* and Szervánszky's *String Serenade* are joined by five of his own pieces in arranged form),[17] or such collections as *Rückblick 1992* and *Signs, Games and Messages*. Quite often, variants of the same piece arise in immediate or close temporal proximity. A good example of this is "Hommage à Szervánszky" (1975) from *Játékok III*, a piece that already appeared in two different versions in that collection (one for piano solo and another for piano four-hands). Besides a version for two cymbaloms (1982) and the arrangements of the two piano versions that entered *Officium breve* (movements III and XII), there exist two other versions from the 1970s: one for violin and cello or viola (1975) and another for guitar, presumably dating from 1977 (see examples 17-1 and 17-2 and plate 17-1). Other examples include "Hommage à Paganini: La nuova campanella" (1974) from *Játékok I*, for which there is a second version for trombone and piano (1976); "Hommage à Petrovics" (1975) from *Játékok III*, which also exists in a version for two violins dating from the same year; and, more recently, "Merrian's Dream" (1998) from *Játékok VII*, of which a version for strings and another for orchestra were written in the same year for his "work in progress" *New Messages* for orchestra, Op. 34b. A special instance is "Virág az ember," a fragment from *Die Sprüche Péter Bornemisza*, Op. 7 (1963–68) that runs through Kurtág's oeuvre in ever-new manifestations like an *idée fixe*, producing what we might call a self-propagating string of pieces.[18]

Various periods in Kurtág's career are present in all these arrangements of his own music, although, given the stylistic homogeneity of his oeuvre, these periods are not always easy to distinguish. Only a comparison of the conflicting versions will shed further light on this subject.

In addition to arrangement, quotation, allusion, and recourse to models, there is another form of deliberate reference in Kurtág's music that one might call "deictic." It is primarily conveyed in a title or subtitle; that is, the

EXAMPLE 17-1 György Kurtág, *Játékok III* [Games III] (1973–78), "Hommage à Szervánszky," version for piano solo (1975). © Editio Musica Budapest.

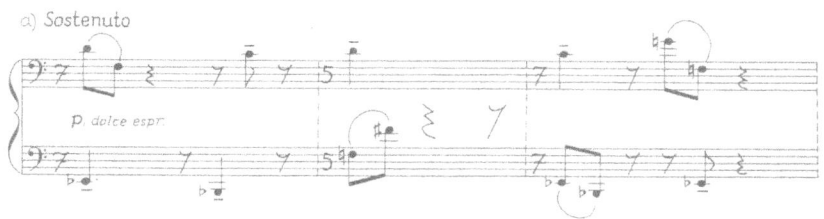

reference, whatever type it may be, is expressly indicated as such. Here I am referring to the series of "Hommages à ..." that have proliferated in Kurtág's oeuvre since 1973, beginning with the first pieces of *Játékok*. Other pieces whose titles refer to composers belong in this same category, such as the still unpublished *Un brin de bruyère à Witold* for piano (1994) or "... humble regard sur Olivier Messiaen" from *Játékok VI*, not to mention the various "Signs" and "Messages" and the countless "in memoriam" compositions. For reasons of space, I will limit myself here to the "Hommages."

To date, Kurtág has written some one hundred such "Hommages," not counting conflicting versions. Some of these are self-contained compositions, such as *Hommage à Mihály* for string quartet, Op. 13 (1977–78), *Omaggio a Luigi Nono*, Op. 19 (1978–79), and *Hommage à R. Sch.*, Op. 15d (1979/1990). Others form parts of collections, especially *Játékok*. The majority originated in the 1970s and were published in volumes I–IV of *Játékok*. These alone amount to forty-seven "Hommages," with another eleven following in V to VII of the volumes published to date.

The "Hommages" fall into three groups according to the person referenced. The first group is made up of composers, the second of musicians (instrumentalists and conductors, including Kurtág's wife Márta), and the third of various other figures: friends, individuals with whom he has worked

PLATE 17-1 György Kurtág, "Hommage à Szervánszky" (1975), version for violin and cello or viola. © Editio Musica Budapest.

PLATE 17-1 (conclusion)

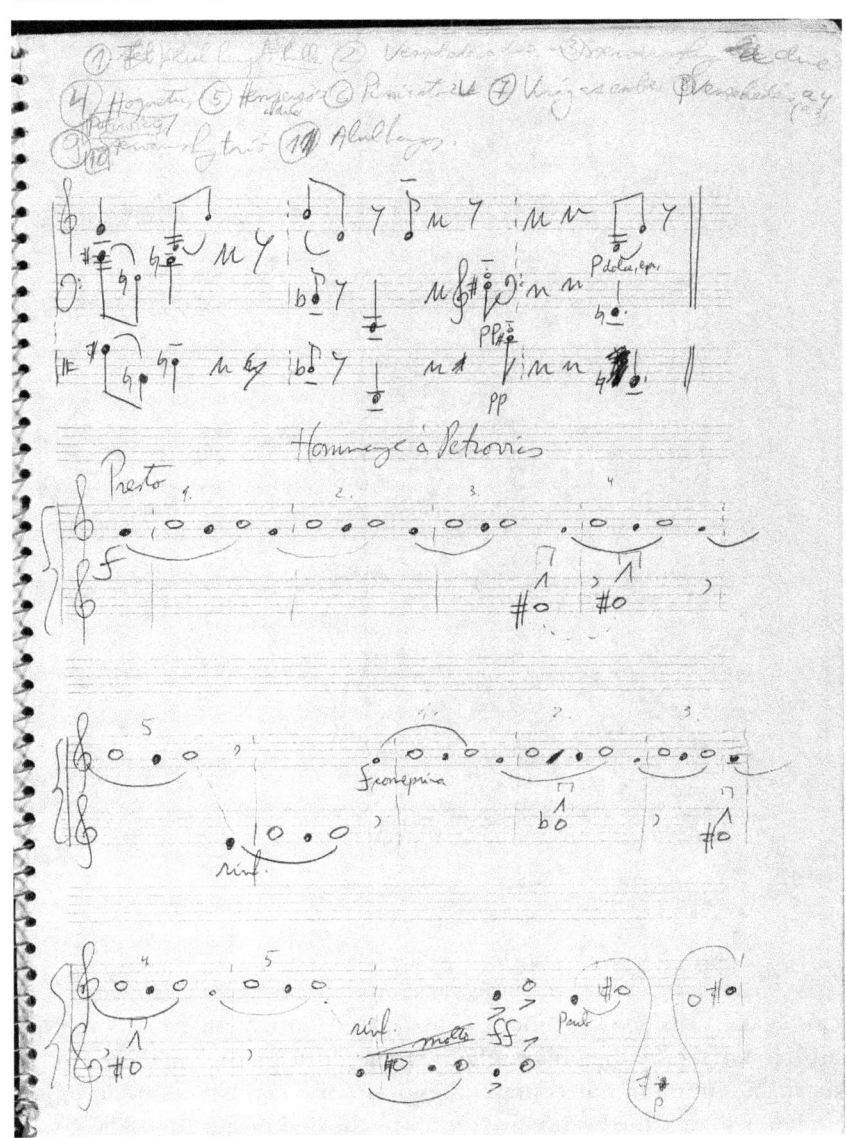

EXAMPLE 17-2 György Kurtág, *Officium breve in memoriam Andreae Szervánszky* (1984–89), Op. 28, for string quartet, movement XII. © Editio Musica Budapest.

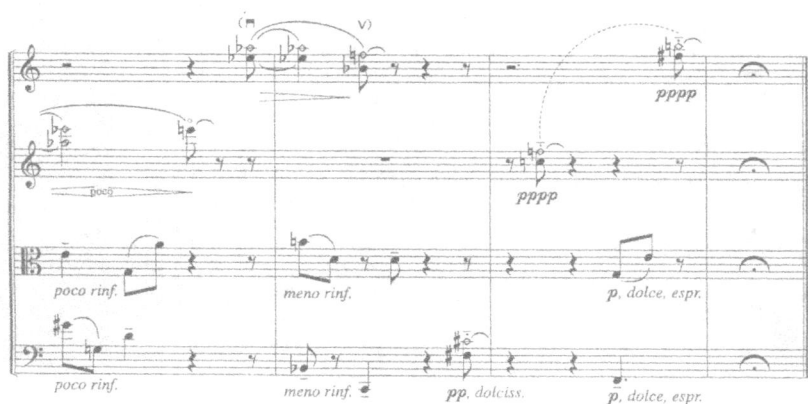

closely on occasion or is otherwise associated, and, as an exception, even an "Hommage" to the philosopher Zenon. Although each of these groups merits attention in our context, the group of composers, amounting to no fewer than some twenty-five pieces by the end of the 1970s, is of special interest, not least with respect to those whose names are missing, *inter alia* Haydn, Mozart, Brahms, and the composers of the Second Viennese School. The extent to which these gaps are accidental or intentional is impossible to determine, at least at present.

Apart from the first "Hommage à Paganini" from *Játékok I*, which is subtitled "La nuova campanella" and refers to Niccolò Paganini's like-named violin concerto and its later transcription as a piano étude by Franz Liszt, the titles of the various "Hommages" to composers do not refer to specific pieces. The names, sometimes reduced to abbreviations such as "J.S.B." or "R. Sch." (themselves references to the corresponding pieces in Volume 3 of Béla Bartók's *Mikrokosmos*), stand for the entire oeuvre of the composer concerned. This does not necessarily imply, however, that Kurtág did not have particular works in mind.

Still, it cannot be taken for granted that an "Hommage" always relates to specific traits of a composer's music—that is, that we are dealing with productive musical assimilation. In any event, there are at least three basic types of reference: allusion to the composer's music, allusion to his personality, or identification of a simple point of departure. A composer's oeuvre and mentality may, simply put, be nothing more than the impulse for Kurtág's own music, a point of departure for his own creativity. One such case, it seems to me, occurs in Kurtág's *Omaggio a Luigi Nono*. Whereas Nono, in his *Omaggio a György Kurtág* (1983–86), refers to the phonemes of Kurtág's name, Kurtág's "Hommage" reveals only very general relations to Nono and his compositional universe, as in the twelve-tone chord at the end of the second movement, the partially serial basis of the compositional fabric, the handling of vocal timbre, and the importance of sound and reverberation. As the reference to the composers in the "Hommages" is stated in the title, the listener inevitably wonders about the relations to the figure thus honoured. It is not always obvious what sort of reference is involved, or indeed if a reference exists at all. And we must assume that there may be hidden allusions waiting to be unveiled, just as a homage may be constructed entirely from Kurtág's own music.

Although a direct point of reference is not clearly discernible in a great many cases, one important referential device in these musical tributes—indeed, perhaps the most important one of all—is allusion. Still, the presence of residues of the past is often reduced to a minimum in these examples, and not infrequently it can only be recognized at all (and thus aesthetically appreciated) from the reference in the title. From a welter of examples I shall choose only a few that all have one feature in common: owing to their brevity, they work with extreme reduction and economy of means. In "Hommage à J.S.B.," one of the "12 neue Mikroludien" in *Játékok III* (see example 17-3), Kurtág works with two types of motion: an oscillating figure consisting of two ascending and one descending fifth (transposed upwards one step at a time) and an irregularly constructed

EXAMPLE 17-3 György Kurtág, *Játékok III* [Games III] (1973–78), "Hommage à J.S.B." © Editio Musica Budapest.

descending *prestissimo* scale spanning six octaves and landing on the piece's initial pitch, B flat, this time, however, in the lowest register of the keyboard. Similar types of motion can be found in Bach's keyboard music, as in Prelude XXI of *WTC I*. The first of these two types can also be read as an allusion to the like-named piece in Bartók's *Mikrokosmos III*.

In the case of "Hommage à Beethoven" from *Játékok I* (see example 17-4), Kurtág evidently focused on two aspects of Beethoven's musical thought that can be viewed as characteristic of his music. The first is the principle of development, in this case the saturation of a diastematic and harmonic space defined by the white keys of the piano, a space explored by transposing the framing interval of a fifth in both hands step by step in contrary motion. The second is the principle of dissection, in this case the systematic reduction of the original five-pitch motif in eighth-note motion to a solitary eighth note, with the kinetic impetus finally vanishing in the arpeggiation of the final chord. We also witness technique reduced to the most elemental aspects of the compositional fabric: verti-

EXAMPLE 17-4 György Kurtág, *Játékok I* [Games I] (1973–78), "Hommage à Beethoven." © Editio Musica Budapest.

cal and horizontal, line and chord, succession and simultaneity. That the title appears in parentheses may have to do with the fact that these aspects are so abstract and universal that they might equally be assigned to other composers.

If Kurtág referred to comparatively abstract aspects in his "Hommages" to Bach and Beethoven, the referential model is more specific and fairly easy to recognize in other pieces. "Hommage à Mussorgsky" from *Játékok III*, for example, obviously alludes to the ending of the final movement of *Pictures at an Exhibition*, even if the *maestoso* character of the original is fractured and its harmonies entirely abandoned. But despite its variable metrical shape, we can still recognize its rhythmic and syntactic structure: the Lombard rhythm and the structure of bar groupings, albeit expanded at one point.[19] In "Hommage à Bartók" from *Játékok I*, the handling of metrical changes and such elementary procedures as contrary motion and stepwise expansion of the tonal compass from a single pitch to three octaves relate to Bartók's *Mikrokosmos*.[20] In "Glocken (Hommage à Stravinsky)" from *Játékok IV*, the point of reference seems to be the final movement of the *Symphony of Psalms*; in "Hommage à Stockhausen" from the "12 neue Mikroludien" in *Játékok III*, it seems to be the piano pieces of the late 1950s, in particular their approach to articulation.

Presence of the Past and Kurtág's Artistic Evolution

Following our brief phenomenology of the forms in which the past appears in Kurtág's music, we now address the question of the reasons for their presence. In his case these reasons, though highly contrasting, are, in the final analysis, always autobiographical. The question can be most easily answered in connection with the many "Hommages" that originated in the aftermath of a profound creative crisis that befell Kurtág with his *Twenty-Four Antiphons* for orchestra, Op. 10 (1970–71), which still remain incomplete. He only found his way out of this crisis with *Játékok*, beginning in 1973—namely, by toying with the music of the past and with piano technique, which not only opened up new possibilities for composition, but enabled him to strike out on a path entirely his own.

In these piano cycles, Kurtág placed himself in a relation to past and present almost excessively using references spelled out in the titles. This approach seems to have had a dual function: first, the psychological function of reassurance by positioning himself in a context; and second, the function of making his position in the musical universe, and the process of its definition, visible to the outside world. These are tributes to composers whose music served Kurtág as guideposts for his own work and/or gave fresh impetus to his creativity. At the same time, he uses them to circumscribe, however incompletely, the major cornerstones of his own musical cosmos. Depending on the circumstances, the instigator is more or less clearly manifested. The very fact that these are not stylistic copies or compositions "*à la manière de* ..."[21] shows that Kurtág's concern was to establish his own position in contrast to others—that is, to find the path to himself through productive reformulation. The emergence of the past is inevitable, especially in those cases where the "Hommages" do not derive from direct encounters with musicians or other figures but relate to composers or their music. Still, what we hear is the past as mirrored in Kurtág, that is, the traces left behind by composers or their music, even if only the impulse to produce something of his own.

That the emergence of the "Hommages" was directly related to overcoming a creative crisis is equally evident in a transformation that came about after 1979.[22] Since then, Kurtág's "Hommages" have no longer arisen solely from an inner urge not readily comprehensible from the outside, but almost entirely from external circumstances—for example, milestone birthdays, personal encounters, or the memory of deceased composers or other figures. Nonetheless, positioning himself in relation to others is a habit that has accompanied his music to the present day. *Officium breve*, Op. 28, should be viewed in this light. Here the quotations have autobiographical significance, fulfilling the function of memory and evocation alike: they point to two composers central to Kurtág's musical universe and artistic biography. At the same time, by arranging five of his own compositions, he erects a personal realm of memory that is, in aesthetic terms, not wholly intelligible, even to listeners well versed in his music—or at least not at the present moment, since two of these pieces still await publication.

If Kurtág deliberately placed a large number of clues in his titles and subtitles beginning in 1973, the situation is quite different in the early works that he himself acknowledges—that is, those around 1960, the years that witnessed the origins of his later Op. 1 and the pieces that followed. Once again, the presence of the past is unmistakable, but it seems to owe its existence less to explicit references to particular works, as in his later periods, than to a compositional and stylistic orientation on Webern, and perhaps still more so on Bartók—two composers who at that time represented what Kurtág considered the cutting edge of composition. Things that obviously struck the ear did not have to be expressly spelled out in an epitext.

Things are different again with the presence of the past in Kurtág's arrangements or transcriptions of music by other composers. Here the reasons are not specifically autobiographical; instead, it is Kurtág the performer expanding his repertoire as a pianist and chamber musician. Since 1973, as far as we can see, the arrangements were created for his own use in concert, or occasionally, judging from a number of dedications, for friends. That Kurtág began to write arrangements for his own instrument at exactly the same time that he was toying with the past and exploring the technical potential of the piano is surely no coincidence. As far as the rendition on the instrument is concerned, as we have seen above, it makes no difference whether the music the performer plays is his own or someone one else's, old or new. Even arrangements establish a relation to the past.

In sum, all the various ways in which residues of the past make their presence known in Kurtág's music have one thing in common: they are essentially autobiographically motivated. The presence has less to do with the general state of cultural history in his age than with his own creative evolution or his artistic livelihood as a performer.

Brief Digression: The "Presence of the Past" in the Work of Other Composers

The presence of the past also plays a central role in the music of many of Kurtág's contemporaries. Among many possible examples, I shall briefly discuss three composers, each roughly a generation apart: Bernd Alois Zimmermann (1919–70), Helmut Lachenmann (1935–) and Wolfgang Rihm (1952–), with Kurtág (1926–) falling between the first two generations. In all three cases, the presence of the past is motivated less by the composer's own life than by cultural history, or more precisely by the history of the media. All three responded in personal ways to the enormous growth in the presence of past music owing to the mechanical reproducibility of sound and the omnipresence of music—especially past music—that resulted from its diffusion in the media. In music, an art form wholly dependent on reproduction, an "imaginary museum" of the sort that André Malraux envisioned for painting and sculpture as a result of photography[23] has long become a reality: an entire universe of music is aesthetically present, or at least accessible, on a constant basis in performances and recordings.

One of the special features of Bernd Alois Zimmermann's final period is his technique of quotation and collage, which plays a key role in such works as *Dialoge* for two pianos and orchestra (1960), the "ballet blanc" *Présence* for violin, cello, and piano (1961), and the ballet *Musique pour les soupers du Roi Ubu* (1966). As Zimmermann put it in a text of 1968 on the subject of the composer's craft, his primary concern in his compositions was to "facilitate the spontaneous inclusion of past or future music, of quotations and collages of quotations."[24] This took place within a proportional structure of temporal layers derived from a constellation of pitches binding for the work in question. Behind his urge to broaden the purview of composition was the aesthetic presence of the past in the form of sounding music. Zimmermann substantiated his own "pluralistic compositional technique" and his notion of the "spherical form of time" (*Kugelgestalt der Zeit*) from the discovery that his own age was marked by the simultaneous presence of music from a great many eras:

> There is no avoiding the fact that we live together in harmony with a huge variety of cultural artifacts from a great many ages, that we exist simultaneously on many temporal and experiential planes, most of which seem derivable from and still connected with each other, and that within this web of many tangled and confusing threads we nevertheless feel, to put it plainly, safe and sound. Thus, one special phenomenon of our existence seems to be that we are capable of constantly experiencing this huge variety, with all the changes brought about by the fact that different threads are being tied together again and again for a fraction of a second.[25]

In his introduction of 1961 to *Présence*, a work pervaded at various points with quotations from Richard Strauss, Sergey Prokofiev, and Karlheinz Stockhausen, Zimmermann vividly summed up the present situation of his own day:

> *Présence*: it is the thin layer of ice on which the foot can tarry only so long before the ice cracks; but while the foot feels that it is resting for a fraction of a second, the layer is already cracking, and the security of

the ice shelf is left behind; we gaze into the future before us with the certainty that the layer of ice will begin to disintegrate over and over again, and that our constant attempts to gain a foothold are inherently absurd. In this sense, *Présence* is the present that links the past and the future.[26]

Zimmermann was intent on integrating quotations—fragments of "intentional objects" from the past—into new contexts. In contrast, a composer of the next generation, Helmut Lachenmann, works with a "real object" in his "music for clarinetist and orchestra" *Accanto* of 1975–76.[27] In *Accanto*, a pre-recorded tape of Mozart's Clarinet Concerto forms the aesthetic point of reference for Lachenmann's own sonic creation. The tape runs without interruption throughout the piece, usually remaining silent in the background but coming to the fore in a few passages with precise structural control, sometimes in a brief flash, sometimes a bit longer and clearly discernible. This procedure can be viewed as a reaction to the undeniable deterioration of sounds through excessive use, a process greatly accelerated by the media.

Since the late 1960s, Lachenmann has sought worlds of sound still untouched by artistic exploitation. In them he hoped to regain the immediacy and power of an aesthetic experience that once stood at the outset of every significant musical innovation—an experience long grown threadbare through centuries of use and sometimes entirely buried by overexposure in the media. He reacted to the state of his age with "determinate negation": he largely excluded conventional sound from his compositions and instead tapped new "extraterritorial" worlds of sound still untouched by artistic exploitation. Nonetheless, he declined to take the path of electronic sound production, preferring to retain conventional musical instruments. In the act of composition, however, each instrument initially mutated into a mere sound generator: the composer explored every conceivable way of producing sound from the instrument, even those shunned in conventional performance as "obstructive" or "ugly." To choose only a few examples, string instruments are bowed not only on the string, but on the body, the tailpiece, or the bridge, each time producing contrasting forms of soft murmurs of varying tinge depending on where the bowing occurs. On the piano, the player cautiously runs his fingernails across the surface of the keys or across the tuning pins inside the instrument to produce soft rippling noises depending on the speed. Having liberated himself from the shackles of conventional usage, the composer now had myriad possibilities for creating sounds on a cello, clarinet, or piano. Finally, the most trenchant were selected and systematized according to their manner of production to form the basis of a composition. Familiar instrumental timbres, though not excluded *prima facie* from this previously unexplored realm of sound, remain only one option among many. Accordingly, the compositions from this period (Lachenmann himself called them *musique concrète instrumentale*) confront us with a wholly transformed timbral guise in which sounds heavily laden with noise predominate.[28] In *Accanto*, the aesthetic strategy of making us aware of the unbridgeable distance separating us from the masterpieces of the past resides in turning the beauty of Mozart's concerto, unattainable today, into a point of reference by sometimes interpolating excerpts from it. As we listen, a sort of window occasionally opens onto the perfect earlier music, born of a moment in history and society that has vanished forever.

Wolfgang Rihm, the youngest of our three composers, belongs to a generation that viewed the growing aesthetic presence of the past as a compositional challenge and a stimulus to creativity from the vantage point of the present—a generation that drew, one might say, the reception-aesthetic consequences of this presence. Rihm figures among a large number of composers who, in the mid-1970s, claimed the right to build not only on the immediately preceding postwar avant-garde (i.e., total serialism and timbral composition), but also on music from the more distant past, including Schoenberg's expressionist period, Berg, and Mahler. Instead of an exclusive art that attempted, as in serialism, to reach an unadulterated core of material through a process of increasing purification, Rihm in the late 1970s advanced the idea of "inclusive composition," an approach "that reached a result saturated with the present by incorporating and embracing every area touched upon and opened up by the imagination and labor economics."[29] Rihm's early works are, accordingly, permeated with allusions and quotations. Examples include the early orchestral piece *Sub-Kontur* (1974–75), with its references to Mahler, Berg, and Richard Strauss; the ballet score *Tutuguri* (1980–81), with echoes of Stravinsky's *The Rite of Spring*; *Musik für drei Streicher* (1976–77), with allusions to Beethoven's chamber music;[30] and *Fremde Szenen I–III* for piano trio (1982–84), with similar allusions to Robert Schumann.

If it was the presence of music by other composers that inspired Rihm in the 1970s and 1980s, the emphasis began to shift to his own music in the early 1990s, but without entirely suppressing the inspirational force of outside creations. Since then, he has produced many arrangements of his own works, sometimes creating entire families of works by means of such contrasting procedures as "overpainting," "contrafactum," and "inscription." This approach is closely related to his poetics of composition, which hinge on the idea of a musical material that can be "taken in hand" in the manner of a sculptor.[31] The notion of a "tactile" musical material to which the composer responds at any given moment—meaning one way today, another way tomorrow—implies an almost dialogic relation between the two.[32] To briefly explain what this means, let us turn to an example. Rihm's *Kolchis* for five instruments (1991), which was originally written for an exhibition of the artist Kurt Kocherscheidt in the Vienna Secession and refers to his wooden sculpture *The Boys from Kolchis*, was inserted into the multi-movement *Frage* for eight instruments (1999–2000) in two forms: an unaltered version and a version altered by an "inscription."[33] The jagged timbral surface of the original, marked primarily by coarse and noisy timbres, was overwritten by a delicate line for cor anglais, bass clarinet, and viola, usually to be played *unisono* and as softly as possible. As a result, two layers of highly contrasting timbre from different periods are present at the same time.[34] Here the past is aesthetically present as a separate layer.

Conclusion

In conclusion, let us return once again to Kurtág. Evidently the "presence of the past" is as important to the three composers briefly introduced above as it is to Kurtág, albeit with a different focus. As contrary as their positions might be, there are nevertheless some surprising parallels: Bernd Alois Zimmermann's amazed discovery, mentioned in the first quotation above, that we are capable of experiencing the huge variety of utterly incompatible things on an aesthetic basis, can be related to Kurtág's treatment of his musical cosmos, whether in his compositions (in works such as *Játékok* and *Officium breve*) or in what he calls his "composed programs," in which he consciously invokes connections among criss-crossing historical threads.[35] Similarly, the motive behind Lachenmann's reaction to the deterioration of past music in the media—namely, his urge to create something different of his own when he hears music by another composer (as he once said with regard to Luigi Nono)[36]—is at least partially at work in Kurtág's music too, as in many of the "Hommages." Finally, both Kurtág and Rihm use extant music, whether their own or someone else's, as a stimulus for their own creative work, even if Kurtág is less willing to flaunt the procedure than Rihm and the layers in the arrangements of his own music do not immediately strike the ear as such. Not least of all, as far as the compositional process is concerned, a study of the sketches reveals that the "hands-on" relation to the material that distinguishes Rihm's work is no less characteristic of Kurtág.

Translated from the German by J. Bradford Robinson

Notes

1. See Roman Ingarden, *Untersuchungen zur Ontologie der Kunst: Musikwerk—Bild—Architektur—Film* (Tübingen: Niemeyer, 1962), especially chapter 6: "Das Problem der Seinsweise des musikalischen Werkes," 101.
2. This is usually true even when these instruments happen to be several centuries old, for only in a tiny minority of cases have such instruments escaped reconstruction and retained their original state.
3. In recent years, "presence" has been the subject of various essays, albeit in the form of cultural critique, which is not of central importance to our discussion. See in particular George Steiner, *Real Presences* (London: Faber and Faber, 1989), and Hans-Ulrich Gumbrecht, *Production of Presence: What Meaning Cannot Convey* (Palo Alto, CA: Stanford University Press, 2004).
4. In the "intentional object," unlike sounding music, all phases exist simultaneously; hence the term "quasi-temporal." See Ingarden, *Untersuchungen*, 11–12.
5. See Jürgen Stenzel's entry on "Anspielung" (allusion) in *Reallexikon der deutschen Literaturwissenschaft*, ed. Klaus Weimar (Berlin and New York: de Gruyter, 1997), 1: 93–96.
6. The composer can adhere to the notation or incorporate other aspects, such as historical combinations of instruments or the use of embellishment. A wide range of gradations is possible with regard to what was notated and what was left unwritten, being part of self-evident usage.
7. See, for example, the arrangements of Henry Purcell's *Examples of Counterpoint and Canon* "Per Arsin & Thesin a 2, 3 and 4," which arose at the same time as *Átiratok Machaut-tól J.S. Bachig*, or the four waltzes for piano four-hands that Kurtág arranged, probably in 1992, from Franz Schubert's *Sechsunddreissig Originaltänze* for piano, Op. 9, D 365 (1816–21).
8. Kurtág follows the original so precisely, even with regard to phrasing and ornamentation, that his arrangement was clearly not based on the relevant volume from the *Neue Bach-Ausgabe* (NBA), although the print of *Átiratok Machaut-tól J.S. Bachig* cites this edition as its source. Rather, it was based on the Old Bach Edition, which at that time was easily accessible and widely available in miniature score. In the NBA volume, which only appeared one year after Kurtág's arrangement originated, the cantata appears in F major rather than E-flat major (to accommodate the ambitus of the recorders) and the phrasing and embellishments clearly differ from the version reproduced in the earlier edition.
9. See Tobias Bleek, "György Kurtág, *Officium breve* op. 28: Eine Studie über musikalische Intertextualität" (PhD diss., Humboldt University, Berlin, 2006), especially his discussion of the cyclic quality at 1: 213–29. I wish to express my warm thanks to Tobias Bleek for allowing me to consult his still unpublished dissertation for my article.

10 Ibid., 1: 144–82.
11 See Mike van Hove, "... *auf eine sehr komplexe Weise einfach* ...": *Die Bedeutung der Játékok für das Oeuvre und den Personalstil von György Kurtág*, Musikwissenschaft an der Technischen Universität Berlin 8 (Berlin: Mensch und Buch, 2007), 189–208.
12 Bleek, "György Kurtág," 1: 76–86.
13 See Christopher A. Reynolds, *Motives for Allusion: Context and Content in Nineteenth-Century Music* (Cambridge, MA: Harvard University Press, 2003), 6.
14 Bleek invokes the criterion, formulated in Reynolds's *Motives* (ibid.), that there must be at least three matching features. Reynolds cites at least three features in each of his examples, it is true, but among them is always one or both of the strong parameters, pitch or duration (i.e., rhythm).
15 See Tobias Bleek, "Eine 'mißverstandene' Kompositionsaufgabe als Ausweg: Zu Kurtágs unpublizierten Klavierstücken 1957/58," *Mitteilungen der Paul Sacher Stiftung* 21 (April 2008): 32–37.
16 These are partly arrangements from the *Kafka-Fragmente*, Op. 24 (1985–87), *Grabstein für Stephan* (1976/1978–9? unpublished), from *Játékok II, Játékok [Verworfene Stücke]* (1974?–1992? unpublished), and *Nagy sirató* for trombone and piano (1976?).
17 *Virág az ember (Turcsányi Tibor emlékére)* for unaccompanied cello (1978) and *In memoriam Baranyai Zsolt* for two woodwinds (recorders, oboes, or clarinets) and harp or keyboard instrument (harmonium, piano, or harpsichord) of 1978(?), both of which remain unpublished, as well as "Hommage à Szervánszky," published in *Játékok III*, and the two pieces "Virág—Garzó Gabinak" for piano (1981?) and "Szoltsányi György emlékezete" (1981?), both published in *Játékok V*.
18 See Mike van Hove, "... *auf eine sehr komplexe Weise einfach* ...," 208–22, and the overview in appendix III, 243. Van Hove provides many other examples of genetic relations among Kurtág's works.
19 Surprisingly, van Hove (ibid., 77) overlooks this connection.
20 On occasion, the *Mikrokosmos* is even cited in the movement titles and must be regarded as a model for *Játékok* as a whole, even though Kurtág himself, in a separately published preface to *Játékok*, insists that the collection is not a piano method. See György Kurtág, "Vorwort zu den 'Spielen für Klavier,'" *Musik der Zeit: Dokumentationen und Studien* 5 (1986): 10.
21 Exceptions are "Les Adieux (in Janáčeks Manier)" from *Játékok VI*, "Fanfare in Mussorgskis Manier," and "Hymne in Strawinskys Manier" from *A kis csáva* for piccolo, trombone, and guitar (1978).
22 It is precisely at this time that Kurtág changed his habits of sketching. Since then he no longer works on *Játékok* in separate sketchbooks, but in the same sketchbooks that he uses for all his other works. See also van Hove, "... *auf eine sehr komplexe Weise einfach* ...," 231.
23 André Malraux, *Essais de psychologie de l'art 1: "Le musée imaginaire"* (Geneva: Skira, 1947); translated by Stuart Gilbert and Francis Price as *Museum without Walls* (London: Secker and Warburg, 1967).
24 Bernd Alois Zimmermann, "Vom Handwerk des Komponisten," in *Intervall und Zeit* (Mainz: Schott, 1974), 35.

25 Ibid.
26 Bernd Alois Zimmermann, "Présence," in *Intervall und Zeit*, 105.
27 Incidentally, Lachenmann was the recipient of a Kurtágian "Hommage" in the form of *Valse*, piece no. 26 from ... *pas à pas ... nulle part* ... for baritone, string trio, and percussion, on texts by Samuel Beckett and Sébastien Roch Nicolas de Chamfort, Op. 36, composed in 1993 and 1995–98.
28 Later Lachenmann increasingly transferred his quest to the unveiling of new aspects in familiar sounds.
29 Wolfgang Rihm, "Der geschockte Komponist," in *Ausgesprochen: Schriften und Gespräche*, ed. Ulrich Mosch (Winterthur: Amadeus; Mainz: Schott Music, 1997), 1: 50–51.
30 See Reinhold Brinkmann, "Wirkungen Beethovens in der Kammermusik," in *Beiträge zu Beethovens Kammermusik: Symposion Bonn 1984*, ed. Sieghard Brandenburg and Helmut Loos (Munich: Henle, 1987), especially 81–83.
31 See Ulrich Mosch, "'Taking Sound in Hand': Wolfgang Rihm and Varèse," in *Edgard Varèse: Composer, Sound Sculptor, Visionary*, ed. Felix Meyer and Heidy Zimmermann (Woodbridge, Suffolk: Boydell, 2006), 433–42.
32 See also Ulrich Mosch, "Taktilität des Klangs—Wolfgang Rihms Poetik," *Österreichische Musikzeitschrift* 63/8–9 (2008): 26–33.
33 The ensemble piece *Frage* is an enlarged version of *In Frage* for the same combination of instruments (1999): besides three newly composed interpolations, Rihm also inserted the unaltered *Kolchis* as a self-quotation even before the arranged version of the same piece.
34 This arranged version later became the second movement of the cycle *Drei Stücke aus Kolchis* (1991, 2000, 2002).
35 Discussed in Tobias Bleek, "György Kurtág," 1: 205–12.
36 Helmut Lachenmann, "Musik als existentielle Erfahrung: Gespräch mit Ulrich Mosch," in *Musik als existentielle Erfahrung*, ed. Josef Häusler (Wiesbaden, Leipzig, and Paris: Breitkopf and Härtel, 2004), 215.

Bibliography

Bleek, Tobias. "Eine 'mißverstandene' Kompositionsaufgabe als Ausweg: Zu Kurtágs unpublizierten Klavierstücken 1957/58." *Mitteilungen der Paul Sacher Stiftung* 21 (April 2008): 32–37.

———. "György Kurtág, Officium breve op. 28: Eine Studie über musikalische Intertextualität." PhD diss., 2 vols. Humboldt University, Berlin, 2006.

Brinkmann, Reinhold. "Wirkungen Beethovens in der Kammermusik." In *Beiträge zu Beethovens Kammermusik: Symposion Bonn 1984*, edited by Sieghard Brandenburg and Helmut Loos, 79–110. Munich: Henle, 1987.

Gumbrecht, Hans-Ulrich. *Production of Presence: What Meaning Cannot Convey*. Palo Alto, CA: Stanford University Press, 2004.

Hove, Mike van. "... *auf eine sehr komplexe Weise einfach ...": Die Bedeutung der Játékok für das Oeuvre und den Personalstil von György Kurtág*. Musikwissenschaft an der Technischen Universität Berlin 8. Berlin: Mensch und Buch, 2007.

Ingarden, Roman. *Untersuchungen zur Ontologie der Kunst: Musikwerk—Bild—Architektur—Film.* Tübingen: Niemeyer, 1962.
Kurtág, György. "Vorwort zu den 'Spielen für Klavier.'" *Musik der Zeit: Dokumentationen und Studien* 5 (1986): 10–11.
Lachenmann, Helmut. "Musik als existentielle Erfahrung: Gespräch mit Ulrich Mosch." In *Musik als existentielle Erfahrung*, edited by Josef Häusler, 213–26. Wiesbaden, Leipzig, and Paris: Breitkopf and Härtel, 2004.
Malraux, André. *Essais de psychologie de l'art 1: "Le musée imaginaire."* Geneva: Skira, 1947. Translated by Stuart Gilbert and Francis Price as *Museum without Walls*. London: Secker and Warburg, 1967.
Mosch, Ulrich. "'Taking Sound in Hand': Wolfgang Rihm and Varèse." In *Edgard Varèse: Composer, Sound Sculptor, Visionary*, edited by Felix Meyer and Heidy Zimmermann, 433–42. Woodbridge, Suffolk: Boydell, 2006.
———. "Taktilität des Klangs—Wolfgang Rihms Poetik." *Österreichische Musikzeitschrift* 63/8–9 (2008): 26–33.
Reynolds, Christopher A. *Motives for Allusion: Context and Content in Nineteenth-Century Music.* Cambridge, MA: Harvard University Press, 2003.
Rihm, Wolfgang. "Der geschockte Komponist." In *Ausgesprochen: Schriften und Gespräche*, edited by Ulrich Mosch, 1: 43–55. Veröffentlichungen der Paul Sacher Stiftung 6. Winterthur: Amadeus; Mainz: Schott Music, 1997.
Steiner, George. *Real Presences.* London: Faber and Faber, 1989.
Stenzel, Jürgen. "Anspielung." In *Reallexikon der deutschen Literaturwissenschaft*, edited by Klaus Weimar, 1: 93–96. Berlin and New York: de Gruyter, 1997.
Zimmermann, Bernd Alois. "Présence." In *Intervall und Zeit*, edited by Christof Bitter, 105–6. Mainz: Schott, 1974.
———. "Vom Handwerk des Komponisten." In *Intervall und Zeit*, edited by Christof Bitter, 31–37. Mainz: Schott, 1974.

EIGHTEEN

"Listening to inner voices": István Anhalt's *Sonance•Resonance (Welche Töne?)*[1]

ALAN GILLMOR

NEAR THE END OF DECEMBER 1988, István Anhalt received a commission from the symphony orchestras of Toronto, Montreal, and Calgary for a new orchestral work. It received its premiere at the opening concert of the 1989–90 Toronto season under the direction of the orchestra's newly appointed director Günther Herbig. The composer was informed that there would be only one other work on the program after the intermission: Beethoven's Ninth Symphony. To share a concert with such an iconic work clearly posed a dilemma, leaving Anhalt with two choices: ignore it or somehow respond to it. After much deliberation, he chose the latter course. The result was *Sonance•Resonance (Welche Töne?)*, premiered on 13 September 1989 at Toronto's Roy Thomson Hall. This paper is an exploration of Anhalt's response to that challenge, based primarily on the musical sketches in the István Anhalt Fonds of Library and Archives Canada, correspondence between Anhalt and the American composer George Rochberg, and personal communications with the author.

Sonance•Resonance is the last of a triptych of orchestral works dating from the late 1980s, each of which explores, in its own unique way, the experience, resonance, and transformation of memory, "those unbidden and unfathomed wisps and fumes of memory that share the mind with all the proud dark images of love and death" (in the poetic words of Thomas Wolfe).[2] Along with its companions—*Simulacrum* (1986–87) and *SparkskrapS* (1987)—*Sonance•Resonance* is a sort of sonic bridge to the composer's past, a recurring trope in his work from this period onward. In a sense, all living art taps into the personal—and collective—past at some level, and the more powerful that resonance, the deeper the response; to cite another novelist, this time the Canadian Robertson Davies, "Of course art isn't emotion; it's evocation and distillation of emotion one has known."[3] Anhalt's creative life has been an ongoing quest for answers to the eternal questions: Who am I? Why am I here? What is my world? *Sonance•Resonance*, as one small fragment of the puzzle, sheds considerable light on the composer's inward journey. It is not simply concerned with memory and remembrance, but more precisely with the subtle transformational processes of the mind itself as it peers into the multiple mirrors that give us occasional glimpses of who we are.

The full score of *Sonance•Resonance* was completed on 12 April 1989, Anhalt's seventieth birthday. It is, of course, a commonplace that with age, and the inevitable intimations of mortality, come deeper reflection and an increased tendency to ponder the strange phenomena of chance, of fate and destiny. And so it is that the story of *Sonance•Resonance* begins, in a sense, in 1938, in Budapest, where the eighteen-year-old music student, oversized score in hand, heard Beethoven's Ninth Symphony for the first time. Although by 1938 there had been several commercial recordings of the Ninth, most notably Fried (1929) and Weingartner (1935),[4] Anhalt had not heard them. For us who inhabit a music-saturated world, with every conceivable kind of music available at the touch of a button, it is very nearly impossible to imagine the excitement of hearing a great musical masterwork for the first time. As chance would have it, his seat-mate on this memorable occasion was a fellow student at the Academy of Music, a young woman by the name of Klára Huszar, who later became a stage director of the Hungarian Opera and the wife of Gábor Devecseri (a noted poet perhaps best remembered in Hungary today for his translations of ancient Greek poetry). It was through Klára, who remained a lifelong friend, that Anhalt was introduced to a group of young intellectuals that he has described as "the Devecseri circle." Here he would meet talented young men and woman from an array of disciplines, among them Sándor Weöres, whose poetry—along with that of Devecseri—he would set in two of his earliest acknowledged works, and János-György Szilágyi, who would become a world authority on Etruscan art and another lifelong friend.[5]

Anhalt's experience of hearing the mighty Ninth for the first time was, not surprisingly, overwhelming: "The impression it made on a first-year composition student," he told an interviewer in 1989, "was almost frightening."[6] When he made the decision that his new orchestral piece should in some way engage, or respond to, the Beethoven at a metaphorical level, the resonance of that Budapest concert of his youth surfaced more than a half-century later, rather "like the scent of the 'Madeleine' in Proust's *Remembrance of Things Past.*"[7] Disregarding the advice of his wife Beate and his good friend George Rochberg to ignore the connection, that the conjunction was irrelevant, Anhalt argued that this occasion struck him as somehow different, weightier, more highly charged. Here was the official Toronto debut of conductor Günther Herbig, a premiere performance by one of Canada's leading orchestras, and then there were those Proustian phantoms—the intriguing music student Klára, the clumsy oversized score, and above all the magnificent music—which insinuated themselves into his imagination and would not relinquish their hold. From the first he was aware of the dangers of creating what he has called (with a nod to Bakhtin whom he had been reading around this time) "a chronotopic juxtaposition"[8] with the Ninth, but by the time he was halfway through the composition of *Sonance•Resonance*, the concerns gradually evaporated. Writing to Rochberg the day after the completion of the new work, Anhalt registered his initial resistance to the idea of responding in some fashion to the Ninth and his gradual realization that he could not avoid it:

> Why should I get entangled in such a situation? I resisted it for weeks and tried other tacks. But to no avail. The idea kept on coming back with more and more justification why I <u>must</u> try to go <u>that</u> way. Finally, and with a sense of uncertainty (fear is too strong a word for it, and it was <u>not</u> that), I gave in and threw myself into the idea and it carried me along to completion in less than 4 months of work, from the first sketches to the finished score.[9]

Speculations about the "meaning" of Beethoven's Ninth Symphony—particularly its revolutionary fourth movement—abound, from Anton Schindler, the composer's secretary-turned-biographer, to the present day. Perhaps the most prevalent view sees the work as an extended metaphor of paradise lost and regained, of alienation and reconciliation, a mythical journey from a lost Arcadia to Elysium, the dream of a new harmony, a new moral unity. In a number of ways, the Ninth Symphony might be seen as Beethoven's "Remembrance of Things Past," a symbol of his own alienation and isolation, the deaf and ailing composer's response to what he perceived to be the trampling of his well-known republican ideals in the reactionary and repressive Vienna of the 1820s, the counter-revolutionary Age of Metternich. We do know that Beethoven had discovered Schiller's 1785 "Ode" in his youth—at least as early as 1793—and had long intended to set it to music. Although the oft-repeated story that Schiller had originally intended his poem as an "Ode to Freedom" (*Freiheit*) has been rejected by most contemporary scholars, Basil Deane nevertheless sees it as "the nearest German equivalent to the hymns and odes to brotherhood, liberty and humanity set to music by the revolutionary composers in France."[10] In many ways Beethoven's last completed symphony—along with its close companion the *Missa Solemnis*—might be considered his last "public" statement before he withdrew into the intensely private inner world of the late string quartets. In the words of the distinguished Beethoven scholar Maynard Solomon:

> Of course we can never know the ways in which the Ninth Symphony was carved out of Beethoven's own experience. But the objects of his desire seem to be quite on the surface here: for the reconstruction of a splintered family, recapture of an idyllic past, achievement of a loving brotherhood, attainment of an extended moment of pure joy, and eternal life … Ever fearful of death (except, it seems, at the very end), prone on occasion to suicide, and preoccupied not only with immortality but with mortality, Beethoven in his last years came to know that the comedy would not last much longer.
>
> In the face of physical decline, and of the emotional chaos that had undermined his psychological integrity for a full decade, Beethoven's creativity may have served to ward off death, to stimulate the will to continue—to provide an imaginative counterbalance against the forces of disintegration.[11]

The very opening of the fourth movement of the Ninth Symphony, coming on the heels of the exalted Adagio, assaults the listener with two dissonant outbursts separated by an episodic recitative-like passage in the cellos and basses. The first is a B-flat appoggiatura over a D minor triad, with the added flat sixth (B flat) piercing through the top of the texture in the oboes and flutes, which momentarily has the effect of pitting D minor and B-flat major against each other. The second (beginning in bar 17) is an even more grating five-note conglomeration of a diminished seventh (F sharp, A, C, E flat) superimposed on a D pedal, which, of course, also outlines a ninth chord (D, F sharp, A, C, E flat). When the gesture returns for the last time (at bar 208), the strings, which had earlier remained silent, add three notes to the texture (C sharp, E, and G) resulting in a crunching dissonance containing all seven notes of the D minor scale, which could be read as a diminished seventh (C sharp, E, G, B flat), which again acts as an appoggiatura, superimposed on its own resolution (the

D minor triad). Even today, it is a startling effect, an emblematic moment that not only signalled a complete break with the past, but one that, in its sheer dissonance, would wait nearly three-quarters of a century for its like in the music of Mahler, Strauss, and others. Little wonder that Wagner famously dubbed this violent gesture the *Schreckensfanfare*, a vivid term that has become permanently inscribed in the hermeneutic lexicon of the Ninth Symphony.[12] Not surprisingly, this was the main trigger that launched Anhalt on his quest:

> The idea that came to mind leaped out of B[eethoven]'s introductory sentence in the brief recitative to the 4th mov[ement]: "O Freunde, nicht diese Töne!" etc. In the sketchbooks one finds: "Nein diese ... erinnern an unsre Verzweifl." What despair did he try to repress? The echo of that resistance almost instantly 'generalized' itself in my mind, and penetrated this whole situation, commission & all. I kept hearing the very opening of the 4th mo[vemen]t: that 'terror-fanfare' (Wagner's term: *Schreckensfanfare*) ... What does that convey? That near *nonpareil* gesture in his output, or, for that matter, in the literature as I (limitedly) know it. I know that he wrestled with the 'technical' aspect of transition (never only 'technical': it required a sort of psychic bridge, a <u>brief</u> justification). But did this occur? Were things left unsaid? Which tones (*Welche Töne*) were left unsung? If at all, no one will ever know. And I am not privy to the secret, either. But what <u>might</u> be possible, I could <u>guess</u> at out of my own head, perhaps, perhaps, so I told myself.[13]

There are around a dozen references to Beethoven—the man, his music, his musical style—in *Sonance•Resonance*. Some are very much on the surface (like the *Schreckensfanfare*, the gruff instrumental recitative that follows shortly thereafter, the Alla marcia [or so-called "Turkish March"], and the Scherzo's main theme) while others are more veiled and oblique. However, it should be noted that none of the musical references are precise quotations, but rather more in the nature of dreamlike echoes, or "resonances," of the German master's music, fragmented, transformed, distorted, some, perhaps, even unconscious. It is analogous to the transformational process of memory itself, the layered filters through which memory grows, decays, and is reborn in an ever-changing kaleidoscope of mental images.

A perusal of the extensive sketches for *Sonance•Resonance* reveals a great deal of the composer's modus operandi.[14] There are numerous pages of row tables, structural guidelines, character indications, rhythmic ideas, even tempo charts for various sections, the kinds of raw material that

Anhalt once referred to as "lattices, jumping-off points, palette-surfaces."[15] For example, early on he sketches a possible structural shape for the work: "Cantilena," "Canon," "Fugue," "Postillon," "Assembly," "Fanfare/March." Close by, he jots down a series of "mood" suggestions: "massive," "calm, peaceful," "dreamlike," "vehement," "terror-stricken," "measured, controlled," "lyrical ('emotional'), loving," "foreboding, dark," "brilliant, sparkling," "cruel, hard," and so forth. Of course, not all of these suggested affects find their way into the final score; it would appear, for example, that the composer's initial impulse was to begin the work with "massive" sonorities before settling on the "calm, peaceful (or flowing)" mood of the soft and delicate opening. Many pages of the sketches are taken up with row tables, eight in all. These range from six- and seven-note sets (series 1 and 6), to eight-note (series 2 and 3), octatonic (series 5), pentachordal ten-note (series 7), and hexachordal twelve-note sets (series 4 and 8). Although not a precise match, it is tempting to speculate that the original six-note row of series 1 (F sharp, F, D, D flat, B flat, A) (plate 18-1) might have been adapted for the opening line in the first violins (F sharp, [G], D, C sharp/D flat, A, B flat) (plate 18-2). In any event, this opening string passage introduces a gesture that links the music, with characteristic subtlety, to the Ninth Symphony. The barcarole-like 12/8 trochaic rhythm of the flowing string lines mirrors the accentuation of *"wel - che tö - ne, wel - che tö – ne."* This would almost certainly go unobserved were it not for the fact that Anhalt notes this correspondence in the sketches for *Sonance•Resonance*. Moreover, the opening gesture in the first violins (which is subtly shadowed by the second violins) outlines the open fifth (in this case G-D), a veiled reference, perhaps, to the celebrated "hollow" opening of the Ninth Symphony, a speculation reinforced by the prominent appearance of the fifth (and its inversion) throughout this opening section.

The mood alters dramatically at bar 77 ("fast, frantically"). Here is an example of a hidden connection to Beethoven, not likely decipherable but for a letter Anhalt wrote to Herbig three weeks before the premiere:

> Concerning the musical substance of the score I should perhaps make one comment here. The passage which begins in bar 77 ("Fast, frantically") was suggested to me by, and it is intended to convey the sense and experience of, this sentence which is contained in the letter Beethoven wrote to Dr. Franz Wegeler on June 29, 1801 [*sic*]: "... meine Ohren, die sausen und brausen Tag und Nacht fort" ["my ears whistle and buzz continually, day and night"]. This imaginary enactment "dissolves," modulates, into the "Allegro appassionato" which begins in bar 113.[16]

"LISTENING TO INNER VOICES" • GILLMOR   377

PLATE 18-1 István Anhalt, "Series 1" from sketches for *Sonance•Resonance (Welche Töne?)* (1989), Library and Archives Canada, MUS 164, D2,37, with kind permission of the composer and of Library and Archives Canada.

PLATE 18-2 István Anhalt, *Sonance•Resonance (Welche Töne?)* (1989), mm. 1–2, with kind permission of the composer.

The simulacrum of Beethoven's tinnitus is captured quite vividly when the loud ringing sounds of the metallophones (pairs of crotales and vibraphones played with hard mallets) enter in bar 83, surrounded by a massive dissonant pedal in the electric organ and the remainder of the orchestra.[17] The frantic gesture gradually dissolves (bars 105–12) into a slower section (beginning in bar 113), which, Anhalt notes in the score, is a remembrance of the final Allegro appassionato of Beethoven's Op. 132 String Quartet, the main theme of which, in a transposed and slightly altered form, Beethoven had originally intended for a purely instrumental finale to the Ninth Symphony, a notion that he had entertained until mid-1823, not long before the work's completion early in 1824.

The composer's "remembrance" of the final movement of Beethoven's Op. 132 String Quartet is just that, not an overt reference, but rather a series of veiled allusions. For example, the stepwise, descending semitone in the second violin underpinned by the double-stopped movement in the viola (example 18-1), which persists, rather like an inner pedal, throughout the first nine bars of the Quartet (and reappears later), is mirrored in Anhalt's chamber-like scoring (pages 21–23), where pairs of solo strings maintain a strikingly similar pattern in the same triple meter (plate 18-3). Reinforcing the connection are the semitone inflections prominent throughout the texture—from woodwinds to double basses—which relate strongly to the second violin passage at the beginning of the Quartet movement. The

EXAMPLE 18-1 Ludwig van Beethoven, String Quartet, Op. 132, Movement 5, Allegro appassionato, mm. 1–19.

most overt reference to the Allegro appassionato is the solo flute line beginning in the last beat of bar 117, which quotes the incipit of the Quartet's first violin melody (A, E, C, A) in a transposed version (C, G, E flat, C) (plate 18-4). Variations of this motif are immediately picked up by the first violins, bringing the first stage of Anhalt's "remembrance" to a close in a grand pause in bar 124—itself a prime Beethovenian dramatic gesture.

Just as the Beethoven movement accelerates and grows in intensity, beginning in bar 125 Anhalt also increases the tempo (*Vivace appassionato*), the dynamic level (*fortissimo*), and the texture (now amplified by the timpani, electric organ, and full brass section). The semitone ostinato in the brass (reinforced by the electric organ) now takes on an aggressive quality, while the ascending scalar sweeps in the woodwinds and strings recall similar passages in the Beethoven Quartet movement. The entire passage (bars 125–69) is a calculated transition leading inexorably to the first statement of the *Schreckensfanfare*. For example, the furious eighth-note, fanfare-like figure that follows on the heels of the initial dissonant chord in the last movement of the Ninth Symphony provides most of the material for this section, as the full orchestra hammers away (*marcato sempre*) at subtle transformations of the

PLATE 18-3 István Anhalt, *Sonance•Resonance (Welche Töne?)* (1989), strings only, mm. 113–16, with kind permission of the composer.

PLATE 18-4 István Anhalt, *Sonance•Resonance (Welche Töne?)* (1989), mm. 117–20, with kind permission of the composer.

Schreckensfanfare material, so that when it finally arrives, it seems but a crystallization of what preceded it. In bar 169 the *fortissimo* brass cut out abruptly, leaving a ghost-like echo in the strings which is immediately shattered by a forceful, and distorted, rendering of the opening fanfare from the last movement of the Ninth Symphony carried by the woodwinds *fortissimo* in high register, reinforced by the brass choir and underpinned by an open-fifth pedal in the low strings (plate 18-5).

The fanfare dissolves—in a rather cinematic way—and relative calm is restored (bar 180). Woodwind figures sound rather like soft reminiscences of the fanfare. The tempo gradually increases, the texture thickens, there are several metric shifts (from triple to duple and back), and finally, at

PLATE 18-5 István Anhalt, *Sonance•Resonance (Welche Töne?)* (1989), mm. 170–74, with kind permission of the composer.

PLATE 18-6 István Anhalt, *Sonance•Resonance (Welche Töne?)* (1989), mm. 227–34, with kind permission of the composer.

bar 225, the music once again dissolves, this time into a dreamlike sequence initiated by an Alberti-like ostinato maintained by a solo piano for some forty bars. As John Beckwith suggests, this "classical passagework" could be perceived as a "resonance" of the world of eighteenth-century sonatas and sonatinas of blessed memory to legions of adolescent pianists.[18] Out of this mysterious sonic image of an eighteenth-century drawing room emerge fleeting reminiscences of the second-movement Scherzo of the Ninth Symphony, first in bars 230–31 with the timpani softly intoning the

PLATE 18-6 (conclusion)

rhythmically dotted downward octave-leap that opens the Scherzo and permeates much of it, followed immediately by a brief recollection of the movement's skittering opening theme (plate 18-6); the gesture is repeated, a semitone downward, in bars 242–43. The timpani keep the Scherzo in the listener's mind with soft interjections of the distinctive falling octave (bars 247, 250, and 257) until the Scherzo theme reappears—again fleetingly—in the high woodwind (bar 260) followed by two last soft statements of the timpani figure (bars 260 and 262). In bar 262 the steady sixteenth-motion of the piano ostinato is broken for the first time into eighth-note patterns, and this shadowy evocation of an eighteenth-century world dissolves in a sustained cluster in the solo piano (A, C, C sharp, F sharp, A, C sharp, F sharp) sounding over a soft haze of strings and high woodwind.

PLATE 18-7 István Anhalt, *Sonance•Resonance (Welche Töne?)* (1989), woodwinds and brass only, mm. 291–97, with kind permission of the composer.

The section beginning in bar 267 ("Slow and calm") acts as a long transition to the *Tempo di marcia* (bar 293), which is clearly an evocation of Beethoven's "Turkish March," complete with crotales, triangle, cymbals, and bass drum. But like previous transitional passages in *Sonance•Resonance*, echoes of Beethoven are never far away. For example, the section begins with the same iambic rhythmic figure that will dominate Beethoven's Alla marcia, so that when the march emerges at bar 293, beginning with a soft "oom-pah" figure in the bass clarinet, bassoons, and contrabassoon, it is as if it were expected (plate 18-7). Finally, we need to remind ourselves that the "Turkish March" is yet another transformation of the "Ode to Joy" theme in Beethoven's expansive variation scheme.

The section that follows (bars 320–37) would seem to inhabit a region similar to the third movement of the Ninth Symphony; the conjunct melody first heard in the upper strings in a flowing 6/8 meter, with its expressive turns (bars 320–26), and the florid violin solo (bars 327–37) tracing arabesques high above the texture (plate 18-8) provide strong reminiscences of Beethoven's Adagio. The violin solo in particular is a close relative to the German composer's equally florid first violin line in the third section of the movement (bars 43–64) (example 18-2).

At bar 338 the full violin choir picks up the fanfare-like figure of the solo violin's final arabesque (bars 335–37), which will subsequently prove to be a prefiguration of the fugue subject that first appears at bar 379.

PLATE 18-8 István Anhalt, *Sonance•Resonance (Welche Töne?)* (1989), mm. 328–30, with kind permission of the composer.

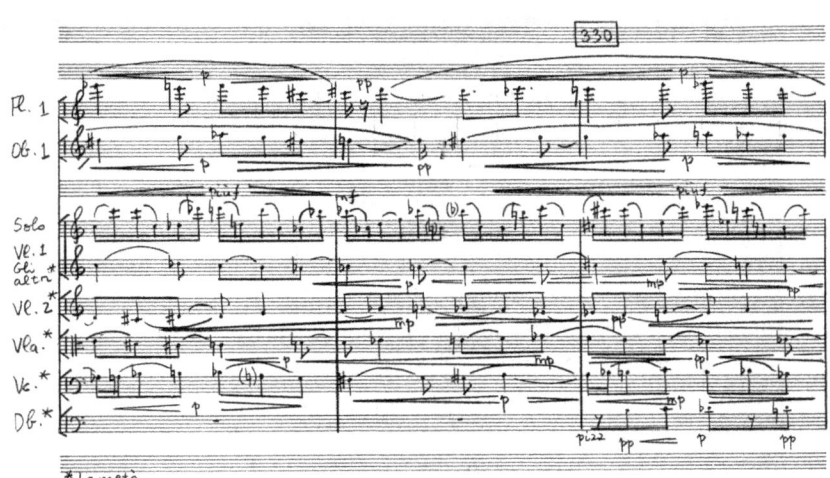

EXAMPLE 18-2 Ludwig van Beethoven, Ninth Symphony, Movement 3, Adagio molto e cantibile (mm. 49–51).

Once again we see a transitional passage functioning as a kind of premonition. The fanfare-like figure (an octave leap by way of the fifth) is heard in close imitation with inversions of itself, an intensely contrapuntal section that is brought to a close with a great thirty-second-note monophonic flourish in the woodwind choir (doubled by one trumpet). It will not go unnoticed that the "modal limbo" of the octave leap by way of the fifth is one of the prime melodic signatures of the Ninth Symphony. Moreover, although it may have been an unconscious connection on Anhalt's part, it is interesting to note that—with slight modification—the opening melodic idea of *Sonance • Resonance* (F sharp, G, D, C sharp) (see plate 18-2) is remarkably similar to the incipit of the fugal passage that begins at bar 379 (D, G, D, C sharp, or G, C, G, F sharp in its transposed version) (plate 18-9). Such are the mysteries of the creative process.

Despite the fact that the interval of the fifth (and its inversion) plays such a central role in the Ninth Symphony, Anhalt's fugue is more in the nature of a generalized response, or homage, to the increased occurrences of fugal passages throughout the third-period works of the German master, including, of course, the fugal passages in the second and last movements of the Ninth Symphony. Anhalt's highly chromatic fugue, with its tritonal entries, though far removed from traditional models, nevertheless invokes in a general way one of the defining characteristics of Beethoven's late musical style. As John Beckwith notes, "a more accu-

PLATE 18-9 István Anhalt, *Sonance•Resonance (Welche Töne?)* (1989), mm. 376–80, with kind permission of the composer.

rate echo, creative reflection, or 'resonance' of third-period Beethoven *ohne Parodie* (without parody, to borrow a phrase from Mahler), would be hard to imagine."[19] Anhalt's fugue builds in intensity until it explodes in a return of the *Schreckensfanfare* (bars 474ff.). After a grand pause and one last furious echo of the fanfare material, the tempo quite suddenly slows into a broad *allargando*, out of which emerges the last overt reference to the Ninth Symphony, a kind of paraphrase of the broad *recitativo* passages that characterize the opening pages of the finale. Preceding the recitative in the string choir (which begins, with an enharmonic twist, in bar 523) (plate 18-10) is an extended solo (bars 498–511) for the euphonium (or baritone, as it is commonly—and aptly—called, and so-named by Anhalt), and one wonders if this is, perhaps, a veiled reference to the fact that the solo baritone voice, echoing the previous instrumental recitatives, is the first vocal sound heard in the Ninth Symphony. The texture thins until the music reaches tonal stasis on a long A pedal, reinforced by the soft beats of the timpani. It is rather like one of those "anti-teleological" moments frequently found in Beethoven's music (including the

PLATE 18-10 István Anhalt, *Sonance•Resonance (Welche Töne?)* (1989), mm. 523–27, with kind permission of the composer.

Ninth Symphony), when forward momentum is temporarily suspended in an expectant hush.

The tempo slows, the A pedal continues, and at bar 547 the composer inscribes "Like a dirge," a mood that will be sustained until the final bars as the music fades on a soft cluster framed by an F natural at the bottom of the texture in the low strings countered by the tritone B natural at the top of the texture in the first violins and second piccolo. Anhalt's detailed instructions in the score at this point are telling. For example, he instructs that the final fermata should last "as long as the crotales are audible," and in the final soft cluster he asks the inner strings (second violins and violas) to glide downward: "shallow (maximum: a whole tone) glides at the threshold of audibility, the effect of a collective sigh." When Anhalt first received the commission for *Sonance•Resonance*, Herbig suggested to the composer that he might consider a "holocaust" piece, perhaps something along the lines of Schoenberg's *Survivor from Warsaw*. Although he has kept his vow that he would never write a "holocaust" piece, *Sonance•Resonance* does contain a private reference to the horrific event, for the "dirge" that brings this music to a quiet and ethereal close brings us back full circle to the composer's native Hungary, where, in a sense, this piece began, in 1938, with the performance of the Ninth Symphony. Four years later, on 1 December 1942, Anhalt was conscripted into a forced labour company of the Hungarian army made up of Jewish men and others deemed unfit for regular service. Anhalt has made it clear that the poignant closing pages of *Sonance•Resonance* serve as a lament for lost companions during these nightmarish years, perhaps most notably László Gyopár, a close friend and fellow student at the Academy of Music, who, too ill to go on, died during a forced march in Poland, almost certainly at the hands of a guard.[20] There is a certain irony in the fact that Gyopár was a Jewish convert to Christianity, whose *Missa* (1942), under Anhalt's urging, was first performed in Budapest in 1994, the fiftieth anniversary of his death. Conversion alone, however, could not save Gyopár, and many others, for in the eyes of the Hungarian authorities of the day he was still "racially" a Jew.

Not long after the premiere of *Sonance•Resonance*, Günther Herbig told the composer that he thought the piece was *zerstückeln* ("disjointed, fragmented"),[21] a curious statement coming from a man who had just conducted the Ninth Symphony, the last movement of which is a glorious amalgam of recitative, chorale, vocal quartet, military march, and fugue, all bound together in a series of expansive variations, with elements of sonata form and rondo, that decisively shattered the mould of symphonic form, with repercussions felt far into the future.[22] Structurally, as Robert Simpson points out, it is "a summing-up of classical possibilities, all expressed in a single huge design with astonishing certainty of touch; it has even the shade of the classical concerto in it." It is, he concludes, "as if Beethoven, like Bach in *The Art of Fugue*, were intent on encompassing everything he knew in one mighty act."[23] Anhalt recalls that in the 1980s he was reading such classics as Pascal's *Pensées*, Novalis's *Fragments*, and Wittgenstein's *On Certainty*, works that resemble one another in that they consist of concatenations of fragments.[24] This suggests a literary source for the collage-like nature of *Sonance•Resonance*, a subtle cross-disciplinary alliance frequently found in Anhalt's multi-layered creative world.

By the composer's own account, *Sonance•Resonance*, like its orchestral companions, is an "'idea' piece."[25] Indeed, so layered and elliptical do the subtexts become at times that these works can appear gnomic and hermetic to the uninitiated. In this regard, it is interesting to note that Beethoven's Ninth Symphony, as Richard Taruskin has written, "poses more questions ... than any other Beethoven symphony—perhaps more than any symphony by anyone else up to the time when composers began purposely loading their symphonies with symbols and sphinxes (this being the tradition that the Ninth 'generated')."[26] Thus Anhalt's *Sonance•Resonance*, not inappropriately, must remain, in some respects, a riddle in response to a riddle, for music's deeper meaning resists translation; it is a multi-faceted source of many possible meanings, and perhaps therein lies the source of its compelling power. As Gadamer tells us, the process of mediation and dialogue is elastic, and never completely transparent.[27] Yet we persist in our search for meaning. Ten years after the composition of *Sonance•Resonance*, Anhalt provided yet another clue in a letter to Rochberg apropos George Steiner's review of the correspondence between Martin Heidegger and Hannah Arendt:

In this review Steiner refers to Heidegger's notion: *"entgegen schweigen"* ... remaining silent 'against,' or 'in the face of something.' Now this set off a loud bell in my head! Wasn't [it] *this* idea, precisely, that fuelled me as I was conceiving of, and composed, my *Sonance•Resonance (Welche Töne?)*? *"Welche Töne?"* A question relating to the Beethovenian opening: *"O Freunde! Nicht diese Töne!"* ... The Heideggerian transformation elicits other, 'unanswered,' questions ... Why the silence? Of course in Heidegger's case one is tempted to guess ... With some hope of success ... Other silences might be more difficult to fathom.[28]

Sonance•Resonance is but one example of a recurring—one is tempted to say obsessive—theme in Anhalt's creative world: the metamorphosis and equivocalness of memory:

This is what I'm interested in, how one lives with memory, how memories are never the same as the first event. There is transformation, distortion. We grow, we remember, we forget. I'm interested in what we are and what the thing remembered means to us at different stages of our life. This is resonance.[29]

Notes

1 I would like to thank Dr. James K. Wright of Carleton University for reading a draft of this essay and making a number of valuable suggestions, especially with regard to some of the theoretical data drawn from Beethoven's Ninth Symphony.
2 Thomas Wolfe, *Of Time and the River* (New York: Charles Scribner's Sons, 1935), 509.
3 Robertson Davies, *The Rebel Angels* (Toronto: Macmillan, 1981), 63.
4 Oskar Fried, Berlin State Opera Orchestra, with the Bruno Kittel Choir and Lotte Leonard (soprano), Jenny Sonnenberg (alto), Eugene Transky (tenor), and Wilhelm Guttmann (bass) (1929); Felix Weingartner, Vienna Philharmonic Orchestra, with the Vienna State Opera Chorus and Luise Helletsgruber (soprano), Rosette Anday (alto), Georg Maikl (tenor), and Richard Mayr (bass) (1935). Both of these historic performances have been reissued a number of times on various labels; see, for example, Naxos Historical CD 8.110929 (Fried) and Naxos Historical CD 8.110863 (Weingartner).
5 An extensive correspondence with both Klára Devecseri and János-György Szilágyi, in Hungarian, can be found in the István Anhalt Fonds (MUS 164), Library and Archives Canada.
6 Quoted in David Barber, "Terrors of the Ninth," *The Whig Standard Magazine* (Kingston), 2 September 1989, 9.
7 Quoted in Jeffrey Reid, "A Short Conversation with a Composer," *Toronto Symphony Times* 2/1 (September 1989): 1.

8   Anhalt to Rochberg, 21 September 1989, in *Eagle Minds: Selected Correspondence of Istvan Anhalt and George Rochberg (1961–2005)*, ed. Alan M. Gillmor (Waterloo: Wilfrid Laurier University Press, 2007), 234. See also Mikhail M. Bakhtin, "Forms of Time and of the Chronotope in the Novel: Notes toward a Historical Poetics," in *The Dialogic Imagination: Four Essays*, ed. Michael Holquist, trans. Caryl Emerson and Michael Holquist (Austin: University of Texas Press, 1981), 84–258.
9   Anhalt to Rochberg, 13 April 1989, in *Eagle Minds*, 227.
10 Basil Deane, "The Symphonies and Overtures," in *The Beethoven Reader*, ed. Denis Arnold and Nigel Fortune (New York: W.W. Norton, 1971), 312–13.
11 Maynard Solomon, "Beethoven's Ninth Symphony: A Search for Order," *19th-Century Music* 10/1 (Summer 1986): 20.
12 The term first appeared in Wagner's 1873 essay "Zum Vortrag der neunten Symphonie Beethoven's," in *Sämtliche Schriften und Dichtungen* (Leipzig: Siegel's Musikalienhandlung, 1907), 9: 231–57. Writing not long after Wagner's death, Sir George Grove referred to the celebrated fanfares in equally vivid terms as "a horrible clamour," a "demoniacal uproar" in *Beethoven and His Nine Symphonies*, 3rd ed. (London: Novello, Ewer, 1898; repr. New York: Dover, 1962), 370–71.
13 Anhalt to Rochberg, 13 April 1989, in *Eagle Minds*, 227.
14 István Anhalt Fonds (MUS 164), Library and Archives Canada. The musical materials relating to *Sonance•Resonance (Welche Töne?)* can be found in Folders D2,37 to D2,42.
15 Anhalt to Rochberg, 14 April 1985, in *Eagle Minds*, 158.
16 Anhalt to Günther Herbig, 24 August 1989, István Anhalt Fonds (MUS 164), Library and Archives Canada. The quotation from Beethoven's letter to Wegeler of 29 June 1800 can be found in Franz Gerhard Wegeler and Ferdinand Ries, *Biographische Notizen über Ludwig van Beethoven* (1838; repr. 1845; repr. Hildesheim: Georg Olms Verlag, 1972), 24, and in English translation in *Beethoven's Letters, with Explanatory Notes by Dr. A.C. Kalischer*, translated with preface by J.S. Shedlock, selected and edited by Arthur Eagflefield-Hull (London and Toronto: J.M. Dent & Sons, 1926; New York: E.P. Dutton, 1926; repr. New York: Dover, 1972), 20. Shedlock translates the passage in question as "the humming in my ears continues day and night without ceasing."
17 Beginning in bar 475, the crotales and vibraphones—again played *fortissimo* with hard mallets—ring through the second allusion to the *Schreckensfanfare* in *Sonance•Resonance*, suggesting that Anhalt may be suggesting a possible connection between "nicht diese Töne" and the well-documented despair of the composer in the face of tinnitus and impending deafness.
18 John Beckwith, "Orchestral Works," in *István Anhalt: Pathways and Memory*, ed. Robin Elliott and Gordon E. Smith (Montreal and Kingston: McGill-Queen's University Press, 2001), 129.
19 Ibid.
20 Anhalt, in conversation with the author, Kingston, Ontario, 13 December 2007.
21 Anhalt, in telephone conversation with the author, October 2006.

22 It is interesting to note that the critic for the *Allgemeine musikalische Zeitung*, in his review of the 7 May 1824 premiere of the Ninth Symphony, although almost ecstatic in his praise ("Art and truth here celebrate their most glorious triumph"), nevertheless referred to the last movement as a "potpourri," concluding that "this truly singular Finale would be all the more imposing if it were drawn together into a more concentrated unity," a view, he has the temerity to suggest, the composer himself would doubtless share "had not cruel fate robbed him of the faculty of hearing his own creations." Quoted in Anton Felix Schindler, *Beethoven as I Knew Him: A Biography*, ed. Donald W. MacArdle, trans. Constance S. Jolly (New York: W.W. Norton, 1972), 280–81.
23 Robert Simpson, *Beethoven Symphonies* (Seattle: University of Washington Press, 1971), 57–58.
24 Anhalt, in telephone conversation with the author, October 2006.
25 Anhalt to Rochberg, 13 April 1989, in *Eagle Minds*, 226.
26 Richard Taruskin, "Resisting the Ninth," *19th-Century Music* 12/3 (Spring 1989): 248.
27 See Hans-Georg Gadamer, *Truth and Method*, trans. and ed. Garrett Barden and John Cumming (New York: Seabury Press, 1975).
28 Anhalt to Rochberg, 19 March 1999, in *Eagle Minds*, 356.
29 Quoted in Reid, 1.

Bibliography

Bakhtin, Mikhail M. "Forms of Time and of the Chronotope in the Novel: Notes toward a Historical Poetics." In *The Dialogic Imagination: Four Essays*, edited by Michael Holquist, translated by Caryl Emerson and Michael Holquist, 84–258. Austin: University of Texas Press, 1981.

Barber, David. "Terrors of the Ninth." *The Whig Standard Magazine* (Kingston), 2 September 1989, 9, 16.

Beckwith, John. "Orchestral Works." In *István Anhalt: Pathways and Memory*, edited by Robin Elliott and Gordon E. Smith, 111–31. Montreal and Kingston: McGill-Queen's University Press, 2001.

Davies, Robertson. *The Rebel Angels*. Toronto: Macmillan, 1981.

Deane, Basil. "The Symphonies and Overtures." In *The Beethoven Reader*, edited by Denis Arnold and Nigel Fortune, 281–317. New York: W.W. Norton, 1971.

Eaglefield-Hull, Arthur, ed. *Beethoven's Letters, with Explanatory Notes by Dr. A.C. Kalischer*. Translated with preface by J.S. Shedlock. London and Toronto: J.M. Dent & Sons, 1926. New York: E.P. Dutton & Co., 1926. Reprint, New York: Dover, 1972.

Gadamer, Hans-Georg. *Truth and Method*. Translated and edited by Garrett Barden and John Cumming. New York: Seabury Press, 1975.

Gillmor, Alan M., ed. *Eagle Minds: Selected Correspondence of Istvan Anhalt and George Rochberg (1961–2005)*. Waterloo, ON: Wilfrid Laurier University Press, 2007.

Grove, Sir George. *Beethoven and His Nine Symphonies*, 3rd ed. London: Novello, Ewer and Company, 1898. Reprint, New York: Dover, 1962.

Reid, Jeffrey. "A Short Conversation with a Composer." *Toronto Symphony Times* 2/1 (September 1989): 1.

Schindler, Anton Felix. *Beethoven as I Knew Him: A Biography*. Edited by Donald W. MacArdle. Translated by Constance S. Jolly. New York: W.W. Norton, 1972.

Simpson, Robert. *Beethoven Symphonies*. Seattle: University of Washington Press, 1971.

Solomon, Maynard. "Beethoven's Ninth Symphony: A Search for Order." *19th-Century Music* 10/1 (Summer 1986): 3–23.

Taruskin, Richard. "Resisting the Ninth." *19th-Century Music* 12/3 (Spring 1989): 241–56.

Wagner, Richard. "Zum Vortrag der neunten Symphonie Beethoven's" (1873). In *Sämtliche Schriften und Dichtungen*, vol. 9: 231–57. Leipzig: Siegel's Musikalienhandlung, 1907.

Wegeler, Franz Gerhard and Ferdinand Ries. *Biographische Notizen über Ludwig van Beethoven*, 1838. Reprint, 1845. Reprint, Hildesheim: Georg Olms Verlag, 1972.

Wolfe, Thomas. *Of Time and the River*. New York: Charles Scribner's Sons, 1935.

NINETEEN

Music Written from Memory in the Late Work of István Anhalt

FRIEDEMANN SALLIS

As an artefact of memory, music has special status by virtue of its temporal and non-representative character (the very things that link it to embodied and emotional modes of being and the very things that make music's powers in relation to memory all the more elusive).

—Tia DeNora[1]

To interpret means to assume the point of view of the producer, to retrace his work in all its trials and interrogations of matter, in its response to and the choice of cues, in its intuition of what the inner coherence of the work wants to be.

—Umberto Eco[2]

Introduction: *Alternative Voices* and István Anhalt's Late Work

Between early 2005 and late 2007, István Anhalt composed *Four Portraits from Memory*, his most recent composition and a moving work, representative of the stylistic and technical tendencies that have marked his creative output for the past twenty-five years. In it, the notion of memory can be examined from at least two distinct perspectives: in the act of writing the music on the one hand and as an integral part of the relationship between form and content on the other. Of course there is nothing new in the fact that music and memory are intimately linked, particularly with regard to art music. Without the emphatic engagement of memory, the listener of this type of music has no hope of apprehending the aesthetic object. Moreover, remembrance as a thematic element has been identified by numerous commentators as a major aspect of Anhalt's late work.[3] In the following we shall examine how notions of memory and remembrance produce a network of musical and extra-musical relationships that are central to the idea of *Four Portraits from Memory*.

Anhalt's late work begins in 1984. In July of that year he retired from his position as professor at Queen's University, bringing an end to a prestigious career as a teacher, a scholar, and an administrator that had begun thirty-five years earlier at McGill University. With regard to Anhalt's creative activity, the mid-1980s also constitute a watershed. In 1983 he completed his second opera, *Winthrop*, on which he had been working since 1975. Shortly after the opera's first performance in September 1986, the composer unexpectedly received two orchestral commissions: the first from Gabriel Chmura, then the conductor designate of the National Arts Centre Orchestra in Ottawa, which resulted in *Simulacrum* (1987), and the second from Alex Pauk, conductor of the Esprit Orchestra in Toronto, for whom Anhalt composed *SparkskrapS* (1987).[4] These two works initiated a series of seven orchestral compositions that are at the core of the composer's production of the past quarter-century.[5]

Nineteen eighty-four is also the year Anhalt published *Alternative Voices: Essays on Contemporary Vocal and Choral Composition*. In it, he discusses the techniques and the interdisciplinary relationships of innovative twentieth-century vocal and choral music, as well as the major recurring surface and "deep" themes in this repertoire. The book focuses on music written after 1945, though the repertoire referred to covers almost the entire century.[6] If reception is any measure of success, the book has done remarkably well. Together with R. Murray Schafer's *The Tuning of the World*, it is one of the few books on music, written and published in Canada, to have achieved a certain international resonance.[7] *Alternative Voices* constitutes a milestone in the composer's career for three reasons. First, it is a summa, culminating a decade of work on vocal music, the voice, and linguistics that Anhalt had been pursuing both as a creative artist and as a scholar.[8] He takes a broad approach, examining vast swaths of knowledge from a musical perspective, including anthropology, ethnomusicology, linguistics (phonetics and psycholinguistics), literature (narratology and prosody), mythology, philosophy (epistemology, semantics, and semiotics), physiology of the voice, depth psychology, religion (esoteric traditions and shamanism), sociology and sociolinguistics, and visual art.[9] The author's remarkable erudition is backed by an extensive bibliography of over 350 authors. At the same time, the book also presents numerous in-depth analyses, notably of Luciano Berio's *Sequenza III*, György Ligeti's *Nouvelles aventures*, and Witold Lutosławski's *Trois poèmes d'Henri Michaux*.

Second, *Alternative Voices* is a child of its time. The book was published during a period marked by the critical rethinking of established practice and conventional wisdom in numerous disciplines, including musicology.[10] Like Jacques Attali's *Bruits: Essai sur l'économie politique de la musique* and Schafer's *The Tuning of the World*, both published just seven years earlier (1977), there is a sense that Anhalt's work was motivated by an underlying unease and dissatisfaction with the reigning theoretical work of the day.[11] Austin Clarkson notes that Anhalt focuses on "music that does not prescribe tempered pitch classes and metred durations" and pointedly observes that he presents a "context for musical ideas that for the most part have been ignored by musical theorists."[12] "Anhalt's theoretical position presents a challenge to mainstream music theory, which is concerned for the most part with nontexted music. In fact, we might conclude that a theorist's position is contingent on the musical genre of choice, and that Anhalt's 'alternative voices' are raised in support of an alternative music theory."[13] Indeed, by the early 1980s Anhalt appears to have grown, if not weary, at least wary of the approaches developed by the hard-edged North American theory establishment during the 1960s and 1970s—that relatively small group of academics who broke away from the AMS, proclaiming new, objective methodologies, but who, by the 1980s, looked more and more like defenders of a new kind of *ars antiqua*. In a letter written to George Rochberg in 1985, Anhalt described this "rebirth of music theory as a mixed blessing ... A fruit of the same old positivist tree ... but then there is in our corner of the woods other vegetation around & various birds (Cage-d or not) that provide other alternatives."[14]

Third, without taking anything away from its erudition and its contextual relationships, the book can also be read as a personal manifesto: an attempt at defining an aesthetic program and identifying issues and problems that Anhalt, as a composer, would encounter on the road ahead. The whole book is focused on introducing and examining new techniques and perspectives which are not only symptomatic of profound change in the way we think and listen to music, but which should lead to an enrichment and rejuvenation of art music that had lost its way in the arid and inexpressive techniques of integral serialism during the postwar period. In his Epilogue, Anhalt underscores the importance of music's expressive potential, which he sought to restore and unleash.[15] Though over twenty years separate the publication of *Alternative Voices* and the composition of

Four Portraits from Memory, the latter can be understood as one of a series of works in which Anhalt attempted to achieve goals set out in his book.

Composition and Performance: Bringing the Work into the World

Each of the *Four Portraits from Memory* was written after the death of a person close to the composer. The pieces were composed between February 2005 and March 2006. The dates of the composition of each *Portrait* are given in the autograph manuscript of the piano version. The following list provides the titles, dedications, and dates as indicated in that document:

- "… Instead … (of answering a letter … a fare-well …) (For Judith Anhalt, my half sister (Jan. 7, 1935–Feb. 23, 2005) with love …)"; 24 February – 29 March 2005 Kingston[16]
- "Dirge (a song of mourning and incomprehension) for George Rochberg … a soul-brother"; 6 June 2005[17]
- "In the memory of András Kelemen – … a friend … 1942–44 … 2005–6 … who lived true to the 'good name' …"; 18 February 2006 Kingston[18]
- "Light … Shade … and in between … (in remembrance of Ingeborg Mohr, painter and friend)"; 27 March 2006[19]

The work exists in three distinct versions, listed below in the order in which they were written:

- for piano solo (with alternate chamber ensemble settings), composed 2005–6, first performed by Charles Foreman, at Calgary, Alberta, on 22 January 2008 (hereafter called the piano version);
- for chamber orchestra, completed 15 September 2007, first performed by the Kingston Symphony Orchestra at Kingston, Ontario, on 4 November 2007 (hereafter called the orchestral version);
- an adaptation of the orchestral version for piano solo, prepared by John Beckwith during the autumn of 2007 ; this version has not yet been performed (hereafter called Beckwith's piano adaptation).

The relationship between these three versions is complicated by the fact that Beckwith's manuscript presents the following title: "Istvan Anhalt, *Four Portraits from Memory* piano solo version, edited by John Beckwith," suggesting that the document represents *the* version for solo piano. In a short preface to his manuscript, Beckwith explains:

This edition originated in a suggestion to the composer after my sight-reading of a copy he kindly sent to me. Though moved by the concept and the intense expression of the work, I found details hard to decipher, the result of problems with his sight (macular degeneration in the left eye) which had plagued Anhalt over a period of some years. I offered to review the score and "correct" dubious values (mainly pitch) by comparing the orchestral version. The task turned out to involve more than mere correction or verification of details: in the orchestral process, Anhalt added dynamic markings, figurations, doublings, and even a few extensions, which had not appeared in the piano solo score. I have tried to render these pianistically as far as possible.[20]

Beckwith was clearly working under the assumption that Anhalt's manuscript of the piano version was an incomplete draft of what had become an orchestral work. Indeed, the fact that the first *Portrait*, written in the winter of 2005, is notated in short score with various instrumental indications certainly reinforces and legitimizes such an interpretation (see plate 19-1).[21]

PLATE 19-1 István Anhalt, *Four Portraits from Memory* (piano version), I, mm. 1–12, with kind permission of the composer.

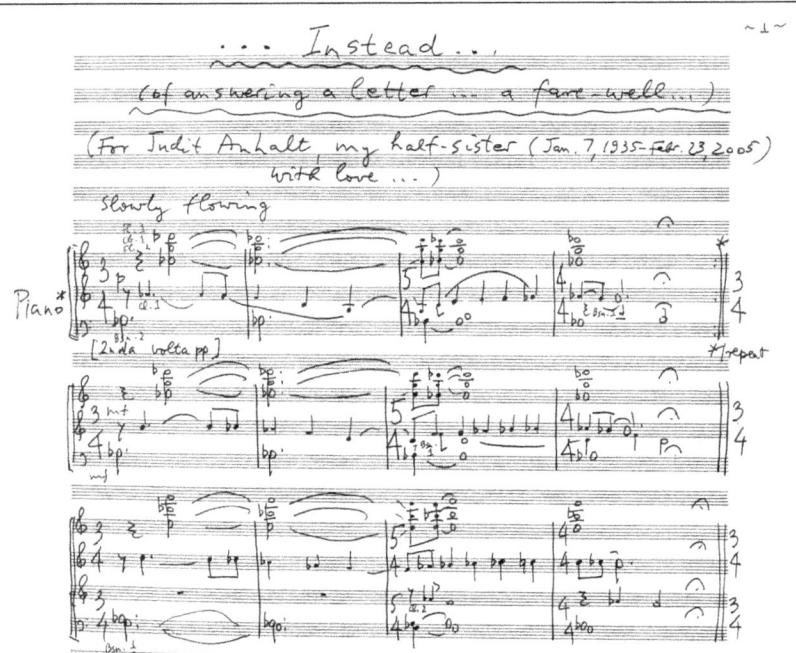

The second *Portrait* was written with the piano in mind (note the pedal indications in the opening bars, see plate 19-2); however, the title page of the manuscript also contains a parenthetical note stating that it can be performed by piano or six strings (2 violins, 1 viola, 2 violoncellos, and 1 double-bass). In fact, the autograph does reveal a polyphonic concept that could easily be set for other instruments.[22]

By contrast, the autographs of the third and fourth *Portraits* contain no mention of alternative settings and are written in a style that is much closer to traditional piano gesture and idiom (see plate 19-3 and plate 19-8).

These examples show that by the winter of 2006 the composer had begun to think of the *Portraits* as part of a cycle of piano pieces, the implication being that the first two *Portraits* were not initially conceived as movements of a larger whole, but rather as individual pieces with differing instrumentation. The single date at the end of the orchestral version (15 September 2006) indicates that what had once been self-standing pieces were now clearly movements of a unified work. However, as shall be shown below, the composer seems to have continued to think of the work as both

PLATE 19-2 István Anhalt, *Four Portraits from Memory* (piano version), II, mm. 1–28, with kind permission of the composer.

a four-movement whole and as a collection of separate pieces even as he was completing the orchestral version in the fall of 2007.

During the summer of 2007 Anhalt agreed that the first performance of the piano version would take place at Calgary. The work was magnificently performed by Charles Foreman on 22 January 2008 as part of the opening recital for the Symposium "Centre and Periphery, Roots and Exile: Interpreting the Music of István Anhalt and György Kurtág." In the fall of 2007, Foreman received copies of all three versions. In consultation with Anhalt, Foreman chose to base his performance on the piano version as it exists in the composer's original manuscript. As noted above, the three versions can be clearly distinguished from one another. In Anhalt's piano version, the last two *Portraits* are shorter than the same movements in the orchestral version, as well as those in the Beckwith piano adaptation, which are identical to the orchestral version: *Portrait* III, the piano version is 110 bars, the orchestral version 112 bars; *Portrait* IV, the piano version is 115 bars, the orchestral version 132 bars. We know that in late 2007 Anhalt did not consider the piano version to be a preliminary draft,

PLATE 19-3 István Anhalt, *Four Portraits from Memory* (piano version), IV, mm. 1–26, with kind permission of the composer.

but rather a version in its own right, independent of the orchestral version because of a correction made to the piano version that the composer enclosed in a letter to this author dated 10 September 2007.

The manuscript shown in plate 19-4 corrects the end of *Portrait* III by providing the penultimate bar that is missing in the initial manuscript of this work (compare plate 19-4 with the last four bars of plate 19-5). Of interest here is what Anhalt *did not* change. If we compare bars 102–3 of the piano version with bars 102–5 of the orchestral version (compare plates 19-5 and 19-6) we note that the orchestral version is expanded by two bars so as to make better use of the sustaining capability of the ensemble. If Anhalt had considered the orchestral version to be the definitive version of the work, he would surely have changed bars 102–3 of the piano version too. As one would expect, Beckwith's adaptation corresponds exactly to the orchestral version (compare plates 19-6 and 19-7).

Plate 19-4 István Anhalt, *Four Portraits from Memory* (piano version), III, correction mm. 107–10, with kind permission of the composer.

Plate 19-5 István Anhalt, *Four Portraits from Memory* (piano version), III, mm. 98–109, with kind permission of the composer.

PLATE 19-6 István Anhalt, *Four Portraits from Memory* (orchestral version), III, mm. 98–112, with kind permission of the composer.

PLATE 19-7 István Anhalt, *Four Portraits from Memory*, adaptation of the orchestral version for piano by John Beckwith, III, mm. 99–112, published with kind permission of both István Anhalt and John Beckwith.

In his letter accompanying the manuscript correction of *Portrait* III, Anhalt wrote, "The enclosed correction in the 'Four Portraits from Memory' occurs at the end of the 3rd piece." In the same letter he also referred to the fourth movement.[23] The choice of words suggests that in September 2007, the work existed in two quite different forms: as a four-movement orchestral work and as a cycle of piano pieces.[24]

Anhalt was not able to be present at the concert in which the piano version received its first performance. However, on hearing the archival recording he was impressed not only with the quality of Foreman's performance but with the work itself. In a letter to Foreman, Anhalt wrote, "It [Foreman's performance captured in the archival recording] is breathtakingly beautiful; poetic, mysterious, full of stunning detail. You, truly joined me as a 'co-creator' with this performance."[25] Foreman's performance clearly provided more than a particularly successful interpretation. Indeed, it should be understood as something akin to musical midwifery in the sense that it convinced the composer that his piano version, if not superior to the orchestral version, was at least of equal status to it and to Beckwith's adaptation.[26]

Portrait III: The Analysis of Compositional Technique versus the Study of Aesthetic Qualities

The initial 56 bars of *Portrait* III can be understood as forming a self-contained unit, marked by a double bar and a change in time signature at bar 57. This first part of the piece is subdivided into four segments: A bars 1–14, B bars 15–22, C bars 23–35, D bars 36–56 (see plate 19-8). Tempo indications, pitch, and rhythm distinguish the first three segments from the fourth. The tempo indication at the beginning is "Unhurriedly and gently," which changes to "Even slower" at bar 36. Anhalt's use of harmony also changes radically at the beginning of segment D. Segments A, B, and C are dominated by an acciaccatura motive and statically repeated dissonant chords in which major sevenths, minor seconds, minor ninths, as well as diminished and augmented octaves predominate. At bar 36 the jolting motion of the acciaccatura motive gives way to an even pulsation in eighth notes. The harmony begins to move, oscillating between E flat and D flat, and abruptly becomes remarkably consonant.

The first four segments are embedded in overlapping mirror symmetrical structures that present Golden Section proportions.[27] The number of quarter notes contained in the four segments is 112.[28] The Golden Section of this number occurs at quarter note 69 ($112 \times .618 = 69$), which falls just one quarter note short of the beginning of segment D (bar 35 first beat). Consequently, segments A, B, and C constitute the greater part (minus one beat) and segment D the lesser part of a Golden Section. However if the same operation is undertaken in the opposite direction we find that the lesser part of the Golden Section falls exactly on the last quarter note of segment B. Thus, in terms of their length, segments A + B and segment D form an almost exact mirror symmetrical structure around segment C (see example 19-1).[29]

Had he been able to examine *Portrait* III, Ernő Lendvai, who first applied the proportional method presented above to Béla Bartók's work, might well have noted the polar opposition between the angular dissonance and the static use of harmony in segments A, B, and C compared with the remarkably consonant harmonic progressions of segment D. As Rachel Beckles Willson points out, Lendvai employed the Gold Section proportions to divide compositions and movements into positive and negative regions: chromatic versus diatonic structures, asymmetry versus periodicity in phrase structure, a proportional versus an acoustic system of harmonic organization, and so forth.[30] He would no doubt have also recognized other Bartókian traits. For example, many of the chords in segment B

PLATE 19-8 István Anhalt, *Four Portraits from Memory* (piano version), III, mm. 1–63, with kind permission of the composer.

EXAMPLE 19-1 István Anhalt, *Four Portraits from Memory* (piano version), III, formal divisions of the first segment of *Portrait* III, mm. 1–56.

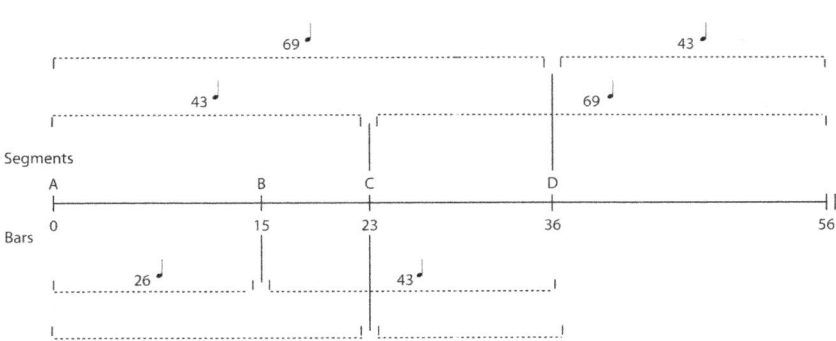

employ simultaneous major and minor thirds (see bars 15–22 in plate 19-8). In all cases, the major third is systematically in the bass voice and the minor third in an upper voice, a characteristic aspect of the so-called "Alpha" chord that Lendvai observed in Bartók's music.[31]

When confronted with the above data extracted from the autograph score, the composer wrote that when he composed *Portrait* III, the Golden Section "was not at all present (at least not consciously) in my mind."[32] This statement was tested against the source material conserved in the István Anhalt Fonds (Library and Archives Canada). With regard to *Portrait* III, the Anhalt Fonds contains 14 half-sheets of staff paper (28 cm wide and approximately 22 cm long) and 4 full sheets (28 by 43.2 cm).[33] The half-sheets and one full sheet contain sketches; the remaining three full sheets present a rough draft of *Portrait* III. This material shows neither explicit reference to the Golden Section nor any mathematical calculations. The rough draft is very close to the fair copy: it contains the same musical material organized in similar sections, though differences in the number of bars per section do occur. For example, between the writing of the rough draft and the fair copy, Anhalt added twelve bars to the first part of the piece: rough draft 44 bars, fair copy 56 bars. Of interest here is the fact that the proportional division of the first part, established between segments A, B, and C on the one hand and D on the other, also obtains in the rough draft. The Golden Section of the first part falls on bar 27 ($44 \times .618 = 27$), which lies just one bar before the beginning of segment D as identified in the fair copy: note the double bar following bar

27 in the draft, indicating that at this stage of the compositional process, bar 27 marked the end of a segment (see plate 19-9).

That the same proportional relationship should obtain in both the draft and the fair copy and that it occurs in two different sets of bar numbers suggests that this aspect of the piece has not been accidentally read into the work by the analyst. The relationship is clearly part of the piece. Whether the composer achieved this result intuitively or consciously is another question. The sources provide no evidence that the composer was counting the number of bars, suggesting that the proportions may well have been intuitively felt, rather than consciously calculated.[34] The working documents also show that *Portrait* III was written in just nine days (10–18 February 2006). During this relatively short period of time, Anhalt appears to have written out the piece from beginning to end with little or no pre-compositional calculations or planning. Of the 14 half sheets containing sketch material 12 are numbered and appear to identify the order in which the pages were used. They open a fascinating window on Anhalt's compositional technique at this late stage in his career. On the first numbered page, the musical ideas of sections A and B respectively are clearly present (see plate 19-10). In both cases Anhalt appears to have conceived these ideas as musical blocks—that is, as static elements with which these sections would be constructed. Like the mature sculptor, Anhalt seems to be forging his musical material based on techniques gleaned from a lifetime of experience, and it is thus entirely possible that the relationships identified in the autograph were in fact worked out in a burst of intensive and spontaneous compositional activity. To paraphrase Marshall McLuhan, the incantatory atmosphere that one finds throughout the *Four Portraits from Memory* is closer to "the magical world of the ear" than "the neutral world of the eye."[35]

But what do the proportional divisions and other stylistic traits of this piece tell us? On the one hand they lead the student of this music back to Anhalt's musical place of origin, Hungary. There is of course nothing intrinsically Hungarian about Golden Section proportion in art and music. From the compositions of Claude Debussy and Erik Satie to those of Karlheinz Stockhausen and John Chowning, the Golden Section, as well as its arithmetic expression in the Fibonacci series, has been observed in the works of numerous composers besides Bartók. Furthermore, Anhalt left Hungary before Lendvai published his findings.[36] Finally, it is also true that there is no mention of Lendvai or his theory in the three major published sources of Anhalt's musical thought: *Alternative Voices*, *Pathways and Memory*, and *Eagle Minds*. Nonetheless, it is inconceivable that he could have

PLATE 19-9 István Anhalt, *Four Portraits from Memory* (piano version), III, draft, Library and Archives Canada, MUS164/2006–10 (Accession)/47, with kind permission of the composer and of Library and Archives Canada.

PLATE 19-10 István Anhalt, *Four Portraits from Memory* (piano version), III, sketch, Library and Archives Canada, MUS164/2006–10 (Accession)/47, with kind permission of the composer and of Library and Archives Canada.

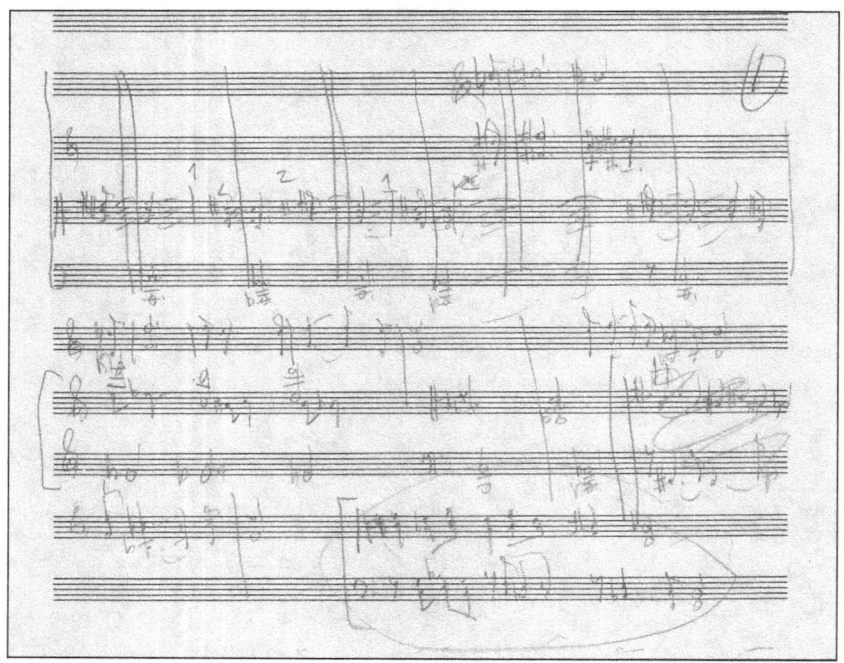

been unaware of Lendvai's findings[37] and of the controversies that accompanied their publication, both in Hungary and abroad.[38] Also, given the fact that *Portrait* III looks back on a friendship that began during the war in Hungary, it seems appropriate that the music should contain traces of musical styles and compositional techniques that can be related to that place. On the other hand, the proportions of the first section provide a rationale for understanding the first 56 bars as a self-contained formal unit. After bar 56 the precise symmetrical relationships that characterize the opening sections of the work disappear. However the music continues to be formed in a series of segments derived from the material of the first part and organized using the principles of balance and symmetry. For example, bars 57–62 are based on a reconfiguration of the pitch material found in bars 1–12 and both segments are made up of exactly 24 quarter notes. Furthermore at bar 63 the appoggiatura motive that dominates the opening segments returns now transposed to D (see plate 19-8). From here until the end we are confronted with similar-sized segments in which material exposed in the first 56 bars comes back in ever-changing forms. Thus, from a precisely calculated point of departure, the second part seems to spread out, ramifying the material presented at the beginning as though the composer were exploring the potential of his initial ideas.

Within this formal envelope, one finds a network of pitch and interval relationships that can be traced back to the opening twelve bars. In bars 7–12 the repeated acciaccatura motive of the first six bars expands to produce a symmetrical tetrachord (E flat, D, B, A sharp; see plate 19-8). This is of course PC-set 4–7, or, if one prefers, a symmetric combination of major and minor thirds within a perfect fourth. A cursory examination of the score reveals that a great deal of the pitch content of *Portrait* III can be derived from this tetrachord, opening the door to a pitch-class analysis of the piece.[39] Such a study would no doubt produce a sophisticated network of relationships. But are these data collection methods (i.e., Allan Forte's pitch-class set analysis or Lendvai's proportional analysis) pertinent to a better understanding of this music? To paraphrase Arnold Schoenberg, while they may be indispensible in understanding *how* the work was composed, do they tell us much about what the work *is*?[40] In reducing the work to a series of measurable units, these analytical approaches may in fact miss or distort those qualities that Anhalt found so compelling in Foreman's performance. From this perspective, the four-note pitch-class set can also be understood as a three-note musical gesture or motive consisting of a large downward movement (the diminished fourth or major third) followed by a smaller interval in contrary motion (the minor third) (see bars 7–12, plate 19-8). One finds numerous examples of this type of gesture in the piece as well. Reading the pitch material in this way creates a tangible link between *Portrait* III and the nineteenth-century character piece. According to Carl Dahlhaus, the hallmark of Romantic piano music is the pregnant and telling motive that sets in motion the musical development and, by remaining in the ear, imparts unity to a piece.[41] Like "Les Sphinxes" of Robert Schumann's *Carnival*, Op. 9, Anhalt's motive and its variants provide *Portrait* III with a tissue of structural relationships out of which its poetic content emerges. We know that the poetic and the mysterious are an integral part of the work because according to Anhalt this is precisely what Foreman was able to compellingly present in his performance of *Four Portraits from Memory*.

The category of the "poetic in music" has remained elusive since Ludwig Tieck identified it as the central idea of Romantic aesthetics in his *Phantasien über die Kunst* in 1799. Schumann sought to define this category negatively by contrasting it with the prosaic: music that "subordinated itself to extra musical purposes that endangered its metaphysical worth or wandered off into empty virtuosity (whether compositional or interpretative) or made itself dependent on programs that provoked petty tone painting."[42] In his *Four Portraits*, Anhalt does not indulge in what Schumann called the merely mechanical. None of the *Portraits* presents trivial displays of external virtuosity. They are also not tied down by specific programs or by obvious musical allusions and quotations. On the contrary, taken individually or as a group, the *Portraits* constitute "a world within itself," as Tieck would have said, and present an example of an autonomous work of absolute music produced in the early twenty-first century.[43]

Music as an Enactment of Remembrance

Memory and remembrance can be related to the third *Portrait* on a number of intersecting levels. First, according to Anhalt, the compositional process was worked out in his mind. The page records what the composer's memory and imagination provided him in terms of ideas, shapes, and gestures that were caught in the act of writing. Second, the compositional technique contains traces of the past: his Hungarian past (the chromatic harmony and symmetric proportions) and the broader past of Western music culture (the nineteenth-century character piece). Third and most important for the composer, each of the four *Portraits* is about death and bereavement. Thus, though the third *Portrait* should be understood as an autonomous work of absolute music, the piece does not lose itself in "tönend bewegte Formen."[44] Rather, in accordance with Schumann's concept of poetic music, it reaches out to the extra-musical world through purely musical means.

As noted above, *Portrait* III opens with a series of rigidly repeated musical gestures organized in groups of three (see the double bars and the fermatas marked "Long" at bars 3 and 6 respectively in plate 19-8). Though this is the most blatant example among the *Portraits*, all four contain similarly repetitive gestures at the outset: see the four-bar frame at the beginning of *Portrait* I (bars 1–4, 5–8, 9–12, etc.) in plate 19-1; the repeated octave Ds in first 14 bars of *Portrait* II in plate 19-2; the repeated minor thirds at the beginning of *Portrait* IV in plate 19-3. Static textures similar to those found at the beginning of *Portrait* III can be found at the beginning of other compositions from Anhalt's late work, notably in the opening bars of *SparkskrapS* (1987), during which we hear thirteen upward leaps of a minor ninth (G-A flat). In his interpretation of this section of

SparkskrapS, William Benjamin observes that it brings to mind "an ancient ceremony in which the Divine is invoked."[45] This observation rings true. In *Alternative Voices*, Anhalt noted that in certain non-Western religious rituals, namely the *nembutsu* of Chinese Buddhism in India and the *dhikr* practices of the Sufi orders of Islam, repeated vocal phrases or mantras are used as a means to achieve mystical understanding through repetition, creating "a state of consciousness which tends to keep down all the ordinary functions of the mind for the purpose of acquiring a most significant insight into the nature of Reality."[46]

The *Portraits* are not so much recollections of individuals as musical representations of commemoration. The ritual-like repetition at the beginning, which one could describe as an instrumental mantra, sets off a process by which the deceased is memorialized. The *Portraits* are musical enactments of memory in which the idea of the deceased is transformed into a kind of personal myth.[47] Within the context of Anhalt's late work as a whole, this aspect of the *Four Portraits from Memory* should be understood not only as a personal gesture of commemoration (as important as this must be for the composer). In *Alternative Voices*, Anhalt observed that the meditative practices that began to be used as models by young composers during the 1960s and 1970s should be understood as the re-emergence of repetition as a central feature in music.[48] At the time, he felt that there was both a cultural and a physiological explanation for the presence of repetitive techniques in the mystical practices of non-Western cultures and certain forms of contemporary music. He believed that research would reveal a shared experience between these two forms of activity, both of which create a psychological "shift from the time-binding, verbal, linear mode of thought into a timeless, oceanic gestalt."[49] If *Alternative Voices* can be understood as a theoretical elaboration of an aesthetic program, then the revitalization of Western art music through a reinforcement of its expressive potential is surely one of the primary goals. *Four Portraits from Memory* is clearly an attempt to achieve this goal.

Notes

1 Tia DeNora, *After Adorno: Rethinking Music Sociology* (Cambridge and New York: Cambridge University Press, 2003), 81.
2 Umberto Eco, *The Open Work*, trans. Anna Cancogni (Cambridge, MA: Harvard University Press, 1989), 163.
3 See, for example, Alan Gillmor, "Echoes of Time and the River," in *Taking a Stand: Essays in Honour of John Beckwith*, ed. Timothy J. McGee (Toronto: University of Toronto Press, 1995), 15–44.

4   Anhalt to Sallis, 18 April 2008. Gordon E. Smith reverses the order in which Anhalt received these two commissions. Anhalt's letter cited here contradicts this information. See Gordon E. Smith, "The Kingston Years (1971–present)," in *Istvan Anhalt: Pathways and Memory*, ed. Robin Elliott and Gordon E. Smith (Montreal and Kingston: McGill-Queen's University Press, 2001), 74–75.

5   Since 1987 Anhalt wrote seven orchestral works: *Simulacrum* (1987), *SparkskrapS* (1987), *Sonance•Resonance (Welche Töne?)* (1989), *Twilight~Fire (Baucis' and Philomen's Feast)* (2001), *The Tents of Abraham (A Mirage-Midrash)* (2003), *... the timber of those times ... (a theogony)* (2005), and the orchestral version of *Four Portraits from Memory* (2005–7). Between *Sonance•Resonance* and *Twilight~Fire* Anhalt wrote four works: a string quartet movement *Doors ... shadows (Glenn Gould in Memory)* (1992); two operas *Traces (Tikkun)* (1995) and *Millennial Mall (Lady Diotima's Walk)* (1999); and a collection of pieces for recorder *Galambabmalag: The Halloween Witch and 24 Other Easy Pieces for Recorder (Solos and Duets)* (1996).

6   The earliest mentioned composition is Arnold Schoenberg's *Pierrot Lunaire*, Op. 21 (1912). Among the latest are R. Murray Schafer's *Ra* (1983) and Anhalt's second opera *Winthrop* (1983). See "List of Compositions," in István Anhalt, *Alternative Voices: Essays on Contemporary Vocal and Choral Composition* (Toronto: University of Toronto Press, 1984), 291–99.

7   R. Murray Schafer, *The Tuning of the World* (New York: Knopf, 1977). The book has recently been republished as *The Soundscape: Our Sonic Environment and the Tuning of the World* (Rochester, VT: Destiny, 1994).

8   Anhalt, *Alternative Voices*, ix.

9   Austin Clarkson, "Between the Keys: Istvan Anhalt Writing on Music," in *Pathways and Memory*, 326.

10 In 1985 Joseph Kerman outlined his vision of a critical approach to the study of music, in opposition to the positivism that still reigned supreme in North America: see Joseph Kerman, *Musicology* (London: Fontana Press, 1985); published in the United States as *Contemplating Music: Challenges to Musicology* (Harvard University Press, 1985).

11 In her Afterword to the English translation of Attali's book, Susan McClary underscored the fact that his book coincided with the emergence of alternative practices and theories of music (what would later come to be known as new musicology). Susan McClary, "Afterword: The Politics of Silence and Sound," in Jacques Attali, *Noise: The Political Economy of Music*, trans. Brian Massumi, Theory and History of Literature, vol. 16 (Minneapolis: University of Minnesota Press, 1985), 156–58. Attili's book was originally published as Jacques Attali, *Bruits: Essai sur l'économie politique de la musique* (Paris: Presses universitaires de France, 1977).

12 Clarkson, "Between the Keys," 325–26.

13 Ibid., 331.

14 Alan M. Gillmor ed., *Eagle Minds: Selected Correspondence of Istvan Anhalt and George Rochberg (1961–2005)* (Waterloo: Wilfrid Laurier University Press, 2007), 155.

15 Anhalt, *Alternative Voices*, 266–68.

16 Judith and István Anhalt shared the same father. Following the war, she remained in Budapest where she made her living as an office worker and a tour guide. The two had last spent an extended period together in 1966, when she and her mother (István's stepmother) visited Anhalt and his family in Montreal. István Anhalt, "About *Four Portraits from Memory*," unpublished typescript dated 16 June 2007, 2. For a thorough presentation of Anhalt's childhood, upbringing, war experiences, and early career in Budapest, see Robin Elliott, "Life in Europe (1919–49)," in *Pathways and Memory*, 3–32.

17 Anhalt met the American composer George Rochberg at an International Conference of Composers held in Stratford, Ontario, during the summer of 1960 and for the next forty-five years they corresponded. For a survey of this friendship and the correspondence, see Alan M. Gillmor, "Introduction," in *Eagle Minds*, xiii–xliii.

18 András Kelemen was Anhalt's closest friend during their time in a forced-labour brigade in Hungary (1942–44). Anhalt recalls that on one occasion Kelemen help saved his life. After the war, Kelemen pursued a distinguished career as a physician in Romania. During the 1990s, he moved to Montreal to be with his son who was suffering from an incurable illness. In 2003 he contacted Anhalt and as a result the two were able to renew their friendship that lasted until the end of Kelemen's life. Anhalt, "About *Four Portraits from Memory*," unpublished typescript, 4.

19 The dedicatee of the fourth *Portrait* is the Canadian painter Ingeborg Mohr. Born in Austria in 1921, she moved to Canada with her husband and three children in 1955. Examples of her work are found in collections conserved by Trent University, the University of Toronto, and the National Gallery of Canada. She died in 2004. (I am grateful to Sara Keane of the Royal Canadian Academy of the Arts for providing me with this information.) The Anhalts' home has several of her paintings. Of one of these, Anhalt wrote the following: "[It shows] a double field of grey and red, between which hovers, precariously, a whitish 'quasi-body' as if suspended in time and space. It is an enigmatic, yet suggestive, painting which reminds one of Ingeborg's favourite poets: T.S. Elliot and Paul Celan. She has worked almost 'to the end.' Her unique smile and expressive silences remain unforgettably in memory." Anhalt, "About *Four Portraits from Memory*," unpublished typescript, 5.

20 John Beckwith, [Preface] to Istvan Anhalt, *Four Portraits from Memory*, piano solo version edited by John Beckwith, unpublished score, 2007, n.p. Permission to publish this text was provided by the author.

21 The autograph of the piano version indicates that the first movement can also be performed by three flutes, two oboes, two clarinets, and two bassoons.

22 Anhalt has since withdrawn the chamber versions of *Portraits* I and II.

23 Anhalt to Sallis, 10 September 2007.

24 This interpretation is further reinforced by the discrepancies between the piano and orchestral versions of *Portrait* IV. In this case the composer added 17 bars and these additions are spread throughout the whole piece. Thus, by the time he began writing out the orchestral score of *Portrait* IV, Anhalt was no longer orchestrating a draft (as he appears to have been doing with *Portraits* I and II). Rather, he was recomposing what had been a complete idea.

25 Anhalt to Foreman, 20 February 2008.
26 Within this context, Beckwith's adaptation should not be understood as an example of a colleague "improving" his friend's music (bringing to mind Nikolai Rimsky-Korsakov's "improvements" to Modest Mussorgsky's *Boris Godunov*). On the contrary, three versions exist because the composer's idea of his work was still evolving in late 2007.
27 The Golden Section divides a line unequally such that the ratio of the smaller part to the larger part is the same as that of the larger part to the whole.
28 The first part of *Portrait* III (bars 1–56) contains no less than 27 fermatas (see plate 19-8). Consequently measuring in continuous quarter notes has nothing to do with the listener's experience of this section of the piece. This method of measuring is nevertheless legitimate, focusing on the composition rather than on the reception of the music.
29 Furthermore, the same mirror symmetrical structure, also based on Golden Section proportions, can be obtained with the segments A, B, and C, again measured in quarter notes. In this case the Golden Section divisions correspond exactly with the end of segment A and the beginning of segment C.
30 Rachel Beckles Willson, *Ligeti, Kurtág and Hungarian Music during the Cold War* (Cambridge and New York: Cambridge University Press, 2007), 57–58. For a full presentation of this aspect of Bartók's music, see Ernő Lendvai, *Bártók's Style*, trans. Paul Merrick and Judit Pokoly (Budapest: Akkord, 1999), 110.
31 Ernő Lendvai, *Bartók and Kodály* (Budapest: Zoltán Kodály Peagogical Institute of Music, 1976), 90–96.
32 Anhalt to Sallis, 18 April 2008.
33 The smaller sheets were halves of the larger sheets that may well have been cut so that the composer could work at the piano.
34 Of course these calculations may well have been made on paper that was then discarded. In ambiguous cases such as these, I am inclined to allow the composer's statement, that he did not consciously calculate these proportions, stand.
35 Marshall McLuhan, *The Gutenberg Galaxy: The Making of Typographic man* (Toronto: University of Toronto Press, 1962), 22.
36 The first publications of Lendvai's analytical and theoretical work with Bartók's music appeared in 1947, the year after Anhalt left Budapest. Ernő Lendvai, "Bartók: As éjszaka zenéje (1926)" [Bartók: The Music of the Night (1926)], *Zenei Szemle* 4 (1947): 216–18. Lendvai's findings concerning the presence and significance of Golden Section proportions in the large-scale structure of works such as the *Sonata for Two Pianos and Percussion* and *Music for Strings, Percussion, and Celeste* appeared for the first time in 1955: Ernő Lendvai, *Bartók stílusa* [Bartók's Style] (Budapest: Zeneműkiadó, 1955). Outside of Hungary, Lendvai's work appeared first in German translation: "Bartók und die Zahl," *Melos* 27 (1960): 327–31. The first English translation of Lendvai's findings was published in 1971: *Béla Bartók. An Analysis of his Music* (London: Kahn and Averill, 1971). Since then English and German translations of his writings have appeared regularly.
37 Anhalt confirmed that he was indeed aware of Lendvai's work, though he added that he "didn't delve into it in any detail." Anhalt to Sallis, 18 April 2008.

38 László Somfai criticized Lendvai's findings, stating that in his examination of Bartók's surviving sketches and autographs, "not a single calculation of the proportions of a composition—with Fibonacci or other numbers—has been discovered." László Somfai, *Béla Bartók: Composition, Concepts and Autograph Scores* (Berkeley: University of California Press, 1996), 81–82. Roy Howat provoked similar protests when he later applied Lendvai's methods to the music of Debussy: Roy Howat, *Debussy in Proportion: A Musical Analysis* (Cambridge and New York: Cambridge University Press, 1983). With regard to Erik Satie's music, see Courtney S. Adams, "Erik Satie and Golden Section Analysis," *Music and Letters* 77/2 (1996): 242–52. For information on Stockhausen's use of the Golden Section and the Fibonacci series, see Robin Maconie, *Other Planets: The Music of Karlheinz Stockhausen* (Lanham: Scarecrow, 2005). Regarding Chowning see Laura Zattra, "'The Assembling of *Stria* by John Chowning: A Philological Investigation," *Computer Music Journal* 31/3 (2007): 50–52.

39 For example the pitch collection used at the beginning of the second part (bar 57) is PC-set 4–7.

40 "I can't utter too many warnings against overrating these analyses, since after all they only lead to what I have always been dead against: seeing how it is *done*; whereas I have always helped people to see what it *is*!" Arnold Schoenberg, *Letters*, ed. Erwin Stein, trans. Eithne Wilkins and Ernst Kaiser (New York: St. Martin's Press, 1965), 164 (Schoenberg's emphasis).

41 Carl Dahlhaus, *Nineteenth-Century Music*, trans. J. Bradford Robinson (Berkeley: University of California Press, 1989), 147.

42 Carl Dahlhaus, *The Idea of Absolute Music*, trans. Roger Lustig (Chicago: University of Chicago Press, 1989), 70.

43 Such an affirmation flies in the face of recent conventional wisdom. According to the few new musicologists *still* among us, the autonomous work was something we were supposed to have left behind sometime in the last century, and yet it continues to produce worry and anxiety to this day. See Richard Taruskin, "Foreword," in Lydia Goehr, *The Imaginary Museum of Musical Works: An Essay in the Philosophy of Music*, revised edition (New York: Oxford University Press, 2007), vii–viii. It may well be that the persistence of this perceived problem in discourse about music and the sustained interest in Schumann's work among composers during the last quarter of the twentieth century are in fact two sides of the same coin.

44 Eduard Hanslick, *Vom Musikalisch-Schönen* (Leipzig: Barth, 1854), 32.

45 William Benjamin, "Alternatives of Voice: Anhalt's Odyssey from Personalized Style to Symbolic Expression," in *Pathways and Memory*, 243.

46 Anhalt, *Alternative Voices*, 180–81.

47 István Anhalt, "On the Way to *Traces*: A Dialogue with the Self," in *Pathways and Memory*, 409.

48 He lists works such as Steve Reich's *Come Out* (1966), Karlheinz Stockhausen's *Stimmung* (1969), and Philip Glass's opera *Satyagraha* (1981). Anhalt, *Alternative Voices*, 181–82.

49 Anhalt, *Alternative Voices*, 182.

Bibliography

Adams, Courtney S. "Erik Satie and Golden Section Analysis." *Music and Letters* 77/2 (1996): 242–52.
Attali, Jacques. *Bruits: Essai sur l'économie politique de la musique*. Paris: Presses universitaires de France, 1977.
Beckles Willson, Rachel. *Ligeti, Kurtág and Hungarian Music during the Cold War*. Cambridge and New York: Cambridge University Press, 2007.
Dahlhaus, Carl. *The Idea of Absolute Music*. Translated by Roger Lustig. Chicago: University of Chicago Press, 1989.
———. *Nineteenth-Century Music*. Translated by J. Bradford Robinson. Berkeley: University of California Press, 1989.
DeNora, Tia. *After Adorno: Rethinking Music Sociology*. Cambridge and New York: Cambridge University Press, 2003.
Eco, Umberto. *The Open Work*. Translated by Anna Cancogni. Cambridge, MA: Harvard University Press, 1989.
Elliott, Robin and Gordon E. Smith, eds. *István Anhalt: Pathways and Memory*. Montreal and Kingston: McGill-Queen's University Press, 2001.
Gillmor Alan M., ed. *Eagle Minds: Selected Correspondence of Istvan Anhalt and George Rochberg (1961–2005)*. Waterloo, ON: Wilfrid Laurier University Press, 2007.
———. "Echoes of Time and the River." In *Taking a Stand: Essays in Honour of John Beckwith*, edited by Timothy J. McGee, 15–44. Toronto: University of Toronto Press, 1995.
Hanslick, Eduard. *Vom Musikalisch-Schönen*. Leipzig: Barth, 1854.
Howat, Roy. *Debussy in Proportion: A Musical Analysis*. Cambridge and New York: Cambridge University Press, 1983.
Kerman, Joseph. *Musicology*. London: Fontana Press, 1985. Published in the United States as *Contemplating Music: Challenges to Musicology*. Cambridge, MA: Harvard University Press, 1985.
Lendvai, Ernő. "Bartók: As éjszaka zenéje (1926)" [Bartók: The Music of the Night (1926)]. *Zenei Szemle* 4 (1947): 216–18.
———. *Bartók and Kodály*. Budapest: Zoltán Kodály Peagogical Institute of Music, 1976.
———. "Bartók und die Zahl." *Melos* 27 (1960): 327–31.
———. *Bartók stílusa* [Bartók's Style]. Budapest: Zeneműkiadó, 1955.
———. *Bártók's Style*. Translated by Paul Merrick and Judit Pokoly. Budapest: Akkord, 1999.
———. *Béla Bartók: An Analysis of His Music*. London: Kahn and Averill, 1971.
Maconie, Robin. *Other Planets: The Music of Karlheinz Stockhausen*. Lanham, MD: Scarecrow Press, 2005.
McClary, Susan. "Afterword. The Politics of Silence and Sound." In Jacques Attali, *Noise: The Political Economy of Music*, translated by Brian Massumi,

Theory and History of Literature vol. 16, 149–58. Minneapolis: University of Minnesota Press, 1985.

McLuhan, Marshall. *The Gutenberg Galaxy: The Making of Typographic Man*. Toronto: University of Toronto Press, 1962.

Mosch, Ulrich. "Zum Formdenken Hans Werner Henzes. Beobachtungen am Particell der 6. Symphonie." In *Quellenstudien II Zwölf Komponisten des 20. Jahrhunderts*, edited by Felix Meyer, 169–204. Winterthur: Amadeus, 1993.

Schafer, R. Murray. *The Tuning of the World*. New York: Knopf, 1977. Republished as *The Soundscape: Our Sonic Environment and the Tuning of the World*. Rochester, VT: Destiny, 1994.

Schoenberg, Arnold. *Letters*. Edited by Erwin Stein. Translated by Eithne Wilkins and Ernst Kaiser. New York: St. Martin's Press, 1965.

Schubert, Giselher and Friedemann Sallis. "Sketches and Sketching." In *A Handbook to Twentieth-Century Musical Sketches*, edited by Patricia Hall and Friedemann Sallis, 5–16. Cambridge and New York: Cambridge University Press, 2004.

Somfai, László. *Béla Bartók: Composition, Concepts and Autograph Scores*. Berkeley: Unviersity of California Press, 1996.

Taruskin, Richard. "Foreword." In Lydia Goehr. *The Imaginary Museum of Musical Works: An Essay in the Philosophy of Music*, revised edition, v–viii. New York: Oxford University Press, 2007.

Zattra, Laura. "The Assembling of *Stria* by John Chowning: A Philological Investigation." *Computer Music Journal* 31/3 (2007): 50–52.

Final Word

TWENTY

On Doubleness and Life in Canada: An Interview with István Anhalt

ROBIN ELLIOTT: Prior to this interview,[1] we both read Lydia Goehr's article "Music and Musicians in Exile: The Romantic Legacy of a Double Life."[2] Perhaps you would like to begin by giving me your initial impressions of what Goehr says in this article.

ISTVÁN ANHALT: Her main point is what she calls, or quotes others as calling, "doubleness."[3] An immigrant composer, when in a new place of residence, experiences a crisis that is characterized by what she calls doubleness. Well, why double? Why not multipleness? A person might have had a complex life, which is not homogeneous; it might have consisted of a number of elements, influences, insights, whatever. So I don't mean to quibble with her use of the word doubleness, but it seems to me that multipleness might be a more appropriate word.

RE: She does use the phrase "more-than-oneness" in this connection ...[4]

IA: Yes, yes, well that I'm much more in agreement with. Another influencing factor, in her case, is her family; especially the three males in her family: the grandfather, Walter, the grand uncle, Rudolf, and the father, Alexander. These were or are all important doers, so her ideas are to a great extent influenced, if not determined, by how her grandfather, for instance, lived a double life as Walter Goehr and George Walter. And even the uncle tried to fit in into his new existence in America by working for the Eastman Kodak Show. But of course the father, Alexander, became the professor of music at Cambridge. In fact, in the year we were there,[5] I remember congratulating him and we spent a very nice evening with Alexander Goehr and his wife. They invited us for dinner and, no surprise for us, he turned out to be a very bright man. He had written an opera, I was working on an opera, and I was also working on *Alternative Voices*. So it was a very interesting evening, but by no means was it any more than just touching on some things, it did not really go very deep. But I came away with very pleasant feelings of an evening well spent, with very generous hosts and so on. So, the other big influence for Lydia is that she is a fourth member of this distinguished family of Goehrs. She admits that she was influenced by that, but beyond her degree of acknowledgement, I understand it to be a very strong determining factor in her life. Or perhaps I should say it is potentially, or might be seen to be, a determining factor, for better or worse. Another important element in her story is the Hollywood syndrome. Hollywood offered income to a number of people and I think even Schoenberg tried to write something for it, if I recall correctly.

RE: Yes, he was approached by a Hollywood producer for a film score, but then he asked for an exorbitant fee, perhaps because he didn't really want to do it, and not surprisingly, the producer wasn't willing to pay the fee. So, nothing came of that project.[6]

IA: So what did Schoenberg do? Schoenberg continued to be Schoenberg, and taught at the University of Southern California for a while, and he retired with a pension of ninety-five dollars. But at least he had a lot of things to sell to libraries; he wasn't starving. So another theme is how these two key figures, Stravinsky and Schoenberg, responded to exile. That's another theme which seemed to loom large in her story, and I think she writes very well about that.

And then there is the Wagner issue. She makes a big deal of what Wagner said, mainly about the Jews. Well, he is not one of my favourite persons; he was not a nice guy, let's face it. He was a genius as a composer, in a way, although I don't think he was the only composer of the late nineteenth century. He was of course a giant, and I think *Die Meistersinger* and *Tristan* are really fabulous achievements. So he is rightfully regarded as one of the giants of the nineteenth century. But I don't think that his politics, his personal loyalties, or his ethics are on the same level of greatness and importance. I think that Lydia Goehr's take on Wagner could have been more nuanced. While giving him credit or acknowledging his enormous achievements, there was another side to Wagner which colours my relationship to him, but I am just only one mind.

RE: How do you see Goehr's comments on doubleness relating to your own experience as a composer during your career in Canada?

IA: I was far from being homogeneous before I became a landed immigrant in Canada upon arriving in Halifax in January 1949; I was pretty much a "multiple" figure in my mind. A survivor of this and a survivor of that. I had very few compositions with me, because I had not yet written very much. First of all there were two whole years during which I didn't touch music. Then I did write a few things in Paris which showed the influence of Bartók, and some influence of Stravinsky, because Nadia Boulanger did her level best to drum Stravinsky into my head. She didn't have a very hard time, I loved Stravinsky. He is one of the giants of the previous century. But by the time I landed in Canada, I was very much interested in Schoenberg. In fact, I was more interested in Schoenberg than I was interested in Stravinsky. Have you heard my Violin Sonata performed by Gisèle Dalbec-Szczesniak and Michel Szczesniak?

RE: I didn't hear the performance in Calgary, but you gave me a compact disc of it, and I have listened to it.

IA: What do you think of it?

RE: The first movement is slower than I imagine it going, but this gives it an elegant wistful quality which I think is very affective. The rest of the performance is more or less as I imagine the work going. It just starts out a little bit more slowly than I had myself thought that it should go. But it is a very convincing performance, beautifully played and very well thought through.

IA: I thought that it was a wonderful performance. I mean, I had to wait for that performance for more than fifty years. And I am very grateful to those players for having achieved that. Now that work was perhaps, in my present-day perception, the most telling of the few chamber music twelve-tone works I have written. And of course there is the Symphony, which is probably the largest thing that I wrote that is strictly twelve-tone, as Bill Benjamin has shown.[7] Well, at one point I thought I had learned enough from working with Schoenberg and his twelve-tone idea, although I don't hear the musical language of the Violin Sonata as being Schoenbergian at all. It is a kind of twelve-tone writing which aims at sonorities that you find also in *Twilight~Fire* or ... *the timber of those times* ...

Coming back to the Goehr book, at one point I simply stopped regarding myself as an immigré composer. I had no first country to hanker back for or to; I just was fascinated by the place where I was living, and tried to learn about the place and I never stopped doing that. And everything that I was writing somehow came out of whatever one remembers from reading, from living here, and having a home right here in Canada. So all the orchestral works, the operas, they all to me are responses to remembering, remembrance, and also to living here and feeling at home here. I don't feel doubleness; I might feel multipleness, but one doesn't have to belabour that. Every single piece of mine, as you know, has a major theme and minor themes. For example, *Sonance•Resonance*, the third work in the first triptych, taps into remembrance and forgetting, and trying to generalize why people want to forget. That is a futile exercise: "I want to forget this memory." The more you want to forget it, the more you have to remember it. *Twilight~Fire*, which I wrote for Beate, taps into another group of concerns. So, cumulatively, all of these contexts and references add up to an account of how one thinks about the world, how one thinks about oneself. Just trying to handle all that as doubleness—well, it seems to me that it is a much more complex thing than that. Goehr might be too influenced by European composers who settled in Hollywood, and how they were influenced by the Hollywood environment. Well I was never anywhere near Hollywood! I went to Montreal, and then came to Kingston. The diversity of how people remember their past, how they make peace with their past, how they can handle things which they are not at peace with, how they see their new environment, these are enormously complex things, and a single word like doubleness doesn't begin to do justice to all the complexity.

RE: There is certainly a focus in exile studies on the German émigré community in Los Angeles because of Thomas Mann, Arnold Schoenberg, Bertolt Brecht, Hanns Eisler, and all those people. But there are two things I think that distinguish the situation in Canada. The first is that there wasn't a large émigré community like the one in California; there were only scattered individuals rather than a community. And the second is that there wasn't a very strong musical culture in Canada, popular or otherwise, to be influenced by. In the United States you did have Hollywood and the popular music industry, which were forces to be reckoned with. Perhaps in some respects this was the antithesis of the traditions that these composers were bringing with them from Europe. In Canada we didn't have a popular music industry, or popular music success stories. We were obviously influenced by American popular music as much as, or more than, most other countries. But at the same time we were aware that it was happening in the United States rather than in Canada. Do you think that those two factors, the lack of a community of émigrés and the lack of a strong musical culture to react against influenced the experience of European émigré composers in Canada?

IA: Yes, I think you are right. I should add one further element to my way of reading Goehr's text, and that concerns the figure of Kurt Weill. Weill, who wanted to fit in, and successfully did fit in, overstated the fact by saying, "Yes, I became a successful American Broadway composer." Well he remained Kurt Weill, in a way a Berlin composer, although I am not negating Weill's American career.

RE: In terms of the American musical, my perception is that Kurt Weill does not have the kind of prominence that Jerome Kern, Irving Berlin, Richard Rodgers, and perhaps half a dozen other composers do. Could I come back to your self-image; do you regard yourself as a Canadian composer?

IA: I regard myself either as a Canadian composer or as a composer living and working happily in Canada. And I hope that cumulatively everything I wrote ends up as part of a composite Canadian musical statement. Now, I should tell you about one anecdote which belongs here. I had a francophone colleague visiting me, and he and I were sitting in the garden, and talking about music, and music in this country. And that person, to my amazement, said, "What Canadian music? There's no such thing as Canadian music. There's Quebec music, but Canadian music, what is that?" It was a non-starter for him. I was astounded. Harry Somers, John Beckwith, Murray Schafer, I said, just to mention a few, were trying to put on paper selected topics and trying to express them in a certain way. He did not think that they share some common attitudes. I was shocked because he was questioning my self-perception. I was trying to be one voice of several in music in this country which cumulatively will add up at one point to something that we can call "Canadian music." These works were, perhaps, more likely to happen in Canada than anywhere else.

RE: I suspect that this composer was a member of the Canadian Music Centre, and his music was broadcast by the Canadian Broadcasting Corporation, and supported by the Canada Council, and performed by orchestras or other musicians across Canada, so if that's not Canadian music, it's hard to know why it isn't or why it shouldn't be.

IA: When the person made reference to these sentiments, unfortunately, the Quebec separatist situation was quite virulent, and he might have been influenced by that. To bring matters home, so to speak, the Kingston Symphony is a local, modest-sized orchestra, but it took me on, at the initiative of Glen Fast, its director, and by now has performed four of my pieces. This made an enormous contribution to my understanding of my ongoing activity as a composer working in this country.

RE: If we could go back to that Quebec composer's comment, just briefly, it does have a slight resonance with the second half of Lydia Goehr's article, when she discusses Wagner, who posited this entity called German music, to which some composers belonged and others didn't, and then he positioned Jewish composers as not belonging to German music. That is one potential danger in saying "This is Canadian music": well then, what's not Canadian music? And this francophone composer saying, "Well there's no such thing as Canadian music," is one way of getting around that problem, but perhaps too drastic a solution. It is always difficult, though, when you try to equate a nation with a musical culture. Musical culture comes out of individuals, and they may take on certain national characteristics to some extent, but then the question of who is included and who is not included does potentially become problematic. I think that maybe this composer was purposefully problematizing the question of Canadian music.

IA: Well, let me ask you this question, Robin. You know as well as anybody else what I have written in music and about music. On a number of occasions, you wrote very appreciative, in fact, probably too appreciative words about me and I was very grateful for that—who would not be? Do you see a connection between my entire musical activity, including writing music and writing words about music, and teaching—because we have to make a living—and this country? Are you at peace if I say that I regard myself as part of the cultural environment of this country?

RE: I like your idea of multipleness, because when I think of you and your relationship to music and my relationship to you, multipleness springs to mind. I first knew you as a neighbour, when you came to a garden party at my parents' invitation back in 1973; you were a neighbour who lived up the road. I also thought of you as a professor at Queen's, as a friend, subsequently, a colleague, a guide, a composer, as someone of Hungarian-Jewish background who has done most of his composing in Canada. I never really thought of you as an émigré, I guess because I never got a signal from you that you considered yourself to be an émigré, so I never considered you an émigré. I just thought of you as someone who was born elsewhere but is living in Canada now, just like my parents, who were born elsewhere and are living in Canada now. I don't think of my parents as émigrés, although they were both born in England. I thought of them as people who were born elsewhere but are living in Canada now, and contributing to the best of their ability to creating a Canada for everybody. Through your teaching, your composition, your writing about music, all of these different aspects, friend, neighbour, teacher, Canadian composer, are all mixed into one. If I were to be rigorous about it, and think, "Let's take all of István Anhalt's output as a composer, just to stick with the composition side of the equation, and let's make a hierarchy from the most Canadian to the least Canadian pieces," well that is an inherently ridiculous kind of thing to attempt to do. Obviously in some pieces you've engaged very closely with the background, traditions, and heritage of Canada, such as *La Tourangelle* ...

IA: Even *Winthrop*.

RE: Even *Winthrop*, as you pointed out, because the New England Puritan mentality had a very strong influence on the Canadian psyche.

IA: Even *Traces*, which is about an immigrant's predicaments. And *Millennial Mall*, which is about living in this commercial culture of ours and how to cope with that.

RE: But then would that make the Violin Sonata a less Canadian piece? I would never think of measuring the Canadianness of a piece in these terms. I'm just interested in all music that has been made, composed, played, received, conceived, and appreciated in Canada as contributing somehow to what it means to be Canadian and a musician or a music lover in Canada.

IA: If someone said, "Anhalt probably can be regarded as having expressed something important related to Canada," but then so does John Beckwith, and Harry Somers, and Murray Schafer, just to mention the usual suspects.

RE: Well let's take John Beckwith. He would be one of the first people to come to mind as being a "Canadian composer," but his situation is much more complex than that. He is a Toronto composer, a University of Toronto composer, a Victoria-born composer; he's somebody who has very strong feelings about belonging to North America, and of that being distinct from Europe. And he loves to travel the world. He has taken in many influences; he was in China last month, on his third trip to that country. He loves to learn about the world.

IA: He and his daughter Robin were here yesterday and we heard quite a bit about his trip to China. But it means he is a Canadian composer his way. If I'm a Canadian composer, I'm a Canadian composer my way. So Lydia Goehr's article touches varied points. Sometimes not quite giving justice to the complexity of things, and sometimes selective in a way which is not difficult to trace because of family relationships and so on. One would have to put it side by side with all the other ways of regarding life stories and productive activities of people who travelled and settled and resettled and unsettled and resettled again. One has to take into account the fact that I left Hungary because I wanted to liberate myself—I was not in exile. I never said to myself, "I'm going into exile." I left a place where I really could not feel at home, and then I found myself at home in this new place.

Notes

1 This conversation with István Anhalt took place at his home, 274 Johnson Street in Kingston, Ontario, in the early afternoon of Sunday, 6 July 2008. Vincent Spilchuk provided a verbatim transcription of the interview, which was then edited by both Robin Elliott and István Anhalt.
2 Lydia Goehr, "Music and Musicians in Exile: The Romantic Legacy of a Double Life," in *The Quest for Voice: On Music, Politics, and the Limits of Philosophy*, the 1997 Ernest Bloch Lectures (Oxford: Clarendon Press, 1998), 174–207. The essay is reprinted in a somewhat modified form in *Driven into Paradise: The Musical Migration from Nazi Germany to the United States*, ed. Reinhold Brinkmann and Christoph Wolff (Berkeley: University of California Press, 1999), 66–91. Lydia Goehr is the granddaughter of Walter Goehr (1903–60), the great-niece of the pianist Rudolf Goehr (1906–81), and the daughter of the composer Alexander Goehr (b. 1932). Walter Goehr was born in Berlin and studied with Schoenberg before fleeing to Britain in 1933, taking with him his wife Laelia, a pianist, and his son Alexander, who was just a few months old at the time. Lydia Goehr was appointed Professor of Philosophy at Columbia University in 1995, three years after the publication of her much-discussed book *The Imaginary Museum of Musical Works: An Essay in the Philosophy of Music* (Oxford: Clarendon Press, 1992; rev. ed. 2007).
3 Goehr, "Music and Musicians in Exile" (1998), cites the philosopher Ernest Bloch's 1939 article "Disrupted Language, Disrupted Culture," in which "he dismissed an exile's suffering from *divided* loyalties and embraced an exile's

celebrating his *double* loyalties" (197, original emphasis). Goehr notes that the condition of doubleness could have "musical, historical, aesthetic, and metaphysical" manifestations (178). Specifically in music, doubleness challenges and probes the limits of two fundamental assumptions: "that music is a language and, relatedly, that creativity is causally or otherwise connected to the condition either of exile or of home" (181). Although her doubleness thesis has philosophical implications that are linked to the ideas of paradox and dialectical reasoning, in its simplest form doubleness relates to the manifold ways that exiled musicians "lived both 'homed' and 'foreign' lives" (182).

4   "The doubling thesis so extended allows us to see ... that *it is less the 'twoness' than the 'more-than-oneness'* that sustains the progressive tendency" (ibid., 203; original emphasis).

5   István and Beate Anhalt spent the 1976–77 academic year in England, and during this time István Anhalt attended Professor J.L.M. Trimm's classes in articulatory phonetics and prosody at Cambridge University. Alexander Goehr was appointed Professor of Music at Cambridge University in 1976 and held this position until 1999.

6   See Sabine M. Feisst, "Arnold Schoenberg and the Cinematic Art," *Musical Quarterly* 83/1 (spring 1999): 93–113, for a complete account of Schoenberg's dealings with Hollywood.

7   See William E. Benjamin, "Alternatives of Voice: Anhalt's Odyssey from Personalized Style to Symbolic Expression," in *Istvan Anhalt: Pathways and Memory*, ed. Robin Elliott and Gordon E. Smith (Montreal and Kingston: McGill-Queen's University Press, 2001), 164–307.

Bibliography

Benjamin, William E. "Alternatives of Voice: Anhalt's Odyssey from Personalized Style to Symbolic Expression." In *Istvan Anhalt: Pathways and Memory*, edited by Robin Elliott and Gordon E. Smith, 164–307. Montreal and Kingston: McGill-Queen's University Press, 2001.

Bloch, Ernst. "Disrupted Language—Disrupted Culture." *Direction* 2/6 (1939): 16–17, 36.

Feisst, Sabine M. "Arnold Schoenberg and the Cinematic Art." *Musical Quarterly* 83/1 (Spring 1999): 93–113.

Goehr, Lydia. *The Imaginary Museum of Musical Works: An Essay in the Philosophy of Music*. Oxford: Clarendon Press, 2007. First published 1992.

———. "Music and Musicians in Exile: The Romantic Legacy of a Double Life." In *The Quest for Voice: On Music, Politics, and the Limits of Philosophy*, the 1997 Ernest Bloch Lectures, 174–207. Oxford: Clarendon Press, 1998.

———. "Music and Musicians in Exile: The Romantic Legacy of a Double Life." In *Driven into Paradise: The Musical Migration from Nazi Germany to the United States*, edited by Reinhold Brinkmann and Christoph Wolff, 66–91. Berkeley: University of California Press, 1999.

THE CONTRIBUTORS

István Anhalt
István Anhalt, the dedicatee of this volume, was born in Budapest in 1919 and emigrated to Canada in 1949 to become a faculty member at McGill University. He moved to Kingston in 1971, served as the head of the Department of Music at Queen's University for ten years, and retired in 1984. A highly respected composer, theorist, and educator, he was made an Officer of the Order of Canada in 2003 and a Fellow of the Royal Society of Canada in 2007. He has produced a substantial body of scholarly and creative work that speaks with force and eloquence about the contemporary human condition. His list of compositions includes electrocoustic, vocal, choral, instrumental, chamber, and orchestral music, and four large-scale operatic works: *La Tourangelle* (1975), *Winthrop* (1986), *Traces (Tikkun)* (1996), and *Millennial Mall* (1999). His life and music are the subject of the book *Istvan Anhalt: Pathways and Memory* (McGill-Queen's University Press, 2001).

John Beckwith
John Beckwith—composer, writer, and music educator—was associated from 1952 to 1990 with the Faculty of Music, University of Toronto, including periods as its dean and as founding director of its Institute for Canadian Music. Some of his later compositions appear on the Centrediscs CDs entitled *Avowals* and *Jalsaghar*. He is the author of *Music Papers: Articles and Talks by a Canadian Composer 1961–1994* (1997) and *Unheard-Of: Memoirs of a Canadian Composer* (Wilfrid Laurier University Press, forthcoming).

Rachel Beckles Willson
Rachel Beckles Willson is associate professor of music at Royal Holloway, University of London. Her research on Eastern Europe and the sociology of Western classical music has been published in two monographs and over twenty book chapters and journal articles and has been presented at conferences worldwide. Recently she has been based at the Humboldt University in Berlin, supported by a Fellowship for Experienced Researchers

from the Alexander von Humboldt Foundation and writing her forthcoming monograph, *Orientalism and Musical Mission: The Case of Palestine*.

William Benjamin
A music theorist and composer, William Benjamin received a PhD in music from Princeton and has taught at the University of British Columbia since 1978. He has published in leading theory journals and collective volumes since the 1970s, with studies of works by several nineteenth- and twentieth-century composers, critiques of present-day analytical method, and contributions to the theories of harmony and meter. More recently, his scholarly work has shifted to the intersection of music theory, cognition, and aesthetics. At present, he is completing a book entitled *Music in Our Heads: Imagined Music as a Determinant of Musical Behaviour, Musical Values, and Musical Culture*.

Rachelle Chiasson-Taylor
Rachelle Chiasson-Taylor détient des doctorats en interprétation musicale et en musicologie de l'Université McGill. Elle poursuit une carrière internationale comme interprète et a enregistré trois CDs de musique ancienne pour clavier chez ATMA. Elle enseigne l'histoire et la littérature musicales à l'Université McGill et sa recherche est publiée au Canada, en Belgique et au Royaume-Uni. Depuis 2002, elle travaille aussi comme historienne et archiviste à Bibliothèque et Archives Canada.

Austin Clarkson
Austin Clarkson, professor of music emeritus, York University, previously held positions at the University of Saskatchewan, Columbia University (where he was founding editor of *Current Musicology*), and Yale University. As general editor of the music and writings of Stefan Wolpe, he has produced many critical editions as well as *On the Music of Stefan Wolpe: Essays and Recollections* (Pendragon) and special Wolpe issues for *Contemporary Music Review* and *Musik-Konzepte*. He recently completed a report on a program that he directs for schoolchildren. www.austinclarkson.ca.

Kenneth DeLong
Kenneth DeLong is professor of music history at the University of Calgary. His research interests principally concern nineteenth-century Czech and English music, opera, and Liszt's piano music. Recent research activities include a conference paper on Liszt's *Il Penseroso* for the Vienna conference of the Word and Music Association, and articles on Schubert and Voříšek for *The Unknown Schubert* and on Sullivan for *Henry Irving*, both

published by Ashgate Press. He is a correspondent and reviewer for *Opera Canada* magazine and for thirty years has been the principal music critic for *The Calgary Herald*.

Robin Elliott
Robin Elliott studied with István Anhalt at Queen's University in Kingston, where he completed a B.Mus. degree in 1978. At the University of Toronto he earned his PhD in musicology in 1990. From 1996 to 2002 he was a faculty member at University College Dublin. He returned to the University of Toronto as the Jean A. Chalmers Chair in Canadian Music in 2002 and was appointed associate dean of the Faculty of Music in 2008.

Julia Galieva-Szokolay
Julia Galieva-Szokolay obtained her doctoral degree in musicology in 1995 at the Russian State Institute for Art Studies, Moscow. After moving to Canada in 1996 she became a faculty member of the Royal Conservatory's Glenn Gould School, in Toronto. Mrs. Galieva-Szokolay combines a teaching career with academic research, specializing in music of Eastern and East-Central Europe. She has published several articles on the works of contemporary composers of Hungary and Russia.

Alan Gillmor
Alan M. Gillmor was educated at the University of Michigan (B.Mus., MA) and the University of Toronto (PhD). He taught at McGill University and Carleton University, from which he retired in 2003 as professor emeritus. Dr. Gillmor's scholarly publications have appeared in professional journals both in North America and Europe, and his monograph on the French composer Erik Satie (1988; 1990) was shortlisted in 1990 for the Ottawa-Carleton Book Award for non-fiction. His most recent publications are *Eagle Minds: Selected Correspondence of Istvan Anhalt & George Rochberg, 1961–2005* (Wilfrid Laurier University Press, 2007) and (with James K. Wright) *Schoenberg's Chamber Music, Schoenberg's World* (Pendragon Press, 2009).

Dina Lentsner
A native of St. Petersburg, Russia, Dina Lentsner received her PhD in music theory from Ohio State University with dissertation on György Kurtág's *Scenes from a Novel*, Op. 19. She is an associate professor of music history, music theory, and composition at Capital University in Columbus, Ohio. Dr. Lentsner's current research focuses on the interpretation of music with text with the emphasis on contemporary music, "spirituality" in music, and music history pedagogy.

Stefano Melis
Stefano Melis graduated in piano performance at the Conservatorio di Musica of Sassari (1988) and in musicology at the Bologna University (1998). As a pianist, he has recorded numerous CDs of contemporary music, notably of works by Sardinian composers Franco Oppo and Antonio Doro. As a musicologist, his research focuses on György Kurtág's music and music pedagogy. Recent publications include "Játékok di György Kurtág. Il primo apprendimento strumentale tra esplorazione, gioco e comprensione musicale" (*Il Saggiatore Musicale*, 2005/1) and "Processus compositionnels et compréhension musicale enfantine dans *Játékok*," in *Gestes, fragments, timbres: la musique de György Kurtág* (L'Harmattan, 2008). He teaches music theory at the Conservatorio di Musica "L. Canepa" of Sassari.

Ulrich Mosch
Ulrich Mosch studied music and German literature in Hannover and musicology at the Technische Universität in Berlin (with Carl Dahlhaus). In 1991 he graduated with a thesis on the aural perception of total serialism and in 2004 was appointed university lecturer (Habilitation) at the Paris Lodron Universität in Salzburg, Austria. Since 1990 he has been a musicologist and curator for music manuscripts at the Paul Sacher Foundation in Basel, Switzerland, and is at present responsible for twenty-five collections of manuscripts, among them documents from Igor Stravinsky, Luciano Berio, Hans Werner Henze, Brian Ferneyhough, and György Kurtág.

Jean-Paul Olive
Jean-Paul Olive est professeur au département de musicologie de l'Université Paris 8 Vincennes–Saint-Denis où il enseigne l'analyse et l'esthétique musicales et dirige le laboratoire « Esthétique, musicologie et créations musicales ». Il a écrit un ouvrage sur l'œuvre d'Alban Berg (*Le tissage et le sens*), un essai sur le montage en musique (*Musique et montage. Essai sur le matériau musical au début du XXe siècle*) et plus récemment un ouvrage sur les écrits musicaux d'Adorno (*Un son désenchanté*). Il dirige la collection « Arts 8 » et est cofondateur de la revue de musicologie *Filigrane*.

Alvaro Oviedo
Né à Córdoba, Argentine, Alvaro Oviedo termine son doctorat, portant sur le geste dans la musique de György Kurtág et de Helmut Lachenmann, à l'Université Paris 8 Vincennes–Saint-Denis. Il a publié des articles sur l'œuvre de ces deux compositeurs et collabore à la revue mexicaine *La Tempestad*.

Il donne actuellement des cours à l'Université Paris 8 Vincennes–Saint-Denis sur la musique vocale du XXe siècle.

Friedemann Sallis
Friedemann Sallis is professor at the University of Calgary. He obtained his PhD in musicology under the direction of the late Carl Dahlhaus at the Technische Universität Berlin. His writings include a book on the early works of György Ligeti, the co-edition of *A Handbook to Twentieth-Century Musical Sketches* (Cambridge University Press, 2004), and numerous articles on twentieth-century music. He has received Fellowship Grants from the Paul Sacher Foundation (Basel) and since 1997 he has been awarded five consecutive research grants by the Social Sciences and Humanities Research Council of Canada.

Florian Scheding
Florian Scheding is lecturer in music at the University of Southampton. He has published articles on the composer Mátyás Seiber, film music, and composers in exile during World War II. A collection of essays, *Music and Displacement: Diasporas, Mobilities and Dislocations in Europe and Beyond*, co-edited with Erik Levi, was published in spring 2010 by Scarecrow Press in the *Europea* series, edited by Martin Stokes and Philip V. Bohlman.

Gorden E. Smith
Gordon E. Smith is professor of ethnomusicology at Queen's University, Kingston, Ontario. Formerly director of the School of Music, he is associate dean in the Faculty of Arts and Science. Co-editor of *Marius Barbeau: Modelling Twentieth-Century Culture* (2008), and *Music Traditions, Cultures, and Contexts* (Wilfrid Laurier University Press, 2010), he is the editor of *MUSICultures*, the Journal of the Canadian Society for Traditional Music / La Société canadienne pour les traditions musicales. His current research includes fieldwork in the Mi'kmaw community of Eskasoni, Cape Breton Island, Nova Scotia.

Gergely Szokolay
Hungarian-born pianist Gergely Szokolay has performed both as a soloist and chamber musician in Europe, North America, and Japan. Currently living in Toronto, he balances a busy schedule of teaching and performing. Equally at home in the vocal and instrumental repertoire, Mr. Szokolay has been collaborative pianist for major festivals and master classes, working with renowned pedagogues like Josef Gingold, Marcel Moyse, Aurèle Nicolet, János Starker, Zoltán Székely, Paul Tortelier, and David Zafer.

Claudio Veress
Claudio Veress studied philosophy and German literature at Bern University and teaches philosophy at a cantonal college. At the same time he is a passionate chamber musician. Since 1992 he has been involved in the scientific and editorial side of the legacy of Sándor Veress, whose chamber music for strings forms one of his specific matters of concern as a violinist and as a viola player.

INDEX

acculturation, 116, 123, 125
acmeism, 282, 296n9
Ádám, Jenő, 259n12
Adorno, Theodore, 3–4, 18n15–17, 105n15, 112, 117, 125n5, 271, 333–34, 343; aura, Walter Benjamin's concept of/conception de Walter Benjamin, 15, 333–34 (*see also* aura; Benjamin, Walter); Debussy, 18n16; on historical determinism, 18n17; *Philosophie der Neuen Musik*, 3–4, 18n17; on tendency of material, 3–4; *Théorie esthétique*, 334
Aeschylus, 111
aesthetics, 106n18, 124, 219–21, 225, 346; as a function of politics, 5; listener's perspective, 13; Romantic, 411; Soviet, 171n48
Agnes Etherington Art Centre, 77, 78, 87n27, 87n31
Akhmatova, Anna, 279–300; allusions to Puskin's poetry in work of, 286; feminine lyricism in work of, 289, 291; poetic debut, 289; Pushkin's legacy in poetics of, 286, 298n22; raising ethical questions through art, 287; relationship with Alexandr Blok, 288–89, 292–93, 298n26; self-presentation, 286, 291, 299n40; and Silver Age, 297n16; as woman poet, 289–90
Allemagne (régime nazi), 210. *Voir aussi* Germany: Nazi/fascist regime
Allik, Kristi, 77
Andrews Sisters, 31
Angleterre, 213n21. *Voir aussi* England
Anhalt, Beate (née Frankenberg – spouse of István Anhalt), 29, 34, 66, 81, 82, 86n22, 373, 426, 431n5
Anhalt, István, 5–13, 15–16, 29–34, 57–71, 73–87, 89–109, 112–27, 175–97, 199–203, 205–211, 219–24, 233–37, 371–92, 395–417; aesthetic views of, 219, 221, 223, 233; allusion in music of, 181, 184, 187, 378, 391n17, 412; in Austria, 33; autobiography, 31, 80, 82, 98–99, 108n35; auto-constructed legacy/auto-construction de soi, 12, 205–9; awards, prizes, recognition, 8,

21n47, 87n31; becomes Canadian citizen, 6; birth, 5; in Canada, 199, 200, 425; car accident, 33; centre vs. periphery, 10, 57, 58, 59–60, 64, 66, 67, 74–75, 101, 175, 176, 177, 178, 179, 187, 194; chamber music, 201, 425; character and personality, 29, 30–31, 32; chercheur/researcher, 202, 396–97; childhood, 60; compositional idiom and technique, 29, 33, 60, 73, 79–82, 95, 98, 100, 101, 102, 106n17, 120–21, 186–87, 193, 375–76, 405–12, 425; as conductor 30, 31–32; contribution to Canadian culture, 20n42; correspondence/correspondance, 30–31, 32–33, 34, 175, 176, 196n14, 196n18, 196n22, 199, 200, 201, 206, 371, 376, 389, 390n5, 415n17; creative imagination, 13, 223–24, 232, 234–35, 237n30; Devecseri circle, 58, 372; dodecaphonic technique, 7, 12, 113, 116, 122, 425; on doubleness/multipleness/more-than-oneness, 423, 425, 426, 428, 430n3; dramatic musical works/operas, 66, 89, 102, 105n15, 176–77, 194, 221–22, 426; electro-acoustic music, 7, 29, 47, 59, 187; on Ernő Lendvai's work, 416n 37; émigré-immigrant, 199, 210; esquisses, brouillons, mises au net/sketches, drafts, and fair copies, 200, 206–210, 375–77, 398–404, 405–6, 408–11; exile/emigration and, 10, 16, 58–59, 65, 73–74, 99, 101, 112, 426, 428–29, 430; on expressive potential of music, 397, 413; French-language reception, 12, 100; Fonds István-Anhalt, 11, 12, 21n50, 31, 68, 196n14, 196n18, 199–203, 205–10, 211n2, 211n5, 371, 390n5, 407; friendship with John Beckwith 29–34; forced-labour brigade, 6, 68, 71n8, 73, 82, 114, 115, 182, 186, 195n2, 388, 415n18; genealogical research, 31, 34, 67; généalogie, 201; Geworfenheit and, 64; grandchildren, of 66, 82, 191; grandfather, of 89; in Greece, 83; health of, 33, 34, 64; and humanism, 90, 96; in Hungary/Hongrie, 5–6, 10, 12, 31, 32, 34, 57, 58, 65, 83, 99, 205, 210, 408–10, 412, 415n18, 416n36, 372, 388, 430; impact de la crise d'Octobre, 205, 209; impact de la Deuxième Guerre mondiale, 199, 205; interest in language, 32, 193, 221; in Israel, 83, 181; in Italy, 83; Jewish identity 6, 11, 12, 13; and Judaism, 89, 90, 92, 104n9, 107n31, 180–81, 196n13; and Kabbalah, 32, 34, 90, 220, 222; and Kingston (Ontario), 6, 11, 20n46, 29, 30, 33, 61, 62, 63, 65, 73–76, 77, 78, 84, 101–3, 205, 210; Kingston Triptych, 11, 65, 73–78, 89, 104n1; late work, 15, 395–98, 413, 414n5; meets György Kurtág, 57; memory and remembrance in music of, 15–16, 395–96, 412–13; in Montreal/Montréal, 11, 12, 29, 30, 59, 61, 74, 76, 99, 100, 108n39, 205, 210, 415n16, 415n18; on music theory, 397; musique de chambre, 201, 425; musique de piano, 201; musique de scène et multi-média, 201; musique d'orchestre, 201; musique électro-acoustique, 199, 202, 205; non-Western religious rituals, 413; orchestral music, 32, 58, 79–84, 86n22, 89, 98, 104n1–2, 181, 371, 426; orchestration, 79–80, 82, 378–80, 383, 385–88, 391n17; in Paris, 6, 11, 59, 76, 114, 122, 425; pedagogue/pédagogue, 7, 201, 205, 206, 209, 234, 428, 429; premières œuvres

INDEX   441

(ca. 1940), 201; and politics, 89, 90, 91, 105n13; professor at/professeur à McGill University, 6, 12, 29, 201; professor at/professeur à Queen's University, 6, 61–62, 64, 76, 77, 84, 86n18, 87n31, 109n44, 180, 200, 201, 396, 428; programmatic elements in music of, 91–92, 95, 98, 106n17, 106n18, 388; racines hongroises de sa culture musicale, 115, 124, 199; réconciliation entre différentes cultures, 206; recourse to models, 99, 117, 386, 413; on repetition in music, 413; and Quebec/Québec, 12, 205, 209–10; sabbatical in Cambridge, 30, 193; scholar/researcher/chercheur, 202, 396–97; sketches, drafts, and fair copies/esquisses, brouillons, mises au net, 200, 206–10, 375–77, 398–404, 405–6, 408–11; studies with Zoltán Kodály, 5, 6, 102, 115, 116; telephone conversations, 32–33, 180, 371; in Turkey, 82, 83; views on Canada 99, 426, 427; views on Palestinian–Israeli conflict, 21n48; views on Israel 90, 99, 104n9, 105n11, 107n25; in Vermont, 30; vocal music, 33–34, 187, 193, 221; World War II, 6, 7, 11, 12, 31, 58, 59, 68, 71n8, 73, 82, 114, 115, 116, 125, 182, 186, 195n2, 223, 388. *See also* creativity: of Anhalt; "I" (in Anhalt's usage); Rochberg, George: correspondence with István Anhalt

Anhalt, István: COMPOSITIONS:
  Cento, 34, 60
  Comments, 65–66
  Concerto (in stilo di Handel), 116
  Doors ... shadows (Glenn Gould in Memory), 414n5
  Electronic Compositions Nos. 2–4, 203

  Fantasia, 29, 60, 116–17, 118, 119
  Foci, 31–32, 60
  Four Portraits from Memory, 15–16, 29, 78, 80, 81–82, 84, 86n20, 87n27, 200, 395–413, 414n5; analysis (Portrait III), 405–12; Bartókian traits in, 405, 407; premiere of piano version, 86n20, 398, 401, 404, 411; creative process, 400–4, 415n24, 416n25; as commemoration, 413; Golden Section proportions in Portrait III, 405–11, 416n28, 416n29, 416n34; premiere of orchestral version, 78, 81–82; versions of, 398–404, 415n21, 416n26
  Galambabmalag: The Halloween Witch and 24 Other Easy Pieces for Recorder (Solos and Duets), 414n5
  La Tourangelle, 31, 60, 65, 66, 100, 105n15, 176, 177, 178, 180, 181, 184, 193, 203, 209–10, 213n25, 221, 429
  Millennial Mall (Lady Diotima's Walk), 66, 81, 104n3, 105n15, 176, 177, 178, 193, 200, 210, 221, 222, 429, 414n5; méta-mémoire, 210
  Simulacrum, 89, 98, 106n18, 196n13, 200, 371, 396, 414n5
  Sonances•Resonance (Welche Töne?), 15, 65, 81, 124, 371–90, 414n5, 426; composition of, 372–73; fugal writing in, 386–87; orchestration in, 378–80, 383, 385–88; premiere of, 371, 389; relation to Beethoven's Ninth Symphony, 65,

371–90; relation to Holocaust, 388, *Schreckensfanfare* in, 375, 379–80, 387, 391n17; sketches for, 375–76, 377
SparkskrapS, 79, 90, 104n2, 106n18, 107n28, 124, 196n13, 200, 371, 396, 412–13, 414n5
Symphony, 30, 31, 60, 89, 116, 119
Symphony of Modules, 60
The Tents of Abraham (A Mirage-Midrash), 11, 33, 65, 78, 79–80, 81, 83, 84, 86n22, 89–103, 200, 414n5; Anhalt's writings on, 83; and Israeli–Palestinian conflict, 90, 91, 103, 107n25, 221; as midrash, 83; portrayal of God in, 95, 96–97, 107n29, 221; orchestration of, 79–80; premiere of, 78; relation to story of Abraham, 81, 83, 91–97, 102, 103
Thisness, 176–77, 195n4, 200
... the timber of those times ... (... a theogony ...), 65, 78, 80, 81, 82–83, 86n22, 200, 414n5, 425; Anhalt's writings on, 82–83; commission of, 78; orchestration of, 80; premiere of, 78
Tikkun (Traces), 12, 66, 89, 105n15, 176, 177, 178, 180–94, 206–11, 221–22, 224, 233, 414n5, 429; Anhalt's description of, 184, 186, 187, 191, 193; autobiographical elements in, 181–82, 186, 191; death portrayed in, 191; libretto of, 184; orchestration of, 186–87, 191, 193; premiere of, 181; techniques d'écriture, 206–9

Twilight~Fire (Baucis'and Philomen's Feast), 65, 78, 79, 81, 82, 84, 86n22, 87n31, 109n44, 221, 414n5, 425, 426; Anhalt's writings on, 82; premiere of, 78; orchestration of, 79
Violin Sonata, 60, 116, 118–19, 120, 425, 429
A Wedding Carol, 200
Winthrop, 30, 66, 102, 105n15, 176, 177, 178, 180, 181, 184, 193, 200, 203, 209–10, 221, 396, 414n6, 429
Anhalt, István: WRITINGS/ÉCRITS: 73, 82–83, 104n9, 105 n.14, 106n17, 107n29, 124, 175, 178, 182, 184, 186, 187, 193, 219–22, 223, 233, 235, 428, 429
Alternative Voices: Essays on Contemporary Vocal and Choral Compositions, 15, 33–34, 197n24, 202, 396–98, 408, 413, 423; as child of its time, 397; as milestone in Anhalt's career, 396–97; as personal manifesto, 397–98
The Bridge: A Parable, 61, 108n37, 202, 206
Kantáta [Délibáb] El patakon, 11, 20n45, 62, 68–70, 73, 85n4
Eagle Minds, 408
libretti 30, 31, 66, 90, 176, 181, 184, 195n4, 196n14, 195n4
An Interim Account of My Search for Genealogical Information Pertaining to My Family's Background, 201
Music: Context, Text, Counter-Text, 202, 223
Oppenheimer [libretto/play], 31, 181, 196n14, 200
A Weave of Life Lines, 202

Anhalt, Judit (Judith) (half-sister of István Anhalt), 87n27, 398, 398, 415n16
Anhalt, Katalin (née Herzfeld; later Somló – mother of István Anhalt), 61, 68, 191
Antal, János, 195n2
anthropology, 74, 75
anti-Semitism, 12, 58, 89, 100, 113, 114
Appadurai, Arjun, 74, 85n8
Archives nationales du Canada, 211n2. *Voir aussi* Bibliothèque et Archives Canada; Library and Archives Canada
Arendt, Hannah, 112, 341, 389
Argentina, 9, 59
ars antiqua, 397
Association canadienne des écoles universitaires de musique/Canadian Association of University Schools of Music, 202
Astaire, Fred, 31
Attali, Jacques, 397; *Bruits: Essais sur l'économie politique de la musique/Noise: The Political Economy of Music*, 397, 414n11
Augustine, Saint, 45; on memory, 45, 51n3
aura, 330–36, 342–43; déclin de, 330–31, 333, 335, 336, 342; définitions, 331–32. *Voir aussi* Adorno, Thedore; Benjamin, Walter
Auschwitz, 6
Austria, 33, 67, 114, 132, 175, 415n19
Austro-German music, 18n16
Austro-Hungarian Empire, 5, 111–12, 114, 117; fall of, 47–48, 296n3
authenticity, 75, 80, 102, 234
auto-citation dans la musique, 339–441. *Voir aussi* Kurtág, György; Rihm, Wolfgang; Veress, Sándor
auto-constructed legacies of composers, 12, 13, 129–49, 279, 281. See also auto-construction de soi

auto-construction de soi, 205–9. *Voir aussi* auto-constructed legacies of composers
avant-garde, 101, 121; interwar, 113, 115, 124; postwar, 7, 117–18, 126n23, 136, 364
Aykroyd, Dan, 86n13

Babbit, Milton, 199
Bach, Johann Sebastian, 137, 335, 349, 358; *Art of Fugue*, 116, 389; Sonatina from *Actus Tragicus* BWV 106, 349; *Das Wohltemperierte Klavier*, 335, 358 (Praeludium XXI); *St. Matthew Passion*, 104n6
Bacon, Francis, 13, 275–76
Bakhtin, Mikhail, 177, 194, 195n6, 373
Balász, István, 257n1
Bali, 59, 65
Bánát (Temesvár Banat, Romania), 279, 296n3; multi-ethnic population of, 296n3
Banks, Don, 114
Bartók, Béla, 19n27, 58, 76, 77, 113, 118, 136, 142–43, 147, 167n17, 169n34, 171n48, 267, 350, 357–58, 359, 361, 405, 407, 408, 416n30, 416n36, 417n38, 425; *Cantata Profana*, 142–43, 170n47; Concerto for Orchestra, 143, 147, 170n48, *Mikrokosmos*, 359, 367n20; (*Mikrokosmos III*) "Hommage à J.S.B.," 357–58; "Hommage à R. Sch.," 357; *Music for Strings, Percussion and Celeste*, 416n36; quotation and parody in music of, 170n48; sketches and autographs, 417n38; *Sonata for Two Pianos and Percussion*, 416n36; Symphony, 136, 169n34
Bashō, Matsuo, 219, 280
Baudelaire, Charles, 327, 330, 331–33; correspondances baudelairiennes, 332
Beard, David, 2
Beckles Willson, Rachel, 20n43, 405

Beckwith, John, 199, 201, 398–99, 401–4, 427, 429–30; car accident, 33; as father/husband, 30, 32, 430; friendship with István Anhalt, 29–34, 430; health of 33; piano adaptation of *Four Portraits from Memory*, 398–99, 401–2, 404, 416n26; writings on István Anhalt, 29, 32–33, 35n1, 80, 100, 116, 122, 125n5, 382, 386–87

Beecroft, Norma, 122

Beethoven, Ludwig van, 3, 18n15, 41–42, 65, 80, 137, 364, 376; *Missa Solemnis*, 374; Ninth Symphony, 81, early recordings of, 372, meaning of, 373–74, premiere of, 392n22, relation to Anhalt *Sonance•Resonance (Welche Töne)*, 371–90, *Schreckensfanfare* of, 374–75, 391n12; Piano Sonata No. 8 in C minor Op. 13 "Pathétique," 41–42; Piano Sonata No. 32 in C minor Op. 111, 18n15; String Quartet in A minor Op. 132, 378–79; tinnitus of, 376, 378, 391n16–17

Benjamin, Walter, 15, 327, 330–35, 341; aura, 15, 330–36, 342–43 (*see also* aura; Adorno); conception radicale du langage, 341; expérience (Erlebnis vs. Erfahrung), 332; manuscrits, 331–32; marxisme, 331; « L'œuvre d'art à l'ère de sa reproductibilité technique », 331, 333; « La petite histoire de la photographie », 331; « Qu'est-ce au juste que l'aura », 331; « Sur quelques thèmes baudelairiens », 332

Benjamin, William E., 80, 104n9, 105n13, 126n17, 413, 425

Berg, Alban, 118, 120, 125n5, 126n18, 364

Berio, Luciano, 201, 223, 397; *Sequenza III*, 397

Berlin, 427, 430n2

Berlin, Irving, 427

Bern Music Society Committee, 47

Bern, 48, 49, 131; old town, 49

Bern, University of, 6

Besard, Jean-Baptiste, 116

Bhabha, Homi, 2

Biasin, Gian-Paolo, 321

Bible, 81, 93, 94, 96, 106n19, 107n21; Genesis 92, 93, 97, 106n19, 107n21–23; 1 Kings, 97

Bibliothèque et Archives Canada (BAC), 199–200, 211n2, 211n5; Fonds István-Anhalt, 199–203, 205–10, 211n2, 211n5; Section de la Musique de la Division des Collections spéciales et archives canadiennes, 211n2. *Voir aussi* Library and Archives Canada (LAC)

Bibliothèque Nationale de France (BNF), 331

Bibliothèque nationale du Canada/ National Library of Canada, 200, 211n2. *Voir aussi* Bibliothèque et Archives Canada; Library and Archives Canada

Biddle, Ian, 2

Binswanger, Ludwig, 276n3

Birtwistle, Harrison, 223

Bleek, Tobias, 351, 367n14

Bloch, Ernest, 430n3

Blok, Alexandr, 282, 283, 284, 285, 288–93, 299n29, 300n45; [Beauty's Terrible, They'll Tell You] Красота страшна, вам скажут, 288

borrowing in music and poetry, categories of: allusion, 15, 347–48, 286, 351–52, 357–58, 391n17, 412; arrangement, 15, 116, 282, 347–50, 352, 366n8; auto/self-quotation, 46, 368n33; quotation, 15, 347–49, 351, 352, 362, 365, 368n33, 368n34; recourse to models, 15, 99, 117, 136, 347, 348–50, 352, 386, 413. *See also* emprunts musicaux

Borsody, Stephen (István), 130–35, 148, 166n11, 168n26; political

INDEX 445

advice to Sándor Veress, 132–33, 167n18
Boston, 66
Boulanger, Nadia, 6, 59, 116, 201, 425
Boulez, Pierre, 4, 117; on serialism, 4, 18n18
Brahms, Johannes, 137, 356
Brájer, Zinaida, 298n19, 298n25
Brecht, Bertolt, 112, 331, 426
Brodsky, Joseph, 282
Brott, Alexander, 77, 78
Buber, Martin, 222, 223, 232, 234, 236n23
Budapest, 5–6, 8, 10, 20n43, 31, 32, 44n9, 48, 57, 58, 76, 83, 113–14, 115, 132, 134, 137, 165n5, 175, 182, 195, 298n19, 303, 372, 373, 389, 415n16, 416n36; Red Army's liberation of, 48; siege of, 134
Burge, John, 77
Busoni, Ferruccio, 346

Cage, John, 4, 199, 201, 397
Calgary Philharmonic Orchestra, 65, 371
Calvinism, 180
Cambridge University, 30, 193, 423, 431n5
Camus, Albert, 112
Canada Council for the Arts/Conseil des Arts du Canada, 78, 427
Canada, 6, 7–10, 21n49, 42, 59, 67, 68, 73–74, 76, 83, 90, 91, 99, 100–1, 102, 103, 114, 116, 117, 121–23, 126n24, 126–27n25, 177, 178, 180, 182, 199, 200, 225, 227, 371, 396, 415n19, 425–29; as former colony of Great Britain, 21n49; 126n25
Canadian Broadcasting Corporation/Société Radio Canada, 65, 79, 100, 213n25, 427
Canadian Jewish Congress/Congrès juif canadien, 89
Canadian League of Composers/Ligue canadienne des compositeurs, 29, 102

Canadian Music Centre/Centre de musique canadienne, 78, 106n17, 427
Canadian music, 78, 101, 427, 428, 429
Canadian Opera Company, 196n14
Canetti, Elias, 329; *Le cœur secret de l'horloge*, 329
canon (of musical culture), construction of, 136, 137
Carroll, Lewis (Charles Lutwidge Dodgson), 315–16, 319; and *Alice's Adventures in Wonderland*, 315, 319; *Through the Looking Glass*, 315, 319
Catholic University of America, 166n6
Catholicism, 180, 221
Celan, Paul, 415n19
centre and periphery, 2–3, 10, 57, 58, 59, 60, 64, 66, 67, 74–75, 101, 175, 176, 177, 178, 179, 187, 194; in musical analysis, 303–4; as a network of possible relationships, 8
Centrediscs, 78, 106n17
Chaillois, Roger, 250–51, 255; taxonomical classification of playing (agon, alea, ilinx, mimicry), 250–52, 255, 260n27, 261n28, 261n29, 261n31
chaosmos, 8–9
Chekhov, Anton (Pavlovich), 39; *Ariadne*, 39
children, 241–46; comprehension of musical form, 257n4; musical mind of, 241, 243–45; perception of rhythmic units, 259n10
China, 430
Chmura, Gabriel, 396
Chopin, Fryderyk, 4, 42; Étude Op. 10 No. 12 "Revolutionary," 42
Chowning, John, 408; Golden Section proportions in music of, 408, 417n38
chronotopes, 67, 81, 177, 193, 194, 195n6, 373

Cixous, Hélène, 221, 321; bodily relationship between reader and text, 321
Clarke, Frederick Robert Charles (F.R.C.), 77
Clarkson, Austin, 397
Clifford, James, 12, 178, 179, 182, 194, 195n1; roots and routes, 12
Cold War, 12, 48, 133
Collegium Hungaricum (Rome), 137
Cologne, 59, 76
colonialism, 112, 126n25
Comenius, Johann Amos, 45; *Orbis sensualium pictus*, 45
Conservatoire national supérieur de musique et de danse de Paris, 59
Constant, Marius, 31
Cornfield, Eitan, 78, 83
Coulthard, Jean, 32
Crawley, Clifford, 77
creative imagination, 13, 223–24, 232, 234–35, 237n30
creativity, 4, 13, 111, 112, 113, 123, 180, 221, 224, 225, 232, 234, 235, 237n29–31, 364, 365; of Anhalt, 11, 13, 20n42, 29, 30, 33, 68, 83, 101, 103, 112, 177, 180, 184, 191, 194, 196n22, 219, 221, 223, 224, 233, 234, 235, 372, 386, 387, 389, 390, 395, 396, 430n3; of Beethoven, 374; of Kurtág, 21n53, 112, 241, 242, 249, 279, 283, 295, 304, 321, 357, 359, 360, 361, 365; of Seiber, 114, 118; of Veress, 47, 50, 51 n7, 135
Crise d'Octobre, 205, 209. *Voir aussi* nationalism: Quebec
Crumb, George, 14, 303–5, 313, 316–21; 14; Kurtág and music of, 304; "Gacela de la muerto oscura," Madrigal No. 2 from *Madrigals, Book III*, 305, 313–21: Carroll and mirror structure in music of, 319–20; Lorca's semantic fields in music of, 316–20;

music as gesture, 316–17, 319–20; musical analysis of, 316–19; musico-poetic analysis of, 319–20; synchronic and diachronic compositional processes in, 317–21; text images in, 313
Crystal, David, 193
Csicsery-Rónay, István, 130–31, 134, 148, 165–66n6, 166n10, 168n26, 171n51; as specialist of Hungarian literature and letters, 148, 171n51
cultural geography, 75
Czechoslovakia, 114

Dahlhaus, Carl, 123, 271, 411; on historical determinism, 3–4; on nationalist histories of music, 3
Dalbec-Szczesniak, Gisèle, 79, 425
Dalos, Rimma, 279, 280, 281–82, 290, 296n5, 300n52, 303, 304, 305–7, 310–12, 320; ["Dream"] "Сон": Kurtág's interpretation of, 308–12; musico-poetic analysis of, 310–12; poetic analysis of, 305–7; search for identity, 281
Dalton, Aaron, 257n1
Darmstadt, 4, 117, 126n14; summer courses at, 4
Davies, Robertson, 372
Deane, Basil, 374
Debussy, Claude, 18n16, 327, 408; Golden Section proportions in music of, 408, 417n38
Deleuze, Gilles, 275–76
DeLong, Kenneth, 257n1
Demény, János, 296n4
Denisov, Edison, 293, 300n48; [Lamentations], 293
Derrida, Jacques, 112, 123
déterminisme historique, 271. *Voir aussi* historical determinism
Devecseri circle, 58, 372
Devecseri, Gábor, 58, 372
Devecseri, Klára (née Huszar), 58, 372, 373, 390n5

Dewey, John, 221
dodecaphony, 7, 116–17, 118, 121–22, 139. *See also* serialism; twelve-tone technique
Donaueschingen, 117, 126n14
Doráti, Antal, 12, 135, 136, 168n27, 169n36; fled Communist Hungary, 136
Dostoevsky, Fyodor, 285
dreaming, as thematic material in music and poetry, 305–12, 313–21

Eastman Kodak Show, 423
Eco, Umberto, 8
École de Vienne, 328. *Voir aussi* Viennese School, Second
Egan, Kieran, 238n51
Eimert, Herbert, 59, 76
Eisler, Hanns, 426
Eliot, T.S., 220, 415n19
Elliott, Robin, 33, 65, 85n1, 116, 180, 202, 428–29
Ellis, Katharine, 212n18
Előpatak (Hungary/Vâlcele, Romania), 68, 73, 85n5
emprunts musicaux: auto-citation, 339–41, citation, 330; référence à des modèles, 329–30, 336. *Voir aussi* Borrowing in music and poetry, categories of
Encounters Chamber Orchestra, 181
England, 29, 47, 122, 178, 429, 431n5. *See also* Great Britain; United Kingdom
Ensemble Intercontemporain, 279
Eötvös, Péter, 285
epitext (titles, mottos, epigraphs), 279, 287, 291, 296nn10, 299n29, 348, 361
Epp, Richard, 176
Eros, 96, 221
Esenin, Sergei, 280, 282, 283, 297n10
ethnomusicology, 5, 74, 180, 196n12; fieldwork in, 180, 196n12
ethnos, 65, 81, 221

ethnoscape, 74–75, 85n8
ethos, 65, 81, 221
Eumée, 276n3
Evtushenko, Evgeny, 297n11
exil, 210. *See also* exile
exile, 7, 10, 19n27, 111, 112, 121, 126n24, 166n6, 175, 177, 178, 210, 281, 282, 424, 426, 430n3; liberation vs., 10; literature on exile theory, 16n4

Fast, Glen, 65, 77, 78, 84, 102, 109n44, 428
Fétis, François-Joseph, 213n20
Fibonacci series, 410, 417n36
Fisher, Alfred, 77
folk song: Hungarian, 5, 139, 147, 293 (*see also* Kodály, Zoltán); Russian, 293
Fonds István-Anhalt/István-Anhalt Fonds (BAC/LAC), 11–12, 21n50, 31, 68, 196n14, 196n18, 199–203, 205–10, 211n2, 211n5, 371, 390n5, 407
Foreman, Charles, 86n20, 398, 401, 404, 411
formalism ("tönend bewegte Formen"), 412
Forte, Allan, 411; pitch-class set analysis, 411
Foucault, Michel, 212n16
Fourestier, Louis, 201
France, 3, 8, 9, 29, 99, 100, 178, 279, 298n18, 298n25, 300n43, 303, 374
Frankfurt, 113, 125n5
Franz Liszt Academy Budapest, 5–8, 37, 39, 44n2, 114, 115, 175, 182, 298n19, 372, 388
Frederick Mann Foundation, 130, 168n27
Freeland, Brian, 32
Freud, Sigmund, 310; *Interpretation of Dreams*, 310
Fricker, Peter Racine, 114, 121–22
Fried, Oskar, 372, 390n4

Gadamer, Hans-Georg, 64, 389; horizon, concept of, 58, 64, 67
Galich, Alexandr, 280, 282
Galieva Szokolay, Julia, 42
Gasparov, Boris, 300n51
George, Graham, 77
Gerlich, Thomas, 139, 165n3
Germany, 3, 4, 9, 29, 59, 100, 134, 137, 147, 167n17, 170n42; Nazi/fascist regime, 4, 113, 114 134, 137, 147, 167n17, 170n42
ghettos and concentration camps, 112
Giegerich, Wolfgang, 234
Gillmor, Alan, 71n6, 80, 200
Glass, Philip, 417n48; *Satyagraha*, 417n48
Glenn Gould Studio (Toronto), 181
Glinka, Mikhail, 18n22
Gloag, Kenneth, 2
global vs. local. *See* universal vs. particular
globalization, 75, 303
Goehr, Alexander, 423, 424, 430n2, 431n5
Goehr, Laelia, 430n2
Goehr, Lydia, 16, 21n58, 430n2; family relationships, 423, 424, 430n2; "Music and Musicians in Exile," 423–24, 426–27, 428, 430n3
Goehr, Rudolf, 423, 430n2
Goehr, Walter (George Walter), 116, 423, 430n2
Golden Section proportions, 405–11, 416n27, 417n38
Gorodetsky, Sergey, 297n9
Gould, Glenn, 20n42, 199, 201
Great Britain, 114, 116, 121, 122, 124, 430n2. *See also* England; United Kingdom
Gumilev, Lev, 283, 293, 297n9
Gyopár, László, 182, 183, 201, 388–89; *Missa*, 201, 389

Haendel, Ida, 77
Harmer, Sarah, 75
Hassidism, 222
Hawkins, John, 31
Haydn, Joseph, 356
Heidegger, Martin, 58, 64, 71n2, 276n3, 389–90
Helms, Hans, 59
Herbig, Günther, 371, 373, 389
Herder, Johann Gottfried, 4; ideas recuperated by totalitarian regimes, 4–5
Hesiod, 81
Hiller, Lejaren, 29
Hindemith, Paul, 118
historical determinism, 4, 18n17, 271
Hitler, Adolf, 113
Hobsbawm, Eric, 1, 112
Hoch Konservatorium (Frankfurt), 113
Hoffmann, Ernst Theodor Wilhelm (E.T.A.), 304; *Lebensanshichten des Katers Murr*, 304
Hölderlin, Friedrich, 341; *Andenken*, 341
Holocaust, 58, 104n9, 115, 124, 125n9, 388–89
Homère, 276n3; « enargeia », 276n3; *Odyssée*, 276n3
Horthy, Miklós, 113, 115
Howat, Roy, 417n38
Hungarian Communist Party, 52n12, 129, 130, 132–34, 167n18
Hungarian emigration, 129–30, 148–49. *See also* Hungary: networks of emigrants; Veress, Sándor
Hungarian Kingdom, 47
Hungarian literature, 148. *See also* Csicsery-Rónay, István
Hungarian music, 47, 113, 115, 124, 137–47, 168n26; anti-Germanic tendencies in twentieth century, 47; folk music, 5, 49, 115, 136, 138–43, 147, 293, 350. *See also* Kurtág, György; Veress, Sándor
Hungarian National Opera, 6, 58, 372
Hungary, 5–9, 12, 19n27, 20n34, 31, 34, 39, 47–48, 51n11, 58, 59, 65, 68, 85n5, 99, 113–14, 115, 116,

124, 129–37, 139, 142–43, 148, 165n5, 165n6, 168n26, 169n39, 170n39, 170n42, 171n48, 171n51, 279, 281, 296n3, 296n5, 296n8, 372, 388, 408, 410, 415n18, 416n36, 430; allied with Nazi Germany, 134–35; Arrow Cross Party, 48; anti-Semitism in, 12; collaboration with Nazi Germany and Soviet Union, 147; cultural renaissance, 6; German occupation of, 48; labour camps, 114, 115, 182, 183, 186, 195n2; networks of emigrants, 130–31, 148–49, 165n6, 171n51 (*see also* Hungarian emigration); proto-fascist regime of Admiral Miklós Horthy, 113; revolution, 15; Smallholders' Party, 130, 165n6; Soviet invasion, 132; Soviet occupation of, 129, 135, 148; Soviet Republic (1919), 132; War of Independence against Austria (1848–49), 132
Hunyadi, Matthias Corvinus, 137, 169n39
Hutchinson, Anne, 66

"I" (in Anhalt's usage)/individuality 57, 58, 60, 66–67, 80, 81, 84, 104n4, 223, 234, 235; Buber's *I–Thou* and, 222, 223, 232, 233; Jungian ideas and, 223, 224
Ingarden, Roman, 346–47; music as intentional object, 346–48, 366n4
intentional fallacy, 105n13, 123–24
Iron Curtain, 7
Isaac the Blind, 220
Islam, 83, 94, 97
Israel, 90, 92, 99, 107n22
István-Anhalt Fonds/Fonds István-Anhalt (LAC/BAC), 11–12, 21n50, 31, 68, 196n14, 196n18, 199–203, 205–10, 211n2, 211n5, 371, 390n5, 407
István Anhalt: Pathways and Memory, 32, 180, 194, 199, 202, 408

Italy, 3, 9, 47, 59, 83 137–38, 167n17; fascist regime in, 167n17

Jackson, Brian, 77, 78
Jakobson, Roman, 321n4
James, William, 221
Jameson, Fredric, 222
Japanese Dynasty, 167n17
Jaspers, Karl, 48; *The Atomic Bomb and the Future of Mankind*, 48
jazz, 99, 101, 113, 115
Joachim, Otto, 122
Jolson, Al, 31
Jonas, Hans, 71n2
Jones, Kelsey, 77
Joyce, James, 8; definition of "chaosmos," 8; *Finnegans Wake*, 8
Judaism, 83, 92, 94, 97, 104n10, 107n31, 108n33, 180–81, 221
Jung, C.G., 221, 223, 224; and active imagination 224; and projection 223; individuation, concept of, 222, 223, 224, 233, 235
Juno Awards, 21n47, 78, 91, 106n16

Kabbalah, 97, 104n10, 107n31, 181; István Anhalt and 32, 34, 90, 97, 104n10, 180–81
Kafka, Franz, 266, 267–68; aphorismes, 266, 267; Odradek, 343; structure binaire des textes, 267
Kagel, Mauricio, 59
Kahn, Erich Itor, 126n23
Kallmann, Hellmut, 199, 200, 201
Kannegisser, Leonid, 299n31
Kant, Immanuel, 52n13
Karinthy, Frigyes, 58
Kasemets, Udo, 33, 122
Kearney, Michael, 303
Kelemen, András, 87n27, 398, 415n18
Kerényi, Károly, 83
Kerman, Joseph, 414n10
Kern, Jerome, 427
Kharms, Daniil, 280, 282
Kingston (Ontario), 6, 8, 11, 16, 20n46, 29, 30, 33, 61, 62, 63, 65,

73–76, 77, 78, 83–84, 99, 101–3, 104n9, 191, 205; history of, 76–77; as István Anhalt's ideal community, 62, 63, 66, 67, 73–74, 210
Kingston Symphony Association, 86n15
Kingston Symphony Orchestra, 34, 65, 74, 77–82, 83, 84, 86n15, 102, 109n44, 398, 428
Kipnis, Igor, 77
Kittay, Eva, 322n6
Knights, Vanessa, 2
Kocherscheidt, Kurt, 365; *The Boys from Kolchis*, 365
Kodály, Zoltán, 5–6, 12, 58, 76, 102, 113, 114, 115, 116, 118, 125n6, 136, 137, 167n17, 169n34, 170n42, 201, 350; contribution to Hungary's cultural renaissance, 6; on inferior foreign music-hall songs, 5; Latin-German influences on Hungarian music, 137–38, 170n42; Symphony, 136, 169n34; "What Is Hungarian in Music?" 137
Koenig, Gottfried Michael, 59
Kolozsvár (Transylvania), 5
Krenek, Ernst, 122, 334
Kristeva, Julia, 111
Kulesha, Gary, 181
Kurtág, György, Jr., 38
Kurtág, György, 5–10, 13–15, 37–44, 112, 241–61, 265–76, 279–300, 303–5, 308–12, 316–21, 328–30, 335–43, 345–46, 348–61, 365–66; and alterity, 281–82, 295; allusion in music of, 15, 298n22, 348, 351–52, 357–58, arrangement 15, 282, 348–50, 352, 366n8; autocitation, 339–41; auto/self-quotation, 352, 365; aphorismes, 335, 337; awards, prizes, recognition, 8; birth, 5; citation, 330; becomes French citizen, 8; becomes Hungarian citizen, 5; composed programs, 365; contraste dans la musique, 267; densité expressive de la musique, 329; dodecaphonic technique, 7; epitexts in work of, 279, 287, 291, 296nn10, 299n29, 348, 361; Editio Musica Budapest, 285, 295n1; ethical questions raised in art, 287; figures musicales, 265, 266, 268–70, 272, 275–76; formes aphoristiques, 329; fragments musicaux, 271–72, 276; gestes expressifs, 3, 30, 272–76; Gyuribácsi, 37, 44n1; homages/hommages in work of, 353–60, 365; Hungarian folk music in work of, 293, 350; and Hungarian literature, 37–38; Hungarian reception of Russian-language works, 281, 296n8; impact of Hungarian revolution on, 6–7; idée fixe, 352; influence de Béla Bartók, 267; influence d'Anton Webern, 267, 328–29, 335; intertextual relationships in music of, 345–46; 348–61, 365–66; Jewish identity, 6; madrigalisms/word painting, 13, 311–12; meets István Anhalt, 57; music as condolence and celebration, 10; music as play, 241, 258n8; musical figure, 13; musical fragments, 7; musical images in work of, 242–46; musical silence, 244; musique folklorique, 273; musique vocale, 265–76; notation, 241, 244; official silence in Budapest, 8; papers, 10, 14; in Paris, 21n53, 300, 351; pedagogue, 7, 10, 13, 39–43, 242, 257, 258n8; performance and interiorization of form, 246–49; period of self-imposed silence, 15, 21n53; as pianist, 15; pieces d'occasion, 349; polyglot, 5, 14, 21n51, 279, 304; professor at Franz Liszt Academy, 7; Pushkin-related images in music of, 298n20; objet volé/objet trouvé dans la musique,

268, 329 (*voir aussi* borrowing in music and poetry); pédagogue, 272–73; quotation in music of, 15, 298n22, 348–49, 351, 352; recourse to models, 15, 336, 348–50, 352; recours aux modèles historiques, 336; and Russian literature, 14, 279–81, 304–5, 308–12; Russian texts in work of, 14, 21n51, 280, 297n10, 304–5; séjour à Paris, 267, 329; sketches and drafts, 296n4, 365–66; studies with Ferenc Farkas, 6, 37; studies with Pál Járdányi, 19n28; studies with Sándor Veress, 5–6; symbolic and expressive communication through music, 249–56; transcription, 347, 349, 357, 361; varietas in music of, 349; vestiges des langages musicaux du passé, 268–71, 335–36; vocal music, 13–14, 279–95, 303–5, 308–12; World War II, 6

Kurtág, György: COMPOSITIONS:
[*And how thy heart*] Как сердечко твое ..., 280
Átiratok Machaut-tól J.S. Bachig, 349, 366n7, 366n8
Un brin de bruyère à Witold, 353
[*Broken love ...*] Разбилась любовь ..., 280
Eight Piano Pieces Op. 3, 39, 352
[*Farewell, my friend ...*] До свиданья, друг мой ..., 280
Four Songs to Poems by János Pilinsky's Poems Op. 11, 296n6
Four Poems by Anna Akhatova [*АннаАхматова: Четыре стихотворения*] Op. 41, 14, 279–95, 295n1, 297n10; Akhmatova as literary subject, biographical person and cultural personage in, 291–92; diatonic and chromatic tonal organization in, 292; impact of Russian folklore (dolnik), 293; music and text, 283–95; vocal style in, 289–90
Games and Messages for Winds, 10
Grabstein für Stephan (1976/1978–79? [withdrawn]), 367n16
Háromgyerekdal: "Примус X" [*Primus X*], 280
Hommage à Mihály András. 12 Microludes for String Quartet Op. 13, 15, 335–41, 342–43, 353; accents populaires, 338; dissonance, 337–38; langage tonal, 336–38; marches dans l'imagination sonore, 336
Hommage à R. Sch. Op. 15d, 352, 353
Hommage à Szervánszky (for violin, viola, and cello), 352, 354–55
[*I felt strange ...*] Как же странно мне было ..., 280
In memoriam Zsolt Baranyai, 367n17
[*It rains again*] И снова дождь, 280
Játékok, 10, 13, 15, 39, 241–61, 266, 272–73, 296n6, 353, 360, 365, 367n16, 367n17, 367n20; micro-structural logic in, 26on23; mnemonic references in, 248–49; pedagogical goals of, 242, 257, 258n8; sound objects in, 242–45, 258n7, 258n8; as voyage into child's mind, 241–42, 257
(*Játékok I*), "Hommage à Bartók," 359; "Hommage à Beethoven," 41–42, 358–59; "Hommage à Csajkovszkij," 39–41, 250; "Hommage à Paganini (La

nuova campanella)," 250–51, 352, 357; "Hoquetus," 350; "Totyogós," 242–49; "Unottan," 252–54, 256–57; "Veszekedés 1," 250

(*Játékok III*), "12 neue Mikroludien," 357, 359; "Hommage à J.S.B.," 357; "Hommage à Mussorgsky," 359; "Hommage à Petrovics," 352; "Hommage à Stockhausen," 359; "Hommage à Szervánszky" (for piano and for piano four hands), 352–53, 367n17; "Hommage à Zenon," 356; "Sirató," 350

(*Játékok IV*), "Glocken (Hommage à Stravinsky)," 359

(*Játékok V*), "Sirató," 350; "Szoltsányi György emlékezete," 367n17; "Virág – Garzó Gabinak," 367n17

(*Játékok VI*), "… humble regard sur Olivier Messiaen," 353; "Les adieux (in Janáčeks Manier)," 367n21

(*Játékok VII*), "Merrian's Dream," 352

Kafka-Fragmente Op. 24, 13, 266, 267–74, 298n20, 343, 367n7; apparitions fantomatiques de la tonalité, 268–69; danses, 268, 273; matériau musical hérité du passé, 268–72, 275–76; multiplicité de liens entre les fragments du cycle, 271–72; pièces « doubles », 272; pièces « in memoriam », 272; présence du corps, 273–74; Sprechstimme, 273

A kis csáva Op. 15b, 296n6, 367n21

[*A letter from Modest to Arseny*] Письмо Модеста Арсению, 280

[*Messages of the Late Miss R.V. Troussova*] Послания покойной Р.В.Трусовой, Op. 17, 279, 280, 288, 290, 291, 297n10, 299n29, 299n36, 299n37

[*A meeting*] Встреча, 280

[*Music for voice and pebbles*] Музыка для голоса и камешек, 280

Nagy sirató, 367n16

New Messages for orchestra, Op. 34b, 352

Officium breve in memoriam Andreæ Szervánszky Op. 28, 15, 349–50, 352, 356, 360, 365

Olyan, Amilyen …, 280

Omaggio a Luigi Nono Op. 19, 280, 300n49, 353, 357

… pas à pas … nulle part … Op. 36, 368n27

[*Proverb*] Пословица, 280

Quasi una fantasia Op. 27, 339–40

[*Requiem for the Beloved*] Реквием по другу Op. 26, 280

Rückblick 1992, 352

[*Scenes from a Novel*] Сцены из романа Op. 19, 14, 280, 298n20, 300n42, 300n49, 305, 308–12; ["Dream"] "Сон": Kurtág's interpretation of, 308–12; musical analysis of, 308–10; musicopoetic analysis of, 310–12; phrase structure of, 308–12; shape of vocal line, 308–11

Signs, Games and Messages for Strings, 10, 352

[*Songs of Despair and Sorrow*] Песни уныния и печали, Op. 18, 280, 288, 294–95, 296n6, 298n19, 300n49

[*A spike of barley*] За колос ячменя, 280
Die Sprüche Péter Bornemisza Op. 7, 354; "Virág az ember," 352
String Quartet Op. 1, 351, 352, 361
Szokolay Cauuanyi első karácsonyára [For Alexander Szokolay's first Christmas], 42–43
Twenty-Four Antiphons Op. 24 (unfinished), 359
Virág as ember (Turcsányi Tibor emlékére), 367n17
Wind Quintet Op. 2, 352
Kurtág, György: WRITINGS: *Játékok: une leçon de György Kurtág*, 241, 257n2, 258n6, 258n8, 259–60n18, 260n21, 260n23, 261n32
Preface to *Játékok*, 249, 260n25, 367n20
Kurtág, Márta (spouse of György Kurtág), 7, 37, 44n3, 353

Lachenmann, Helmut, 15, 345, 361, 363–64, 365, 368n27, 368n28; *Accanto*, 363–64; musique concrète instrumentale, 364
Lanz, Doris, 139
Laver, John, 193
LeCaine, Hugh, 29, 59
Leibowitz, René, 126n23
Le Moyne, Jean, 20n42
Lendvai, Ernő, 405, 407, 410, 411, 416n36; proportional analysis of Bartók works, 405, 416n30, 416n36
Leningrad/Petrograd, 283, 286
Lentsner, Dina, 296n4
Lermontov, Mikhail, 280, 285
Library and Archives Canada (LAC), 11, 12, 31, 68, 196n14, 196n18, 371, 407; István-Anhalt Fonds, 11–12, 21n50, 407. *Voir aussi* Bibliothèque et Archives Canada (BAC); Bibliothèque nationale du Canada
Ligeti, György, 7, 19n27, 20n34, 59, 100, 201, 327, 397; *Nouvelles aventures*, 397
Ligue canadienne des compositeurs/Canadian League of Composers, 29, 202
Liszt, Franz, 42, 106n17, 356
Liverpool, 75
London, 6, 113–14, 115, 116
Lorca, Federico García, 14, 303–5, 313–20; "Gacela de la muerto oscura," from *Diván del tamarit*, 305, 313–20: musico-poetic analysis of, 310–12; poetic analysis of, 313–16; symmetrical structures in, 314; synchronic and diachronic reading of, 315
Lotman, Yuri, 14, 304–5, 313; [*Analysis of the Poetic Text*] *Analiz poeticheskogo teksta*, 304–5
Lugoj (Hungary/Lugos Romania), 5, 279, 296n3
Luria, Isaac, 220–21
Lutosławski, Witold, 397; *Trois poèmes d'Henri Michaux*, 397
Lutyens, Elisabeth, 122

McClary, Susan, 414n11
MacDonald, James Edward Harvey (J.E.H.), 224; *The Beaver Dam*, 224–25; viewer response to, 225
Macdonald, John A., 76
McGill University, 6, 12, 29, 59, 61, 76, 77, 122, 201, 395
Machaut, Guillaume de, 346
McLuhan, Marshall, 2, 20n42, 408
McMorrow, Kathleen, 32, 34
MacNaughton, Doug, 181
Mahler, Gustav, 4, 77, 364, 375, 387
Mailing, Phyllis, 176
mainstream vs. margin, 2–4, 17n14
Malcolm, Ryan, 75
Malinowsky, Bronislaw, 33

Malraux, André, 362
Mandelstam, Osip, 280, 282, 283, 285, 289, 295, 297n9
Mann, Thomas, 37, 426; *Tonio Kröger*, 37
Marie de l'Incarnation (née Marie Guyart), 60, 66, 102, 180, 184, 209–10
Marlboro (US), 298n18
Massey, Doreen, 178
Mather, Bruce, 122, 201
Mathews, Max, 29
Mayakovsky, Vladimir, 283
Melnikova, Natalia, 298n18
mémoire, 268, 329–330, 332; mémoire involontaire, 332, 333; méta–mémoire, 210; remémoration, 332, 338, 342. *Voir aussi* memory
memory, 9, 14–16, 29, 45, 51n3, 68, 80, 87n27, 89, 98, 103, 104n2, 121, 177, 178, 179, 181–82, 184, 194, 221, 248, 279, 362, 371, 372, 375, 382, 390, 395–96, 398, 412–13, 415n19, 426. See also mémoire
Memphis, 75
Mercure, Pierre, 201
Messiaen, Olivier, 95
midrash, 83, 92, 93, 106n19; *Genesis Rabbah*, 106 n19–20, 107n21, 107n23
migration, 16, 16n4, 22n58, 111, 115, 122, 123, 124–25, 126n24, 194, 423; as career trajectory, 8; mass, 1–2
Mihály, András, 335
Mikuli, Karol, 42
Milhaud, Darius, 2, 17n10
Minneapolis Symphony Orchestra, 168n27
Minneapolis, 12, 130, 131, 135, 137, 138, 166n10, 168n27, 169n36
modernism, 98, 99, 101, 103
Mohr, Ingeborg, 87n27, 398, 415n19
Montreal Symphony Orchestra, 371

Montréal/Montreal, 8, 11, 12, 29, 30, 59, 61, 74, 76, 99, 100, 108n39, 126n25, 205, 210, 415n16, 415n18
Mozart, Wolfgang Amadeus, 80, 115, 356; Clarinet Concerto, 363–64
Munich, 130, 165n5
music (ideas of): as aesthetic experience, 13; as autobiography, 45–51, 51n7, 136–37, 148–49, 360–61; based on diatonic scale, 52n20; and displacement, 1–2, 11–12, 89, 111, 112, 123, 124, 125, 178, 179, 181, 184, 194; as iconic image 244, 245–46; as intentional object, 346–48, 366n4 (*see also* Ingarden, Roman); memory and remembrance, 9, 14–16, 395–96, 412–13; as messages of condolence and celebration, 10; and mourning, 398; in multicultural contexts, 1–2; national/regional identity, 2–4, 9; and pedagogy, 13, 242, 258n8; and place, 1–3, 8–9, 11–12, 14, 16, 74–76, 99, 121; as play, 48–49, 50, 241, 258n8; and politics, 4–5, 18n22; as putatively autonomous, 136; as relic of past (scores and recordings), 345–48; and religious identity, 2, 17n10; score as script to be performed, 252; as sensory-motor image, 243–46; social status of, 2; as sound image, 242, 245–46; sound objects, 242–45, 258n7; as tactile image 245–46, 260n19; and text, 13–14; as transitory object, 346; as voyage of discovery, 241
musicologie: d'antiquitaire, 204, 213n20; archéologie musicale, 213n20; archivistique, 203–5; et nouvel historicisme, 212n16; science de la musique, 213n20. *Voir aussi* music (ideas of); musicology
musicology: construction of a musical canon, 136, 137; popular music

studies, 5, 16n4, 75. *See also* musicologie
Musil, Robert, 194
musique: autobiographique, 272; comme langage, 271, 275–76, 327–30, 342–43; formes, 328, 329–30; geste expressif, 272–76, 330; et identité nationale et régionale, 209–10; image figurative, 265–76; et langage, 265–66; langage tonal, 327, 336–37; et lieu, 209–10 (*voir aussi* music: and place); matériau(x) de la, 265–72, 275–76, 329–30, 335, 338; matériau hérité du passé, 329–30 (*voir aussi* Kurtág, György: vestiges des langages musicaux du passé); et mémoire, 268–71; processus de réification, 272, 276, 328; et texte, 265–76
Mussolini, Benito, 167n17
Mussorgsky, Modest, 280, 298n20, 416n26; *Boris Godonov*, 298n20, 416n26; *Pictures at an Exhibition*, 359
mythology, 81, 82–83, 87n34, 102, 111, 221, 373

Nabokov, Vladimir, 295n2
Nagy, Ferenc, 166n6
Narbut, Vladimir, 297n9
National Archives of Canada, 21. *See also* Archives nationales du Canada (ANC), Bibliothèque et Archives Canada (BAC), Library and Archives Canada (LAC)
National Gallery of Canada/Musée des beaux-arts du Canada, 415n19
National Library of Canada/Bibliothèque nationale du Canada. *See* Library and Archives Canada (LAC); Bibliothèque et Archives Canada (BAC)
National Research Council Canada/Conseil national de recherches Canada, 59

nationalism, 2, 3, 99, 100–1, 108n35, 108n40,136, 138; vs. cosmopolitanism, 4–5; German, 136; in musicological discourse, 3–5, 17n13, 18n16 (*see also* Dahlhaus, Carl); Quebec, 100, 108n35
nationality, as métissage, 2
NATO (North Atlantic Treate Organisation), 48
Nedobrovo, Nikolai, 299n31
neoclassicism/néo-classicisme, 116, 296n9, 335
Neue Bach-Ausgabe, 366n8
New England, 178, 429
New France/Nouvelle-France, 100, 178, 210
new music, 8, 59, 73, 74, 75–76, 98, 100–1, 103
New York City, 75, 285
Niagara-on-the-Lake (Ontario), 76–77
Nono, Luigi, 357, 365; *Omaggio a György Kurtág*, 357
Nørgård, Per, 201
North America, 9, 13, 17n13, 34, 76, 77, 99, 101, 102, 130, 177, 178, 180, 182, 414n10, 430
Nouvelle France/New France, 100, 178, 210
Novalis (Georg Friedrich Freiherr von Hardenberg), 333, 389; *Fragments*, 389

Old Hall (manuscrit/manuscript), 213n21
Oliveros, Pauline, 237n33
Oppenheimer, J. Robert, 181. *See also* Anhalt: Writings: *Oppenheimer*
Ordukhanyan, Margarit Tadevosyan, 295n2
Ottawa, 29, 31, 34, 59, 79, 196n14, 196n18, 396
Ottoman Empire, 111
Ovid, 81, 82, 87n31, 221

Paganini, Niccolò, 357
Papineau-Couture, Jean, 100, 199, 201

Papp, Márta, 300n43
Paris, 6, 11, 21n53, 57, 59, 76, 100, 114, 116, 122, 267, 300n48, 329, 351, 425
Pascal, Blaise, 389; *Pensées*, 389
passé au sein du présent, 335. *Voir aussi* presence of the past
Paul Sacher Foundation, 10, 14, 150, 165n4, 168n27, 171n55, 296n4; Antal Doráti Collection, 168n27; György Kurtág Collection, 10, 14, 296n4; Sándor Veress Collection, 150, 165n4
Pauk, Alex, 396
pedagogy of transformation, 219, 224, 225, 233–35; case studies in, 226–33; exercises in, 226
Pennsylvania College for Women (now Chatham University), 130, 166n7
Pentland, Barbara, 126n25
Pépin, Clermont, 201
performance: as choreography, 245; of Anhalt's Violin Sonata by Gisèle Dalbec-Szczesniak and Michel Szczesniak, 425; of *Four Portraits from Memory* by Charles Foreman, 86n20, 398, 401, 404, 411; as gesture, 39, 241, 243–45, 252, 254; improvisation in, 250, 261n32; as re-enactment of past, 346–47
Piaget, Jean, 234; construction of reality, 258n8
Pittsburgh, 130
place and displacement, 1–2, 10–12, 16n4, 178; and identity, 12; in musicological discourse, 2–5
poetic structure, analysis of, 304–5
Poland, 67
Polanyi, Michael, 260n20
popular music, 99, 114, 426–27
Post-modernisme, 335
Prado Museum, 223
presence of the past: authorship, 348; in architecture, 345; in visual arts, 345; in music 344–66, 412–13. *See also* passé au sein du présent

presence, concept of, 345–48, 366n3
Proctor, George, 120
Prokofiev, Sergey, 362
Proust, Marcel, 333, 373; *Remembrance of Things Past*, 373
Purcell, Henry, 349; *Fantasia upon One Note*, 349; *Examples of Counterpoint and Canon "Per Arsin & Thesin a 2, 3 and 4,"* 366n7
Puritanism, 221
Pushkin, Alexander, 283, 285–88, 298n29; *Boris Godunov*, 298n20; *Eugene Onegin*, 298n19, as Protean genius, 286

Québec/Quebec (province), 12, 60, 100–1, 108n35, 108n37, 109n43, 205, 209–10, 427–28
Québec/Quebec City, 76
Queen's University, 6, 32, 61–62, 64, 76, 77, 84, 86n18, 87n31, 109n44, 180, 200, 201, 396, 428
Quran, 92, 94, 106n20

Rackin, Donald, 319
Ranke, Leopold von, 203, 212n13
Ranran, Matsukura, 280
Reading University, 193
reception of art and music, 13, 75: as aesthetic experience, 13; French language reception of Anhalt's work, 12; triangular relation (work, context, receiver), 13
Reed, Henry, 237n34
refugee, 1, 111–12
Reich, Steve, 417n48; *Come Out*, 417n48
Rembrandt, 77
Ricoeur, Paul, 220
Rihm, Wolfgang, 15, 345, 361, 364–65; auto/self-quotation, 364–65, 368n33, 368n34; contrafactum, 365; *Drei Stücke aus Kolchis*, 368n34; *Frage*, 365 368n33; *Fremde Szenen I–III*, 364; *In Frage*, 368n33; inscription, 365; *Kolchis*, 365, 368n33; *Musik für drei Stre-*

icher, 364; overpainting, 365; sketches 365–66; *Tutuguri*, 364
Rilke, Rainer Maria, 39; *Letters to a Young Poet*, 39
Rimsky-Korsakov, Nikolai, 416n26
Rochberg, George, 20n46, 30, 31, 87n27, 196n18, 199–201, 206, 373; correspondence with István Anhalt 30, 73, 98, 196n18, 196n22, 237n45, 371, 373, 375, 389–90, 397, 398, 415n17
Rodgers, Richard, 427
Rogers, Ginger, 31
Romania, 5, 52n11, 85n5, 114, 296n3, 415n18
Rome, 58, 137, 167n17, 170n40
roots, 12, 57, 65, 99, 175, 176–82, 184, 194, 221; and routes, 175, 177, 178–79, 194, 195n1
Rosbaud, Hans, 126n23
Rostal, Max, 117
Roy Thomson Hall (Toronto), 371
Royal Canadian Academy of the Arts/Académie royale des arts du Canada, 87n31, 415n19
Rufer, Josef, 17n14
Russia, 9, 111, 281, 282, 283, 297n9; eschatological era of Russian history, 294; Imperial 282; pre-Revolutionary era, 289
Russian language, 279, 281–82, 288, 298n19, 304–5; in Cyrillic script, 295n1; Hungarian reception of Kurtág's Russian-language works, 281, 296n8; prosody, 14
Russian literature and poetry, 279–82, 283, 293, 285–86; archetypal Russian idioms, 293, 300n46; as marginal to Western European traditions, 281–82; Silver Age, 297n16; translation and transliteration of poetry, 305–7

Said, Edward, 112, 121
Saint-André-de-Cubzac (France), 298n18, 298n25, 300n43
Saint Lawrence River valley, 8

Saint-Saëns, Camille, 346
Salesian Order, 176, 194, 195n2
Sallis, Friedemann, 34, 57, 71n9, 83, 85n1, 212n15, 257n1, 296n4
Sampih, 65–66
Sandler, Stephanie, 286
Satie, Erik, 408; Golden Section proportions in music of, 408, 417n38
Schaeffer, Pierre, 76
Schafer, R. Murray, 74, 95n10, 199, 201, 223, 397, 427, 429; *Ra*, 414n6; *The Tuning of the World*, 396, 397, 414n7
Schiller, Friedrich von, 373–74
Schindler, Anton, 373
Schoenberg, Arnold, 14–15, 17n14, 21n53, 76, 116, 117, 118, 121, 122, 125n5, 327–28, 330, 364, 411, 424, 425, 426, 430n2, 431n6; expression artistique, 328; on analysis, 411, 417n38; *Erwartung*, 106n18; expressionist period, 364; *Le style et l'idée*, 327; *Pierrot lunaire*, Op. 21, 414n6; *Survivor from Warsaw*, 388; technique de composition, 327
Scholem, Gershom, 97, 104n10, 107n31, 181
Schubert, Franz, 42, 366n7; *Sechsunddreissig Originaltänze* Op. 9 D365, 366n7
Schubert, Giselher, 5
Schumann, Robert, 4, 346, 411–12, 417n43; *Carnival*, Op. 9, 413; *Frauen-liebe und Leben*, 291; poetic vs. prosaic in music, 414
Schütz, Heinrich, 137
Schwartz-Bart, André, 66
Schwarzenegger, Arnold, 87n34
Schweizer, Gottfried, 118
Searle, Humphrey, 122
Seattle, 75
Seiber, Mátyás, 11–12, 111–26; biography 113–15; as conductor 114; as composition teacher 114, 115, 121; compositional idiom 113,

114, 115–16, 117, 118, 120–21;
move to UK, 21n49
Seiber, Mátyás: COMPOSITIONS:
Besardo Suites, 116
Divertimento, 113
Elegy, 124, 126n14
Fantasia, 116
Fantasia Concertante, 117, 119, 126n14
Improvisation, 118
Jazzolettes, 115
3 Morgenstern Songs, 126n14
Permutazioni a cinque, 126n14
Quartetto Lirico, 119
String Quartet No. 1, 115
Tre pezzi, 116
Ulysses, 119, 120, 126n14
Violin Sonata, 116
sémiologie musicale, 212n16
Serbia, 296n3
serialism, 4, 12, 114, 117, 122, 125, 364, 397; integral/total, 4, 364, 397. See also dodecaphony; twelve-tone technique
Shankar, Ravi, 77
Shelemay, Kay Kaufman, 74–75, 85n10
Shostakovich, Dmitri, 170n48; Seventh Symphony, 170n48
Simon Fraser University, 74, 238n51
Simpson, Robert, 389
Smith, Gordon E., 65, 179–80, 202, 414n4
Smolenskaya Icon of the Mother of God, 293,
Société de Musique Contemporaine du Québec, 100
Société Radio Canada (SRC), 213n25. Voir aussi Canadian Broadcasting Corporation (CBC)
sociology, 75, 220, 396
Solomon, Maynard, 374
Somers, Harry, 122, 427, 429
Somfai, László, 417n38
Somlyó, Zoltán, 58
Soós, Géza, 130–31, 165n5, 166n11; founding member of the Reformed Church of the Hungarian Diaspora, 165n5
Soviet aesthetics, 171n48
Soviet Union, 4, 48, 132, 147; proletarian State, 282, Red terror, 299n31; Siberian labour camps, 283
Spanish Civil War, 303; Fascists in, 303
Spanish literature and poetry, 303–7; translation and transliteration of poetry, 305–7
Spilchuk, Vincent, 430n1
SS United States, 48
Stalin, 48
Stanislavski, Constanin, 37; An Actor Prepares, 37
State University of New York at Buffalo, 201
Stein, Marianne, 21n53
Steiner, George, 389–90
Stockhausen, Karlheinz, 59, 117, 193, 201, 223, 362, 408; Golden Section proportions in music of, 408, 417n38; Stimmung, 417n48
Stratford (Ontario), 417n17; International Conference of Composers in, 31, 196n18
Strauss, Richard, 77, 106n17, 362, 364, 375
Stravinsky, Igor, 39, 77, 118, 364, 424, 425; Petrouchka, 39; The Rite of Spring, 364; Symphony of Psalms, 359
Stravinsky, Soulima, 59, 116
Strohm, Reinhard, 3
surréalisme, 333
Switzerland, 6, 7–9, 12, 20n34, 129, 136, 148, 149, 150, 166n9, 296n4
symbolism, 296n9
synesthesia, 259n16; networks of, 245–46
Szabó, Csaba, 350
Szczesniak, Michel, 425
Székely, István, 182, 183
Szervánszky, Endre, 350; Serenade for string orchestra, 350, 352

Szesztay, Sári, 37
Szilágyi, János-György 58, 372, 390n5
Szokolay, Alexander, 42
Szokolay, Balázs, 39
Szokolay, Gergely (György Kurtág's godson), 37
Szokolay, Sándor, 37, 43, 44n2, 350; *Vérnász*, 44n2
Szokolay, Sophia (Sonia), 10, 42

Taruskin, Richard, 281, 389
Taubner, Ödön, 182, 183
Tchaikovsky, Pyotr Illich, 106n17; First Piano Concerto, 39
technology, 1; impact on culture, 2, 9
Télémaque, 276n3
Théberge, Paul, 20n42
Tieck, Ludwig, 412; *Phantasien über die Kunst*, 412
Tinguely, Jean, 48–49
Tokyo, 167n17
Torah, 93, 94, 220–21
Toronto Symphony Orchestra, 371
Toronto, 10, 11, 30, 31, 32, 34, 79, 100, 117, 126n25, 181, 371, 373, 396, 429
totalitarianism, 222
Tovey, Donald, 213n20
Tragically Hip, The, 75
Transylvania, 5, 52n11, 73
Traub, Andreas, 52n13, 130, 136, 139, 170n43
Treaty of Trianon, 48, 51n11
Tremblay, Gilles, 201
Trent University, 415n19
Trimm, John Leslie Melville (J.L.M.), 193, 431n5
Tsvetaeva, Marina, 283, 321
Turner, William, 47
twelve-tone technique, 50–51, 52n20, 60, 95, 113, 116, 117, 122, 136, 139, 157, 425. *See also* dodecaphony; serialism

Ulysse, 276n3
United Kingdom, 9, 21n49. *See also* England; Great Britain

United States, 12, 16n4, 29, 48, 123, 126n24, 129, 130–31, 135, 148–49, 165–66n6, 168n26, 171n51, 414n10, 426–27
universal vs. particular/global vs. local, 2–5, 17n13; globalization and Euclidean space, 303
Université de l'État de New York à Buffalo, 201
Université McGill, 201. *Voir aussi* McGill University
Université Queen's, 200, 201. *Voir aussi* Queen's University
Université Western Ontario, 202
University of Calgary, 9, 57, 85n1, 86n20, 98, 125
University of Chicago, 74
University of Edinburgh, 193
University of Maryland, 166n6
University of Southern California, 424
University of Toronto, 29, 415n19, 429; Press, 33
urban studies, 75
University of Western Ontario, 202
Uritsky, Moisei, 299n31; head of Bolshevik secret police, 299n31
utopia, 48, 222

Vâlcele, Romania. *See* Előpatak
Valéry, Paul, 276
Vámos, Júlia, 280
Vancouver New Music Society, 176
Varèse, Edgard, 201
Velázquez, Diego, 223; *Las Hilanderas (The Spinners)*, 223
Venice, 51n10
Verdi, Giuseppe, 78
Veress, Claudio (son of Sándor Veress), 45, 165n1, 170n41
Veress, Endre (father of Sándor Veress), 47, 137, 166n14, 169–70n40
Veress, Sándor the elder (grandfather of Sándor Veress), 48
Veress, Sándor, 5–10, 12, 45–52, 129–64; on American idealism, 148; Aryan origin, 134;

ambivalence towards science and technology, 48; attempts to immigrate to US, 12, 48, 129–35, 148; autobiographical statements, 129, 130–35, 150, 167n15; auto-constructed legacy, 12, 129–49; auto/self-quotation, 46; awards, prizes, recognition, 7; becomes Swiss citizen, 7, 171n51; Bern, 48, 49, 131; birth, 5; Cold War, 12, 48, 133; collaboration with Fascist regimes during World War II, 167n17; correspondence, 12, 130–35, 148, 150, 165n4, 166n7, 166n11, 168n25, 168n27, 170n41; declarations of political allegiance, 133–35; dodecaphonic technique, 7; early émigré years, 130, 165n3; England, 47; as exile, 7, 10; on exile in Switzerland, 20n34, 129; family history, 132, 169n40; fascination with precise mechanisms, 48–49, 50; György Kurtág's teacher, 5–6; helping Jews during Nazi period, 167n17; Hungarian folk music in work of, 136, 138–43; Hungary, 5–6, 7, 8, 12, 47–48, 129–37, 139, 142–43, 148; ideal of freedom, 50; on Italian art and culture, 47, 51n10; juror at Llangollen Eisteddfod, 47; as liberal social democrat, 132; in London, 6; on living in Bern, 49; on marxism, 48; mechanism vs. teleology, 48; member of Hungarian Communist Party, 52n12, 129, 130, 132–34, 167n18; member of Hungarian emigration, 129–30, 148–49; music as play, 48–49, 50; pedagogue, 7, 19n29, 50; as polyglot, 150; professor at University of Bern, 6, 166n9; on Soviet Socialism, 48; on spiritual and moral collapse of Europe, 148; student at Collegium Hungaricum (Rome), 137; studies with Zoltán Kodály, 5; and Suvini Zerboni, Edizioni, 136; on time, 45; twelve-tone technique, 50–51, 52n20, 136, 138–39; and Universal Edition, 167n17; views on Western democracy, 133, 135; World War I, 5, 48, 51n11; World War II, 6, 48

Veress, Sándor: COMPOSITIONS:
  Concertotilinkó (unfinished fragment), 51n6
  Geschichten und Märchen (unfinished fragment), 51n6
  Orbis Tonarum, 10, 45–51; as autobiography, 45–51, 51n7; auto-quotation in music, 46; folk-music-like bicinium, 49; irony in, 50
  I. Quartetto per 2 Violini, Viola e Violoncello, 46
  Sinfonia Minneapolitana, 12, 130, 131, 135–49, 165n4, 169n36; as putatively autonomous music, 136; commissioned, 130, 168n27; Hungarian folk-music, 136, 138–43; as autobiographical statement, 136–37, 148–49; as exploration of twelve-tone technique, 136, 138–39; Italianate title, 137–38; as narrative of national history, 138–42, 147; as pivot between Europe and America, 148; as purely musical form, 136; thematic contrast (between twelve-tone and folk-like themes), 138–47, 170n46
  Symphony No. 1 "Hungarian Greetings on the 2600th Anniversary of the Japanese Dynasty," 167n17
  Tromboniade, 51n6

Veress, Sándor: WRITINGS: Autobiographic statements (unpublished typescripts), 151–57, 159–64
Veress-Blake, Enid (spouse of Sándor Veress), 47, 133; British citizenship, 133
Victoria (British Columbia), 429
Vienna, 76, 121, 122, 373
Viennese School, Second (*see also* École de Vienne), 356
voyage of discovery, as personal metaphor, 241, 257n2

Wagner, Richard, 375, 391n12, 424, 428
Walsh, Stephen, 291
Washington (DC), 130, 165n5, 171n51
Wathey, Andrew, 203–4, 213n21
Weber, Carl Maria von, 201; *Obéron*, 201
Webern, Anton, 119, 120, 122, 267, 328, 329, 335, 343, 349–50, 351, 361; expressionisme atonal, 328; *Five Movements for String Quartet*, Op. 5, 351; formes aphoristiques, 328, 335; intensification du discours, 328; intensité expressive de l'œuvre, 328; période atonale, 335; refus d'héritage tonal, 328; *Sechs Bagatellen/Six bagatelles pour quatuor à corde*, Op. 9, 328, 343, 351; Second Cantata, Op. 31, 349, 352; String Quartet, Op. 28, 351; Symphony, Op. 21, 119
Wegeler, Franz, 376
Weill, Kurt, 427

Weiner, László, 182, 183
Weingartner, Felix, 372, 390n4
Weinzweig, John, 32, 122, 201
Weissman, John, 7
Wellesz, Egon, 122, 126n23
Weltanschauungsmusik, 104n1
Weöres, Sándor, 38, 372; "Orbán," 38
Wigmore Hall, 117
Winthrop, John, 66, 102, 180, 184, 210
Wishart, Trevor, 193
Wittgenstein, Ludwig, 389; *On Certainty*, 389
Wolfe, Thomas, 371
Wood, Hugh, 114
World War I, 5, 48, 51n11, 108n31, 111–12
World War II, 3, 6, 7, 11, 12, 31, 48, 58, 59, 73, 82, 103, 112, 114, 115, 116, 121, 122, 125, 182, 186, 195n2, 223; American and British radio broadcasts to Hungary, 133, 134
Wright, James K., 390

York University, 237n33
Yugoslavia, 114

Zagorinskaya, Natalia, 285, 297n17
Zenkevich, Michael, 296n9
Zhdanov, Andrei, 18n22
Zimmermann, Bernd Alois, 15, 345, 361, 362–63, 365; *Dialoge*, 362–63; *Musique pour les soupers du Roi Ubu*, 262; *Présence*, 362; spherical form of time, 362; quotation in music of, 362
Zionism, 90, 102

www.ingramcontent.com/pod-product-compliance
Lightning Source LLC
Chambersburg PA
CBHW070042080526
44586CB00013B/881